What Man Believes:
A Study of the World's Great Faiths

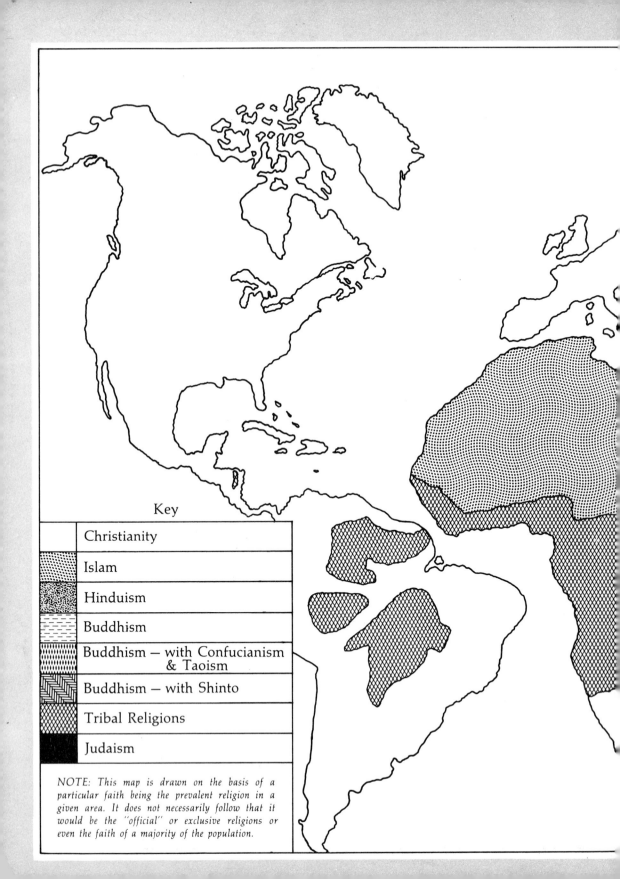

Key

	Christianity
	Islam
	Hinduism
	Buddhism
	Buddhism — with Confucianism & Taoism
	Buddhism — with Shinto
	Tribal Religions
	Judaism

NOTE: This map is drawn on the basis of a particular faith being the prevalent religion in a given area. It does not necessarily follow that it would be the "official" or exclusive religions or even the faith of a majority of the population.

Religions of the World

What Man Believes:
A Study of the World's Great Faiths

by

Allan S. Evans
Head
History Department
Emery Collegiate Institute
Weston, Ontario

Riley E. Moynes
North York Board of Education
Seconded to the Royal Ontario Museum
Queen's Park,
Toronto, Ontario

Larry Martinello
History Department
Emery Collegiate Institute
Weston, Ontario

McGraw-Hill Ryerson Limited
Toronto   Montreal   New York   London
Sydney   Johannesburg   Mexico   Panama   Düsseldorf
Singapore   New Delhi   Kuala Lumpur   São Paulo

ISBN   0-07-077440-4
Library of Congress Catalogue Card Number 73-7047

Printed and bound in Canada

5 6 7 8 9 10 D 2 1 0 9 8

Preface

The study of religion in its various manifestations offers an illuminating view of man's development historically, socially, intellectually and spiritually. *What Man Believes* has been written in the hope that it will contribute not only to a deeper understanding of, but also to a greater tolerance and respect for, the religions of all peoples.

In the interests of flexibility, clarity and thoroughness, the book is organized basically on the survey principle. However, provisions have also been made for those who prefer a biographical, conceptual, inquiry or interdisciplinary approach. To make the most effective use of *What Man Believes* the authors recommend reference to the Instructor's Guide which accompanies this book, courtesy of the publisher.

In preparing the manuscript, the authors worked in consultation with the following:

J. Don Fulton — Committee on Publication for Ontario of the Church of Christ, Scientist;
Professor J. Webster Grant — Professor of Church History, Emmanuel College in Victoria University, University of Toronto;
Dr. L. Clayton Kitchen — Associate Professor (Ret.), McMaster University, Hamilton;
Mr. C. Lalonde — President of the Toronto Stake of the Church of Jesus Christ of Latter-Day Saints;
Dr. D. C. MacDonald — Clerk of Assembly of the Presbyterian Church in Canada;
Mr. Arnold W. MacNamara — Assistant Branch Manager, Toronto Branch of the Watch Tower Bible and Tract Society;
Mr. M. Muinuddin — Editor, *Islam Canada*;
Rev. Lorne Shook — President, Pontifical Institute of Medieval Studies, St. Michael's College in the University of Toronto;
Rev. Peeter Vanker — Church of the Good Shepherd (Lutheran), Toronto;
Rev. Ronald F. Watts — General Secretary of the Baptist Convention of Ontario and Quebec;
Rabbi I. E. Witty — Executive Director of the Board of Jewish Education for Metropolitan Toronto.

We would also like to thank:

Mr. Veerendra D. Adhiya — President, Know India Cultural Society;
Brother Alexander — The Process;
Ms. Barbara Arnott — Secretary of the Canadian Unitarian Council;
Rev. Roger Cann — Secretary of the Department of Communications, Baptist Convention of Ontario and Quebec;
Miss A. Hedderick — Librarian, Anglican Church House, Toronto;
Jayadvaita dasa brahmacari — Editor, ISKCON Press (A division of the International Society for Krishna Consciousness);
Rev. B. G. Levman — The Church of Scientology;
Dr. Helen Milton — Theology Department, University of Windsor;
Mr. R. Vezina — Editor, *Catholic Register*, Toronto;
The Indian-Eskimo Association of Canada.

We wish to express our sincere thanks to these individuals for their sound and scholarly advice. The Ontario Human Rights Commission has also assisted by reading the manuscript to ensure objectivity and freedom from prejudice. However, in a book of this nature, several matters of judgment and interpretation are bound to arise. In such instances we accept sole responsibility for the viewpoints expressed.

We also wish to thank the following for their efforts on our behalf:
Mr. M. Hussain; Mrs. Neda Leipen, Curator of the Greek and Roman Department, Royal Ontario Museum; Dr. N. Millett, Curator of the Egyptian Department, R.O.M.; Mrs. Dorothy Poynter; Miss A. Westley of Catholic Extension.

Excerpts from the King James version of the Holy Bible are reprinted by permission of Oxford University Press.

Special thanks are extended to our wives Marjorie, Yvonne and Donna who encouraged us in our efforts and were patient during the long period of manuscript preparation.

A.S.E.
R.E.M.
L.F.M.

Contents

The Beginnings of Man's Beliefs

Chapter One

The Foundations of Religion

I<small>T</small> is said that Truth is one, though wise men call it by different names. Truth, however, is often subject to interpretation, and from the differences of such interpretations the world religions were born.

Since the forms of man's religion and his religious experience are endless, we find diverse ways by which religious truth has manifested itself to various individuals. Moses found it one day in a burning bush on Mount Horeb; *Mohammed** received it in a desolate cave in an Arabian desert; the *Buddha* saw it in contemplation of poverty, old age, sickness and death. Such was the power and magnetism of these spiritual leaders that they were able to persuade other men, by the millions, to follow their unique path to salvation.

The variety of reasons that draw man to religion have been operative for as long as man has existed. Anthropologists, archaeologists and other scientists continue to unearth evidence which supports the presumption that man has always worshipped. In countless forms, in countless communities, man still worships.

Even if societies had existed in the past without religion, they would form so insignificant a part of the total picture that it is valid to assume the phenomenon of religion has always been universal. From this vantage point, if, as has often been claimed, man is a rational being, it is equally fair to call him a religious being.

1. The Nature of Religion

Function. Man worships for a variety of reasons, and every religion confers a number of benefits on its followers. Religion sustains man in time of troubles; it strengthens him in time of fear; it offers the path of a meaningful life in this world and the hope of a better life in the next. Religion performs many more functions, both social and spiritual, but they are probably secondary to the prime consideration which motivates the individual in religious worship: the comfort provided by the belief that there is a power greater than man which at times aids and sustains him in his struggle against a generally hostile environment and the ultimate reality of death. It is this relationship — honour and worship on the part of man in expectation of assistance from the Power he worships — which forms the basis of religion.

Historian Will Durant summarizes the ageless and pervasive function of religion in these terms:

> To the unhappy, to the suffering, the bereaved, the old, it has brought supernatural comforts valued by millions of souls as more precious than any natural aid. It has helped parents and teenagers to discipline

*Italics indicates word is listed in glossary.   2

the young. It has conferred meaning and dignity upon the lowliest
existence and through its sacraments has made for stability by transforming human covenants into solemn relationships with God. It has
kept the poor (said Napoleon) from murdering the rich. For since the
natural inequality of men dooms many of us to poverty or defeat, some
supernatural hope may be the sole alternative to despair.[1]

The Meaning of Religion   What is the universal phenomenon we call
religion? As many volumes have been written in answering this question as in
describing the various religions themselves. In some ways it is a more difficult
task.

The word "religion" is derived from *religio,* a word of Latin origin
meaning "to bind", as in the sense of binding man to the spirits. It was originally
used to express the sense of awe or fear which people experienced in the
presence of forces they felt to be superior or supernatural. The word has a much
broader meaning today, but it is extremely difficult to arrive at an agreement on
exactly what that meaning is. There are several reasons for this.

One point of view maintains that religion is primarily an emotional
experience:

> I took a day to search for God,
> And found Him not. But as I trod
> By rocky ledge, through woods untamed,
> Just where one scarlet lily flamed,
> I saw His footprint in the sod.
> Bliss Carman[2]

Another viewpoint stresses the dependency of man on God:

> Religion may be defined . . . as the relationship between man and the
> superhuman power he believes in and feels himself to be dependent on.
> Hans-Joachim Schoeps[3]

The philosopher Hegel attempted to undermine this proposal by
pointing out that if this feeling of dependency were truly the essence of religion,
then dogs would be the most religious beings since they exhibit this quality to
perfection.

Others tend to stress the intellectual aspects of religion:

> Religion is a mental faculty or disposition, which, independent of, nay
> in spite of, sense and reason, enables man to apprehend the Infinite
> under different names and under varying guises.
> Max Müller[4]

However this definition also would appear too narrow, since it over-
looks the possibility of genuine religious experiences of the kind which
transformed Moses, Gautama and other religious leaders.

The relationship between religion and morality is emphasized by
others:

> Religion is the recognition of all duties as divine commands.
> Immanuel Kant[5]

Some reject this view on the basis that man's "duties" — moral or
ethical — may be separate from religious considerations. Buddhism in its early

stage, for example, did not profess belief in any God, though it is among the richest of religions in moral and ethical content. Indeed there are some who maintain that even the idea of God is not essential to religion:

> Real religion may exist without a definite conception of divinity.
> N. Soderblom[6]

Again, Buddhism can be cited as an example to support this definition. It should be noted however that, with this one exception, every major religion holds the idea of God as central to its beliefs.

A definition of a different sort emphasizes the importance of individual experiences:

> Religion . . . shall mean for us the feelings, acts, and experiences of individual men in their solitude, so far as they apprehend themselves to stand in relation to whatever they may consider the divine.
> William James[7]

The opposing viewpoint places the emphasis on the role of the community:

> Religion is a unified system of beliefs and practices relative to sacred things — things set apart and forbidden — beliefs and practices which unite into a single moral community called a Church, all those who adhere to them.
> Emile Durkheim[8]

Finally, there are those explanations which attempt to include all possible elements:

> By religion is meant the life of man in his superhuman relations; that is, his relation to the power on which he feels himself dependent, the authority to which he deems himself responsible, and the unseen being with whom he is capable of communing. In the ideal of religion, dependence, responsibility and communion belong together.
> William Adams Brown[9]

Obviously each of these points represents only one aspect of the definition and function of religion. As such they may express inadequately the precise meaning religion holds for each individual. Indeed, it seems impossible to arrive at an all-inclusive definition of religion and perhaps the most valid approach may be to allow each individual to work out the meaning on the basis of his personal religious beliefs.

2. The Elements of Religion

While it is difficult to achieve unanimity on what religion *is*, it is possible to some extent to delineate areas of common interest in most of the world's largest living religions. Among the most common and most important areas to be touched upon here are: the idea of God, the soul, the ethical question of man's relationship with other men and the nature of religious leadership.

A. The Idea of God

The idea of God is as old as man. From earliest times men have worshipped spirits or powers which they believed to be superior to themselves, and in some way responsible for the existence and functioning of the world around them. At first this concept took the form of *animism*, a belief in countless numbers of nameless, shapeless spirits who existed in nature and were rather fearsome in character.

In the course of the historical development of religion this gave way to *polytheism*, the belief in many gods. These gods could be identified by name; they possessed individual characteristics; and they usually had a specific role or function to perform in nature. In ancient times for example, the sun god was thought to be responsible for the daily rotation of the sun around the earth and was worshipped accordingly.

Last in development was *monotheism*, the concept of a single Supreme Being as the creative principle of the universe and the object of man's worship.

Traditionally the debate over God has centred on two main questions: Does God exist? What is the meaning and nature of God? With the exception of early Buddhism, all the great religions of the modern world adhere to the belief in the existence of an all-powerful Essence. Beyond this one general agreement it is virtually impossible to arrive at a consensus on the nature of God. Even among those faiths which belong to the same religious tradition, such as Judaism, Christianity and Islam, there are notable differences.

The Eastern View   The religions of the Eastern tradition, and we are referring here principally to Hinduism, Confucianism, Buddhism and their offshoot branches, reject the Western image of a personal deity, but it is difficult for most Westerners to comprehend the Eastern concept of God.

Traditionally Buddhism entertains no conception of God; however, if the idea of God is taken at its widest possible definition, the Buddhist concept of *Nirvana* (the ultimate state of "nothingness", the final end of man) may represent something approaching the idea of God. The Buddha himself refused to identify Nirvana, calling it "incomprehensible, indescribable, inconceivable, unutterable".

Hinduism, too, disclaims the possibility of mere mortals describing or comprehending adequately the nature of *Brahman*, the ultimate reality. That task would be akin to expecting an insect to understand the Theory of Relativity. Nevertheless some attempts to explain Brahman have been made, particularly in the Hindu sacred writings, the *Upanishads*:

> 1. Verily, this whole world is *Brahman*, from which he comes forth, without which he will be dissolved, and in which he breathes. Tranquil, one should meditate on it.
>
> 2. He who consists of mind, whose body is life, whose form is light, whose conception is truth, whose soul is space, containing all works, containing all desires, containing all odours, containing all tastes, encompassing this whole world, being without speech and without concern.
>
> 3. This is my self within the heart, smaller than a grain of rice, than a

barley corn, than a mustard seed, than a grain of millet or than the
kernel of a grain of a millet. This is myself within the heart, greater
than the earth, greater than the atmosphere, greater than the sky,
greater than these worlds.

4. Containing all works, containing all desires, containing all odours,
containing all tastes, encompassing this whole world, without speech,
without concern, this is the self of mine within the heart; this is
Brahman. Into him, I shall enter, on departing hence. Verily, he who
believes this, will have no more doubts.

. . . But the self *(atman)* is not this, not this. He is incomprehensible
for he is never comprehended. He is indestructible for he cannot be
destroyed. He is unattached for he does not attach himself. . . .[10]

The Western View   The God of Western tradition is an all-powerful eternal
Being, a Creator-God from whom all things spring. He revealed himself to
Moses as "I am that I am"—in a sense the source of all existence. He is some-
times spoken of in human terms, and indeed is believed to have conversed with
Moses and Jesus in human voice.

Some Christian churches, notably Catholicism, have permitted images
of God in human form to be made, such as in the beautiful paintings by
Michelangelo in the Sistine Chapel. Other Christian denominations, together
with Judaism and Islam, forbid any such representation of God, taking literally
the commandment: "Thou shalt not make unto thee any graven image or any
likeness of anything that is in heaven above or that is in the earth beneath."
The mental image is far more difficult to eradicate however; it is still quite
common in Western religious tradition to conceive of God as having human
form, usually as an old man with a long white beard. Writing 2,500 years ago
the Greek Xenophanes remarked on the universality of this concept among men.

But mortals deem that the gods are begotten as they are, and have
clothes like theirs, and voice and form. Yes, and if oxen and horses or
lions had hands, and could paint with their hands, and produce works
of art as men do, horses would paint the forms of the gods like horses,
and oxen like oxen, and make their bodies in the image of their several
kind.

The Ethiopians make their gods black and snub-nosed; the
Thracians say theirs have blue eyes and red hair.[11]

The God of Western tradition is also a personal God. He has made a
covenant or agreement with men whereby they promise to keep his laws and
worship him in return for his protection, justice and salvation:

13. Thou shalt fear the Lord thy God, and serve Him and shalt swear by
his name.

"The Head of the Creator" by Michelangelo. This painting from the Sistine Chapel is symbolic
of the Christian concept of God.

Miller Services Ltd.

14. Ye shall not go after other Gods, of the gods of the people which are about you;

15. (For the Lord thy God is a jealous God among you) lest the anger of the Lord thy God be kindled against thee, and destroy thee from off the face of the earth.

16. Ye shall not tempt the Lord thy God as ye tempted him in Massah.

17. Ye shall diligently keep the commandments of the Lord your God, and his testimonies, and his statutes, which he hath commanded thee.

Deuteronomy 6: 13-17

Like a father with his children, God can also be merciful toward men, even though they may be undeserving. In this way, even sinners can hope for forgiveness and salvation. Islam, which places stress on the concept of a God who exacts justice for wrong-doing, maintains that the quality of mercy is one of God's chief attributes. The Moslem view is beautifully summarized in this passage from the holy book, the *Koran:*

He is God;
There is no god but He.
He is the knower of the Unseen and the Visible;
He is the All-merciful, the All-compassionate.
He is God;
There is no god but He.
He is the King, the All-holy, the All-peaceable,
the All-Faithful, the All-preserver,
the All-mighty, the All-compeller,
the All-sublime.
Glory be to God, above that they associate!
He is God;
the Creator, the Maker, the Shaper.
To Him belong the Names Most Beautiful.
All that is in the heavens and the earth magnifies Him;
He is the All-mighty, the All-wise. (LIX, 23-5.)[12]

Christianity added a further dimension to the concept of God — the idea of the Trinity. This doctrine maintains that while there is only one God, he is at the same time three different persons: the Father, the Son and the Holy Ghost. Christianity holds this doctrine to be a mystery, partly beyond the power of man to understand, but to many non-Christians it appears that Christians reject the idea of monotheism.

Reference to the Trinity comes mainly from the New Testament:

Go ye therefore and teach all nations, baptizing them in the name of the Father, and of the Son, and of the Holy Ghost.

Matthew 28: 19

For there are three that bear record in heaven, the Father, the Word, and the Holy Ghost: and these three are one.

I John 5: 7

The Deist (Rationalist) View   A quite different concept of God emerged during the seventeenth and eighteenth centuries, as the rationalist movement swept Europe and America. The philosophy of *deism*, espoused and propagated by leading thinkers such as Voltaire and Diderot, applied the principles of reason to religion, and ended by rejecting many of the previously accepted attributes of the Supreme Being, particularly those held in the Judeo-Christian-Moslem tradition.

Deists believe in an all-powerful Supreme Being who created the world and set the laws of the universe in motion; but once the act was completed God severed himself from the mechanical, physical universe, and no longer interfered in its operation. In the deist view, this would make useless such acts as prayers, services, ritual and sacrifice, and would make impossible miracles, revelations, Holy Scriptures, prophets and Messiahs. God's only gift to man is reason.

The following is from Thomas Paine's defence of the deist position:

It is only by the exercise of reason, that man can discover God. Take away that reason, and he would be incapable of understanding any thing; and, in this case it would be just as consistent to read even the book called the Bible to a horse as to a man. How then is it that those people pretend to reject reason?

Canst thou by searching find out God? Yes; because in the first place, I know I did not make myself, and yet I have existence; and by *searching* into the nature of things, I find that no other thing could make itself; and yet millions of other things exist; therefore it is, that I know, by positive conclusion resulting from this search, that there is a power superior to all those things, and that power is God.

Canst thou find out the Almighty to *perfection?* No; not only because the power and wisdom He has manifested in the structure of the Creation that I behold is to me incomprehensible, but because even this manifestation, great as it is, is probably but a small display of that immensity of power and wisdom, by which millions of other worlds, to me invisible by their distance, were created and continue to exist.

The two questions have different objects; the first refers to the existence of God, the second to his attributes; reason can discover the one, but it falls infinitely short in discovering the whole of the other. . . .

The true Deist has but one Deity, and his religion consists in contemplating the power, wisdom, and benignity of the Deity in his works, and in endeavouring to imitate him in every thing moral, scientifical, and mechanical. . . .

From whence then could arise the solitary and strange conceit, that the Almighty, who had millions of worlds equally dependant on his protection, should quit the care of all the rest, and come to die in our world, because, they say, one man and one woman had eaten an apple! And, on the other hand, are we to suppose that every world in the boundless creation, had an Eve, an apple, a serpent and a redeemer? In this case, the person who is irreverently called the Son of God, and sometimes God himself, would have nothing else to do than to travel from world to world, in an endless succession of death, with scarcely a momentary interval of life.[13]

B. The Question of God's Existence

Fundamentally, those who profess a belief in God, whatever his attributes might be, maintain his existence can be apprehended either through the power of faith and revelation, or through the use of reason. Traditionally, the majority of the great religions have adopted their doctrines of God through the former process; however, many subsequently developed rational proofs to support their beliefs.

Opposing this view are individuals who maintain that God does not exist, or at least that knowledge of his existence is beyond the powers of human understanding.

The Case for God's Existence   The classic defence of the case for the existence of God through the use of reason and logic was probably provided by the medieval Catholic theologian, St. Thomas Aquinas (1225 to 1274). Aquinas devised the famous "five proofs" for the existence of God:

> The existence of God can be proved in five ways.
>
> The first and more manifest way is the argument from motion. It is certain and evident to our senses that some things are in motion. Whatever is in motion is moved by another, for nothing can be in motion except it have a potentiality for that towards which it is being moved. By "motion" we mean nothing else than the reduction of something from a state of potentiality into a state of actuality. Nothing, however, can be reduced from a state of potentiality into a state of actuality, unless by something already in a state of actuality. . . .
>
> It is therefore impossible that from the same point of view and in the same way anything should be both moved and mover, or that it should move itself. Therefore, whatever is in motion must be put in motion by another. . . .
>
> Therefore it is necessary to arrive at a First Mover, put in motion by no other; and this everyone understands to be God.
>
> The second way is from the formality of efficient causation. In the world of sense we find there is an order of efficient causation. There is no case known (neither is it, indeed, possible) in which a thing is found to be the efficient cause of itself; for so it would be prior to itself, which is impossible. . . .
>
> To take away the cause is to take away the effect. Therefore, if there be no first cause among efficient causes, there will be no ulti-mate cause, nor any intermediate. If in efficient causes it is possible to go on to infinity, there will be no first efficient cause, neither will there be an ultimate effect, nor any intermediate efficient causes; all of which is plainly false. Therefore it is necessary to put forward a First Efficient Cause, to which everyone gives the name of God.
>
> The third way is taken from possibility and necessity, and runs thus. We find in nature things that could either exist or not exist, since they are found to be generated, and to corrupt; and, conse-quently, they can exist, and then not exist. It is impossible for these always to exist, for that which can one day cease to exist must at some time have not existed. Therefore, if everything could cease to exist, then at one time there could have been nothing in existence. If this were true, even now there would be nothing in existence, because that

which does not exist only begins to exist by something already existing. Therefore, if at one time nothing was in existence, it would have been impossible for anything to have begun to exist; and thus even now nothing would be in existence — which is absurd. . . .

Therefore we cannot but postulate the existence of some being having of itself its own necessity, and not receiving it from another, but rather causing in others their necessity. This all men speak of as God.

The fourth way is taken from the gradation to be found in things. Among beings there are some more and some less good, true, noble, and the like. But "more" and "less" are predicated of different things, according as they resemble in their different ways something which is in the degree of "most," as a thing is said to be hotter according as it more nearly resembles that which is hottest, so that there is something which is truest, something best, something noblest, and, consequently, something which is uttermost being; for the truer things are, the more truly they exist. What is most complete in any genus is the cause of all in that genus; as fire, which is the most complete form of heat, is the cause whereby all things are made hot. Therefore there must also be something which is to all beings the cause of their being, goodness, and every other perfection; and this we call God.

The fifth way is taken from the governance of the world; for we see that things which lack intelligence, such as natural bodies, act for some purpose, which fact is evident from their acting always, or nearly always, in the same way, so as to obtain the best result. Hence it is plain that not fortuitously, but designedly, do they achieve their purpose. Whatever lacks intelligence cannot fulfil some purpose, unless it be directed by some being endowed with intelligence and knowledge; as the arrow is shot to its mark by the archer. Therefore some intelligent being exists by whom all natural things are ordained towards a definite purpose; and this being we call God.[14]

The Case against God's Existence   While there are no known human societies which lack religious beliefs, there have always been individuals in every society possessed of the firm belief that there is no God. Such individuals are commonly termed *atheists*. One of the leading spokesmen for *atheism* was the nineteenth-century German philosopher, Friedrich Nietzsche, who coined the phrase "God is dead":

After the Buddha was dead people showed his shadow for centuries afterwards in a cave, an immense frightful shadow. God is dead: but as the human race is constituted, there will perhaps be caves for milleniums yet, in which people will show his shadow. — And we — we have still to overcome his shadow! . . . When will all these shadows of God cease to obscure us? When shall we have nature entirely undeified! When shall we be permitted to naturalise ourselves by means of the pure, newly discovered, newly redeemed nature?[15]

The Middle Position   At some position between those who believe with certainty in God' existence and the atheists who believe with equal certainty that there is no God, are *agnostics* who profess ignorance in the question of God's existence: perhaps God exists, perhaps he does not; in any case the question is pointless since man can never have the true answer. Such is the agnostic position.

> . . . When I reached intellectual maturity and began to ask myself whether I was an atheist, a theist, or a pantheist; a materialist or an idealist; a Christian or a freethinker; I found that the more I learned and reflected, the less ready was the answer; until, at last, I came to the conclusion that I had neither art nor part with any of these denominations, except the last. The one thing in which most of these good people were agreed was the one thing in which I differed from them. They were quite sure they had attained a certain "gnosis," — had, more or less successfully, solved the problem of existence; while I was quite sure I had not, and had a pretty strong conviction that the problem was insoluble.
>
> Thomas Huxley[16]

> *What Is an Agnostic?*
> An Agnostic thinks it impossible to know the truth in matters such as God and the future life with which Christianity and other religions are concerned. Or, if not impossible, at least impossible at the present time.
>
> *Are Agnostics Atheists?*
> No. An atheist, like a Christian, holds that we *can* know whether or not there is a God. The Christian holds that we can know there is a God; the atheist, that we can know there is not. The Agnostic suspends judgment, saying that there are not sufficient grounds either for affirmation or for denial. At the same time, an Agnostic may hold that the existence of God, though not impossible, is very improbable.
>
> Bertrand Russell[17]

C. The Idea of the Soul

The idea of the soul is in some ways as important a concept in religion as the existence of God. The idea of an afterlife, Heaven, Hell, the worship of God, and indeed much of religion itself would be futile without the added belief that some part of man too is immortal and is ordained for eternal happiness.

The idea of the soul was present in ancient Egypt, one of the world's oldest societies, but it is quite likely that, even earlier, prehistoric man entertained some notion of the existence of souls. It has since become common to virtually all religions.

The problem consists of defining the nature and function of the soul. Primitive groups liken it to, or even equate it with, man's shadow:

> To understand the popular conceptions of the human soul or spirit, it is instructive to notice the words which have been found suitable to express it. The ghost or phantasm seen by the dreamer or the visionary is in unsubstantial form, like a shadow or reflection, and thus the familiar term of the *shade* comes in to express the soul. . . . The Basutos not only call the spirit remaining after death the *seriti* or

"shadow", but they think that if a man walks on the river bank, a croco-
dile may seize his shadow on the water and draw him in. . . .[18]

Possibly the classic definition of the soul in Western philosophy was
provided by the Greek sage Plato, who viewed the soul as a distinct spiritual
substance, superior to the body which imprisons it, and immortal. The Greek
idea is of added importance because it significantly influenced the Christian view.

Plato presents his case in the form of a dialogue or discussion between
the master, Socrates, and his pupil, Cebes:

> Yet once more consider the matter in another light: When the soul and
> the body are united, then nature orders the soul to rule and govern,
> and the body to obey and serve. Now which of these two functions is
> akin to the divine? and which to the mortal? Does not the divine appear
> to you to be that which naturally orders and rules, and the mortal to
> be that which is subject and servant?
>
> True.
>
> And which does the soul resemble?
>
> The soul resembles the divine, and the body the mortal —
> there can be no doubt of that, Socrates.
>
> Then reflect, Cebes: of all which has been said is not this;
> the conclusions — that the soul is in the very likeness of the divine,
> and immortal, and intellectual, and uniform, and indissoluble, and un-
> changeable; and that the body is in the very likeness of the human, and
> mortal, and unintellectual, and multiform, and dissoluble, and change-
> able. Can this, my dear Cebes, be denied?
>
> It cannot.
>
> And it is likely that the soul, which is invisible, in passing to
> the place of the true Hades, which like her is invisible, and pure, and
> noble, and on her way to the good and wise God, whither, if God will,
> my soul is also soon to go, — that the soul, I repeat, if this be her
> nature and origin, will be blown away and destroyed immediately on
> quitting the body, as the many say? That can never be, my dear
> Simmias and Cebes. The truth rather is, that the soul which is pure at
> departing and draws after her no bodily taint, having never voluntarily
> during life had connection with the body, which she is ever avoiding,
> herself gathered into herself; — and making such abstraction her per-
> petual study — which means that she has been a true disciple of
> philosophy; and therefore has in fact been always engaged in the
> practice of dying? For is not philosophy the study of death? —
>
> Certainly —
>
> That soul, I say, herself invisible, departs to the invisible
> world — to the divine and immortal and rational; thither arriving, she
> is secure of bliss and is released from the error and folly of men, their
> fears and wild passions and all other human ills, and for ever dwells,
> as they say of the initiated, in company with the gods. Is not this true,
> Cebes?
>
> Yes, said Cebes, beyond a doubt.[19]

Plato also believed that until the soul was released of sin and
imperfection, it was destined to suffer through continual rebirths, or reincarna-
tions, before being allowed reunion with God. This is remarkably similar to the

Hindu view, which also maintains a belief that the soul undergoes a cycle of rebirths until it is pure enough to return to Brahman.

In Western tradition there is a greater tendency to view the relationship between body and soul as one of harmonious unity. The Jewish view particularly stressed that the living person was an essential blend of spiritual and physical elements. This philosophy was necessary to the view of the afterlife which held that both body and soul were resurrected.

The function of the soul is also in dispute. In early Judaism it was agreed that the soul is the essential spiritual principle of life, truly the breath of life:

> And the Lord God formed man of the dust of the ground, and breathed into his nostrils the breath of life; and man became a living soul.
>
> Genesis 2:7

The Christian outlook was more deeply influenced by Greek philosophy. To the Jewish view, Christianity added the belief that souls are separate entities created by God and placed in physical bodies. The imperfect body tends to corrupt the soul, thus impairing its chances of salvation and reunion with God.

Some Christian denominations dispute the means of the soul's salvation. Some view the soul as having a free will, and thereby having the capacity to determine its own salvation. Others view salvation as a gift from God and hold that the soul is powerless of itself to work out its own salvation. The extension of this argument is *predestination*, the belief that some souls are selected for salvation and others for damnation even before birth. The debate continues in Christian circles.

D. Ethics

Religion concerns itself in great part with the nature of the relationship between man and God. Most religions are also concerned with the proper conduct of man in relation to his fellow men. The study of man's moral behaviour is called *ethics*. In the most simple terms, to act morally or ethically means to act rightly. Of course moral codes vary from society to society; for example, euthanasia is considered acceptable in some societies while the majority in our society appears to condemn it. Whatever form they may take, moral principles exist in every society.

It is entirely possible for men to have ethical standards without the necessity of a religion, but many religions not only prescribe *how* a man should act, they also show him *why* he should act this way.

Each religion has a different approach to this question, hence it would be improper to apply a narrow classification which would find the Eastern religions pitted against those of the West. There are, however, several areas of legitimate contrast.

Essentially, the religions of the West maintain that there is a close or even identical relation between religion and ethics. They regard both their religious and ethical codes as being divinely ordered as, for example, were the Ten Commandments.

On the whole, the Eastern religions, especially Buddhism and Confucianism, tend to avoid attaching a divine will to ethical codes.

The Western religions also emphasize the involvement of man in the world, which they view as basically good. The Eastern religions, though also stressing that right living involves love of one's fellow-man, believe at the same time that man can only achieve happiness through self-discipline, and in some cases self-denial. The physical universe places obstacles in the path of this objective, so it is viewed as a distinct hindrance. This doctrine implies a withdrawal from the affairs of the world and it is one reason why monks and ascetics seem to flourish in the Eastern world.

The lessons given by the great religious leaders in this respect are instructive for the insight they give in understanding the approach taken by the religions they founded:

Buddhist Ethics

103. If one were to conquer a thousand thousand in the battle — he who conquers self is the greatest warrior.

104, 105. Self-conquest is better than other victories, neither god nor demi-god, neither Mara nor Brahma, can undo the victory of such a one, who is self-controlled and always calm.

110. Better than a hundred years of impure and intemperate existence is a single day of moral, contemplative life.

141. Nor nakedness, nor matted hair, nor dirt, nor fastings, nor sleeping in sanctuaries, nor ashes, nor ascetic posture — none of these things purifies a man who is not free from doubt.

165. Thou art brought low by the evil thou has done thyself: by the evil thou has left undone art thou purified. Purity and impurity are things of man's inmost self; no man can purify another.

169. Follow after virtue, not after vice. The virtuous live happy in this world and the next.

197. O Joy! We live in bliss; amongst men of hate, hating none. Let us indeed dwell among them without hatred.

198. O Joy! In Bliss we dwell; healthy amidst the ailing. Let us indeed dwell amongst them in perfect health.

202. There is no fire like lust; no luck so bad as hate. There is no sorrow like existence: no bliss greater than Nirvana [rest].

211. Take a liking for nothing; loss of the prize is evil. There are no bonds for him who has neither likes nor dislikes.

212. From attachment comes grief, from attachment comes fear. He who is pure from attachment knows neither grief nor fear.

214. From pleasure comes grief and fear. He who is freed from pleasure knows neither grief nor fear.

216. From desire comes grief and fear. He who is free of desire knows neither grief nor fear. . . .

223. By calmness let a man overcome wrath; let him overcome evil by

good; the miser let him subdue by liberality, and the liar by truth.

224. Speak the truth, be not angry, give of thy poverty to the suppliant: by these three virtues a man attains to the company of the gods.

386. Him I call Brahmin who is meditative, clean of heart, solitary, who has done his duty and got rid of taints, who has reached the goal of effort. . . .

400. He is the Brahmin who does not give way to anger, who is careful of religious duties, who is upright, pure, and controlled, who has reached his last birth.[20]

Confucian Ethics

Fan Ch'ih asked about humanity. Confucius said: "Love men." (xii, 22).

Tzu Chang asked Confucius about humanity. Confucius said: "To be able to practise five virtues anywhere in the world constitutes humanity." Tzu Chang begged to know what these were. Confusius said: "Courtesy, magnanimity, good faith, diligence, and kindness. He who is courteous is not humiliated, he who is magnanimous wins the multitude, he who is of good faith is trusted by the people, he who is diligent attains his objective, and he who is kind can get service from the people." (xvii, 6.)

Confucius said: "Without humanity a man cannot long endure adversity, nor can he long enjoy prosperity. The humane rest in humanity; the wise find it beneficial." (iv, 2.)

Confucius said: "Only the humane man can love men and can hate men." (iv, 3.)[21]

Jewish Ethics

1. And God spake all these words, saying,

2. I *am* the LORD thy God, which have brought thee out of the land of Egypt, out of the house of bondage.

3. Thou shalt have no other gods before me.

4. Thou shalt not make unto thee any graven image, or any likeness *of any thing* that *is* in heaven above, or that *is* in the earth beneath, or that *is* in the water under the earth:

5. Thou shalt not bow down thyself to them, nor serve them: for I the LORD thy God *am* a jealous God, visiting the iniquity of the fathers upon the children unto the third and fourth *generation* of them that hate me;

6. And shewing mercy unto thousands of them that love me, and keep my commandments.

7. Thou shalt not take the name of the LORD thy God in vain; for the LORD will not hold him guiltless that taketh his name in vain.

8. Remember the sabbath day, to keep it holy.

9. Six days shalt thou labour, and do all thy work:

10. But the seventh day is the sabbath of the LORD thy God: *in it* thou shalt not do any work, thou, nor thy son, nor thy daughter, thy manservant, nor thy maidservant, nor thy cattle, nor thy stranger that *is* within thy gates:

11. For *in* six days the LORD made heaven and earth, the sea, and all

that in them *is*, and rested the seventh day: wherefore the Lᴏʀᴅ blessed the sabbath day, and hallowed it.

12. Honour thy father and thy mother: that thy days may be long upon the land which the Lᴏʀᴅ thy God giveth thee.

13. Thou shalt not kill.

14. Thou shalt not commit adultery.

15. Thou shalt not steal.

16. Thou shalt not bear false witness against thy neighbour.

17. Thou shalt not covet thy neighbour's house, thou shalt not covet thy neighbour's wife, nor his manservant, nor his maidservant, nor his ox, nor his ass, nor any thing that *is* thy neighbour's.

Exodus 20:1-17

Christian Ethics

1. And seeing the multitudes, he went up into a mountain: and when he was set, his disciples came unto him:

2. And he opened his mouth, and taught them, saying,

3. Blessed *are* the poor in spirit: for theirs is the kingdom of heaven.

4. Blessed *are* they that mourn: for they shall be comforted.

5. Blessed *are* the meek: for they shall inherit the earth.

6. Blessed *are* they which do hunger and thirst after righteousness: for they shall be filled.

7. Blessed *are* the merciful: for they shall obtain mercy.

8. Blessed *are* the pure in heart: for they shall see God.

9. Blessed *are* the peacemakers: for they shall be called the children of God.

10. Blessed *are* they which are persecuted for righteousness' sake: for theirs is the kingdom of heaven.

11. Blessed are ye, when *men* shall revile you, and persecute *you*, and shall say all manner of evil against you falsely, for my sake.

Matthew 5:1-11

38. Ye have heard that it hath been said, An eye for an eye, and a tooth for a tooth.

39. But I say unto you, That ye resist not evil: but whosoever shall smite thee on thy right cheek, turn to him the other also.

40. And if any man will sue thee at the law, and take away thy coat, let him have *thy* cloak also.

41. And whosoever shall compel thee to go a mile, go with him twain.

42. Give to him that asketh thee, and from him that would borrow of thee turn not thou away.

43. Ye have heard that it hath been said, Thou shalt love thy neighbour, and hate thine enemy.

44. But I say unto you, Love your enemies, bless them that curse you, do good to them that hate you, and pray for them which despitefully use you, and persecute you;

Matthew 5:38-43

36. Master, which *is* the great commandment in the law?

37. Jesus said unto him, Thou shalt love the Lord thy God with all thy heart, and with all thy soul, and with all thy mind.

38. This is the first and great commandment.

39. And the second *is* like unto it, Thou shalt love thy neighbour as thyself.

Matthew 22:36-39

E. Religion and Sacred Literature

The veneration of sacred literature is common to all world religions. Literature of this type may include books, hymns, chants, poems, letters and any other form of expression which a particular religious community considers integral to its beliefs. Some, like the Moslem Koran, may have been compiled by one individual over a relatively short span of time; others, like the Bible, may have had dozens of contributors and have taken nearly a thousand years to compile.

Sacred writings encompass at least three main areas: they may represent the direct words of God to man; they may represent the words of religious founders and prophets, or revelations made by God through these prophets; or they may record the forms of worship, laws, traditions and historic development of a religious community, at least during its formative period.

The high importance of sacred literature in organized religion is assured for several reasons: for one, it enables the community to unite around a given set of accepted rules and minimizes the chances of doctrinal distortions or squabbles; for another, it guarantees as much as possible the accuracy of the original laws given by God and his prophets to man; again, the presence of such writings enables the community to preserve and pass on their religious traditions from generation to generation, thereby ensuring the continuity of the religion.

It is not possible to deal here with other aspects of sacred writings, such as their significant role in the public education systems of many countries, or their influence on art and literature, which has also been considerable; nor indeed with the bitter controversy in meaning and interpretation they have at times unwittingly spawned. It is safe to conclude they remain among the important elements of most religions.

While the sacred writings of each religion differ greatly in content and scope, it is instructive to discover also many areas of similarity among them.

It may thus prove useful to examine one story common to the religious heritage of many of the world's religions.

The Flood Narratives   The story of a great Flood occurs in the narratives of many of the world's religions, from those of primitive societies to the world faiths. The content and detail of these narratives are in some cases remarkably similar:

The Greek Narrative

> On his return to Olympus, Zeus in disgust let loose a great flood on the earth, meaning to wipe out the whole race of man; but Deucalion, King of Phythia, warned by his father Prometheus the Titan, whom he had visited in the Caucasus, built an ark, victualled it, and went aboard with his wife Pyrrha, a daughter of Epimetheus. Then the South Wind blew, the rain fell, and the rivers roared down to the sea which, rising with astonishing speed, washed away every city of the coast and plain; until the entire world was flooded, but for a few mountain peaks, and all mortal creatures seemed to have been lost, except

Deucalion and Pyrrha. The ark floated about for nine days until, at last, the waters subsided, and it came to rest on Mount Parnassus or, some tell, on Mount Aetna; or Mount Athos; or Mount Othrys in Thessaly. It is said that Deucalion was reassured by a dove which he had sent on an exploratory flight.

Disembarking in safety, they offered a sacrifice to Father Zeus, the preserver of fugitives, and went down to pray at the shrine of Themis, beside the river Cephissus, where the roof was now draped with seaweed and the altar cold. They pleaded humbly that mankind should be renewed, and Zeus, hearing their voices from afar, sent Hermes to assure them that whatever request they might make would be granted forthwith.[22]

The Hindu Narrative

1. In the morning they brought to Manu water for washing, just as now also they (are wont to) bring (water) for washing the hands. When he was washing himself, a fish came into his hands.
2. It spake to him the word, "Rear me, I will save thee!" "Wherefrom wilt thou save me?" "A flood will carry away all these creatures: from that I will save thee!" "How am I to rear thee?"
3. It said, "As long as we are small, there is great destruction for us: fish devours fish. Thou wilt first keep me in a jar. When I outgrow that thou wilt dig a pit and keep me in it. When I outgrow that, thou wilt take me down to the sea, for then I shall be beyond destruction."
4. It soon became a *ghasha* (a great fish); for that grows largest (of all fish). Thereupon it said, "In such and such a year that flood will come. Thou shalt then attend to me (i.e. to my advice) by preparing a ship; and when the flood has risen thou shalt enter into the ship, and I will save thee from it."
5. After he had reared it in this way, he took it down to the sea. And in the same year which the fish had indicated to him, he attended to (the advice of the fish) by preparing a ship; and when the flood had risen, he entered into the ship. The fish then swam up to him, and to its horn he tied a rope of the ship, and by that means he passed swiftly up to yonder northern mountain.
6. It then said, "I have saved thee. Fasten the ship to a tree; but let not the water cut thee off whilst thou art on the mountain. As the water subsides, thou mayest gradually descend!" Accordingly he gradually descended and hence that (slope) of the northern mountain is called "Manu's descent." The flood then swept away all these creatures, and Manu alone remained here.[23]

The Persian Narrative

Man of Shurruppak, son of Ubar-Tutu,
Tear down (this) house, build a ship!
Give up possessions, seek thou life.
Despise property and keep the soul alive.

Aboard the ship take thou the seed of all living things.
The ship that thou shalt build,
Her dimensions shall be to measure.
Equal shall be her width and her length.

On the fifth day I laid her framework.
One (whole) acre was her floor space,
    Ten dozen cubits the height of each of her walls,
Ten dozen cubits each edge of the square deck.
I laid out the shape of her sides and joined her together.
I provided her with six decks,
Dividing her (thus) into seven parts.
Her floor plan I divided into nine parts.

On the seventh day the ship was completed.

Whatever I had of all the living beings I laded upon her.
All my family and kin I made go aboard the ship.
The beasts of the field, the wild creatures of the field,
    All the craftsmen I made go aboard.

Six days and six nights
Blows the flood wind, as the south-storm sweeps the land.
When the seventh day arrived,
    The flood (-carrying) south-storm subsided in the battle,
Which it had fought like an army.
The sea grew quiet, the tempest was still, the flood ceased.
I looked at the weather: stillness had set in,
And all of mankind had returned to clay.
The landscape was as level as a flat roof.
I opened a hatch, and light fell on my face.
Bowing low, I sat and wept,
Tears running down my face.
I looked about for coast lines in the expanse of the sea:
In each of fourteen (regions)
    There emerged a region (-mountain).
On Mount Nisir the ship came to a halt.
Mount Nisir held the ship fast,
    Allowing no motion.

[For six days the ship is held fast by Mount Nisir.]
When the seventh day arrived,
I sent forth and set free a dove.
The dove went forth, but came back;
There was no resting-place for it and she turned round.
Then I sent forth and set free a swallow.
The swallow went forth, but came back;
There was no resting-place for it and she turned round.
Then I sent forth and set free a raven.
The raven went forth and, seeing that the waters had diminished,
He eats, circles, caws, and turns not round.
Then I let out (all) to the four winds
    And offered a sacrifice.
I poured out a libation on the top of the mountain.[24]

The Biblical Narrative

13. And God said unto Noah, The end of all flesh is come before me;
for the earth is filled with violence through them; and, behold, I will
destroy them with the earth.

14. Make thee an ark of gopher wood; rooms shalt thou make in the ark, and shalt pitch it within and without with pitch.

15. And this *is the fashion* which thou shalt make it *of:* The length of the ark *shall* be three hundred cubits, the breadth of it fifty cubits, and the height of it thirty cubits.

16. A window shalt thou make to the ark, and in a cubit shalt thou finish it above; and the door of the ark shalt thou set in the side thereof; *with* lower, second, and third *stories* shalt thou make it.

17. And, behold, I, even I, do bring a flood of waters upon the earth, to destroy all flesh, wherein *is* the breath of life, from under heaven; *and* every thing that *is* in the earth shall die.

Chapter 7

1. And the LORD said unto Noah, Come thou and all thy house into the ark; for thee have I seen righteous before me in this generation.

2. Of every clean beast thou shalt take to thee by sevens, the male and his female: and of beasts that *are* not clean by two, the male and his female.

3. Of fowls also of the air by sevens, the male and the female; to keep seed alive upon the face of all the earth.

4. For yet seven days, and I will cause it to rain upon the earth forty days and forty nights; and every living substance that I have made will I destroy from off the face of the earth.

5. And Noah did according unto all that the LORD commanded him.

6. And Noah *was* six hundred years old when the flood of waters was upon the earth.

7. And Noah went in, and his sons, and his wife, and his sons' wives with him, into the ark, because of the waters of the flood.

8. Of clean beasts, and of beasts that *are* not clean, and of fowls, and of every thing that creepeth upon the earth,

9. There went in two and two unto Noah into the ark, the male and the female, as God had commanded Noah.

10. And it came to pass after seven days, that the waters of the flood were upon the earth.

11. In the six hundredth year of Noah's life, in the second month, the seventeenth day of the month, the same day were all the fountains of the great deep broken up, and the windows of heaven were opened.

12. And the rain was upon the earth forty days and forty nights.

13. In the selfsame day entered Noah, and Shem, and Ham, and Japheth, the sons of Noah, and Noah's wife, and the three wives of his sons with them, into the ark;

14. They, and every beast after his kind, and all the cattle after their kind, and every creeping thing that creepeth upon the earth after his kind, and every fowl after his kind, every bird of every sort.

15. And they went in unto Noah into the ark, two and two of all flesh, wherein *is* the breath of life.

16. And they that went in, went in male and female of all flesh, as God had commanded him: and the LORD shut him in.

17. And the flood was forty days upon the earth; and the waters increased, and bare up the ark, and it was lift up above the earth.

18. And the waters prevailed, and were increased greatly upon the earth: and the ark went upon the face of the waters.

19. And the waters prevailed exceedingly upon the earth; and all the high hills, that *were* under the whole heaven, were covered.

20. Fifteen cubits upward did the waters prevail; and the mountains were covered.

21. And all flesh died that moved upon the earth, both of fowl, and of cattle, and of beast, and of every creeping thing that creepeth upon the earth, and every man:

22. All in whose nostrils *was* the breath of life, of all that *was* in the dry *land,* died.

23. And every living substance was destroyed which was upon the face of the ground, both man, and cattle, and the creeping things, and the fowl of the heaven; and they were destroyed from the earth: and Noah only remained *alive,* and they that *were* with him in the ark.

24. And the waters prevailed upon the earth an hundred and fifty days.

Chapter 8

1. And God remembered Noah, and every living thing, and all the cattle that *was* with him in the ark: and God made a wind to pass over the earth, and the waters asswaged;

2. The fountains also of the deep and the windows of heaven were stopped, and the rain from heaven was restrained;

3. And the waters returned from off the earth continually: and after the end of the hundred and fifty days the waters were abated.

4. And the ark rested in the seventh month, on the seventeenth day of the month, upon the mountains of Ararat.

5. And the waters decreased continually until the tenth month: in the tenth *month,* on the first *day* of the month, were the tops of the mountains seen.

6. And it came to pass at the end of forty days, that Noah opened the window of the ark which he had made:

7. And he sent forth a raven, which went forth to and fro, until the waters were dried up from off the earth.

8. Also he sent forth a dove from him, to see if the waters were abated from off the face of the ground;

9. But the dove found no rest for the sole of her foot, and she returned unto him into the ark, for the waters *were* on the face of the whole earth: then he put forth his hand, and took her, and pulled her in unto him into the ark.

10. And he stayed yet other seven days; and again he sent forth the dove out of the ark;

11. And the dove came in to him in the evening; and, lo, in her mouth *was* an olive leaf pluckt off: so Noah knew that the waters were abated from off the earth.

12. And he stayed yet other seven days; and sent forth the dove; which returned not again unto him any more.

13. And it came to pass in the six hundredth and first year, in the first *month,* the first *day* of the month, the waters were dried up from off the earth: and Noah removed the covering of the ark, and looked, and behold, the face of the ground was dry.

14. And in the second month, on the seven and twentieth day of the month, was the earth dried.

Genesis 6:13-17; 7:1-24; 8:1-14

Miller Services Ltd.

Noah's Ark. The ark rests on Mount Ararat as the receding waters signify the end of the Flood.

F. Religious Personalities

Another aspect of the phenomenon of religion is the presence of great leaders and personalities. This common factor often tends to influence or direct the path a particular religion will take, hence it must be counted as an essential element of religion.

The Priest   On the most basic level is the "priest", or his equivalent, who acts as the religious representative of a specific community. His function normally is to interpret doctrines and Scriptures, and to lead the faithful in their religious services, but sometimes also he is called upon to act as judge, missionary, teacher, confessor, financial expert and arbitrator in domestic quarrels. His presence until most recently has tended to perpetuate the most conservative elements in religion; in conjunction with sacred literature, the role of the priest has been instrumental in preserving the traditional forms of worship of his religion. The Jewish service, the oldest in the world, has remained substantially unchanged for over two thousand years and much credit for this must go to the presence of scribes and rabbis who over the years have preserved Jewish tradition against at times seemingly impossible odds.

The Reformer   On a different level are those rare religious personalities who might genuinely be identified as reformers, prophets or even founders. Often the roles are identical or interchangeable: Mohammed and Jesus may be regarded as prophets, and along with the Buddha they might also be considered as reformers and founders of separate faiths.

Reformers, such as Martin Luther and John Calvin, remain essentially within the religious tradition to which they belong — in this case Christianity — but at the same time they recognize certain areas within this tradition which they feel have stagnated or become corrupt, and which require wholesale reform or change. If the established church rejects or resists these reforms, the result most often is a separation of the original body into several distinct groups or denominations. The Christian church, with two separate Catholic churches (Roman and Orthodox) and numerous Protestant churches, is the most notable example of this phenomenon, but similar splits have occurred in virtually all the world's major religions.

The Prophet   The prophet interprets divine messages which he has received usually in mystical experiences such as dreams or sometimes direct revelations from God. The whole history of Jewish prophecy, from Moses to Jesus has been in this tradition. As the mouthpiece of God, the prophet sounds warning and doom, and where necessary seeks to reform his church:

> 8. Then the Lord put forth his hand, and touched my mouth. And the Lord said unto me, Behold, I have put my words in thy mouth.
> 9. See, I have this day set thee over the nations and over the kingdoms, to root out, and to pull down, and to destroy, and to throw down, to build and to plant.

> 16. And I will utter my judgments against them touching all their wickedness, who have forsaken me, and have burned incense unto other gods, and have worshipped the work of their own hands,
>
> Jeremiah 1:8-9, 16

The Founder   Most important is the religious founder. With the exception of Hinduism, each of the world's great modern faiths began as the personal religious experience of some individual who was able to convey his message to a great number of followers. Of course, the originator of the new faith exercises a great influence in the early development of his religion. Usually he is fortunate in having about him outstanding disciples who are able to spread the message after the death of the founder.

Only one founder — Jesus — has ever claimed to be divine; none-theless, cults which worship their founders have also developed in Buddhism, Confucianism, and to a slight extent, Islam. Judaism alone among the great religions has not developed a founder-cult. As befits the object of such veneration, great legends have grown about the life and personality of the founder, particularly in the prophetic circumstances surrounding his birth. Witness the following two examples:

Buddha

Now the future Buddha had become a superb white elephant, and was wandering about at no great distance, on Gold Hill. Descending thence, he ascended Silver Hill, and approaching from the north, he plucked a white lotus with his silvery trunk, and trumpeting loudly, went into the golden mansion. And three times he walked round his mother's couch, with his right side towards it, and striking her on her right side, he seemed to enter her womb.

On the next day the queen awoke, and told the dream to the king. And the king caused sixty-four eminent Brahmanas to be summoned . . .

"Be not anxious, great king!" said the Brahmanas; "a child has planted itself in the womb of your queen, and it is a male child and not a female. You will have a son. And he, if he continue to live the household life, will become a universal monarch; but if he leave the household life and retire from the world, he will become a Buddha, and roll back the clouds of sin and folly of this world."

From the time the future Buddha was thus conceived, four angels with swords in their hands kept guard, to ward off all harm from both the future Buddha and the future Buddha's mother.

. . . Throughout the whole of Lumbini Grove the scene re-sembled Chittalata Grove in Indra's paradise, or the magnificently dec-orated banqueting pavilion of some potent king.

When the queen beheld it she became desirous of disporting herself therein, and the courtiers therefore took her into it. And there in the flowering Lumbini Grove her son, the future Buddha, was born.

At that very moment came four pure-minded Maha-Brahma angels bearing a golden net; and, receiving the future Buddha on this golden net, they placed him before his mother and said,

"Rejoice, O queen! A mighty son has been born to you." Then the Brahma angels, after receiving him on their golden net, delivered him to the four guardian angels, who received him from their hands on a rug which was made of the skins of black antelopes, and was soft to the touch, being such as is used on state occasions; and the guardian angels delivered him to men who received him on a coil of fine cloth; and the men let him out of their hands on the ground, where he stood and faced the east. There, before him, lay many thou-sands of worlds, like a great open court; and in them, gods and men, making offerings to him of perfumes, garlands, and so on, were saying,

"Great Being! There is none your equal, much less your superior."[25]

Jesus

26. And in the sixth month the angel Gabriel was sent from God unto a city of Galilee, named Nazareth,

27. To a virgin espoused to a man whose name was Joseph, of the house of David; and the virgin's name *was* Mary.

28. And the angel came in unto her, and said, Hail, *thou that art* highly favoured, the Lord *is* with thee: blessed *art* thou among women.

29. And when she saw *him*, she was troubled at his saying, and cast in her mind what manner of salutation this should be.

30. And the angel said unto her, Fear not, Mary: for thou hast found favour with God.

31. And, behold thou shalt conceive in thy womb, and bring forth a son, and shalt call his name JESUS.

32. He shall be great, and shall be called the Son of the Highest: and the Lord God shall give unto him the throne of his father David:

33. And he shall reign over the house of Jacob for ever; and of his kingdom there shall be no end.

34. Then said Mary unto the angel, How shall this be, seeing I know not a man?

35. And the angel answered and said unto her, The Holy Ghost shall come upon thee, and the power of the Highest shall overshadow thee: therefore also that holy thing which shall be born of thee shall be called the Son of God.

36. And, behold, thy cousin Elisabeth, she hath also conceived a son in her old age: and this is the sixth month with her, who was called barren.

37. For with God nothing shall be impossible.

38. And Mary said, Behold the handmaid of the Lord; be it unto me according to thy word. And the angel departed from her.

Luke 1:26-38

Finally, the very life of the founder becomes a focal point of instruction. His career and personality become examples to his followers as ideals in this life. They serve as signposts pointing the road to salvation.

Conclusion

Religion is a universal phenomenon; yet of the hundreds of religions which have emerged since the beginning of time only six — Islam, Christianity, Judaism, Hinduism, Buddhism and Confucianism — can be termed truly universal religions. Only these have been able to burst the limitations of geographical boundaries and exert their appeal to many nations and many races. We have already examined several of the factors responsible for this; it is evident that these religions each share in the essential elements of religion, and while they differ in approach, their objectives remain the same. It is written: "It is a function of religion to help man to want only what he deserves and to enjoy what he gets as being his ultimate value." How the world religions have achieved this goal will be seen in subsequent chapters.

Suggestions For Further Study

1. God has sometimes been depicted as an old man with a white beard. Discuss why this representation of God has been so common in Western religious tradition.

2. The soul has sometimes been defined as "the breath of life". Discuss the possibility that other (non-human) animal, or vegetable, life may also possess souls.

3. Some religions possess a system of ethics without at the same time professing a belief in God. Debate the proposition that a prescribed code of moral and ethical conduct is meaningless without a belief in God and an afterlife.
4. The Flood narrative is but one of several stories common to many religions. Compare other stories, such as that of the Creation, which appear to have their counterparts in the literature of other world religions.
5. In the literature and oral legends of many religions, great stories have developed about the life of the founders. Discuss the similarities in the stories concerning the birth and death of Gautama, Zoroaster, Jesus and Mohammed.

Notes

1Will and Ariel Durant, *The Lessons of History*. New York: Simon and Schuster, 1968, p. 43. © 1968 by Will and Ariel Durant. Reprinted by permission of Simon and Schuster.
2Bliss Carmen, "Vestigia" from *Poems*. Toronto: McClelland and Stewart, 1959, p. 217; New York: Dodd, Mead & Company, 1931; reprinted by permission of The Canadian Publishers, McClelland and Stewart, and Dodd, Mead & Company, and by special permission of the Bliss Carmen Trust, The University of New Brunswick, Canada.
3Hans-Joachim Schoeps, *The Religions of Mankind*. Garden City: Anchor Books, Doubleday & Co., Inc., 1968, p. 6.
4Robert Hume, *The World's Living Religions*. New York: Charles Scribner's Sons, 1952, pp. 7-8. Copyright 1924 Charles Scribner's Sons; renewal copyright 1952 Laura Caswell Hume.
5*Ibid.*, pp. 7-8.
6Schoeps, *op. cit.*, p. 12.
7Hume, *op. cit.*, pp. 7-8.
8E. Durkheim, *The Elementary Forms of Religious Life*. Translated by J. W. Swain. Glencoe, Ill.: The Free Press, Inc., 1948, p. 47.
9Hume, *op. cit.*, p. 8.
10Chandogya Upanishad, III, 14, 1-4; Brihad-Aranyaka Upanishad, IV, 2, 4 as cited in *The Principal Upanishads*, translated by S. Radhakrishnan. New York: Humanities Press, Inc., 1953; London: George Allen and Unwin Ltd., 1953.
11W. H. Auden, *The Portable Greek Reader*. New York: Viking Press, 1963, pp. 68-9.
12*The Holy Koran*, translated by A. J. Arberry. London: George Allen & Unwin Ltd., 1953, chap. LIX, pp. 23-5.
13Thomas Paine, *The Age of Reason*, 1793, as cited in Wm. Sahakian, *Philosophies of Religion*. Cambridge, Mass: Schenkman Publishing Co., 1965, pp. 176-8.
14*"Summa Theologica" of St. Thomas Acquinas*, translated by the Fathers of the English Dominican Province. New York: Benziger Brothers, 1911.
15Friedrich Nietzsche, *Joyful Wisdom*, Thomas Common, trans., from the German *Die fröhliche Wissenschaft*, 1882, as cited in Sahakian, *op. cit.*, pp. 91, 93.
16Thomas H. Huxley, *Science and Christian Tradition*, 1894, *Ibid.*, p. 125.
17Bertrand Russell, *Ibid.*, p. 145.
18E. B. Tylor, *Religion in Primitive Culture*. New York: Harper Torchbook, 1958, p. 14; London: John Murray Ltd., 1871.
19Plato, *Phaedo*, Benjamin Jowett, trans., as cited in Sahakian, *op. cit.*, pp. 295-6.
20The *Dhammapada* as cited in W. D. C. Wagiswara and K. J. Saunders, *The Buddha's Way of Virtue*. London: John Murray, 1912.
21*The Analects* as cited in W. T. de Bary *et al*, eds., *Sources of Chinese Tradition*. New York: Columbia University Press, 1960, pp. 24-5, 28-31. With permission of Columbia University Press.
22Robert Graves, *The Greek Myths*. London: A. P. Watt & Son, 1958, p. 139. By permission of Robert Graves.
23Julius Eggeling, *Sacred Books of the East*, XII. Oxford: Oxford University Press, 1882, pp. 216-18.
24"Akkadian Myths and Epics", translated by E. A. Speiser in James B. Pritchard *Ancient Near Eastern Texts Relating to the Old Testament*, 3rd rev. edn., with Supplement (copyright © 1969 by Princeton University Press), pp. 93-5. Reprinted by permission of Princeton University Press.
25Introduction to the *Jataka* as cited in Henry Clarke Warren, *Buddhism In Translations*, Harvard Oriental Series, Vol. 3. Cambridge, Mass.: Harvard University Press, 1896, 1963. Reprinted by permission of Harvard University Press.

Chapter Two

The Origin of Religion

Any study of man's religious experiences throughout the ages must inevitably come to grips with the problem of the origin of religious belief. How did religion originate? Why does man believe and worship as he does? Ours is by no means the first generation to seek an answer to this important question, for among the early Greeks and Romans there were inquisitive minds grappling with the problem. The answers they found were not always complimentary or flattering to the institution of religion. Some believed religion was born out of the fears and superstitions of men. Others, like the Roman philosopher-poet Lucretius, saw in religious beliefs the roots of many of the social ills which plagued mankind and complained that "religion has persuaded man to many evils".

Yet despite such early attempts to discover a meaning or pattern to religion, it was not until the nineteenth century that a preliminary study was carried out on the origins of religious belief. The wave of enthusiasm for studies in religion coincided dramatically with the new discoveries in the field of science, but the co-existence of science and religion was not to prove peaceful. Skirmishes broke out along several fronts, setting learned scholars from both sides against each other, and culminating in the famous Scopes "monkey trial" of 1925. This trial, which pitted the question of the literal truth of the Bible against the right to present scientific evidence for evolution in schools, was to end in a victory for the scientific community.

But science has also proved useful to religious studies. The work of anthropologists and archaeologists has verified the essential truth of many stories once considered pure fable, such as the Biblical story of the Flood, and has thereby helped fortify the religious beliefs of many people.

New archaeological discoveries have also given rise to new theories of religious origins which can at best be termed speculative. The most famous of these is provided by Erich von Däniken, whose *Chariots of the Gods* suggests the possibility that the earth was visited in prehistoric times by spacemen from other galaxies. These spacemen were then worshipped by primitive earthmen as gods, and in this way religion was born. This view has a certain attraction for those fascinated by the mysteries of unexplained phenomena, though many scholars dismiss it as pure guesswork.

It will be worthwhile to examine other theories concerning the origin of religion to help further our understanding of the roots of religious development.

1. The Impact of Darwinism

Apart from Christianity, religions in other areas of the world had varying answers to the question of the origin of the earth and man. The Hindus, for example, thought the earth began millions of years ago. Still others considered the question of so little importance that they were not troubled by it.

But in the realm of Christianity the publication of Charles Darwin's

The Origin of Species in 1859 was of monumental importance not only for the study of science, but also for a new approach to the study of religion. In 1650 the Biblical scholar, Bishop James Ussher, had computed the creation of the earth, according to the Book of Genesis, as occurring in the year 4004 B.C. To be precise, the process was calculated to have begun on Monday October 23, at exactly 9:00 A.M. For the many who placed implicit trust in the words of Genesis and Bishop Ussher's calculations, the question of the origins of the earth and man was of little interest, since the answer was given so obviously in Genesis.

However, new discoveries in the fields of geology, biology and other sciences cast increasing doubt on an interpretation of the Bible which considered the earth of such recent origin. While many devout Christians, preferring to place their trust in tradition, ignored such objections, the community of scholars was not as easily satisfied.

Darwin's publication was of importance not simply for his theory of evolution, which had already been widely guessed at before his time, but because, for the first time, the theory was supported by a foundation of solid, demonstrable evidence.

Significantly, the book created a furor in the religious community and caused some scholars to undertake a fundamental re-assessment of deeply-rooted beliefs and conceptions of religion.

Evolutionism   Out of this re-appraisal grew a new school of religious thought sometimes known as *evolutionism*. It was an outgrowth of the evolutionary thought of Darwin and Herbert Spencer, and was based on the supposition that the principles of scientific inquiry, especially as related to evolution, could be applied to the study of religion as well. Darwin's theory, briefly stated, purports that:

> 1. Evolution follows a uniform development, obeying similar laws and passing through similar stages, though not at a similar rate.
> 2. Evolution progresses very slowly in time.
> 3. Evolution proceeds in all cases from lower to higher forms.

Applying these principles, the evolutionists concluded that the origin and development of a particular religion could be discovered, and that a similar process of development could be supposed of all the religions of the world. Arranged on an evolutionary scale, all religions were thought to follow a common growth proceeding from primitive stages to the final development of the higher modern faiths.

While it is obvious that religions, like all institutions, develop or change, it is highly questionable whether all religions follow inevitably the lock-step stages prescribed for them by the evolutionists. For example, the tremendous impact of a religious leader such as Moses or Mohammed changes the whole course of a particular religion, and shatters the principle that religions develop by slow and minute steps as the evolutionists claim. Other objections raised on similar evidence have effectively discredited evolutionist philosophy today.

The evolutionist school is nonetheless of importance to the study of religion, particularly in an historical sense, because it inspired a whole generation of students of religion to seek an affirmation of its principles through direct research in the field. The explorations of Europeans in previously unknown areas of the world had brought the religions of other peoples to the attention of the Western world long before Darwin's time, but intensive research in this area did not begin until the latter part of the nineteenth century. Much of what we know of the religions of the world, in both their primitive and modern context, is the product of this time and the study of the origin of religion can properly be said to have had its beginnings with the evolutionist school.

2. The Religion of Prehistoric Man

Recent and continuing work by archaeologists and anthropologists has provided insights into man's ancestral origins more than two million years ago at a time when a primitive, man-like creature *Australopithecus* [*australo* means southern; *pithecus* means ape] began to assert a tenuous existence in Africa. While these creatures, and other successive species in the first one and a half million years of human evolution, have shown traces of a primitive culture, there is as yet no evidence that "religious awareness" formed part of this culture.

Homo Erectus   An exception to this may be a more advanced species known as *Homo erectus* [*homo* means man; *erectus* means upright]. Found near Peking, China, and dated approximately 500,000 B.C. *Homo erectus* is believed by at least a few experts to provide the first indication of human actions based on religious motivations. The evidence for this theory is entirely circumstantial; it lies in the fact that *Homo erectus* practised cannibalism. Other subsequent species, including modern man, have also been known to indulge in this grisly custom, but in the case of *Homo erectus* the truly unusual aspect of this trait concerns the portion of the body he consumed — the brain! It is not known, of course, whether this early cannibalism was for nutritional or religious reasons, but in recent times cannibalism has tended to have magical or religious motivations, and it is thus argued that *Homo erectus* must have had similar motives for his cannibalism. It should be noted that this is not a widely accepted theory.

Neanderthal Man   The first concrete evidence of what we have termed "religious awareness" occurs with the advent of the *Neanderthal* species, whose remains date back to more than 100,000 B.C. Although the species mysteriously disappeared about 30,000 years ago, in the intervening period it developed a culture which reveals a fuller conception of religion through a particular religious rite.
    The evidence for this conclusion is based on more substantial proof than the admittedly doubtful claim of *Homo erectus*; it lies in the burial customs of Neanderthal man. The practice of burying the dead is quite unique to man; while several other species share with man the awareness of the finality of death, no other species is inclined to dispose of their dead in this manner. The common procedure in the animal kingdom is simply to abandon the dead, although some primates give the appearance of mourning the dead for a very brief period.

Burial Customs   Individual burial customs have of course varied with each society and during the different stages of history. Both archaeology and written documents make available a wealth of information on the burial practices of past civilizations. These sources reveal complex, often extravagant, procedures not

Miller Services Ltd.

Indian burial grounds c. 1550. The similarities between these Indian burials and those of prehistoric man are striking.

only in the preparation of the body for burial, but also in the construction of huge sepulchres for its preservation. Perhaps the most perfect examples of these mausoleums are the pyramids of Egypt. In Egypt and many other ancient societies concern for the dead became a preoccupation which consumed much of the time and energy of the living; indeed, our own society is not exempt from indulging in elaborate and costly procedures for the burial of our dead.

Like later societies, Neanderthal man did not bury his dead merely to dispose of them, nor did he bury them haphazardly; it is clear that some form

of ritual probably of religious significance was involved. From excavation of
Neanderthal grave sites in Europe, the Near East, and elsewhere, a pattern of
burial procedures becomes evident. Typical of this pattern is the example of one
of the first Neanderthal finds, a grave discovered at Le Moustier in southern
France in 1908. The remains found were those of a young man, perhaps sixteen
or seventeen years old, who had been carefully buried in a shallow, circular pit.
He had been placed on his side, with his head cushioned on a pile of flints and
resting on his right arm in a typical sleeping position. His legs had also been
bent at the knees, and alongside the body were found carefully worked stone
tools and animal bones. Succeeding excavations at other sites revealed individuals and, in some cases, whole families, buried in a similar fashion.

In the "culture" of *Cro-Magnon man*, the first representative of true
man (*Homo sapiens*) in 30,000 B.C., the burial rites first practised by the
Neanderthals were continued and even refined. The Cro-Magnons, too, covered
the body with ornaments, weapons and food, but of particular interest is their
practice of painting the dead with a colouring substance, red ochre. In some
instances, the grave appears to have been uncovered after burial and the bone
remains then covered with this matter.

Importance   What is the significance of these rites? The answer to this must
naturally be based on speculation, but it is nonetheless possible to make reasonable inferences from the facts available. We may state with some certainty that
the burial rituals had a primarily religious motivation. Perhaps burial merely
provided a convenient way of disposing of the body before decomposition set
in, with all its accompanying problems including that of attracting dangerous
predators, but the weight of the evidence seems to suggest a deeper purpose to
this well-planned and widespread custom. In the first place the discovery of
tools, weapons and food in the grave indicate that prehistoric man believed in
some form of afterlife; the articles were obviously placed in the grave because
it was felt the dead would be in need of them.

If preparation for the afterlife was indeed the purpose of burial, and
physical death was not considered the end of man's existence, what form did
this afterlife take? Again, the artifacts found in the graves provide a clue. The
tools and weapons suggest an existence similar to the one the dead man had
recently departed, since these tools would obviously be used in the same way
and for the same purpose; the animal remains were probably intended to serve
as food in the transitional period from this life to the next; the red pigment may
possibly have had a magical significance. The ochre resembles the colour of
blood; hence, to cover the body in this fashion suggests an attempt to restore
some life-giving vitality to the body for the afterlife.

Secondly, the position of the body in itself may be of some significance.
Many of the bodies discovered had been carefully placed in an east-west
position facing the rising sun, which would indicate that, symbolically, they
expected the body would, like the sun, be resurrected at some point in the future.

Also, the position of the body suggests that prehistoric man may have
conceived of death as a form of sleep — a temporary rather than permanent
state. The taut, flexed body of the deceased would not be arranged in this
manner merely to save space, since land for burial purposes was available in
unlimited quantities.

A third possibility can be suggested: the flexed position of the body appears to simulate the prenatal position of an infant in the mother's womb; if this hypothesis were to be extended, it might very well indicate that the dead were placed in the womb of the earth for future rebirth.

Fear of the Dead   There is also evidence that in some cases the corpses were tightly bound before burial. There are primitive societies today which practise similar rites; the purpose of securely binding the body is to ensure against the return of the dead in some spiritual form. Fear of the dead, of their possible return to haunt the living, plays a large role in the religious thinking of many primitive societies today. While this fear is of the return of the ghost or spirit of the dead, rather than his physical being, the ritual binding of the body at the time of burial is felt to be a deterrent to the return of the spirit as well. A similar motive may have impelled prehistoric man to perform the same rituals on the bodies of his dead. On the basis of this evidence of funeral rites, we may conclude that prehistoric man had a belief in the afterlife.

Prehistoric Gods   Prehistoric man's gods are equally shrouded in conjecture and uncertainty. The fragmentary evidence available on this subject comes principally from two sources: cave paintings and sculptured figurines. The figures represented by prehistoric "artists" shared several common traits of considerable importance: in the first place, all the figures depicted are female; secondly, without exception, the facial features are entirely omitted, and the maternal attributes, the breasts, hips and navel, are emphasized and, indeed, exaggerated. As it is obvious that these figurines, whimsically called "Venuses", are not representative of individual women, it must be assumed that they represent an abstract principle, perhaps motherhood.

It is presumed that since prehistoric life was so brief, and death so certain, the promise of a rebirth or another life must have dominated early man's religious thinking; indeed, it is still an essential factor in religion today. It is in this context that the principle of birth or continuing life is important, for the evidence suggests that the first deity worshipped by mankind was in fact female.

Further weight is lent to this argument when we consider that the male's role in procreation is scarcely found in prehistoric art. This implies that either prehistoric man was ignorant of the male function in procreation, or that he did not attach equal importance to it in comparison with the female role. The latter suggestion appears on the whole to be more plausible.

Early Magic   The element of magic is another facet of the religious awakening of early man. Much of his cave art is preoccupied with the depiction of dead or wounded animals of all types, their bodies pierced successfully by spears and arrows. That these animals do not merely represent a list or tally-sheet of successful hunts is apparent: the time, effort, and resources expended on each painting would make it impossible for a cave artist, or even a fleet of them, to keep pace with the hunters by depicting each new animal brought back to the cave.

The purpose of this artistic exercise was, in all probability, magical. Each painting was a magical hunting rite, designed to ensure the success of each new hunt and to maintain or increase the supply of their game animals. If prehistoric man conceived of a male deity at all, it was most probably in connection

The famous "Venus" of Laussels. The exaggerated proportions suggest her functions were those of a fertility goddess.

Courtesy of the American Museum of Natural History, New York

Prehistoric cave artists at work. Cave paintings had magical rather than decorative purposes.

with the hunting ritual, and this god may have been represented as possessing a combination of human and animal characteristics.

Recent evidence has tended to confirm that these paintings were not intended for public display. Most of the cave paintings found were located in the deepest, darkest, most inaccessible regions of the cave itself, hardly an ideal spot if the artist had intended them to be seen and admired by the rest of the cave-dwelling community.

Furthermore, the most famous of the cave paintings, those at Lascaux, France, have deteriorated badly since the cave was opened for public view. Experts feel that the mysterious green algae which have been eating away at these paintings have developed, for some unknown reason, because of increasing visits of large numbers of people. Similar results are occurring elsewhere, and it must be supposed that their preservation in excellent condition since their creation some 15,000 to 20,000 years ago is somehow directly related to the lack of a large viewing public in prehistoric times. It begins to appear quite likely that few people, beyond the artist himself, had access to the paintings.

The Coming of Modern Man   The evidence of excavations dating from the New Stone Age (10000 to 3000 B.C.) indicates a more widespread and sophisticated religious culture in the human community. Burials appear to have been conducted with more ceremony and, in some cases, included the burial of wives and servants of the dead. For the first time, also, elaborate structures were carved out of sheer rock or caves for the entombment of the dead. Although the evidence is not conclusive, it also appears that enormous stone structures, similar to Stonehenge, were erected to serve some ritual function, perhaps worship or sacrifice.

There is unmistakable evidence as well that a form of nature worship was practised, for the relics found from this period are predominantly concerned with the veneration of the sun, moon, stars and trees.

With the inception of writing, about 4000 B.C., our knowledge of the religious beliefs of early historic societies can be based on some written records. It is, in relative terms, a short span of time until the emergence of the major religions of the modern world. Between the simple primitive rites of prehistoric man and the complex beliefs and rites developed by these religions there exists a large gulf, but it is worthwhile to pause at this point and reflect upon the origins of man's religious awareness.

Conclusion

While no completely accurate conclusions can be drawn concerning the nature and beliefs of these early religions, it is possible to infer some legitimate theories from the available evidence. In summary, it might be said that prehistoric man's religion was designed principally to alleviate his concern and fear in three main areas: birth, death and food supply. The bewildering mysteries of birth and death led in the first case to the conception of a mother goddess who symbolized fertility, in the latter case to a belief in life after death and the development of burial rites. The need for a constant food supply probably accounts for the elaborate cave paintings designed to ensure the success of the hunt through magical means.

It should be re-emphasized that these theories of the origins of religion, based primarily on archaeological research, are by no means the only ones advanced on this subject. In fact, every major religion today has, as part of its cosmology or world view, its own teaching concerning the origins of man and religion. The archaeological view does provide the earliest evidence available. But because of its obvious incompleteness, it leaves certain basic questions unanswered, or at best only partially answered, and, in spite of the phenomenal growth of archaeological research, it is unlikely that archaeological study by itself will ever be able to provide the answers. When did the first religious thought occur? How was it expressed? Of even greater importance, why did man begin to worship? Some scholars feel that the answers lie in the mysterious rituals and practices of primitive people of today, and it is to their study that we now turn.

3. The Religions of Primitive People

The many theories concerning the origin of religion have as their basis the belief that a parallel exists between the religion of primitive societies in the modern world, and that of prehistoric times. The term "primitive" will be used in this book to refer to those contemporary societies which still lack the level of technology generally present in most parts of the world today, and no attempt should be made to impose a moral or ethical judgment on these cultural communities through the use of this term.

Influence of Modern Society   It is in some respects futile to attempt to draw a comparison between the religion of prehistoric man and that of primitive societies of today. There is certainly no society existing today which can exactly parallel that stage of development attained by prehistoric societies. There are several reasons for this.

Prehistoric man was not likely to imagine a culture superior to his own, because in his time none existed; even in the remote possibility that one did, his relative isolation from other groups made him immune to the influx of new ideas, whether political, economic or religious in nature.

Such isolation is unlikely today. There is virtually no primitive society today, regardless of how small or remote, which has not had some degree of contact with the industrialized world. In the jungles of the Philippines, anthropological expeditions have recently made contact with small groups that had been isolated from outside influence for centuries, but these may well be the last outposts of such isolation.

Cargo Cult   More representative of the true nature of the situation was a recent story which emerged from the jungles of New Guinea. The story contains elements of pathos, and is indicative of the extent to which modern society has influenced even the most primitive of religions. Combining loyal devotion to traditional rituals, with faith in the Christian God to whom they had been introduced by Europeans, several thousand New Guinea tribesmen developed a new cult: the Cult of the Cargo. This cult hinges on the belief that the wealth possessed by the white man is due primarily to special ritual practices he performs for his God, and that if the members of the cult could only discover these rituals, the treasures of the earth would open for them also. To ensure their success, the tribesmen began to imitate the white man's practices, without a true understanding of their significance; in one area, they staked out an airfield in the middle of the jungle, convinced that now hundreds of transport planes would land and deliver to them a precious cargo of assorted tools and weapons. The results have proved disappointing, but have not as yet diminished the following of the cult.

The tribesmen have no knowledge of assembly lines or machine technology, consequently they reason that it must be God who brings these gifts to men once the magic formula is found. In pursuance of this belief, the cultists have built banks, hoping that money would magically appear; they have raised thousands of dollars hoping to buy the President of the United States; they have sought at various times to purchase Queen Elizabeth and the Pope, and in several locations in New Guinea and Australia have raised monuments to ensure the arrival of the cargo. All these ventures have met with repeated failure, but the cult's spirits and hopes remain undaunted. This is but one of many examples which serve to indicate the deep influence of the modern world on primitive conditions and beliefs.

After this point has been clarified, it is still possible to draw some general principles from the religion of primitive peoples which may be instrumental in answering the fundamental questions posed earlier in this chapter. In studying the various theories of the origin of religion, certain beliefs may suggest parallels with the great religions of today. It is not intended that the following synopsis be regarded as an attempt to portray a neat scheme in the evolution of religion from a primitive to a higher stage; this sort of evolutionary classification of religions has been rightfully discredited.

The noted Dr. Samuel Johnson thought the study of primitive
religions for this purpose an exercise in futility; he once asked an acquaintance:

> And what account of their religion do you suppose to be learnt from
> the savages? Only consider sir, our own state. Our religion is in a
> book: we have an order of men whose duty it is to teach it: we have
> one day in the week set apart for it, and this in general pretty well
> observed; Yet ask the first ten gross men you meet, and hear what
> they can tell of their religion.[1]

There is some truth in this. It may be difficult, if not impossible, for us
to understand fully the structure and function of primitive man's religion.
Nevertheless, if we are to understand properly the great religions of today, it is
essential to have a basic knowledge of the forces which first gave rise to the
idea of religion.

Characteristics of Primitive Religion   It is possible to say of primitive peoples
in various parts of the world that they share certain common characteristics, and
that among these is the need to act in unison with the group or society to which
they belong, particularly where social customs or religious beliefs are concerned.
While there are innovative individuals in this as in every other cultural community, it is a general trait of primitive man that he submits to the beliefs of
the group at large and in this connection tradition and custom are most important. This may help us to understand why change comes slowly to primitive
societies, and why their mode of life has remained substantially unchanged for
centuries.

The attachment of such importance to traditional customs and beliefs
and rituals, may also aid us in understanding the nature of primitive man's
religious beliefs. His religion is an integral part of his culture, and while it may
have no clearly rational basis to him, as part of his overall beliefs, it serves on
one level at least to provide satisfactory answers to his psychological needs. It
seems to provide stability, security and defence against fear of pain, death or
the unknown.

It should be remembered when studying the common features of
primitive religions that no matter how unusual or imaginative these beliefs may
appear to us, they have a practical value which enables primitive man to cope
with the external forces in his life.

A. Psychological Origins

Role of Fear   Was it fear that first created in man the need for religion? Confronted with this question two thousand years ago, the Roman Petronius
concluded affirmatively that "fear created the gods". This view echoes the
commonly held opinion that fear of unknown powers, mysterious events,
hunger and, most of all, eventual death is a natural horror to man. There is an
obvious element of truth in this; prehistoric man was confronted with an
imposing series of obstacles, environmental and psychological, over which he
exercised relatively little control. Existence in such conditions was in itself
fortuitous, and fear of an untimely end to this fragile hold on life may well have
been predominant in his thoughts. Primitive societies today display to some
degree a similar inability to control the environment about them, and it may be

fair to assume that fear of external forces forms an important part of primitive man's psychological makeup. Does religion then serve to calm these fears and to provide man with answers to the uncontrollable and unexplainable powers which confront him daily? Recognizing the scientific limitations which face primitive man, we may readily assert that religion provides the most satisfactory explanation for these mysterious forces which he is able to devise.

Lucretius, writing in Roman times, attributed the rise of religious beliefs to the fear and ignorance of men:

> They observed how the array of heaven and the various seasons of the year came round in due order, and could not discover by what causes all that came about. Therefore their refuge was to leave all in the hands of the gods, and to suppose that by their nod all things were done. They placed the gods' habitation in the sky, because through the sky the night and the moon are seen to revolve, and the . . . sun, rain and snow, winds, lightning and hail, rapid roarings and threatening throes of thunder. . . . O unhappy race of mankind, to ascribe such doings to the gods and to add thereto bitter wrath! What groans did they then create for themselves, what wounds for us, what tears for generations to come![2]

Modern science has managed, to a large extent, to narrow the circle of what at one time were such "unexplainable" phenomena. In this manner, many of the sources of insecurity and fear, which may well have given rise to religious feelings, have been eliminated. It is no longer usual for people to think of thunder or lightning as being directly caused by the gods.

Nonetheless, man has not succeeded in eliminating fear, though perhaps it exists in more subtle forms. In most societies, religion still serves to comfort man and provide him with a sense of security. Since it functions in those areas where science for the most part has yet to find the answers, religion is not, as some suggest, used as a "crutch" to support human frailty. In this sense it bridges the gap between what is known and what is merely guessed at. In this sense too, there is a similarity between modern industrial society and that of the primitive.

Bronislaw Malinowski, who believes that fear is an essential element in religions, summarizes the two positions:

> The call to religion arises out of an individual crisis, the death which threatens man or woman. Never does an individual need the comfort of belief and ritual as in the sacrament of the viaticum (rite given to a person in danger of death), in the last comforts given to him at the final stage of life's journey — acts which are well-nigh universal in all primitive religions. These acts are directed against the overwhelming fear, against corroding doubt, from which the savage is no more free than the civilized man. These acts confirm his hope that there is a hereafter, that it is not worse than the present life; indeed, better.[3]

There are nevertheless serious flaws in this argument and it may be presumptuous to overestimate the importance of the role which fear of death plays in religious determination.

It may be argued for example that before there can be fear, there must exist something which is the object of that fear, something possessing powers greater than man himself. Clearly these powers exist beyond the physical level, dwelling perhaps in the realm of the spiritual or psychological; in any case, they are beyond the level at which man can cope. In primitive religions, these ultra-physical powers which man has conceived, which he fears and which he worships, are now commonly referred to by a term originating with the Melanesians of the Pacific — *mana*.

B. Mana

The word mana, though Melanesian in origin, is used to describe an element of belief existing in many primitive religions around the world. Basically mana is an invisible, powerful force which can exist in anything (animal, vegetable or mineral) acting as an independent force or in conjunction with the ordinary powers already possessed by the object in which it exists.

A scientist might describe it as potential energy, or electricity, ever ready to act, and capable of being transmitted to another object. A man might possess mana himself if he is especially skilled at a particular task; for example, if a quarterback consistently throws the football skilfully and accurately he might be said to possess mana. A manufacturer who continues to produce high-grade hockey sticks which perform well might also possess this power. Conversely, this special power might exist in inanimate objects, the football or the hockey sticks themselves, in which case the mana would have been transmitted to these objects from their maker or user. It should be understood that mana is not a "spirit" or "being", and has no will of its own. It is merely that power existing in some object which enables it to achieve a high degree of excellence in the special task for which it has been designed.

As early as the nineteenth century, a European observer living with the Maoris in New Zealand gave this description of mana:

> Virtue, prestige, authority, good fortune, influence, sanctity, luck are all words which, under certain conditions, give something near the meaning. . . . mana sometimes means a more than natural virtue or power attaching to some person or thing, different from and independent of the ordinary natural conditions of either. . . . I once had a wild pig which, before heavy rain, would always cut extraordinary capers and squeak and run like mad. . . . all the Maori said it was . . . a pig possessed of mana: it had more than natural powers and could foretell rain.[4]

Source of Mana   To the primitives, the source of mana is not usually of importance. Some cults believe the power flows from gods or spirits, others that it simply exists naturally as an independent force; still others believe that proper ritual observances will succeed in obtaining mana for themselves. The matter of common importance to all cults, the test of whether an object possesses mana, is if it works. As a hypothetical example, a primitive may find a stone of unusual shape, and, believing it to possess mana, will bury it in his fields; if the next crop is bountiful, the object's power will have been proven, since it has transmitted this power to the fields or the crops. It is a situation analogous to a hockey coach who wears a new hat to a game; if his team happens to win, there will be a strong tendency to wear the same hat to all subsequent games, particularly if the team makes a habit of winning.

Of course mana can degenerate into mere superstition or belief in luck. The distinction is this: that in the mana cults this belief gives rise to certain powerful religious feelings and sensations which help to influence man's decisions and determine his behaviour. The so-called Cargo Cults described earlier in this chapter may be seen as a social manifestation of the belief in the power of mana. There are indeed scholars who claim that religion may have had its origins in a powerful impulse such as the belief in mana.

Among these, Professor William Howells states:

> There is probably no better example of how a basic religious feeling — a sense of the special, the supernatural — takes form as a religious belief than in the idea of mana.[5]

C. The Sacred

Another phenomenon which may explain the origin of religion is a feature common to many primitive beliefs: the reverence, fear, or respect which many primitives have for "sacred" or "holy" objects. The German religious scholar Rudolf Otto introduced the idea of the "sacred" by outlining his belief in the theory that man first comprehended God through a direct emotional experience; that is, man was moved by some force exterior to himself to grasp the concept of God. Objects which had a demonstrable connection with God would then also become sacred or holy. Like mana, holiness is not confined to any particular object. To primitives, gods are holy, but so are the priests and prophets who serve them, the trees, caves and temples where they dwell, or even the ground on which they walk. The Bible itself includes many examples of the "holiness" of certain objects because of their connection to God. In one, Moses, facing the burning bush, is warned:

> Come no nearer! Remove the sandals from your feet, for the place where you stand is holy ground.

Similarity to Mana   There is indeed a striking resemblance between Otto's idea of the sacred and the primitive concept of mana, tne chief distinction being Otto's belief that God is the source of holiness or sacredness, whereas mana is self-existent. Others argue, however, that it is quite possible to have a reverence for the holiness of certain objects without simultaneously holding a concept of God; this very point has in fact been observed of several primitive religions. One author has noted that

> Real religion may exist without a definite conception of divinity . . . but an idea of God without the conception of the holy is not a religion.

D. Animism

Another belief similar to, though quite distinct from, mana, generally prevalent among primitives is termed *animism* [Lat. *anima* means soul]. This belief proposes that all sorts of objects, living and non-living, have spirits or souls in them. An early student of primitive religion, E. B. Tyler, popularized the term animism and defined it as "the belief in spiritual beings". Tyler believed that animism may have been the phenomenon responsible for the origin of religious belief. He argued that the unsophisticated primitive would have been struck by the significance of death; particularly puzzling would have been the difference between a corpse and a living being, and he must have concluded that the latter contained some vital element which gave it life — perhaps a soul.

Dreams   Secondly, the primitive would be puzzled by the mystery of dream experience. In dreams he might see himself performing acts perhaps great distances away from where he actually lies sleeping; when he awakens, he realizes

The belief in "ghosts" is prevalent in modern as well as primitive societies. In this case trick photography was used by spirit photographer William Hope to give a ghostly impression.

Miller Services Ltd.

it was not his material self which performed these acts, and would therefore conclude that a spiritual or "ghostly" representation of himself was responsible.

Souls   According to Tyler then, primitive man developed his idea of the soul from his experiences of dreams, visions and death. It was but a simple step to project this concept to animals and other natural objects, a step which probably led to nature worship. Also, since the souls of the departed still existed after the death of the body, a special regard had to be shown them, and this too led to a phenomenon very common to primitive societies: ancestor worship. The tendency to believe in ancestor worship, and in particular nature worship, is easily understood in view of the strong identification of the primitive with his environment, and his natural inclination to view external objects such as trees and stones as possessing an existence similar to his own. Tyler indeed stated that in the mind of the primitive, "all nature is possessed, pervaded, crowded with spiritual beings".

Animism, as distinct from mana, represents a belief that the soul can have a shape, a will, purpose and feelings. In fact, souls are quite like people in their range of moods and sentiments; they can be in turn charitable, capricious, angry, violent, vain, loyal or generous, and one must always be careful to remain in their good graces, or suffer the consequences.

E. Totemism

An important aspect of the widespread concept of spirits is the belief that spirits exist in stones, plants and animals. This belief, sometimes known as *totemism*, carries with it a number of religious variations. In some cases, the objects themselves are actually worshipped; in others, it is the spirits of the objects which are worshipped, or perhaps the objects may simply be symbols of the power which is truly worshipped. In most cases, the object or animal is not worshipped at all, but merely venerated or respected. It is difficult at times to draw a distinction between worship and veneration, but perhaps some modern examples may clarify the point: in Roman Catholic services the religious images, or icons, are not worshipped in themselves, but rather venerated as symbolic representations of Christ or the saints. The Moslems profess a similar reverence for the Black Stone housed in the Kaaba at Mecca, although this respect falls short of worship.

Respect for Nature   The close relationship in primitive thought between man and animal may be evident even in our modern society; our own mythology abounds with favourite stories of bird-women, vampires, mermaids, minotaurs, etc. In many areas of the Christian world, hunters and farmers still ask forgiveness of the animal they are about to kill, or the tree they are about to fell. We have only to recall the all-too-familiar scene in the typical Western movie where the bereaved cowboy bids a last farewell to his dying horse with the promise they will meet again "at the last roundup". It should not be surprising that in other parts of the world snakes, lizards and dragons are the focus of similar regard.

The high veneration of nature may eventually have led the individual, or a whole tribe, to ally itself with a particular animal or plant, such as a bear, a turtle or a maple tree, which then became the *totem* of that tribe. In many

cases the totem came to be regarded in future generations as the ancestor of the
tribe and its protector, and exerted an influence on its social and economic
attitudes as well. The Australian aboriginals, for example, must select their
wives from tribes outside their own totem group; also it is forbidden of a tribe
to kill or eat their totem animals, although normally it is permitted to hunt the
totem animal of another clan.

Freud   Some eminent scholars believed the concept of *totemism* might be the
key in explaining the origin and development of religion. Among these was the
noted psychoanalyst Sigmund Freud, who proposed a complex and unusual
theory of how the idea began. According to Freud, in the first social stages of
man, the leader of the clan kept all the eligible women to himself, and discouraged any interest in the females among his sons. The sons then staged a
revolt, murdered the hapless father, and (says Freud) *ate* him! The sons
presently became aware of their guilt for performing such a foul deed, and
were forced to seek a new father-figure, in an animal form. They were also
forced to renounce their father's women, thereby making it necessary to find
their mates from outside the group. One author has unkindly suggested that
while this might be good Freud, it is wretched anthropology.

   While some religious students still hold to the importance of the
concept of totemism, more likely it is a corollary or an outgrowth of the more
widespread belief in animism.

   We have examined some, though by no means all, of the most important theories concerning the origin and growth of religion. Whatever form this
origin may have taken, primitive man was, and still is, concerned with harnessing
this religious force so it will exercise its power on his behalf. As a result he has
developed certain rituals and practices designed to aid him in achieving his goal.
Several of the many practices instituted by man to control this power follow
below.

F. Tabu

Tabu or Taboo, another term of Melanesian origin, is among the most common
of the ritual beliefs connected with primitive religion. In the modern sense, it
has come to mean something forbidden, but for the primitive, it has a much
greater significance. Normally, tabu is associated with the force of mana or the
powers exhibited by the spirits in animism, and refers to the special awe or
reverence in which certain acts or individuals are held. A person especially
charged with sacred mana, usually a chief, must be treated as tabu and all
profane persons, those not of the same status, must keep a proper and respectful
distance. This is true of many Polynesian and African tribes, where the chief is
in fact treated with such reverence, and a similar phenomenon may even be
observed among the Hindus of India, where an outcaste, or a member of the
lower-caste, must avoid contact with Brahmins, those of the upper-caste.

Victims   In the former cases particularly, it is felt that this special individual
is so charged with power that to touch him or his belongings is not only
dangerous, but perhaps fatal. So real is the fear of these individuals among the
common people, in fact, that there have been many recorded cases of men and
women dying of sheer fright on having learned that they had unwittingly been

desecrated by a person who was tabu. Such incidents would then serve to further reinforce the belief among the rest of the community.

Not only are special individuals or objects considered tabu, but often unclean or impure objects as well. Members of certain social classes are automatically considered tabu, as for example the Hindu outcastes noted above. Individuals might become impure by receiving an overdose of mana, perhaps as a result of having trod on the same ground upon which the chief set foot. Among objects or special occurrences likewise considered tabu might be a newborn baby, a recently widowed woman, sharp weapons, hair, blood and certain foods. Indeed, the list is virtually endless, and it requires an alert mind and a vigilant eye to avoid committing daily some transgression against tabu.

Purification   For those unlucky enough to be the victims of tabu, or to have come in contact with a forbidden object, the usual means of breaking the curse is through some form of purification rite. This commonly takes the form of fasting, shaving the hair or washing the body, but may also involve painful rituals such as walking on fire, opening wounds in the body, and where an entire tribe feels threatened because of a particularly serious offence, the death penalty may be imposed on the offending individual.

A further means of avoiding personal disaster may be sought through possession of certain objects which may best be described as "good-luck" charms. Such objects, perhaps an unusually shaped stone or piece of wood, are thought to possess special powers in themselves to ward off misfortune for their owners. In religious terms, these charms are usually known as *fetishes*. In the Western world, a comparable situation exists for those individuals who seriously believe that a rabbit's foot can bring good luck. Of course, in our society such individuals tend to be very limited in number, whereas in primitive societies they would constitute a majority of the community.

It may be seen that to the primitive, the existence of tabu forms a very real and very serious danger to his well-being. It should be noted in closing that tabu in some form or other exists in virtually all societies, including our own, particularly in the form of superstitions which may be regarded either in jest or in earnest, but which are a part of our daily reality nevertheless.

G. Magic

So deeply rooted is the idea of magic as a function of primitive religion that at one time it was thought to explain the very origin of religion. Few would maintain this today, but magic remains possibly the best-known and least understood aspect of primitive religion. In a very broad sense, we may define magic as the attempt to control the power of spiritual beings or the course of events by the performance of special acts or the utterance of specific words. This definition makes a distinction between magic and ordinary prayer in that the latter merely requests the aid of some power, while magic attempts to force the cooperation of this power.

Types of magic   Very generally, magic may be classified under two broad categories: productive (or sympathetic) magic, and destructive (or black) magic. The former, which may include as its function success in such things as hunting, farming, fishing, rain-making and love could be performed either by individuals for their own private purposes, or by special magicians where the tribe or community as a whole is concerned. A typical example of hunting magic would be the cave paintings of prehistoric man in which the magic ritual consisted of imitating the desired effect, that is, the killing of the game animals; similar hunting rituals, including pre-hunt ceremonies and feasts, are still practised in various parts of the primitive world. In an example of farming magic, if a farmer wished his grain to grow very tall, he might stand in the middle of his fields, speak to the budding plants, then jump as high as he is able, thereby encouraging the plants to grow at least as high as he has jumped.

The following is a typical rain-making ritual practised among aborigines of Australia:

> It is universally believed by the tribes of the Karamundi nation, of the Darling River, that rain can be brought down by the following ceremony. A vein in the arm of one of the men is opened and the blood allowed to drop into a piece of hollow bark until there is a little pool. Into this is put a quantity of gypsum, ground fine, and stirred until it has a consistency of a thick paste. A number of hairs are pulled out of the man's beard and mixed up with this paste, which is then placed between two pieces of bark and put under the surface of the water in some river or lagoon and kept there by means of pointed stakes driven into the ground. When the mixture is all dissolved away, the blackfellows say that a great cloud will come, bringing rain. From the time that this ceremony takes place until the rain comes, the men are tabooed from their wives, or the charm will be spoiled, and the old men say that if this prohibition were properly respected, rain would come every time that it is done. In a time of drought, when rain is badly wanted, the whole tribe meets and performs this ceremony.[6]

Black Magic   The second form, black magic, generally has as its aim destruction of property, or personal injury, sickness and death. Black magic may also be performed by individuals or specialists, but most often such acts are not approved by the community, and the magician or sorcerer who performs such acts is commonly ostracized from the group. In Western society, until the eighteenth century, the magician or witch who practised black magic was not merely banished, but often punished or killed, as the infamous Salem witch trials and hangings of the seventeenth century attest.

Black magic also employs imitative actions to produce the desired results. We are all familiar with the sorcerer who makes an image of his enemy, perhaps of mud or wax, and ritually sticks it with pins, or twists an arm, hoping to produce similar effects in the living individual. In some parts of the world, this is commonly known as voodooism, in others, witchcraft.

Reasons for Success   The most amazing aspect of all is that this practice will, on frequent occasions, actually produce the desired results. Often, it is sufficient for the sorcerer to merely inform the victim of what is about to happen to him for the luckless individual to actually begin to suffer the terrible things which were described.

A question persists regarding magical practices: why are they still believed in when they must so often be doomed to failure? Why will the farmer continue to practise magic on his field if on several occasions his grain does not grow to the desired height?

Basically there are four reasons for this. In the first place, the desired results occur with enough frequency to keep many people believing in the power of magic, even if in reality these results were achieved because of other reasons; secondly, some deception or trickery may be played by the magician on the rest of the community; thirdly, even with the large number of failures, it is the tendency of the mind to remember more clearly and emphasize the successes rather than failures; finally, the magician can always claim that the proper ritual procedures or incantations were not followed.

Several of these defences may be seen in a typical story reputed to have occurred in Papua and witnessed by several Europeans. A sorcerer attempted to bring a dead dog back to life, but failed. To the Europeans present, this was a clear example of the failure of magic; however, the magician argued that the proper rituals had not been observed. He was supported in this argument by other Papuan natives who suggested that the dog was indeed returning to life when an uninvited guest appeared, spoiling the result, and rendering the dog again to its lifeless state. Despite the obvious failure, neither side really changed opinion for common sense prevailed in both cases. To the Papuan, the failure of the magic was due to very logical reasons — the breaking of the ritual; to the Europeans, the failure could also be explained logically, though the reasons and conclusions were of course very different. Thus through logic, or fear or whatever other motives may be at work, magic continues to exert great influence in primitive religion today.

Voodoo initiates must trace this diagram on the site where they are to make sacrificial offerings. They must first taste the blood of the sacrificial animal, then place it in the centre of the cross, to be burned.

H. Shamanism

A third method used to control the powers of the spirit world is through the practice of *shamanism*. A *shaman* is a medium (not to be confused with an ordinary priest or medicine man, each of whom has a specific role to perform in his society) who has special contact with the spirit world. Shamanism is widespread among Eskimos and North American Indians, as well as many African tribes. The modern shaman is the equivalent of the Celtic Druids before the Roman occupation of Britain over two thousand years ago. Among their tribes, the Druids were expected to serve in the multiple role of priests, doctors, judges and teachers and to perform a host of other minor duties; the shaman basically carries out similar functions in his community today.

It is believed that the shaman, because of some special powers he possesses, is capable of visions wherein he is able to convey the wishes and commands of the spirit world to humans. He may be required also to contact the spirits of the dead for certain families, and to carry back the messages of the dead to their living kin, much as certain mediums in our society are presumed to do.

A shaman in action. Shaman Ntopa, holding a python in one hand, swallows fire which feeds his "controlling spirits".

Miller Services Ltd.

The power possessed by the shaman does not of course prevent his accepting payment for his services. He is generally well-paid and often among the wealthiest men in the community. Among the North American Indians, the shaman often doubled as a medicine man as well, particularly when the official medicine man was unable to cure illnesses thought to be caused by evil spirits, and hence beyond the power of ordinary medicine. The following excerpt outlines the ritual undergone by a typical shaman in performance of his function. The speaker is a shaman of the Gitksan Indians of British Columbia explaining his role in curing an illness:

> My first patient was a woman, the wife of chief Gitemraldaw. . . . She was seriously ill, had been for a long time, and she had been treated before by other medicine men, but without avail. I was called in to see if I could do something for her. So I went into her house and instructed the people there to light a fire first. As I began to sing over her, many people around me were hitting sticks on boards and beating skin drums for me. My canoe came to me in a dream and there were many people sitting in it. The canoe itself was the Otter. The woman whom I was doctoring sat with the others inside this Otter canoe. By that time about twenty other halaaits (medicine men) were present in the house. . . . I told them "Spread the fire out, into two parts, and make a pathway between them." I walked up and down this path four times while the other halaaits kept singing until they were very tired. Then I went over to the couch where the sick woman was lying. . . . I placed my hand on her stomach and moved round her couch, all the while trying to draw the canoe out of her. I managed to pull it up very close to the surface of her chest. I grasped it, drew it out, and put it in my own bosom. This I did. Two days later, the woman rose out of bed; she was cured.[7]

The state of ecstasy experienced by this shaman is typical of the self-induced state of euphoria frequently employed by most shamans. In some tribes, this condition is induced by means of drugs, while in others no external stimulant is required. Whether or not the shaman is actually responsible for the visions or the cures, he personally has no doubt that he has been visited by spirits and that his performance has been directly responsible for warding off the evil spirits which cause the disease of his patients. Consequently, among such communities, the shaman is an individual of special significance, one whose high talents are frequently employed by the ordinary mortal so that he might avoid the natural or supernatural calamities which would otherwise befall him.

4. Case Studies in Primitive Religion

For a more complete understanding of the nature of primitive religion, it would be most useful to glance at a specific religion and relate the various aspects of primitive belief to one another. A brief analysis of the religions of the North American Indians and Eskimos will largely serve this purpose.

A. North American Indians

Many of the individual characteristics of primitive religion are evidenced in the
beliefs and rituals of certain North American Indian religions, particularly those
of the pre-Columbian period, before the pervasive influence of the white man
was felt in full.

With regard to the origins of the earth and man in Indian mythology,
there are as many legends as there are tribes. Some legends explain that the
Indian came from beneath the ground, or from the sunset in the west; others,
that he came down from the sky by means of a ladder, or from the bowels of
a volcano. The Ojibways of Canada, in their version of the genesis, believe that:

> The Muskrat swam down into the waters of the universe and gathered
> together bottom mud until an island rose to the lapping waves, and
> thus the earth was made.[8]

The Winnebago Indians also have a creation myth:

> What it was our father lay on when he came to consciousness we do
> not know. He moved his right arm and then his left arm, his right
> leg and then his left leg. He began to think of what he should do and
> finally he began to cry and tears began to flow from his eyes and fall
> down below him. After a while he looked down below him and saw
> something bright. The bright objects were his tears that had flowed
> below and formed the present waters. . . . Earthmaker began to think
> again. He thought: "It is thus, If I wish anything it will become as I
> wish, just as my tears have become seas." Thus he thought. So he
> wished for light and it became light. Then he thought: "It is as I
> supposed; the things that I have wished for have come into existence
> as I desired." Then he again thought and wished for the earth and
> this earth came into existence. Earthmaker looked at the earth and he
> liked it but it was not quiet. . . . (After the earth had become quiet) he
> thought again of how things came into existence just as he desired.
> Then he first began to talk. He said, "As things are just as I wish them
> I shall make one being like myself." So he took a piece of earth and
> made it like himself. Then he talked to what he had created but it
> did not answer. He looked upon it and he saw that it had no mind or
> thought. So he made a mind for it. Again he talked to it, but it did not
> answer. So he looked upon it again and saw that it had no tongue.
> Then he made it a tongue. Then he talked to it again but it did not
> answer. So he looked upon it again and saw that it had no soul. So he
> made it a soul. He talked to it again and it very nearly said something.
> But it did not make itself intelligible. So Earthmaker breathed into its
> mouth and talked to it and it answered.[9]

While it is difficult to discover any consistent pattern in these myths
which might be applied to Indian religion as a whole, it is possible to find some
common underlying themes such as the widespread story of the great Flood,
similar in outline to the Flood story preserved in the tradition of many European
and Asian religions. However, it is in the Indian concept of the supernatural and
the relationship of man to the spirits that the similarities in Indian religion
become more evident.

Numerous Indian tribes believed in a sacred power or force very much similar to the Melanesian concept of mana. To the Sioux, this power was described as *wakan*, while the Iroquois termed it *orenda*, and the Algonkians *manitou*. Anything acting out of the ordinary or displaying unusual qualities was considered to have this power, and indeed the terms could be applied to the sun, the stars, trees or even spirits. Most tribes believed in specific gods as well, with the sky god usually supreme among the Plains Indians, while among some others the sun god held a similar role:

> Every object in the world has a spirit and that spirit is *wakan*. Thus the spirits of the tree or things of that kind, while not like the spirit of man, are also *wakan*. *Wakan* comes from the *wakan* beings. These *wakan* beings are greater than mankind in the same way that mankind is greater than animals. They are never born and never die. They can do many things that mankind cannot do. Mankind can pray to the *wakan* beings for help. There are many of these beings but all are of four kinds. The word *Wakan Tanka* means all of the *wakan* beings because they are all as if one. *Wakan Tanka Kin* signifies the chief or leading *Wakan* being which is the Sun. However, the most powerful of the *Wakan* beings is *Nagi Tanka*, the Great Spirit who is also *Taku Skanskan*. *Taku Skanskan* signifies the Blue, in other words, the Sky. . . . Mankind is permitted to pray to the *Wakan* beings. If their prayer is directed to all the good *Wakan* beings, they should pray to *Wakan Tanka*; but if the prayer is offered to only one of these beings, then the one addressed should be named. . . . *Wakan Tanka* is like sixteen different persons; but each person is *kan*. Therefore, they are only the same as one.[10]

The Afterlife   Many tribes held a concept of an afterlife, one very similar to an earthly Heaven or Hell. They believed that man possessed an immortal soul which would receive its just rewards or punishments in the afterworld. For individuals who had faithfully followed the customs of their society, the rewards were attractive:

> The rewards to which they look forward consist principally in feasting, and their chastisement in the privation of every pleasure. Thus they think that those who have been faithful observers of their laws will be conducted into a region of pleasures, where all kinds of exquisite viands will be furnished them in abundance, that their delightful and tranquil days will flow on in the midst of festivals, dances, and women; in short, they will revel in all imaginable pleasures.[11]

On the other hand, the punishment for the unfortunate lawbreakers was most unpleasant:

> [They] will be cast upon lands unfruitful and entirely covered with water, where they will not have any kind of corn, but will be exposed entirely naked to the sharp bites of mosquitoes, that all Nations will make war upon them, that they will never eat meat, and have no nourishment but the flesh of crocodiles, spoiled fish, and shell-fish.[12]

The Sun Dance   Among some tribes it was believed that each male had a guardian spirit (often animal) with whom he sought to communicate by way of a personal vision. In order to induce this vision, males, both adolescent and adult, frequently resorted to chewing on the narcotic cactus root, the peyote, or to physical endurance tests such as prolonged fasting, repeated cold baths or vigorous physical activity to the point of exhaustion, followed by long periods of solitude from other humans.

Some Plains tribes, like the Cheyenne, went to the extreme of self-torture in their version of the Sun Dance. This dance, requiring three days' preparation, usually lasted from two to four days, during which time the dancer, in order to induce a vision, fasted and sometimes offered some blood sacrifice from his own flesh such as a finger or a toe.

Canadian Plain Indians also had a version of the Sun Dance, a ritual which was made illegal by the Canadian government after the Riel Rebellion of 1885. The Sun Dance however, continued to be popular, and was celebrated secretly, until the Canadian government finally lifted the ban in the revision of the Indian Act in 1951.

The Mandans   One further example of the intensity of religious fervour experienced by some Indian groups will suffice. George Catlin, an American painter passing through the West in the 1830's, observed rituals similar to the Sun Dance among the Mandans, a highly sophisticated tribe. Every year among the Mandans when a number of their young men were prepared to be initiated to full manhood, they were forced to undergo a four-day religious ritual called *okipa.*

In a large building in full view of other adults, the initiate allowed his flesh to be pierced and ropes skewered through the flesh both in his chest and back; he was then hoisted high above the ground and left hanging by his flesh; at this point, several warriors on the roof of the building would twist the ropes by which the candidate was suspended, causing him to spin until he became unconscious. The initiate was now allowed to fall to the ground, and here he lay until regaining consciousness. The ordeal was far from over; he was now forced to crawl to an area where the medicine man ritually chopped off one of his fingers with a hatchet; this was followed by several warriors who proceeded to pull the initiate around the room by the ropes until they tore through the flesh, at which point he was officially admitted to manhood.

As an amazing footnote to this, Catlin remarks that those initiated in this fashion appeared to feel no pain whatever throughout their ordeal.

It appears that this practice was not restricted to North America alone. Observers have noted the similarity between the nineteenth-century Mandan ritual and similar practices among Hindu devotees of the God Shiva in some parts of India in this century.

Whether the initiates performed in a religiously induced state of self-hypnosis or another reason exists for this stoic self-control, it does point out the immense power the force of religion can exert over the mind and spirit of the individual.

The Navaho   Among North American Indians today, the Navaho of the south-western United States is the most numerous, and one of the most religious. "Religion enters every phase of Navaho life," writes an anthropologist. "It is scarcely out of their mind from the time they are old enough to understand anything about it."

If one of the functions of religion is to provide the individual with a sense of security, the Navaho religion serves its purpose well. To the Navaho, the insecurity of illness is a constant in his life, although his concept of illness goes beyond the purely physical. A doctor might term some of this illness psychosomatic. The causes of illness are numerous indeed: vicinity to lightning or an object struck by lightning; hunting certain animals; mischievous spirits of the dead; evil witchcraft. All these and many more are, to the Navaho, reasons for illness. The discovery of the specific cause and the cure of the illness lies at the root of Navaho religious ritual.

There are dozens of chants and ceremonials calculated to retain good health and dispel disease, but most of them centre around the power of the local shaman or medicine man. It takes many years for a person to reach the status of full-fledged shaman (known as a "singer" among the Navaho), but the occupation can be highly rewarding in a monetary as well as spiritual sense, as a shaman may receive up to five hundred dollars per case for his services. The actual ritual involved in curing a sick person is much the same as that outlined earlier by the Gitskan shaman, including similar perfunctory trances and chants.

The average Navaho is much concerned about his religion, and observers have noted that the men spend almost one-third of their waking hours, and perhaps twenty per cent of the family income on religion, or activities connected with religion. As with most other religious groupings, it is most difficult to assess Indian religion or to say exactly why certain practices exist, but in substance the characteristics of their religious practices display a remarkable blend of primitive traits with features which can compare favourably with those held by most of the modern world faiths.

B. Eskimos

Most Eskimos of today populate the northern coast of North America from Labrador in the east to Alaska in the west, although a small group inhabits the Siberian region of Asia. The religion of the North American Eskimo can most accurately be described as animistic, although, as in most other areas, the arrival of the white man's society has resulted in the breakdown and blending of Eskimo society with that of the newcomer. This is especially true in the area of religion; consequently, it is becoming increasingly difficult to reconstruct a true picture of the original, undiluted Eskimo belief. A story related by one of the first missionaries to the Eskimos illustrates the point: the missionaries told the Eskimos the biblical story of Creation; many of the Eskimos at first refused to accept this, stating that one of their deities, Raven, had created the world. After much debate, a compromise was finally struck when one Eskimo was reported to have said "Very well, God made the world, but Raven made it first."

Basically, Eskimo religious activity centres about the attempt of the individual or the group to exert some control over the power of the spirits. To achieve this control it was necessary to develop elaborate rituals and ceremonies. Since hunting forms such a dominant part of Eskimo life, these religious rituals are especially concerned with the relationship between the hunter and the animals he hunts. Indeed, an observer has noted that "much of what might be termed religion . . . lay in attempts to placate, cajole, compel, or otherwise to influence the animal in question."

Eskimos do, however, have a prescribed set of religious beliefs, myths and deities. According to one such myth, the world is flat, and is supported by four pillars, one in each corner; it is believed stray hunters or boats fall off the edge at times. Although there appears to be no solid concept of the underworld among more contemporary beliefs, older sources suggest that this belief may have originally been present; in some cases it was believed that the aurora borealis was the underworld, or the abode of the spirits. Generally, however, Eskimos rarely concern themselves with the beyond since it is this world which is of importance.

In Eskimo religion it is believed that man possesses two distinct spirits or souls in his body. The first, the immortal spirit, remains in the body until death, then departs forever to the spirit world; the second, the "name" soul, also leaves the body at death for the spirit world for a time, but returns to the body of a descendant. It is also believed that illness is caused by the temporary loss of these souls, and the principal function of the Eskimo shaman is to recover these souls for the owner. It is interesting to note that among many North American Indian tribes a similar belief existed, although here there was by no means a standard number of souls per person, and as many as three or four souls could inhabit the body at the same time. In both cases, it was believed that souls could be lost or stolen by sorcerers or witches, and also that at death, the souls permanently left the body.

The Eskimos also believe in major deities, of which three are of importance: *Sila*, lord of the air, who has the power, like fate, of punishing man's sins; *Sedna*, goddess of the water, who is queen of the sea mammals and grants luck in hunting when the proper ritual has been performed in her honour; finally there is the God of the Moon, who has various powers including the granting of success in hunting.

Shaman   To control the powers of these deities, the Eskimo shaman is of unsurpassed importance. In Eskimo terms, the shaman is primarily concerned with curing illness, but may also be called upon to foretell the future, find lost articles or missing persons, revive the dead, control the weather or practise black magic and murder. Because of the sort of influence, both positive and negative, which the shaman has tended to wield, some efforts have been made by government authorities to undermine his power or to banish him altogether from Eskimo society. This has been more easily accomplished where Christianity has taken root, but in other areas, his power remains effective.

The Eskimo shaman works much in the same manner as shamans of other religions, relying principally on chants, rituals and trances to cure diseases. Since it is believed that illness is brought on through temporary loss of the soul, the function of the shaman's ritual is to induce the soul to return. Some individuals who believe the "name" soul is to blame for sickness even go to the extent of changing names, hoping thereby to pick up a "name" soul which may help them avoid or get rid of the sickness. When the shaman is called in for help, and if he succeeds, he is normally paid a substantial fee, usually geared to the income of the patient; if he fails he is still usually offered a token payment, since it is believed that the shaman has the power to cause illness as well as to cure it, and few wish to risk his anger.

The shaman inspires confidence in his powers through a collection of magic tricks which include pulling a long rope out of one's mouth, ventriloquism

Catholic Truth

Eskimo children making the sign of the cross. The influence of Christianity has greatly eroded much of the traditional Eskimo religion.

to prove conversation with the dead, bleeding from non-existent wounds and elaborate seances. To ordinary mortals, no further proof of the shaman's validity is usually required.

In sum, we may say that the religion of the Eskimo places a great stress on the rigours of daily living, and while the powers of the spirits are very real, he attaches greater value to the problems of this earth. Because of his great identification with nature, the cycle of birth and death is a natural, non-mysterious process, and we are not surprised to learn that while he exhibits a natural fear of death, this fear is neither excessive nor hysterical.

Like the North American Indian, the culture of the Eskimo has been eroded by the influence of the white man. Despite some recent signs of resurgence and the fact that many groups have clung proudly and tenaciously to their traditional beliefs, Indian and Eskimo religious culture is in part extinct. Much of what we have noted already belongs to history.

Conclusion

The validity of studying primitive religions as a key to understanding the origin of religion may be questioned in some areas, especially as each of the great religions of the modern world have their own teachings to explain this origin.

Equally, it may not be valid to compare the religion of modern primitives with that of early man for the purpose of deciding how religion began, since the two societies may be vastly different. Nevertheless, a study of the theories summarized in this chapter may be invaluable in providing clues from which the origins of religious beliefs may ultimately be discovered. At the very least they provide a framework for a better understanding of our own religious values and practices.

Suggestions For Further Study

1. Lucretius believed fear and ignorance were responsible for the origins of religion. To what did Homer, Hesiod, Ovid and other Greek and Roman scholars attribute its origins?
2. Some scholars seriously doubt that fear of death is among the important elements in religious motivation. What arguments would support this view? Are there some societies in which fear of death is less prevalent than in others?
3. Animal and nature-worship is still evident in modern societies, though perhaps not in such obvious forms. List some of the different ways in which modern society practises these beliefs.
4. Is is possible to equate modern man's persistent tendency to superstitious practices with primitive man's belief in magic and fetishes? In what respects are the two different?
5. Select a Canadian Indian tribe, modern or historic, and analyse its religious beliefs.
6. Account for the importance of the shaman or medicine man in virtually all primitive societies.

Notes

[1]H. L. Shapiro, ed., *Man, Culture and Society*. New York: Oxford University Press, 1960, p. 316.
[2]Lucretius, *De Rerum Natura*, pp. 1183 ff. Translated by W. H. D. Rouse. Cambridge, Mass.: Loeb Classical Library, Harvard University Press, 1924.
[3]B. Malinowski, *Magic, Science and Religion*. London: The Society for Promoting Christian Knowledge, 1954, pp. 60-61. Reprinted by permission of the Society for Promoting Christian Knowledge, London.
[4]Shapiro, *op. cit.*, p. 316.
[5]W. Howells, *The Heathens*. New York: Doubleday & Co., 1948, p. 25.
[6]A. W. Howitt, *The Native Tribes of South-East Australia*. London: The Macmillan Co., 1904, pp. 396-7.
[7]M. Barbeau, *Medicine Men on the North Pacific Coast*. Ottawa: Information Canada, 1958, pp. 45-8. Reprinted by permission of Information Canada.
[8]F. Symington, *The Canadian Indian*. Toronto: McClelland and Stewart, 1968, p. 18. Reprinted by permission of The Canadian Publishers, McClelland and Stewart Limited, Toronto.
[9]Paul Radin, "The Winnebago Tribe", in 37th *Annual Report of the Bureau of American Ethnology*, Smithsonian Institute, Washington, D.C., 1963, pp. 212-13.
[10]J. R. Walker, "The Sun Dance and Other Ceremonies of the Oglala Division of the Teton Dakota", American Museum of Natural History, Anthropological Papers, vol. XVI, part II. New York: American Museum of Natural History, 1917, pp. 150-3.
[11]From the book *Man's Rise to Civilization As Shown By the Indians of North America from Primeval Times to the Coming of the White Industrial State* by Peter Farb, p. 158. Copyright © 1968 by Peter Farb. Published by E. P. Dutton & Co. Inc. and used with their permission.
[12]*Ibid.*, p. 158.

Chapter Three

The Religions Of
The Ancient World

THE religions of the ancient world, like the empires in which they thrived, no longer exist. Two thousand years have passed since the worship of Osiris and Zeus was witnessed among men. Even in their time the ancient faiths of Egypt, Greece and Rome were inadequate to carry out the role of moral leadership which is a function of great religions that have endured. So, obsolete, they died.

Their study is included in this volume because they were instrumental in preparing the soil in which some of the major religions — particularly Judaism, Christianity and Islam — were to flourish.

Further, they may be viewed as case studies of religions which evolved from primitivism, to polytheism, to an early concept of monotheism. They provide, in this sense, examples of religious evolution.

As these religions began to lose their primitive characteristics, they exerted an appeal beyond the purely local or tribal level. They became important national religions with the ability to facilitate the social and political, as well as religious, unification of large numbers of people.

Among the many ancient religions which provided transitional links from the stage of primitive religion to that of some of today's world religions are those of Egypt, Greece, Rome and Persia, which will be examined in this chapter.

The religion of Persia, Zoroastrianism, is in many ways unlike the other state religions of its time: it developed, through the medium of prophetic revelation, a belief in monotheism, a moral and ethical creed, and it survives to this day to a limited extent. It is included here because, more than any other ancient faith, it made significant and lasting contributions to Judaism, Christianity and Islam.

1. The Religion of Egypt

Origins "For beneath and above everything in Egypt was religion," observes one author in describing the life-cycle of one of the world's oldest societies. In recent times we have become accustomed to excluding religion from other sectors of daily activity; the separation of church and state in many Western societies is now an established fact. To the people of the ancient world, and most especially to the Egyptians, such a separation was unthinkable. Five thousand years ago, every sphere of Egyptian life — social, political and economic — was directly dependent on religion and the will of the gods.

As with most ancient religions, that of Egypt was the offspring of primitive elements. The Egyptian attributed god-like qualities to the elements of nature — trees, stones, rivers — and worshipped accordingly. In the dry, parched climate in which he lived, life was most difficult and hence most precious to the Egyptian. He held all forms of life to be sacred, even the lowly vegetable, and represented each of these in the form of a god. Indeed, there were, in total, over three thousand gods in ancient Egyptian religion.

The most popular of these early gods were the animal forms of bulls, crocodiles, goats, cats and dogs. Anubis, god of the dead, for example, was represented as a jackal; Thoth, a god of wisdom, was a baboon; Horus, the sky-god, was a falcon. The Egyptians in fact retained their reverence for animals throughout their history, and with the exception of the pig, they were hesitant to use animals as sacrificial victims at any time.

As time passed, the Egyptian became more knowledgeable about the world around him. As the mechanics of nature became less mysterious, his appreciation of man increased. The physical representation of the gods was affected by this new outlook: man and nature became fused in one form. Anubis, for example, retained his jackal's head, but now had a human body; human bodies were likewise given to Thoth, Horus and many other deities. In time, the important gods such as Ra and Osiris became entirely human in form, although this evolution was slow in developing. This process of change from *zoo-morphism* (animal shape) to *anthropomorphism* (human shape) evolved over thousands of years.

Myths   The Egyptians developed the earliest myths for which there is documented evidence. Myths can be defined as the attempt by people to explain the world around them by ascribing the phenomena of nature to supernatural or immortal beings, or mortal but superhuman heroes. Myths exist in virtually every culture, but are most prevalent in those societies that lack a scientific knowledge of the universe.

The Egyptians had several legends to explain the creation of the universe and man. According to one myth, in the beginning only the sky existed, and from the sky god all the gods and other forms of life came. On the earth at first there was only the ocean, but Ptah, "Lord of the Truth" and the creator-god of ancient Egypt, created an egg from which came the sun and the moon. From the sun-god, Amon-Ra, came the air, from the air came the earth, from the earth came the Nile, and from the Nile, Egypt. Thus was Egypt, in religion and in fact, "the gift of the Nile".

The Gods   The sun and the Nile gave life to Egypt, so it is not surprising to find Egypt's chief deities connected with these forces. In most areas of Egypt, in various forms and under various names, the sun-god was of pre-eminent importance. Amon, Aton, Ra — all these were names for the god who was the giver of life to Egypt. Like the cycle of life and death, the sun was reborn in the east each morning, and according to mythology, died in the west each night. It was for this reason that the dead in Egypt were buried in the lands west of the Nile.

Most communities in Egypt retained their loyalty to local gods, in the same sense perhaps that many European Christian communities today have patron saints. However, so powerful and necessary was the influence of the sun, that the cult of the sun-god absorbed the chief gods in most of these communities. However, other names were not totally erased, which helps to explain the various names by which Ra is called.

In the royal palace the worship of the sun was especially prominent.

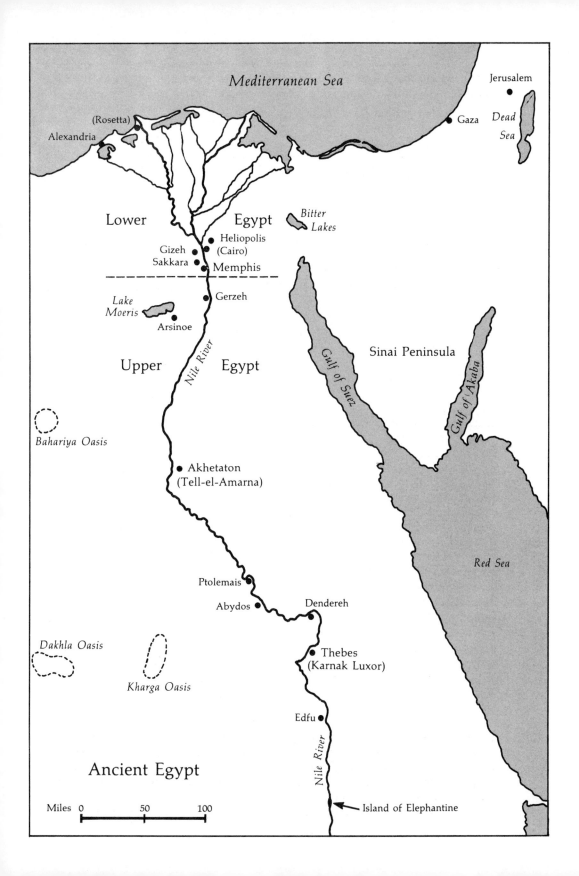

Mediterranean Sea

Jerusalem

(Rosetta)

Alexandria

Gaza

Dead
Sea

Lower   Egypt

Bitter
Lakes

Heliopolis
(Cairo)

Gizeh
Sakkara

Memphis

Gerzeh

Lake
Moeris

Arsinoe

Gulf of Suez

Sinai Peninsula

Gulf of 'Akaba

Upper   Egypt

Nile River

Bahariya Oasis

Akhetaton
(Tell-el-Amarna)

Red Sea

Ptolemais

Abydos

Dendereh

Dakhla Oasis

Kharga Oasis

Thebes
(Karnak Luxor)

Edfu

Ancient Egypt

Nile River

Miles   0   50   100

Island of Elephantine

Each morning the Pharaoh was awakened by the chanting of hymns to Ra, and
in the temples similar hymns were sung:

> Hail to thee, Ra, Lord of Truth
> whose shrine is hidden, Lord of the gods;
> the Creator in his boat:
> at whose command the gods were made:
> Atum [Aton], maker of men:
> supporting their works, giving them life.
>
> Lord of wisdom whose precepts are wise:
> at whose pleasure the Nile overflows:
> Lord of mercy most loving:
> at whose coming men live:
> opener of every eye:
> proceeding from the firmament:
> causer of pleasure and light:
> at whose goodness the gods rejoice.[1]

Osiris   The worship of the Nile is connected with the cult of Isis and Osiris, a
myth which personified also the eternal conflict between life and death, good
and evil, creation and destruction. It exercised a profound influence on every
Egyptian from peasant to Pharaoh.

Osiris, as the son of Heaven and Earth, succeeded to the throne of
Egypt. He took his sister Isis as his wife; Egyptian ethics accepted as normal
procedure the wedding of brother and sister in the royal family. Although
Osiris governed his country wisely, he aroused the jealousy of his brother Seth,
who slew him and cut the body into twelve pieces, scattering them throughout
Egypt. The faithful Isis collected the parts, except for the generative organ, and
brought him back to life. However, because he had lost the power to reproduce
life, Osiris was forced to abdicate the world of the living, and descend to the
Underworld where he became the god of the dead and the judge of souls.
Horus, the son of Isis and Osiris, avenged his father's death by slaying Seth
and taking for himself the position of Pharaoh, ruler of the earth.

The myth of the death and resurrection of Osiris was of great religious
importance: other religions subsequently adopted the idea of resurrection as
part of their own beliefs. The Egyptians also drew the parallel between the
resurrection of Osiris and the annual flooding of the Nile, and thereby linked
Osiris as god of the Nile.

The myth also profoundly influenced the mortuary beliefs of the
Egyptians themselves. In life, each Pharaoh assumed the symbol of Horus, and
in death he expected to become an Osiris. At his death the priests prayed:

> As Osiris lives, so shall he also live;
> as Osiris died not, so shall he also not die;
> as Osiris perished not, so shall he also not perish.

The Afterlife   The world of the dead ruled by Osiris was not conceived by
the Egyptians as a gloomy or desolate place. Indeed, if anything, they expected
to lead a life more glorious than on earth. More than any other people known
to history, the Egyptians were preoccupied with the idea of death, and spent a
good portion of their lives preparing for it.

It was believed in early times that each individual possessed a body and two souls. The true soul, the *ba*, was depicted as a human-headed, bearded bird which lived in the heart and departed the body at death. The body was also animated by the *ka*, sometimes thought of as the person's "double", which also left the body at death.

Both the ba and the ka were expected to return to the body in order to escort it to the underworld. As the soul's return might be months or even years after death, it was essential that the body be preserved in some way to make it recognizable. In early times the procedure was simple: the body was laid on its left side in a shallow grave in the sand. Remarkably, because of the hot, dry sands, the bodies were preserved for a long time. Indeed, some bodies buried in this manner have retained their skin and hair to this day. Unfortunately, because the graves were so shallow, and because the deceased's valued possessions were buried with him, the graves were frequently plundered.

Among wealthier Egyptians, graves became increasingly more complex structures, starting with stone shafts and culminating with the building of the enormous pyramids for the Pharaohs. At the same time, new measures had to be taken to preserve the body; in this way the process of embalming, or mummification, began.

Herodotus, a Greek historian, gives a vivid description of this procedure:

> . . . as much as possible of the brain is extracted through the nostrils with an iron hook, and what the hook cannot reach is rinsed out with drugs; next the flank is laid open with a flint knife and the whole contents of the abdomen removed; the cavity is then thoroughly cleansed and washed out, first with palm wine and again with an infusion of pounded spices. After that it is filled with . . . every other aromatic substance with the exception of frankincense, and sewn up again, after which the body is placed in natrum, covered entirely over, for seventy days. . . . When this period, which must not be exceeded, is over, the body is washed and then wrapped from head to foot in linen cut into strips and smeared on the other side with gum. . . . In this condition the body is given back to the family, who have a wooden case made, shaped like the human figure, into which it is put. The case is then sealed up and stored in a sepulchral chamber, upright against the wall. . . .[2]

Judgment of the Dead   The Egyptian view of the afterlife is of immense significance: it provides possibly the world's oldest concept of Heaven, Hell and the "Day of Judgment". The enchanted fields for deserving souls were thought to exist far to the west or in the Milky Way, a formation resembling a "heavenly Nile" to the Egyptians. There the land was fertile, and filled with shade trees; the manual work was done by slaves and the grain grew yearly to great heights.

Not all souls were deserving, however, and these were destined to a terrible fate; those which were not devoured by savage animals were thrown into a pit of fire where they suffered greatly.

The decision as to whether the soul merited reward or punishment was made on the Day of Judgment and depended on the individual's earthly conduct. This belief that individuals had to answer in the afterlife for their conduct in this one was developed in Egypt centuries before Israel or Persia conceived a similar idea.

The Judgment of the Dead. The gods Anubis and Horus weigh the heart (on left) against the Feather of Truth. If the heart proved to be the heavier of the two, it was condemned to punishment.

On the Day of Judgment the dead were brought before the throne of Osiris, and forty-two other judges who were to decide their fate. Each soul was to proclaim its virtue, after which the god Anubis placed the soul on a scale against the weight of a feather. If the soul proved to be the heavier of the two, it was deemed guilty by Osiris.

Magical symbols and rites were connected with the Day of Judgment. Among Egyptians, the favourite magical token was the scarab beetle. It was thought that if one of these ornaments was placed on the body, the soul would be guaranteed a happy judgment. Because the magic spells and incantations were easily available to most Egyptians, it was believed that the great majority of souls received a favourable judgment.

In proclaiming its virtue, the soul was expected to declare the "negative confessions" before Osiris and the other judges. These confessions, together with the whole collection of spells and prayers, is known as the "Book of the Dead". The following give some idea of these confessions:

1. I have not acted sinfully towards men.

2. I have not oppressed the members of my family.
3. I have not done wrong instead of what is right.
4. I have known no worthless folk.
20. I have not defrauded the gods of their cakes.
23. I have not polluted the sacred waters of the god of my city.
32. I have not fished with bait made of the bodies of fish.
33. I have have not stopped water when it should run.
35. I have not extinguished a fire when it should burn.[3]

Religion and Ethics   Egyptian religion possessed a great deal more ethical content than other religions of the period, and certainly more so than that of the later Greeks and Romans. That the Egyptians did not always live up to their beliefs was due then as now to the shortcomings of human nature rather than of the religion. In their everyday conduct, Egyptians believed that a system of truth and justice was operative in the world, and if man did not transgress against the rules of society, good order would be established. This principal rule of conduct was called *maat,* and its precepts are clearly seen in the Book of the Dead. The same faults of conduct condemned in the modern world were also penalized by the gods of Egypt. Among these are:

murder
    16. I have not committed murder.
    17. I have not given an order to cause murder.
theft
    10. I have not filched the property of the lowly man.
lies
    42. I have not uttered falsehood.
adultery
    47. I have not lain with another man's wife.
blasphemy
    9. I have not belittled god.

Beyond these are other commandments which can be considered acts of mercy:
    14. I have not permitted any man to suffer hunger.
    6. I have not made excessive work to be done for me on any day.[4]

It may be seen that the Egyptians had a highly developed ethical code, the breaking of which would lead directly to eternal punishment for the transgressor. In the Egyptian scheme of things, personal morality, social justice and religious beliefs were already inseparable practices.

Akhenaton   At some time in the fourteenth century B.C., a profound religious revolution transformed Egypt under the rule of the Pharaoh Akhenaton. During his reign the Pharaoh outlawed all other gods in Egypt with the exception of the sun-god, Aton, and thereby launched possibly the first venture into monotheism in the history of man. It was to prove of short duration.

The sun-god had always been highly regarded in Egypt and his worship had always been linked with the most prosperous periods in Egyptian history. Akhenaton, however, at some point became convinced not only that Aton was the chief god of Egypt, but the only god.

He replaced his given name Amenhotep, "Amon rests", with the name
by which he is known to posterity, Akhenaton, which means "Spirit of Aton."

He also aroused the anger of the priests of Egypt by going to the
point of removing the names of all other gods from the monuments and temples
under his dominion, and erecting a great new capital city in honour of Aton.

The nature of Akhenaton's spiritual attachment to Aton may be seen
in his eloquent hymn of praise. Indeed, there is a striking resemblance between
Akhenaton's hymn in praise of Aton, and the later Jewish 104th psalm:

The dawning is beautiful in the horizon of heaven
O living Aton, beginning of life!
When thou risest in the eastern horizon of heaven
Thou fillest every land with thy beauty;

When thou settest in the western horizon of heaven,
The world is in darkness like the dead.
Thou makest darkness and it is night
Wherein all the beasts of the forest do creep forth.

Every lion cometh forth from his den,
All serpents they sting.
Darkness reigns,
The world is in silence,
He that hath made them has gone to rest in his horizon.
The young lions roar after their prey;
They seek their meat from God.

Bright is the earth,
When thou risest in the horizon.

The two lands are in daily restivity,
Awake and standing upon their feet,
And thou hast raised them up.
Their limbs bathed, they take their clothing;
Their arms uplifted in adoration to thy dawning.
Then in all the world they do their work.
The sun ariseth, they get them away,
And lay them down in their dens.
Man goeth forth unto his work,
And to his labour until the evening

How manifold are all thy works!
They are hidden from before us,
O Lord, how manifold are thy works!
While thou wast alone:
O thou sole god, whose powers no other possesseth.
Thou didst create the earth according to thy desire.
Men, all cattle large and small,
All that are upon the earth,
That go about upon their feet;
All that are on high,
That fly with their wings.

> In wisdom hast thou made them all;
> The earth is full of thy creatures.[5]

The Final Stage   There have been some attempts to show a direct relationship between Akhenaton's concept of monotheism and that developed by the Hebrews; however, there is no concrete evidence to support such a conclusion. Moreover, Akhenaton's religious reformation did not outlive him. With his death, the priests of Egypt reverted to their former polytheistic practices and eradicated the memory of Akhenaton's short-lived reforms.

The old religion reclaimed its former dominant status, although it remained in gradual decline until the advent of Christianity in the first century A.D. eclipsed it forever. In its time, it served its function in society admirably. It also left an important legacy of religious concepts to the religions yet to develop.

As exemplified by the cult of Osiris, the religion of Egypt "had a longer history than that of any other religious faith. . . . It continued as an effective force down to the official suppression of paganism by the Roman Emperor Theodosious (A.D. 379 to 395). . . . And it is perhaps not surprising that, when the cult of Osiris finally disappeared from the world, it was succeeded by the religion of Christ, the new saviour-god, who had also died and rose to life again.[6]

2. The Religion of Greece

The religions of the ancient Greeks and Romans are extinct. They now belong to history, literature, music and museums. Today, no one on earth worships the Olympian gods: Zeus, Apollo or Venus. Yet, since they flourished in a time and place which was to prove of great significance for Christianity they merit our further study. Of additional importance, they provide interesting cases of religions which were beginning to slip the bonds of their primitive ancestry, but for reasons which will become clear, were unable to evolve into truly great or lasting faiths.

Origins   Greek religion was essentially a blending of the beliefs of a nomadic, warlike people from the north who invaded Greece sometime during the twelfth century B.C., and those of an agricultural and domestic native society whose gods reflected its own peaceful attitudes. As these two cultures settled down, merged and blended, the patterns of a new religion began to emerge.

There was in reality no such thing as a "national" religion, since each city-state in Greece worshipped its own deity and had its own beliefs. Greek religion displayed certain characteristics that indicate the fundamental differences between this early semi-primitive religion and the more complex modern faiths.

To begin with, Greek religion was basically polytheistic: literally scores of major and minor gods were worshipped, and each city had at least one patron god. In addition, Greek religion possessed no sacred writings or books equivalent to the Bible, nor was there a professional clergy in the true sense, although there were numerous prophets and official priests who conducted public ceremonies.

Further, there was no evidence of a moral or ethical code designed to regulate the behaviour of man, although such a code was operative in Greece independent of religion. Finally, Greek religion was unique in its failure to advocate the existence of an evil power or the presence of evil spirits in the world. Even Hades, god of the Underworld, was not represented as an evil being.

The religion which the majority of Greeks finally came to accept was based on the writings of Homer (ninth century B.C.?) and Hesiod (eighth century B.C.). The Greek historian Herodotus gives credit to these two poets for composing the generations of the gods:

> It was only the day before yesterday that the Greeks came to know the origin and form of the various gods, and whether or not all of them had always existed; for Homer and Hesiod, the poets who composed our theogonies . . . described the gods for us, giving them all their appropriate titles, offices, and powers.[7]

Homer   Homer achieved this effect chiefly in his two epic poems the *Iliad* and the *Odyssey*, tales concerned with the Trojan War and its aftermath. These long poems both contain memorable accounts of the gods — their appearance, activities, likes and dislikes, and general conduct — as well as passages describing exemplary modes of conduct among men. Homer's tales can be regarded as the Greeks' "sacred writings", although they lack the content, purpose and effect of the Bible or the Koran.

Hesiod   Of only slightly lesser importance were the writings of Hesiod. In the *Theogony* he tried to explain the origins of the world and of the gods and thus bring a system of order to the numerous gods. In *Works and Days* he sought to bring a moral order to men by emphasizing the importance of daily work and the necessity for justice, peace and virtue among men.

Mythology   Probably to a greater extent than any other religion known to man, the religion of the Greeks, and the Romans who copied them, had a foundation based on myth and legend. This is an indication that, in the early stages at least, these societies lacked a true religious base, and their level of scientific knowledge remained at the same time in a fairly primitive stage.

In answer to the basic questions which have always puzzled man, ("What is the origin of the earth? of man?" "Why does it rain?") imaginative, often poetic stories called *myths* evolved. Frequently these myths had roots in historical reality: the many amorous affairs of the god Zeus with various young ladies of both heavenly and earthly origin, for example, probably represents the actual union of the early Aryan invaders of Greece with the native peoples of the country. As well, the exciting archaeological discoveries at Troy, Mycenae, Crete and elsewhere indicate the substantial reality of many stories once considered pure fiction; but, in the Greek experience at least, it is probably fair to say that myths are ". . . neither conscious poetry nor valid science, but the common root and raw materials of both".

Greek mythology and, to a lesser extent, Roman, has had a deep influence on Western civilization. The stories continue to inspire authors, musicians and artists as they have done through the ages.

The Creation Myths   The Greeks did not conceive of a time when nothing existed, consequently they took as their starting point the existence in the universe of a formless void, *Chaos*. From Chaos all things came:

> In the beginning was Chaos, and next broad-bosomed Earth. From Chaos came Erebus and black Night, and of Night and Erebus were born Air and Day. And Earth bore the starry Heaven to cover her and become the home of the blessed gods. She also bore the unharvested Sea. Later to Earth and Heaven was born Cronus [father of Zeus] the cunning youngest and most fearful of her brood.[8]

But there is a later Creation myth which carries an amazing resemblance to the Biblical account of the Creation of earth and man:

> Others say that the God of All Things — whoever he may have been, for some call him Nature — appearing suddenly in Chaos, separated earth from the heavens, the water from the earth, and the upper air from the lower. Having unravelled the elements, he set them in due order, as they are now found. He divided the earth into zones, some very hot, some very cold, others temperate; moulded it into plains and mountains; and clothed it with grass and trees. Above it he set the rolling firmament, spangling it with stars, and assigned stations to the four winds. He also peopled the waters with fish, the earth with beasts, and the sky with the sun, the moon, and the five planets. Lastly, he made man — who, alone of all beasts, raises his face to heaven and observes the sun, the moon, and the stars — unless it be indeed true that Prometheus, son of Iapetus, made man's body from water and clay, and that his soul was supplied by certain wandering divine elements, which had survived from the First Creation.[9]

The Gods   While Cronus was the king of the gods, at some point in time his six offspring, led by Zeus, the youngest, overthrew their father and divided the heavenly estate among them. As his portion Zeus took the sky and the title king of the gods, and from this point all the gods made their home on the peak of Mount Olympus. (*See* genealogy chart, p. 68.)

In keeping with the Greek belief that there was "nothing more wonderful than man", the Greek gods were anthropomorphic, that is, they had the features and qualities of humans, both in physical and moral characteristics.

Morally, the actions ascribed to the gods were as varied as those of the men who worshipped them. Zeus, king of the gods, was constantly henpecked by his domineering and jealous wife, Hera:

> "What goddess," she asked, "has been scheming with you now, you arch-deceiver? How like you it is, when my back is turned, to settle things in your own furtive way. You never of your own accord confide in me."[10]

Zeus for his part devoted much of his time to extra-marital pursuits, and at times beat his wife; Hera's son advises her:

> "Be patient and swallow your resentment, or I that love you may see you beaten here in front of me."[11]

The other gods were also subject to the frailties of human nature: Ares, the god of War, was a drunken bully for example, and Aphrodite, the beautiful goddess of love, was promiscuous.

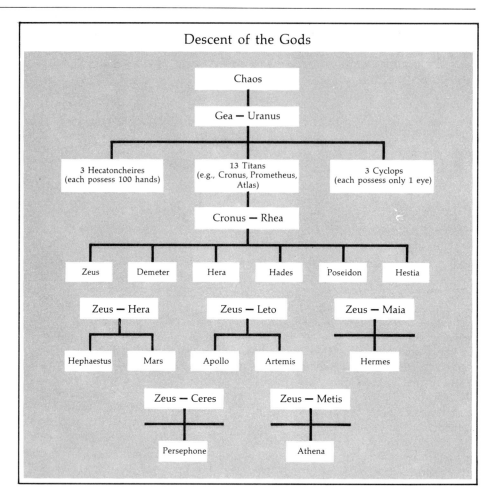

Descent of the Gods

Physically, the main distinction between gods and men appears to be that the gods were immortal, although like humans, they could be hurt and bleed. In general they tended to be pictured as more beautiful than humans, hence they became the subjects of some of the most splendid sculptures in the history of the world.

Religion and the Individual   To the average Greek, for whom life was most difficult, the gods must have appeared fickle indeed. So it was with fear and awe that he worshipped his gods, and not with love. Thus, in the worship, it was the ritual itself which was of importance rather than the sentiment behind it. Throughout the country, rituals had a similar format and every Greek worshipped in much the same way as every other Greek. The Greeks sacrificed food to the gods before every meal at a special altar for this purpose found in every home; before drinking wine, they would pour a few drops on the floor as a libation; and every meal was preceded and followed by a prayer to Hestia, goddess of the hearth.

The Afterlife   Nor was there much consolation in the afterlife. Particularly for ordinary mortals Hades, the Underworld, was conceived of as a cheerless place. Hades was thought to consist of three separate areas, and the mortal's final destination was determined not by the quality of his moral life, but by the pleasure of the gods.

It was thought that ordinary folk were placed on dreary plains and lived a shadowy, gloomy existence. Those who had offended the gods were placed in the caverns of *tartarus* where they were made to suffer cruel and unusual punishment. The great heroes, kings and warriors whom the gods favoured faced a pleasant existence in the *Elysian Fields*, "The Isles of the Blest". Poets described them as "peaceful and happy by night and by day", where men "are happy, for ever and ever".

However, something closer to the true Greek attitude emerges when, in the *Odyssey*, we hear Achilles, the greatest of Greek heroes, exclaim in dejection:

> Speak not to me of anything fine about death. Better to be alive as a poor man's slave than rule among the dead as king of them all.[12]

The Festivals   Aside from the purely individual rituals, each Greek city-state had numerous public rituals or festivals in honour of a particular god. Like our Saturdays and Sundays, they came about primarily as rest days for the working populace. In Athens, the two great festivals were the *Panathenaea*, in honour of Athena, and the *Dionysia*, the festival of Dionysus, god of wine.

The festival of Dionysus was especially notable: it was celebrated over a six-day period in April or May and it was during this festival that the Greek theatre was born. It was the occasion for the première performances of the tragedies of the playwrights Aeschylus, Sophocles and Euripides, and the comedies of Aristophanes.

Festivals were also held in other parts of Greece, such as the Olympic games at Olympia which were held in honour of the gods. These took the form of athletic contests which were the forerunners of the modern Olympics.

The Oracles   An interesting aspect of both public and private worship was the existence in many parts of Greece of *oracles*. The oracles were means by which the Greeks found out the wishes of the gods and the most famous of these was located at Delphi.

Inside the shrine of Apollo at Delphi sat the prophetess (*Pythia*), a woman of pure character who had been blessed with the power to foretell the future. Before seeking an interview, the pilgrim had to first wash himself in the sacred spring and offer prayer and sacrifice to Apollo.

The Pythia, who awaited in a cave-like inner shrine, chewed on narcotic laurel leaves, inhaled the fumes of burning laurel, and sat on a golden tripod over a crack in the earth from which vapour rose. The combination of these elements put the Pythia in a trance, during which time she uttered unintelligible words. Her priests, in return for a suitable offering from the visitor, would then translate the message in terms the visitor could understand.

These replies were usually of such a nature that they had at least two meanings, so that the oracle was able to maintain its reputation of infallibility. Nevertheless, the prophecies were taken seriously by the visitors, and frequently state decisions were based on them. One example will suffice: Croesus of Lydia,

Miller Services Ltd.

The Temple of Apollo at Delphi. It was here that the Pythia made her famous prophecies.

a rich and powerful king, asked the oracle whether he should go to war against the empire of Persia; the oracle replied: "If you go to war, a great empire will be destroyed." Spurred on by dreams of glory, Croesus went to war only to suffer a disastrous defeat and have his own empire destroyed.

To hear such messages from the oracle, visitors flocked to its temple from all over the known world.

The Mysteries   As the formalized worship prevalent in Greek religion devoted little attention to the spiritual or emotional needs of the individual, it was inevitable that new cults would arise to fill this void. One such cult was known as the *Mysteries*. As the name implies, the beliefs and rituals were extremely secretive, and to this day, little is known of the actual practices of the cult. Candidates participated in night-long ceremonies involving drinking, wild dancing and revelries which were supposed to heighten the religious experience and permit individual communication with God.

In a positive light, some of the more thoughtful cults developed a belief in the soul, an afterlife determined by one's moral behaviour and a new attitude toward man's ethical behaviour. Indeed, many of the doctrines and beliefs embraced by later Christians appear to have had a substantial following among devotees of the mystery cults. Among these, the doctrines of Heaven, Hell and purgatory, the nature of the soul, the belief in the Resurrection of a slain god, and the ritual eating of the body and blood of a god-symbol may have had a direct or indirect influence in the development of early Christianity.

Religion and Philosophy   The outlet which provided the Greek with an opportunity to release his intellectual energy lay in the realm of philosophy. By the fifth century B.C. the Greek thinkers had harnessed the rational force of philosophy to religion, and produced some important religious concepts. Indeed, the wedding of religion and philosophy is among the greatest of the contributions of Greek civilization to posterity.

The two foremost philosophers who addressed themselves to this area were Plato (427 to 347 B.C.) and his pupil Aristotle (384 to 322 B.C.). Plato's ideas concerning God and the nature of the soul greatly influenced many of the Fathers of the early Christian church, particularly St. Augustine. Plato believed in a Supreme Being, whom he identified with the Good. The Creator conceived of other perfect forms from which ultimately he created the physical universe including man and his soul:

> Did the universe always exist, or was it created? Since it is visible and tangible and has material substance we conclude that it was created. What is created must necessarily be created by a cause. . . .
>
> God did not make material first and soul afterwards; in origin and value he made the soul prior to material in order to rule it. . . .
>
> . . . the universe has became a creation expressing the Creator, who is the image of the intellectual, the greatest, the most beautiful, and the best.[13]

Aristotle, more concerned with natural phenomena, attempted to formulate an idea of God through the use of the science of physics:

> Evidently there is a first cause. Since continuous motion exists, there must be something eternal that first imparts motion, and this must itself be unmoved. And insofar as it is necessary, it is good. Such a principle governs the heavens and the natural world.[14]

Through similar logic, he also attempted to define the nature of God:

> God is always in that state of contemplation which is most pleasurable and best. Life belongs to God; for the existence of thought is life, and God is that existence, and God's essential being is life most good and eternal. So we say that God is a being eternal and perfect, and that life and continuous duration belong to God.[15]

On the purely ethical level the opposing philosophies of *Stoicism* and *Epicureanism* also developed a moral code which, though separate from the religious sphere, were both emotionally and intellectually satisfying for many Greeks. The following is from the Epicurean philosophy:

> Pleasure is an original and natural good, but we do not choose every pleasure. Sometimes we eschew pleasures when a greater pain follows them; and many pains we consider preferable to pleasure when they lead eventually to a greater pleasure. Self-sufficiency is to be sought. Luxuries are hard to get, but natural things are easy and give us much pleasure.

> When we say that pleasure is the purpose of life, we do not mean the pleasures of the sensually self-indulgent, as some assert, but rather freedom from bodily pain and mental disturbance. The life of pleasure does not come from drinking or revels, or other sensual pleasures. It comes from sober thinking, the sensible investigation of what to choose and to avoid, and getting rid of ideas which agitate the soul. Common sense is our best guide. It tells us that we cannot live happily unless we live wisely, nobly, and justly; nor can we live wisely, nobly, and justly without being happy. The virtues are inseparably linked with pleasure. For whom do you rate higher than the man who has correct beliefs about God, who has no fear of death, who has understood the purpose of Nature, who realizes that pain does not last long, and that Necessity, which some people consider the directing force of the world, is partly a matter of luck and partly in our power?

> Gods exist, but they are not as they are popularly thought to be. To destroy the gods as they are commonly thought to be is not impious; actually it is impious to have such distorted notions. The divine powers, blessed and incorruptible, neither are troubled themselves nor do they feel anger or gratitude towards men.

> Accustom yourself to think that death means nothing to us. For what is good and bad is a matter of sensation, and death is an end of sensation. Grasping this principle makes human life pleasant, not by giving us any promise of immortality, but by freeing us from any desire for immortality. For there is nothing in life to be afraid of for a man who understands that he need not be afraid of its extinction. So death, usually regarded as the greatest of calamities, is actually nothing to us; for while we are, death is not, and when death is here, we are not. So death means nothing to either the living or the dead, for it has nothing to do with the living and the dead do not exist.

> Justice is a bargain based on self-interest, which we make so as to avoid being injured by others or injuring them.[16]

Conclusion

By the fifth century B.C., the Greeks had developed a highly elaborate, ritualistic-oriented religion, which, though rich in mythology, art and literature, lacked the emotional appeal to sustain its practice among the majority of the people. For the educated minority, the slack was taken up by the genius of philosophy, then in full flower in Greece.

For the majority, the traditional Homeric faith slowly ceased to function, as it was eclipsed in turn by the popular Eastern cults, and subsequently by Christianity. To Christianity, in the area of both art and ideas, the Greeks contributed a great deal.

The Olympian Gods

Greek Name	Function	Roman Name
Zeus	King of the Gods	Jupiter
Hera	Queen of the Gods	Juno
Athena	Goddess of Wisdom	Minerva
Apollo	God of the Sun, Prophecy, Music and Medicine	Apollo
Artemis	Goddess of the Hunt and the Moon	Diana
Hermes	Messenger of the Gods	Mercury
Hestia	Goddess of the Hearth	Vesta
Hephaestus	God of Fire	Vulcan
Hades	God of the Underworld	Pluto
Aphrodite	Goddess of Love	Venus
Demeter	Goddess of Agriculture	Ceres
Dionysus	God of Wine & Drama	Bacchus
Poseidon	God of the Sea	Neptune
Persephone	Goddess of the Underworld	Proserpina

3. The Religion of Rome

Origins Like early Greek religion, the religion of the Romans developed essentially from a blending of the beliefs of the native peoples with the gods of the surrounding civilizations that they conquered. The most important of the influences were those of the Etruscans to the north of Rome, and the Greeks in southern Italy.

In time, as Rome's imperial thrust spread to Asia and Africa, the religions of these conquered areas were also imported and amalgamated with the existing religions in Rome. It is a tribute to the Roman sense of practicality and religious toleration that each new cult, with the notable exception of Christianity, was received with open arms rather than with fear and persecution.

Early Rome The religion of the Romans, like others at that time, retained many aspects of its primitive ancestry. The Romans believed they were surrounded by invisible spirits and powerful forces which they called *numina*. The numina were present everywhere in nature: in the air, trees, groves, springs and fountains, rivers and hilltops.

To the practical-minded Roman, the immediate task facing him was to identify these forces and harness their power in his behalf. Consequently, all worship, whether of a public or private nature, assumed the form of a contract between man and gods: prayer and worship were to be offered dutifully in return for services rendered. In only the rarest of cases was worship of the gods imbued with the sentiment of love.

As befits an agricultural society where the basic unit is the family, the majority of spirits came to be identified with some aspects of the farming household. Chief among these were the *Lares*, guardians of the household, and the *Penates*, guardians of the pantry or cupboard. Each family had a shrine containing images of these spirits in the home, and according to tradition a candle was kept perpetually burning before the shrine.

Equally important to the family were: Vesta, goddess of the hearth or fireplace which was used to heat the home, and Janus, guardian of the gateway. It is said that Janus was always the first god mentioned in any prayer, and for this reason to him went the honour of having the first month of the year, January, named in his behalf.

Another early belief, important though difficult to grasp, was the Roman concept of the *genius*, the true spirit of man, or his spiritual double. The genius was thought to reside in every male and was the inspiration behind each man's deeds. It was in fact the genius, rather than the man himself, which was honoured when a feast or banquet was held for an individual. Today we usually mean something quite different when we speak of a certain person's genius, but our usage had it origin in this early Roman concept.

The New Gods   As the Roman conquests spread across the Mediterranean, a whole spectrum of foreign deities came into favour in Rome. From Egypt came the popular cult of Isis and Osiris; from Phrygia in Asia Minor came Cybele, the Earth Mother, who was imported during the wars against Carthage and according to tradition was instrumental in the defeat of Hannibal by the Romans; from Persia came the cult of Mithras the sun-god, which exerted an immense appeal to Roman manhood through its emphasis on honour, courage and combat.

Most important of all, however, were the Greek gods who, with all the elaborate mythology which enshrouded them, were especially attractive to the educated segment of Roman society. With only minor changes, the Romans absorbed most of the major Greek gods into their pantheon. (See chart on p. 73.) In some cases, Apollo for example, the Romans even retained the original Greek name.

Augury   From the Etruscans, the Romans learned the secrets of augury. It was thought that the will of the gods could be discovered if one carefully followed certain ritual practices. For the Romans this meant the precise observations of the entrails of birds or the eating habits of chickens. In time, this ritual became so important that no significant personal or state function would ever be undertaken until the approval of the auspices, the "forecasts", was secured. For those who ignored the practice there was always the risk of repeating the tragic experience of Flaminius, whose army was destroyed when he disregarded the auspices, or Publius Claudius, the skeptical naval commander,

> . . . Who, when the poultry were let out of the coop and would not feed, ordered them to be thrown into the water, and joking even upon the Gods, said with a sneer, "Let them drink since they will not eat;"

Miller Services Ltd.

The Roman Pantheon. Typical of Roman toleration of all religions was this impressive edifice, erected in honour of all the gods.

which piece of ridicule, being followed by a victory over his fleet, cost him many tears and brought a great calamity on the Roman people.[17]

Another medium of prophecy, also imported from the Etruscans, centred about the oracles of the Sybil, or prophetess, of Cumae. The oracles were contained in three books and formed the entire sum of what might be called Rome's sacred writings. They were the most honoured of Rome's religious relics, but the actual content of these books is a mystery to this day, since none of them survived the destruction of the Empire.

The Priests and Priestesses   The art of augury was not left to ordinary individuals. Only priests were permitted to practise it. No special training was given to these priests, however, as in most cases the position was a reward for loyal service to the state. Even the position of High Priest, the *Pontifex Maximus*, was an elected office and was considered only a first step to more important political positions. Indeed, Julius Caesar, who was elected Pontifex Maximus in 63 B.C., was an agnostic who was sceptical of both the gods and religion.

The chief duties of the Pontifex Maximus and his assistants were to make the offerings to the gods, take the auspices for important state occasions, take care of the Sacred Law, and keep records of religious feasts and holidays, which in the Roman calendar totalled one hundred and four days.

They were aided in these duties by the six priestesses of the Temple of Vesta, the Vestal Virgins. By reputation the Vestals were of aristocratic birth, beautiful and unmarried. They were selected between the ages of six and ten, and served in the temple for the next thirty years.

Those selected spent the first ten years learning their duties, the next ten practising them, and the last ten teaching the young novitiates. At the end of this period they could leave the temple to marry, but there are few recorded cases of this actually happening. The Vestals also took a vow of chastity for the duration of their service, and the penalty for breaking this oath was severe: the offender was flogged, then buried alive. In the one thousand years of Roman history, there are only twelve recorded cases of this punishment actually being carried out.

Festivals   Roman religion, like others of this period, was sustained among the ordinary people through its numerous festivals. These varied in theme from the somber mood of the *parentalia,* in which the souls of dead ancestors were commemorated, to the light and festive mood of the *saturnalia.* For the duration of this latter festival, the traditional roles of master and slave were reversed, and the slaves were waited on by their owners.

Festivals such as these were instrumental in giving the common labourer a much-needed break from his daily work routine. This tradition was carried on by the Catholic Church among others during the Middle Ages in the form of holy days, while in the modern world this function has been assumed by the state, which celebrates periodic national holidays.

Emperor Worship   After the death of Julius Caesar there was strong pressure within the Roman state toward emperor-worship. At first, this took the form of worship of dead rulers. Augustus Caesar had resisted all attempts to make him a god while still alive. However, he was deified after his death, and beginning with Caligula, later emperors became living gods. The irony of this situation was touched upon by one dying emperor when he commented with some humour on his expected demise, "I feel myself becoming a god."

The practice of emperor-worship had the dual effect of providing a unifying symbol for Rome's scattered subjects in the far-flung empire, as well as instituting an official head for the Roman state religion.

Decline of the Old Religion   By the first century B.C. however, it was already evident that the old religion was essentially discredited by its failure to provide moral and ethical sustenance. Being ritualistic in form and content, it could ill provide the much-needed ethical and moral guidance for the vast majority of the people. So long as the ideal of empire and conquest had been maintained, the desire to serve Rome had replaced religious ideals; when the empire was consolidated and retrenched, the traditional virtues also declined, and there was no meaningful religion to replace them. Perhaps the spiritually poor religion of Rome leaves this lesson to be learned.

The great orator Cicero appealed persuasively, though in vain, for the abolition of superstition from the core of religious beliefs:

> I want it clearly understood that I do not want religion destroyed along with superstition. For it is the wise man's business to protect ancestral institutions by retaining the old rites and ceremonies. That some eternal supreme being exists, and that the human race ought to revere and admire Him is an admission to which the beauty of the universe and the orderliness of the celestial bodies compel us. Therefore, just as religion . . . ought to be propagated, so every root of superstition ought to be weeded out.[18]

The answer for many Romans did not lie in the purification of religious observances or the importation of foreign cults, but in new philosophies dealing with ethical behaviour. As in Greece whence they originated, the most influential of these were Epicureanism and Stoicism. Epicureanism, with its emphasis on the pursuit of pleasure and avoidance of pain, attracted many of the young Roman nobles, but it was Stoicism which captivated the greatest intellects of the Empire, including the emperor, Marcus Aurelius.

> Every morning repeat to thyself: I shall meet with a busybody, an ingrate, and a bully; with treachery, envy, and selfishness. All these vices have fallen to their share because they know not good and evil. But I have contemplated the nature of the good and seen that it is the beautiful; of evil, and seen that it is deformity; of the sinner, and seen that it is kindred to my own — kindred, not because he shares the same flesh and blood and is sprung from the same seed, but because he partakes of the same reason and the same spark of divinity. How then can any of these harm me? For none can involve me in the shameful save myself. Or how can I be angered with my kith and kin, or cherish hatred towards them?
>
> For we are all created to work together, as the members of one body — feet, hands, and eyelids, or the upper and nether teeth. Whence, to work against each other is contrary to nature; — but this is the very essence of anger and aversion. . . .
>
> Why suffer the incidence of things external to distract thee? Make for thyself leisure to learn something new of good, and cease this endless round. — And here beware lest the wheel only reverse its motion. For fools, too, are they who have worn out their lives in action, yet never set before themselves a goal to which they could direct every impulse — nay, every thought.
>
> Thou mayest search, but wilt hardly find a man made

wretched through failing to read another's soul; whereas he who fails to ponder the motions of his own must needs be wretched.

Let me ever be mindful what is the nature of the universe, and what my own; how the latter is related to the former, and what part it is of what whole. — And forget not that there is none that can forbid thee to be ever, in deed and word, in harmony with the nature whereof thou art part. . . .

God views the minds of all men in their nakedness, stripped of the casings and husks and impurities of the material. For, solely in virtue of the intellectual part of Himself, He touches directly the human intellect that emanates from Him and has flowed into these bodies of ours. So train thou thyself to do likewise, and thou shalt be quit of this sore distraction of thine. For he who has no eyes for our fleshly covering surely will not trouble himself with the contemplation of a man's house, raiment, fame, or aught else of these outer trappings and stage decorations. . . .

I have often marvelled how it is that every one loves himself more than the rest of human kind, yet values his own opinion of himself less than that of others. At all events, were some god or some sage to stand by a man and bid him entertain no idea, no thought, within himself without simultaneously uttering it aloud, he could not abide the ordeal for a single day. So true it is that we have more respect for our neighbours and their thoughts of us than we have for ourselves.[19]

For the ordinary Roman, there was little consolation. Even the attempt to amalgamate the various religious cults through the institution of emperor-worship was a failure. What was needed was a faith which could appeal to men on an individual basis and set before them new goals and challenges. Increasingly throughout Rome and its western empire after the first century A.D, that religion was Christianity.

4. Zoroastrianism

In the religious history of man no period is of greater significance than the sixth century B.C. Consider the amazing series of coincidental events: in different corners of the world at about the same time in history, three of the great religions had their beginnings, while two others underwent profound changes.

In the Near East, the Babylonian Captivity destroyed the Jewish state, and the hardships suffered during the period of exile forced the Jews to reassess their rituals and practices. Many of the rites of modern Judaism had their origin in this period.

In Greece, the old Homeric theology was being challenged and eventually supplanted by the rise of philosophy, which was to achieve in time the concept of monotheism and develop certain codes for man's earthly conduct.

In northern India in 567 B.C. Gautama, the Buddha, was born, who was destined to found one of the great religions of modern man. At about the same time in China, Confucius preached a religion the base of which was the proper conduct of man and which still numbers millions among its adherents today.

At the same time also, there arose among shepherd tribes in Iran a religion which became in time the state religion of the great Persian Empire. Zoroastrianism, the religion inspired by the prophet Zarathustra, or Zoroaster, has few followers today, but from its beginning it was destined to exercise a significant influence on the beliefs and practices of many of the world's living religions.

Origins Before the advent of Zoroaster, the Persians worshipped many gods. Among these were helpful nature spirits such as the god of rain, or the sun-god. These nature-gods they called *Daevas*, the origin of our own word "devil".

To aid in the worship of these gods was a Persian priestly class called the *Magi*. It is three Magi of this sort who are referred to in the New Testament as having visited the infant Jesus. It is also from this name that the term "magic" is derived, and indeed the rites used by these priests to influence their gods were frequently touched with magical practices.

It was this polytheistic religion which Zoroaster sought to purify by turning man to the worship of one God.

Zoroaster Had he lived six centuries later at the time of Jesus under a jurisdiction so powerful and cosmopolitan as the Roman Empire, or had he been as fortunate as to inspire Apostles with the zeal and talent of Peter and Paul, it is conceivable that today Zoroaster rather than Jesus might be honoured as the founder of the religion which swept the ancient world of the Mediterranean. For his life, as we shall see, significantly resembles in many details that of Jesus.

Various dates have been offered for Zoroaster's life, but the years 660 to 583 B.C. appear to be the most acceptable. Confusion on this matter is due to the fact that little is known of Zoroaster's personal life except what is registered in the *Gathas*. The Gathas, or "hymns", form a part of the *Avesta*, the sacred book of Zoroastrianism, and are believed to have been written by the prophet himself. However, since they deal more with religious matters than with biographical material, even these do not document satisfactorily Zoroaster's activities. Only fragments now remain of the Gathas; however, the original writings were reputed to have been etched in gold characters on the hides of twelve thousand oxen. These originals for the most part were destroyed by the invading armies of Alexander the Great in the fourth century B.C. Because the remains are so fragmentary, there are some scholars who doubt Zoroaster ever lived. The same might be said of Jesus.

The outline of Zoroaster's life will sound remarkably familiar to those who have any knowledge of the life of Jesus. According to Persian belief, Zoroaster (the Greek form of his actual Persian name Zarathustra) was born of a fifteen-year-old virgin who conceived miraculously through union with a flash of light. His ancestry was traced back through forty-five generations to Gayomart, the Persian equivalent of the biblical Adam. He appears to have been an unusually serious and precocious child and even in his early teens was supposed to have engaged wise men in religious debates.

At the age of thirty, Zoroaster, like Moses before him and Jesus and Mohammed after, went into the desert wilderness where he lived for several years in a cave and spent much time in meditation on the causes of human misery, injustice, conflict and evil. During this period he became convinced of the failure of the polytheistic religion of Persia to provide solutions to these problems, and waited patiently for a revelation which might disclose to him the nature of the true religion.

At last, through a vision, the revelation came. Zoroaster made reference to this in the Gathas:

> As the Holy One I knew Thee, Ahura Mazda, when Good Thought came to me and asked me, Who art thou? — Whose art thou? — By what sign wilt thou appoint the days for questioning about thine and thee? — Then I said to Him: First, Zarathustra am I, true hater of the false man to the uttermost of my power, but to the righteous would I be a powerful support, that I may win the future things of the Infinite Kingdom, according as I praise and sing Thee, O Mazda.
>
> As the Holy One I knew Thee, Ahura Mazda, when Good Thought came to me. To His question, For what wilt thou make decisions? — I made reply: At every offering of reverence to Thy fire, I will bethink me of right so long as I have power. Then show me Right, upon whom I call.[20]

In the following years, his mission to convert the tribes of Persia to the worship of Ahura Mazda, the one true God, met with public failure. In desperation he pleaded:

> To what land shall I go to flee? wither to flee? — From nobles and my peers they sever me, nor are the people pleased with me, nor the untruthful rulers of the land. How am I to please Thee, Ahura Mazda? I know wherefore I am without success; because few cattle are mine, and for that I have but few folk. I cry unto Thee, see Thou to it, Ahura, granting me support as friend gives to friend. Teach me by the right how to acquire Good Thought.[21]

Failure was followed by temptation from the Evil Spirit, Angra Mainyu, or Ahriman, whom Zoroaster was to identify as the source of all evil in the world. At last, ten years after his initial revelation, Zoroaster had his first convert, a cousin. From this point his success began to mount, aided no doubt by the fact that he managed to convert a powerful king to his faith. The religion spread rapidly throughout nomadic and farming communities, and within a century, Zoroastrianism became the official state religion of the Persian Empire. Zoroaster did not live to see this success as he died of unknown causes at the age of seventy-seven.

His Teachings   The message Zoroaster preached to the world focused upon a simple theme: devotion to the one true God, whom he called Ahura Mazda. At the same time, Zoroaster was faced with a theologically puzzling question: if God is essentially good, why does evil exist in the world? This question was to plague other religions as well, and satisfactory answers were seldom to be found. Zoroaster's answer was radically novel: there existed alongside the true God an Evil Spirit who was the source of all misfortune and evil in the world. The Evil One, Ahriman, had co-existed with Ahura Mazda from the very beginning, and operated independently of him. Perhaps history's first conception of the devil is described thus:

> Now the two primal Spirits, who revealed themselves in vision as Twins, are the Better and the Bad in thought, word and action. And between these two the wise ones choose aright the foolish not so. And

Courtesy of the Oriental Institute, University of Chicago

Symbol of Ahura Mazda, the God of Zoroastrianism, on door of the Council Hall at Persepolis, Iran.

when these twain Spirits came together in the beginning, they established Life and Not-Life, and that at the last the Worst Existence [Hell] shall be to the followers of the Lie, but the Best Thought [Paradise] to him that follows Right. Of these twain Spirits, he that followed the Lie chose doing the worst things; the holiest Spirit chose Right.[22]

Thus conflict between good and evil has existed from the beginning of time, and it exists as well in each man's soul. Zoroaster believed man had been endowed with a free will whereby he could choose between the two. One could easily distinguish the two types. The good man always spoke the truth, carried out his duties faithfully, and worshipped Ahura Mazda; the evil man shunned the truth, did no honest work and followed Ahriman.

Afterlife   The rewards for the good man were outlined by Zoroaster in a description of Paradise which was depicted as a place of eternal bliss, where the sun always shone, and the righteous enjoyed happy companionship.

The evil man fell into one of the many levels of a Hell reminiscent of Dante's *Inferno*; the punishment coincided with his degree of wickedness. Here, alone, he was destined to suffer darkness, terror, eternal fire and pain forever.

For those who had sinned, but had also performed a sufficient number of good works, Zoroaster taught that there was a Purgatory or place of purification where, after twelve thousand years of suffering, they would be admitted into Heaven.

Judgment   The Judgment of souls was divided into two stages: individual Judgment after death, and a final Judgment for all souls at the end of the world.

At death, each soul was escorted to the Bridge of the Separator which spanned the abyss of Hell. On the far side was Heaven, below lay Hell. At the centre of the bridge, the soul's past was read out. If the individual's good actions outweighed the evil, he was escorted to Heaven by Zoroaster himself. Those condemned would be unable to continue:

> Their own Soul and their own Self shall torment them when they come to the Bridge of the Separator. To all time will they be guests for the House of the Lie.[23]

Zoroaster also preached a final Day of Judgment which was to take place at the end of the world. The world order would come to an end three thousand years after the birth of Zoroaster, at which time "The dead shall rise . . . forever and ever."

Zoroastrians also believed in a Saviour, or at least three Saviours, each one the posthumous offspring of Zoroaster, coming at one-thousand-year intervals. The last one would usher in the end of the world and the final Judgment.

Other Teachings   Believing Ahura Mazda to be the only God, Zoroaster thought him too great and powerful to be represented by images. He wished the religion to remain as uncomplicated in ritual as it was in its belief. Fire, the purest of the elements, which the prophet associated with Ahura Mazda, was used frequently at prayers and offerings, but the ceremony on the whole remained simple. It was inevitable that after the death of Zoroaster the Persians who had long been accustomed to more exotic and elaborate religious rituals would reintroduce many of their former practices. The ceremony today is once again simple, but impressive.

Zoroastrianism also came close to adopting a belief in the equality of God and the Devil. Indeed, each was given his own army: Ahura Mazda with his Seven Good Spirits, the Immortal Holy Ones, and Ahriman with the evil spirits, the Daevas. Zoroaster himself was convinced however, that in the end Ahriman and his host would be destroyed by Ahura Mazda and the forces of good, hence the religion he preached remained essentially monotheistic.

It may be seen from the preceding that Zoroaster was in many ways far ahead of his time in the development of religious concepts. Many in fact became important cornerstones of some of the the world's great religions.

Contributions   Zoroastrianism exerted very little influence outside Persia, and it has almost ceased to exist as a living religion, hence it cannot truly be classified as a world-religion. Nevertheless, it has made great and lasting contributions to world-religions, principally the religions of the West: Judaism, Christianity and Islam.

Judaism   When the Jews returned to Israel from their prolonged exile in Persia they had already come into direct contact with Zoroastrianism. How much they borrowed from the Persian faith is open to debate, although Zoroastrian influence is apparent in at least three areas:

1. *The Concept of Satan*   In Jewish literature before the exile, Satan is rarely mentioned. When he does emerge he appears, though evil, as the servant and instrument of God. There are references to Satan in this light in the Book of Job:

> 6. Now there was a day when the sons of God came to present themselves before the Lord, and Satan came also among them.
> 7. And the Lord said unto Satan, Whence comest thou? Then Satan answered the Lord and said, From going to and fro on the earth, and from walking up and down in it.
> 8. And the Lord said unto Satan, Hast thou considered my servant Job, that there is none like him in the earth, a perfect and upright man, one that feareth God, and escheweth evil?
> 9. Then Satan answered the Lord and said, Doth Job fear God for nought?
> 10. Hast thou not made an hedge about him, and about his house, and about all that he hath on every side? thou hast blessed the work of his hands, and his substance is increased in the land.
> 11. But put forth thine hand now, and touch all that he hath, and he will curse thee to thy face.
> 12. And the Lord said unto Satan, Behold, all that he hath is in thy power; only upon himself put not forth thy hand. So Satan went forth from the presence of the Lord.
>
> Job 1:6-12

In later passages, Satan becomes truly the adversary, the opponent of God, and the instigator of man's misfortunes:

> And he shewed me Joshua the high priest standing before the angel of the Lord and Satan standing at his right hand to resist him.
> 2. And the Lord said unto Satan, the Lord rebuke thee O Satan; even the Lord that hath chosen Jerusalem rebuke thee: is not this a brand plucked out of the fire?
>
> Zachariah 3:1-2

2. *The Concept of Two Spirits*   With the spectacular discovery of the Dead Sea Scrolls in 1949 re-emerged the Doctrine of the Two Spirits. This indicates that in the world there exist two opposing spirits — good and evil — represented as Light and Darkness. A battle would rage for the soul of every man between these two forces, but after a lengthy struggle the Spirit of Light was expected to win.

> And he assigned to Man two Spirits in which he should walk until the time of his visitation. They are the spirits of Truth and Perversity: Truth born out of the spring of Light, Perversity from the well of Darkness. The dominion of all the children of righteousness is in the hands of the Prince of Lights so that they walk in the ways of Light, whereas the government of the children of perversity is in the hands

of the Angel of Darkness, to walk in the ways of Darkness. The purpose of the Angel of Darkness is to lead all the children of righteousness astray, and all their sin, their inequities, their guilt and their
rebellious works are the results of his domination, in accordance with
God's mysteries until His appointed time. And all their stripes and
seasons of affliction are consequent upon the rule of his [Satan's]
hostility.[24]

3. *The Concept of Angels.*   While a concept of angels clearly existed before
the exile of the Jews, it was only after the contact with Zoroastrianism that a
hierarchy of angels was developed, along with an increasing list of specific
functions to be performed by individual angels. At the top of the hierarchy was
the Angel of the Lord, followed by the Archangels, Michael, Gabriel and
Raphael, from which were descended other "levels" of angels, including angels
representing nations, or individual guardian angels.

Christianity   The debt of Christianity to Zoroastrianism is more in doubt, since
it is difficult to tell whether some Christian doctrines came directly from
Zoroastrianism or passed first through Judaism.

However, several parallels to Zoroastrian doctrine can be discerned in
the New Testament:
1. The concept of the virgin birth was an essential doctrine of the early
Christian church and remains so for most Christian denominations today.
2. The idea of the Seven Angels of God found in the Book of Revelations or
Apocalypse has its counterpart in the Seven Immortal Spirits of Zoroastrianism.
3. The Christian idea of the Last Judgment at the end of the world seems to
have many parallels with its Zoroastrian counterpart. A description of Judgment
Day comes from the Gospel of Matthew:

31. When the Son of Man shall come in his glory, and all the holy
angels with him, then shall he sit on the throne of his glory.
32. And before him shall be gathered all nations; and he shall separate
them one from another, as a shepherd divideth his sheep from the
goats.
33. And he shall set the sheep on the right hand, but the goats on the
left.
34. Then shall the King say unto them on his right hand, Come ye
blessed of my Father, inherit the kingdom prepared for you from the
foundation of the world.

Matthew 25:31-34

4. The concept of purgatory as an abode of temporary punishment is still
maintained by numerous Christian denominations.
5. The concept of a redeeming Saviour, prominent in Zoroastrian doctrine is
common to both Judaism and Christianity.

Islam   As with Christianity, it is difficult to ascribe a direct relationship
between some Islamic beliefs and similar Zoroastrian ideas because of the
significant influence of both Judaism and Christianity on Islamic doctrine.

Among the many similarities are:
1. The concept of purgatory, common also to Christianity.
2. The Bridge of the Separator of Zoroaster finds an echo in a similar bridge to separate good and evil souls in Islam.
3. In Zoroastrianism the soul meets the personification of its good or evil deeds in the form of a young maid or an old hag. In Islam a similar personification takes the form of a young man.

These are but a few of the numerous influences on Western religions exerted by the faith first taught by Zoroaster twenty-six centuries ago.

Today Zoroastrianism remained as the official state religion of Iran or Persia until A.D. 652 when Moslem invaders overthrew the existing government, forced the gradual extinction of the old religion and replaced it with Islam. Today, the religion of Zoroaster is kept alive by two small communities: 20,000 Parsees in Iran and about 120,000 more in India. As well, there are several thousand Parsees living in Canada and the United States. One of the reasons its numbers have remained so small is that, unlike some other faiths, Zoroastrianism is not a missionary religion. Indeed, there is but one way a person may become a Zoroastrian, and that is to be born one. Children of mixed marriages are considered to be Parsees only if the fathers are. In India, Persia, and wherever else they reside, the followers of Zoroaster have built a reputation for honesty and charity in both their public and private transactions.

Zoroastrianism was never to achieve the status of a world-religion, but in another sense its influence was world-wide, since its legacy had such a deep effect on some of the other great religions of the world.

Suggestions For Further Study

1. Examine the construction of the pyramids. Was their function greater than to simply serve as elaborate tombs for the Pharaohs?
2. In what respects is the Osiris legend similar to Christian beliefs in the Resurrection and the Day of Judgment?
3. Read the Greek play *Oedipus Rex*. To what extent did Greeks believe their fate was determined by the gods?
4. Many Greek politicians based their decisions on the prophecy of the Oracle of Apollo. How are "oracles" still prominent in our society?
5. Despite their tolerance of most religions, the Romans persecuted the early Christians. Are there non-religious reasons to explain the Roman attitude toward Christianity?
6. Do further research into the Parsees of India. To what extent do they follow the original teachings of Zoroaster? Can you account for the limited number of followers among these two groups?

Notes

[1] E. K. Milliken, *The Cradles of Western Civilization.* London: George C. Harrap & Co. Ltd., 1968, p. 60.
[2] Herodotus, *The Histories.* Translated by Aubrey de Selincourt, (Penguin Classics). Harmondsworth: Penguin Books Ltd., 1968, p. 133. Reprinted by permission of Penguin Books Ltd.
[3] E. A. Wallis Budge, *From Fetish to God in Ancient Egypt.* London: Oxford University Press, 1934, pp. 296-300.
[4] *Ibid.*

[5]J. H. Breasted, *A History of Egypt.* New York: Charles Scribner's Sons, 1967, pp. 312-15. Reprinted by permission of Charles Scribner's Sons. Copyright 1909 Charles Scribner's Sons; renewal copyright 1937 Imogene Breasted.

[6]*History Today*, Sept. 1960, p. 597.

[7]Herodotus, *op. cit.*, p. 124.

[8]W. R. Agard, *The Greek Mind.* New York: Van Nostrand Reinhold Ltd., 1957, p. 89. Reprinted by permission of W. R. Agard.

[9]Robert Graves, *The Greek Myths.* London: A. P. Watt & Son, 1958, p. 34. By permission of Robert Graves.

[10]Homer, *The Iliad.* Translated by E. V. Rieu, (Penguin Classics). Harmondsworth: Penguin Books Ltd., 1964, p. 37. Reprinted by permission of Penguin Books. Ltd.

[11]*Ibid.*, p. 38.

[12]Homer, *The Odyssey.* Translated by E. V. Rieu, (Penguin Classics). Harmondsworth: Penguin Books Ltd., 1963.

[13]Agard, *op. cit.*, pp. 115-16.

[14]*Ibid.*, pp. 116-17.

[15]*Ibid.*, p. 117.

[16]Cicero, *On Divination* as cited in H. C. Boren, *The Roman Republic.* New York: Van Nostrand Reinhold Ltd., 1965, p. 135.

[17]Cicero as cited in Paul MacKendrick, *The Roman Mind at Work.* New York: Van Nostrand Reinhold Ltd., 1958, p. 153.

[18]Agard, *op. cit.*, pp. 161-2.

[19]Knowles and Snyder, *op. cit.*, pp. 152-5.

[20]A. C. Bouquet, *Sacred Books of the World.* Harmondsworth: Penguin Books Ltd., 1954, pp. 106-7. © A. C. Bouquet, 1954.

[21]*Ibid.*, pp. 106-7.

[22]*History Today*, April 1963, p. 253.

[23]J. B. Noss, *Man's Religions.* New York: The Macmillan Co., 1964, p. 470.

[24]J. M. Allegro, *The Dead Sea Scrolls.* Harmondsworth: Penguin Books Ltd., 1956, p. 124. © John M. Allegro, 1956.

The Eastern Religions

Chapter Four

Hinduism

Founded:
Hinduism evolved over a long period of time, beginning around 1500 B.C.

Founder:
No one person established Hinduism.

Place:
India

Sacred Books:
The main Hindu Scriptures are the *Vedas* (the oldest), plus the *Brahmanas* and the *Upanishads*. In addition, there are two great epics, the *Ramayana* and the *Mahabharata*, and such lesser texts as the *Puranas*, the *Tantras* and the *Laws of Manu*.

Number of Adherents:
Approximately 470 million.

Distribution:
India, and to a lesser extent, Bali, Ceylon, and Indonesia. Africa and North America also have small numbers of Hindus.

Hindus In Canada:
Approximately 15,000.

Sects:
Hinduism has many sects, which tend to centre around favourite deities and around different methods of attaining salvation.

The ancient symbol of Om. (Om is the most sacred mantra or syllable in the Vedas, and is used in meditation and prayer. A mantra embodies in sound some type of supernatural power.)

* A wandering beggar, deep in meditation in a cave high in the Himalayas

* A group of worshippers prostrating themselves before the image of a monkey-god

* A young man collapsing from exhaustion after several delirious hours of dancing in honour of his favourite goddess

* A woman preparing a banquet of flour for ants on a temple floor

* A holy man by the banks of the River Ganges, balancing on one foot, with back arched, arms extended forward and back, motionless for several hours in an apparent trance

* A group of young women parading around a sacred tree, reciting Scriptures and praying for fertility

* A man bathing and feeding the image of a god as a child would tend a toy doll

ALL these people are Hindus and, on any given day, all these religious activities, and many more, can be observed where Hinduism is practised by significant numbers of people.

Hinduism is the oldest of the great religions of man, and may well be older than any other organized religion alive today. With more than 450,000,000 adherents, it also is the third largest religion, after Christianity and Islam. Like Buddhism, *Jainism* and *Sikhism*, the Hindu faith was mothered by India, whose population is now approximately seventy-five per cent Hindu. Most of the world's remaining Hindus are to be found in nearby countries such as Indonesia, Ceylon, Nepal and, to a lesser extent, in East Africa and certain Pacific islands. The word "Hindu" is derived from "Indus", the name of the river by which the early Hindus lived.

In many ways Hinduism is a unique religion. It has no founder, no uniform dogma, no hierarchical clergy, no direct divine revelation and no rigidly prescribed moral code. It has evolved from primitive animism to polytheism to *monism* (belief in a single, underlying reality), in each case without totally rejecting the previous stage. Therefore some Hindus today worship demons, spirits and assorted gods, while others engage in the most profound philosophical speculation.

Historically, its response to the challenge of competing faiths has been to absorb rather than attack them, thereby adding to the multitude of ideas and values which a Hindu can accept.

To an outside observer, therefore, Hinduism may appear to be a shapeless, directionless faith, full of mystery and contradictions, and thus very difficult to understand, or at times even to respect. The Hindu might reply that his faith is the fountainhead of all religion, made richer by the diverse elements it contains. More likely, he would chide such critics for their narrow-minded concern with petty details and offer the argument that there is but One Truth, sought by all men, and reachable in a number of equally valid ways. Each man chooses the way that suits him best. This is the common denominator that ultimately rationalizes the complexities of Hinduism, and explains the Hindu's belief that all other religions are simply varying manifestations of his own all-encompassing faith.

1. The Evolutionary Development of Hinduism

Modern Hinduism was not founded by a particular individual at a certain point in history, but rather has been built up over a period of thousands of years. During this time, it has undergone numerous changes.

Influencing Factors   This evolutionary process has been influenced by several factors. For example, India is susceptible to both droughts and torrential rainfall, and thus alternately to famine and floods. Consequently, Hinduism began with the deification of the forces of nature, and with rituals designed to please them.

Moreover, the Indian people are a mixture of many races, including Dravidians, Aryans, Mongols, Scythians, Arabs and various aboriginal peoples. This situation, combined with the fact that India has been invaded (mainly through the Himalayan mountain passes) by several peoples of different religions, helps to account for the complexity and especially the diversity of Hindu beliefs. Because of the almost infinite variety of religious concepts it contains, Hinduism is sometimes described as a "museum" of religion.

The Religion of Early India   Archaeologists have discovered the ruins of Dravidian settlements in the Indus River Valley which date back to at least 3000 B.C. While there is no specific knowledge about their religion, it was probably quite similar to that of contemporary civilizations in Egypt and Mesopotamia.

Sometime around 1500 B.C., the Dravidians of the arid Punjab region were conquered by Aryan invaders from the northwest, who brought with them certain prayers, in the form of hymns or chants, which later became known as *Vedas*.

The religious notions of the early Vedas were strongly animistic, and also contained many evidences of the influence of ancient Greek religious ideas. The deities personified various natural forces and phenomena, and their worship involved animal sacrifices and other rituals. The latter sometimes included the consumption of *soma*, a liquid produced from the leaves of an unknown plant, and having hallucinatory, mind-expanding capacities similar to LSD. The language of the Aryans became the prototype for *Sanskrit*, the sacred language of the Hindu Scriptures.

The Growth of Brahmanism   By the time many of the Aryans had moved to the fertile Ganges Valley, perhaps around 1000 B.C., the Vedas had begun to grow in volume and complexity. This process subsequently accelerated, and the resultant need for guidance in sacred rituals and interpretation of the holy writings led to the development of a class of priests called *Brahmins*.

From approximately 800 to 200 B.C., two other collections of holy writings emerged — these were the *Brahmanas* and the *Upanishads*. The former concentrated on regulating sacrifices to the gods and interpreting prayers, while the latter contained unsystematic philosophical commentaries dealing mainly with the ideas of the Vedas. In both of these new texts, the idea emerged of the existence of a supreme god, *Brahma*, who was the personification of the eternal, unchanging, cosmic force, *Brahman*, which was believed to underly all existence. This doctrine, known as *Brahmanism*, argued that the goal of every person should be to achieve union with Brahman.

However, there was a great divergence of opinion as to how this could be done. The Brahmanas maintained that the priests, with their prescribed rituals and sacrifices, held the key. The Upanishads, on the other hand, suggested that each individual must achieve the goal on his own, through rigorous self-denial, or asceticism, and meditation. Most Hindus, illiterate and unconcerned with fine distinctions, found Brahmanism too complex and impersonal, and continued with their nature worship and primitive animism.

The Emergence of Popular Hinduism   In time, Brahmanism was caught up in a flood of new doctrines and sects. Some of these were prompted by the arrival, over a period of several hundred years, of competing religions such as Buddhism, Christianity and Islam. In addition to new interpretations of existing Scriptures, there also emerged new collections of sacred writings. Chief among these were the enormous epics, the *Ramayana* and the *Mahabharata*. Lesser texts included the *Puranas* (poems addressed to prominent, popular gods) and the *Tantras* (instructions on how to win the favour of the gods). New emphasis was placed on salvation through passionate devotion (*bhakti*) to one or more gods.

Most Hindus were attracted by the stress on intimate worship of personal deities representing forces that were easily comprehended, and relevant to their immediate lives. Innumerable sects have since arisen around these deities so that, today, Hinduism is a phantasmagoria of seemingly divergent practices and beliefs. At present, about eighty per cent of India's Hindus are so-called "village Hindus"; they are concerned mainly with worshipping their personal deities and hardly at all with the philosophical complexities of Hinduism. Most rites and ceremonies are designed to control or appease these spirits, and thereby escape their anger.

Thus, to the question "What is Hinduism?" one cannot accurately answer more specifically than B. P. Lamb, who remarked: ". . . it is a wide variety of beliefs held together by an attitude of mutual tolerance and by the characteristically Hindu conviction that all approaches to God are equally valid."[1] As for the individual Hindu, he is in effect free to believe, or disbelieve, what he wants.

2. The Sacred Writings of Hinduism

The Vedas   The word "Veda" can be translated as "truth" or "knowledge". Basically, the Vedas are collections of Aryan hymns, chants, incantations, charms and the like, which tradition has arranged into four groups. For centuries they were preserved orally, but eventually they were written down, mainly during the period 1500 to 500 B.C., after the invading Aryans had settled in northern India. The oldest text is the *Rig-Veda*, which is a collection of 1,028 poetic hymns in ten books. In the main, the hymns take the form of praise or requests addressed to the gods, most of which personify great forces in nature, such as the sun, rain, wind, fire and so on. The hymns reflect man's concern for health, prosperity and security, as can be seen in the following passage:

> I worship by hymns Agni [the personification of fire], the high priest of the sacrifice, the deity, the sacrificial priest who presents oblations to the deities and is the possessor of great riches.
>
> May Agni, lauded by the ancient and modern Rishis, conduct the deities hither.
>
> Through Agni, the worshiper comes by wealth which multiplies daily, which is the source of fame and which secures heroes.
>
> O Agni, the sacrifice, around which thou residest, is unimpeded and reaches the celestials in heaven.
>
> May Agni, the presenter of oblations, the attainer of success in works ever truthful, highly illustrious for many noble deeds, divine, come hither with the celestials.
>
> Whatever good, O Agni, thou mayest confer upon the giver of oblations, that, indeed, O Angiras, belongs to thee.
>
> Bowing unto thee mentally, O Agni, we approach thee daily, both morning and evening.
>
> Thee, the radiant, the protector of sacrifices unobstructed by Rakshasas [demonic powers], the perpetual illuminator of truth and increasing in thine own room.
>
> Like unto a father to his son, O Agni, be easily accessible unto us; be ever present with us for our well-being.[2]

The *Sama-Veda* consists mainly of chants to be used at sacrificial ceremonies. Liturgy, or prose formulas to be used by priests assisting at various rites, are laid down in the *Yajur-Veda*. This is essentially the RigVeda, rearranged with musical notations to facilitate chanting. Finally, the *Atharva-Veda* is a somewhat later collection of charms, incantations and assorted magical formulas, mainly in prose form.

The Brahmanas and Aranyakas   To a great degree, all subsequent Hindu writings are explanations, interpretations or other forms of elaboration upon the Vedas. The Brahmanas emerged over a long period of time, and consist chiefly of detailed instructions for priests conducting various ceremonies, and of explanations of the meaning of the Vedic prayers. They also serve to illustrate desirable moral qualities. The *Aranyakas* are yet another body of commentary upon the Vedas. They add new insights into the nature of the gods and the meaning of sacrifices.

The Upanishads   Probably the best known writings, both to Hindus and outsiders, are the *Upanishads*. These represent a new and higher level of religious thought, and contain many of the basic ideas to which most of today's Hindus subscribe. The Upanishads shift the emphasis from outward activity — the learning and performing of assorted rites — to inward personal contemplation. Although they are quite disorganized and even seemingly self-contradictory, as a body they contain some of man's most profound philosophical speculation upon fundamental questions such as the meaning of his life and his ultimate fate.

The Evolution of Hinduism And Its Sacred Writings

Name of Scriptures	Approximate Time of Formulation	Basic Nature or Contents	General Trend Reflected
The Vedas	1500 to 800 B.C.	— polytheistic and animistic — containing philosophy, ritual and magic	— in early sections, a primitive, nature-worshipping faith; later, changed toward philosophical speculation, and Brahmanism
The Brahmanas	800 to 200 B.C.	— interpretation of Vedic rituals — detailed instructions for various ceremonies	
The Upanishads		— philosophical commentaries, mainly on the Vedas — speculation on the nature of the universe, the soul, and salvation — stress on asceticism as best path to Nirvana	— full development of complex, impersonal concept of Brahman as the underlying cosmic source with which all souls seek reunion
The Sutras		— an attempt to interpret and summarize the Upanishads	
The Epics (Mahabharata and Ramayana)	200 B.C. to A.D. 300	— further elaboration on the Vedas — illustrated, in popular terms, Hindu ethical and social values	— an effort to take religion back to the people, with exciting, human interest stories that made the gods warm, benevolent and personal, rather than coldly abstract
The Puranas	A.D. 300 to 750	— a form of mass entertainment and religious education through ancient tales about Creation, and the gods and heroes of Hinduism	— led to resurgence of Hinduism, and to the rise of numerous cults

BHAGAVAD - GITTA

The Upanishads were developed from about 800 to 500 B.C. by religious sages, who passed them on to groups of disciples. There is a Upanishad for every Veda and for every Brahmana. Various attempts were made to organize and record these teachings, with the result that Hindu tradition recognizes the authority of one hundred and eight Upanishads, though many more writings given the same name are in existence. About a dozen of the Upanishads are regarded as having special importance. Numerous efforts have been made to interpret the Upanishads systematically. The *Sutras,* developed between 500 and 200 B.C., are an example of this. They are basically a set of rules and axioms. Collectively, the philosophy contained in the Upanishads, and as later expressed in recognized schools of interpretation, is called *Vedanta* (the "end" or culmination of the Vedas).

The Epics   Yet another shift in emphasis in Hindu thinking is discernible in the period 200 B.C. to A.D. 300, when several epic stories developed. Among the most important of these are the Ramayana and the Mahabharata, which are known and loved by virtually every Hindu.

Consisting of 24,000 couplet verses, the Ramayana recounts the exploits of the heroic figure Rama, a righteous prince who is unjustly banished from his kingdom and forced to take refuge in the forests. Through numerous adventures, he displays superior virtues (courage, modesty, selflessness and so on) and ultimately conquers the forces of evil, personified by Ravana, the chief of demons.

The Mahabharata, at 100,000 verses, is probably the longest story in existence. It takes the form of an allegorical conflict within man's soul between good and evil, and its timeless, universal appeal lies in its theme of individual conscience conflicting with the rules of society. The values of loyalty, truthfulness and bravery are greatly stressed. As in the Ramayana, justice is finally done as the forces of righteousness win out.

The best known section of the Mahabharata is the *Bhagavad-Gita* (The Song of the Adorable One) which is revered by all Hindus and seems to typify the religious feeling of most of them. It has been translated into many languages, and read by tens of millions of people over the centuries. The Bhagavad-Gita further develops the doctrine of a universal soul or being, with which individual souls will finally be re-united. Moreover, at a time when Buddhism was threatening to win over large numbers of converts from Hinduism, the Gita opened a path to salvation which was feasible and attractive to the great majority of Hindus, namely that of *bhakti* or intense devotion to a personal saviour god. This was specifically encouraged by the portrayal of the god Krishna as a loving, compassionate, benevolent deity, as reflected in this passage:

> Take my last word, my utmost meaning have!
> Precious thou art to me; right well-beloved!
> Listen! I tell thee for thy comfort this.
> Give me thy heart! adore me! serve me! cling
> In faith and love and reverence to me!
> So shalt thou come to me! I promise true,
>
> For thou art sweet to me! . . . Fly to me alone!
> Make me thy single refuge! I will free
> Thy soul from all its sins![3]

Because it provides a microcosmic view of all the major types of Hindu religious thinking, the Bhagavad-Gita is sometimes referred to as the "gospel" or "New Testament" of Hinduism.

Considerable insight into the Hindu view of life is provided in the following excerpt from the Gita, in which the hero, Arjuna, faces decisive battle and is appalled by the prospect of the slaughter. He is counselled by the god Krishna to do his duty and not concern himself with the relatively minor matters of life and death.

> . . . The truly wise mourn neither for the living nor for the dead. There was never a time when I did not exist, nor you, nor any of these kings. Nor is there any future in which we will cease to be.
>
> Just as the dweller in this body passes through childhood, youth and old age, so at death he merely passes into another kind of body. The wise are not deceived by that.
>
> Feelings of heat and cold, pleasure and pain, are caused by the contact of the senses with their objects. They come and they go, never lasting long. . . . Bodies are said to die, but That which possesses the body is eternal. It cannot be limited, or destroyed.
>
> . . . You ought not to hesitate, for, to a warrior, there is nothing nobler than a righteous war. . . . Die, and you win heaven. Conquer, and you enjoy the earth. . . . Realize that pleasure and pain, and gain and loss, victory and defeat, are all one and the same; then go into battle. Do this and you cannot commit any sin.[4]

In general, the epics single out certain gods for special attention and praise by Hindus, and encourage proper conduct even in the face of adversity, since good and bad fortune in this life, and one's fate in the hereafter, are affected by one's thoughts and deeds in this present life.

Other Holy Writings   A number of other collections of sacred texts deserve brief attention. The Sutras, mentioned previously, are interpretations of the Upanishads. The *Laws of Manu*, dating from around the time of Christ, lay down certain laws for social and religious life, and help to justify the well-known *caste system*. The Puranas, or ancient tales, were developed between A.D. 300 and 750, and are great favourites with Hindu villagers to this day. These contain stories, sometimes highly erotic, about creation, theories about the age of the world and legends concerning the gods. To summarize, Hindus believe that all their religious texts contain divinely inspired truth. No single text is regarded as definitive of the faith, and thus Hindus are free to give special attention to whichever Scriptures, or portions thereof, they find most appealing.

3. Hindu Beliefs

Cosmology   Hindus believe that the only ultimate reality is Brahman. This concept is monistic in nature and can best be explained as the cosmic spirit which underlies all existence and embraces all phenomena. It is partially described in this passage from the Upanishads:

Thou [Brahman] art woman. Thou art man. Thou art the dark-blue bee and the green [parrot] with red eyes. Thou hast the lightning as thy child. Thou art the seasons and the seas. . . . Thou dost abide with all-pervadingness, Wherefrom all things are born.[5]

All forms of existence, including this present world and everything in it, are temporary and illusory and are referred to as *maya*. The goal of every Hindu is to break free of this imperfect world and achieve blissful reunion with Brahman. Hinduism is essentially an optimistic faith, in that it contends that everyone will eventually attain this goal. There is no threat of permanent Hell or damnation.

Hindus believe the universe presently in existence to be vast and filled with countless worlds, each with its own Heaven and Hell. A universe, they believe, endures for approximately 4,320,000,000 years, before being destroyed by fire or water and replaced by another universe. In their belief, this cycle of creation has always existed and will go on forever. Moreover, the substance of these creations has always existed also and will continue to do so — it merely changes form from time to time. From these notions, Hindus have developed a concept of time as a circle, in the sense that everything that happens has happened before and will happen again; this contrasts with the tendency of Western man to regard time more as a straight line, with a clear beginning (Creation) and a steady progression to some future goal.

Since Hindus believe that this present life is so fleeting, insignificant and unreal, there is little value in attempting, and less hope of achieving, any social or material progress here on earth. This idea has contributed to India's relative backwardness in technology and in social reform. Yet it has also contributed to a unique aura which exists in Hindu life and which has been aptly described by N. W. Ross:

There is among Hindus in general, and in spite of the deep timeless sadness one so often feels in their presence, a capacity for joyful, even euphoric, participation in life that is one of their most arresting qualities. No Westerner who has ever shared a dawn with the simple country people of India is likely to forget the moving sight, the reassuring experience of men, women, and children — often carrying flowers — greeting the new day with song and homage; walking to temple tanks for the morning purification bath, to the fields with bullocks, to and from the wells with water. In the midst of the poverty, deprivation, sadness, ignorance, superstition and even, one might fairly say, neurosis of this very old people, there endures a vital living force among them, a capacity for the worshipful acceptance of life itself — quite apart from all theological dogma and religious constructions — that is without parallel in the modern world.[6]

Brahman   What is Brahman? It is literally everything. It is night and day, heat and cold, goodness and evil, matter and spirit, life and death, being and non-being. Nothing exists of a material, physical, spiritual or even conceptual nature that is beyond Brahman; all things come from, and ultimately return to Brahman. The importance of a Hindu realizing this truth is explained in the *Bhagavad-Gita*:

Who sees his Lord
Within every creature
Deathlessly dwelling
Amidst the mortal:
That man sees truly. . . .

Who sees the separate
Lives of all creatures
United in Brahman
Brought forth from Brahman,
Himself finds Brahman.[7]

The Soul   Hindus believe that every living thing has an essential core to its
life — a soul, as it were, which is called an *atman*. But the individual atman
is simply a temporarily separated part of the cosmic or world soul, known as
Paramatman (The Supreme Atman), which of course is a dimension of Brahman.

Gods   In the Hindu religion, there are tens of thousands of deities. A Hindu
can believe in one, a few, or many. It does not matter, because all gods (like
everything else) are simply manifestations of Brahman. The tendency is for
educated Hindus to attempt direct meditation on Brahman itself, while the
followers of "village Hinduism" prefer to worship less abstract, more personal
gods, which are expressions of Brahman. Among the more popular of such gods
are Shiva, Vishnu and Brahma. The latter functions as the creator of universes;
Vishnu protects and sustains them; and Shiva finally destroys them.

Perhaps because the functions of Shiva and Vishnu have more bearing
on their daily lives, most Hindus pay much greater attention to them than to
Brahma. India's major temples and religious festivals are devoted to the worship
of one or both of these popular deities. Followers of Shiva are known as
Shaivites, and can be identified by the horizontal bands of paint across their
foreheads. Members of the cult of Vishnu are called *Vaishnavites*, and wear
three vertical lines of paint on their foreheads. These are two of the largest
of Hinduism's many sects.

Shiva   Shiva is usually depicted with six arms, each with a different function
to perform. Among his roles are those of destroyer and restorer of life, symbol
of the reproductive forces of nature, philosopher and sage. His third eye
signifies wisdom or higher consciousness, and his blue throat is the result of
his having swallowed the full cup of man's sins. His rather terrifying overall
appearance is appropriate to his role of the enemy of evil spirits. Worship of
Shiva includes fertility rites, and veneration of the symbols of male and female
sex organs. Some Hindus imagine Shiva being in deep meditation high in the
Himalayas. In spring, his frozen locks melt, releasing the waters of the sacred
Ganges River, which itself is regarded as a goddess. A bath in the holy mother
Ganges is believed to wash away all the sins of this earth; to achieve this is a
cherished once-in-a-lifetime dream for millions of Hindus.

Vishnu   Vishnu, the preserver, is understandably portrayed as a much more
amiable, kindly deity than Shiva. He loves, forgives and tries to lead all men
toward salvation. An interesting feature of the cult of Vishnu is the belief that
this god has a number of incarnations, called *avatars*. When necessary, an avatar

Miller Services Ltd.

A Brahmin, bedecked in floral garlands. The markings on his forehead indicate that he is a devotee of Vishnu.

of Vishnu appears on earth, in either human or animal form, for purposes suggested in this passage from the *Bhagavad-Gita:*

> When goodness grows weak,
> When evil increases,
> I make myself a body.
>
> In every age I come back
> To deliver the holy,
> To destroy the sin of the sinner,
> To establish the righteous.[8]

There are, in fact, ten chief avatars of Vishnu. One of the earliest of these was a giant sea turtle who saved mankind by lifting the earth above a primeval flood. The seventh and eighth avatars of Vishnu were Rama and Krishna, the heroes of the epics previously described. Gautama, the founder of Buddhism, was the ninth. The tenth, known as Kalkin, generates some controversy. Most Hindus believe that, as a saviour who will rid the world of evil and restore it to purity, he is yet to come. But there are Hindus who believe that he has already come; some think he was Christ, others that he appeared only recently as Mahatma Ghandi, the twentieth-century pioneer of non-violence who believed in the universal brotherhood of man. A significant point to note is that, through this concept of avatars which are manifestations of Brahman, Hinduism has defended itself against, and to some extent even absorbed, other major religions with which it has come in contact in India.

The Trimurti   As Shiva and Vishnu, and to a lesser extent Brahma, have become aggrandized by their respective followers, sometimes to the point of each being hailed as the greatest god, there has developed a tendency to merge these three deities into a *trimurti*. This represents a synthesis — the three gods or functions merged into a single concept.

The trimurti is frequently depicted as a single body, with three heads, or with three faces emerging half-way from a single head.

Female Gods   There are numerous female deities in Hinduism. The essential idea here is that of a mother goddess, who takes several forms, each of which has a different name. Among these are Parvati, the consort of Shiva, within whom resides the feminine creative spark, called *Shakti*. Durga (The Inaccessible One) and Kali (The Black One) represent forces of mystery and fear. In temple paintings they are depicted as cruel deities, with fierce eyes, mouths dripping blood. Kali has a particularly large following in rural India, especially in Bengal, where villagers make all sorts of sacrifices and other offerings to avert her wrath.

To summarize, the most popular of all Hindu gods are Shiva, Vishnu and Parvati (in any one of her several forms). The tendency is for a Hindu to worship only one deity, and to look upon all the others as expressions of the one he worships.

The Nature of Man   One of the most fundamental ideas in Hindu thought is that human life has no ultimate significance, but rather is only a small part of the vast, unending and essentially meaningless cycle of life, death and rebirth.

To repeat, every living thing has an atman or soul, which is an expression of the Paramatman or world soul. Each atman is in a process of evolution spanning countless cycles of time, whereby it seeks, through successive rebirths, to reach upward to ultimate reunion with the Paramatman, which is Brahman. Thus, Hinduism believes in *reincarnation*, and in the *transmigration of souls*. When this reunion occurs, a being has achieved paradise — it is free from the cycle of rebirths and will dwell in Brahman forever. As a higher form of life, man is further up the ladder toward this paradise than most other creatures. How long his final salvation takes depends on the path he chooses to the goal, and the earnestness with which he follows it.

Reincarnation   The form which any living thing assumes in this maya (unreal) life of sense and feeling, time and space, is determined by the *karma*, or accumulation of good and evil, of its previous life. Each creature has its own *dharma* or religious duty, which it must follow in order to gain merit. Man, for example, must live righteously according to his station in life, which is defined as his caste. Whatever karma he accumulates determines whether he will be reborn in a higher or lower caste, or indeed as some lower form of life such as a dog, crow, worm or whatever. Conversely, an animal may rise to human status in stages, or in exceptional cases all at once. The latter could occur as a result of the animal in question performing some significant service for a human of high caste.

Particularly evil karma could result in rebirth in Hell, or prolonged wanderings through space and time as a bodiless spirit, yearning for rebirth in order to begin again the long ascent through various levels of existence to a level from which salvation can finally be reached.

Insights into the accumulation and functioning of karma are provided by these passages from the sacred writings:

> According as one acts, according as one conducts himself, so does he become. The doer of good becomes good. The doer of evil becomes evil. One becomes virtuous by virtuous action, bad by bad action.[9]

> This is the sum of all ... righteousness —
> In causing pleasure or in giving pain,
> In doing good or injury to others ...
> A man obtains a proper rule of action
> By looking at his neighbour as himself.[10]

> A man is the creator of his own fate. .... A man cannot fly from the effects of his own prior deeds. .... A man gets in life what he is fated to get, and even a god cannot make it otherwise. .... A man dies not before the appointed time. ...
>
> ... Life is transitory. Transient are the youth and opulence of a man. Wives, children, friends and relations are but passing shadows. .... Only virtue and good deeds endure.
>
> Ah, what is the end of life? What does glory, fame or honour signify? Death with his attendants Day and Night is perpetually travelling the world in the guise of Old Age, and is devouring all created beings, as a serpent gulps down a gust of wind.[11]

Man's Goals   Hindus believe that one of the greatest insights a man can achieve is the realization of the truth expressed in the last passage quoted above. The fact is that man has several levels of aspiration, but only one of these will lead him to true happiness, or salvation.

First, humans tend to seek pleasure. This is natural and thus part of man's dharma. It should, however, be indulged in cautiously, with moderation. Eventually, the seeking of pleasure becomes boring, because it is trivial and shallow. Thus, man turns to more lasting satisfactions, which he thinks he can find in "success", represented by fame, money, power, social status and so on. But even this will not suffice. One never seems to have enough of these things, and must sooner or later come to the realization that they are selfish goals which, even if attained to some degree, cannot last. The frustrating treadmill of accelerating pursuit of material rewards which bring only diminishing contentment is well known in the Western world today.

Man begins to make real progress toward realization of the true goal of life when he turns outward from himself and undertakes service to others in his community. Yet even though there is greater merit and satisfaction in giving than in receiving, the individual is still confronted with the fact that his works, however noble, kind or useful, are impermanent, even if they survive his own particular death. Further discouragement stems from Hindu scepticism about the possibility of significantly altering the world or its inhabitants.

Salvation   Then, how can one be happy? Hindus believe that life essentially is suffering, brought on the individual by his own actions and ignorance. He can escape only by breaking *samsara*, the tedious cycle of rebirth that holds him in bondage and by merging his own atman with the Paramatman. This freedom, or release from the limitations and difficulties of earthly existence, is called *moksha*, and the subsequent loss of personal identity or self in the Great Cosmic Self is called *Nirvana*.

This condition has been variously described, but is generally agreed to involve total absence of sensations, emotions or needs. It translates as "annihilation" suggesting the extinguishing of all traces of ego. Loss of individuality is an idea repugnant to most Westerners but, for a Hindu, to achieve the state of Nirvana is the highest possible goal. It is also the most difficult of all objectives to attain.

The Stages of Life   Hindus believe that there are four basic stages in a normal life, which tend to encourage the evolution of a man's objectives in the pattern outlined above. To each such stage, certain attitudes and activities are appropriate.

First, one should be a student, from the time of initiation into the Hindu faith (sometime between the ages of eight and twelve) for the next twelve years. At the rite of initiation, a male youth receives the sacred thread, which he retains for life and which marks his spiritual rebirth. This interval should be a time of learning, in the company of a *guru* or religious teacher.

The second stage, that of the householder, begins with marriage. Here the individual is occupied with the tasks of establishing and maintaining a household, raising children and possibly progressing above the goals of pleasure, wealth and status to the idea of service to others.

By the time of retirement, or the third stage, of which the arrival of the first grandchild is often a signal, the wise man will have sensed the inadequacy of his previous goals and achievements, and will withdraw from the world to meditate seriously on fundamental questions. Hopefully, these contemplative efforts will produce a breakthrough to Nirvana, after which one's physical death becomes a totally insignificant occurrence. People who are believed to have attained Nirvana are often called "the silent ones"; they have no sense of personal identity, no further ambitions of any kind, and seem completely indifferent to their surroundings. Many of them spend their remaining years as wandering holy men, called *sadhus*.

In practice, this model life is possible only for Hindus of the highest class. Many Hindus, because of their environment, die at a relatively young age or, because of their social and financial situation, have never been able to afford the luxury of "retirement" from the daily grind of eking out a living. Moreover, many people simply lack the intellect required to fully understand, let alone meditate upon, the concept of Brahman. Consequently, Hinduism accommodates all of its followers by offering four paths to salvation.

Although Hindus are encouraged to at least attempt all four, they are assured that any one will do, and that all four are equally valid means of achieving the commonly desired goal.

Yoga   *Yoga,* roughly translated from Sanskrit, means discipline or, more specifically, a method of training designed to achieve the desired union of one's atman with the Paramatman. Thus, the yoga of a Hindu is his path to salvation. One who practises one of the four recognized paths to this goal is called a *yogin.* Each of the four yogas is especially suited to a particular kind of person.

4. The Paths to Salvation

Jnana Yoga   For persons of high intellect and a tendency toward philosophical speculation, *jnana yoga,* The Way of Knowledge, is recommended. Such an individual will pursue the idealized Hindu life described above, which emphasizes religious teaching from a guru and prolonged periods of intense meditation, as well as thorough study of the holy Scriptures, particularly the Vedas and Upanishads. True knowledge about Brahman, derived from the guru's teaching and from one's own reflections, will release one's soul for union with the Paramatman. The sort of people who follow this path tolerate the habits of the masses in venerating images, performing sacrifices and so on, but tend to look down upon them.

Karma Yoga   An easier, but lengthier, way to salvation is The Way of Action. Through good works and good intentions, a person can accumulate karma which will cause him to re-enter life at a higher level when he is born again. Generally, the path of *karma yoga* is followed by adhering to the rules of one's caste, performing the required rituals and prayers and practising Hinduism's teachings on ethics and morals. The demands of the latter vary, according to a person's station in life. For example, certain actions may be prohibited for a person of high caste, but quite in order for those of lesser status.

To generalize again, Hindus are sympathetic to the basic sentiment of the "Golden Rule". They particularly abhor violence, blasphemy and sacrilege; some high caste Hindus also oppose the killing of any living thing, a belief that is reflected in their vegetarianism. Further insights can be derived from these excerpts from the Laws of Manu:

> Wound not others, do no one injury by thought or deed, utter no word to pain thy fellow creatures.

> He who habitually salutes . . . the aged obtains an increase of four things: length of life, knowledge, fame and strength. . . .

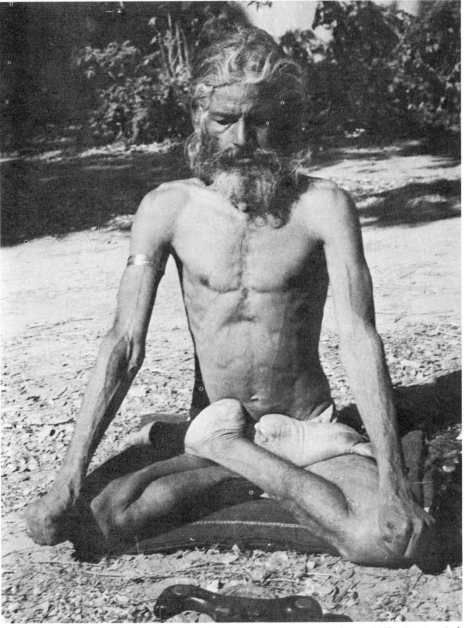

A yogin in meditation demonstrates a basic position of yoga.

Depend not on another, but lean instead on thyself. . . . True happiness is born of self-reliance. . . .

By falsehood a sacrifice becomes vain; by self-complacency the reward for austerities is lost; by boasting the goodness of an offering is brought to naught. . . .

One should speak the truth. . . .

There is no fault in eating flesh, nor in drinking intoxicating liquor, nor in copulation, for that is the occupation of beings, but cessation from them produces great fruit. . . .[12]

Bhakti Yoga Another of the easier paths is that of *bhakti yoga*, The Way, Devotion (or love). Hindus can earn salvation through total surrender of their own self-interest in favour of devotion to a particular god. This is taken as an expression of love, the most powerful of emotions. Vishnu is a principal recipient of such devotion, which is clearly expressed in the Bhagavad-Gita. Krishna, avatar of Vishnu, speaks:

> Whoever serve Me — as I show Myself —
> Constantly true, in full devotion fixed,
> These hold I very holy. But who serve —
> Worshipping Me, the One, the Invisible,
> The Unrevealed, the Unnamed, Unthinkable,
> Uttermost, All-pervading, Highest, Sure —
> Who thus adore Me, mastering their sense,
> Of one set mind to all, glad in all good,
> These blessed souls come unto me.[13]

Bhakti yoga is very popular among Hindus, because of the opportunity to demonstrate emotion, and to identify with a god on a personal, rather than an intellectual level. The actual method of worship stressed by the devotee is of little importance; it could be ritual prayer, strict asceticism or even sexual orgies to celebrate the reproductive prowess of Shiva. Each person may choose the way which best suits him. The important point is the sincerity of the commitment.

Raja Yoga The Way of Meditation is, at least in part, what Westerners first think of when they encounter the word "yoga". *Raja yoga* is the most uniquely Hindu path to salvation, but ironically it enjoys the least popularity, perhaps because it is very difficult to practise. Its followers conceive of man as a four-layered being: within the obvious physical exterior there exists a personality, aware of its own identity; inside this is the subconscious, which is normally concealed; at the core of a man's being is a man's atman or soul, which longs to return to Paramatman, the World Soul. The goal is, through the most intense, concentrated meditation, to break through to knowledge of Brahman, and thereby achieve Nirvana.

The discipline required even to approach such total concentration is exacting to say the least. As a preparatory measure, the devotee must free himself from the distractions of this life by abstaining from lying, stealing, greed, violence and sensuality. Next, he must demonstrate his devotion by practising personal cleanliness and self-control, by learning to be content, and by studious contemplation.

Postures must then be learned, so that the yogin can remain motionless yet comfortable for long periods of time. Five basic postures or *asanas* are employed. Of these, the "lotus" position is best known; in this, a person sits, legs crossed, with feet resting on opposite thighs. The back is erect, the hands rest in the lap, palms up, one resting on top of the other, and the eyes remain half-closed, concentrating on a single point, such as the tip of the nose, or the navel. It is also necessary to develop the ability to control one's breathing, so that it becomes very regular, and as light as possible. Any sneeze, cough or even a sigh can break the spell of concentration.

The next two steps are virtually inseparable. To cut off all information coming from the senses, the yogin must fix attention on one thing — the object itself is of no consequence. Once in this deep trance, the yogin can begin to meditate upon the Supreme Being, Brahman. The final two stages of raja yoga are the most difficult to describe, and probably to achieve as well. Somehow, the mind must cease to think of itself as being separate from the object of its thought. If this can be done, the individual, now lacking all awareness of his personal self, will experience *samadhi*, the trance state of final absorption in the Ultimate (Brahman), when the mind is emptied of all content and is one with the One. In effect, the object being studied disappears as the observer is absorbed into it. The genuine ascetics who choose this path are among the most highly respected people in Hindu society.

In summary, most Hindus practise bhakti yoga, and attempt to follow karma yoga as well. Furthermore, their faith encourages them to give jnana and raja yoga a try; the more studious among them do so, no doubt attracted by the intellectual challenge and the promise of faster attainment of Nirvana offered by these yogas. The Upanishads promise: "They who seek the Atman by austerity, chastity, faith and knowledge . . . they do not return."[14]

5. Other Hindu Practices

The Caste System   Although primarily associated with the Hindu religion, the caste system has also been an integral part of social, political and economic life in India. The Sanskrit word for caste means colour, suggesting that early Indian society was socially divided along racial lines, with the light-skinned Aryan conquerors claiming supremacy over their darker-skinned Dravidian subjects. Later, caste divisions represented differentiations on the basis of occupational groups.

Essentially, the system consists of four main castes, with membership being determined by birth. The highest caste is that of the *Brahmins*, whose members have been the priests, philosophers and religious teachers of Hindu society. Next in stature and authority are the *Kshatriyas*, or rulers and soldiers. These are followed by the *Vaishyas* (merchants and farmers) and then by the *Sudras* (peasants and servants). From these four basic groups an elaborate system of some 3,000 sub-castes has developed. In a highly popular hymn, dedicated to a primal man, Purusha, whom the gods sacrificed, the Rig Veda explains the origin not only of the caste system, but of the entire universe:

> When they divided Purusha, in how many different portions did they arrange him? . . . His mouth became the Brahmin; his two arms were

made into the rajanya [Kshatriya]; his two thighs the Vaishyas; from his two feet the Sudra was born. The moon was born from the mind, from the eye the sun was born; from the mouth Indra and Agni, from the breath the wind was born. From the navel was the atmosphere created, from the head the heaven issued forth; from the two feet was born the earth and the quarters (cardinal directions) from the ear. Thus did they fashion the worlds.[15]

One of the tragic consequences of the caste system has been the development of a class known as the *Untouchables*. This status is usually the result of one's having broken the bonds or rules of one's own caste. The penalty for this very serious offence is to be expelled by one's own peer group. Excluded and ignored by their own caste, such unfortunate people must earn their living by performing what Hindus regard as the lowest of tasks — cleaning latrines, removing garbage, handling animal carcasses, repairing shoes and so on. Ultimately, this outcaste status has become hereditary.

The Significance of Caste   Until recent times, the caste system virtually dictated a person's way of life in India. For example, it determined one's diet, style of dress, neighbourhood, time of prayer, mate in marriage and many other basic considerations. The first three castes were referred to as the *"twice-born"*, a reference to their physical birth and their later initiation into the Hindu faith with the presentation of the sacred thread. The lowly Sudras were denied this privilege, and could only hope for improved status in a later incarnation. Indeed, it was forbidden that they should study the Vedas, and any unfortunate who accidentally heard these most sacred Scriptures being recited would have his ears filled with molten lead!

Whatever a person's caste, it was possible for him to be polluted, usually through some improper type of exposure to someone of a lower caste or an Untouchable. A Brahmin, for example, was not to drink water that had been carried, touched or otherwise polluted by an Untouchable. He could be polluted by the shadow of an Untouchable falling across his own, or even by the presence of his own son at the same dining table, before the boy had received a sacred thread in the initiation rite. There were minimum distances, measured in paces, which a person of lower caste had to maintain between himself and a person of higher caste, to avoid polluting the latter. Often, Untouchables were required to beat wooden clappers to warn of their approach, and they were forbidden to use public roads, lest their shadows defile any of the "twice-born" passing by. The development of sub-castes created bizarre situations, as in the case where the potter using a large wheel feared pollution by a fellow potter using a smaller wheel! (The larger wheel connoted greater privilege and status.)

Although the concept of Untouchability has been officially outlawed by the Indian government, it is still quite strong, particularly in the rural areas of southern India, as are many other features of the caste system.

The Role of Women   Traditionally, Hinduism has downgraded the role of women. The Laws of Manu offer these guidelines for their conduct:

No act is to be done according to her own will by a young girl, a young woman, or even by an old woman, though in their own houses. In her childhood a girl should be under the will of her father; in her youth, of her husband; her husband being dead, of her sons; a woman should never enjoy her own will. She must never wish separation of her self from her father, husband, or sons, for by separation from them a woman would make both families contemptible. She must always be cheerful and clever in household business, with the furniture well cleaned, and with not a free hand in expenditure.

The good wife of a husband, be he living or dead, if she desire the world where her husband is, must never do anything disagreeable to him. But she may at will, when he is dead, emaciate her body by living on pure flowers, fruits and roots. She may not, however, when her husband is dead, mention even the name of another man. She must be till death subdued, intent, chaste, following that best law which is the rule of wives of a single husband.

But the woman who, from desire of offspring, is unfaithful to her dead husband, meets with blame here and is deprived of her husband's place in the next world. She who, being restrained in mind and speech and body, is not unfaithful to her husband, attains the abode of her husband, and is called virtuous by the good. A twice-born man must burn a wife of such behaviour and of the same caste, if dying before him, by means of the sacred fire and sacrificial vessels, according to rule.

Having used the fires for the last rites to his wife dying before him, he may marry again, and again establish the sacred fires also.

. . . The wives of all the four castes must always be most carefully guarded. . . .

Wife, son and slave, these three are said to be without property: whatever property they acquire is his to whom they belong.[16]

Hindu Worship A devout Hindu feels compelled to purify himself with water before he performs worship. Then, his devotions can take several forms. Frequently, he will perform *tarpana*, which is the offering of food, flowers or other appropriate commodities to the particular god he is honouring. *Japa*, another type of worship, entails the repetitious chanting of the name of a favourite deity, or of sacred phrases, known as *mantras*. The latter are mystical formulae, usually given to an initiate by his guru. *Homa* is the placing of offerings (often, clarified butter known as "ghee") into fire that has been blessed by a priest. It is common for Hindus to rub the ashes from such fires onto the forehead, as a further sign of devotion. Most Hindus engage in the everyday ritual of greeting the rising sun.

Hindus may worship individually or in groups, and in great temples or the privacy of their own homes. Every home has its place of worship, or *puja place*, complete with a small shelf for images of gods and incense burners. To worship properly, a Hindu must know the correct use of water, lights, fire and flowers, as well as of various scents and sounds. At temple ceremonies, the

Miller Services Ltd.

Part of a gathering of millions of pilgrims on the banks of the River Ganges.

services of trained priests are often required, but it should be remembered that their role is to ensure the proper carrying out of rituals, and not to act as intercessors between worshippers and their gods.

Group Observances   Many festivals and holy days are observed by Hindus. Such occasions mark birthdays of great gods and saints, seasonal changes, and so on. Another type of group observance found in Hinduism is the pilgrimage.

The goals of some of these treks are the various great temples which have survived the ravages of man and nature over the centuries. Among the great temples still in existence are Badrinath, Divarka, Jagannath and Rameswaram, dedicated respectively to Shiva, Krishna, Vishnu and Rama. Srirangam (in Madras) is one of the largest temples in the world.

The goal of other pilgrimages is the sacred mother Ganges, whose purifying waters are believed capable of curing all human maladies as well as washing away sin. One such gathering occurs every twelve years at the junction of the Ganges and Jumna rivers, and attracts Hindus from all over the world. In 1954, this location was the scene of the death of five hundred zealots who were killed in the rush of the crowd to reach the holy waters. Most pilgrims carry home water from the Ganges, for use in subsequent family rituals. Many holy men, ascetics who have withdrawn from the world to meditate and seek Nirvana, dwell in the rugged countryside of the upper reaches of the Ganges.

Benares   The city of Benares has a special place in the Hindu religion. Sanctified by its location on the Ganges, Benares is the place which Hindus attempt to visit at least once in their lifetime, and where they hope to die. Some of them believe that to die there guarantees immediate transfer to the presence of Shiva, who is enthroned in a Himalayan paradise. Because death means either final release of the soul bound for union with Paramatman, or the prelude to subsequent rebirth, it does not call for great mourning. The dead are cremated on the banks of the Ganges, and their ashes scattered on its waters. The funeral pyres of Benares burn night and day. Only the holiest of men, who are believed to have achieved Nirvana, are not cremated; their bodies are weighted and dropped into the river, symbolizing their reunion with Brahman. The rite of *suttee*, in which a widow placed herself on her husband's funeral pyre in an attempt to share his fate, has been outlawed in India, and is rarely practised nowadays.

It is believed that, while the body of a person is burned, his soul survives, and will eventually re-appear in the body of another human being or lesser animal, or in the form of a tree, stone — whatever is appropriate to his karma. Some Hindus think that the soul of a particularly good person, while awaiting rebirth, resides in a sort of paradise. However, if a person has committed a particularly serious sin, his soul may go to Hell for a period of time appropriate to the offence, but not forever. For example, the soul of a Brahmin who has eaten the flesh of a cow will languish in Hell for as many years as the cow has hairs, according to the Scriptures.

Sacred Animals   For various reasons, Hindus single out particular creatures for special favour. Offerings are made to cobras because of their alleged potency to engender fertility. Monkeys also are honoured, because the epic Ramayana tells of the aid given to Rama by Hanuman, the god of monkeys. The symbol of fidelity, these creatures can be found boldly roaming through the streets and temples of Indian cities. Bulls are symbols of procreativity; elephants are believed to bring rain and general good fortune. Indeed, Hindus tend to see God in all living things — hence their reluctance to take a life of any kind.

Cows are revered above all other animals, however, for reasons which are apparent in this quotation from the Atharva-Veda:

> Worship to thee, springing to life, and worship to
>   thee when born!
> Worship, O Cow, to thy tail-hair, and to thy
>   hooves, and to thy form! . . .
> By whom the heaven, by whom the earth,
>   by whom these waters are preserved. . . .
> Forth from thy mouth the songs came,
>   from thy neck's nape sprang
>   strength, O Cow.
> Sacrifice from thy flanks was born, and
>   rays of sunlight from thy teats.
> From thy forequarters and thy thighs
>   motion was generated, Cow!
> Food from thine entrails was produced,
>   and from thy belly came the plants. . . .
> She hath become this universe: all that the
>   Sun surveys is she.[17]

Miller Services Ltd.

Sacred cows block the main street of Jaipur, India, forcing all types of traffic to go around them.

Because of writings such as these, the consumption of beef is regarded as a sacrilege. Cows wander freely in most Indian towns and cities, and are accorded special honours in certain religious festivals. To help accumulate good karma for themselves, wealthy men sometimes provide funds to establish asylums for the care of aging cows.

6. Challenges to Hinduism in India

Although it is the faith of the great majority of the people of India, and has been for the past 3,000 years, Hinduism has been challenged periodically, and in varying degree, by certain other religions. The earliest and perhaps most serious of these tests was presented by the origination, within India itself, of the religion of Jainism and Buddhism. Both of these were essentially protest movements against contemporary Hindu practices and beliefs, such as the great power and wealth of the Brahmin priests, and the institution of the caste system.

Jainism   The man who contributed the most toward the development of

Jainism was Vardhamana, who lived from approximately 599 to 527 B.C. He is commonly referred to as "Mahavira', meaning "Great Man" or "Hero", because he is believed to have conquered the weaknesses and ignorance which plague most men. The term *Jina* or "Conqueror" is applied to him, and to those who share his beliefs.

Since the first written record of Mahavira's life appeared about a thousand years after his death, any biographical details are legendary in nature. It seems that he was born into the Kshatriya class, the son of a minor king. Around the age of thirty, he renounced his comfortable life to become an ascetic, and in this capacity experienced *moksha* or release from false ideas, sometime in his early forties. The rest of his life he devoted to founding an order of monks, and to spreading his views.

Jainism is atheistic in nature, but is a religion in the sense that it represents an attempt by man to find The First Principle or Ultimate Truth about himself and the world. Because Jains believe that the universe is eternal, and that each soul must work out its own salvation, they find the concept of a God who is a creator and protector to be irrelevant and unnecessary. Jains believe in the existence of an infinite number of *jivas* or souls. Accepting the Hindu ideas of karma and rebirth, they argue that every physical object is inhabited by a jiva, which survives the death or destruction of that object and then finds itself another temporary home, the nature or quality of which is determined by the karma created by the previous existence.

The Jain Temple, Calcutta   *Mr. L.C. Kitchen, Hamilton*

The goal, the Jain equivalent of Nirvana, is moksha, which is the release of the soul from the grip of karma and subsequent blissful escape from the tedious cycle of rebirth.

The way to this goal is through right thought and right action. All Jains must take five vows:

1. to practise *ahisma* (avoidance of doing harm to any living thing)
2. to be absolutely truthful
3. not to steal
4. to practise continence (chastity for a monk, fidelity for others)
5. to renounce pleasure in material things.

Clearly, then, the life-style most admired by Jains is that of the ascetic who embraces poverty and masters his physical appetites. Such virtues build good karma and enhance the possibility of becoming a true *Jina*, or conqueror, while failure to live up to these values produces bad karma which acts as a weight to pull the *jiva*, or soul, down to a lower form of existence in its next life.

The doctrine of non-violence is highly stressed, and is carried to extremes with such practices as wearing masks to avoid inhaling flying insects, carrying whisks to brush bugs away from clothing and furniture and so on. Jains teach that man's greatest enemy is himself, and the highest conquest is to master the self, an ideal epitomized by Mahavira's death by self-imposed starvation.

Buddhism   Buddhism, which is described in detail in the next chapter, is like Jainism in some respects. It too claims a legendary founder, Siddhartha Gautama (563 to 483 B.C.), who became known as the "Buddha" or "Enlightened One". Like Mahavira, Buddha was born into a noble family but rejected a life of luxury and ease to seek the truth through a regimen of asceticism and meditation. He too achieved a special insight, which he spread to a host of disciples in a lengthy career of preaching and teaching. While it accepted the ideas of dharma, karma and reincarnation, Buddhism varied significantly from Hinduism on a number of major questions and thus became a unique religion in its own right.

Despite its well-deserved reputation for broadmindedness and flexibility regarding religious beliefs, Hinduism found both Jainism and Buddhism unacceptable, and in effect branded them as unorthodox. Part of the reason for this was undoubtedly the criticism these new faiths levelled against the all-powerful Brahmin class. The latter substantiated their criticism of these two "heresies" with the indisputable charge that they both rejected the authority of the sacred Vedas, an unthinkable position for any devout Hindu.

But, true to their nature, the Hindus generally refrained from active persecution of these religions, so that today there are approximately 2,000,000 Jains in India, and an even larger number of Buddhists. Buddhism, of course, expanded dramatically into other parts of Asia, so that today it ranks as one of the world's major faiths. Moreover, both religions have had substantial effects on Hinduism.

Jainism, for example, has caused numerous Hindus to become vegetarians, and has contributed to Hindu traditions of asceticism, mysticism and non-violence. Jains tend to be well educated, prosperous and quite influential in their communities. Buddhism, which was the "official" religion of India in law but not in fact during the reign of the Emperor Ashoka in the third century B.C., exerted a considerable influence on Hindu art, education and religious thought.

Islam The Moslem faith struck India by way of three successive waves of invading peoples: the Arabs, Turks and Turkish-Afghans in the eighth, twelfth and sixteenth centuries respectively. Unlike previous invaders, who had settled down in India and eventually adopted Hindu religious and social values, the Moslems had a strong and distinctive culture of their own, which survived and clashed with that of the native inhabitants. The fabulous Mogul Empire which the Moslems ultimately established in northern India, while it achieved political control over most of the Indian subcontinent, was unable to break Hinduism's control over the everyday life of the vast majority of the people.

7. Modern Developments in Hinduism

The Sikh Movement The Sikh movement was founded by Nanak (1469 to 1538) at a time when Islam had begun to make significant gains in northern India. Though originally a Hindu, Nanak was opposed to many of the beliefs and practices of that religion, such as its caste system, worship of idols, polytheism, asceticism and discrimination against women.

In effect, Nanak blended the monotheism of Islam with the basic ethical values and world view of Hinduism. He urged his followers to rise above petty debates over doctrine and ritual, and to devote themselves instead to serving the one true universal God. Despite this emphasis by its founder, Sikhism gradually developed its own doctrine and rituals. These are based on the *Granth*, the holy Scriptures of Sikhism, which were compiled mainly from Hindu and Moslem writings, and from the thoughts of outstanding Sikh holy men. Still more ironic is the fact that the Sikhs later adopted many of the caste practices of Hinduism.

In its early years, the Sikh community was markedly peaceful and non-violent. However, it was transformed in the seventeenth century into a tough military society by Govind Singh, who was determined to make the Sikhs capable of vigorous self-defence. To this day, each member of the warrior class, which is world-renowned for its valour, traditionally takes the name of Singh or "lion".

At present, there are over 6,000,000 Sikhs; they are found mainly in the Punjab. They believe in a common God of all mankind, and preach religious toleration. The Sikhs continue to be strongly influenced by Hinduism, and tend to side with India in its political disputes with neighbouring Pakistan. Many of them would like to see a separate state of Sikhistan created.

Recent Trends With the advent of French and British imperialism, beginning in the seventeenth century, India came under the increasing influence of Western Christianity. Although hundreds of missions were set up throughout the country, to this day less than five per cent of the population is Christian. However, the "Christian" community in India tends to have influence beyond its numbers, primarily because the science, education and general secularism of the West have had greater impact than its religion. Together, all of these Western influences produced reform movements in the Hindu religion and, in time, social reforms in Indian life.

Religious Reform Movements One such movement was led by Swami Dayanand Sarasvati (1824 to 1883), who emphasized the validity of the truth revealed in the Vedas. A conservative, he called for a return to the old, pure

Hindu children in a public school saying prayers before lunch. Mass public education is a key part of the drive to raise living standards in India.

United Nations

Hindu faith. Another religious teacher, Ramakrishna (1836 to 1886), who has achieved the status of a Hindu saint, studied several major religions and declared them to be different but equally valid paths to the same ultimate goal. One of his disciples, Swami Vivekananda (1863 to 1902), founded the Ramakrishna Mission, an organization which stressed social, economic and educational reforms, and spoke out against the caste system. Today, the Ramakrishna Mission contributes much needed services such as health clinics, day nurseries, orphanages and the like.

Social Reforms The efforts of such men, and their twentieth-century counterparts like Mahatma Gandhi, finally forced the outlawing of discrimination by the caste system in India. As part of the same general movement of progress and social reform, certain other traditional Hindu practices, such as child marriage, the rite of suttee, and the doctrine of Untouchability, have also been banned, though not completely eradicated. The status of women is gradually rising, as is evidenced by their increasing opportunities in education and employment, and their growing prominence in medicine, politics and other key professions. These changes have been most extensive in the cities, where public education is helping to overcome illiteracy, and the barriers of conservatism and superstition. But eighty per cent of the Indian population still lives in rural areas where change is, and will continue to be, very slow.

Summary

Hinduism has been the dominant force in the social, cultural and religious life of the majority of people on the Indian subcontinent almost from the beginning of that religion's recorded history. It has shaped manners, morals, customs and art, as well as many other aspects of life. Even today, the people of countless isolated villages in India, Ceylon, Burma, Thailand, Cambodia, Indonesia, Malaysia and other Southeast Asian lands enjoy attending plays, puppet shows and dances based on the Ramayana and the Mahabharata, or listening to travelling minstrels recite and sing these epic poems.

Over the ages, Hinduism has demonstrated a remarkable capacity to absorb new ideas and to adapt to changing conditions. It has successfully withstood the challenges of three of the world's biggest and fastest-spreading religions, namely Buddhism, Christianity and Islam. Therefore, it is almost certain to continue to flourish. Part of the secret of its apparently eternal quality is revealed in these words of Ramakrishna:

> God has made different religions to suit different aspirants, times and countries. All doctrines are only so many paths; . . . Indeed, one can reach God if one follows any one of the paths with whole-hearted devotion. . . .
>
> The Saviour is the messenger of God. . . . It is one and the same Saviour that, having plunged into the ocean of life, rises up in one place and is known as Krishna and diving down again rises in another place and is known as Christ. . . .
>
> People partition off their lands by means of boundaries, but no one can partition off the all-embracing sky overhead. . . . So common man in ignorance says, "My religion is the only one, my religion

is the best." But when his heart is illumined by true knowledge, he knows that above all these wars of sects and sectarians presides the one indivisible, eternal, all-knowing bliss. . . .[18]

Suggestions For Further Study

1. Along with the idea of reincarnation, the concepts of karma and dharma are central to Hindu philosophy. What advantages and disadvantages for Indian society are associated with their acceptance by the great majority of Hindus today?

2. What are some essential differences between the ways in which Hinduism and Western religions view life?

3. The Hindu sage, Shri Ramakrishna, remarked: "He who tries to give an idea of God by mere book learning is like the man who tries to give an idea of the city of Benares by means of a map or picture."[19] What is the main point of this remark? How else, other than through books, could a person come to "know God"?

4. What factors would explain why Hindus are so tolerant of other religions? How did they rationalize their social intolerance, as reflected in their class consciousness?

5. Although there are over 2,000,000 Jains in India, none of them are farmers. How do you account for this?

6. India today faces some gigantic problems, one of which is controlling its population. What Hindu ideas might be contributing to the relatively slow acceptance of birth control?

7. The Communist party is one of the largest political parties in India, but it has never won control of the central government. Would the continuing strength of Hinduism among the masses of the people tend to work for or against the chances of a Communist election victory in India? Why?

8. Other peoples who had been exposed to Islam found such ideas as one God, a loving and protective God, the equality and brotherhood of all believers, and so on to be very attractive. Why, then, would Islam make so little headway in India, with its confusing array of deities, rigid caste system and chronic political disunity?

9. The following are remarks attributed to the Reverend Mr. D. O. Allen, a nineteenth-century American missionary who visited India in the 1830's:

> Such customs and credulity show the superstition, the ignorance, and the wretched moral and intellectual state of the greater part of the people of India. Who can contemplate them as rational beings, and not pity them? What Christian can view them as immortal beings and not pray for them?
>
> Nothing is too foolish or absurd to be taught by the Brahmans [Brahmins] or to be believed and practised by the ignorant and superstitious Hindoos. I endeavoured to direct their minds to God, as the only proper object of worship. . . .
>
> I found it was of little use to attempt reasoning with them so bigoted were they in their opinions and so positive in vindication of them.[20]

        To what aspects of Hindu faith and practice might the Rev. Mr. Allen have been referring? Why would he react this way? How do you react to his remarks? Why? Is there anything ironic about them? How do you think a Hindu would react? Why?

10. In the Bhagavad-Gita, Krishna says to Arjuna: "Gaze [upon me]. I manifest for thee those hundred thousand thousand shapes that clothe my mystery."[21] What basic Hindu idea is expressed here?

Notes

[1]B. P. Lamb, *India, A World In Transition*. New York: Frederick A. Praeger, Inc., 1963, p. 97.

[2]The *Rig-Veda*, I, 1.

[3]The *Bhagavad-Gita* as cited in Lucille Schulberg and the Editors of Time-Life Books, *Historic India*. New York: Time Incorporated, 1968, p. 121.

[4]The *Bhagavad-Gita* as cited in the Editors of the National Geographic Society, *Great Religions of the World*. Washington, D.C.: The National Geographic Society, 1971. Reprinted by permission.

[5]The *Upanishads* as cited in the Editors of Life, *The World's Great Religions*, Vol. I: Religions of the East. New York: Time Incorporated, 1955, p. 19.

[6]Nancy Wilson Ross, *Three Ways of Asian Wisdom*. New York: Simon and Schuster, Inc., 1966, p. 76. Copyright © 1966 Nancy Wilson Ross. Reprinted by permission of Simon and Schuster; London: (*Hinduism, Buddhism, Zen: An Introduction to Their Meaning and Their Arts*) Faber and Faber Ltd., 1968. Used with permission.

[7]*The Song of God: Bhagavad-Gita*. Translated by Swami Prabhavananda and Christopher Isherwood. Hollywood: Vedanta Press, 1972. Reprinted by permission of Vedanta Press, Hollywood, California.

[8]*Ibid.*

[9]The *Upanishads* as cited in *Great Religions of the World, op. cit.*, p. 163.

[10]The *Mahabharata, ibid.*

[11]The *Garuda Purana*, 113, 115 as cited in *The World's Great Religions, Vol. I: Religions of the East, op. cit.*, p. 39.

[12]*The Laws of Manu, ibid.*

[13]The *Bhagavad-Gita* as cited in *The Song Celestial*. Translated by Edwin Arnold. London: 1885, chap. XII, lines 5-13.

[14]The *Prasna Upanishads*, 1, 10 as cited in A. C. Bouquet, *Comparative Religion*. Harmondsworth: Penguin Books Ltd., 1962, p. 131.

[15]The *Rig-Veda*, X, 90 as cited in *Great Religions of the World*.

[16]*The Laws of Manu* as cited in *The World's Great Religions, Vol. I: Religions of the East, op. cit.*, p. 42.

[17]The *Atharva-Veda* as cited in *Great Religions of the World, op. cit.*, p. 162.

[18]Huston Smith, *The Religions of Man*. New York: New American Library, 1958, pp. 86-7.

[19]Ross, *op. cit.*, p. 11.

[20]*The Missionary Herald*, May, June and August, 1837, pp. 207-12, 233-6, 332-4.

[21]The *Bhagavad-Gita* as cited in *Historic India, op. cit.*, p. 120.

Chapter Five

Early Religions Of China and Japan

Taoism

Founded:
Sixth century B.C.

Founder:
According to tradition, the philosopher Lao Tzu (about 604 to 524 B.C.). Some historians challenge this view.

Place:
China

Sacred Books:
The Tao Teh Ching (The Way and Its Power)

Number of Adherents:
Probably around 50 million, but impossible to pinpoint because Taoists might also be Buddhists and/or Confucianists.

Distribution:
Most Taoists are found in China.

Taoists In Canada:
A negligible number.

Sects:
Very numerous.

The Chinese character above represents the "Tao" or "Way". It can be used as a symbol of both Taoism and Confucianism. To Confucianists "Tao" came to mean the way of morality, and to the Taoists the way of nature.

Confucianism

Founded:
Sixth century B.C.

Founder:
K'ung Fu Tzu, later known as Confucius (about 551 to 479 B.C.)

Place:
China

Sacred Books:
These include the Wu Ching (Five Classics), the Ssu Shu (Four Books), the Analects and the Meng-Tze (Book of Mencius).

Number of Adherents:
Approximately 375 million, but as with Taoism, the precise figure is impossible to determine.

Distribution:
Confucianists are found mainly in China.

Confucianists In Canada:
Between five and ten thousand.

Sects:
None.

Shinto

Founded:
Time uncertain, but several centuries before Christ, in the earliest stages of Japanese history.

Founder:
Unknown.

Place:
Japan

Sacred Books:
The Kojiki (Records of the Ancients), Nihongi (Chronicles of Japan), and the Yengishiki (Hymns and Prayers).

Number of Adherents:
Approximately 20 million.

Distribution:
The vast majority of Shintoists are Japanese.

Shintoists In Canada:
A negligible number.

Sects:
Shinto has a great many sects.

Throughout the eighteenth and nineteenth centuries, and even up to the early 1960's many people in the West adopted a rather condescending attitude toward the cultures of the Far East, and to those of China and Japan in particular. This superiority complex was based partly on the knowledge that, in terms of wealth, technology and military power, the major Western nations had clearly surpassed their counterparts in Asia. However, in the past few years this smugness has begun to be replaced by a new-found respect for, and desire to learn about, the peoples and cultures of the East.

One of the best ways to learn about a particular people is to study their religion, since a religion has a broad impact on the society in which it exists, not only on moral values and laws, but also on social structure, the arts and even political and economic life. Thus, for example, a study of the beliefs of Confucius can be valuable both for their intrinsic merits and for the insight they afford into the thoughts of the contemporary Chinese, a people comprising almost one-fourth of humanity. For this purpose, an understanding of Confucianism might very well be as instructive as a study of Marxism, or the thoughts of Chairman Mao Tse-tung.

Finally, before examining Eastern religions, and especially those of China and Japan, it is wise to keep in mind that they differ from the more familiar faiths of Judaism, Christianity and Islam in several important ways. For example, they do not necessarily all believe in one God or in any god; their concept of God, if they have one, may not be as a person or Saviour; they may not believe in a soul, an afterlife, a fixed moral code or in any connection between ethical conduct and its reward or punishment in the hereafter. Nonetheless, they deserve to be called religions because they seek ultimate truth as an answer to the fundamental questions of life.

1. Chinese Religious Thought

Introduction

The religion of Western man is centred around the concept of God. Indeed, many of us might be inclined to define religion simply as "belief in God". Generally speaking, however, the Chinese think of the divine not as a Supreme Being, who is the Creator and Protector of man, but as nature itself, of which God or gods are a part. Moreover, they do not share our tendency to regard man as the most important part of Creation.

Looking at this world, which they regard as real rather than illusory (as some religions such as Hinduism do), the Chinese are inclined to be very practical and down-to-earth. They seek happiness primarily in *this* life instead of emphasizing preparation for something better in the hereafter. Consequently, they do not agree that man's goal should be complete submission to the will of a supernatural God; rather, he should make the best of what life brings, and accept human nature as basically good, yet not perfectible. Until the Communists took over in 1949, the Chinese traditionally were tolerant of different religious beliefs, probably because there never was a single, closely-knit orthodox faith, and no established "church" with a priestly hierarchy.

Early Animism   Reverence for nature was evident even in the early religions of China which was, as in many other primitive cultures, strongly animistic. The Chinese worshipped the forces of nature, and revered the spirits of departed ancestors in order to bring good fortune to themselves. They sensed the great forces at work in the world of nature, as in the changing of the seasons, the growth of crops, the operation of the tides and so on, and placed great stress on living in harmony with these forces, lest calamity occur in the form of floods, war, disease, famine or whatever.

Accordingly, they paid homage to a whole host of gods and goddesses, of the sky, earth, sea, wind, thunder, river and so on. They also believed in ghosts, of departed emperors and heroes mainly, which they attempted to please with various offerings, and to consult for advice concerning future activities.

Festivals, fertility rites and blood sacrifices were among the many rituals conducted by an assortment of priests and shamans. Even today, few Chinese festivals are complete without lanterns, fierce dragons, loud gongs or cymbals, firecrackers and other devices for frightening away evil spirits.

Yang and Yin   As they observed nature, and life in general, Chinese sages perceived that phenomena exist in pairs of opposites, and that a pattern of ebb and flow runs between them, maintaining a delicate, almost miraculous balance. For example, there are strong and weak, dry and wet, hard and soft, good and evil, active and passive, male and female, ad infinitum. The Chinese came to regard this principle as the life-generating force in nature. The term *yang* was used to suggest the positive and initiating force, with which they associated the male, strength, heaven, spring, light, etc.; and the term *yin* had the opposite connotations, such as female, weakness, earth, autumn, darkness and so on.

Beginning somewhere around 1000 B.C., Chinese religious thought began to evolve, from primitive animism emphasizing fear of spirits to a higher, philosophic level concerned more with understanding man and devising standards for human conduct and relationships. This important change in direction paved the way for the emergence of two native Chinese religions, Taoism and Confucianism, and for the later acceptance of Buddhism, which was imported from India.

The Bah-Kua, ancient symbol of yang and yin, a concept that is fundamental to Chinese philosophy.

A. Taoism

The Origin of Taoism   According to legend, the religion of Taoism was
founded by Lao Tzu, a Chinese sage of the sixth century B.C. Actually, many
scholars suspect that no such person ever lived, and that the beliefs and writings
attributed to him really were the combined work of two or three philosophers
of a later era. In any event, tradition suggests that Lao Tzu, whose name means
"Grand Old Master", was born around 604 B.C. He avoided attempting to
convert followers, but won over many disciples by the powerful example of his
own lifestyle, and later in life he reluctantly compiled a small record of his
beliefs, before dying at the age of eighty-seven.

Important Writings   The core of Taoist thought is contained in a small book of
eighty-one short poems, known as the *Tao Teh Ching*, (The Way and Its Power).
This allegedly was written by Lao Tzu, but a later and very prominent Taoist
scholar, Chuang Tzu, contributed additional writings, in which he attempted to
elaborate on the ideas found in the Tao Teh Ching by means of essays and
parables. In time, as Taoism broke up into a number of widely divergent sects
and cults, the amount of new literature mushroomed, and finally topped one
thousand volumes. In the interest of clarity, only those ideas expressed in the
Tao Teh Ching will be dealt with here.

The Tao   Lao Tzu's basic teaching was that man, and all other forms of life,
should follow *Tao*, or "The Way". Supposedly, this concept could be sensed
intuitively, but not totally comprehended. Lao Tzu claimed: "The Tao which
can be conceived is not the real Tao." He also wrote: "How unfathomable is
Tao — like unto the emptiness of a vessel, yet, as it were, the honoured ancestor
of us all. Using it we find it inexhaustible, deep and unfathomable. How pure
and still is the Way! I do not know who generated it. . . .[1] Still, most analysts
agree that what it refers to is the natural order of the universe, the single
principle, reflected in yang and yin, that underlies all existence. The world of
nature seems to have its own rhythm — the order of planets, their movement
around the sun, the earth's rotation upon its axis, the coming and going of the
seasons, life and death, drought and flood, etc. By suggesting that men follow
Tao, Lao Tzu meant that they should live in harmony with this natural order,
and not attempt to upset or alter it.

Wu-Wei   To achieve this ideal, men must practise *wu-wei*, which means "not
doing". Actually, this was not intended to suggest complete lethargy, but rather
that a person "tune in" to the natural rhythm of the universe, and then avoid
those things which cause disharmony. Here are but a few illustrations of the
point: chasms were not meant to be spanned, trees to be chopped down, the air
to be dirtied, nor man to be restricted by complex rituals, rules and laws of
various kinds. In an effort to convey the spontaneity, and adaptability to
circumstance he was recommending, Lao Tzu drew an analogy with water:

> As the soft yield of water cleaves obstinate stone,
> So to yield with life solves the insoluble:
> To yield, I have learned, is to come back again.
> But this unworded lesson,
> This easy example,
> Is lost upon men.

Man at his best, like water,
Serves as he goes along:
Like water he seeks his own level,
The common level of life,
Loves living close to the earth,
Living clear down in his heart,
Loves kinship with his neighbours,
The pick of words that tell the truth. . . .[2]

God   In Taoism, there is no personified divine Being, or God. Underlying all existence is the eternal, unchanging principle of Tao. Thus it follows that man has no one to pray to for protection, forgiveness, aid or salvation; even if there were such a being, prayer would be useless, because Tao operates independently, without interference. Lao Tzu did not object to, but neither did he advocate, the traditional Chinese practice of paying respects to the spirits of ancestors and of nature. Presumably, he regarded such activity as consistent with Tao, in that it helped to promote good feeling and harmony within the universe.

Man and His Fate   Like everything else, man is an expression of Tao. He is not a special, favoured creature, and he should accept his limitations, including his mortality. On the subject of death, Chuang Tzu, a later Taoist philosopher, had this to say:

> . . . in death no strange new fate befalls us. In the beginning we lack not life only, but form. Not form only, but spirit. We are blended in the one great featureless indistinguishable mass. Then a time came when the mass evolved spirit, spirit evolved form, form evolved life. And now life in its turn has evolved death. For not nature only but man's being has its seasons, its sequence of spring and autumn, summer and winter. If some one is tired and has gone to lie down, we do not pursue him with shouting and bawling. She whom I have lost [his wife] has lain down to sleep for a while in the Great Inner Room. To break in upon her rest with the noise of lamentation would but show that I knew nothing of nature's Sovereign Law. That is why I ceased to mourn.[3]

Man must work out his own life as best he can, following Tao if he is wise, and not concerning himself about unanswerable questions such as the existence of an afterlife. The latter sentiment is reflected in this passage from the Tao Teh Ching:

> . . . And who can tell exactly to which qualities heaven objects?
> Heaven does nothing to win the day,
> Says nothing —
> Is echoed,
> Orders nothing —
> Is obeyed,
> Advises nothing —
> Is right:
> And which of us, seeing that nothing is outside the vast
> Wide-meshed net of heaven, knows just how it is cast?[4]

Conduct   Although Lao Tzu did not believe in complicating man's life with
elaborate rules and restrictions, many of his remarks in the Tao Teh Ching deal
with types of motives and actions of which he approved or disapproved. Since
Taoism does not believe in God, there is no dictum about obeying the will of
God, and thus no concept of sin, at least in our sense of the word; instead, there
is an impression of the type of conduct which is "wise", because it is in
accordance with Tao. Here are some examples:

> . . . Perfect politeness is not artificial; perfect duty to one's neighbour
> is not a matter of calculation; perfect wisdom takes no thought; perfect
> charity recognizes no ties; perfect trust requires no pledges. Discard
> the stimuli of purpose. Free the mind from disturbances. Get rid of
> entanglements to virtue. Pierce the obstructions to Tao. Honours,
> wealth, distinction, power, fame, gain — these six stimulate purpose.
> Mien, carriage, beauty, arguments, influence, opinions — these six
> disturb the mind. Hate, ambition, joy, anger, sorrow, pleasure — these
> six are entanglements to virtue. Rejecting, adopting, receiving, giving,
> knowledge, ability — these six are obstructions to Tao. The key to
> which is inaction.[5]

He who knows others is learned;
    He who knows himself is wise.
He who conquers others has power of muscles;
    He who conquers himself is strong.
He who is contented is rich,
    He who is determined has strength of will.
He who does not lose his centre endures;
    He who dies yet [his power] remains has long life.[6]

Those who would take over the earth
And shape it to their will
Never, I notice, succeed.
The earth is like a vessel so sacred
That at the mere approach of the profane
It is marred
And when they reach out their fingers it is gone.
For a time in the world some force themselves ahead
And some are left behind,
For a time in the world some make a great noise
And some are held silent,
For a time in the world some are puffed fat
And some are kept hungry,
For a time in the world some push aboard
And some are tipped out:
At no time in the world will a man who is sane
Over-reach himself,
Over-spend himself,
Over-rate himself.

Which means more to you,

You or your renown?
Which brings more to you,
You or what you own?
And which would cost you more
If it were gone?
The niggard pays,
The miser loses.
The least ashamed of men
Goes back if he chooses:
He knows both ways,
He starts again.

There is no need to run outside
For better seeing,
Nor to peer from a window. Rather abide
At the center of your being;
For the more you leave it, the less you learn,
Search your heart and see
If he is wise who takes each turn:
The way to do is to be.

Those who know do not tell,
Those who tell do not know.
Not to set the tongue loose
But to curb it,
Not to have edges that catch
But to remain untangled,
Unblinded,
Unconfused,
Is to find balance,
And he who holds balance beyond sway of love or hate,
Beyond reach of profit or loss,
Beyond care of praise or blame,
Has attained the highest post in the world.[7]

     In these passages from the Tao Teh Ching, Lao Tzu was suggesting that the pursuit of selfish goals, and the attempt to impose one's own ego or will are against Tao; as such, they are unnatural, unwise and certain to have unpleasant consequences. One should cease striving. Time spent in mystical contemplation on the Tao will make it possible to overcome the illusion of desire. Such a position leads to the conclusion that efforts to reform human beings, or society at large, should not be undertaken.

     In fact, Lao Tzu believed that his own civilization of the sixth century B.C. was already far too complicated, and thus out of harmony with Tao. States, he felt, should be kept as small as possible and governed with a minimum of regulations by a ruler who knows how to follow Tao. Life in this ideal state should remain simple and agrarian in nature. Machines, which degrade men and make them dependent, should be banned. People should make their own clothes, grow their own food and be content in their self-sufficiency. And, as with the individual person, the state should not strive to impose its ways on neighbouring countries by pressures of various kinds, and particularly not by war. As Lao Tzu put it:

> When people lost sight of the way to live
> Came codes of love and honesty,
> Learning came, charity came,
> Hypocrisy took charge;
> When differences weakened family ties
> Came benevolent fathers and dutiful sons;
> And when lands were disrupted and misgoverned
> Came ministers commended as loyal.
>
> Rid of formalized wisdom and learning
> People would be a hundredfold happier,
> Rid of conventionalized duty and honor
> People would find their families dear,
> Rid of legalized profiteering
> People would have no thieves to fear.
> These methods of life have failed, all three,
> Here is the way, it seems to me:
> Set people free,
> As deep in their hearts they would like to be,
> From private greeds
> And wanton needs.[8]

Evolution of Taoism   In time, Taoism became recognized as one of the "Three Pillars of Thought", along with Confucianism and Buddhism. However, like many other founders of religion, the teachings of Lao Tzu were broadened and distorted by later disciples and scholars. What was originally a fairly simple philosophy gradually became a popular religion featuring a host of gods, a huge quantity of writings and an amazing range of practices and beliefs. Perverted forms of the faith emerged, masquerading under the name of Taoism; they included priestcraft, sorcery, alchemy and occultism.

However appalling these developments might have been to the original Taoists, they at least were more appealing to the Chinese masses than Lao Tzu's idealistic urging to renounce personal gains and ambitions.

A number of the secret societies for which China was well known in earlier times also were associated with Taoism. Some of these were involved in the abortive Taiping Rebellion, which attempted to expel the Western imperialist powers in the mid-nineteenth century.

Taoism Today   It is extremely difficult to assess the present strength of Taoism in China. Undoubtedly it has deteriorated, as it inevitably would have done in the face of increasing competition from Western secular ideas, and sweeping changes have been transforming the country under the Communist regime. Its decline has been hastened by the intense persecution it has experienced at the hands of Mao Tse-tung's government, which is attempting to obliterate most traditional values in China, religious or otherwise.

Taoism, in various forms, probably lives on among some members of the rural community, particularly in the more remote areas. It also survives in

part through Buddhism, and especially Zen, which it greatly influenced.
Finally, Taoism helped to shape the Chinese character; traits such as patience,
tolerance, conservatism, endurance and even pacifism, which most of the people
of China still demonstrate, are living testimony to its legacy.

B. Confucianism

The Life of Confucius   (551 to 479 B.C.). Confucianism, which originated in
the sixth century B.C., was the strongest single influence on Chinese life and
thought until the dawn of the twentieth century. Its founder, K'ung Fu Tzu
(Confucius), was a real person whose existence has been positively established.
In fact, there is a considerable amount of information concerning him. He was
born into an impoverished family in what is now Shantung province. Married at
nineteen, but divorced at twenty-three, he devoted his life to teaching, first as a
hired tutor and later as an adviser to rulers.

     In his fifties, he became a travelling sage, and then returned home to
spend his last years writing, teaching youth, editing the classics and acquiring
many followers. Despite this long and busy life, Confucius remained relatively
unknown during his lifetime, but the elaboration of his ideas by many disciples
helped to slowly spread his reputation. In time, he came to be regarded as *the*
authority on customs and morals and, with government sponsorship, by the
second century A.D. he had attained the status of a god.

His Character   From the many stories pertaining to his life, it is possible to
construct a fairly reliable impression of the nature and personality of Confucius
Tolerance, compassion, modesty and candor seem to have been among his
outstanding characteristics. Though firm and dignified with his students, he was
also friendly and encouraging. It is clear that he was no "stuffed shirt", but
rather a person who loved life and believed in enjoying, in moderation, what it
had to offer. In the sayings attributed to him, there are hints of an earthy sense
of humour which undoubtedly helped him withstand the abuse and humiliation
to which he was periodically subjected on his travels. Above all, however,
Confucius is noteworthy for his integrity and his profound practical wisdom.

Confucianist Writings   The essential Confucianist writings are contained in
two main units: the *Wu Ching* or "Five Classics" and the *Ssu Shu* or "Four
Books". The *Wu Ching* consist of classical Chinese writings of legends, history,
metaphysics, behaviour, etc. edited by Confucius, plus the writings of Confucius himself. The *I Ching* (Book of Changes) includes a fascinating series of
diagrams, with instructions and commentary, which comprise a unique means
of foretelling the future that is becoming increasingly popular in North America.
     The *Ssu Shu* are later elaborations of the principles of Confucianism.
The Analects, for example, consist of fragmentary recollections about Confucius and his sayings, which disciples converted from oral to written versions
years after his death. The *Meng-Tze* is the Book of Mencius, who was perhaps
the greatest of all Confucian scholars.

The Ideas of Confucianism   Confucius never claimed or desired to be an
innovator. During his lifetime, China was beset by a host of troubles. The
country had no effective central government, and had split up into numerous

feudal states in which corruption and oppression were rampant and among which warfare was almost perpetual. Neighbouring tribes posed an additional threat. Confucius believed that such times called for the restoration of peace and harmony through the re-establishment of proper rules of conduct prescribed by earlier sages. Thus, he saw himself basically as a transmitter of ancient wisdom.

Confucius accepted some Taoist ideas, including the fundamental goodness of man, and the supremacy of nature. Like Taoism, Confucianism adopted certain well-established features of early Chinese religion, such as ancestor worship and the concept of yang-yin. But Confucianism was unique in China for its unprecedented heavy emphasis on solving the real, everyday problems of government, family and social life. The core of Confucianist philosophy is found in the principles of conduct and classic virtues described below.

Basic Virtues   The highest of all virtues is *jen,* which is a combination of compassion and goodwill. Confucius believed that only rare individuals could fully achieve such nobility of spirit, and confessed that he personally had never met such a person. If anyone did attain perfect jen, he would surely die to preserve it. Accompanying attitudes would of necessity be love, respect for life, courtesy, charity, selflessness and a genuine benevolence toward others. *Hsin* is the vitrue of truthfulness, including the connotation of sincerity.

Perhaps the most famous of all Confucian virtues is that of *li,* the idea of propriety. Confucius believed that tradition had established proper conventions for conducting all aspects of social and public life, whether they be matters of family, state or religion. Rituals were valuable in themselves, and also because their faithful repetition gave a vital sense of continuity and solidarity to society. Time-honoured relationships between people should be maintained for similar reasons. The most important of these relationships were those of father and son, husband and wife, elder and younger brother, older and younger friend, and ruler and subject.

In each case the first position is superior to that of the second. Accordingly, the father should receive reverence from his son, the husband obedience from his wife, the elder brother humility and respect from the younger, the older friend deference from the younger, and the ruler loyalty from his subject. However, each relationship is reciprocal, because the superior person must *demonstrate* his virtue and magnanimity to deserve his preferential treatment. Hence, the father must show love, the husband righteous behaviour, the elder brother gentility, the elder friend consideration, and the ruler benevolence. The virtue of li is in action, when people observe these conventions and carry out official functions in the traditionally prescribed manner.

Yet another Confucian goal, difficult to attain, was the ideal of *chih,* or wisdom. This embraces all other virtues and, when possessed, makes a person into a *chun-tzu,* a gentleman in the broadest sense of the term. Such a man would display every good attribute, and observe every convention, but in a completely natural, graceful and unassuming way. Such a man would be truly worthy of great power and prestige. More important, he could act as a model to inspire others.

The following sayings attributed to Confucius serve to illustrate his main values:

A man who lacks reliability is utterly useless.

Great Man's attitude toward the world is such that he shows no preferences; but he is prejudiced in favor of justice.

Great Man cherishes Excellence; Petty Man, his own comfort.

If a man has rendered himself correct, he will have no trouble governing. If he cannot render himself correct, how can he correct others?

Great Man is dignified but not proud. Petty Man is proud but not dignified.

Great Man complains about his own inabilities, not about people's ignorance of himself.[9]

Do not do to others what you would not want others to do to you.

Requite injury with justice, and kindness with kindness.[10]

To these words of the master himself should be added a comment by Mencius on the fundamental goodness of Man:

We see that no man is without a sense of compassion, or a sense of shame, or a sense of courtesy, or a sense of right and wrong. The sense of compassion is the beginning of humanity; the sense of shame is the beginning of righteousness; the sense of courtesy is the beginning of decorum; the sense of right and wrong is the beginning of wisdom. Every man has within himself these four beginnings, just as he has four limbs. Since everyone has these four beginnings within him, the man who considers himself incapable of exercising them is destroying himself.[11]

Finally, Confucius summarized the *point* of his ethical teachings this way:

If there be righteousness in the heart, there will be beauty in the character.
If there be beauty in the character, there will be harmony in the home.
If there be harmony in the home, there will be order in the nation.
If there be order in the nation, there will be peace in the world.[12]

Implications for Society   It is quite clear that Confucius believed in a hierarchical class structure. However, he was opposed to the organization of class lines on hereditary grounds. Rather, he preferred that class membership, and thus roles in society, be determined by the degree of energy, ability and especially wisdom that each individual possessed.

He gave top ranking to scholars, because of their knowledge of the classics, which afforded them the best chance to attain the ideals of jen and chih. Next came the farmers, who provided the means for sustaining the life of the community, and then the craftsmen, whose skills made other goods and services possible. Lower down the scale were merchants, who only traded the things grown or made by others. At the very bottom of the social order were soldiers, virtual outcasts who dealt in death and destruction, and whose services were required only when men, abandoning virtue, sank to their lowest animal depths.

World View   In keeping with his respect for ancient teachings, Confucius did not attempt to contradict the traditional Chinese view that the universe consisted of a Heaven (where the spirits of ancestors resided), earth and the "ten thousand things", (the material world and all things living therein). He seems to have accepted worship of ancestors and nature spirits as established customs, and hints at the possible existence of a supreme god of the sky, known to the Chinese as *T'ien*. Furthermore, Confucius believed that there was a force at work in the universe on the side of good. This is consistent with his conviction that man should follow his natural inclination, which is to do the right thing.

But the overall position of Confucius on the question of God and Heaven must be described as agnostic. He is supposed to have remarked: "While you cannot serve men, how can you serve the gods? While you do not understand life, what can you understand of death?"[13]

Thus, believing metaphysical speculation to be futile, Confucius urged men to concentrate on regulating their affairs and improving life here on earth. "Devote yourself to the proper demands of the people, respect the ghosts and spirits but keep them at a distance — this may be called wisdom."[14]

Salvation   If man could not *rely* on an afterlife, he could at least study the classics, in which he could find comfort, wisdom and happiness. Beyond this, he should maintain the link with past generations through ancestor worship, and raise children who will revere his name when he is gone. If it turns out that there is no hereafter, at least he can hope to live on in the affectionate memory of succeeding generations.

Brief History of Confucianism   Although Confucianism was gradually emerging from obscurity in the decades following the death of its founder in 479 B.C., it really did not achieve national recognition in China until the period of the Han Dynasty (206 B.C., to A.D. 220). Around 195 B.C, the emperor, Liu Pang, offered the first known imperial sacrifice at the tomb of Confucius. Before long, temples were being erected in his honour. His writings became an integral part of the curriculum of all schools, and mastery of them compulsory for all persons seeking major public office. (This latter requirement remained in effect until 1912!)

Confucianism had become the state religion of China. This is not surprising, because the basic teachings of Confucius emphasized loyalty and obedience to superiors and were thus extremely useful for maintaining the position of the ruling family. Accordingly, the government of the emperor, having a vested interest in the sustenance and growth of Confucianism, developed a state cult around its founder. Confucius was declared a god, regular sacrifices prescribed in temples and schools throughout the land, and annual festivals established to mark such important events as the sage's birthday.

After the first century A.D., both Taoism and Confucianism were confronted with the challenge of Mahayana Buddhism. The latter's ideas about

Miller Services Ltd.

The Temple of Good Years, part of the large Temple of Heaven complex in the Forbidden City, Peking. This might host various religious ceremonies, including those of Confucianist nature.

saviour gods and a spiritual afterlife had an appeal which the native faiths could not seem to match. However, rather than competing, the three religions tended to complement one another, each bringing its own unique dimensions to the needs of Chinese society, so that it was by no means uncommon for a Chinese to think of himself as a follower of all three faiths: a Confucianist in his outward, public life; a Taoist in his inner thoughts; and a Buddhist in time of personal crisis.

Bolstered by continuing government support, Confucianism maintained a strong position in China right into the twentieth century. Indeed, in 1906 the last Manchu emperor elevated Confucius to a plateau on a par with Heaven and Earth, the highest objects of worship in the official state religion.

Confucianism's Influence on China   For almost 2,500 years, Confucianism was the strongest single influence on Chinese civilization. As such, it also affected Korea, Japan and other areas to which Chinese culture spread. Quite clearly, Confucianism determined the nature of family life, influenced politics and philosophy, and totally dominated education in China. Its ethical values not only shaped Chinese character but, by contributing to long periods of domestic order and tranquility, helped make possible some of the great periods of Chinese art.

On the negative side there is no doubt that Confucianism contributed mightily, through its emphasis on revering the past and not seeking new knowledge, to the eventual stagnation of Chinese civilization and thus to the regrettable humiliation of China by modern Western powers in the nineteenth century.

Confucianism Today   As was the case with Taoism, Confucianism was fated to decline seriously in the twentieth century, as China was confronted with the challenge of Western imperialism, industrialism and secular philosophy. Since the advent of Communism, the traditional rites and ceremonies of Confucianism have been largely eradicated, although they can still be found on the island of Taiwan. Some analysts, including Arnold Toynbee, believe that Confucianism is too deeply ingrained to be erased altogether from Chinese life, but the strength of Mao Tse-tung's government, and its determined efforts to totally reshape the thoughts and lives of the people of China, make the future of Confucianism appear very bleak.

2. Shinto

Introduction

Shinto is the native religion of Japan. Its origins are obscure, but can be said to go back to the earliest stages of Japanese history, several centuries prior to the Christian era. It began as a collection of animistic practices and beliefs, and has not evolved much beyond that point, although it has developed a collection of official Scriptures and a large number of divergent sects.

Fundamentally, it is a set of rituals and customs ingrained into the Japanese way of life, primarily through the institutions of the family and the state, and not a separate, independently organized church.

Of Japan's current population of approximately 105 million, about 16 million are said to be Shintoists, as opposed to 83 million Buddhists. However, these statistics can be rather misleading for several reasons. First, as in other countries in the Far East, many people in Japan embrace two or even more religions concurrently, regarding them as complementary rather than mutually exclusive in nature. Thus, many Japanese who classify themselves as "Buddhist" still observe many of the rites of Shinto. Secondly, the rapid industrialization of Japan, and the attendant influx of Western ideas, has created a significant degree of disaffection for traditional religious beliefs, particularly among Japanese youth.

Thus, as in North America, although many families officially number themselves among the followers of the established faiths, their real commitment to them could be questioned. It would be reasonable to say, nonetheless, that over half of the Japanese people pay some attention, however scant, to the time-honoured ways of Shinto.

Important Writings Shinto existed for centuries before its followers began recording its rites and beliefs in scriptural form. The decision to do so seems to have been prompted by the flood of Chinese religious ideas, particularly those of Confucianism and Mahayana Buddhism, beginning in the sixth century A.D. The key documents are the *Kojiki* and the *Nihongi*, published in the early eighth century, and the *Yengishiki*, which appeared about two hundred years later. In these texts are compiled the rites and beliefs of Shinto, plus important events in Japanese history, both legendary and real.

Basic Beliefs Shinto [Shin-toe] is actually a Chinese term meaning "the way of the gods", used to describe the non-Buddhist religion which the Chinese discovered when they came to Japan. (The first contacts were probably made around the first century A.D., five hundred years before Buddhism gained a foothold in Japan.) This was a religion of gods, demons, mystical rites and most of the other trappings commonly found in primitive animism.

The following excerpts from a third-century official Chinese history provide random glimpses of some features of Japanese life reflecting Shintoist influence:

> . . . When a person dies, they [the Japanese] prepare a single coffin, without an outer one. They cover the graves with earth to make a mound. When death occurs, mourning is observed for more than ten days, during which period they do not eat meat. The head mourners wail and lament, while friends sing, dance, and drink liquor. When the funeral is over, all members of the family go into the water to cleanse themselves in a bath of purification.
>
> When they go on voyages across the sea to visit China, they always select a man who does not comb his hair, does not rid himself of fleas, lets his clothing get as dirty as it will, does not eat meat. . . . This man behaves like a mourner and is known as the "mourning keeper". When the voyage meets with good fortune, they all lavish on him slaves and other valuables. In case there is disease or mishap, they kill him, saying that he was not scrupulous in observing the taboos. . . .
> . . . In their worship, men of importance simply clap their hands instead of kneeling or bowing. . . . Ordinarily, men of importance have four or five wives; the lesser ones, two or three. . . . There is no theft, and [legal action] is infrequent. In case of violation of law, the light offender loses his wife and children by confiscation; as for the grave offender, the members of his household and all his kinsmen are exterminated. . . .
> . . . She [the empress] occupied herself with magic and sorcery, bewitching the people. . . .[15]

At this early stage, the most important gods and goddesses personified the sky, earth, sea and the various forces of nature. The sun, an obviously vital part of nature, was taken as the national symbol, which it remains to this day. The Sun Goddess, Amaterasu, was highly exalted, and regarded as the ancestress of the Japanese emperor. This concept was part of an elaborate myth of Creation, which is outlined below. The Japanese also believed in spirits, mainly of

ancestors, heroes, former emperors and so on. These spirits usually were regarded as beneficient and were the objects of sacrifices and other forms of
worship designed to guarantee their friendliness and support for earthly
ventures.

The sun is the symbol of the Shinto goddess of the sun, and is the
national symbol of Japan.

World View   According to Shinto mythology, creation can be traced to a huge
egg, which divided to form Heaven and earth. Somehow, various gods and
goddesses appeared, and from the union of one couple, Izanagi and Izanami,
were produced the sacred islands of Japan, whose first inhabitants also
were of divine birth. For example, the Japanese emperors are believed to
have descended from the Great Sun Goddess, Amaterasu. The line of succession,
allegedly unbroken through 2,600 years of history, stretches from Jimmu, the
semi-legendary first emperor who ruled in the seventh century B.C., to Hirohito,
the present emperor. This belief persists among some Japanese to this day,
despite the fact that in 1946 Emperor Hirohito renounced any claim to divine
ancestry.

Significantly, this mythology encouraged the belief, still not extinct,
that the Japanese islands were the centre of the earth, blessed by the gods, and
their people superior to all others in the world.

Some of these ideas are expressed in the following Shinto document
from the early thirteenth century:

> Japan is the divine country. The heavenly ancestor it was who first laid
> its foundations, and the Sun Goddess left her descendants to reign
> over it forever and ever. It is true only of our country, and nothing
> similar may be found in foreign lands. That is why it is called the
> divine country. . . .
>
> . . . It [Japan] is also called the country of the great eight
> islands. This name was given because eight islands were produced
> when the Male Deity and the Female Deity begot Japan. . . .
>
> The beginnings of Japan . . . tell of the world's creation from
> the seed of the heavenly gods. . . . In our country the succession of the

throne has followed a single undeviating line since the first divine ancestor. . . . Only in our country has the succession remained inviolate, from the beginning of heaven and earth to the present.[16]

These traditional beliefs were revived and exploited by the militarists who ruled Japan in the 1920's and 1930's, to the point where many Japanese were convinced that their cause was right, but also that it was invincible, since it enjoyed divine protection. Understandably, their defeat in World War II was a traumatic experience for the Japanese people and dealt a shattering blow to the Shintoist revival.

Gods   The idea of deities is embraced in the larger concept of *kami,* which includes mana, spirits, gods — in fact, any type of supernatural being or force. Shintoists believe that the universe is full of kami-beings. Among the more important, in addition to Amaterasu, are Susanowo (goddess of storms), and Tsuki-yomi (the moon-god). Many Shintoists also worship natural phenomena such as Mount Fujiyama, and the Japanese islands themselves, as kami-beings.

Man and His Fate   Like other living beings, man is believed to have both a physical and a kami, or spiritual, element in his nature. After his physical death, a person's kami being will survive, and dwell either in Heaven or Hell, depending on which fate he deserves.
    Thus, the Shintoist has two motives for observing the required rituals and rules of conduct: first, to please the spirits and so secure good fortune in this life; secondly, to assure himself of a place in Heaven when he dies.

Ritual   Shinto requires both "do's" and "don't's" of those who hope to join their ancestors and the gods in the spirit world. A devout Shintoist performs daily rites before a *kami-dana,* or god-shelf, in his own home, which serves as an altar on which he keeps various religious artifacts. These may include a mirror or some other symbol of Amaterasu, a figurine of some prominent deity, emperor or ancestor. Acts of devotion range from a simple bow or prayer, to the lighting of lamps and the offering of flowers, food or sacred wine. The more important the occasion, the more elaborate the ceremony. Funerals are among the most important services. It is not uncommon for a family to observe the required rituals before their kami-dana, and then retire to another room, where a Buddhist priest they have hired will make additional efforts on behalf of the departed soul.
    Besides these domestic activities, Shinto also features elaborately staged ceremonies conducted by state-appointed priests throughout the country. In all, there are over 100,000 national shrines, the most important of which is located at Ise and dedicated to Amaterasu. Services are conducted daily in her honour by several dozen priests. Special festivals, closely related to seasonal changes, are held here in February, June, October and December; on such occasions, the emperor despatches a personal representative to make offerings and prayers for the welfare of the Japanese people and nation. Most Shinto shrines are relatively simple, and are designed to blend in with their natural surroundings.

Taboos   Failure to observe prescribed rituals is only one way by which a Shintoist may invite the wrath of the kami-world. Over the centuries, a number of taboos developed, some of which are still accepted by a few Shinto sects. Many of these taboos involve the idea of pollution. If a person becomes polluted, through contact with unclean persons or things (for example, blood is regarded as a polluting agent), he must undergo purification — by fasting, walking on hot coals, reciting Shinto Scriptures or some other rite.

Conduct   Observance of rituals and taboos is much more important than ethical conduct in determining one's fate in the hereafter. In terms of "do's" and "don't's", the predominant theme of Shinto is "keep out of trouble" rather than "do good to others". This is illustrated in the following behavioural precepts:

1. Do not transgress the will of the gods.
2. Do not forget your obligations to your ancestors.
3. Do not transgress the decrees of the state.
4. Do not forget the profound goodness of the gods, whereby misfortune is averted and sickness is healed.
5. Do not forget that the world is one great family.
6. Do not forget the limitations of your own person.
7. Even though others become angry do not become angry yourself.
8. Do not be slothful in your business.
9. Do not be a person who brings blame to the teaching.
10. Do not be carried away by foreign teachings.[17]

To a Shintoist, the greatest shortcoming in an individual is disloyalty. Through his thoughts, words and actions a person should remain steadfastly loyal to, and fulfil the expectations of, his family, ancestors, emperor, country and Shinto beliefs. An interesting facet of Shinto is the ingenious way in which it has interwoven these loyalties so that they work *with* rather than against each other.

Most people in the West are familiar with *hara-kiri*, the practice of ritual suicide. This is performed by an individual who believes that he has failed to meet this standard and wishes to prove his sincerity and continuing loyalty, to redeem whatever honour has been lost and to assure himself perpetual life among his distinguished ancestors. The *kamikaze* pilots, named after the "divine wind" which destroyed a Mongol invasion fleet in the thirteenth century, expected to earn immortality by crashing their planes into American naval vessels during the latter stages of World War II.

A Brief History of Shinto   Shinto monopolized the religious field in Japan until the establishment of firm contacts with China. By the sixth century A.D., commerce and travel between the two countries were so extensive, and the impact of the vastly superior culture of China so irresistible, that Shinto found itself confronted with an apparent challenge in the form of the great missionary faith of Buddhism, which already had swept through much of Asia.

However, Shinto had the built-in advantages of state support, because of its emphasis on loyalty to the emperor, and of being deeply ingrained in the life of the masses. Moreover, the form of Buddhism which had reached China, and hence Japan, was Mahayana Buddhism, a tolerant, flexible branch of the faith which could adapt itself readily to local needs and conditions. Accordingly, Buddhism tended to complement Shinto, providing, as it had in China, the

Japan Information Centre, Consulate General of Japan, Toronto

A Shinto wedding ceremony at the Meiji shrine in Tokyo. The mixture of Eastern and Western ways in Japanese life is reflected in the traditional ceremonial kimono of the bride and the morning clothes of her husband.

encouraging concepts of saviour gods and eventual salvation for everyone. To further discourage competition between the two religions, they were gradually intermingled to some extent. For example, it was alleged that Amaterasu had pronounced Shinto and Buddhism to be different forms of the same faith. Shinto deities were declared to be *bodhisattvas* (enlightened persons working to save unenlightened men), and Buddhist temples were attached to some Shinto shrines. Chinese artists and architects were hired to design and decorate Shinto shrines, some of which were used to house imported statues of Buddha himself.

Concurrent with this Buddhist influence from China came certain elements of Confucianism which could be fitted into the Japanese way of life. Most important of these were the concepts of filial piety and the five relationships, although the Japanese dropped the emphasis on reciprocal duties of superiors to inferiors. Periodic attempts by Japanese nationalists to remove the Buddhist and other Chinese influences from the life of the country proved futile.

In the nineteenth century, as Japan became one of the many targets of Western imperialism, the nationalistic elements in Shinto again came to the fore, and helped to rally the country's resistance to foreign exploitation. Through rapid modernization, featuring industrialization on a gigantic scale, Japan was able not only to free itself of outside domination, but also to undertake an ambitious program of imperial expansion of its own — a venture which culminated in the invasion of China and ultimate defeat in World War II. The impact of this unbelievable (to the Japanese) setback partially discredited Shinto, but it is now making a modest comeback in the wake of the recovery of Japanese industry and pride.

Today, the youth of Japan are faced with basically the same challenges to traditional religious convictions as are their peers in all other countries, and the extent to which these beliefs will survive cannot be predicted. At the moment, Shinto seems to be losing ground to a strong Buddhist revival, and to the secular ideas of socialism and materialism. But it should be remembered that Shinto is as old as Japan itself. Furthermore, it has traditionally been associated with the Japanese state, and has flourished in periods of nationalistic fervor. Most experts agree that Japan is on the verge of another such age.

Suggestions For Further Study

1. In the introduction to this chapter, it is claimed that people in the West have a newly found respect for, and curiosity about, the peoples and cultures of the Far East. What factors account for this development?

2. According to one author, there are amazing similarities between the thoughts attributed to Lao Tzu in the Tao Teh Ching and sayings of Jesus Christ in the New Testament. Test the validity of this view by comparing passages from the written literature.

3. To some extent, Taoism was a protest movement against Confucianism. With which Confucianist ideals and practices does Taoism disagree?

4. What, in your opinion, would Lao Tzu think of twentieth-century North American society? Why? Could any of his suggestions be realistically applied to our situation? Explain your answer.

5. It is frequently said that, in success, a Chinese is a Confucianist, and in time of failure a Taoist. What is the point behind this thought?

6. Confucius allegedly said: "The duty of children to their parents is the fountain from which all virtues spring." How does this compare with current practice in the West? Why did Confucius put such emphasis on "filial piety"?

7. Confucius contributed to the traditional Chinese belief that old age is preferable to youth. How does this compare to North American thought? Which viewpoint do you think has greater merit?

8. Confucianism taught that women were decidedly inferior. Study *The Analects* to discover how Confucius expressed himself on this point. Investigate the effects which this view had on the subsequent position of women in Chinese society.

9. It is the opinion of some analysts that Confucianism actually made it easier for Mao Tse-tung and his Communists to gain control of China. In what ways might this have been true?

10. Elaborate on the ideas that a Chinese could embrace Confucianism, Taoism and Buddhism at the same time. (Buddhism should be studied before attempting to deal with this question.)

11. Why is it possible that a Shintoist does not experience any conflict of loyalty among his familial, state and religious duties? Why would most North

Americans find this unusual today? What are the possible advantages and dis-advantages of the Shintoist's situation?

12. Herman Kahn of the Hudson Institute of Strategic Studies, in an interview for *Newsweek* magazine, said he believed that, of all the world's great peoples, the Japanese, by cultural and ethical tradition, would have the least compunction about *using* nuclear weapons. What elements in Shinto might tend to confirm this judgment? What other elements or circumstances in Japanese life might argue *against* this view?

Notes

[1]Nancy Wilson Ross, *Three Ways of Asian Wisdom*. New York: Simon and Schuster, Inc., 1966, p. 141. Copyright © 1966 Nancy Wilson Ross. Reprinted by permission of Simon and Schuster. London: (*Hinduism, Buddhism, Zen: An Introduction to Their Meaning and Their Arts*) Faber and Faber Ltd., 1968. Used with permission.
[2]*The Way of Life: According to Lao Tzu*. Translated by Witter Bynner. New York: The John Day Company, Inc., 1944, p. 53. Copyright 1944 by Witter Bynner. Reprinted by permission of The John Day Company, Inc., publisher.
[3]Arthur Waley, *Three Ways of Thought in Ancient China*. London: George Allen and Unwin, 1939, pp. 6-7. New York: Barnes and Noble, 1939.
[4]Bynner, *op. cit.*, p. 72.
[5]The Estate of Dr. S. G. Champion for selections from *Readings From World Religions* by S. G. Champion and Dorothy Short. London: C. A. Watts Co., 1951. Reprinted by permission of Mrs. B. C. Briault.
[6]*The Wisdom of China*, edited by Lin Yutang, p. 602. Copyright 1942, renewed 1970 by Random House, Inc. Reprinted by permission of the publisher. London: Michael Joseph Ltd., 1944. Used with permission.
[7]Bynner, *op. cit.*, pp. 60-61.
[8]*Ibid.*, p. 35.
[9]*The Sayings of Confucius*, translated by James R. Ware. Copyright © 1955 by James R. Ware. Reprinted by arrangement with the New American Library, Inc., New York, New York.
[10]*The Analects* as cited in the Editors of the National Geographic Society, *Great Religions of the World*. Washington, D.C.: The National Geographic Society, 1971, p. 167. Reprinted by permission of the National Geographic Society.
[11]*The Book of Mencius, ibid*, p. 167.
[12]Huston Smith, *The Religions of Man*. New York: The New American Library, 1958, p. 169.
[13]Ross, *op. cit.*, p. 141.
[14]*The Analects* as cited in *Great Religions of the World, op. cit.*, p. 167.
[15]Tsunoda, de Bary, and Keene: *Sources of Japanese Tradition*. New York: Columbia University Press, 1958, pp. 6-8, as adapted from Tsunoda and Goodrich: *Japan in the Chinese Dynastic Histories*, pp. 8-16. Reprinted by permission of Columbia University Press.
[16]*Ibid.*, pp. 274-9.
[17]Champion and Short, *op. cit.*

Chapter Six

Buddhism

Founded:
Sixth century B.C.

Founder:
Siddhartha Gautama, otherwise known as the Buddha (The Enlightened One), about 565 to 483 B.C.
563

Place:
India

Sacred Books:
The oldest and most important Scriptures are the *Tripitaka,* or The Three Baskets of Wisdom. Literally hundreds of later volumes of sacred writings have been added since the compilation of the Tripitaka.

Number of Adherents:
Probably about 200 million close adherents, although some estimates surpass the 600 million mark. Precision is impossible because the exact impact of the Chinese Communist government's anti-religion policy is unknown, and because many Buddhists profess to be Confucianists and/or Taoists as well.

Distribution:
Buddhism is the predominant faith in Burma, Ceylon, Thailand and Indo-China. It also has many followers in China, Korea, Mongolia and Japan.

Buddhists in Canada:
Upwards of 10,000

Sects:
The two principal schools are Mahayana and Theravadin (or Hinayana) Buddhism.

The eight-spoked wheel, the Buddhist symbol of the Noble Eightfold Path.

THE figure of Buddha is one of the best-known images in the world. It has long been a symbol of the East, and can now be found in almost every country on earth, in a wide variety of forms — from the gigantic (135-ton Amithabha Buddha of Kamakura, Japan) and the exquisite (Golden Buddha of the Wat Bornives monastery in Bangkok, Thailand) to the mundane (bookends by the thousands of pairs) and even the bizarre (plastic containers for a well-known North American after-shave lotion!).

The religion founded by the Buddha is also widespread, being practised, in one form or another, on all six continents. It claims approximately 600 million nominal followers, of whom perhaps 200 million could be termed devout or active practitioners. Moreover, at 2,500 years of age, Buddhism clearly ranks as one of the oldest living religions of man, and certainly it is the oldest of the three great missionary faiths. No doubt it is this combination of circumstances that has caused one noted author to assert that Buddha has reached more people than Christ.

Although we in the West are quite familiar with its outward symbol, most of us lack adequate information regarding Buddhism's basic tenets. This situation is unfortunate in that it separates us from a unique philosophy and from one of the noblest ethics yet devised by man. It is likewise dangerous, in that it severely limits our understanding of the culture and outlook of Asia, at a time when such understanding is so obviously important for political, economic and other reasons.

1. The Origin of Buddhism

Its Founder Buddhism was founded by Siddhartha Gautama, an Indian prince born around the year 565 B.C. to the ruler of a small kingdom in what is now southern Nepal. As with a number of great religious figures, many legends subsequently arose concerning Gautama's life. Some of these pertain to Gautama's birth itself. Buddhist writings describe this as a miraculous event, the consequence of his mother being immaculately impregnated by a sacred white elephant, who touched her left side with a lotus flower. The Scriptures claim:

> Now the instant the Future Buddha was conceived in the womb of his mother, all the ten thousand worlds suddenly quaked, quivered and shook. And the Thirty-two Prognostics appeared, as follows: an immeasurable light spread through ten thousand worlds; the blind recovered their sight, as if from desire to see this his glory; the deaf received their hearing; the dumb talked; the hunchbacked became straight of body; the lame recovered the power to walk; . . . the fires went out in all the hells. . . . Diseases ceased among men. . . . In all quarters of the heavens the weather became fair. . . .The rivers checked their flowing . . . and the whole ten thousand worlds became one mass of garlands of the utmost possible magnificence. . . .[1]

At birth, the future Buddha supposedly talked and walked, lotus blooms forming in his footprints.

Yet another Buddhist legend suggests that Gautama's father was told by a sage that the boy was destined for greatness — either as a powerful emperor or as a religious leader who would devise a path to salvation for all mankind. Preferring the first of these possibilities, the father resolved to isolate his son in the luxury of palaces, in order to prevent him from venturing forth into the outside world, where he might "see how the other half lived" and perhaps derive some special religious inspiration.

The "Four Signs"   But complete seclusion proved to be impossible, and the bright, inquisitive Gautama eventually saw the "four sights" which would, if experienced, as the sage foretold, lead the young prince to a religious life. These sights, referred to by Buddhists as the "Four Signs" were, in turn, a sick man covered with terrible sores, an old man, a corpse and a wandering monk. Understandably, the high-living prince was moved to reflecting upon the suffering and inevitable death which comes to all men, great and small, and upon deeper questions such as the meaning of life and the ultimate fate of man. As time passed, he became increasingly dissatisfied with the shallow, dissolute life of the royal court. This malaise turned to outright disgust after a particularly wild party in which he was a participant. Thus at twenty-nine years of age, though married to a beautiful wife and father of a young son as well as being heir to a rich throne, he forsook everything to become a travelling holy man.

Gautama's Search for Truth   Despite his most strenuous efforts, Gautama frustrated for almost seven years in his search for the ultimate truth about life. He studied the Hindu Scriptures, but found them lacking. Various gurus were unable to answer his questions satisfactorily. But if Hinduism could not provide the solution to his dilemma, at least it offered him a means by which to pursue his goal; this was raja yoga, the art of meditation. Sensing that perhaps his sacrifices were not yet great enough, Gautama plunged into asceticism, scourging and starving himself virtually to the point of death. But this too seemed futile, both because no deeper insight came, and because if he did die, he would certainly be defeating his original purpose. Consequently, Gautama determined to follow a "middle way" between asceticism and self-indulgence, and furthermore to continue the quest for truth strictly on his own, with no outside assistance. Both of these principles later became key points in his teachings.

Enlightenment and Buddhahood   The experience which transformed Siddhartha Gautama into the Buddha ("Enlightened One") and thus gave birth to the religion of Buddhism began at dusk on Gautama's thirty-fifth birthday. While meditating under a tree, (the Bodhi-Tree of Wisdom or Enlightenment) he sensed that a breakthrough was imminent. Here again, legend takes over — in the face of the strongest efforts of Māra, the Evil One, who tempted him with beautiful goddesses, and attacked him with tempests, flaming rocks and other devices, Gautama held fast. Eventually, at dawn, his mind "pierced the bubble" of the universe, enabling him to realize the essential truth about life, and about the path to salvation. In the introduction to the *Jataka*, part of Buddhist Scripture, the event is described as follows:

It was before the sun had set that the Great Being thus vanquished the army of Māra. And then, while the Bo-tree in homage rained red, coral-like sprigs upon his priestly robes, he acquired in the first watch of the night the knowledge of previous existences; in the middle watch of the night, the divine eye; and in the last watch of the night, his intellect fathomed Dependent Origination.

. . . And when the Great Being, at the dawning of the day, had thus made the ten thousand worlds thunder with his attainment of omniscience, all these worlds became most gloriously adorned. Flags and banners erected on the eastern rim of the world let their streamers fly to the western rim of the world; likewise those erected on the western rim of the world, to the eastern rim of the world;

. . . When thus he had attained to omniscience, and was the centre of such unparalleled glory and homage . . . he breathed forth

Buddha. (Although this particular likeness is Japanese, it still reflects strong Indian influences in design. What are these influences, and what is the significance of Buddha's "third eye" and elongated ear lobes?)

United Nations

that solemn utterance which has never been omitted by any of the Buddhas:

"Through birth, and rebirth's endless round,
    Seeking in vain, I hastened on,
    To find who framed this edifice.
    What misery! — birth incessantly!

O builder! I've discovered thee!
    This fabric thou shalt ne'er rebuild!
    Thy rafters all are broken now,
    And pointed roof demolished lies!
    This mind has demolition reached,
    And seen the last of all desire!"[2]

Thus, Gautama became the Buddha. Enraptured, he remained rooted to the spot for seven days, and in a trance-like state for several more weeks. The experience filled him with a desire to share his insight with others, and this he did, with great effectiveness, as a preacher and teacher until his death around 483 B.C. The site of Buddha's enlightenment became a sacred place to his followers, and remains to this day a destination of many devout Buddhist pilgrims. It is located in northern India, near the city of Gaya.

The Founding of the Buddhist Religion   As soon as he was able, Buddha left his place of meditation, and began walking to Benares, which was more than one hundred miles to the north-west. Near the city, he encountered five ascetics who had previously abandoned him for his unorthodox views. In a speech to them, he outlined his enlightened thoughts and converted them as his first disciples. In time, they helped him to found the *Sangha*, the monastic brotherhood of Buddhism. Within a few short years, monasteries were springing up all over India. A new religion had been established.

2. Buddhist Scriptures

How They Developed   Unlike most of the other world religions, Buddhism makes no official attempt to insist upon orthodoxy of belief, and has no single book of divinely inspired revelation. The Buddha himself apparently wrote nothing. According to Buddhist tradition, this fact prompted five hundred of the leading monks to hold the first Great Council, immediately after Buddha's death, to formulate authoritatively his teachings. Subsequently, these were preserved orally in the Buddhist monasteries, which had come to number in the hundreds.

A century later, a second Great Council was necessary to settle numerous doctrinal disputes that had developed. A third Great Council was called by the emperor Ashoka for exactly the same purpose. The fourth Great Council, held on the island of Ceylon in the first century A.D., saw the first formal attempt to organize, in the *Pali* tongue (a language much like Sanskrit) the massive sections of hitherto memorized teachings. As well as these original teachings, some Buddhists accept the validity of the commentaries and views of later sages, so that today, Buddhist Scriptures, if all bound together, would fill a thousand library shelves.

The Tripitaka   Of all the scriptural passages known to Buddhists, the ones commonly revered are known as *The Tripitaka* (The Three Baskets). The Tripitaka is almost ten thousand pages long and is the principal source for the life and teachings of Gautama. It has three main divisions: the *Vinaya Pitaka* is a collection of rules for the Sangha; the *Sutta Pitaka* contains discourses between Buddha and his disciples, which constitute the main body of Buddhist beliefs; and the *Abhidhamma Pitaka* contains views on the nature of the universe.

3. The Basic Beliefs of Buddhism

Relation to Hinduism   In the sixth century B.C., northern India seethed with religious as well as political turmoil. There was a growing disenchantment with certain features of Hinduism, particularly the oppressive caste system, and the exalted place of the priestly caste of Brahmins within that system. Although he was a prominent member of the second-ranking Kshatriya caste, Gautama nonetheless rejected the notion of human inequality based on mere hereditary distinctions. His scepticism concerning the elaborate, secretive rituals of the priesthood, and other Hindu practices, is reflected in this comment attributed to him:

> It is not the knotted hair and the sprinkling of ashes that make a Brahmin but the practice of truth and love. . . . Neither abstinence, nor going naked, nor shaving the head, nor a rough garment, neither offerings to priests, nor sacrifices to gods, will cleanse a man who is not free from delusions.[3]

The Buddha likewise rejected the contemporary Hindu fatalism that suggested salvation could be attained only by a chosen few. He believed that it was a mistake to insist that Sanskrit remain the language of religion, since it was unintelligible to the vast majority of Hindus. Furthermore, he concluded that the magic and sorcery creeping into Hinduism was a sham — a trend encouraged by corrupt Brahmins who were profiting handsomely by playing on the superstition and credulity of the masses. In short: "Religion had become a technique for cajoling or coercing innumerable cosmic bellhops to do what you wanted them to."[4] Such criticisms, plus his unwillingness to accept the total authority of the Vedas and Upanishads, caused Buddha to be branded a heretic by the official Hindu community. But this did not necessarily mean persecution, and in fact the Buddhists were allowed to practise their beliefs, largely unmolested, for centuries. Ironically, Buddhism subsequently disappeared almost entirely in India, for reasons that will be explained later in this chapter.

Despite these differences, however, it must be noted that Buddhism did not, or could not, free itself entirely from its Hindu background. Gautama accepted the traditional Indian beliefs of reincarnation, dharma and karma, and although his concept of it was somewhat different, he also believed in Nirvana. Moreover, as previously indicated, he was a devotee of raja yoga, the profound meditation which held the key to enlightenment, and thus to the salvation of Nirvana.

The Core of Buddhism   Buddha himself expressed the kernel of his philosophy when he said: "I teach only two things, O disciples, the fact of suffering and the possibility of escape from suffering."[5]

These fundamental ideas are enlarged upon in the famous "Four Noble Truths" and "Eightfold Path", which Buddha initially revealed in his first sermon to the five ascetics, referred to earlier. This version is taken from the "Mahavagga" (a section of the *Vinaya Pitaka*):

> There are two extremes, brethren, which he who has given up the world ought to avoid. What are these two extremes? A life given to pleasures, devoted to pleasures and lusts — this is degrading, sensual, vulgar, ignoble and profitless. And a life given to mortifications — this is painful, ignoble and profitless. By avoiding these two extremes, brethren, I have gained the knowledge of the Middle Path which leads to insight, which leads to wisdom, which conduces to calm, to knowledge and to Supreme Enlightenment. . . . It is the Noble Eightfold Path, namely: right views, right intent, right speech, right conduct, right means of livelihood, right endeavour, right mindfulness, right meditation. . . .
>
> This, brethren, is the Noble Truth of Suffering: birth is suffering; decay is suffering; illness is suffering; death is suffering; presence of objects we hate is suffering; separation from objects we love is suffering; not to obtain what we desire is suffering.
>
> In brief, the five aggregates which spring from grasping are painful.
>
> This, brethren, is the Noble Truth concerning the Origin of Suffering: verily, it originates in that craving which causes the renewal of becomings, is accompanied by sensual delight, and seeks satisfaction now here, now there; that is to say, craving for pleasures, craving for becoming, craving for not becoming.
>
> This, brethren, is the Noble Truth concerning the Cessation of Suffering: verily, it is passionlessness, cessation without remainder of this very craving; the laying aside of, the giving up, the being free from, the harbouring no longer of, this craving.
>
> This, brethren, is the Noble Truth concerning the Path which leads to the Cessation of Suffering: verily, it is this Noble Eightfold Path. . . .
>
> And this knowledge and insight arose in my mind: the emancipation of my mind cannot be shaken; this is my last birth; now shall I not be born again. . . .[6]

The Four Noble Truths   To summarize, the "facts of life" as Buddha sees them are as follows:

1. Life is *dukkha.* (suffering)
2. The cause of suffering is *tanha.* (desire)
3. The way to end suffering is by overcoming desire.
4. To overcome desire, one must follow the Eightfold Path.

Buddha taught that man is a slave to his ego. He wishes pleasure, wealth, happiness, security, success, long life and a myriad of other things for himself and for his loved ones. However, pain, frustration, sickness and decrepitude are more likely to be his lot, and death is inevitable. By clinging to the "wheel of life", we condemn ourselves to an endless cycle of rebirths, with all its attendant miseries. The only way we can avoid these evils is by eliminating all desires — in other words, to extinguish our own egos altogether, as we would snuff out candles. In this way, the sting of illness, old age and even death is removed, because these "developments" do not interfere with any of our plans or goals. This is true wisdom, and can be attained by following the Eightfold Path, a set of philosophical and ethical guidelines that should be pursued in ascending order.

The Eightfold Path

1. *Right Knowledge.*   This is basically the Four Noble Truths, and is more likely to be achieved if one associates with a trained holy man, to absorb his wisdom and his spirit of compassion and love.

2. *Right Aims.*   Above all, one must *resolve* to make progress toward salvation.

3. *Right Speech.*   Our speech reflects our character. We must especially avoid speaking false, obscene, slanderous and belittling words.

4. *Right Conduct.*   Five precepts constitute the core of Buddhism's moral code: no killing, stealing, lying, committing of illicit sexual acts or consuming of intoxicants.

5. *Right Livelihood.*   One's line of work should not make it impossible to observe the moral code. Some specific occupations which Buddha condemned included the slave dealer, butcher, prostitute and the trader in lethal weapons and substances.

6. *Right Effort.*   One must have the will power to curb his desires and develop the required virtues.

7. *Right Mindfulness.*   Buddha told his followers that what a person is stems from what he thinks. We must examine our behaviour, and the thoughts from which it stems. By improving our thoughts, we should become more virtuous. Thus, our ignorance, the real cause of our sins, can be overcome.

8. *Right Meditation.*   By this Buddha meant the practice of raja yoga in which, after proper mental and physical preparation, the truly devoted person breaks through to Nirvana.

Emphasis on Individual Effort   Some people tend to criticize Buddhism on the grounds that it seeks to suppress and indeed annihilate individualism. It is true that Buddhists believe the idea of a single, separate self to be false. Rather, they conceive of the universe consisting perpetually of the same materials, which are constantly re-assembling in a process of unending flux. Thus, a "person" is merely a tiny collection of hopes, fears, thoughts, feelings, physical matter, etc., which is changing with every passing moment. They see no tragedy in the person attempting to identify or associate with ultimate reality rather than himself. To draw an analogy, the significant thing is not the drop of water entering the ocean, but the ocean itself. Moreover, it can be clearly seen that, in seeking this broader identity or salvation through the Eightfold Path, the Buddhist is urged to rely on his own efforts. Buddha stressed the idea that each person was responsible for his own salvation, as indicated in this remark: "By one's self the evil is done, by one's self one suffers; by one's self the evil is left undone, by one's self one is purified. The pure and the impure stand and fall by themselves, no one can purify another."[7]

Buddha's constant advice to his followers was: "Look within, *thou* art the Buddha." On his death-bed, he is purported to have said:

> . . . Therefore . . . be ye lamps unto yourselves. Rely on yourselves, and do not rely on external help. Hold fast to the truth as a lamp. Seek salvation alone in the truth. . . . Those who, either now or after I am dead, shall be a lamp unto themselves, relying upon themselves only and not relying upon any external help, but holding fast to the truth as their lamp . . . it is they . . . who shall reach the very topmost height![8]

Is Buddhism A Religion? *

There are those who, rather than criticize Buddhism as a religion, prefer to argue that it is not, in fact, a religion at all. Assuredly, Buddha had no use for sacrifices, worship, prayers or rituals of any kind, and just as adamantly rejected the principle of authority in religious matters. As he advised his followers:

> Believe nothing just because you have been told it, or it is commonly believed, or because it is traditional or because you yourselves have imagined it. Do not believe what your Teacher tells you merely out of respect for the Teacher. But whatsoever, after due examination and analysis, you find to be conducive to the good, the benefit, the welfare of all beings — that doctrine believe and cling to, and take as your guide.[9]

Buddha also revealed his disbelief in the supernatural with flat condemnations of sorcery, divination and the like. He gave this warning: "By this ye shall know that a man is not my disciple — that he tries to work a miracle."[10]

*(Review Chapter One, The Nature of Religion, p. 2.)

Most significantly, Buddha doubted the existence of a human soul, (this is the *anatta,* or no-soul doctrine) and of a god in the sense of a personified father-figure who created and presides over the universe. He never claimed to do miracles, nor did he encourage people to regard him as a god, or a saviour of any kind. He merely said he was "awake", or enlightened, and thus in a position to *point the way* toward salvation, a difficult path which the individual would have to walk on his own.

Of course, Buddhism's claim to the status of a religion is based mainly on its attempt to examine the meaning of life and the universe, and to provide man with an ethical standard and an overall goal beyond this life. Also, despite Buddha's wishes, he was deified after his death by some of his followers. This step was only the beginning of Buddhism taking on many of the usual trappings of a major religion, including sacrifices, temple worship and various other rituals, plus elaborate Scriptures and complex doctrines.

Buddhism's World View   Because of his overriding concern with the problems of this life, and how to cope with them, Buddha did not bother to develop a precise or detailed cosmology. However, a few basic views on this subject do emerge from his teachings. The universe, he believed, consists of a vast number of worlds, on many of which there could be life, and it is composed of two essential elements: *prakriti* (matter) and *purushas* (spirits). Buddha rejected the Hindu belief that matter is maya, or illusory and unreal. The physical world, and the suffering it produces, are only too real. An individual human being is a purusha (of which there are an infinite number), who has been reborn into his present existence because of past karma. His ignorance, which causes him to crave pleasure, wealth and other things of this material world, and to commit evil deeds, is the chain that binds him to the wheel of rebirth. This idea is further expanded in Buddhist Scriptures, as in the following excerpt from Buddha's reflections on "Dependent Origination" while under the Bodhi Tree:

> On ignorance depends karma;
> On karma depends consciousness;
> On consciousness depend name and form;
> On name and form depend the six organs of sense;
> On the six organs of sense depends contact;
> On contact depends sensation;
> On sensation depends desire;
> On desire depends attachment;
> On attachment depends existence;
> On existence depends birth;
> On birth depend old age and death, sorrow, lamentation, misery, grief and despair.[11]

Buddha argued that no rituals, gods or any type of outside power could save man. The only salvation lies in the realization of the Four Noble Truths and the diligent pursuit of the Noble Eightfold Path.

Karma
> Nor grain, nor wealth, nor store of gold and silver,
> Not one amongst his women-folk and children,

Nor slave, domestic, hired man,
Nor anyone that eats his bread,
Can follow him who leaves this life,
But all things must be left behind.

But every deed a man performs,
With body, or with voice, or mind,
'Tis this that he can call his own,
This with him take as he goes hence.
This is what follows after him,
And like a shadow ne'er departs.

Let all, then, noble deeds perform,
A treasure-store for future weal;
For merit gained this life within,
Will yield a blessing in the next.[12]

The above passage reveals Buddhism's view of karma, and its debt to
Hindu thinking on this theme. The following words of Buddha on the same
topic are interesting for their phraseology, which is somewhat reminiscent of
an Old Testament saying:

That which ye sow, ye reap. See yonder fields!
The sesamum was sesamum, the corn
Was corn. The Silence and the Darkness knew!
So is a man's fate born.
He cometh, reaper of the things he sowed. . . .[13]

Conduct   Generally speaking, the fundamental ethics of Buddhism are
spelled out in the Noble Eightfold Path. As in the case of many other religions,
Buddhism looks up to its founder as the ideal in human conduct. Above all, the
humane qualities of Gautama are stressed. Buddhist Scriptures are filled with
stories illustrating the compassion, charity and non-violence which he preached
and practised. For example, there is the occasion when he broke society's convention to speak to a wretched, terrified outcaste and ended up by admitting the
man into his religious order.
    The following passages shed further light on Buddha's definition of
"goodness":

Let a man overcome anger by love, let him overcome evil by good; let
him overcome the greedy by liberality, the liar by truth. Shame on him
that strikes; greater shame on him who, stricken, strikes back.[14]

Brethren, there are two ethical teachings. . . . What two? "Look at evil
as evil" is the first teaching. "Seeing evil as evil, be disgusted therewith,
be cleansed of it, be freed of it" is the second teaching. . . . Brethren,
there are these three persons found existing in the world. What three?
The one who is like a drought, the one who rains locally, and the one
who pours down everywhere.

And how, brethren, is a person like a drought?

Herein, brethren, a certain person is . . . no giver of food and drink, clothing and . . . bed, lodging and lights to . . . the wretched and needy beggars. . . .

And how, brethren, is a person like a local rainfall? In this case a person is a giver to some, but to others he gives not. . . .

And how, brethren, does a person rain down everywhere? In this case a certain person gives to all. . . .

Brethren, even if one should seize the hem of my garment and walk behind me step for step, yet if he be covetous in his desires, fierce in his longing, malevolent of heart, of mind corrupt, careless and unrestrained, not quieted but scatterbrained and uncontrolled in his sense, that monk is far from me and I am far from him. . . .[15]

Hatred does not cease by hatred at any time; hatred ceases by love. . . . As rain breaks through an ill-thatched house, passion will break through an unreflecting mind. . . . As a solid rock is not shaken by the wind, wise people waver not amidst blame and praise. Wise people . . . become serene. . . . If one man conquer in battle a thousand times a thousand men, and if another conquer himself, he is the greatest of conquerors. . . . Not even a god could change into defeat the victory of a man who has vanquished himself. . . . Let no man think lightly of evil, saying in his heart, "It will not come nigh unto me." Even by the falling of water drops a water pot is filled; the fool becomes full of evil, even if he gather it little by little. . . . There is no fire like passion; there is no evil like hatred; there is no pain like this bodily existence; there is no happiness higher than peace. Hunger is the worst of diseases, bodily demands the greatest evil; if one knows this truly, that is Nirvana. . . . Those who are attached to nothing, and hate nothing, have no fetters. . . . The fault of others is easily perceived, but that of oneself is difficult to perceive; a man winnows his neighbour's faults like chaff, but his own fault he hides, as a cheat hides an unlucky cast of the die. . . . A man who has learned little grows old like an ox; his flesh grows, but his knowledge does not grow. . . . Earnestness is the path of Nirvana, thoughtlessness the path of death.[16]

Nirvana   Periodically, Buddha was pointedly questioned about the potential for, and nature of, a life after death. For a person who did not achieve enlightenment in his present life there would be a later rebirth in a form appropriate to the karma accumulated by that person. But what of the *arhat*, or holy man, who had achieved the ideal of the Eightfold Path and had extinguished all desire? On this point the Buddha equivocated somewhat, but his remarks tend to the conclusion that, once enlightened, the arhat escapes the cycle of rebirth and attains perfect freedom and bliss, the precise nature of which cannot be defined by man. Buddha's own death, and subsequent passage to Nirvana, is portrayed in this excerpt from the Scriptures:

Then the Lord addressed the brethren, "Well then, brethren, I now exhort you. Impermanent are compound things; strive with earnestness!" These were his last words. Then the Lord reached the first Ecstacy, and ascending from the first he reached the second, from the second he reached the third, and from the third he reached the fourth. From the fourth he reached the abode of infinite space. . . . When the Lord attained Nirvana, at the time of Nirvana, there was a great shaking of the earth, terrifying and frightful, and the drums of the gods resounded. . . .[17]

When pressed on speculative questions dealing with such matters as Creation, the existence of a Supreme Power, and the nature of the afterlife, Buddha became non-committal. Basically, he tried to discourage what he considered to be idle guesswork because he doubted the possibility of definitive answers and felt the time could be better spent attempting to deal with the harsh realities presented by life in the here and now. When a monk threatened to leave the Sangha unless he received some straight answers to his questions about the hereafter, Buddha allegedly replied:

Whether the dogma obtains, Malunkyaputta, that the world is eternal, or that the world is not eternal, there still remain birth, old age, death, sorrow, lamentations, misery, grief and despair — for the extinction of which in the present life I am prescribing.[18]

Thus, any detailed formulations in Buddhist thought on such questions cannot be reliably attributed to Buddha himself. This reservation should be kept in mind when reading such passages as this one, in which one scholar, Edward Conze, summarizes the attributes of Nirvana as described in Buddhist Scriptures:

. . . Nirvana is permanent, stable, imperishable, immovable, ageless, deathless, unborn, and unbecome, that it is power, bliss and happiness, the secure refuge, the shelter, and the place of unassailable safety; that it is the real Truth and the supreme Reality; that it is the Good, the supreme goal and the one and only consummation of our life, the eternal, hidden and incomprehensible Peace.[19]

The Place of Women   There is no doubt that in Buddhist doctrine the place of women is an inferior one. This stems from the traditional cultural and social values of Asia, and specifically from the influence of the Hindu environment from which Buddhism grew. It is true that Buddha permitted both men and women of any caste to become monks and to join the Sangha, or brotherhood of believers. But being a monk did not automatically guarantee enlightenment, and Buddhist Scriptures create the impression that females, although they can accumulate good karma, can only rarely attain Nirvana, and usually must await rebirth as a male before they can take this ultimate step.

Toleration   Although theirs is a missionary religion, Buddhists as a general rule have not forced their beliefs on other people. They rely more on setting an example which others might emulate and on providing in their excellent schools and libraries the background for those who wish it.

But the key to how Buddhists look upon other religions is found in these words spoken by Buddha when asked about the validity of the faiths of other men:

> . . . in whatever doctrine and discipline the noble eightfold path is not found, therein also is not found the monk of the first degree, nor the monk of the second degree, nor the monk of the third degree, nor the monk of the fourth degree. . . . Now in this Doctrine and Discipline, O Subhadda, the noble eightfold path is found; and therein alone, O Subhadda, are found the monk of the first degree, and the monk of the second degree, and the monk of the third degree, and the monk of the fourth degree. Destitute of true monks are all other creeds.[20]

4. Buddhist Practices

The Monastic Ideal   Since Buddhism emphasizes the desirability of self-removal from the turmoil of everyday life, it understandably came to be an essentially monastic religion. Buddha advised his followers to seek out men of wisdom and to remain close by them. This of course encouraged the growth of communities around Buddhist sages — in effect monasteries whose members shared a common goal, the attainment of Nirvana through enlightenment. Buddha cautioned that membership in the Sangha did not guarantee success in this quest, but it at least represented the best chance for success.

Today, there are thousands of Buddhist monasteries throughout the world and their membership constitutes the "hard core" of the faithful. In some countries, such as Burma, Thailand and Ceylon, virtually every young male spends at least a few weeks of his life in a monastery.

Typically, he will be initiated in an elaborate ceremony around the age of four. To symbolize the life of Gautama, he will first be dressed in fine garments, then stripped of these, have his head shaved, and be given a begging bowl and a plain, saffron-coloured robe — the traditional symbols of the Buddhist monk. Most likely, he will spend the next night in a monastery, before returning to his family and regular life. Around the age of twenty, a male spends several weeks in a monastery, and may then decide to remain permanently as a full-fledged monk; however, most return ultimately to a lay life.

For those who do become monks, a life of poverty, celibacy and "inoffensiveness" is prescribed. Before gaining admittance to the brotherhood, a would-be monk must make this declaration of faith: "I go to the Buddha for refuge; I go to the Dhamma [religious law] for refuge; I go to the Sangha for refuge."[21] In so doing, the devotee gives up his civic rights, such as voting and being eligible for public office. Moreover, few sects permit monks to marry. In return for renouncing this world, the monk gains the deep respect of laymen, and exemption from trial in courts of law except in cases involving serious offences.

Miller Services Ltd.

A five-year-old "mini-monk" performs a fire ritual, watched by the adult members of a Buddhist seminary.

A monk is allowed only a few personal possessions; these include the aforementioned robe and begging bowl, plus utensils such as a needle, razor, filter for straining insects from drinking water (so as not to inadvertently swallow them and thus break the rule of no killing) and a string of beads to count while meditating on the qualities of Buddha. In begging for food, a monk must obey certain rules, chief of which are: do not eat after the noon-hour, do accept whatever is offered, and make no reply when it is offered. The Buddhist view is that the *donor* should offer thanks — for the opportunity to show generosity and thus accumulate good karma. In return for being sustained by the community, the members of a monastery provide services for laymen, such as performing ceremonies at temples, assisting at weddings and funerals, and educating the young in religious matters. But their primary concern is meditation and, in the case of some, missionary work.

The monastery itself, in addition to acting as a school, often functions as a community centre, a hotel for travellers and a refuge for the sick, the poor and the elderly. Moreover, the monastic communities in predominantly Buddhist countries have often played an active role in political affairs, as has recently been demonstrated in the case of the war in Vietnam. Conversely, in some Southeast Asian countries, such as Burma, it is not uncommon for leading political figures to withdraw to the relative seclusion of a monastery for a prolonged period of rest and meditation.

It should be remembered, however, that the majority of Buddhists are laymen and, as such, occupy themselves with the tasks of daily life, hoping to accumulate enough good karma and earn salvation by good works or at least a higher existence in the next rebirth. In fact, because of the relatively slow advance of public education in parts of Asia until recent times, significant numbers of the common people pay little more than lip service to the ideals of Buddhism and they practise what amounts to a thinly veiled animism.

Other Practices   Contrary to the exhortations of Gautama, Buddhists have, over the centuries, evolved both complicated doctrines and elaborate rituals, and some have even deified Buddha himself, so that Buddha has become the world's best known idol. Correspondingly, temples of worship have come into existence, and the monks have become, to some extent, a priestly class.

In addition to their usual devotions in the temples, some Buddhists engage in pilgrimages. For example, Shri Pada, a mountain in Ceylon, is visited by over 300,000 pilgrims annually, because at its peak are markings believed to be footprints of the Buddha. Other major targets are the *stupas*, or sacred shrines. These are in the shape of towers or domes, and supposedly contain relics of Buddha or his disciples. By walking around a stupa, presenting offerings such as food or flowers, and meditating upon Buddha's teachings, both monks and laymen accumulate good karma. Such merit also can be earned by anyone who helps to clean and otherwise maintain temples, stupas and other important Buddhist institutions.

5. Growth and Division

History of Expansion   Even within Gautama's own lifetime, Buddhism had gained a significant foothold in India, the land of its origin. Dozens, and later hundreds, of monasteries sprang up, and it was from these centres that the message of Buddha was spread. Its expansion was no doubt facilitated by the contemporary dissatisfaction, at least on the part of some people, with certain aspects of Hinduism. In contrast, Gautama was a great popularizer of religion, as he avoided the elaborate, esoteric ideas of the Upanishads and communicated a simple, ritual-free path of salvation, open to all believers, in a language that the common people could understand.

Another key factor in the early expansion of Buddhism was its acceptance in the third century B.C. by the great emperor, Ashoka, who promoted its growth throughout most of India and helped its spread into Ceylon and parts of Southeast Asia. Within a short time, Buddhism was making headway in Burma, Thailand, Vietnam, Cambodia and Laos. By the sixth century A.D. it had spread even further, into Nepal, Sikkim, Tibet, Mongolia, China, Korea and Japan. In all of these countries, Buddhism profoundly influenced the social and cultural, as well as the religious, life of the people it touched. Ironically, however, Buddhism all but disappeared in India itself, due principally to the flexibility and revitalization of Hinduism, unfortunate attacks by Moslems on Buddhist schools and monasteries, and the gradual infiltration of luxury and other abuses into the life of some monasteries.

The Development of Sects   Like every other world religion, Buddhism has been fragmented into sects. This was caused by disputes over translation and interpretation of Buddha's teachings, by the impact of various native cultures upon Buddhism as it reached them, and simply by the passage of the centuries. But in spite of their many and considerable differences, these sects retain as a common denominator their acceptance of Buddha's essential message: the Four Noble Truths and the Eightfold Path.

The Big and Little Rafts   Two of the largest and most important Buddhist sects are Hinayana and Mahayana Buddhism. The word "yana" means ferry or raft, and reflects Buddha's view of his teachings as being a vehicle for crossing the sea of life to the tranquil shore of Nirvana. The terms "Mahayana" and "Hinayana" means the "greater" and "lesser" way respectively, and refer to differing degrees of flexibility in approach to doctrinal questions, and in the interpretation and practice of Buddhist ideas.

Hinayana Buddhism   Hinayana Buddhism is really more properly referred to as Theravada (The Way of the Elders). This is a conservative school of Buddhist thought which claims to represent the original and true teachings of the Buddha (so does every other sect). Theravadins emphasize the idea that each individual must save himself. Their ideal is the arhat, or holy man, who renounces the world, seeks Nirvana through diligent meditation and adheres strictly to monastic rules as well as to the established doctrines of his sect. The latter are based on the very earliest Buddhist texts.

For Theravadins, the key virtue is *bodhi*, or wisdom. Buddha is not worshipped as a god but revered as a great teacher and saint. They avoid metaphysical speculation, believing it to be unnecessary, and futile in any case. Life is suffering; Buddha has indicated the path of escape, and a man must walk it alone. Thus it can be argued that Hinayana Buddhism is a relatively austere, rational faith, offering intellectual challenge, but little companionship or emotional solace. Nonetheless, it has had great success in Burma, Thailand and Ceylon, where it predominates, and is also fairly strong in Laos, Cambodia and parts of Vietnam.

Mahayana Buddhism   The "Greater Vehicle" is bigger not only in the sense of a more liberal interpretation of Buddhist doctrine, but also in terms of numbers of adherents. It began to develop about two hundred years after the death of Buddha. Mahayana Buddhists stress the fact that Buddha demonstrated great selflessness when, after achieving supreme *bodhi* and becoming the Buddha, he turned his back on the salvation he had earned to show others the way. Thus, for Mahayanists, the ideal is the bodhisattva (one whose essence is bodhi) who

Miller Services Ltd.

In the garden of the monastery to which he belongs, a monk engages in quiet study.

follows the example of Buddha and remains in the world to serve his fellows. They believe there have been many such figures and will be many more to aid in the eventual salvation of every person. As Buddhism expanded into lands of different religious beliefs, the idea of the bodhisattva became a convenient bridging device, since important local deities and sages could be regarded as bodhisattvas and thus retain some significance when Buddhism was adopted.

Mahayana Buddhism has not spurned metaphysics, and so has developed an elaborate world view, featuring many Heavens and Hells, and a rather materialistic concept of Nirvana, as the following passage indicates:

> [It is a place] surrounded by radiant beams and brilliant jewels of un-told price. In every direction the air resounds with harmonious tunes, the sky is full of radiance, large heavenly birds of paradise are flying to and fro. . . . [Amitabha] Buddha sits on a lotus seat like, a gold mountain in the midst of all glories, surrounded by his saints.[22]

Some Mahayanists believe that spirits, while awaiting rebirth, reside in these Heavens or Hells, depending upon their accumulated karma. Buddha is worshipped as a god, and as such is the recipient of prayers and sacrifices of various kinds. Mahayanists also reject the idea that a man's salvation is strictly in his own hands. They point to Buddha's claim that there really are no individual selves as a suggestion that each person's fate is bound up with that of everyone else. Finally, the Mahayana sect accepts all Buddhist texts as equally authoritative, and by being somewhat less strict in its demands about following rules and discipline holds out hope of salvation to a greater number of people — the average person as well as the brilliant monk, the female as well as the male, the layman as well as the holy man. Mahayanists are the leading Buddhist sect in Mongolia, Tibet, Korea, China and Japan.

Because of its greater flexibility and permissiveness, Mahayana Buddhism has been more susceptible to the influence of local religions and cultures. This is reflected in its wide variety of practices and doctrines. Periods of worship may coincide with local festivals. Forms of worship strongly reflect local customs, and may include the use of incense, candles, flowers, holy water or other embellishments. Most important, fundamental doctrinal differences within the Mahayana school have produced numerous sub-sects, some of which deserve special attention.

Tibetan Lamaism   A unique form of Buddhism has evolved in Tibet. Around A.D. 750 an Indian monk appeared in that country, preaching *Tantrism;* this combined certain features of Mahayana Buddhism with some of the magical, mystical elements of popular Hinduism. Tantrism, after mingling with Tibet's own beliefs in demons and sorcery, was transformed into what is known as Tibetan Lamaism. Tibet's rulers, the Dalai Lamas, came to be regarded as god-kings — the living incarnations of previous holy beings and thus the highest possible representation of divine power in a human condition. The followers of this faith have been severely persecuted since 1950 by the Chinese Communists and have seen the current Dalai Lama exiled.

Shin Buddhism   Buddhism came to China from India around the first century A.D. Because of the strength of the native philosophies of Taoism and Confucianism, its growth was fairly slow. But beginning in the sixth century, an increasing number of missionary monks of the Mahayana sect arrived in China,

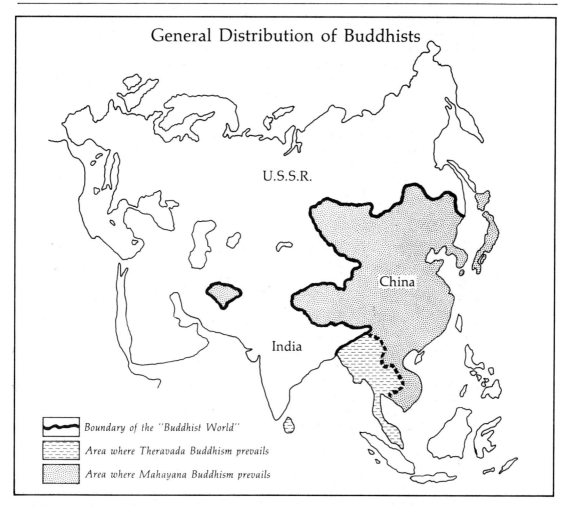

General Distribution of Buddhists

U.S.S.R.

China

India

Boundary of the "Buddhist World"

Area where Theravada Buddhism prevails

Area where Mahayana Buddhism prevails

and their teachings about a compassionate saviour and a life after death attracted a significant number of followers. Buddhism's cause was greatly strengthened by the flexibility of Mahayana doctrines, which enabled it to adapt itself to Chinese life. Its official recognition by later Chinese emperors as one of the "Three Great Truths" led to rather unique situations. For example, a Chinese peasant might follow Taoist principles as a farmer, structure his family life around Confucianist ideals, and pray to Buddha in times of stress, such as at funerals, during illness, and so on.

    Shin Buddhism developed as a major Buddhist sect in China. Its key variation is the concept of Amida Buddha. He is the supreme Buddha, and the compassionate saviour of mankind. All bodhisattvas, and even Gautama himself, are regarded as manifestations of Amida, who sent them to reveal his truth in different places at different times (a notion reminiscent of the avatars of Hinduism). Since men are imperfect, and incapable of achieving Nirvana on their own, they can seek and rely on the aid of Amida Buddha's saving grace. Nirvana is depicted as a place, to which saved souls go, and where they survive as separate and conscious beings.

Along with many other aspects of Chinese civilization, Shin Buddhism was "exported" to Korea, and to Japan in the seventh century A.D.; today, almost half of Japan's 35 million Buddhists are members of the Shin sect. Because it invites men to accept the unearned gift of salvation from their saviour, Amida Buddha, Shin is frequently referred to in Japan as "the easy way". The "hard way", which attracts almost as many followers, is known as *Zen*.

Zen Buddhism   Although it originated in China, the unique and fascinating philosophy of Zen has been most successful in Japan, where it was introduced around the twelfth century. "Zen" means a technique of meditation. It takes its inspiration from a legendary act of Buddha. On one occasion, he supposedly was presented with a golden flower, and asked to speak on his beliefs; instead, he merely held it aloft and looked at it without saying a word. The interpretation derived from this by advocates of Zen is that the Buddha meant people to reject philosophical discourse and speculation in favour of intense personal reflection on life itself. Consequently, Zen monks disregard doctrine, Scriptures, prayer, ritual worship, and even the reverence of Buddha himself and devote themselves to their own peculiar brand of meditation. "Cleanse your mouth of the word Buddha"[23] is an old Zen saying. Images of Buddha and bodhisattvas in Zen temples are not there to be worshipped, but rather to serve as reminders that enlightenment lies within the grasp of any truly earnest seeker. Zen's only real link with Buddhism is that it follows Gautama's advice to seek ultimate knowledge and to "Look within, thou are the Buddha".

The followers of Zen believe that enlightenment comes in a brilliant flash of inspiration known as *satori*. This experience is the goal of all devotees. Initiates begin a program of training under the guidance of a monk who has already achieved his satori. It is generally agreed that this training period, which involves both physical and mental discipline, must last at least ten years. During this time, the initiate is presented with his own special *koan*, which is a puzzle or riddle which he then attempts to fathom. There are about 1,700 koans in all, of which only a small number are in use. Here are a few, as illustrations:

> What was your original face — the one you had before your parents gave birth to you?

> You can make the sound of two hands clapping. Now what is the sound of one hand?

> What is that which makes you answer when you are called?[24]

The Zen trainee may meditate on a single koan until satori comes, or more often, work with different koans from time to time. Periodically, he consults with his teacher, suggesting answers to his koan and receiving "encouragement" which takes very unusual forms, such as a fierce shout, a slap in the face, a clout over the shoulder with a stick or some other exhortation.

The attainment of true satori is very difficult, and quite rare. It cannot be done by sheer intellectualizing, no matter how profound the thought, however clearly expressed. This is what the koans are supposed to illustrate. The Zen trainee is being driven toward an impasse; ideally, a point will be

reached where the trainee meets the stubborn challenge and difficulty of his
koan with all the strength of his will and, at the precise moment of impact, he
has his satori. He realizes there was nothing in the koan after all. The experience
has been known to produce uproarious laughter. Here is one description of
satori:

> Ztt! I entered. I lost the boundary of my physical body. I had my skin,
> of course, but I felt I was standing in the center of the cosmos. . . .
> I saw people coming toward me, but all were the same man. All were
> myself. I had never known this world before. I had believed that I was
> created, but now I must change my opinion: I was never created: I was
> the cosmos; no individual . . . existed.[25]

There are various degrees of satori, and thus it can be partially
experienced on several occasions. If a person attains complete satori, he becomes
an accredited Zen master.

There are no gods, no saviours, no separate selves, but only temporary
expressions of the Universal One. Human beings come into existence, live and
pass away, only to reappear as someone or something else, like waves in the
sea. This is the reality to be appreciated, and once it is, then personal worries
and ambitions will fall away. Faith and good works cannot lead one to satori
any more than reason can. There are no formal rituals to follow, no doctrines
to accept; just float along with the stream of life, accepting the experiences it
brings and, above all, appreciate every moment, especially those spent in the
simplest everyday activities — watching the flight of a bird, walking, doing the
dishes, cutting the grass and yes, sitting in the middle of a traffic jam. The
beauty and wonder of the most common experiences and of the world of nature
are expressed in this passage from Zen writings:

> How marvelous, how miraculous,
> I draw water,
> I gather fuel.
>
> The water-fowl
> Lays its beak in its breast
> And sleeps as it floats.
>
> An old pine tree preaches wisdom
> And a wild bird is crying truth.[26]

One should not try to manage or plan one's life, because not all the
goals will be reached, and only needless frustration will result. Take interest
only in the present, and enjoy it fully.

In a sense, Zen is amoral, because it puts the individual beyond good
and evil, reward and punishment; the chances of the murderer and the rapist
attaining satori are no better or worse than those of the most humane, compassionate person. However, neither does it encourage harmful or cruel acts;
rather, it prompts people to look on one another as brothers, having a common

substance and being fellow travellers through life. On the subject of life and death, Zen has this to say:

> When this realization [that there is no true distinction between life and death] is completely achieved, never again can one feel that one's individual death brings an end to life. One has lived from an endless past and will live into an endless future. . . . At this very moment one partakes of Eternal Life — blissful, luminous, pure.[27]

The Influence of Zen   Zen has had a profound impact on Japanese life. Indeed, it was the most important and influential factor until the recent introduction of elements of Western culture. Some of the arts for which Japan is most famous take their inspiration from Zen, and many are related to the well-known tea ceremony, the origin of which can be found in Buddhist legend.

One day, according to one such legend, Buddha became irritated at his own drowsiness during a prolonged period of meditation and finally cut off his eyelids. Where they fell to the ground, tea plants took root. For centuries, the rejuvenating powers of tea were enjoyed in Zen monasteries, and a formal ceremony was devised for the serving of that beverage.

Today, the tea ceremony is practised mainly by Japanese laymen, who see in it an opportunity for calm reflection in a peaceful, secluded environment. The latter is provided by the tea house, whose delicacy, simplicity and proportion is enhanced by the restful, beautifully landscaped garden that surrounds it. Inside, a modest flower arrangement and perhaps a single beautiful painting provide a touch of warmth to the basically austere design of the house, and serve as elegantly simple reminders of Zen's emphasis on the appreciation of lovely things. The same qualities of simplicity, naturalness, tranquility, spontaneity and balance are reflected in Japanese poetry, music, brush-drawing, drama, pottery-making and architecture.

The martial arts of Japan also are rooted in Zen. Kendo, the art of ceremonial swordsmanship, and judo, the art of unarmed self-defence, feature strict rules and techniques based on Zen principles. For example, one such principle is *wu-wei,* or inaction, derived from the observation of supple tree-branches surviving by bending under the weight of snow, rather than resisting rigidly and being snapped off. Similarly, in judo the expert awaits attack and then uses the opponent's own strength and momentum to defeat him. So, in life, one can defeat himself through striving. The samurai, or warrior class of feudal Japan, adapted their sword-fighting technique along the same lines, stressing alert anticipation of attack and meeting it with spontaneous parries and thrusts, destroying the enemy with a clean, decisive blow — just as one would experience satori.

Today, some Japanese business corporations offer Zen training to their employees because experience has shown that it can reduce strain, fatigue and inefficiency in workers. This can even contribute to a feeling of pride in intuitive mastery of necessary skills and thus leads to job satisfaction and increased productivity.

While it is true that Western culture continues to have considerable impact on Japan, it is likewise true that Zen is growing in popularity in the West. It clearly has influenced the thoughts of such prominent intellectuals as Martin Heidegger, Jean-Paul Sartre and Aldous Huxley. Psychoanalysts see it as a possible way to release the tensions, created particularly in North American

Japan Information Centre, Consulate General of Japan, Toronto

The Daitokuji Temple and garden in Kyoto, Japan. (The spread of white sand represents the sea; the trimmed trees at the corners symbolize mountains.)

cities, where some individuals unnaturally suppress tensions which can lead to various forms of physical and mental illness. Many people are taking up Zen meditation, some for its religious value, others simply as a means of relaxation. Dogen, a Zen master of the thirteenth century, offered these guidelines for meditation:

> To attain the blessedness of meditation you should begin the practice with a pure motive and a firm determination. Your room for meditation must be clean and quiet. Take your regular meal sparingly, and shut out all noises and disturbances. Do not let the mind dwell in thought on what is good or what is bad. Just relax and forget that you are meditating. Do not desire to become a Buddha. If you do, you will never become one.
>
> Sit down in a chair with a large cushion in a manner as comfortable as possible. Wear the clothing loosely, and remove your shoes, but keep your feet in a pair of warm slippers.

Put your right hand on your left thigh, palm up, and let it hold the four fingers of your left hand so that the left thumb may press down the right thumb. Hold your body straight. Lean not to the left nor the right. Do not tip forward nor bend to the back. Your ears should be at right angles to your shoulders, and your nose must be on a straight line with the navel. Keep your tongue at the roof of your mouth and close your lips and teeth firmly. Keep your eyes slightly open, and breathe through your nostrils.

Before you begin meditation, move your body from right to left a few times, then take several slow, deep breaths. Hold your body erect, allowing your breathing to become normal again. Many thoughts will crowd into your mind. . . . Just ignore them and they will soon vanish. . . . In other words, think nothing. . . .

In your meditation you yourself are the mirror reflecting the solution of your problems. The human mind has absolute freedom within its true nature. You can attain your emancipation intuitively. Do not work for emancipation . . . but allow the work itself to be emancipation.

When you wish to rest, move your body slowly and stand up quietly. Practise this meditation in the morning, or in the evening, or at any leisure time during the day. You will soon then realize that your mental burdens are dropping away from you one by one, and that you are gaining a sort of intuitive power hitherto unnoticed. . . . Constant practice of mind culture will lead anyone to the realization of truth.

In Oriental countries there have been thousands upon thousands of students who have practised Zen meditation and obtained its fruits. Do not doubt its possibilities because of the simplicity of its method. If you cannot find the truth right where you are, where else do you expect to wander in finding it?

Life is short and no one knows what the next moment will bring. Cultivate your mind while you have the opportunity, thereby gaining the treasures of wisdom, which in turn you can share abundantly with others, bringing them happiness.[28]

6. The Importance of Buddhism — Past and Present

Its Historical Significance   There is no doubt that Buddhism elevated the level of religious life and thought in most of Asia. This is true even of those areas where Hinduism predominated, because it forced that religion to remedy some of its abuses and revitalize its teachings. Moreover, it had an incalculable effect upon the philosophy, education, literature and art of South and Southeast Asia. For example, Buddhism contributed enormously to the achievements of the Gupta period in India (A.D. 320 to 544 approximately). It inspired the "golden age" of China during the T'ang Dynasty (A.D. 618 to 907) and virtually intro-

Japan Information Centre, Consulate General of Japan, Toronto
A likeness of Buddha painted on the wall of a tenth century temple in South Korea.

duced civilization to Japan. The contributions of Zen Buddhism in particular
have been noted already.

Buddhism Today   Buddhism is not actually winning a lot of new converts
these days, but it is showing signs of rejuvenation in areas where it has long
existed. The Fifth and Sixth Great Councils, held in Burma in Mandalay (1871)
and Rangoon (mid-1950's) respectively, contributed somewhat to this trend.
Moreover, the movement of increasing numbers of Buddhists to the West, and
particularly to North America, is at least causing the thoughts of Buddha to be
spread over more parts of the globe. There are approximately 180,000 Buddhists
in Canada and the continental United States, and Buddhism is the predominant
religion in the state of Hawaii. Naturally, Buddhists are most numerous in cities
having substantial Chinese or East Asian populations, such as Vancouver,

Toronto, San Francisco and New York. Buddhist societies also flourish today in England, Belgium, Holland, Switzerland, Finland and Sweden.

As in the case of Hinduism, the views of Buddhism have to some extent discouraged social progress and reform in lands where it is the principal faith. Ideas such as the elimination of desire and material goals, the promise of eventual salvation for all, and the acceptance of life as basically problematical and full of suffering, do not produce great concern regarding poverty, illiteracy, illness, pollution, the population explosion, or any of the other momentous issues facing humanity today.

The perpetuation of these problems in Buddhist Asia has, of course, increased the opportunities for the spread of Communism. At the time of the Communist takeover of China in 1949, about one-third of the Chinese people were Buddhists. Mao Tse-tung's regime immediately nationalized the monasteries and all sources of Buddhist revenues, and sent the monks either to work in fields and factories or even, in some cases, to fight in the Korean War. The policy of persecution has since been partially eased, and some Buddhist scholars, if their political views are "correct", are permitted to write and occasionally to travel or study abroad.

Western concern regarding the spread of Communism has been reflected in many ways, including the fighting of the war in Vietnam. At one time, some experts regarded Buddhism as a natural ally of local nationalism in the struggle against the spread of Communism. However, the Buddhists' belief in non-violence somewhat limits their effectiveness in this role. Indeed, small numbers of monks have been converted to Marxism, in which they see certain parallels to their own views. And the tragically impressive self-immolations of Vietnamese Buddhist monks, so highly publicized in the West, have been as much protests against Western imperialist interference in Asian life as they have been against Communist aggression. Whether or not Buddhism will be able to retain its hold on countries facing the gigantic problems of the late twentieth century, only time will tell.

Suggestions For Further Study

1. If the Buddha believed that life was suffering, why would he not advocate committing suicide?

2. Buddhism withered in its own soil (India) but took root elsewhere. Why? In what other religions has a similar phenomenon occurred?

3. Buddhism acknowledges the ultimate validity of no other religion, and yet Buddhists have a distinguished record of toleration toward people of other faiths. How can this be explained?

4. Would it be true to say that some Buddhist sects are atheistic, while others are not? Explain.

5. How do you account for the fact that Theravada Buddhism is strong in Buddhist lands close to India, while Mahayana Buddhism predominates in those farther away?

6. In what way was the growth of Mahayana Buddhism similar to the development of the bhakti cults in Hinduism? Has this trend appeared in any other major religion?

7. Statues of the Buddha show a small proturberance in the centre of the fore-head — it is round, and looks somewhat like a bead. What is its significance?

8. In what ways does Marxism coincide *and* clash with Buddhism?

9. The wheel is an ancient Indian symbol. How is it appropriate to Hinduism? to Buddhism? What significance is there in the fact that an eight-spoked wheel is a Buddhist symbol?

Notes

[1]*The Sacred Writings*, as cited in *The Wisdom of Buddha*. New York: The Philosophical Library, 1968, p. 14.

[2]The *Jataka, ibid*, pp. 29-30.

[3]Nancy Wilson Ross, *Three Ways of Asian Wisdom*. New York: Simon and Schuster, Inc., 1966, p. 81. Copyright © 1966 Nancy Wilson Ross. Reprinted by permission of Simon and Schuster. London: (*Hinduism, Buddhism, Zen: An Introduction to Their Meaning and Their Arts*) Faber and Faber Ltd., 1968. Used with permission.

[4]Huston Smith, *The Religions of Man*. New York: The New American Library, 1958, p. 102.

[5]Ross, *op. cit.*, p. 81.

[6]The *Mahavagga* as cited in the Editors of Life, *The World's Great Religions, Vol. I: Religions of the East*. New York: Time Incorporated, 1955, p. 75.

[7]Ross, *op. cit.*, p. 114.

[8]The *Maha-Parinibbana-Sutta* as cited in *The World's Great Religions, Vol. I: Religions of the East, op. cit.*, p. 74.

[9]Ross, *op. cit.*, p. 80.

[10]Smith, *op. cit.*, p. 105.

[11]The *Mahavagga* as cited in *The Wisdom of Buddha, op. cit.*, p. 31.

[12]The *Samyutta-Nikaya, ibid*, p. 84.

[13]Ross, *op. cit.*, p. 114.

[14]The Editors of the National Geographic Society, *Great Religions of the World*. Washington, D.C.: The National Geographic Society, 1971, p. 97. Reprinted by permission of the National Geographic Society.

[15]*The World's Great Religions, Vol. I: Religions of the East, op. cit.*, p. 76.

[16]*Ibid.*, p. 70.

[17]The *Maha-Parinibbana-Sutta, ibid.*, p. 74.

[18]Ross, *op. cit.*, p. 113.

[19]Conze, Edward, *Buddhism: Its Essence and Development*. New York: The Philosophical Library, 1951, p. 40.

[20]*The Wisdom of Buddha, op. cit.*, pp. 48-9.

[21]D. G. Bradley, *A Guide to the World's Religions*. Campden, N.J.: Prentice-Hall, Inc., 1963, p. 115.

[22]*The World's Great Religions, Vol. I: Religions of the East, op. cit.*, p. 64.

[23]Ross, *op. cit.*, p. 145.

[24]*Ibid.*, p. 178.

[25]*Zen Notes*, Vol. I, No. 5, p. 1. New York: The First Zen Institute of America, Inc. Reprinted by permission of The First Zen Institute of America, Inc.

[26]Ross, *op. cit.*, p. 148.

[27]R. F. Sasaki, *Zen: A Religion*. New York: The First Zen Institute of America, Inc., 1958, p. 12. Reprinted by permission of The First Zen Institute of America, Inc.

[28]N. Senzaki and R. S. McCandless, *Buddhism and Zen*. New York: The Wisdom Library, 1953, pp. 25-7. Reprinted by permission of The Philosophical Library, Inc., New York.

Part C

The Western Religions

Chapter Seven

Judaism

Founded:
Thirteenth century B.C.

Founder:
Moses, who emancipated the Jews from slavery in Egypt and later established a "covenant" between his people and Yahweh on Mount Sinai.
Traditionally it is held that Abraham and his descendants established Judaism before Moses; however, the Ten Commandments are now considered by many to be the foundation upon which Judaism rests.

Place:
Palestine (sometimes called Canaan); now Israel

Sacred Books:
The Old Testament, which consists of the Five Books of the Law, the historical books, the Prophets, and other writings. The most sacred books are the Five Books of the Law (the first five books of the Bible), sometimes called the Torah.

Number of Adherents:
About fourteen and one half million

Distribution:
Jews are found throughout the world. Nearly three million live in Asia with the heaviest concentration in Israel. There are about four million in Europe, and seven million in North and South America. Of these, nearly six million are in the United States.

Jews In Canada:
about 350,000-400,000

Sects:
The major sects are Orthodox, Conservative and Reform; there are also sects and divisions within each major sect.

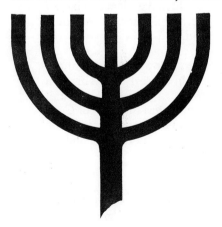

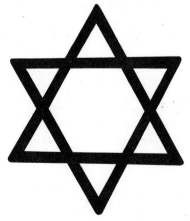

The Menorah   The Star of David (See pages 214-15)

Less than one half of one percent of the world's population is classified as being Jewish. Statistically, they should barely be seen and certainly not heard. Yet, the Jewish contribution to the list of the world's great names in religion, science, literature, music, finance and philosophy is immense. Over ten per cent of all Nobel prizes in physics, chemistry and medicine have been awarded to Jews. From this people came Jesus Christ, acclaimed Son of God by the largest religious body in the world with over 850 million adherents. The organizer of the Christian Church, Paul, was a Jew. Over one billion Communists venerate another man of Jewish lineage, Karl Marx, whose writings form the philosophic basis of a new world order. Albert Einstein, another Jew, ushered in the atomic age and opened a path to the moon with his theoretical physics. Sigmund Freud, a Jewish psychoanalyst, radically altered man's ideas of himself and the relation between mind and matter. Centuries earlier, yet another Jew, Baruch Spinoza inserted a wedge between philosophy and mysticism and thus opened the way to rationalism and modern science. Great nations which appeared at the same time as the Jews have totally disappeared; the Jews, with no homeland for 2,000 years, survive and thrive.

Inevitable questions spring from information like this. How *did* they survive with no homeland for over 2,000 years, not to mention the savage persecution inflicted on them from time to time? Why are their contributions so disproportionately large for their numbers? What do the Jews believe in that can remain so dynamic in these days of religious lethargy? Questions like these form the basis of the following chapter.

1. Origins

The Jewish story begins around 2,000 B.C., on the northern border of the Arabian desert, with a group of people called *Semites*. They were wanderers, ruled by an elder or patriarch. They worshipped stones and pillars, for large ones were thought to be the homes of gods. Springs were considered sacred, as was perhaps natural for a desert people; gods could make them dry up if they so desired. Nature was the centre of their interest and most of the gods were connected in one way or another with the land.

Abraham   Into this Semitic group was born, in Ur, a boy named Abraham who was later to become a tribal leader.* Sometime in his early life Abraham changed from being a *polytheist* to being a *monotheist,* and he put all his faith in the god of the mountains, "El-Shaddai". Believing it was the wish of God, or perhaps because there had recently been many invasions of different peoples into the Ur area, Abraham and the group he now led decided to leave and look for a new home in Canaan. This event occurred about 1900 B.C.

*NOTE: Abraham is the first Old Testament figure to be called a Hebrew. The name was given by the people of Canaan who called him and his followers *Ibri* and *Ibris* (Hebrews), meaning: "From across" — the people who came across the Tigris and Euphrates Rivers. Abraham's descendants were commonly called after his grandson Jacob, or Israel, and thus bore the name *Children of Israel* or *Israelites.* This last name is preferred by some recent scholars to *Hebrews.*

Arriving in Canaan these followers of Abraham soon established themselves, and when Abraham died, his son Isaac and grandson Jacob continued his leadership. Shortly thereafter, (about 1800 B.C.) a famine devastated Canaan. The Israelites, or Hebrews, resumed their travels, this time arriving and settling in the area of the Egyptian empire called the Land of Goshen. Their settlement there is told in the Biblical story of Joseph in Genesis 37-50, and took place in approximately 1700 B.C. At this time, the Hyksos invaders had conquered Egypt and were ruling that land (1750 to 1550 B.C.); they were very tolerant, and allowed the Israelites to live there in peace and to worship their own God, despite the fact that the Egyptians were polytheists in the extreme. During this time, the Israelites thrived.

Before long, though, this situation changed for the worse. About 1500 B.C. the resurgent Egyptians mastered the technique of chariot fighting and used their knowledge to dislodge the Hyksos (invaders who had previously conquered the land). For a time, the Hebrews were allowed to carry on their tranquil life. Later Pharaoh Rameses II, came to the throne. He had a passion for building, and for such jobs needed manpower; the Hebrews were enslaved and put to work. They remained in a state of bondage until the Exodus in about 1300 B.C.

Moses   In order to prevent the Hebrews from remaining apart from the rest of the Egyptians, and to prevent their plotting against the government, the Pharaoh decided to kill all the boys born to Hebrews. Then the girls would have to marry Egyptians and become like the Egyptians themselves. A baby named Moses was born shortly after this law was passed and, by the law, he should have been drowned. But his mother could not do it; neither could she keep him. Therefore she put her child in a basket and let it float down the Nile. The story of his survival is told in chapters of Exodus [Exodus I: 8-10, 22; II: 1-10].

Then one day after he had become a man, Moses killed an Egyptian who had beaten a fellow Hebrew. Then he fled beyond the Red Sea to Midian, where he married Zipporah, the daughter of a priest named Jethro, and settled down to tend Jethro's flocks of sheep. On these long days and nights, Moses began to find himself thinking more and more of the Hebrews in bondage in Egypt and how he might help them. According to the Bible, while Moses was tending the flocks one day, God called him to lead his people to the "land of milk and honey":

1. Now Moses kept the flock of Jethro his father-in-law, the priest of Midian: and he led the flock to the back side of the desert, and came to the mountain of God, *even* to Horeb.

2. And the Angel of the LORD appeared unto him in a flame of fire out of the midst of a bush: and he looked, and, behold, the bush burned with fire, and the bush *was* not consumed.

3. And Moses said, I will now turn aside, and see this great sight, why the bush is not burnt.

4. And when the LORD saw that he turned aside to see, God called unto him out of the midst of the bush, and said, Moses, Moses. And he said. Here *am* I.

5. And he said, Draw not nigh hither: put off thy shoes from off thy feet, for the place whereon thou standest *is* holy ground.

6. Moreover he said, I *am* the God thy father, the God of Abraham, the God of Isaac, and the God of Jacob. And Moses hid his face; for he was afraid to look upon God.

7. And the LORD said, I have surely seen the affliction of my people which *are* in Egypt, and have heard their cry by reason of their taskmasters; for I know their sorrows;

8. And I am come down to deliver them out of the hand of the Egyptians, and to bring them up out of that land unto a good land and a large, unto a land flowing with milk and honey: unto the place of the Canaanites, and the Hittites, and the Amorites, and the Perizzites, and the Hivites, and the Jebusites.

9. Now therefore, behold, the cry of the children of Israel is come unto me: and I have also seen the oppression wherewith the Egyptians oppress them.

10. Come now therefore, and I will send thee unto Pharaoh, that thou mayest bring forth my people the children of Israel out of Egypt.

11. And Moses said unto God, Who *am* I, that I should go unto Pharaoh, and that I should bring forth the children of Israel out of Egypt?

12. And he said, Certainly I will be with thee; and this *shall* be a token unto thee that I have sent thee. When thou hast brought forth the people out of Egypt, ye shall serve God upon this mountain.

13. And Moses said unto God, Behold, *when* I come unto the children of Israel, and shall say unto them, The God of your fathers hath sent me unto you; and they shall say to me, What *is* his name? what shall I say unto them?

14. And God said unto Moses, I AM THAT I AM: and he said Thus shalt thou say unto the children of Israel, I AM hath sent me unto you.

15. And God said moreover unto Moses, Thus shalt thou say unto the children of Israel, The LORD God of your fathers, the God of Abraham, the God of Isaac, and the God of Jacob, hath sent me unto you: this *is* my name for ever, and this *is* my memorial unto all generations.

Exodus 3:1-15

In this passage God is called *Yahweh* or *Jehovah* for the first time. Of course, previously to Abraham, Isaac and Jacob, he had been *El-Shaddai*. The word "Yahweh" can be translated in various ways, all of which have the same basic meaning: "I will be what I will be", or "I am who I am" or "I am he that causes to be", that is, the Creator. Jews have for a long time considered the word too holy to pronounce and when coming upon it in their reading, they say instead "Adonai", Lord.

Exodus After this confrontation with Yahweh, Moses became active and set about instituting the Lord's plan. Various stories embellish this exciting period of history and make it difficult to know with certainty the exact sequence of events. We do know that Moses went to the Pharaoh and demanded freedom for the Hebrews and that he was refused. Exodus 12 tells of plagues, presumably of the Lord's instigation, ravishing Egypt and causing chaos in the land; it also tells how the Lord "passed over" the Hebrews and killed the first born of the Egyptians. (See pp. 203-4.) During the chaos, the Israelites were collected by Moses and began their escape from the Pharaoh; the Bible story of the crossing of the Red Sea is known to most, and certain recent studies have made it seem a little more plausible.

Historically, it does seem conceivable that the Israelites could have escaped at that time (about 1300 B.C.) for there is evidence to suggest that the Pharaoh could not afford to send enough men to prevent the Exodus, or escape. Egypt was threatened from the north by pirates who were sailing up the Nile from the Mediterranean and destroying cities in their wake. At the same time, enemies from Libya were threatening from the west, the total effect of which may well have been to distract the Egyptians' attention from the relatively small group of people leaving the country. Perhaps these were the plagues spoken of in the Bible or perhaps they came in addition to those mentioned in the Book. At any rate, the Exodus had been achieved.

2. Historical Development

Covenant at Sinai   Perhaps the fact of the Exodus is not as important as the event which transpired shortly thereafter. In the desert to which they had escaped, the followers of Moses were confronted by their Lord, Yahweh, in a development that firmly established the basis of the Jewish religion. Called to Mount Sinai by the Lord, Moses returned to his people forty days later, armed with what has become the basis of the covenant between Yahweh and the Hebrews: the Ten Commandments, of which we possess today a highly polished version [Exodus 34: 17-26]. By the covenant the Jews agreed to adhere to God's Commandments and God promised never to forsake them, regardless of their unworthiness at times.

The significance of the covenant cannot be overestimated. By its nature, all Jewish people became priests in their own religion:

> 5. Now therefore, if ye will obey my voice indeed, and keep my covenant, then ye shall be a peculiar treasure unto me above all people: for all the earth *is* mine.
>
> 6. And ye shall be unto me a kingdom of priests, and an holy nation. These *are* the words which thou shalt speak unto the children of Israel.
>
> Exodus 19:5-6

The Jewish people were to abide by the laws of Yahweh because he helped them escape from Egypt; otherwise they would be punished. And punished they have been, time and time again.

This has been the interpretation attributed to the Babylonian captivity after the destruction of the first Temple when the Jews were forcefully dispersed throughout the Near East, to the exile and dispersion after A.D. 70, and to the unforgettable persecution of World War II and many other tribulations..

Chosen People   But despite the burden of obedience and the threat of punishment, there is an overwhelming love displayed in the covenant. It is, for example, unbreakable; each side has contracted forever. It is almost a parent-child relationship, in which everlasting patience and love remain despite the fact that it is often not deserved. But the most important part of the covenant is the concept of the "chosen people". Yahweh had chosen these people to be the instruments of his will, to show mankind what he desired us to be like, to be examples that all people could follow. To be chosen implies a definite favouritism or love, but it also implies a definite responsibility as can be seen in this passage from Deuteronomy:

6. For thou *art* an holy people unto the LORD thy God: the LORD thy God hath chosen thee to be a special people unto himself, above all people that *are* upon the face of the earth.

7. The LORD did not set his love upon you, nor choose you, because ye were more in number than any people; for ye *were* the fewest of all people;

8. But because the LORD loved you, and because he would keep the oath which he had sworn unto your fathers, hath the LORD brought you out with a mighty hand, and redeemed you out of the house of bond-men, from the hand of Pharaoh king of Egypt.

9. Know therefore that the LORD thy God, he *is* God, the faithful God, which keepeth covenant and mercy with them that love him and keep his commandments, to a thousand generations:

10. And repayeth them that hate him to their face, to destroy them: he will not be slack to him that hateth him, he will repay him to his face.

11. Thou shalt therefore keep the commandments, and the statutes, and the judgments, which I command thee this day, to do them.

12. Wherefore it shall come to pass, if ye hearken to these judgments, and keep and do them, that the LORD thy God shall keep unto thee the covenant and the mercy which he sware unto thy fathers:

13. And he will love thee, and bless thee, and multiply thee: he will also bless the fruit of thy womb, and the fruit of thy land, thy corn, and thy wine, and thine oil, the increase of thy kine, and the flocks of thy sheep, in the land which he sware unto thy fathers to give thee.

Deuteronomy 7:6-13

According to Jewish belief, a covenant exists between God and all mankind; the Jews were chosen to be symbols of mankind only and nowhere is it stated that only they will achieve salvation. According to Judaism, Noah is the ancestor of all mankind and God promised him that humanity would never

be destroyed totally as it had been at the Flood. In return, men must obey the
moral law and forsake idolatry. In effect then, salvation is open to all if they
obey the laws of righteousness. Converts to Judaism then are particularly
precious not only because of the religious aspects (they could achieve salvation
in their own religion), but also because they take upon themselves the special
burden of Jewish destiny and obligation.

Hebrew Kings   After the Exodus, the Hebrews wandered in the desert for
about forty years before feeling strong enough to re-enter Canaan. Under
Moses' successor, Joshua, Jericho was taken, and the walls came tumbling down.
Over the next two hundred years, more and more of Canaan was taken and the
problem then became one of holding the land in opposition to the Moabites and
Philistines. Under their first king, Saul, the conflict with the Philistines
heightened; under his successor David, the Philistines were routed. David
then captured Jerusalem, made it his capital and planned a Temple to house
the Ark of the Covenant, that is, the container made for the stone tablets
received by Moses. David's son, Solomon, whose wisdom is legendary, carried
out the construction of the first Temple.

     In 586 B.C. the Babylonians invaded Judah, destroyed the cities, burned
the Temple, took the Ark of the Covenant which was never found again and
carried thousands of Hebrews away to captivity in Babylon. The Kingdom of
Israel had disappeared without a trace, the Kingdom of Judah was destroyed and
the Children of Israel taken away. At this point, the story of the Hebrews
seemed to have ended — the last page had, it seemed, been turned. But not quite.

Babylonian Captivity   Since the Babylonian captivity is regarded as being a
punishment for the sins of the Hebrews, we might ask, "What had they done
between the Exodus and the captivity to deserve such a fate?" Basically it was
believed that they were being punished for adopting the Canaanite religion and
the worship of the *Baals,* which were basically nature gods. Festivals based on
the agricultural cycle were important to the Canaanites, and the Hebrews began
to follow them more and more closely. In this worship and in the orgies associated with the festivals, the Hebrews were breaking some of the Ten Commandments, and therefore the Covenant. The prophet Hoseah wrote:

> 11. Whoredom and wine and new wine take away the heart.
>
> 12. My people ask counsel at their stocks, and their staff declareth
> unto them: for the spirit of whoredoms hath caused *them* to err, and
> they have gone a whoring from under their God.
>
> 13. They sacrifice upon the tops of the mountains, and burn incense
> upon the hills, under oaks and poplars and elms, because the shadow
> thereof *is* good: therefore your daughters shall commit whoredom, and
> your spouses shall commit adultery.
>
> 14. I will not punish your daughters when they commit whoredom,
> nor your spouses when they commit adultery; for themselves are
> separated with whores, and they sacrifice with harlots: therefore the
> people *that* doth not understand shall fall.
>
> Hoseah 4: 11-14

Actions like these were almost inviting punishment — the Babylonian captivity was seen as that punishment.

11. And I will make Jerusalem heaps, *and* a den of dragons; and I will make the cities of Judah desolate, without an inhabitant.

12. Who *is* the wise man, that may understand this? and *who is he* to whom the mouth of the LORD hath spoken, that he may declare it, for what the land perisheth *and* is burnt up like a wilderness, that none passeth through?

13. And the LORD saith, Because they have forsaken my law which I set before them, and have not obeyed my voice, neither walked therein;

14. But have walked after the imagination of their own heart, and after Baalim, which their fathers taught them:

15. Therefore thus saith the LORD of hosts, the God of Israel; Behold, I will feed them, *even* this people, with wormwood, and give them water of gall to drink.

16. I will scatter them also among the heathen, whom neither they nor their fathers have known; and I will send a sword after them, till I have consumed them.

Jeremiah 9:11-16

Synagogues and Rabbis   Sacrifices could be offered only in Jerusalem; thus, while in captivity, any approach to Yahweh seemed to be denied. But there evolved from this situation the institutions known as *synagogues*. Here scrolls and writings could be studied; the custom of sermons was begun to provide interpretations and explanations of parts of the sacred books; and in these synagogues, traditions were written down so that those sincerely devout would not forget their heritage. The Torah, of which more will be said later, also was read and studied.

The *rabbis* (teachers) of the synagogues filled a real need; they were chosen not by wealth or birth, but by recognition that they were the authentic receivers and transmitters of the Torah. The rabbis in effect transformed Judaism into a faith not needing one place or even one land; the presence of Jerusalem became desirable, but not essential to the religion. Further, the rabbis changed the basic liturgy so that, although the prayer book is never "complete", (that is, it is being added to at intervals) Jews in Babylon in the sixth century B.C., in fourteenth-century Spain, and twentieth-century Poland have been united by words, thoughts and prayers, which have overcome the disintegrating effects of time and space. Besides this, the rabbis also spelled out in detail all aspects of the Law and made it the key to Jewish life. Finally, the rabbis decreed that whenever ten men gather in God's name, there he would cause his presence to descend, and this prerequisite to certain types of public worship exists in synagogues today.

Persian Period   In 583 B.C. Cyrus of Persia conquered Babylonia and allowed the Jews to leave. Many stayed on since they were doing well; thousands more returned to Jerusalem, where they rebuilt the Temple and began to hold morning and evening sacrifices.

Jews remained free until 322 B.C., when Alexander the Great passed through Palestine en route to Egypt and Persia. Hellenistic culture was spread by example rather than force, and the result was that many Jews adopted Greek ways — from the naming of their children to the practice of their religion. Those who held back from embracing the new culture were mostly rabbis and the common folk referred to as *Hasidim* or "pious ones".

Greek and Syrian Period   After the death of Alexander, Antiochus Epiphanes, the King of Syria, tried to force Hellensic religion on the Jews — especially the worship of Zeus, of whom the king claimed to be the worldly manifestation.

Therefore they were forbidden to keep their Sabbath, to own copies of the sacred writings, or to practise circumcision; all of this was on pain of death. Further, they were forced to sacrifice pigs. A priest, Mattathias, killed a Syrian officer when told to sacrifice a pig, and a revolt began. With five sons and many followers, Mattathias began a war that was carried on by his sons with great success. One son, Judas Maccabeus, defeated four Syrian armies. By 160 B.C. most of Jerusalem had been recaptured and purified and the Syrians had been forced out of Judea. Other sons and grandsons of Mattathias carried on until they had regained a land very close in size to the empire of David. The independence thus gained lasted until 63 B.C. when civil war broke out among the Jews themselves.

Jewish Parties   The influence of Greek culture and the Persian religion, Zoroastrianism, led to the formation of Jewish parties. The *Sadducees* were the wealthy, aristocratic Jews who kept away from the emotion of the masses. They believed in the written Law and generally thought well of the Greek intellectuals and writers. Religiously they opposed the then spreading belief in angels and the idea of the Resurrection of the body to full consciousness in the after-life. As mentioned earlier, the Hasidim were the "pious ones" whose sole passion was the Jewish religion. They came very quickly to help Judas Maccabeus in the war for independence, had no interest in politics and were opposed to the large influence of Greek culture. From this group sprang the *Pharisees*. Generally, scribes and rabbis made up this party which believed that the Sadducees were lost souls, doomed to destruction. They embraced the new concepts of Resurrection of the dead and the Last Judgment, and they believed that on this earth one must obey both written and unwritten Law. Therefore they tended to study Scripture and tradition and attempted to be morally pure and obedient.

SADDUCEES
PHARISEES
HERODIANS
ZEALOTES
ESSENES

Problems arose when Maccabean successors to Mattathias became over-sympathetic to the Sadducees. The previous support of these rulers by the Pharisees turned to opposition and sporadic revolt, which led to violent suppression and bloody massacre. When given the opportunity, the other side did the same thing. Before long, the cruel war had reached a stalemate and Pompey was sent from Rome to arbitrate. Upon his arrival in 63 B.C. the country was made a Roman province.

civil war

Roman Period to A.D. 70   A man named Antipater was made a Roman citizen and procurator of Judea by Julius Caesar. Although nominally a Jew, he was an Idumean and therefore racially unacceptable to the Jews; despite these objections, he was superior to the high priest. In 40 B.C., his son Herod was chosen by

Augustus to be King of Judea. Despite peace, prosperity, and the fact that he remodelled the Temple, he too was despised by the Jews and on his death in 4 B.C. (the same year as the birth of Jesus), there was universal rejoicing by the Jews.

During the Roman control, three new Jewish political parties came into existence and complemented those already established parties mentioned earlier.

The *Herodians* supported the house of Herod and came into existence in A.D. 6 when Augustus accepted the Jewish recommendation that Herod's son be deposed and replaced by a Roman procurator. Basically this party wanted home rule.

The *Zealots* were opposed to Rome and wanted to instigate rebellion against her; this party began in A.D. 6 when a revolt was put down viciously. If Roman rule was accepted, they said, God was forsaken; by taking the sword they believed the Messiah might be more likely to appear.

Thirdly, there were the *Essenes*, who were not interested in politics; rather they withdrew from the corruption of society to await the Messiah's arrival. They were very strict about observing established rituals and existed until dispersed by Rome in A.D. 68. Then, of course, in addition to all of these, there were the unorganized common people, ignoring some rituals, preserving others and not belonging to any particular party.

Great Dispersal   Roman control of this part of the empire was never well received. From A.D. 6, when the first revolt erupted, the story is mainly one of revolt, retribution and very little peace. Politically the Romans divided Palestine into four parts: three were ruled by sons of Herod, the fourth by a Roman procurator who resided at Caesarea. Religiously they were very diplomatic and tolerant. They never brought imperial standards or images of Caesar to Jerusalem; they never demanded that a statue of the emperor be erected and worshipped in the Temple; and they accepted the Jewish promise to do a daily sacrifice for the emperor.

But the Jews were very touchy, it seems, and complained continually. They complained, for example, when Pilate took Temple funds to build a new aquaduct extension into Jerusalem. Things eased slightly for a time under Caligula and Claudius, but by A.D. 66 the situation was one of definite open rebellion. Under Vespasian, his son Titus was appointed to subdue the Jews. After a very bitter siege and almost superhuman resistance, Jerusalem fell: slaughter, rape, looting and burning went on for days. A victory arch was built in Rome to commemorate the event and Titus was granted the supreme compliment — a triumph in Rome.

The consequences of the Roman victory of A.D. 70 were vital to the religion of the Jews. The second Temple was destroyed and the religion was again decentralized; priests, Sadducees, Zealots, Essenes and Herodians disappeared forever. Only the rabbinic party, the Pharisees, remained along with a small rebel sect called Christians. Jews were dispersed over the entire empire and beyond: Babylonia, Arabian Desert, Syria and Asia-Minor.

Not until the victory over the Arabs in the Six Day War of 1967, were the Jews to control the wall of the old Temple in Jerusalem.

Thus, from A.D. 70 until the creation of the state of Israel in 1948, the world's Jews had no homeland. Spread throughout the world, they had little in common but their religion as symbolized by their holy writings and the influence of the rabbis.

3. Holy Writings

After the Great Dispersal of A.D. 70, the Jews survived as a religious body by maintaining a religious and cultural cohesion, by pursuing a form of non-violent resistance, by the leadership of those intellectual and moral stalwarts, the rabbis, and by a devout reading of the holy works of Judaism. In this section discussion will centre around this holy literature.

Torah The major function of the synagogues of the world today, is to provide a place for Jews to gather in order to read, interpret and study the Torah. To this day the central act of every public worship is the removal of the Scroll of the Torah from the Ark, and the reading of parts of it. On the Sabbath, there is

An open ark in a synagogue; the Torah scrolls are visible. Note also the Sabbath candles burning.

Miller Services Ltd.

a regular cycle of readings from the Torah. The Torah *is* the most important
Jewish Scripture.

In the narrowest sense, the Torah consists of the *Five Books of Moses*
(sometimes called the *Pentateuch*) which are the first five books of the Bible,
written on a parchment scroll in ancient form by hand, and kept in the Ark (a
special box container) of the synagogue. Orthodox Jews believe these five books
to be the literal word of God. In a wider sense the term "Torah" is often
applied to a combination of the Pentateuch and *Talmud*, the Talmud being a
compendium of the faith including legends, traditions, laws and customs which
enlarge upon and explain the Torah. In the widest sense, the Torah consists of
every act or word which reveals the power and the presence of God, from the
preachings of the prophets to simple statements of a shepherd.

Here is the beginning of the Torah service:

There is none like You among the mighty, O Lord, and there are no
deeds like Yours. Your kingdom is an everlasting kingdom and Your
dominion endures forever. The Lord is King, the Lord was King, the
Lord shall be King for ever and ever. May the Lord give strength to
His people; may the Lord bless His people with peace.

Father of compassion, may it be Your will to favor Zion with
Your goodness and to rebuild the walls of Jerusalem. In You alone we
trust, O King, high and exalted God, Lord of the universe.

Blessing after the Reading:

Praised are You, O Lord our God, King of the universe, who gave us
a Torah of truth, endowing us with everlasting life. Praised are You,
O Lord, Giver of the Torah.[1]

While not impossible to follow, the Torah provides a detailed set of
guidelines and ideals of the type outlined in the Ten Commandments, which in
fact comprise part of the Torah. As stated in Deuteronomy:

11. For this commandment which I command thee this day, it *is* not
hidden from thee, neither *is* it far off:

12. It *is* not in heaven, that thou shouldest say, Who shall go up for
us to heaven, and bring it unto us, that we may hear it, and do it?

13. Neither *is* it beyond the sea, that thou shouldest say, Who shall go
over the sea for us, and bring it unto us, that we may hear it, and do it?

14. But the word *is* very nigh unto thee, in thy mouth, and in thy
heart, that thou mayest do it.

Deuteronomy 30:11-14

By following the Torah a man will be guided to righteousness. Regarded in the correct light, the Torah to the Jew is *life*.

Besides the Torah's use as a commandment, it also serves as a
repository of great wisdom. In its widest interpretation, it is the entirety of the
sacred tradition, and on more than one occasion in the Bible, study of the Torah
is commanded.

The following passage shows what wisdom can come from the study of the Torah:

> Whoever occupies himself with the study of the Torah with no ulterior motive merits many things. Furthermore, the entire world is indebted to him. He is called beloved friend [of God]. He loves God and mankind, and he causes God and mankind to rejoice. The Torah clothes him with humility and fear of the Lord, and it prepares him to be just, pious, upright and faithful. It keeps him far from sin and it brings him near to virtue. Through him men enjoy counsel and sound wisdom, insight and strength, as it is written, "I have counsel and sound wisdom, I have insight, I have strength" [Prov. 8:14]. [In that chapter of Proverbs, wisdom, or Torah, is speaking.] It gives him sovereignty and dominion and discerning judgment. The secrets of the Torah are revealed to him; he becomes like a neverfailing spring and like a river which never halts. He becomes modest, patient and forgiving of insult; it magnifies him and exalts him above all the works of creation.[2]

Of great significance to Jews then and now was the fact that in ages past when only a few could read, illiteracy was virtually unknown among the Jews — they had to read and study as part of their religion and way of life. Thus learning was always among the most highly prized of all possessions. Much of this attitude towards learning is rooted in the Jewish faith.

Talmud The Talmud is the second most important source of Jewish Law and lore, which complements and interprets the Torah and applies Scripture to everyday life and observance. In A.D. 69 while Titus was at the gates of Jerusalem, a rabbi named Johanan ben Zakkai escaped to the town of Jamnia where he established a school or "house of learning"; his goal was to save Judaism by systematizing its laws and doctrines and adapting interpretations to meet changing conditions. Gradually this school and the men in it became recognized as the authority on Judaism and could pronounce on the true meanings and right practices of the faith. The elder of the school was known as the "patriarch" and was officially recognized by the Romans (until A.D. 425) as the leader of all Jews in the Roman Empire.

The school made a detailed study of the written Law, the Torah; recorded and defined previously unwritten Law called the *Halakah*, which had been passed down through the years by word of mouth; and, added to this the interpretations of these traditions by learned rabbis. This effort produced a mass of written material that had to be sorted out.

With further repression under Hadrian, the scrolls of Jerusalem were removed to schools in Galilee, where the task continued. Rabbi Meir and Rabbi Judah (known as Judah the Prince) ultimately produced a systematized code called the *Mishnah* (in six sections), which was to interpret the original Torah in the light of second-century A.D. conditions. Because it was so relevant to the time, it was considered by many Jews to be on the same level of importance as the Torah. It concerned itself with a wide range of subjects stretching from seasonal festivals to the rights of the poor, to laws regarding marriage and divorce, to civil and criminal law; it was completed around A.D. 200.

About a hundred years later, intellectual leadership of Judaism shifted from Galilee to Babylon. Here the work of consolidation and interpretation continued. Scholars here decided that the Mishnah was useful, but that further elaboration was needed in applying it to everyday affairs and in spelling out the details of ritual observance. Since the Mishnah was primarily devoted to the unwritten parts of the Law, the Halakah, and contained relatively little of the oral traditions which the Jews called *Haggadah*, that is, the historic, religious and moral instructions of the rabbis, therefore (in Babylon) it was the latter part of Jewish lore that was added for the first time. When completed, the now enlarged efforts on the Haggadah were combined with those already done on the Halakah to form the *Gemara*. This was the magnum opus, the great contribution of the Babylonian Jewish schools.

Finally then, the *Gemara* was combined with the Mishnah to form the *Talmud*. This was completed by the end of the fifth century. Comprising the six major parts decided upon earlier, and a total of 63 volumes, the Talmud served as a constant source of light to the Jews during the black ordeal of the Middle Ages, and probably was a major factor in their survival. Though some of their fellows were burned, torn and placed on the rack, the majority of Jews clung tenaciously to the Talmud for in it there is, according to Jewish tradition, wisdom that derives from God.

But there are other basic texts as well as the Torah and Talmud. The other books of the Old Testament (besides the Pentateuch), the Weekday Prayer Book, commentaries on the Law, and mystical writings and sayings of inspired teachers through the ages also are part of the Jewish faith. Doubtless, the Torah and Talmud tower above the others as the Christian Bible towers above other works, but in the same way as Christianity, these other writings are significant. In simplest terms, as Jews themselves explain, the Torah is the golden rule; all else is commentary.

4. The Prophets

Often throughout history there have been occasions on which rules or traditions have been either distorted or ignored. Almost always there have come individuals or groups who consider it their responsibility to remind people of the rule or tradition being ignored and to guide them back to the straight and narrow path. They are referred to as prophets; Judaism, as well as Christianity and Islam, has had many of them in its midst.

In Judaism they appear as far back as 1000 B.C. in the book of Judges. Frequently at that time they were ecstatics who went into frenzied trances. Later they were more rational and were quite well trained, particularly in their knowledge of the Torah. Many prophets made significant contributions to Judaism including Elijah, Elisha, Hosea, Micah, Zephania, Habakkuk and Nahum, but in this section we will centre on four who were perhaps most important: Amos, Isaiah, Ezekiel and Deutero-Isaiah.

Amos   Amos was a herdsman who lived in the eighth century B.C. in Judah, where, it will be remembered, the worship of Yahweh was much more faithfully carried out than it was in the Northern Kingdom of Israel. While driving his herds in this Northern Kingdom, Amos saw that the people there were

religiously and morally lax, that integrity, mercy and spiritual health were
rapidly disappearing. His teachings accordingly were, in essence, that doom was
descending over the north, that Yahweh was tired of the laxness of the people,
and that the children of Israel would be forced to pay for their sins unless they
repented quickly.

4. For thus saith the LORD unto the house of Israel, Seek ye me, and
ye shall live:

5. But seek not Beth-el, nor enter into Gilgal, and pass not to Beersheba: for Gilgal shall surely go into captivity, and Beth-el shall come
to nought.

6. Seek the LORD, and ye shall live; lest he break out like fire in the
house of Joseph, and devour it, and there be none to quench it in
Beth-el.

21. I hate, I despise your feast days, and I will not smell in your
solemn assemblies.

22. Though ye offer me burnt offerings and your meat offerings I will
not accept them; neither will I regard the peace offerings of your fat
beasts.

23. Take thou away from me the noise of thy songs; for I will not hear
the melody of thy viols.

24. But let judgment run down as waters, and righteousness as a
mighty stream.

Amos 5:4-6, 21-24

But besides prophecy Amos, as well as other prophets, contributed
to the religion in a different way. While encouraging people to repent, he
presented Yahweh in a light not shown before that time; Yahweh would send a
foe to attack the north. The implication was that Yahweh had an unlimited
power over nature and could bring drought, flood, plagues and earthquakes to
any place on earth. Yahweh ruled the world. This concept, more far-reaching
than any before it, was integrated into the fabric of Judaism.

Isaiah   Isaiah came on the scene perhaps 25 years after Amos, about 720 B.C.
He too was from the Southern Kingdom, and taught the need for confidence in
Yahweh. Although it appeared that those in the Northern Kingdom were
breaking the Law and not being punished, Isaiah implied that they would be;
have confidence, he said in effect, for the Lord will be true to his Word.
In 722 B.C. when the Northern Kingdom was destroyed by the Assyrians and
they were at the walls of Jerusalem, Isaiah continued to teach confidence in the
Lord. Miraculously the siege was lifted — some say a plague hit the Assyrians,
other sources say they were paid a ransom; whatever the cause, the Southern
Kingdom remained while the Northern one was destroyed. Isaiah's prophecy
seemed to have come true.
        Again, beyond the prophecy, the prophet contributed to Judaism.
Surely Yahweh was the moving force behind history, not blind fate. He surely

would punish evil. But Yahweh punished out of a deep pity and love of mankind, and the purpose of punishment was not for its own sake, but rather to purge and purify the soul. This concept of a loving God was crystallized by Isaiah.

> 18. Come now, and let us reason together, saith the LORD: Though your sins be as scarlet, they shall be as white as snow; though they be red like crimson, they shall be as wool.
>
> 19. If ye be willing and obedient, ye shall eat the good of the land:
>
> Isaiah 1:18-19

An important theme in Isaiah is the concept of "the remnant", that is, those who had remained true to Yahweh enjoying eternal peace, prosperity and health after the day of judgment and doom.

> 1. The word that Isaiah the son of Amoz saw concerning Judah and Jerusalem.
>
> 2. And it shall come to pass in the last days, *that* the mountain of the LORD's house shall be established in the top of the mountains, and shall be exalted above the hills; and all nations shall flow unto it.
>
> 3. And many people shall go and say, Come ye, and let us go up to the mountain of the LORD, to the house of the God of Jacob; and he will teach us of his ways, and we will walk in his paths: for out of Zion shall go forth the law, and the word of the LORD from Jerusalem.
>
> 4. And he shall judge among the nations, and shall rebuke many people; and they shall beat their swords into plowshares, and their spears into pruning-hooks: nation shall not lift up sword against nation neither shall they learn war any more.
>
> 5. O house of Jacob, come ye, and let us walk in the light of the LORD.
>
> Isaiah 2:1-5

Considering the destruction of the Northern Kingdom it is not surprising that he should long for this peace; it was certainly not to come about for a long time. But the concept was there, complete with the Messiah who would spring from the family of King David, and it provided hope for many.

> 1. And there shall come forth a rod out of the stem of Jesse, and a Branch shall grow out of his roots:
>
> 2. And the Spirit of the LORD shall rest upon him, the spirit of wisdom and understanding, the spirit of counsel and might, the spirit of knowledge and of the fear of the LORD;
>
> 3. And shall make him of quick understanding in the fear of the LORD: and he shall not judge after the sight of his eyes, neither reprove after the hearing of his ears:
>
> 4. But with righteousness shall he judge the poor, and reprove with equity for the meek of the earth: and he shall smite the earth with the

rod of his mouth, and with the breath of his lips shall he slay the wicked.

5. And righteousness shall be the girdle of his loins, and faithfulness the girdle of his reins.

6. The wolf also shall dwell with the lamb, and the leopard shall lie down with the kid; and the calf and the young lion and the fatling together; and a little child shall lead them.

7. And the cow and the bear shall feed; their young ones shall lie down together: and the lion shall eat straw like the ox.

8. And the sucking child shall play on the hole of the asp, and the weaned child shall put his hand on the cockatrice' den.

9. They shall not hurt nor destroy in all my holy mountain: for the earth shall be full of the knowledge of the LORD, as the waters cover the sea.

10. And in that day there shall be a root of Jesse, which shall stand for an ensign of the people; to it shall the Gentiles seek: and his rest shall be glorious.

Isaiah 11:1-10

Ezekiel   Ezekiel, the son of a priestly family, was carried off to Babylonia in 597 B.C. While in exile, he regarded himself as the watchman of Israel, and constantly considered methods of reviving and restoring his people. A major theme of his writings thus became the conducting of services in the restored Temple after the people had returned to their home. He was sure that the Temple and the services within it had to be restored, and therefore outlined in minute detail the intricacies of the service — a contribution which greatly influenced later Judaism.

He combined the new emphasis on individual worship and responsibility, propounded by Jeremiah, with a refined vision of Yahweh. The Lord, he said, would not gush forth with love and forgiveness at the first sign of remorse on the part of sinners. His exalted position demanded an extremely humble, sincere, devout and chastened approach by people gathering in the Temple in a state of emotional and physical purity. Only then — maybe — would he, the Lord, listen.

Beyond this he saw his job as being one which showed that Yahweh was more than *just* the loving protector of his people:

22. Therefore say unto the house of Israel, Thus saith the Lord GOD; I do not *this* for your sakes, O house of Israel, but for mine holy name's sake, which ye have profaned among the heathen, whither ye went.

23. And I will sanctify my great name, which was profaned among the heathen, which ye have profaned in the midst of them; and the heathen shall know that I *am* the LORD, saith the Lord GOD, when I shall be sanctified in you before their eyes.

Ezekiel 36:22-23

Deutero-Isaiah   Of this prophet, nothing is known except that he wrote during the Babylonian captivity and that his prophecies are contained in the later part of the book of Isaiah. Despite our lack of knowledge of him, we do know that his prophesy was of vital significance not only to Judaism but also to Christianity. His major theme was, "Why had so much disaster befallen the Hebrews?" The old answer was that it was payment for sins in the past; but all could see that the people of Babylon were as bad as, if not worse than, the Jews. This prophet's answer was that Israel's role was that of a messenger to the world at large:

> 6. I the LORD have called thee in righteousness, and will hold thine hand, and will keep thee, and give thee for a covenant of the people, for a light of the Gentiles;
>
> Isaiah 42:6

That is, they had been chosen *not* to be the recipients of unearned favours, but rather to set an example so that in their actions and words, the nations of the world would see the presence of Yahweh. To this the Jews had been blind. Thus disasters had befallen them, not so much to pay for sins, although that was part of it, but mainly to refine and purify the people, to make them see their true purpose on earth. The suffering had not been in vain; it served a purpose.

> 3. Strengthen ye the weak hands, and confirm the feeble knees.
>
> 4. Say to them *that are* of a fearful heart, Be strong, fear not: behold your God will come *with* vengeance, *even* God *with* a recompence; he will come and save you.
>
> 5. Then the eyes of the blind shall be opened, and the ears of the deaf shall be unstopped:
>
> 6. Then shall the lame *man* leap as an hart, and the tongue of the dumb sing: for in the wilderness shall waters break out, and streams in the desert.
>
> Isaiah 35:3-6

This concept was an important one to Judaism, and became a part of the fabric of Judaic belief and remained such through World War II, and in fact down to the present.

The offshoot of this suffering for mankind went in two directions. Firstly, it meant that redemption and salvation was universal; you did not have to be a Jew to be saved. This is a much more tolerant view than that of some Christian churches. Secondly, the idea of the few suffering for mankind was slightly changed later by Christians who considered that Jesus, a Jew, had sacrificed himself for humanity. This concept, then, can be seen as being significant to Judaism *and* Christianity.

5. Basic Concepts of Judaism

> **God**   In Judaism, as in some other religions, God (or Yahweh, or Jehovah or the Lord) is the focus of everything. Everything in Judaism either centres upon, or

is created by God. To Jews, God is not something that must be proven — he
exists and all else proceeds from that. God started the world: "In the beginning,
God created the heavens and the earth" [Genesis 1:1]. And beyond creating the
earth, he cares for it intensely and for all things that live on the earth:

1. The LORD is my shepherd, I shall not want.

2. He maketh me to lie down in green pastures: he leadeth me beside
the still waters.

3. He restoreth my soul: he leadeth me in the paths of righteousness
for his name's sake.

4. Yea, though I walk through the valley of the shadow of death, I
will fear no evil: for thou *art* with me, thy rod and thy staff they comfort me.

5. Thou preparest a table before me in the presence of mine enemies;
thou anointest my head with oil; my cup runneth over.
6. Surely goodness and mercy shall follow me all the days of my life,
and I will dwell in the house of the LORD for ever.

Psalm 23

In return for God's favour, man should approach him with gratitude,
humility and reverence. The following is a psalm of Thanksgiving.

Sing praises, O you servants of the Lord;
Praise the glory of the Lord. Halleluyah!

Praised is the glory of the Lord, now and always;
From sunrise to sunset, praised is the Lord.

Supreme over all nations is the Lord;
His glory is high over all the heavens.

Who is like the Lord our God, enthroned on high,
Yet bending low to survey all heaven and earth?

He raises the poor from the dust;
He lifts the needy from the ash heap.

He places them in the seats of the noble;
He seats them with the princes of His people.

He transforms the childless mistress of a home
Into a joyous mother of children. Halleluyah![3]

God is one. There is only one — other gods are false gods, and idolatry
is forbidden. For this principle untold numbers of Jewish martyrs have died

throughout the ages. The following selections from Holy Scripture illustrate
this concept.

> 4. Hear O Israel, the Lord our God, the Lord is one.
>
> > Deuteronomy 6:4

> 2. I *am* the Lord thy God, which have brought thee out of the land of
> Egypt, out of the house of bondage.
>
> 3. Thou shalt have no other gods before me.
>
> 4. Thou shalt not make unto thee any graven image, or any likeness *of
> any thing* that *is* in heaven above or that *is* in the earth beneath, or
> that *is* in the water under the earth:
>
> 5. Thou shalt not bow down thyself to them, nor serve them: for I
> the Lord thy God *am* a jealous God, visiting the iniquity of the fathers
> upon the children unto the third and fourth *generation* of them that
> hate me;
>
> 6. And showing mercy unto thousands of them that love me, and
> keep my commandments.
>
> 7. Thou shalt not take the name of the Lord thy God in vain: for the
> the Lord will not hold him guiltless that taketh his name in vain.
>
> > Exodus 20:2-7

Yahweh is a moral god; he creates good and evil but demands good
from man and will punish those who are evil.

> 6. And the Lord passed by before him, and proclaimed, The Lord,
> The Lord God, merciful and gracious, long-suffering, and abundant in
> goodness and truth,
> 7. Keeping mercy for thousands, forgiving iniquity and transgression
> and sin, and that will by no means clear *the guilty;* visiting the in-
> iquity of the fathers upon the children, and upon the children's chil-
> dren, unto the third and to the fourth *generation.*
>
> > Exodus 34:6-7

Lastly, it was and is man's purpose to serve and love God. This was
done by imitating his ways and by absolute devotion — to the death, if
necessary.

> And thou shalt love the Lord thy God with all thine heart, and with all
> thy soul, and with all thy might.
>
> > Deuteronomy 6:5

> Praise the Lord, all nations. Lord Him, all peoples. Great is His love for
> us; everlasting His faithfulness. Halleluyah![4]

Chosen People   This concept has been explained earlier (see pp. 174-5) and it
is only necessary to reconfirm it here. They believed that God had chosen the

Children of Israel to light the way for all mankind, not to receive undeserved favours or to make them special. This was the basic significance of the covenant with Moses and the Hebrew people in the desert at Sinai. If anything, to be the chosen people brought more responsibilities and more burdens than those borne by others. Conversely, if the duties were carried out properly, to have been in the forefront of bringing God's will to fulfilment would be an honour indeed. This concept is rejected by many Jewish theologians.

℘ **Messiah**   The term, Messiah, means "anointed one". Kings and priests were anointed in ancient times to set them apart as specially designated leaders of society. Jews believe that the "anointed one" will bring redemption to this world. It will be a time of true happiness, unparalleled in human existence. It will not be a *new* world; rather it will be this world brought to perfection. Universal peace, tranquility, lawfulness and goodness will prevail, and all will acknowledge the unity and sovereignty of God.

Traditional Judaism believes in the coming of the great hero, anointed for leadership — a descendant of the House of David, who will lead the world out of chaos. He will be of flesh and blood, a mortal sent expressly by God to fulfil the glory of his people. The traditional belief is that man must work to better the world and help bring forth the Messiah. The idea that man by *himself* will progress to such an era is inconceivable. Rather, a supernatural gift to mankind, in the person of the Messiah, will be required to bring the world to this pinnacle of glory.

God, they say, will directly intervene to prevent the world from rushing into darkness, and will bring redemption through a human personality. The Messiah, though supernaturally introduced to humanity, will not be a divine personality. He will bring only the redemption granted by God; he will have no power to bring that redemption himself. He will have no miraculous powers and by himself will not be able to atone for the sins of others. He will have no superhuman relationship to God. He will however be an exalted personality of extreme ability and will usher in the rehabilitation of the Jewish people and the subsequent regeneration of all mankind.

How the Messiah will come and how we will be able to identify him has evoked imaginative suggestions throughout the ages. Similarly the time of his coming has aroused much conjecture. Some answers are based on biblical interpretation; others are traditional beliefs; others remain wild speculation. There are no clear answers to these questions.

In doctrine, the basic conflict between Judaism and Christianity has centred around this concept of the Messiah. To Jews, awaiting the Messianic Age, Jesus was a pretender; Christians, believing Jesus to have been God incarnate and the true Messiah, are awaiting the second coming and the ensuing Judgment.

Role of Jesus in Jewish Belief   Jesus was born a Jew and was fully conversant with all aspects of Jewish life; and to Jews he was no different from many Jews before him and after — he was a preacher and teacher. He was not the Son of God, and did not become so, even to Christianity, until almost a century after his death when the gospels were being written presenting this interpretation. This is a point that must be kept in mind to understand the Jewish belief: the Jesus of that period was not the Jesus of today. A whole body of beliefs, ritual and dogma has been consructed around his person throughout the centuries that did not exist at the time of his death. His major contribution was an ability to crystallize ideas and statements made by many people before his time. Isaiah, for example, presented many of Jesus' beliefs (using different words) many years earlier; the Sermon on the Mount also falls into this category. Rather than making contributions to belief, Jesus drew people around his person.

Also it should be noted that, despite the fact that the cross has become the symbol of Christianity, crucifixion was not invented for Jesus; it was a common Roman method of execution. Jesus was put to death by the Romans for political, not religious, reasons; he was not murdered by the Jews.

To the Jews, Jesus remained in death as in life a preacher and teacher. To early Christians unfamiliar with the Rabbinic teachings which Jesus propounded in his unique way, he became the founder of a new faith and the incarnation of a Messiah.

Man and His Importance   "Judaism knows no accepted catechism" but on the other hand it is not just a string of legal commandments divorced from faith. While a portion of Jewish theology is definable in terms readily understood by the Western mind, certain aspects of it reveal the universality of Jewish faith.

Dignity of Man   Since God is merciful and man is made in his image, man must strive to achieve that quality. Beyond this, as God made an orderly world, so must man work for a just world. This may help to explain the fact that many Jews are very active in government, law, medicine and public works; more than a personal interest, it is part of their religious heritage and therefore a part of their life.

Another part of the doctrine of the dignity of man is that, despite the fact that man can sink very low, he is not, in God's eyes, irretrievable from sin. Conversely, because man had something to offer the world, man should not renounce the world. He should hallow and purify life on a basic level and attempt to raise it to a higher level. Accordingly, there is no asceticsm in Judaism as there is in Christianity.   *self denile*

Responsibility of Man   According to Judaism, all things are foreseen by God; at the same time though, man has free will — and can do what he wants:

> Everything is foreseen by God, and freedom of choice is given to man; the world is judged with goodness, and all depends upon the preponderance of good or evil deeds.[5]

To this classic dilemma, there is no attempt to give a reply — only the assertion that man has freedom, but also is responsible for the results of this freedom.

Man's responsibility goes one step further. Individuals are responsible not only for their own actions but also for those of all mankind. The corollary of this is that there must be laws, and respect for government. In this way, by following the law, society at large will be protected from individual members who disobey laws. Only if a government transgresses universal or moral law has an individual the right to oppose that government.

Sin and Repentance   Sin, in Judaism, is equal to rebellion against God; beyond that, it is a debasement of man's nature. Punishment therefore is not intended primarily as retribution or revenge; rather, it is a chastisement aimed at reminding man of his proper dignity. Not surprisingly then, the word for "repentance" in Hebrew is *teshuvah* which means "returning", that is, man is returning to God and to his basic human nature when he repents. The following selection from the Scriptures reinforces this view:

> 30. Therefore I will judge you, O house of Israel, every one according to his ways, saith the Lord God. Repent, and turn *yourselves* from all your transgressions; so iniquity shall not be your ruin.

> 31. Cast away from you all your transgressions, whereby ye have transgressed; and make you a new heart and a new spirit: for why will ye die, O house of Israel?

> 32. For I have no pleasure in the death of him that dieth, saith the Lord God: wherefore turn *yourselves* and live ye.
>
> Ezekiel 18:30-32

Suffering   As men often failed to follow the full covenant, sin and the necessary corollary, suffering, were something that had to be faced. In Judaism, this was heightened, for even those who had led exemplary lives expected to suffer, sometimes for the sins of others, even of their forefathers. As the chosen people, Jews expected to suffer for all mankind, and they have endured much suffering for centuries. But suffering was not useless, although at times it surely appeared to be so since the meaning was often hidden.

This concept is shown in the following passage which concludes *The Last of the Just*, Andre Schwartz-Bart's novel about Jewish suffering through the ages, culminating in the Nazi death camps:

> The building resembled a huge bathhouse. To left and right large concrete pots cupped the stems of faded flowers. At the foot of the small wooden stairway an S.S. man, mustached and benevolent, told the condemned, "Nothing painful will happen! You just have to breathe very deeply. It strengthens the lungs. It's a way to prevent contagious diseases. It disinfects." Most of them went in silently, pressed forward by those behind. Inside, numbered coathooks garnished the walls of a sort of gigantic cloakroom where the flock undressed one way or another, encouraged by their S.S. cicerones, who advised them to remember the numbers carefully. Cakes of stony soap were distributed. Golda begged Ernie not to look at her, and he went through the sliding door of the second room with his eyes closed, led by the young woman and by the children, whose soft hands clung to his naked thighs.

There, under the showerheads embedded in the ceiling, in the blue light of screened bulbs glowing in recesses of the concrete walls, Jewish men and women, children and patriarchs were huddled together. His eyes still closed, he felt the press of the last parcels of flesh that the S.S. men were clubbing into the gas chamber now, and his eyes still closed, he knew that the lights had been extinguished on the living, on the hundreds of Jewish women suddenly shrieking in terror, on the old men whose prayers rose immediately and grew stronger, on the martyred children, who were rediscovering in their last agonies the fresh innocence of yesteryear's agonies in a chorus of identical exclamations: *"Mama! But I was a good boy! It's dark! It's dark!"* And when the first waves of Cyclon B gas was billowed among the sweating bodies, drifting down toward the squirming carpet of children's heads, Ernie freed himself from the girl's mute embrace and leaned out into the darkness toward the children invisible even at his knees, and he shouted with all the gentleness and all the strength of his soul, "Breathe deeply, my lambs, and quickly!"

When the layers of gas had covered everything, there was silence in the dark room for perhaps a minute, broken only by shrill, racking coughs and the gasps of those too far gone in their agonies to offer a devotion. And first a stream, then a cascade, an irrepressible, majestic torrent, the poem that through the smoke of fires and above the funeral pyres of history the Jews — who for two thousand years did not bear arms and who never had either missionary empires nor colored slaves — the old love poem that they traced in letters of blood on the earth's hard crust unfurled in the gas chamber, enveloped it, vanquished its somber, abysmal snickering: "SHEMA YISRAEL ADONOI ELOHENU ADONOI ECHOD . . . Hear, O Israel, the Lord is our God, the Lord is One. O Lord, by your grace you nourish the living, and by your great pity you resurrect the dead, and you uphold the weak, cure the sick, break the chains of slaves. And faithfully you keep your promises to those who sleep in the dust. Who is like unto you, O merciful Father, and who could be like unto you . . .?"

The voices died one by one in the course of the unfinished poem. The dying children had already dug their nails into Ernie's thighs and Golda's embrace was already weaker, her kisses were blurred when, clinging fiercely to her beloved's neck, she exhaled a harsh sigh: "Then I'll never see you again? Never again?"

Ernie managed to spit up the needle of fire jabbing at his throat, and as the woman's body slumped against him, its eyes wide in the opaque night, he shouted against the unconscious Golda's ear, "In a little while, *I swear it!"* And then he knew that he could do nothing more for anyone in the world, and in the flash that preceded his own annihilation he remembered, happily, the legend of Rabbi Chanina ben Teradion, as Mordecai had joyfully recited it: "When the gentle rabbi, wrapped in the scrolls of the Torah, was flung upon the pyre by the Romans for having taught the Law, and when they lit the fagots, the branches still green to make his torture last, his pupils said, 'Master, what do you see?' And Rabbi Chanina answered, 'I see the parchment burning, but the letters are taking wing.'" — *"Ah, yes, surely, the letters are taking wing,"* Ernie repeated as the flame blazing in his chest rose suddenly to his head. With dying arms he embraced Golda's body in an already unconscious gesture of loving protection, and they were found that way half an hour later by the team of *Sonderkommando* responsible for burning the Jews in the crematory ovens. And so it was for millions, who turned from *Luftmenschen* into *Luft*. I shall not translate. So this story will not finish with some to be visited in memoriam. For the smoke that rises from crematoriums obeys physical laws like any other: the particles come together and disperse according to the wind that propels them. The only pilgrimage, estimable reader, would be to look with sadness at a stormy sky now and then.

And praised. *Auschwitz.* Be. *Maidanek.* The Lord. *Treblinka.* And praised. *Buchenwald.* Be. *Mauthausen.* The Lord. *Belzec.* And praised. *Sobibor.* Be. *Chelmno.* The Lord. *Ponary.* And praised. *Theresienstadt.* Be. *Warsaw.* The Lord. *Vilna.* And praised. *Skarzysko.* Be. *Bergen-Belsen.* The Lord. *Janow.* And praised. *Dora.* Be. *Neuengamme.* The Lord. *Pustkow.* And praised . . .

Yes, at times one's heart could break in sorrow. But often too, preferably in the evening, I can't help thinking that Ernie Levy, dead six million times, is still alive somewhere, I don't know where. . . . Yesterday, as I stood in the street trembling in despair, rooted to the spot, a drop of pity fell from above upon my face. But there was no breeze in the air, no cloud in the sky. . . . There was only a presence.[6]

Death and the Afterlife   On death, the body returns to the earth ("dust to dust") but the soul returns to God who gave it. This doctrine of the immortality of the soul is affirmed not only by Judaism but also by other religious and secular philosophies. Judaism, further, believes in the eventual Resurrection of the body, which will be reunited with the soul at a later time. The human form of the righteous of all ages, buried and long since decomposed, will be resurrected at God's will. Though perhaps appearing incredible to the contemporary mind, some Jews ask why it is more miraculous than birth. The adhesion of sperm and egg, the subsequent fertilization and development in the womb culminating in the birth of the astoundingly complex network of tubes and glands, bones and organs, their incredibly precise functioning and the unbelievably intricate human brain that guides them is surely a miracle of the first magnitude.

The belief in bodily Resurrection is one of many reasons why it is required that the body be interred in the earth and not cremated — it expresses a faith in future Resurrection. Of course, the all-powerful God could recreate the body whether buried, drowned or burned. Yet wilful cremation signifies an arrogant denial of the possibility of Resurrection. The body and its limbs — whether amputated before death, or during a permissable post-mortem — must be allowed to decompose as one complete organism by the process of nature, not by man's mechanical act.

Three basic ideas of Judaism are symbolized by the belief in a physical Resurrection. One is that man does not achieve this ultimate redemption by virtue of his inherent nature. He will not *inevitably* be resurrected. Rather it is God's grace and mercy which reward the deserving and revive those who sleep in the dust.

Secondly, Resurrection is not only a bonus for the righteous person, but also it is a corporate reward; *all* of the righteous of *all* of the ages will be revived.

Thirdly, physical Resurrection affirms clearly that man's soul *and* his body are the creations of the holy God. In Christianity and oriental religions there is a tendency to see the body and soul as separate, with the body being regarded as inferior. This accounts for the asceticism evident in some religions. On the contrary, Judaism has always stressed that the body, like the soul, is a gift of God and belongs to him. To care for the body is a religious command of the Bible. Resurrection thus affirms that the body is of value because it came from God and will be revived by God.

The specific virtues that might guarantee a person Resurrection are open to debate. The method of Resurrection is an open question also. While the details of the after-life are speculative, many Jews suggest that the traditional idea that God will revive the righteous dead and leave the wicked in the dust must serve to illuminate a dark subject.

The meaning of death to the Jewish faith depends very much on the meaning of life. If life is absurd and man is forever bound and chained by fate without any freedom, then death is a welcome release. But, if life is the creation of a benevolent God, if man has a soul and a body and if he tempers his passions with the moral commands of an eternal omnipotent God, then death is a return to the Creator and the gift of life after death is the only possibility for a just and merciful God. If life has any significance, and Judaism teaches that it has, then man knows that someday his body will be replaced just as his soul unites with eternal God.

Nevertheless, Judaism is basically a "this world" religion. Whereas some religious groups, including some of the early Christian martyrs, looked to death as something almost to be desired, Judaism has little but contempt for suicides. The person who commits suicide in effect denies God's supreme lordship over him when he decides that he is the lord of his own soul. He is then committing not only violence, but also an act of sacrilege. Judaism believes that the foundations of the next life are to be laid in this life — the next world will reward the efforts of men here. Every day then must be lived to the fullest.

This may help to account for the fact that so many of the rites and observances of the faith deal with everyday affairs including details of food, drink, laws of the market place and personal hygiene.

6. Modern Rites

More than some other religions, Judaism places great emphasis on ceremony and tradition. These rituals, believed to be capable of focusing attention on the Lord, were largely responsible for preserving the faith of individuals during difficult periods for Judaism. No group worship with fellow Jews in a central location was possible, and families were thrown on their own. Thus many of the rites still practised in Judaism are not necessarily relevant to modern society but serve a vital function by reminding Jews of their past trials and tribulations.

Practices and Institutions

Charity   Whereas in other religions charity is optional for individual members, to Jews it is a legally binding obligation; it is part of the Torah:

> 10. And six years thou shalt sow thy land, and shalt gather in the fruits thereof:
>
> 11. But the seventh *year* thou shalt let it rest and lie still; that the poor of thy people may eat; and what they leave the beasts of the field shall eat. In like manner thou shalt deal with thy vineyard, *and* with thy oliveyard.
>
> Exodus 23:10-11

Since charity begins at home, the Jews are very tightly knit and helpful to each other. They have learned from bitter experience that they can seldom rely on others.

The United Jewish Appeal which runs each year in the fall raises money for the Jewish community and the money is almost totally raised from within that community. Old age homes and community centres built from the proceeds then serve the needs of the Jewish community.

The phrase "Love thy neighbour" is a well-known one in rabbinic teaching and is, in reality, another way of stating the golden rule. The significance of this concept in Judaism cannot be over-estimated as shown by the following selection:

> 18. Thou shalt not avenge, nor bear any grudge against the children of thy people; but thou shalt love thy neighbour as thyself: I *am* the Lord.
>
> Leviticus 19:18

Marriage and Children   According to Judaism, the family is the basic unit of society and therefore its existence and integrity must be protected. Both husband and wife have obligations to each other; some of the wife's are described in the following:

> A wife must do the following for her husband: grind flour, bake bread, wash clothes, cook food, give suck to her child, make ready his bed and work in wool. If she brought him one maidservant [from her father's house], she need not grind or bake or wash. If she brought two maidservants, she need not cook or give her child suck. If she brought three maidservants, she need not make ready his bed or work in wool. If four, she may sit all day and do nothing. Rabbi Eliezer says: Even if she brought one hundred maidservants he should force her to work in wool, for idleness leads to unchastity.[7]

Usually a wedding ceremony is performed today by a rabbi, although technically any Jew can perform it. The giving of a ring, or any object said to be of value, from groom to bride is sufficient to validate the marriage as long as the ceremony is witnessed by any other two adult male Jews. The following is a portion of the text of the Jewish wedding ceremony:

You that come in the name of the Lord are blessed.

May He who is supreme in might, blessing and glory bless this bridegroom and bride.

A cup of wine is filled and held by the officiant as he recites:

Praised are You, O Lord our God, King of the universe, Creator of the fruit of the vine.

Praised are You, O Lord our God, King of the universe, who sanctified us with Your commandments, and commanded us concerning forbidden marriages, who forbade us those to whom we are not married, and permitted us those married to us by means of the wedding ceremony and the bridal canopy. Praised are You, O Lord, who sanctifies Your people Israel through the wedding ceremony beneath the bridal canopy.

The cup of wine is presented first to the bridegroom and then to the bride.

The bridegroom then places the ring on the finger of his bride, and says:

By this ring you are consecrated to me as my wife in accordance with the law of Moses and the people of Israel.

The cup of wine is refilled, and held by the officiant as he recites:

Praised are You, O Lord our God, King of the universe, Creator of the fruit of the vine.

Praised are You, O Lord our God, King of the universe, who created all things for Your glory.

Praised are You, O Lord our God, King of the universe, Creator of man.

Praised are You, O Lord our God, King of the universe, who created man and woman in Your image, fashioning woman in the likeness of man, preparing for man a mate, that together they might perpetuate life. Praised are You, O Lord, Creator of man.

May Zion rejoice as her children in joy are restored to her. Praised are You, O Lord, who causes Zion to rejoice at her children's return.

Grant great joy to these beloved companions, as You did to the first man and woman in the Garden of Eden. Praised are You, O Lord, who grants joy to bride and groom.

Praised are You, O Lord our God, King of the universe, who created joy and gladness, bride and groom, mirth, song, delight and rejoicing, love and harmony, peace and companionship. O Lord our God, may there be heard in the cities of Judah and in the streets of Jerusalem voices of joy and gladness, voices of bride and groom, the jubilant voices of those joined in marriage under the bridal canopy, the voices of young people feasting and singing. Praised are You, O Lord, who causes the groom to rejoice with his bride.[8]

The ceremony is performed under a canopy, which symbolizes the home that will be made together. At the end of the ceremony, the groom shatters a drinking glass under foot — a reminder of the destruction of the Temple. This introduces the Jewish concept that there is always sorrow amid joy.

That a prime reason for marriage is to bring forth children is indicated by the following selection from the Mishnah:

> No man may abstain from fulfilling the commandment "Be fruitful and multiply" [Genesis 1:28], unless he already has children. According to the School of Shamai, "children" here means two sons, while the School of Hillel states that it means a son and a daughter, for it is written, "Male and female created He them" [Genesis 5:2]. If he married a woman and lived with her for ten years and she bore no child, he is not permitted to abstain from fulfilling the commandment. If he divorced her she may marry another, and the second husband may live with her for ten years. If she had a miscarriage, the period of ten years is reckoned from the time of the miscarriage. The duty to be fruitful and multiply is incumbent upon the man but not upon the woman. Rabbi Johanan ben Baroka says: Concerning them both it is written: "God blessed them and God said to them: Be fruitful and multiply" [Genesis 1.28].[9]

Children are admonished to honour and love their parents. But rabbinic writings say that such love is to be shown equally to father *and* mother, a perhaps surprising concept for the period of history in which it was written. Perhaps more surprising still was the idea that parents had specific duties toward their children; it was definitely a two-way responsibility.

"Cursed be he who dishonours his father or his mother" [Deuteronomy 27:16]. But at the same time,

> A father is obligated to see that his son is circumcised, to redeem him [if he is the first-born], to teach him Torah and a craft and to find a wife for him. Some say that he must teach his son to swim. Rabbi Judah said: Whoever does not teach his son a craft is considered as having taught him thievery.[10]

Circumcision   Circumcision is the oldest of Jewish rituals and remains today as it did thousands of year ago.

> 9. And God said unto Abraham, Thou shalt keep my covenant therefore, thou, and thy seed after thee in their generations.
>
> 10. This *is* my covenant, which ye shall keep, between me and you and thy seed after thee; Every man-child among you shall be circumcised.
>
> 11. And ye shall circumcise the flesh of your foreskin; and it shall be a token of the covenant betwixt me and you.
>
> 12. And he that is eight days old shall be circumcised among you, every man-child in your generations, he that is born in the house, or bought with money of any stranger, which *is* not of thy seed.
>
> 13. He that is born in thy house, and he that is bought with thy money, must needs be circumcised: and my covenant shall be in your flesh for an everlasting covenant.

14. And the uncircumcised man-child, whose flesh of his foreskin is not circumcised, that soul shall be cut off from his people; he hath broken my covenant.

Genesis 17:9-14

The significance of the ritual is explained as being "a sign of the faith in the flesh". Originally intended as a means of showing a bodily sign of spiritual belief, some believe that the hygienic reasons were also significant. One Conservative rabbi however says that this is reading too much into it, and gives too much credit to the early Jews. Surely the hygienic aspects are valid today; but today circumcision is practised by many — not only Jews.

Dietary Laws   Sometimes called *Kashruth*, the dietary laws are among the most pervasive of all Jewish rituals. They are observed by the faithful in the very act of eating to sustain life. The reasons for the laws are probably many; however, there are two which crop up more often than any others in the traditional writings. One theory is that by providing certain restrictions, they curb the animal instincts of man. That is, by controlling what goes into one's mouth, hopefully the words which come out will also be controlled. It is primarily an exercise in self-discipline. Secondly, the laws set the Jews apart from others in day-to-day affairs and this may have been another reason for their institution. As with so many rituals of the Jews and others, these cannot be explained or defended logically; they must be accepted as part of the whole fabric of life. Regarding adherence to the laws, the most devout usually tend to be members of Orthodox Judaism; often Conservatives follow some and not others: Reform Judaism has rejected them almost totally.

A certificate of Kashruth found in a Toronto butcher shop. Notice the certificate is also printed in Hebrew.

Riley E. Moynes

Chosen from the holy writings of Judaism, the following are some of
the restrictions:

32. Therefore the children of Israel eat not *of* the sinew which shrank,
which *is* upon the hollow of the thigh, unto this day: because he
touched the hollow of Jacob's thigh in the sinew that shrank.
Genesis 32:32

31. And ye shall be holy men unto me; neither shall ye eat any flesh
that is torn of beasts in the field; ye shall cast it to the dogs.
Exodus 22:31

2. Speak unto the children of Israel, saying, These *are* the beasts which
ye shall eat among all the beasts that are on the earth.

3. Whatsoever parteth the hoof, and is cloven-footed, *and* cheweth the
cud, among the beasts, that shall ye eat.

4. Nevertheless these shall ye not eat of them that chew the cud, or of
them that divide the hoof: *as* the camel, because he cheweth the cud,
but divideth not the hoof; he *is* unclean unto you.

5. And the coney, because he cheweth the cud, but divideth not the
hoof; he is unclean unto you.

6. And the hare, because he cheweth the cud, but divideth not the
hoof; he is unclean unto you.

7. And the swine, though he divide the hoof, and be cloven-footed, yet
he cheweth not the cud; he *is* unclean to you.

8. Of their flesh shall ye not eat and their carcase shall ye not touch;
they *are* unclean to you.
Leviticus 11:2-8

9. These shall ye eat of all that *are* in the waters: whatsoever hath
fins and scales in the waters, in the seas, and in the rivers, them shall
ye eat.

10. And all that have not fins and scales in the seas, and in the rivers,
of all that move in the waters, and of any living thing which *is* in the
waters, they *shall be* an abomination unto you:

11. They shall be even an abomination unto you; ye shall not eat of
their flesh, but ye shall have their carcases in abomination.
Leviticus 11, 9-11

10. And whatsoever man *there be* of the house of Israel, or of the
strangers that sojourn among you, that eateth any manner of blood; I
will even set my face against that soul that eateth blood, and will cut
him off from among his people.

11. For the life of the flesh *is* in the blood: and I have given it to you upon the altar to make an atonement for your souls: for it *is* the blood *that* maketh an atonement for the soul.

12. Therefore I said unto the children of Israel, No soul of you shall eat blood, neither shall any stranger that sojourneth among you eat blood.

13. And whatsoever man *there be* of the children of Israel, or of the strangers that sojourn among you, which hunteth and catcheth any beast or fowl that may be eaten; he shall even pour out the blood thereof, and cover it with dust.

14. For *it is* the life of all flesh; the blood of it *is* for the life thereof: therefore I said unto the children of Israel, Ye shall eat the blood of no manner of flesh: for the life of all flesh *is* the blood thereof: whosoever eateth it shall be cut off.

Leviticus 17:10-14

This last decree is the scriptural basis for the fact that before meat can be labelled "kosher" or fit for Jews to eat, a rabbi should be present to be sure that this decree, as well as the one regarding the blood being drained, is followed exactly.

Again there are those who believed that many of these laws may have more than a religious raison d'être. Although one rabbi plays down the health considerations, they may have been present. For example, in days before refrigeration pork in particular was subject to spoilage despite being salted; therefore it may have been dangerous to eat. No one suggests that these reasons overshadow the religious ones or even that there is much consistency in the selection of animals; however, the health consideration could be a valid one.

Bar Mitzvah   At the age of thirteen, a Jewish boy becomes *Bar Mitzvah*, a Son of the Commandment. It is the pinnacle of boyhood and the beginning of manhood and usually takes place on the Saturday following the thirteenth birthday. Preparation for the day begins much earlier; in fact from the ages of six or seven to thirteen, a boy may attend Jewish school some days after regular school and on Sunday. At school, many learn to read from the difficult Torah scroll in the year prior to their Bar Mitzvah. The boy is counted as one of the ten needed for communal prayers; for the first time, he becomes part of the Jewish *minyan*, a group of ten men in public prayer together.

Bar Mitzvah day usually involves a large family reunion and feast. But first comes the ceremony in the synagogue. Following the morning service the Torah is lifted from the Ark and is unrolled. The boy is then honoured with an *aliyah*, a call to come forward and recite a portion of the Word. He recites a blessing and reads a portion from the Torah. As he reads, the boy, in an Orthodox ceremony, wears a prayer shawl and skull cap as he does at all prayer; in some Reform ceremonies he may wear neither. Besides these trappings, the boy is expected to begin wearing the *T'fillin* on his forehead and arm during weekday services as a physical reminder of the spiritual responsibilities of manhood. T'fillin are black leather straps laced to the body, usually used in the weekday morning worship.

Courtesy Rabbi I.E. Witty

A rabbi teaching his son how to put on his Phylacteries (T'fillin) in preparation for his Bar Mitzvah. Note that the rabbi wears a large prayer shawl (Tallit) with a silver Atarah or decoration. Both are wearing the Kipa (skull cap) and the T'fillin for the hand (Shel Yad) and for the head (Shel Rosh).

The Reform synagogues ignore the trappings because they say that the Torah was God-inspired rather than God-given and therefore do not accept the traditional 613 *mitzvot* or commandments as Divine Law. A further change they have made is to allow men and women to sit together in the synagogue (Conservative temples often do the same); Orthodox congregations still insist that male and female sit separately; in some instances women sit behind a partition called a *mechitza*; others provide a special area for the women. Some Reform and Conservative temples now have the Bas Mitzvah for girls at age thirteen, although maturity is really achieved at twelve years plus a day.

The final part of the ceremony may see the boy, now the man, proceed to the pulpit to deliver a Bar Mitzvah address in which, among other things, he vows to be a good Jew. Then the family celebration begins; it sometimes is a very lavish affair.

Prayer   Prayer provides a direct contact between man and God and as such is a very important part of the Jewish faith. It can be used to speak to God, to beseech, to experience nearness or express gratitude to God. God on his part hears human prayer and answers it; but this does not mean that he always gives the answer that man wants, for the ways of God are different from the ways of man. The following selection stresses these statements: "The Holy One, praised be He, longs for the prayers of the righteous".

In the synagogue, on the Sabbath there is a prescribed cycle of readings from the Torah. There are consecutive readings from the Five Books of Moses each Sabbath during the year. At all other times, the reading is from the Five Books of Moses and is something appropriate to the occasion. On Sabbaths and festivals a complementary section is read from Prophets (Haphtorah).

The *Shema* is the daily prayer of Judaism:

4. Hear, O Israel: The Lord our God is one God.

5. And thou shalt love the Lord thy God with all thine heart, and with all thy soul, and with all thy might.

6. And these words, which I command thee this day, shall be in thine heart.

7. And thou shalt teach them diligently unto thy children, and shalt talk of them when thou sittest in thine house, and when thou walkest by the way, and when thou liest down and when thou risest up.

8. And thou shalt bind them for a sign upon thine hand, and they shall be as frontlets between thine eyes.

9. And thou shalt write them upon the posts of thy house, and on thy gates.

Deuteronomy 6:4-9

Besides the prescribed prayers and services which are insisted upon, private devotion is also encouraged. Thousands of prayers may be chosen; the following is one:

God, it is true, before You there is no night, and the light is with You, and You make the whole world shine with Your light.

The mornings tell of Your mercy, and the nights tell of Your truth, and all creatures tell of Your great mercy and of great miracles.

Each day You renew Your help, O God! Who can recount Your miracles? You sit in the sky and count the days of the devout, and set the time for all Your creatures. Your single day is a thousand years and Your years and days are unbounded.

All that is in the world must live its life to an end, but You are there, You will always be there, and outlive all Your creatures.

You, God, are pure, and pure are Your holy servants who three times every day cry, "Holy," and sanctify You in heaven and on earth:

You, God, are sanctified and praised. The whole world is filled with Your glory for ever and ever.[11]

7. Major Festivals

Passover The Passover celebration glorifies the significant moment of God's intervention in human history, when he allowed the Exodus from Egypt through Moses; in arranging the escape, God is believed to have sent a plague to strike the Egyptians, but "passed over" the homes of the Hebrews, thus sparing them. Furthermore it is a ritual celebration of individual and group liberation and renewal in all periods, beginning with the Exodus and continuing through history.

"Seven days shall there be no leaven found in your houses" [Exodus 12:19] and so, there is a traditional candlelight search throughout the house for leavened bread, that is, bread with leaven which causes it to "rise". Pots and pans which are untouched by leaven are used, and *matzah* (unleavened bread) is eaten to remind Jews of the time when they could not wait for the bread to rise as they fled from the Pharaoh.

14. And this day shall be unto you for a memorial; and ye shall keep it a feast to the Lord throughout your generations; ye shall keep it a feast by an ordinance for ever.

15. Seven days shall ye eat unleavened bread; even the first day ye shall put away leaven out of your houses: for whosoever eateth leavened bread from the first day until the seventh day, that soul shall be cut off from Israel.

16. And in the first day *there shall be* an holy convocation, and in the seventh day there shall be an holy convocation to you; no manner of work shall be done in them, save *that* which every man must eat, that only may be done of you,

17. And ye shall observe *the feast of* unleavened bread; for in this self same day have I brought your armies out of the land of Egypt: therefore shall ye observe this day in your generations by an ordinance for ever.

18. In the first *month*, on the fourteenth day of the month at even, ye shall eat unleavened bread, until the one and twentieth day of the month at even.

19. Seven days shall there be no leaven found in your houses: for whosoever eateth that which is leavened, even that soul shall be cut off from the congregation of Israel, whether he be a stranger, or born in the land.

20. Ye shall eat nothing leavened; in all your habitations shall ye eat unleavened bread.

Exodus 12: 14-20

On the eve of the Passover, the Seder Feast, at which the entire family gathers, is celebrated. Prescribed symbolic foods are set at the table: roasted eggs remind Jews of the ancient Temple offerings; shank bone of the pascal lamb sacrificed in the Temple. Haroset (made of apples, nuts and wine) reminds

Jews of the mortar used to construct the Pharaoh's cities; the dipping of the herbs in haroset evokes their oppressed life. Greens in salted water signify the acts of free men who ate greens this way in early times.

In answer to the youngest male's question, "Why is this night different from other nights?", the father answers that matzah is eaten to represent their forefathers' bread of affliction and that bitter herbs are eaten to remind Jews of their early days as slaves. Songs are then sung and the real evening meal is served. Then the door is opened and Elijah, the hoped-for forerunner of the Messiah is invited to enter and drink from the "Elijah cup" which had stood untouched on the table during the preceding ceremony. Finally the service ends and the rejoicing aspects of the evening come to the fore.

Sabbath   From these restrictions have come many interesting questions for today's Jew: Orthodox Judaism forbids travel by automobile on the Sabbath (which falls on Saturday); Reform Judaism permits it. Conservative Judaism generally permits it solely for the purpose of attending synagogue. The prohibition of making a fire has led to discussions regarding the switching on and off of lights on the Sabbath and the use by some of time switches (on some appliances) set before the Sabbath.

But the impression should not be of the Sabbath as a day of restrictions only. It is also a day of physical and spiritual refreshment, when people can let their everyday cares and problems wait. It is

A Jewish family the Passover "Seder" meal. Note the roasted eggs, the shank bone and the matzah.

Miller Services Ltd.

a day for family togetherness, for discussion, for meeting friends, for study and for praising God, Creator of man and the universe. It is a happy day — the positive, rather than negative, features are in the forefront.

Shavuot   On the fiftieth day after the Seder Feast, there is a day of rejoicing set aside to commemorate the first fruits of the spring wheat harvest. Called *Shavuot* (or the Pentecost, or the Feast of Weeks) it is significant because it is regarded as being the anniversary of the giving of the Torah at Sinai. Thus Shavuot is connected with both the Passover and Sukkot (page 208) in that all three are intimately associated with the Exodus.

It has become customary on Shavuot to read in the synagogue from the book of Ruth. Ruth's loyalty is legendary and the symbolism of Israel's loyalty to the Torah is made clear in this way. Further, this day is associated with Ruth's "conversion" or acceptance of the Torah; thus to read from the book of Ruth is appropriate for a ceremony commemorating the giving of the Torah and its acceptance by Moses.

Rosh Hashanah   In September or early October, the High Holy Days begin. Starting with *Rosh Hashanah* and concluding with the solemn Day of Atonement (Yom Kippur), a period of ten days are observed.

Rosh Hashanah is New Year's Day — "a day of blowing the horn" [Leviticus 23:23-5], and so the *shofar* is used as a vital part of the holiday. Usually a ram's horn, symbolic of the ram sacrificed in the place of Abraham's son Isaac, it is considered meritorious to use a curved one to symbolize submission to God. There are numerous theories for the use of the horn — at least ten are considered reasonable. Among these are that as trumpets are sounded at coronations so is God heralded as king this day. Another theory is that there is scriptural basis for it — Isaiah (27:13) speaks of the shofar heralding the messianic age.

At the festive meal, it is customary to dip a piece of bread into honey as a token of the sweet year it is hoped will come. The sending of greeting cards is now a widespread practice though not supported by Jewish tradition. But Rosh Hashanah is the Day of Judgment and as such is a very solemn day. God's overwhelming power and glory is remembered, and it is hoped that, in his omnipotence and might, he will have mercy on undeserving humans, remembering the strengths and attributes of Jewish forefathers rather than the weakness and sinfulness of those living today. Symbolic of the realization of God's supremacy is the fact that this is the only day of the year on which a Jew falls to his knees before God in the synagogue.

The Jewish year 5733 was celebrated in 1973, Christian era. The exact dating is again open to discussion. Some Jews believe that it dates back to the Creation of the earth; others suggest that it may be from the date at which "man first achieved an awareness of a Creator".

Yom Kippur   After ten days of repentance dawns the most solemn day of the Jewish year, the Day of Atonement, *Yom Kippur*. On this day there is to be no eating, no drinking, no wearing of leather shoes (which are considered to be very comfortable), no sexual intercourse and no anointing (that is, no bathing, no showering, no makeup, no hairspray, etc.). Jews are to spend almost all of their waking hours in prayer; to serve God not as men but analogous to angels,

Courtesy Rabbi I.E. Witty

Three young men testing their skills in blowing the shofar in preparation for Rosh Hashanah services. On the right is a cloth covering the reader's desk.

by putting aside as many human endeavours as possible. This is symbolized in part by the cantor's wearing of white in the synagogue — white being the colour of purity.

The essence of the day is stated clearly in Leviticus (16:30): "For on this day shall atonement be made for you, to cleanse you; from all your sins shall ye be clean before the Lord." And so it is a day of purification for those who confess their guilt and iniquity. On the eve of the day there is usually a family feast part of which is the asking of forgiveness of others. On this day it is said, Satan has no power; this is a day of pardon and forgiveness.

Other celebrations have come to be associated with the day. It is said to be the anniversary of the day on which the second tablet of commandments was given to Moses. Also it is the anniversary of the circumcision of Abraham. The importance and significance of this day to Jews throughout the world can scarcely be over-estimated.

Following is a selection from the "confession" to be recited ten times on Yom Kippur. The wording is interesting in that there are obviously more sins included than the greatest of all sinners could have committed; also, the plural is used, indicating a responsibility of each man for the sins of all.

We have trespassed, we have betrayed, we have robbed, we have spoken slander. We have perverted what is right, we have wrought wickedness, we have been presumptuous, we have done violence, we have forged lies. We have given evil counsel, we have spoken falsely, we have scoffed, we have revolted, we have blasphemed, we have been rebellious, we have been perverse, we have transgressed, we have

An Orthodox Jewish youth engrossed in prayer at Jerusalem's Wailing Wall on the eve of Yom Kippur, the Day of Atonement. The Wailing Wall — one of Judaism's most revered holy places — is in Old Jerusalem, formerly held by Jordan; but since the Six Day War in 1967, it has again been in Israeli hands.

Religious News Service Photo

oppressed, we have been stiff-necked. We have acted wickedly, we have acted corruptly, we have committed abomination, we have gone astray, we have led others astray.[12]

Sukkot   Five days after Yom Kippur comes *Sukkot*, the eight-day Feast of Booths. In early days, the celebration was in honour of the fall fruits and the harvest and came to be called the "Feast of the Lord". At this time, people would often move to the fields and live in tents in an effort to finish their work

An Orthodox Jew choosing etrog for Sukkot.

Israel Government Tourist Office

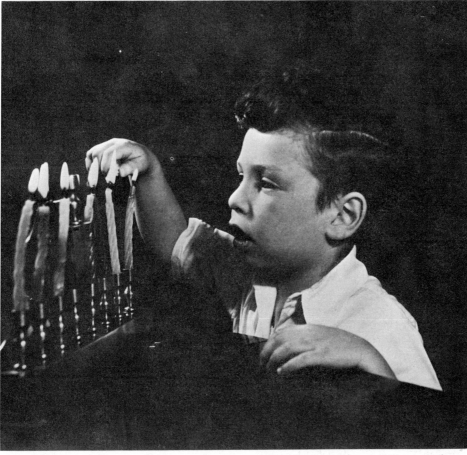

A Jewish youngster lights the Hanukkah candles.

ɔefore the winter rains. Historically it is associated with the temporary housing
necessitated by the years of wandering in the wilderness after the Exodus
[Leviticus 23:42-3]. A main festival of the year, it is celebrated in connection
with the consecration of Solomon's Temple in Jerusalem.

The booths built are decorated with fruits and other ornaments. Four
traditional fruits of Palestine are carried together, especially on the first day of
the festival. These are a citron (*etrog*), and palmn branches (*lulav*) bound with
branches of myrtle (*hadasim*) and willow (*aravot*). Those who can, erect booths
or tabernacles beside their homes and then eat their meals there during the
eight-day festival. Some who are even more dedicated sleep in them. For those
who cannot build their own, there are often booths erected outside synagogues.

Hanukkah   In December Judaism celebrates an eight-day Festival of Lights. On
the first day there is one candle lit in the home and synagogue; on the second
day, two, and so on until on the eighth day when all the candles are burning. This
festival in part commemorates the rededication of the Temple in 165 B.C. by

Judas Maccabeus after he had defeated the Seleucid oppressors of Israel. (See page 177.)

Josephus, a Jewish historian, called it the Festival of Lights because, he said, the right to serve God came to the people unexpectedly, like a sudden light. During this period of happiness, it is forbidden to eulogize the dead or to fast. For the children, the period, falling usually very close to the Christian Christmas celebrations, is a time for receiving and opening gifts. It is not surprising now to see "Christmas" and "Hanukkah" lights illuminating the homes of Christian and Jewish neighbours at this time of the year.

8. Modern Judaism

Jews in the Middle Ages   From A.D. 70, Jews have been scattered throughout the world. Of necessity they were influenced by other religions, and in the Middle Ages Christianity and Islam were those in closest contact with Judaism.

Christianity and Judaism were not always in harmony. Christians always hoped that Jews would come to accept their idea of Jesus; in fact, for nearly 2,000 years the effort has gone on, although Jews always opposed the pressure. St. Paul, for example, carried the message to the Greeks who immediately began interpreting Jesus in a very liberal way and saw him as more than just the Son of God – instead he was interpreted as being part of the cosmological setting of Greek philosophy. But the Talmud demanded a strict interpretation of the Messiah. This split widened in A.D. 312 with the conversion of Constantine to Christianity and later when Christianity became the official religion of the empire. Later still, especially in the Middle Ages as church bishops became more powerful, they became less and less tolerant; violence and anti-Semitism became more widespread.

Islam, a more tolerant religion than Christianity, showed such tolerance in their dealings with Judaism. In the Moslem Empire, Jews were protected from Christians and Zoroastrians; culturally, racially and religiously Jews and Moslems have a number of similarities. Rabbinical schools thrived in Babylon and the *exilarch*, the Prince of the Exile, was a powerful figure at the Moslem court at Baghdad; Jewish traders followed Moslem soldiers to all parts of the Mediterranean.

Then when the Turks took over the Moslem Empire, this attitude changed and the Jews were once again oppressed. Therefore in the tenth and eleventh centuries, Jewish Babylonian scholars moved to Spain where the "golden age" of Jewish science, religion and philosophy ensued.

Karaite Heresy   The "Children of the Text", or Karaites, were founded by Anan ben David of Baghdad. In effect he said that the sole authority was what we call today the Old Testament and not the Talmud. The Karaites were very literalistic and strict in the following of the commandments. They forbade the eating of *any* meat and said that recourse to physicians was proof of lack of faith. They were individuals who insisted on singular interpretation of the texts; however, without any unifying force they became fragmented and their numbers declined though a few still exist in Russia today.

The significance of this "heresy" was that it shook Orthodox Jews from their complacent acceptance of a strictly logical deduction from Divine Law and stimulated a re-examination of the Talmud's indebtedness to the Old Testament in which much mysticism is evident.

Moses Maimonides   Moses Maimonides (A.D. 1135 to 1204) was probably the most outstanding of all Jewish philosophers. He wrote two great works, one ultimately reducing the basic articles of Jewish faith to thirteen cardinal principles; the second was a virtual rewriting of the Talmud in an attempt to simplify and condense rabbinical law. His most significant philosophical work was the *Guide to the Perplexed* which has been quoted in this chapter. It was a rational explanation of the Jewish faith, affirming that man's rational mind was of prime importance, though revelation was needed to supplement it. Miracles then could be explained rationally, and Genesis was viewed as an allegory. By using one's understanding in this fashion, Maimonides believed that the highest truth of God could be known. Many Jewish scholars disagreed so vehemently that some of his works were publicly burned; they believed that religion was mystical and that some things simply could not be understood by man.

Dark Ages   Throughout the Middle Ages life for Jews was filled with hazards and persecution. Crusades aroused emotions against the "infidels" and it mattered little whether they were Moslem or Jew; many were butchered, others were expelled from villages and towns, especially in Germany. Jews were expelled from England in A.D. 1290 and were denied residence in France in A.D. 1394. After the expulsion of the Moors, Spain became inhospitable and those who had not been converted to Roman Catholicism were expelled by Ferdinand and Isabella in A.D. 1492.

Many fled east to Syria, Palestine or Turkey; others headed north to Poland and Russia. Those who stayed in Europe (in Italy, Austria and Germany), were forced to live in ghettos; usually the Roman Catholic Church enforced the thirteenth-century law forbidding a Jew, on pain of death, to be in the streets without his "Jew badge" — some identifying mark like a star of David sewn prominently onto his clothing. Almost invariably the ghetto gates were actually locked at night.

The Reformation initially seemed to herald a better life for the Jews of Europe. Luther was originally sympathetic to Judaism and in 1523 wrote a pamphlet entitled "Jesus Was Born a Jew" which was most favourable toward the faith.

However, when they would not be converted to Lutheranism, he changed his attitude and was loudly anti-Jewish, accusing them of all kinds of treachery, including murdering children to obtain blood for their Passover ritual. In effect then, the Reformation brought virtually no improvement in their treatment; indeed the sixteenth and seventeenth centuries were very trying for European Jews.

Jews in the Eighteenth and Nineteenth Centuries   The general trend of these years was a slow liberation from civil disabilities and a return to everyday life.

The justice of this trend was admitted by most writers of the Enlightenment, and it was put into effect by the revolutionary upheavals of this period in France and Germany. At the same time, many intellectuals were opposed to religion in general and therefore worked at breaking down the religious and social barriers that had previously existed in European centres of culture. One effect of this was to allow Moses Mendelsohn, a philosopher and the grandfather of the composer Felix Mendelsohn, one of the greatest Jews of modern times, to play a major role in the intellectual life of Berlin.

The growth of democracy and liberalism in Europe and the United States at last brought freedom. In the later stages of the French Revolution, the Jews of France were granted the rights of full citizenship. Napoleon destroyed many ghettos and set Jews free to live amidst the society of the time although his reason was the hope of assimilating the Jews rather than the desire to set them free in the usual sense. After Napoleon, a reaction set in and many ghettos were re-established, but only for a short time. Finally the revolutions of 1848 brought virtually complete freedom before the law for all Jews in Europe. Universities were then thrown open to Jews, and since that time they have made significant contributions in this area.

9. Twentieth-Century Judaism

Zionism   In the last half of the nineteenth century, many Jews achieved economic and professional success. However, there still existed much anti-Semitic feeling and action, especially in Russia and Germany, and the Dreyfus affair in France also had ugly anti-Semitic overtones. Many Jews became convinced, in the face of this, that real security and opportunity rested solely in the re-establishment of a national home in Palestine. A book published in 1896 called *The Jewish State* by Theodore Herzl, crystallized this view and led directly to the establishment of an international Jewish movement called *Zionism*, whose goal was to obtain a homeland for the world's Jews.

Balfour Declaration   The next development was the Balfour Declaration expounded during World War I. This statement said, in part, that the British government looked favourably upon the "establishment in Palestine of a national home for the Jewish people" and would seek to "facilitate the achievement of this object". This statement changed the movement from a relatively weak one into a dynamic, healthy one in a very short period of time. In the next years, thousands of Jews settled in Palestine under the British Mandate and established the roots of the present-day state of Israel.

The Nazi atrocities of World War II, however, intensified the pressure to establish a Jewish state, and this feeling was shared by many nations of the world. Some say this was the result of world-wide guilt or sorrow at the genocide of the Hitler era. Final victory was achieved in 1947 with the United Nations' decision to partition Palestine and establish the Jewish state of Israel. Even with the establishment of this state, problems for Jews have not ended. The constant friction between Arab and Israeli, culminating in the Six-Day War in 1967, continues apace.

Other Recent Developments Judaism, as most other religions, is less than united on all aspects of faith, daily life and prayer. As the Anglican Church is divided into Low Anglican, Middle Anglican and High Anglican, so is Judaism. Although there are more than three divisions in Judaism, the major ones are Orthodox, Conservative and Reform.

Reform Judaism Reform Judaism is the most liberal wing of the faith. Reform congregations tend to simplify and modernize synagogue worship. The Sabbath service is condensed from the Conservative version, and both the songs and the service are carried on in the vernacular. Many references to the Messiah, the Resurrection of the dead, the re-establishment of Jewish nationality and the sacrificial rites of ancient Palestine are stricken from the Reform services. Most moderates and left-wing radicals of the faith are members of this wing of Judaism which is presently strongest in the United States. According to these people, Judaism has always been a religion of change, a religion which adapted itself to new and changing situations. Further changes must be made now, they say, in order to preserve the integrity and dynamism of the faith — a faith which has survived for almost four thousand years by recognizing the need for modernization.

Orthodox Judaism Orthodox leadership rejects arguments such as those put forth by Reformers. Orthodoxy believes that the innovations incorporated into Reform liturgy, the use of organ music, prayers in the vernacular instead of in Hebrew, violate talmudic law. Furthermore, realizing that these reforms were only the beginning of other larger changes, Orthodoxy reacted with an all-out effort to preserve the status quo. The slightest tampering with tradition was condemned, for attempts to adjust Judaism to "the spirit of the time" are believed to be utterly incompatible with the entire thrust of normative Judaism, which holds that the revealed will of God rather than the values of any given age are the ultimate standard.

To Orthodox Jews, it is probably fair to say, the practices or the rites are of almost equal importance with the beliefs of the faith. One does not have to believe exactly as the rabbis do, for example, but one *must* adhere strictly to the practical parts of the Law of Moses as interpreted by the Talmud. As closely as possible, one must cling to the practices of the old days. Thus it is in practice and ritual rather than in belief that Orthodoxy is different from other groups.

Conservative Judaism Conservative Judaism despite the name, attempts to bridge the gap between the other two. Whereas Reform Judaism has totally thrown out some of the ritual and Orthodox Jews cling tenaciously to ritual, Conservatives have attempted a middle path. In some cases they are closer to Reform; for example, men and women sit together. In others they are closer to Orthodoxy; heads are covered in the synagogue. In Conservative Judaism, riding to the synagogue on the Sabbath is usually acceptable, although riding for pleasure or business is not. Riding on the Sabbath is forbidden by Orthodox Jews, as is even the act of turning on lights — both are regarded as forbidden activities. Reform Jews would hardly stop to think about riding to the synagogue and then going shopping afterwards.

Conservative Jews affirm the end of the "ghettoization" of the Jews and their emancipation in Europe as a positive good; they hail the Westernization of Jews in manner, education and culture. They know, of course, that some changes are inevitable in the Jewish mode of life and they affirm that these changes can be valid in the light of biblical and rabbinic precedent, for they view all of Jewish history as a succession of changes. They emphasize Judaism throughout the ages as an organism that refreshed its living spirit by responding creatively to new challenges. Thus they stand for change as it becomes essential under new, different conditions; they do not make changes just for the sake of change as Reform Jews are sometimes accused of doing.

10. Final Comments and Observations

Most consistently in Jewish history before disaster has struck, it seems that the means to survive the disaster have been provided. Some Jews accept this as part of the "chosenness" of the group; others believe it is merely chance. The fact is that it seems to have happened regularly. Before the punishment meted out by the Lord for ignoring the covenant, Prophets were sent to attempt to return the people to the proper path. During the exile many of their writings which added to the faith, were used to help hold the faith together. Before the destruction of the first Temple, rabbis were sent to provide a nucleus for Judaism during the long harsh years of the Babylonian captivity.

Before the decline of Babylonia in the ninth century A.D., Torah centres arose in North Africa and western Europe to perpetuate the society and faith of the Jews. Before being exiled from Spain in A.D. 1492, eastern Europe witnessed a vibrant statement of Jewish life. Interestingly, when Jews in western Europe were liberated after the French Revolution, many of them decided to remain in those nations and become Frenchmen or Germans first, and Jews second. However, in eastern Europe no liberation came from the tsars, and it was from here that the loudest voice came for the establishment of the Jewish state — Theodore Herzl's book has been mentioned in this context.

Lastly, it is believed that during the holocaust of Hitler, the Jews were given the strength of will to persevere and survive. In fact, far from failing to destroy Judaism, the persecutions seem to have inspired a renaissance of Jewishness in many parts of the world.

More so than most religions, Judaism combines faith and history to an almost inseparable extent. The relationship between the Exodus and the covenant at Sinai is self-evident. This helps account for the Jews' interest in their own past. At the same time, more than many religions, Judaism is a religion of today — much of Jewish faith deals with the Jew in society. Whereas many religions are intensely philosophical, Judaism is a practical faith — certain conditions are admitted to make the practice of some rites impossible. Whereas the majority of adherents to other religions are united by religious beliefs alone, there is a certain racial and cultural homogeneity associated with the Jews. Thus, in many ways the Jews are a unique people.

The Star of David and the Menorah   The six-sided Star of David is also known known as the Shield of David or the Shield of Solomon. Its origins are uncertain, but it is known that it was not a Jewish invention. Some say that it was originally a magical pagan emblem used to ward off evil, and originated sometime in the seventh century B.C. Others say that it was adopted, and used by King David on the shields of his soldiers to symbolize their goal: equality. Both triangles which make up the symbol are equilateral triangles thus stressing the theme of equality. It later became a sign of the coming Messiah who it was believed would come from the House of David. Still others say that the six sides symbolize universality — the universality of God. The six sides symbolize north, south, east, west, the land above and the world below. Today it appears, among other places, on the flag of Israel.

Despite the Star of David's position on the flag, the Menorah is today the symbol of the state of Israel and is described in the Old Testament – first in Exodus (25 : 31,32). God commanded Moses to make a candlestick of gold with six branches plus the main stem, and to place it in the tabernacle. Upon the stock and the six branches were to be placed golden lamps which were to be made immovable and in which was to be placed oil and cotton. In many Jewish homes, the candlestick for the Hannukah lights is fashioned in the form similar to that seen in the picture. The lights in many synagogues emanate from lamps fashioned in the form of a menorah.

Tourists climbing Mount Sinai to the spot where it is believed Moses received the Ten Commandments.

Israel Government Tourist Agency

Suggestions For Further Study

1. A large number of prominent people, in all walks of North American life, are Jewish. Find the names, and investigate the careers of as many as possible. Wayne and Schuster, Jack Benny and Mark Spitz are just a few.

2. Certain archaeological evidence uncovered in the last few years suggests that the Red Sea may have in fact parted as the Bible states. Research this theory. Talk to an archaeologist for his views.

3. Read *The Jewish Way in Death and Mourning*, by Maurice Lamm (Jonathan David Publishers, N.Y.). What are some of the key differences between Jewish and Christian burial ritual?

4. Read James Michener's *The Source*. It is an interesting study of the changes that came to the Jews in the Holy Land as the political situation ebbed and flowed. It is also engrossing reading.

5. What factors enabled numerous prophets to have such influence over Jewish communities? Name men who today are considered by some to be prophets. What factors enable them to gather such large followings?

6. What examples can you use to suggest that anti-Semitism exists in Canada today? What are the reasons, either real or imagined, for such feelings?

7. Which of the three basic sections of Judaism (Orthodox, Conservative, Reform) has the largest number of followers? the least? How do you account for these facts? What significance, if any, do you attach to these figures?

8. "The Jews have never had it so good — nor have they ever been in such danger of extinction." What did Rabbi Rosenberg of Toronto mean by this statement? Do you agree with it?

9. Many Jewish expressions and phrases have now been adopted by others and are a part of the language. See McGraw-Hill's *Yiddish-English Dictionary* for examples. What factors have led to this development?

Notes

[1]*Weekday Prayer Book*, Rabbinical Assembly of America, 1961, as cited in Arthur Hertzberg, ed., *Judaism*. New York: George Braziller, 1962, p. 236.
[2]The Mishnah Avot 6, *ibid.*, p. 76.
[3]Psalm 117 from the *Weekday Prayer Book*, Rabbinical Assembly of America, 1961, *ibid.*, p. 48.
[4]*Ibid.*, p. 48.
[5]The Mishnah Avot 3:15, *ibid.*, p. 184.
[6]Andre Schwarz-Bart, *The Last of the Just*. New York: Atheneum Publishers, Inc., 1960; Paris: Editions du Seuil, 1959; London: Martin Secker & Warberg Ltd., 1961. Copyright © 1960 by Atheneum House, Inc. Copyright © 1959 by Editions du Seuil, Paris. Reprinted by permission of the publishers.
[7]The Mishnah Ketubot 5:5, as cited in Hertzberg, p. 89.
[8]The Marriage Service, *ibid.*, pp. 96-7.
[9]The Mishnah Yebamot 6:6, *ibid.*, p. 90.
[10]The Kiddushim 29a, *ibid.*, p. 99.
[11]The Sefer Hassidim, *ibid.*, p. 246.
[12]The High Holy Day Prayer Book, *ibid.*, pp. 145-6.

Chapter Eight

Early Christianity

Founded:
About A.D. 30

Founder:
Jesus of Nazareth; called "Christ" (about 4 B.C. to about A.D. 30)

Place:
Palestine (sometimes called Canaan); now Israel

Sacred Books:
The Old and New Testaments; to these, large segments of Christianity add the *Apocrypha*. The Old Testament is the same (except for order) as the Hebrew Scriptures. The New Testament consists of the story of Jesus as told in the *Four Gospels*, the formation of the church as told in the *Acts* and the *Epistles*, and the prophetic book of *Revelation*. The *Apocrypha* consists of fourteen miscellaneous works which form a bridge between Old and New Testaments.

Number of Adherents:
925,000,000

Distribution:
Christians are found in numbers all over the world. However, they predominate in North and South America and Europe.

Christians In Canada:
18,000,000

Sects:
Christianity is divided into Greek Orthodoxy, Roman Catholicism and Protestantism. There is a total of some 250 Protestant denominations.

The fish

Christ (in Greek)

See pages 222-3 for Symbolism in Christianity.

WANTED

JESUS CHRIST

ALIAS: THE MESSIAH, THE SON OF GOD, KING OF KINGS,
         PRINCE OF PEACE, ETC.

Notorious leader of an underground liberation movement

Wanted for:
* practising winemaking, food distribution and medicine without a license
* interfering with businessmen in the temple
* associating with known criminals, radicals, subver-
  sives, prostitutes and street dwellers
* claiming the authority to make people into God's
  children

APPEARANCE: typical hippie type — long hair, beard, robe, sandals;
              hangs around slum areas; often sneaks out into the
              desert

BEWARE: This man is extremely dangerous. His inflammatory mes-
          sage is particularly dangerous to young people who
          have not yet been taught to ignore him. He changes men
          and claims to set them free.

WARNING: HE IS STILL AT LARGE

So reads the message of a modern underground newspaper in words amazingly similar to those that might have been used by the Romans nearly 2,000 years ago. The words describe the man who, perhaps more than anyone else ever born, altered the course of world history. If the present "Jesus revival" is sincere, then to a very great extent today the spirit of the man lives on; and more than ever it seems in the minds and hearts of the young. Today, Christianity is the world's largest single religion claiming a following of about *one billion — nearly one-third of the world's population.*

But behind the present success and religious revival are some very humble beginnings and some sobering facts that must be kept in mind when studying Christianity. To a greater extent than most other religions, it is rooted firmly in history; much of its development is connected with political events. More often than many like to admit, significant developments within the religion were the results of primarily political decisions. There is not always the obvious divine guidance some may expect or at least look for.

Secondly and more important in studying Christianity, one must forget for the moment the rational — the logical. Whether you believe, for example, in the miracles attributed to Jesus during his short ministry is of little consequence; the important thing is that people at the time did. Whether you believe in the Resurrection of Jesus (either physically or spiritually) again matters little — more important is that some people, then and now, *do* believe.

Lastly it must be borne in mind that there is a great difference between Jesus the man and Jesus the legend. One must remember that the Resurrection was the unique aspect of this new faith — not the man who was the instrument of God's will. The gospels of the New Testament tell us very little about Jesus the man before he began his ministry; and when they do discuss the ministry, it is the theological Jesus rather than Jesus the individual who is examined. If one approaches the situation keeping these things in mind, it will probably seem quite clear; otherwise one may well become bogged down in comparing one's personal faith with that of the Christian church.

1. Relation To Judaism

Christianity is closely linked to Judaism — some see it as the fulfillment of Judaism — a point made clear by the fact that the Apostles saw no dichotomy between their belief in the resurrection of Jesus and their Jewish faith. After the eastern Mediterranean was conquered by Rome, she attempted to impose the Hellenistic concept of the unification of diverse peoples under one (Roman) rule. However, the Jews had felt the yoke of Assyria, Babylonia, Persia, Greece and now Rome, and longed to be allowed to develop their own "separateness". The only way this seemed possible, given the conditions of the time, was for the Messiah to come and initiate the Kingdom of Heaven — NOW.

In Galilee around the time of Jesus' birth, Herod Antipas (the son of Herod the Great) ruled. He hoped to fuse the diverse elements of the territory into one and began to rebuild the cities of the area on the Greek model. But, in order to do so, he raised the taxes of the Jews. Not only were their taxes raised, but would be used to pursue an ideal of racial integration that would destroy their very existence. Needless to say, the Jews were dead set against these new taxes. Nevertheless salt taxes, bridge and harbour taxes and others were levied. Then in A.D. 6 a census was conducted so that (according to the Jews) the specific number of people who *should* pay taxes would be known. This led to a Jewish insurrection, led by the so-called Zealots who fought for the principle of: "No God but Yahweh, no tax but on the Temple, no friend but the Zealot."

Inevitably the revolt was squashed; Varus used two legions to do so, and then crucified and burned thousands of Zealots. Jesus was about twelve years of age at the time.

The view was widespread among Jews that the last days had arrived; that out of the disorder, the chaos, the killing, and the suppression would come the Lord to usher in the new Kingdom of God. The book of Isaiah makes numerous references to these days in the Old Testament, and the Gospel of Mark refers to it also and implies that the end is *very* near:

1. And he said unto them, Verily I say unto you, That there be some of them that stand here, which shall not taste of death, till they have seen the kingdom of God come with power.

Mark 9:1

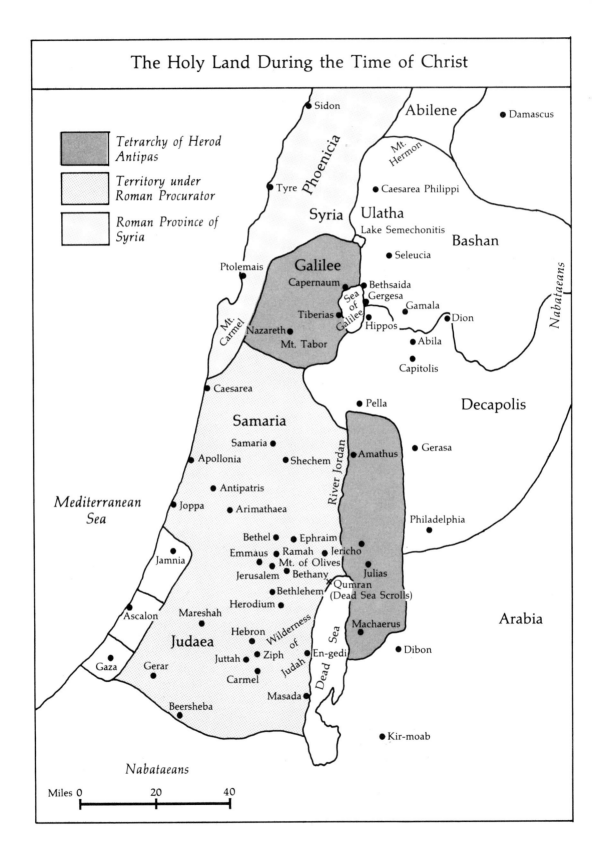

The Holy Land During the Time of Christ

Tetrarchy of Herod Antipas

Territory under Roman Procurator

Roman Province of Syria

Sidon

Abilene

Damascus

Mt. Hermon

Phoenicia

Tyre

Caesarea Philippi

Syria

Ulatha

Lake Semechonitis

Bashan

Ptolemais

Galilee

Seleucia

Capernaum

Bethsaida
Gergesa

Sea of Galilee

Gamala

Mt. Carmel

Tiberias

Hippos

Dion

Nazareth

Mt. Tabor

Abila

Capitolis

Caesarea

Pella

Decapolis

Samaria

Samaria

Gerasa

Apollonia

Shechem

Amathus

River Jordan

Antipatris

Mediterranean Sea

Joppa

Arimathaea

Philadelphia

Bethel

Ephraim

Emmaus

Ramah

Jericho

Mt. of Olives

Jerusalem

Bethany

Julias

Jamnia

Bethlehem

Qumran (Dead Sea Scrolls)

Herodium

Ascalon

Mareshah

Machaerus

Arabia

Hebron

Wilderness of Judah

Dead Sea

Judaea

Juttah

Ziph

En-gedi

Dibon

Gaza

Gerar

Carmel

Masada

Beersheba

Kir-moab

Nabataeans

Miles 0   20   40

In chapter thirteen Mark goes further. In answer to a question posed by the disciples Peter, James, John and Andrew as to the signs of the end being near Jesus answered: ". . . nation will make war upon nation. . . . there will be famines. . . . you will be flogged in synagogues. . . . Brother will betray brother to death. . . . the sun will be darkened, the moon will not give her light. . . ." [Mark 13:3-23]. And when will all this happen? "I tell you this: the present generation will live to see it all" [Mark 13:30].

Obviously then, the Messianic hope was reaching a fever pitch.

Jesus was born and raised in this environment, and it is against this background that his life and death must be viewed.

2. Our Sources of Knowledge About Jesus

Almost all of our firsthand information about Jesus comes from the first four books of the New Testament. These are the sources that have survived and apparently once circulated among Christians in the first two centuries after Jesus' death. Sometimes these books are referred to as *gospels*. This word is a rendering of the Greek word "evangelion" which is the opening word of the book of Mark — it means "glad tidings". The glad tidings were that the Messiah had come and that the Kingdom of God was at hand. All these authors, it should be noted, shared with the Roman historian Sallust the concept that history was a vehicle for moral ideas. Most historians today reject this concept.

The Gospels of Matthew, Mark and Luke were all written in "popular" language and are not models of grammar or literary polish. However, they are direct and forceful in expressing deep feelings, and are thus fascinating reading. The Gospel of Mark was probably written between A.D. 65 and 70, that is, between 35 and 40 years after Jesus' death. It is based on the *Logia* (the words of Christ) and is, according to Albert Schweitzer, "genuine history" in its essentials. The Gospel of Matthew was probably written between A.D. 85 and 90. It borrows from Mark and tries to convert Jews by stressing the miracles performed by Jesus. It attempts to show the Jews that the Old Testament prophecy of the coming of a Messiah was fulfilled in Jesus. The Gospel of Luke is later still; it was probably written between A.D. 90 and 100. It borrows from Mark and Matthew and tries to reconcile and co-ordinate these two earlier gospels with itself. It is written in an effort to convert Gentiles to Christianity, not Jews. The Fourth Gospel, that is, that of John, does not purport to be a biography of Christ as do the others. Rather, it looks at Christ from the theological point of view as the divine redeemer of mankind. These diverse sources are our main support in studying the life and death of Christ, as well as his teachings and beliefs.

Symbolism In Christianity

One of the early symbols was the fish.

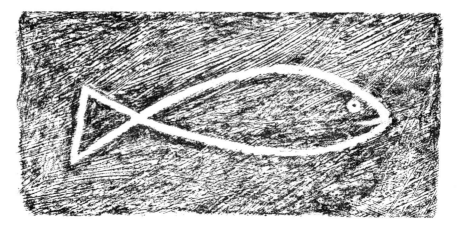

In Greek, it is pronounced "ichthys" and forms an acronym for "Jesus Christ, Son of God, Saviour"
that is:

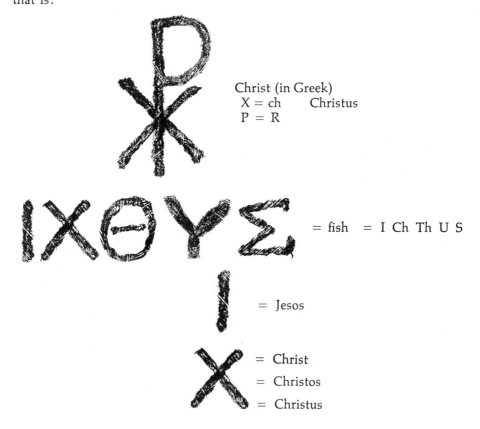

Christ (in Greek)
X = ch   Christus
P = R

= fish   = I Ch Th U S

= Jesos

= Christ
= Christos
= Christus

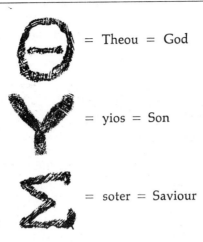

= Theou = God

= yios = Son

= soter = Saviour

Other symbols evident around A.D. 200 were the dove, which symbolized the soul freed from the prison of life; the phoenix, rising from the ashes of death, symbolizing Resurrection; the palm branch announcing victory; and, the olive branch announcing peace.

3. Role of Jesus

A. Basic Concepts and Beliefs

Most Biblical scholars agree that Jesus was born sometime in 4 B.C. Dates including April 18, May 20 and November 17 have been advanced; in A.D. 354 the church decided on December 25 because it was believed (erroneously) that this was the winter solstice, that is, the shortest day of the year, the date we know to be December 21. The strangeness of Jesus being born in 4 "B.C." is explained by the fact that we know that Herod the Great was still alive; he died in 3 B.C. Not until the sixth century A.D. did the church begin to use the terms B.C. and A.D. The discrepancy in dating stems from the miscalculation of the winter solstice.

Though born in Bethlehem, Jesus lived in Nazareth for most of the first thirty years of his life. His parents were peasants who were deeply religious and Jesus was brought up within the Jewish framework. The Gospel of Mark (6:3) suggests that Jesus had brothers and sisters although not all Christian denominations accept this. During his first twelve years of life we know that he helped his father and learned the carpentry trade; we also know that he was a religious person and knew about the background to the Zealot uprising over the taxes. Almost nothing is known about his youth from the ages of twelve to thirty. We hear of Jesus next when John the Baptist bursts onto the scene.

John the Baptist was a prophet in the mould of Amos, Isaiah and Jeremiah. He was sure that the present age was about to end and that the Messiah was coming very soon to bring the day of wrath upon those who lived an evil life. His goal was to baptize people and thus wash away their sins *before* the Judgment Day. After baptism, they were to await the end doing good deeds and attempting to save others.

Jesus was attracted to John's preaching as Mark tells us in chapter one of his gospel. Having been baptized, Jesus retired to the Judean wilderness for a period said to be forty days in order to think and decide what he must do. The baptism of Jesus marked the beginning of his ministry and the beginning of his *historical* interest.

In the Wilderness   Several decisions were made by Jesus in the wilderness, all of which were to be significant in later days. He decided no longer to work for a living but rather to depend on the charity of others. He decided not to force God's hand — he would not use spectacular methods to draw attention to himself. Thirdly, he decided against the pursuit of political power — to do so he believed would be to compromise with Satan. Thus Jesus rejected the *Zealot* approach as being futile and self-destructive. The *Pharisees* were rejected also. This group was the largest political-religious party in Galilee and was composed mainly of highly trained rabbis. They were well organized and ran fine schools with outstanding teachers. They tried to live as closely to their prescribed way of life as conditions would allow. Very conservative and traditional, they tried to hasten the coming of the Messiah and to save Judaism by a scrupulous adherence to every detail of everyday life. This was the point on which Jesus differed with them. As explained in Matthew 23, they were concerned about the wrong things: they were concerned, according to Jesus, with dietary restrictions, etc., when they should have been concerned with justice and mercy.

This decision of Jesus also meant that he would not join the *Sadducees*. They were a smaller group than the Pharisees and were even more conservative than the latter. The Sadducees believed that the old ways and the Torah were unchangeable. With these people, Jesus had little contact. And finally, he did not join the *Essenes*. Opposed to violence on general principle, they waited patiently for the Messiah in very severe, austere surroundings. Adhering strictly to the Law, they lived the type of life not generally associated with Jesus' enjoyment of feasts, meetings and contact with allegedly unclean people.

Jesus' Ministry   Emerging from his period of introspection, Jesus embarked upon his short but famous ministry. The first followers were Simon Peter, Andrew, James and John — all fishermen, for Jesus began his ministry in the area around the Lake of Galilee. At first he spoke in synagogues but as the crowds grew larger he was forced to speak in large open areas, in one case even from a boat to those on the shore.

Much is made in this context of the miraculous healings attributed to Jesus. Mark especially stresses this aspect of the ministry (e.g., Mark 1:29-34; 40-44; 4:35-41), but this is not the key. Jesus never tried to gain acceptance by performing miracles; on the contrary, most of these acts took place away from large public gatherings and were performed, as Jesus himself said, *not* by him but by the faith of the individual. Certainly by today's standards these acts were unusual, but the same type of faith healing has been attributed to Oral Roberts, among others. He too maintains that the person's faith did the healing, not he. Whatever the explanation, it is once again imperative to note that whether one today believes these things to have happened does not matter; what does matter is that people then believed these events to be miraculous and this belief influenced their attitude towards Jesus.

Basic Teachings   The kernel of Jesus' teachings can be stated rather briefly. The major point was God's overwhelming love for man. The second

Israel Government Tourist Office

The Mount of Beatitudes. This is the location where it is believed Jesus gave his "Sermon on the Mount." Today many tourists visit the site and look over the surrounding countryside.

key was the need for man to receive this love and in turn to let it flow out to his neighbours. But here rests the problem for man; we often feel love should somehow be based on a person's *due*: Jesus felt it should be based on his *need*. We find it difficult to give love when it is not deserved, but we must fulfil Jesus' teachings. A more detailed study of Jesus' teachings can be found in the Sermon on the Mount [Matthew 5-7].

But these teachings, taken individually, are not new. Almost totally they were part of the Torah of the Jews. Their success was primarily due to the fact that Jesus spoke in simple language that the uneducated masses could understand; he also spoke with authority and held peoples' interest.

These two bases of Jesus' teachings had many implications, some of which we will now examine.

B. Religious Teaching

At the time under study, no one doubted that God was alive and well; their questions were: "What is He like?" "What will He do?" To Jesus, God was the absolute sovereign of the universe and the moving spirit behind the course of history. He never departed from perfect justice in determining the course of events or the destiny of an individual. He was also forgiving, merciful and deeply concerned with human redemption. Jesus implied that God gives man free choice to do evil (or good) and that he loves them through the redemptive process of suffering and punishment that must follow their evil; he will also forgive them when they return to the fold. The corollary to this is that since God is utterly good and holy, man must trust without doubt and seek spiritual enlightenment through prayer. A major problem with man, according to Jesus, was that man seeks food and clothing *first*; if, however, he chose to seek the Kingdom of God first, then all else would come in time. *This is God's plan, and a major key to Jesus' faith.*

Jesus, unlike some churchmen of later times, never suggested that the body was inherently corrupt or that the soul was foully imprisoned in the flesh; on the contrary, and in Jewish fashion, he saw the body as being functionally integrated with the mind. The body may be an agent of evil but it may also become a temple for the Holy Spirit. Man's first job was to do God's will — and all men are capable of doing it. There were no exceptions to this law of love; it was interracial and international. Thus Jesus' teachings are universal — in this he breaks free from the more restricted view held by the Pharisee Jews.

The Kingdom of Heaven   Along with other Jews, Jesus shared the expectation of the Messianic Kingdom. It should not be forgotten that he lived his whole life at a time when this feeling was vibrant. Jesus however altered the narrowly conceived Jewish Messianic Kingdom and made it the universal Kingdom of the father of all men; the "elect" were not only Jews, they were from the world at large: "Many, I tell you, will come from east and west to feast with Abraham, Isaac, and Jacob in the Kingdom of Heaven" [Matthew 8:11-12]. Entrance to the Kingdom was not limited to those who kept the Law of Moses; broader considerations existed: "How blest are those who have suffered persecution for the cause of right; the Kingdom of Heaven is theirs" [Matthew 5:10]. Furthermore, Jesus lessened the tension associated with the coming of the Messiah by saying that in the real sense, many of the elements of the Kingdom were already present. By so doing he may have been trying to play down the expectation of earth-shaking events associated with the coming of the Messiah.

The question of the relation of Jesus to God seems to be one which is more important to us than it was to him. To be sure, Jesus felt a very close intimacy with God; but this is not surprising given his religious interest from youth and his Jewish upbringing. It seems clear that he was convinced that he had been "sent"; he was sure God had commissioned him to establish his Kingdom. This belief probably accounts for Jesus' confident attitude in choosing his followers, preaching, teaching and working with the masses. He believed sincerely the passage from Isaiah: "The spirit of the Lord is upon me." Today, of course, the relation between Jesus and God is interpreted differently by various groups; more will be said about this in Chapter Ten.

C. Ethical Teaching

To Jesus there was a great overlap of the religious and the ethical aspects of his teaching; in the interests of clarity, however, we shall separate the two. It should first be noted then that once a person committed himself to Jesus' religious beliefs, Jesus expected a complete commitment to himself and more important to the Kingdom of Heaven:

> 59. And he said unto another, Follow me. But he said, Lord, suffer me first to go and bury my father.
> 60. Jesus said unto him, Let the dead bury their dead: but go thou and preach the kingdom of God.
>
> Luke 9:59-60

People were to place moral obligations *above* social, legal or ceremonial demands, and this was the reason for Jesus' dislike of the ceremony associated with the Pharisees. They carried out the ritual devotedly, but he felt that in so doing, they overlooked some major moral questions like justice, integrity and honesty.

Golden Rule   Once a person accepted his religious teachings, Jesus demanded that man be concerned with the *inner* and not the *outer* self. And here there is a very close connection with the idea of love being given because it is needed, not because it is earned. This teaching is as basic to Christianity as it is to Judaism:

> Always treat others as you would like them to treat you: that is the Law and the prophets.
>
> Matthew 7:12

> . . . the Pharisees met together; and one of their number tested him with this question: "Master, which is the greatest commandment in the Law?" He answered, "Love the Lord your God with all your heart, with all your soul, and with all your mind. That is the greatest commandment. It comes first. The second is like it: Love your neighbour as yourself. Everything in the Law and the prophets hangs on these two commandments."
>
> Matthew 22:35-40

Thus this important idea is stated; it was left to the individual to apply it as various situations arose.

In all this, as has been observed by many, "Nothing is new except the arrangement". Many prophets before had taught the same basic lesson. (See Chapter Seven, Judaism.) To his followers, Jesus was the Messiah; but they believed he would radically alter the unbearable political situation. When he did not, they began to fall away. Will Durant states it so well, "His achievement lay not in ushering in a new state, but in outlining an ideal morality."

D. Opposition, Trial and Death

As Jesus' amazing popularity spread, the voices of conservatism within Judaism (that is, the Pharisees and Sadducees) were raised against him and they began to send "spies" to listen to Jesus and to heckle him. In effect, they tried to force him into breaking a Torah Law and thus show that he was not worthy of being believed. They heckled him on one occasion when his disciples picked wheat in the fields on the Sabbath, thus seemingly breaking one of the Ten Commandments; they heckled when he healed people on the Sabbath, for such work was forbidden; and they heckled when his disciples on occasion did not wash before eating.

But what really angered these groups was Jesus' re-interpretation of the Jewish Law. By what authority had he the right to do so? This was the sacred Law of Moses and the Prophets! But he did so anyway particularly in his Sermon on the Mount:

> 38. Ye have heard that it hath been said, An eye for an eye, and a tooth for a tooth:
> 39. But I say unto you, That ye resist not evil; but whosoever shall smite thee on thy right cheek, turn to him the other also.
> Matthew 5:38-39

It should be noted that Jesus did not consider that he was abolishing the Hebrew Law; rather he thought that he was fulfilling it:

> 17. Think not that I am come to destroy the Law, or the Prophets: I am not come to destroy, but to fulfil.
> Matthew 5:17

Zealots also opposed Jesus for his teachings that those who live by the sword shall also die by the sword. Thus with the followings of these three groups now opposed to him, the number of Jesus' supporters dwindled, and those who were carried merely by a casual interest or attachment began to fall away, particularly as whispered threats against his life began to be heard. Jesus thus thought it prudent to retire to the north towards Tyre and Sidon and thence

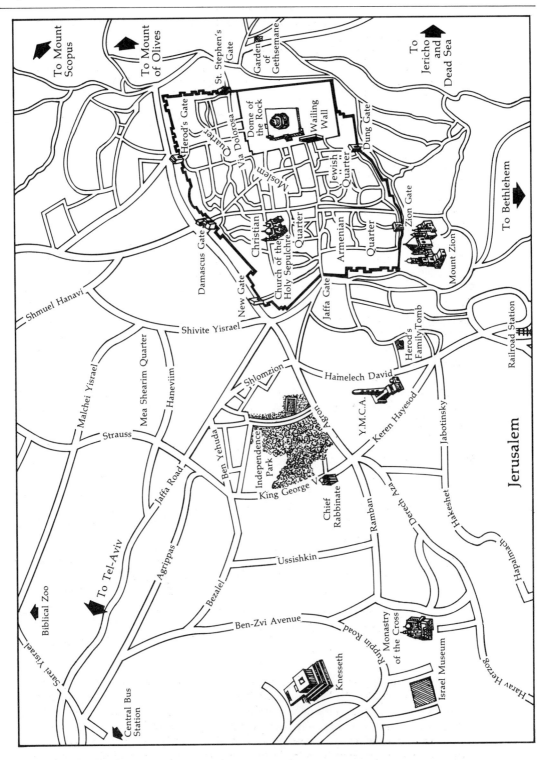

To Mount Scopus

To Mount of Olives

To Jericho and Dead Sea

St. Stephen's Gate

Garden of Gethsemane

Herod's Gate

Dome of the Rock

Wailing Wall

Dung Gate

Via Dolorosa

Moslem Quarter

Jewish Quarter

Zion Gate

To Bethlehem

Damascus Gate

Christian Quarter

Church of the Holy Sepulchre

Quarter

Armenian Quarter

Mount Zion

New Gate

Jaffa Gate

Shmuel Hanavi

Shivite Yisrael

Herod's Family Tomb

Railroad Station

Shlomzion

Hamelech David

Ben Yehuda

Haneviim

Mea Shearim Quarter

Malchei Yisrael

Strauss

Independence Park

Agron

Y.M.C.A.

Keren Hayesod

Jabotinsky

Jerusalem

Jaffa Road

King George V

Chief Rabbinate

Ramban

Derech Aza

Hakeshet

Agrippas

Bezalel

Ussishkin

To Tel-Aviv

Biblical Zoo

Sarei Yisrael

Ben-Zvi Avenue

Ruppin Road

Monastry of the Cross

Knesseth

Israel Museum

Hapalmach

Harav Herzog

Central Bus Station

into southern Syria to think, to plan and to evaluate his next moves. Also at this time Jesus began to prepare his disciples for what he was sure would follow:

> 27. And Jesus went out, and his disciples, into the towns of Cesarea Philippi: and by the way he asked his disciples, saying unto them, Whom do men say that I am?
>
> 28. And they answered, John the Bapist: but some *say*, Elias; and others, One of the prophets.
>
> 29. And he saith unto them, But whom say ye that I am? And Peter answereth and saith unto him, Thou art the Christ.
>
> 30. And he charged them that they should tell no man of him.

Wending their way through the streets of Jerusalem, nuns, priests and other tourists retrace the route of Christ on Good Friday when forced to carry his Cross to the site of execution.

Israel Government Tourist Office

31. And he began to teach them, that the Son of man must suffer many things, and be rejected of the elders, and *of* the chief priests, and scribes, and be killed, and after three days rise again.

32. And he spake that saying openly. And Peter took him, and began to rebuke him.

33. But when he had turned about, and looked on his disciples, he rebuked Peter, saying, Get thee behind me, Satan: for thou savourest not the things that be of God, but the things that be of men.

Mark 8:27-33

Shortly thereafter, Jesus and his disciples headed back to Jerusalem for the Passover.

Holy Week   In Jerusalem the week before Passover were many thousands of Jews; the Roman procurator Pontius Pilate was there and so was Herod Antipas who had come from Galilee for the festivities. On Sunday (Palm Sunday) after a much publicized entry into the city, Jesus went to the Temple. The events of the week are well known and are recounted in Matthew, Mark, Luke and John: the overturning of the tables in the Temple; the attempts by the Pharisees to entrap Jesus in his own words; his loss of public support through his refusal to absolve people of their tax obligations (Render unto the Lord . . . render unto Caesar . . .); the Last Supper and his prediction of betrayal; the scene in Gethsemane; the condemnation to death for no religious crime but for the political one of blasphemy, stemming from his threat to destroy the Temple; the attempt by both Pilate and Herod to avoid the situation; Pilate's attempt at justice by releasing a prisoner (as was the custom at Passover); the mob's demand for the Zealot guerilla Barabbas; and, the final tragic scene of Jesus under a bloody crown of thorns struggling with his own Cross. All of these are part of the Judaeo-Christian heritage.

An Attempt to Save Jesus?

Who was responsible for Jesus' death? Although the Gospels tend to blame the Jews of Jerusalem, Christian Biblical scholars generally agree that the Evangelists underplayed Roman responsibility. Now, Israel Supreme Court Justice Haim Cohn, an expert in the history of Jewish legal traditions, argues that not only did the Jews have no part in the trial of Christ, but also that the Sanhedrin, Judaism's high court, actually tried to save him from death.

Judge Cohn's thesis, which has intrigued Christian Scriptural experts in Jerusalem, is contained in an article in the current issue of the *Israel Law Review*. Analyzing the Gospel accounts of the Passion in the light of known facts about legal customs and traditions of Jesus' time, Cohn insists that Jesus was tried and condemned for the political crime of insurrection — a charge that could be handled only by the Roman Procurator and not by a Jewish court. The Justice supports this suggestion by reference to the Gospel texts: when Jesus was asked by Pilate if he was King of the Jews, he answered "You have said so" — in effect says Cohn, a *nolo contendere* admission of guilt.

Recouping Prestige. On Legal grounds, Cohn insists that there is neither reason nor precedent behind the Gospel statements that the Sanhedrin examined Jesus on the night before his Crucifixion, condemned him, and turned him over to the Romans for a speedy trial and death. For one thing, it is most unlikely that the Sanhedrin would have undertaken any kind of fact-finding investigation on behalf of the hated bloody-handed Pontius Pilate. Just as improbable would have been a trial after sundown — especially on the eve of Passover, when most members of the Sanhedrin would have been busy with ritual preparations for the feast. Still, if they had met, under Jewish law any condemnation would have required the sworn testimony of at least two trustworthy witnesses. Even according to the Gospels, none could be found.

Why, then, did the Jewish authorities summon Jesus? Their motive, Cohn believes, may well have been a desire to recoup their waning popular prestige by saving a prophetic teacher beloved by the masses of Jerusalem. In Cohn's reconstruction of the events, the Sanhedrin first examined witnesses not to condemn Christ but to find men who would convincingly testify in his favor before the Romans. When it could find none, the high court attempted to persuade Jesus to plead not guilty before the Romans; he refused. The buffeting that *Matthew* says Jesus received from Sanhedrin members was thus not punishment for blasphemy but simply the product of bitter frustration. "Jesus had refused to cooperate and to bow to their authority," says Cohn, "and there was nothing that could be done to prevent the trial from taking its course."[1]

Death and Burial   At about 3:00 P.M. on that first Good Friday, after six agonizing hours on the Cross Jesus cried, "My God, my God, why hast thou forsaken me?" and died. Despite Pilate's surprise at death coming so quickly, especially since his legs had not been broken, the order was given to have Jesus taken down, and he was then buried in a tomb offered by a man named Joseph of Arimathaea. Here, then, as in so many cases before, it seemed that the death of the leader would bring the death of his teachings. To be sure, even the most devout of his followers were deeply demoralized on the Friday and Saturday — their beliefs had been shattered. Jesus was only human after all; perhaps their faith had been misplaced; perhaps they had been deceived. It seemed to be over.

E. The Importance of the Belief in Resurrection

But it wasn't over! The earliest written account of the Resurrection was in A.D. 52 when Paul wrote to the Corinthian Church [I Cor. 15:1-8, 42-44, 50]; this was about twenty years after the event, and in this example Paul spoke of a spiritual rather than a physical Resurrection: "It is a physical body that is sown, it is a spiritual body that is raised." This is not what Luke or John say,

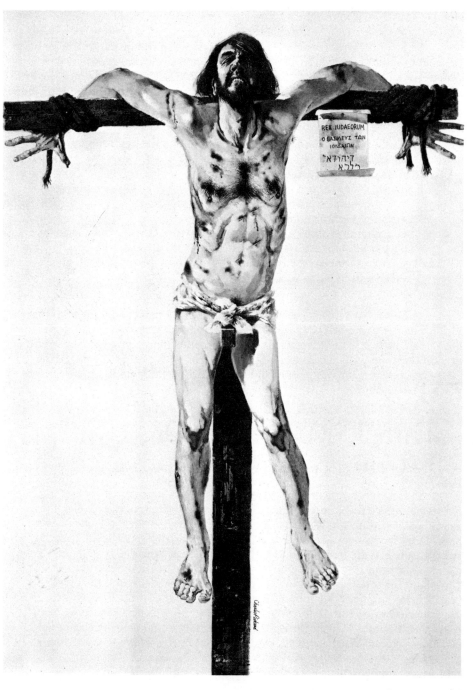

REX IUDAEORUM
Ο ΒΑΣΙΛΕΥΣ ΤΩΝ
ΙΟΥΔΑΙΩΝ
דיהודיא
מלכא

Miller Services Ltd.

This drawing reconstructs what the execution of Jesus may well have looked like. As a check the artist actually manoeuvered himself into this position and reported that the pain lasted for days afterward. Notice the inscription in Latin, Greek and Hebrew.

and certainly not what all Christian churches teach today. Again the important thing is not whether one believes the story or any part of it; the important thing is that the disciples at the time did.

The idea was irresistible! While alive Jesus symbolized total goodness; the belief in the Resurrection symbolized total power of total goodness over death. To the disciples, it was conclusive proof that nothing could block God's will — not even death. With this renewed faith came further confirmation when the Holy Spirit apparently came to them at Pentecost (the Jewish holiday *Shebuot* coming fifty days after Passover):

> 1. And when the day of Pentecost was fully come, they were all with one accord in one place.
> 2. And suddenly there came a sound from heaven, as of a rushing mighty wind, and it filled all the house where they were sitting.
> 3. And there appeared unto them cloven tongues, like as of fire, and it sat upon each of them.
> 4. And they were all filled with the Holy Ghost, and began to speak with other tongues, as the Spirit gave them utterance.
> 5. And there were dwelling at Jerusalem Jews, devout men, out of every nation under heaven.
>
> Acts 2:1-5

Fully re-vitalized and absolutely sure that Christ had risen and then visited them, the disciples exploded into the world to spread the good news, the gospel: all must prepare themselves for the second coming when the Lord will reward the good with everlasting life and the evil with everlasting perdition. "Repent, change your ways, you can be saved!" The religion was to sweep the world like wildfire.

4. Early Development Of The Church (to A.D. 500)

The teachings of the Apostles and other followers were tolerated in Jerusalem, for almost unanimously these people kept the provisions of the Jewish law and considered themselves to be good Jews; furthermore it was believed that they would soon lose their zeal since they had lost their leader. This group later became known as the *Ebionites* or Nazarenes. However another group of Christians, or followers of Christ, had some different ideas, and they were the ones who triumphed. The followers of Peter believed that the Holy Spirit came to all men, not just the circumcised and they were not as firm regarding Jewish dietary restrictions. They believed baptism to have equal value with circumcision as a sign of faith and membership in the church. This group was fiercely persecuted throughout the empire for a time, and none was a more devoted persecutor than Saul (later Paul) of Tarsus.

A. Paul's Role

The son of a Pharisee, Saul was present and probably participated in the death by stoning of Stephen, the first Christian martyr who was put to death for his disrespect for the Jewish Law. While travelling to Damascus in A.D.31 to search for and arrest more Christians, Saul, an educated product of Greek-Hebrew culture and a Roman citizen, underwent a deeply spiritual experience which transformed him from a hunter into a member of the hunted sect. While on the road and tired from the long, hot journey which must have taken its toll on the frail and possibly epileptic body, he believed he heard Jesus say, "Saul, Saul, why do you persecute me?" After recovering from the experience, he began to work for Jesus — his contribution was so great that he justifiably has been called the "second founder of Christianity". This story is recounted in Acts 9: 2-19.

Paul, as he then became known, taught the gospel at Antioch, Damascus and the surrounding area as well as in distant lands covered during his famous and hazardous travels. Far from being journeys of ease these trips involved constant danger, as he explained in his second letter to the church at Corinth:

> 24. Of the Jews five times received I forty *stripes* save one.
> 25. Thrice was I beaten with rods, once was I stoned, thrice I suffered shipwreck, a night and a day I have been in the deep;
> 26. *In* journeyings often, *in* perils of waters, *in* perils of robbers, *in* perils by *mine own* countrymen, *in* perils by the heathen, *in* perils in the city, *in* perils in the wilderness, *in* perils in the sea, *in* perils among false brethren;
> 27. In weariness and painfulness, in watchings often, in hunger and thirst, in fastings often, in cold and nakedness.
>
> II Corinthians 11: 24-27

Paul's importance can scarcely be over-emphasized. Primarily he made Christianty acceptable to the Gentile, that is, the non-Jewish, world. He also was instrumental in establishing and organizing many churches and then, in his letters to them, was a major force in establishing the theology which would guide them. By defending the divinity of Jesus, (that is that Jesus was the Son of God), and the fact that his righteousness was more important than the righteousness of the Law — in fact that Jesus was the fulfillment of the Law — he cast aside the restrictiveness of the Law to (as he saw it) free the spirit. No longer was there a need for circumcision, dietary restrictions and distinctions between clean and unclean. This was the crucial break with Judaism, one that made the new faith available to millions.

Sovereignty of Jesus   The sovereignty of Jesus was stressed by Paul as being more important than his Messiahship. This was an original contribution of Paul, one taken for granted today: Christ was a divine Being who possessed the nature of God but who humiliated himself by dying on the Cross for our sins, to rise again in victory over death [Colossians 1: 19-20]. This was what captivated the Gentiles, this idea of redemption — the idea that Jesus had made it possible for man to be saved by dying for his sins. Paul offered immortality through a union with Christ; he provided the means of salvation from guilt and sin *in this life*. It was irresistible: simply too good to turn down.

Paul's Death   Later Paul was arrested, probably for flouting the emperor's laws and claiming that there was a rival king — Jesus [Acts 17:7]. As a Roman citizen he was sent to Rome for trial where he was held and later, it is believed, executed as a troublemaker. He was forgotten for about 100 years after his death. But

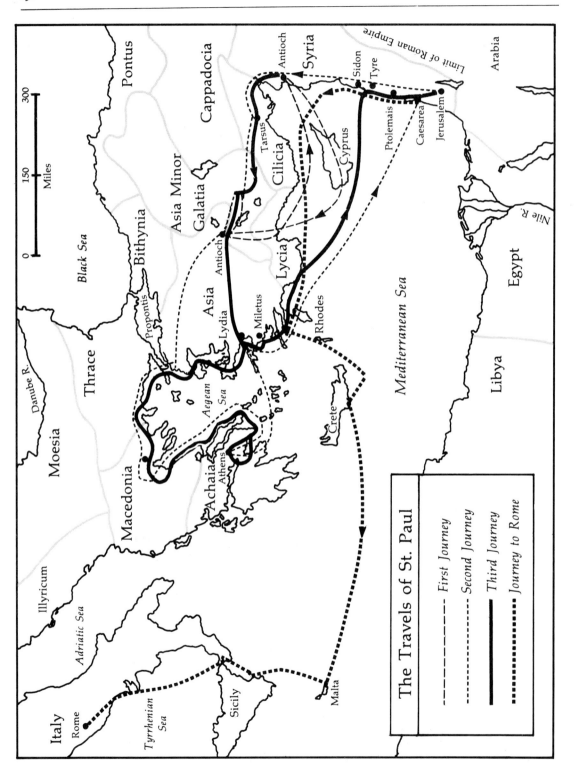

The Travels of St. Paul

- – – – – First Journey
- .... Second Journey
- ———— Third Journey
- ▪▪▪▪▪ Journey to Rome

when the first generation of Christians passed away, the oral traditions of the Apostles began to fade, and a hundred heresies confused the situation, the letters (epistles) of Paul provided the framework for a stabilizing system of belief that united the scattered congregations in the soon-to-be powerful Christian church.

B. Beginning of Organization and Doctrine

The years from Jesus' death to approximately A.D. 200 present no clear view of developments; indeed it has been said that to try to understand the history of Christianity during this period is like plunging into a tunnel — one emerges at the end, but did not see much along the way. Needless to say, with the vaguenesses spoken by Jesus (what, for example, was the nature of the Kingdom of Heaven?), there were many interpretations, and often people of the same belief would form small groups; the number of such groups is unknown, but must have been very large. One of the major developments of the period was the organization of the authority of the church, in an attempt to defend itself against the many heresies, as well as the formation of a scriptural canon and doctrine — in other words, the formation of the "true faith".

A major factor in establishing this authority was the centralized organization of the church. The development of a hierarchy was a slow matter and, in growing, it followed the lines of the Roman imperial administration. In each Roman municipality (from the second century on) the bishop was regarded as being the supreme clerical authority. As the church grew in size and power, lower orders of clergy came into existence: priests administered sacraments and cared for the spiritual welfare of their followers, and deacons were in charge of financial affairs. All were under the authority of the bishop.

In order to establish uniformity of belief and practice and to enforce discipline over isolated communities, a higher authority was needed. By the fourth century A.D. all the bishops of a given province of the empire were meeting with some regularity and the bishop of the provincial capital who presided at these councils was recognized as being the supreme bishop in the province with the title of *metropolitan* or archbishop. In the fifth century the bishop of Rome was elevated to a position of supremacy in the Western church and the title "pope" came to be applied to him.

Thenceforth the Church of Rome began to consolidate its pre-eminent position. Having taken a leading role in framing the Apostles' Creed and in formulating the New Testament, it was looked up to by others. In A.D. 450 the bishop of Rome stated that since St. Peter was first among the disciples, so should his church be first among churches. Also there was a verse in Matthew which said:

> 18. And I say also unto thee, That thou art Peter, and upon this rock
> I will build my church; and the gates of hell shall not prevail against it.
>   Matthew 16:18

This verse gave rise to the Petrine Theory that the successors of Peter were first among bishops. These things combined then to establish the bishop of Rome as the supreme church ruler — a position generally recognized by the fifth century under Leo the Great (440 to 461), the first "pope".

Together with this administrative organization went a development of doctrine and belief, and before this could take place there had to be writings upon which to base the faith. This was made more urgent by the dual development of first generation Christians dying and the failure of Jesus to make his second appearance. Some written records of the master's life and teachings were essential. Certainly the Epistles of Paul were useful, as were the Gospels of Matthew, Mark, Luke and John. As can be seen by closer study, these four men differed in their opinions of certain things; but it must not be forgotten that they were all written at least a generation after Jesus' death. Despite the weaknesses of the accounts, despite the variations and omissions, they still do provide the framework of Christian holy literature.

With these writings to go by (the New Testament was largely decided upon by A.D. 180), the church could then decide whether various beliefs were heretical, for the Apostles were considered by the church to have had perfect knowledge of the gospels. Therefore, those ideas not in agreement with the gospels or the epistles were obviously incorrect and therefore unacceptable and heretical. The Apostles' Creed came to be used to sum up this belief and to destroy some early heretical sects including the Gnostics and the Marcionites.

For millions on millions of Christians the central convictions of their faith are expressed in the 110 words below. This is the Apostles' Creed, repeated countless thousands of times every day in every part of the world by Christians of many churches. As a formal statement of belief it is used by Roman Catholics, Anglicans, Presbyterians, Lutherans, Methodists and many other Christians with only slight variations in wording (e.g., "Creator" for "Maker," "Spirit" for "Ghost," "living" for "quick"; this version is one widely used by Protestants). Some groups, the largest being Baptists and Congregationalists, accept no binding creed.

The earliest Christian statements of belief began when followers of Jesus had their converts answer questions concerning faith at the time they were baptized. These were not formalized at once; this creed, which legend later attributed to the Apostles, developed slowly, between the second and eighth centuries. It finally became the creed in many churches. For the individual Christian, who has concern for salvation, saying the creed is now — as it always has been — a personal avowal in historic words of the faith that man is saved through God's grace and Christ's life and death.

The Apostles' Creed

I believe in God the Father Almighty maker of heaven and earth: And in Jesus Christ His only Son our Lord: Who was conceived by the Holy Ghost, born of the Virgin Mary: suffered under Pontius Pilate, was crucified, dead, and buried: He descended into Hell; the third day He rose again from the dead: He ascended into heaven, and sitteth on the right hand of God the Father Almighty: from thence He shall come to judge the quick and the dead.

I believe in the Holy Ghost: the holy Catholic Church: the communion of saints: the forgiveness of sins: the resurrection of the body: and the life everlasting.

Amen.

C. Arian Heresy and Nicene Creed

In the third century A.D. came the best example of the increasing power of the church in its early history, and the most famous heresy. Arius, a priest of Alexandria, believed and stated that God and Jesus were of different substance — Jesus was created and therefore not eternal. Another priest Athanasius declared they were one substance. The church was split. A church council was therefore called at Nicaea in A.D. 325 and after much wrangling the Nicene Creed was issued, a creed still in use today. Thus one major heresy was stopped, but it was a constant battle for more were always springing up.

> *Nicene Creed*
> We believe in one God, Father Almighty, maker of all things, visible and invisible. And in one Lord Jesus Christ, the Son of God, begotten of [literally, "out of"] the Father, as His only Son, that is, from the substance of the Father, God from God, light from light, true God from true God, *begotten, not made, of the same substance [homo-ousios] with the Father*, through whom all things in heaven and earth were made; who for us men and our salvation came down and was made flesh, became man, suffered, and rose on the third day, ascended to heaven, and is coming to judge the living and the dead. And (we believe) in the Holy Spirit.

While these doctrines were being hammered out, politics too was influencing the church's development. As early as A.D. 64 persecutions were known. Because of the mysterious nature, signs and behaviour of these Christians, the Roman authorities were worried. Most Christians disassociated themselves from worldly interests including the army and imperial administration. Rumours spread about their cannibalism (". . . this is my body . . . this is my blood . . ."); they often refused to offer incense to the emperor and to take an oath to his "divine spirit". Generally, to the Roman mind, they were troublemakers; and there is really little reason for surprise at their being persecuted.

Importance of Constantine However, despite the periodic repressions, their numbers grew. Marcus Aurelius (Caracalla), Septimus Severus, Maximus and Diocletian all persecuted them; in A.D. 250 a law stated that all citizens must have a certificate declaring that they had sacrificed to the emperor. Without such a certificate, the penalty was death. Many were tortured, many gave in and many died as martyrs. But the movement grew. Then came Constantine who allegedly saw a cross in a dream the night before a battle, and won the battle the next day. He then made Christianity a religion equal in stature to other religions (A.D 313). Further, he made the Christian Sabbath a legal holiday and built numerous churches for the faith. Finally in A.D. 383 Christianity was made the official religion of the empire: it had arrived. Now all energies could be devoted to acquiring converts; no more energy had to be expended in defence as had always been the case before.

D. St. Augustine

Lastly, in this section, mention must be made of the contribution of St. Augustine (A.D. 354 to 430). He has been called by some "the greatest personality of the ancient Catholic Church". After a rather wild early life he was converted by St. Ambrose while in Rome and then returned home to Hippo in North Africa to found a monastery. As bishop at Hippo, he lived there the rest of his life and wrote voluminously.

He contributed greatly to the theology of the early church. He viewed Adam as a symbol of man's depravity, and saw all men as being in a state of Original Sin. From this sin, man cannot escape alone — he needs God's help. The church, according to Augustine, was divinely appointed to perform the sacraments which were instituted by God and which are the means of achieving grace. These ideas, of course, are still basic to the thought of many Christians today.

Augustine's greatest masterpiece, though, was an epic called *The City of God*, written while Rome was being sacked by invaders. He saw all human history as a struggle between the earthly city (Rome being equivalent to evil) and the heavenly, spiritual City of God (goodness). The City of God, he said, would win in the end, and those having chosen salvation in it would be saved by divine grace. In addition to this book, he wrote many others in which he discussed nearly all important religious problems concerning man. While not all of his writings influenced the church, many did and also helped to win intellectuals to the faith.

5. The Church In The Middle Ages (A.D. 500 to 1500)

With the final collapse of Rome, western Europe was split into a staggeringly minute patchwork-type of organization — some autonomous states were smaller than Toronto's Exhibition Park. No one authority was strong enough to impose authority over the whole fabric, but warfare was seemingly continual in the efforts of some to do so. Into this situation the church was able to bring some semblance of order. Being international, in that much of Europe and England was converted (or soon would be), the church did possess some of the essentials of centralized power. This being the case, it is not surprising that the institution played much more than a strictly religious role during the period. As all scholars agree, to separate the church from politics, economics, social welfare, art and architecture is simply impossible. It is not however within our scope to attempt a history of the church in the Middle Ages; others have done that very well. Our concern is to examine the religious development of the church, only relating politics, etc., where the two are so closely bound as to be, in effect, one.

A. Establishment of Authority

It seems fair to say that the period under discussion was not generally significant from the point of view of extremely important theological developments; the real importance of the time is that it provided the church the opportunity to solidify and deeply root its already well-established position. The fact that the church could harness the energy and co-operation of so many political leaders and countries for its own ends is testimony to its strength.

An example of this capacity was the Crusades (1095 to 1204) which were organized by popes for the alleged purpose of ridding the Holy Land of the menace of Islam, and many people became involved out of deeply religious motives. Others of course were more mercenary, but the organization and the moving spirit of the Crusades was initiated by the church. Witness what Will Durant refers to as the "most influential speech of mediaeval history", one delivered by Pope Urban II in November of 1095 to gain support for the First Crusade:

> O race of Franks! race beloved and chosen by God! . . . From the confines of Jerusalem and from Constantinople a grievous report has gone forth that an accursed race, wholly alienated from God, has violently invaded the lands of these Christians, and has depopulated them by pillage and fire. They have led away a part of the captives into their own country, and a part they have killed by cruel tortures. They destroy the altars, after having defiled them with their uncleanliness. The kingdom of the Greeks is now dismembered by them, and has been deprived of territory so vast in extent that it could not be traversed in two months' time.
>
> On whom, then, rests the labor of avenging these wrongs, and of recovering this territory, if not upon you — you upon whom, above all others, God has conferred remarkable glory in arms, great bravery, and strength to humble the heads of those who resist you? Let the deeds of your ancestors encourage you — the glory and grandeur of Charlemagne and your other monarches. Let the Holy Sepulcher of Our Lord Saviour, now held by unclean nations, arouse you, and the holy places that are now stained with pollution. . . . Let none of your possessions keep you back, nor anxiety for your family affairs. For this land which you now inhabit, shut in on all sides by the sea and the mountain peaks, is too narrow for your large population; it scarcely furnishes food enough for its cultivators. Hence it is that you murder and devour one another, that you wage wars, and that many among you perish in civil strife.
>
> Let hatred, therefore, depart among you, let your quarrels end. Enter upon the road to the Holy Sepulcher; wrest that land from a wicked race, and subject it to yourselves. Jerusalem is a land fruitful above all others, a paradise of delights. That royal city, situated at the center of the earth, implores you to come to her aid. Undertake this journey eagerly for the remission of your sins, and be assured of the reward of imperishable glory in the Kingdom of Heaven.[2]

B. Conflict: Pope vs. Emperor

Other more worldly activities occupied the minds of mediaeval popes too. A major trial of strength was brewing between popes and kings of fledgling nation states. In the early 1070's Pope Gregory VII informed Henry IV, the Holy Roman Emperor of the Germanic states that the power to appoint bishops was

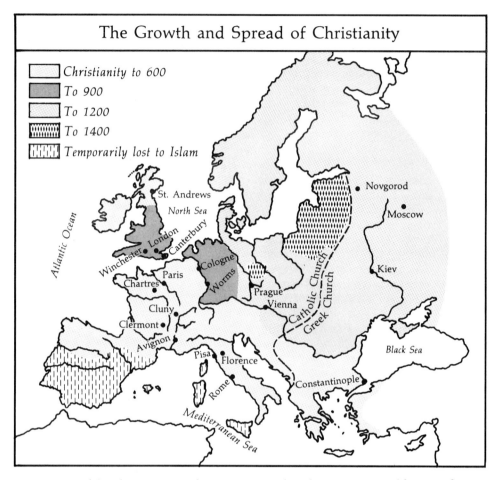

The Growth and Spread of Christianity

Christianity to 600
To 900
To 1200
To 1400
Temporarily lost to Islam

one reserved for the pope, not the emperor, and at the same time told married German bishops to give up their wives. Henry rejected the pope's authority; in retaliation, Pope Gregory excommunicated Henry, thus releasing all of his subjects from their feudal oaths of loyalty to him. Henry's position of course was based on the fact that people did owe feudal obligations to him — without it he was not an emperor. The culmination was that in 1077 Henry IV went to Canossa in the Alps in the winter, barefoot and penitent, to apologize to the pope; having done so, it was clear that religious authority at the time excelled political authority.

But the mediaeval papacy reached its height of prestige, leadership and power under Pope Innocent III (1198 to 1216). In addition to his organization of the Fourth Crusade, he claimed further power over political leaders. After victory in war his power seemed complete; but it was unwritten, unofficial power. Pope Innocent decided to legalize and formalize the situation. He said:

> As God, the creator of the universe, set two lights in the firmament of heaven, the greater light to rule the day and lesser light to rule the night, so He set two great dignities in the firmament of the universal

Conflict Between Church and Empire

I. *Holy Roman Empire:*
   Developed from German part of Charlemagne's empire
   — a fanciful imitation of the ancient Roman Empire
   — conflict developed between emperors and popes
      (*temporal* vs. *spiritual* authority)

II. *Pope Gregory VII and Emperor Henry IV:*
   — Pope claimed both spiritual and temporal authority (superior to emperor)

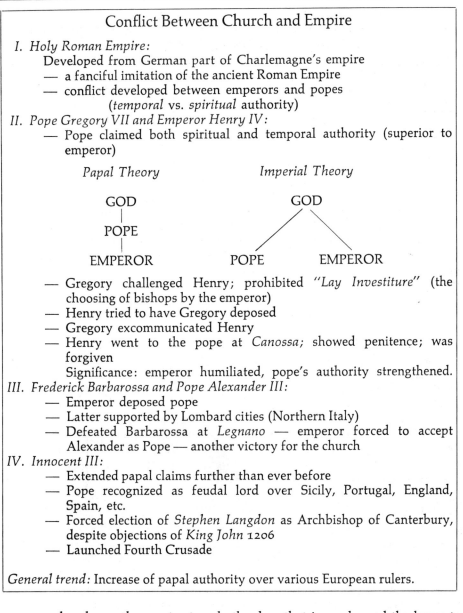

Papal Theory   *Imperial Theory*

GOD   GOD
| / \
POPE   POPE   EMPEROR
|
EMPEROR

   — Gregory challenged Henry; prohibited *"Lay Investiture"* (the choosing of bishops by the emperor)
   — Henry tried to have Gregory deposed
   — Gregory excommunicated Henry
   — Henry went to the pope at *Canossa;* showed penitence; was forgiven
      Significance: emperor humiliated, pope's authority strengthened.

III. *Frederick Barbarossa and Pope Alexander III:*
   — Emperor deposed pope
   — Latter supported by Lombard cities (Northern Italy)
   — Defeated Barbarossa at *Legnano* — emperor forced to accept Alexander as Pope — another victory for the church

IV. *Innocent III:*
   — Extended papal claims further than ever before
   — Pope recognized as feudal lord over Sicily, Portugal, England, Spain, etc.
   — Forced election of *Stephen Langdon* as Archbishop of Canterbury, despite objections of *King John* 1206
   — Launched Fourth Crusade

General trend: Increase of papal authority over various European rulers.

church . . . the greater to rule the day, that is, souls, and the lesser to rule the night, that is bodies. These dignities are the papal power and the royal power. And just as the moon gets her light from the sun, and is inferior to the sun in quality, quantity, position, and effect, so the royal power gets the splendour of its dignity for the papal authority.

   He then proceeded to prove his point, by intervening in the internal affairs of most principalities and states of Europe.
   In 1206 he conflicted with King John of England over the election of

the Archbishop of Canterbury. Pope Innocent arranged that Stephen Langdon be elected; John refused to accept him. Pope Innocent then slapped John with an excommunication. Finally under this and other threats, John capitulated and recognized Pope Innocent as his feudal overlord and England as a papal fief. It was Pope Innocent's greatest victory and served to show the close connection between religion and politics *and* the fact that the popes were only too willing to become involved in some rather worldly pursuits. As the final feather in his cap, Pope Innocent is credited with the establishment of a very organized, centralized and strong church administration — the type of thing needed for best results in any organization.

C. Monasticism: Dominicans and Franciscans

The church's establishment of strong roots in the life of the times was not limited to political victories over kings. Others saw that the close connection of religion and politics had led to some abuses of power, and attempted to bring reform from within. They felt that to purify the church and themselves, they would have to withdraw from this worldly society. They were *in* this world but not *of* it. Though not exclusively so, the most notable expression of this trend was that practised by the Dominicans and Franciscans.

The Dominicans (the black friars) went as preachers throughout the area of western Europe in imitation of the Apostle Paul. Drawn particularly to university towns, they attempted, through their devotion to learning, to win converts among the educated and therefore higher classes. Organized in a centralized way, the master general was the head. Beneath him were provincial priors and beneath them were priors or prioresses of individual monasteries or nunneries.

The Franciscans (grey friars) were organized by St. Francis of Assisi and were more successful in winning converts among the poor. "Married to Lady Poverty", the grey friars possessed no property, ate plain food, worked or begged for their meals and worked among the same types of social outcast as did Jesus. They became organized along Dominican lines in their later history.

St. Francis   St. Francis (1181 to 1226) had been content to base his Rule on a few simple precepts from the gospels. After his death, however, more detailed regulations, still based on St. Francis' essential beliefs, were drawn up. This Franciscan Rule, a few extracts from which follow, was approved by Pope Honorius III in 1223.

> In the Lord's name thus begins the way of life of the brothers minor. The rule and life of the brothers minor is this, to observe the holy Gospel of our Lord Jesus Christ, living in obedience, without property, and in chastity....
>
>   ... If any wish to take up this life and they come to our brothers, the latter shall send them to their provincial ministers. ... And the ministers shall carefully examine them concerning the Catholic faith and the sacraments of the Church. ... the ministers shall bid them, in the words of the holy Gospel, to go and sell all their goods and carefully distribute all to the poor. ... And when the year of probation is over, they shall be received into obedience, promising ever to observe

this life and rule. . . . And those who have promised obedience shall have one gown with a hood and, if they wish, one without a hood. And those who really need them can wear shoes. And all the brothers shall wear poor clothing, which they may repair with sack cloth and other scraps, with God's blessing. And warn and exhort them not to despise or judge men whom they see clothed in soft and coloured raiment or enjoying rich food and drink; but each shall rather judge and despise himself.

I strictly command all the brothers never to receive coin or money either directly or through an intermediary. The ministers and guardians shall make provision, through spiritual friends, for the needs of the infirm and for other brothers who need clothing, according to the locality, season or cold climate. . . .

The brothers shall possess nothing, neither a house, nor a place, nor anything. But, as pilgrims and strangers in this world, serving God in poverty and humility, they shall confidently seek alms, and not be ashamed, for the Lord made Himself poor in this world for us. . . .

. . . And [the brothers] shall not attempt to teach the illiterate, but shall strive for that which they should desire above all things, to have the spirit of the Lord and its holy working, ever to pray to Him with a pure heart, to have humility and patience in persecution and infirmity, and to love those who persecute and censure and revile us, for the Lord says "Love your enemies. . . ."

These groups and others like them were evidence of the existence of the church and proof of the concern of the church for all people. Since the church helped people in all aspects of their lives, it is clear why it became so important, necessary and powerful in the Middle Ages.

St. Thomas Aquinas   In any discussion of the Mediaeval church, mention must be made of the contribution of St. Thomas Aquinas. From about A.D. 800 education became increasingly important in cathedrals and monasteries. This development was based primarily, though not solely, on Augustine's precept that "Faith seeks the support of the intelligence." Thomas Aquinas contributed greatly to the meshing of the two. Two of his major works are still standard theological guides in Roman Catholicism — his *Summa Contra Gentiles* and, more famous, his *Summa Theologica*. He believed that to reconcile reason with revelation and philosophy with theology was essential. He did not believe they were separate and unrelated. Basically his argument was that they were simply two different levels of the same thing, but that they were complementary. Both levels were essential to a "complete" faith. And he applied the same two-level theory to the sacraments: the material element (that is, wine and bread) and the spiritual element (the blood and body of Christ) together formed an organic whole and a means of grace.

Aquinas' significance then is that in addition to helping formulate Roman Catholic theology, he also contributed significantly to the fact that many intellectuals became church members, attracted by his intellectual and learned writings.

D. Decline of the Papacy

After the pontificate of Innocent III the power of the church gradually declined
until the time of the Protestant Reformation. A number of reasons help account
for the trend. A major one was that nation states were beginning to re-emerge
with considerable strength; later popes were not so adept as was Innocent III
in recruiting military support. Another was the wide-spread worldliness and
corruption of church officials from nuns and priests to cardinals and popes —
people saw, and could not respect, an institution which allowed this to happen.
Lastly, stories of the Crusades, Marco Polo, Columbus, Magellan, the growth of
trade and cities, increasing education — all combined to cause a serious
questioning of the old ways. Thus practices as diverse as the sale of indulgences,
papal taxation for the performance of marriage and baptism ceremonies, and the
prohibition of individual interpretation of the Bible all came to be questioned
strongly, particularly in northern Europe. Men like John Wycliffe, John Hus,
Erasmus of Rotterdam and Martin Luther were heard. All were members of
the church, all anxious to bring reform from within. And the church itself
recognized certain of the evils and took steps to deal with some of them — such
was the purpose of the Councils of Constance and Basel in the first half of the
fifteenth century. As we shall see though, reform came in too small doses and
too late.

E. The Split between East and West

Even before the well-known split in Western Christianity took place, a major
division had already been made in Christianity. A long-smouldering dispute
between Eastern and Western wings of the church, dating back to A.D. 726
finally was made absolute in A.D. 1054. Though numerous issues were at stake,
one of the major ones was the dispute over whether or not the pope's claims
to spiritual authority over the whole church were valid. The Christian church
in the East refused to accept this doctrine and the unity of Christianity was
ruptured. Tensions were made worse when Crusaders sacked and pillaged
Constantinople, the centre of the Eastern church, in A.D. 1204.

   Today the Eastern Orthodox Church has about 200 million adherents
and includes the Churches of Albania, Bulgaria, Georgia, Greece, Poland,
Romania, Russia, Serbia and Sinai, although the first allegiance to the faithful
of these national churches is the Eastern Orthodox Church. With a few
significant exceptions the Eastern Orthodox Church is very close to the Roman
Catholic Church in its beliefs. However, substantial differences are evident in
ceremonies and other rituals.

Key Differences The Eastern Churches tend to be somewhat more mystical
than do their Roman Catholic counterparts — their emphasis is the life-giving
incarnation of God in Christ as conveyed by the seven sacraments. But whereas
the Roman Catholic Church feels that the seven sacraments fulfil the function, to
Easterners a large role is attributed to icons; these too convey divine grace.
Further key differences are present within the sacraments. The Eastern church
conducts baptism in infancy by triple immersion; in the West it is performed
in infancy usually by sprinkling oil. Confession in the East is to be done only
after reconciliation has been achieved with those wronged; in the West, this

Greek Orthodox priest (one of the caretakers at the Church of the Nativity, Bethlehem) lighting candles by the Grotto (right) where, according to tradition, Jesus was born.

proviso is not compulsory. Eastern marriage ceremonies are conducted with the bride and groom both wearing crowns of flowers; such is not the case in the West. In the Eastern church extreme unction (last rites) may be given in serious illness to encourage recovery *and* (as in the West) if death is near. In the East, lower-rank clergymen may marry if they are content to remain in the lower echelons; such is not the case in the West.

On the question of authority, the Eastern church is not as dogmatic as the Roman Catholic Church sometimes tends to be. For example, the Eastern still repudiates the pope's claim to complete supremacy; they believe that the Apostles were equal and that Peter was not the most important — thus all major bishops are equal in power to the bishop of Rome, the pope. Hence the pope is not infallible with regard to statements on faith and morals (as is claimed by the Roman Catholic Church), and he is not superior to church councils. Along the same line the Eastern church allows much more personal, individual interpretation of what is acceptable belief than does the Roman Catholic Church. While Roman Catholic dogma comes from the pope, the Eastern church believes that truth comes from "the conscience of the church", that is the consensus of Christians in general as expressed in ecumenical councils.

Despite this seemingly large number of divisive beliefs, certain developments can be cited to suggest a thawing in the rather icy relations between the two. In 1964, for example, the Senior Prelate of the Eastern Orthodox Churches, Patriarch Athenagoras I of Constantinople, met with Pope Paul in Jerusalem — the first time such a meeting had been held since the split in 1054. The next year (1965), the mutual excommunications decreed each upon the other in 1054 were annulled simultaneously in Rome and Constantinople. Perhaps there is hope for closer ties in the future.

6. The Reformation

Many Protestants refer to the movement begun by Martin Luther in 1520 as the "Protestant Reformation", the implication being that things were improved — and this is accurate to an extent. Roman Catholics have been heard to refer to it as the "Protestant Revolution" with connotations of evil or futility. Whatever name one applies to the event, it certainly was of utmost importance. By Luther's actions Western Christianity was severed in two and, in turn, splinter groups broke from and developed independently of Luther. From that time until this the trend has been, for the most part, a further splintering and cracking of a once united Christian church. Today, however, there is evidence of a reverse trend, but more will be said of that later.

Reasons   Why did Luther break with the Christian church? The reasons are many, and they are by no means all religious in nature. At this time, about 1510 to 1520, religion was inextricably bound with politics, economics, sociology, social work, education and other things so that it is simply impossible to separate them. However, we do know that there were some religious factors present — and these were abuses well known to all living at the time. Many of the clergy were unable to read the Latin of the Mass they celebrated and some openly ignored the rule of celibacy. Some of the higher church officials lived in luxury, thus openly ignoring their vow of poverty and their alleged concern for spiritual above material things.

The sale of religious positions was a well-known fact. High church posts were known to be sold on occasion to the highest bidder who would then charge high rates for his services in order to turn a profit.

Dispensations, which were exemptions from a vow or church law previously accepted, were for sale. So were indulgences, which were remissions of all or part of the worldly punishment for one's sins. According to the theory of the "Treasure of Merit", Jesus and the saints, having on earth more goodness than was necessary, accumulated in Heaven an excess amount on which a pope could draw for the benefit of common men. Originally indulgences were given (not sold) for works of charity, a pilgrimage, or Crusade and were dependent on a person being truly sorry and repentent for his sins. Later, however, the sale of indulgences was turned over to travelling salesmen called "pardoners" who received a salesman's commission on all the forgiveness sold. Often these pardoners had false relics for sale, — a relic being an object supposed to have been used by Jesus, Mary or the saints, in some cases bones of their bodies — which was believed to have miraculous healing power. Of course once all the real relics were sold, the sale should have ceased, but did not. Poor ignorant people, deeply devoted to their faith, were easy prey for the hucksters. The outstanding Catholic churchman Erasmus noted at the time that there were enough chunks of the alleged true Cross to build a battleship. Equally important was the problem of church doctrine in general. The argument raged between acceptance of the theories of St. Augustine (see pp. 239-40), or those of St. Thomas Aquinas (the Thomist doctrine) (See p. 245).

Luther, an austere Augustinian monk was not the first to see the abuses. Much earlier John Wycliffe in England attacked abuses and doctrine. In Czechoslovakia, John Hus followed Wycliffe's theories and was burned at the stake for his troubles (1415). In Luther's time, Erasmus of Rotterdam was critical of aspects of church doctrine and worked hard for reform. And Luther himself originally desired to see reform from within the church.

Originally looking only for an opportunity for debate, Luther posted the "Ninety-Five Theses" on the door of the university church at Wittenburg, Germany on October 31, 1517. Several of these were:

> 5. The Pope has neither the will nor the power to remit any penalties except those which he has imposed by his own authority, or by that of the canons.

> 6. The Pope has no power to remit any guilt, except by declaring and warranting it to have been remitted by God; or at most by remitting cases reserved for himself; in which cases, if his power were despised, guilt would certainly remain.

> 21. Thus those preachers of indulgences are in error who say that by the indulgences of the Pope a man is freed and saved from all punishment.

> 27. They preach mad, who say that the soul flies out of purgatory as soon as the money thrown into the chest rattles.

> 32. Those who believe that, through letters of pardon, they are made sure of their own salvation, will be eternally damned along with their teachers.

> 36. Every Christian who feels true compunction has of right plenary remission of pain and guilt, even without letters of pardon.

Again politics became involved in religion and vice versa, the final result being that Leo X excommunicated Luther, declared 41 of the 95 theses heretical and condemned him to be tried as a heretic.

> Arise, O Lord, and judge thy cause. A wild boar has invaded thy vineyard. Arise, O Peter, and consider the case of the Holy Roman church, the mother of all churches, consecrated by thy blood. Arise, O Paul, who by thy teaching and death hast and dost illumine the

Church. Arise, all ye saints, and the whole universal Church, whose interpretation of Scripture has been assailed. We can scarcely express our grief over the ancient heresies which have been revived in Germany. . . . Our pastoral office can no longer tolerate the pestiferous virus of the following forty-one errors. . . . We can no longer suffer the serpent to creep through the field of the Lord. The books of Martin Luther which contain these errors are to be examined and burned. . . . Now therefore we give Martin sixty days in which to submit, dating from the time of the publication of this bull in his district. Anyone who presumes to infringe our excommunication and anathema will stand under the wrath of Almighty God and of the apostles Peter and Paul.

Dated on the 15th day of June, 1520.

Protected by a powerful friend, no danger came to his person but he was no longer a member of the accepted church. Through the rest of his life he studied and formulated ideas basic to some Protestant groups today.

A. Luther's Ideas

It would be fair to say that much of Lutheran doctrine was a reaction against the (now) Roman Catholic Church. He had originally attempted to reform from within, but now he was attacking the church by denying the truth or value of many of its doctrines. After much thought and soul-searching Luther was able to formulate his own beliefs. Probably foremost is the belief in "justification by faith alone". While the Roman Catholic Church decreed that to be justified in going to Heaven a man must have faith, do good deeds, partake of the sacraments and generally fulfil a number of church demands, Luther accepted the words of Romans 1:17:

17. For therein is the righteousness of God revealed from faith to faith: as it is written, The just shall live by faith.

Good works will not get one into Heaven; they are nice if done out of willingness, but not as a means of attaining salvation. If one has faith, he will be saved.

Because he decided that the church was far away from its Scriptural basis, and because he saw in Rome many scandalous things, he decided that the "true" church was not any particular ecclesiastical organization but rather comprised those who were faithful and whose head was Christ. Thus each person could read the Bible and would be guided to understanding by the Holy Spirit — a direct contradiction to Catholic dogma where the faithful were not to read and interpret the Bible for themselves. From this same argument came the idea of the "priesthood of all believers". Again there is a great difference between this idea and the stand of the Catholic Church which indicates that only a trained and ordained priest can perform these functions.

He introduced further change. He favoured services being conducted in the vernacular and being made clearer to the faithful; this reform was introduced into Roman Catholic ceremony after Vatican II in 1962. He allowed priests

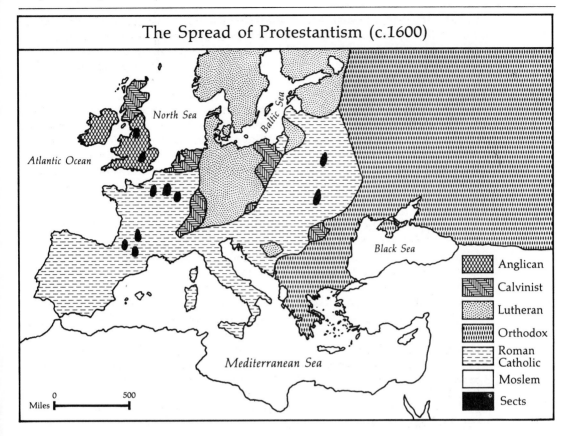

The Spread of Protestantism (c.1600)

North Sea

Baltic Sea

Atlantic Ocean

Black Sea

Mediterranean Sea

▨	Anglican
▦	Calvinist
▒	Lutheran
▥	Orthodox
▤	Roman Catholic
☐	Moslem
■	Sects

Miles   0   500

to marry; he himself married an ex-nun and fathered five children. He rejected five of the seven church sacraments. Only baptism and Holy Communion were kept, and even they were said to have no supernatural effect in bringing divine grace from Heaven. The Bible was the sole and final authority — no pope or church council could dictate doctrine. An individual could read and find for himself.

> I say, then, neither pope, nor bishop, nor any man whatever has the right of making one syllable binding on a Christian man, unless it be done with his own consent. Whatever is done otherwise is done in the spirit of tyranny. . . . I cry aloud on behalf of liberty and conscience, and I proclaim with confidence that no kind of law can with any justice be imposed on Christians, except so far as they themselves will; for we are free from all.

To help with the task he translated first the New Testament and then the entire Bible into German (1534) and really put the word of God into the hands of the common man. Finally he rejected the Catholic doctrine of *trans-substantiation*, that is, the belief that at Communion the bread and wine are changed into the actual body and blood of Christ; in its place he substituted the theory of *consubstantiation*, that is, the belief that the body and blood of Christ are present during the reception of the Eucharist, along with the bread and wine.

But for all his changes, he was not a radical at heart. True, he did reject such religious practices as fasts, pilgrimages, veneration of relics, etc., but on the other hand he preserved many other traditions. He was very fond of the teachings of St. Paul and St. Augustine; the opposite was true of the teachings of Aristotle and St. Thomas Aquinas. He maintained the use of candles, the crucifix, the organ and some elements of the Roman Mass. Socially and politically too his ideas were conservative in nature, though a discussion of these is outside the scope of this work.

Luther's ideas spread quickly in northern Europe and so did the concept of breaking from the establishment. As Luther broke with the Roman Church, so did other groups do the same, so that the reform movement was not a united one for long. In Zurich, Ulrich Zwingli established a church more austere than Luther's. Anabaptists gathered converts with their idea that adult baptism was the only logical one; in Geneva, John Calvin ruled the entire city as a theocracy in very austere style — the goal of Christians he said was to "indulge oneself as little as possible" as well as to show "unflagging effort" to cut "all show of superfluous wealth, not to mention licentiousness".

Henry VIII of England broke with the pope and established the Church of England, the Anglican Church. Divisions and subdivisions took place with bewildering speed giving birth to such diverse groups as the Quakers, the Methodists, the Unitarians, Puritans, Baptists, Congregationalists and many more. Some of these sects will be examined more closely in the next chapter.

B. Counter Reformation

Reverberations of Luther's actions were felt strongly in the Roman Church. Suddenly it was realized how severe the need for reform really was, and with much interest the church set about to right itself — a development sometimes referred to as the Counter-Reformation. Most significant was the Council of Trent (1545 to 1563) which reconfirmed some beliefs (seven sacraments; church alone can interpret Scripture; justification by faith *and* good works) and made numerous reforms (stricter regulations issued regarding issuance of indulgences and veneration of saints; bishops and priests told to become more actively involved with the people they were trying to save). An index was also issued prohibiting the reading of certain publications.

Jesuits   Besides the Council of Trent, other measures were beginning to help the church recover. The Inquisition was re-organized for church-wide operation (1542) and was a means of punishing heresy and of returning wayward members to the straight and narrow path. But probably the most important element of the Counter-Reformation was the establishment in 1540 of the "Society of Jesus", the Jesuits by Ignatius Loyola.

Society of Jesus: Foundation Charter (August, 1539)
        The Jesuit Order, the work of St. Ignatius Loyola (1491 to 1556) and his small group of friends, encountered difficulties from the jealousy and disapproval of older orders both in its inception and during its existence. This document is the draft charter which, with difficulty promoted at Rome by Cardinal Contarini, was formally embodied by Paul III in his Bull *Regimini Militantis Ecclesiae* of September, 1540. [*Translated from* Monumenta Ignatiana *Vol. 1, pp. 14-16;* Monumenta Historica Societatis Jesu, *Vol. 63 (Rome, 1934).*]

> First: All those who want to fight under the banner of God in our Society, which we wish to designate with the name of Jesus, and who are willing to serve solely God and his vicar on earth, shall after a solemn vow of chastity resolve their minds as follows. They will be part of a community instituted for this supreme purpose; they will employ themselves principally in the propagation of the faith by the ministry of the Word, by spiritual exercises, and by works of charity, and more specifically in teaching Christianity to children and the un-educated; and they will endeavor to have always before their eyes first of all God and secondly the reason of this their membership (which is a way to God), and to attain with all their power to the end set them by God. Each man, that is to say, according to the grace granted him by the Holy Spirit and the proper degree of his vocation (so that no one shall use [excessive] zeal), but not according to human understand-ing. The assessment of their individual degree [of vocation] and the allocation and distribution of offices shall be entirely in the hands of a provost or prelate to be elected by us, so that a decent order, necessary to a community well designed in all things, may be observed. . . . [The provost shall be assisted by a Council.]
>
> Second: All members shall be aware — and that not only at the time of their first profession but as long as they live, and shall daily keep it in mind — that this entire Society and its members serve as soldiers in faithful obedience to the most holy lord Paul III and his successors. We are subject to the rule and divinely instituted authority of Christ's vicar to such a degree that we not only obey him according to the general duty owed by all the clergy but are so tied to him by the bond of an oath that whatever His Holiness may ordain for the profit of souls and the propagation of the faith we are bound to carry out instantly, as far as in us lies, without any evasion or excuse: whether he send us to the Turks, or into the New World, or to the Lutherans, or into any other realms of infidels or believers. . . .
>
> Third: All individuals shall swear to be obedient to the pro-vost of the Society in all matters concerning the observation of our Rule. He in his turn shall order such things as he shall see are necessary for the construction of the purpose put before him by God and the Society; in his leadership he shall always remember Christ's benignity, gentleness and love, as well as the injunctions of Peter and Paul. Both he and the Council shall pay special attention to this rule; they shall take particular care over the instruction of children and the unlearned in the Christian doctrine of the Ten Commandments and other like rudiments, so far as they think suitable, allowing for the condition of persons, places and times. . . .

Rilel E. Moynes

Built on the hillside overlooking the now restored Sainte-Marie (Jesuit headquarters for their work among the Hurons) Martyrs' Shrine at Midland, Ontario is a memorial and a testimonial to North America's first canonized saints. Between 1646 and 1649 at least six Jesuits were killed by Indians of the area.

Their purpose was to translate in their lives the life and spirit of Christ, and by strict discipline, spiritual exercises and absolute obedience to do anything in their power to serve the pope. Traditionally associated with missionary work, they were particularly successful in India, China and Japan under Francis Xavier and in South America, the St. Lawrence and Mississippi Valleys of North America, Mexico and California. Accepting only the very intelligent, they often attained positions of political power, too, particularly in Spain, Portugal, France and Austria. Traditionally associated also with education and teaching, some of the finest Catholic institutions of learning in the world today are run by the Jesuits, including Notre Dame in Indiana.

By the middle of the sixteenth century, Christian unity in Europe had been shattered. The continent was divided among increasingly hostile sects who incited numerous religious conflicts. Roman Catholics, Lutherans, Calvinists and a host of others distrusted each other deeply. Many years of warfare followed, and the scars of some of these battles are yet to be healed. Many people fled the continent in search of religious freedom in North America and here many new groups were begun.

Israeli Government Tourist Agency

At Golgotha where Jesus was crucified (John 19:16-18) there was a garden, and in the garden a new tomb, not yet used for burial. There, because the tomb was near at hand, and it was the eve of the Jewish Sabbath, Jesus was buried. This photo was taken in the garden.

The seventeenth, eighteenth and nineteenth centuries also saw major developments which affected religion. The "Scientific Revolution" produced new theories as to the nature of God — some theories denied his existence. The horizons of the world were broadened by courageous explorers; new knowledge about the universe and its diversity led to alterations in long held beliefs regarding the nature of the world, the nature of man and the nature of God, and God's relationship to man and the universe.

Charles Darwin's *The Origin of Species* threw a literal interpretation of the book of Genesis into question and encouraged much theological speculation. One of the gravest questions was how a person was to reconcile science with religion — questions which are, if anything, more pertinent today than in Darwin's time. The answers to such questions are presently being sought by contemporary Canadian churches; Chapter Ten attempts to deal more fully with these current developments.

Suggestions For Further Study

1. How do the Gospels of Matthew, Mark, Luke and John differ regarding:
    a. Attention to life span of Jesus
    b. Divinity of Jesus
    c. Miracles wrought

2. Why were the Gnostics and the Marcionites declared heretical?

3. Why was it considered so essential to both popes and kings that *they* control the appointment of bishops?

4. Were the Crusades primarily religious or worldly?

5. Why did it develop that northern Europe was more critical of the church than southern Europe?

6. "As Judea had given Christianity its ethics and Greece had given its theology, so now Rome gave its organization" (*Caesar and Christ*, Durant, p. 610). To what extent is this statement correct?

7. In the following sources there is reference to the coming of the end of the world, the nature of heaven, etc:

Mark 14:25	Luke 13:30
Matthew 10:23	Mark 13:32
Matthew 16:28	Matthew 24:6-12

Why are these references so vague?

8. Jesus has been interpreted in many different ways. One view is that he was a social revolutionist and that the Kingdom was a Communist utopia. The following passages have partially been responsible for this view:

Mark 10:23
Matthew 6:25
Luke 16:13
Matthew 19:15

To what extent do these and other passages support such a theory?

9. *The Passover Plot*, a Bantam book by Dr. W. J. Schonfeld, is an interesting book which presents a rather unorthodox view of Jesus. Among other things, it suggests that Jesus did not die on the Cross. Read this book and discuss the major theses it puts forth.

Notes

[1]"The Bible: An Attempt to Save Jesus?" *Time*, November 10, 1967. Reprinted by permission from TIME, The Weekly Newsmagazine; Copyright *Time*, Inc.

[2]Will Durant, *Caesar and Christ*. New York: Simon and Schuster, Inc., 1950, p. 587. Copyright © 1950 Will Durant. Reprinted by permission of Simon and Schuster, Inc.

Chapter Nine

Islam

Founded:
A.D. 622

Founder:
Mohammed (about A.D. 570 to 632)

Place:
Mecca, Saudi Arabia

Sacred Books:
The Koran

Number of Adherents:
Over 550 million

Distribution:
Islam is the predominant faith in the Near and Middle East, Pakistan and North Africa. Considerable numbers of Moslems also are found in Malaysia, Indonesia, the Soviet Union and central Africa.

Moslems In Canada:
Approximately 30,000

Sects:
Although it has a very strong sense of the brotherhood of all believers, Islam still has its internal divisions. The two main schools are the Sunnites and the Shiites each of which is subdivided into numerous sects.

La Ilaha Illa Allah; Muhammed Rasul Allah. This is the Shahada, expressed in Arabic. It expresses the very kernel of the Islamic faith.

"LA ILAHA ILLA ALLAH; MUHAMMED RASUL ALLAH."

Ι̇т is possible that the Arabic phrase above, which in English means "There is no God but Allah; Mohammed is the Prophet of Allah", could be spoken over one billion times on any given day. This is because it is the cardinal statement of the faith of Islam which, having almost 600 million believers, is today the world's second largest religion. Approximately one human being out of every seven is a Moslem, a follower of Islam. This fact is all the more impressive when one considers that Islam is also the youngest of the world's major faiths.

From its founding in Arabia by the prophet Mohammed in the seventh century A.D., the great missionary religion of Islam spread with almost incredible speed to the north, east and west, spanning three continents and thus becoming a true world religion within one hundred years of its birth. Although this pace has since slowed, Islam has continued to demonstrate both durability and vitality, and is still winning converts daily in far-flung parts of the world. It is the predominant faith in a broad swath of territory that stretches from north-west Africa, east to the Bay of Bengal. It also is strongly established in Malaysia and Indonesia. Every race and all six continents are represented in its following. Thus, no one can question the success of Islam; but to understand its appeal, one must examine its basic principles, and the circumstances surrounding its origin.

1. The Birth of Islam

A. Pre-Islamic Arabia

Early Arab Society   One can come to understand the rise of Islam partly by looking at the conditions which existed in Arabia during the sixth century A.D. The Arabian peninsula consists of approximately one million square miles, much of which is desert. The word "Arab" means nomad, and nomadic is certainly an appropriate term to describe the life of the Bedouin tribes that roamed the desert wilderness, eking out a bare existence from the hostile environment.

No single tribe dominated the entire peninsula. Rather, individual tribes or allied groups of tribes established power in a region of the country, and then schemed to maintain their position. Lacking a unified government, this society was plagued by inter-tribal warfare, blood feuds and general political instability. It had no science or art to speak of, and its literature consisted mainly of poetic fables, passed on from one generation to the next in stories and songs.

Arab Religion   The religion of early Arabia could best be described as poly-theistic paganism. The Bedouins had literally hundreds of gods and goddesses, and worshipped such elements of nature as trees and stones, which they regarded as the dwelling places of powerful spirits. They also believed in demons which they called *jinns*.

There were small communities of both Christians and Jews in Arabia; although they had no significant political power, it is possible that they were exerting some religious influence because, despite the numbers of their gods, the Arabs had developed the concept of a chief god and creator, whom they called *Allah*.

However, the fact that brawling, gambling, drinking and sexual promiscuity were widespread would suggest that religion generally had little effect on how the Arabs conducted themselves. Moreover, there were signs that many people were restive in these circumstances and perhaps ready to embrace a more demanding faith.

Mecca   In western Arabia, near the coast of the Red Sea, there were three towns in a mountainous region known as the Hijaz. Two of these towns, Mecca and Yethrib (later known as Medina) became the originating centres of a new religion. Mecca, set in a ravine and surrounded by barren mountains, was the largest and most important of the three towns.

Dominated by a powerful tribe known as the Quraysh, Mecca was situated at the crossroads of major caravan and pilgrimage routes and thus prospered from a brisk trade. Among their other enterprises, the Quraysh were the guardians of the *Kaaba*, a small rectangular shrine to which many Arabs made pilgrimages because it housed scores of gods and the mystical *Black Stone*. (This small rock, believed by some scientists to be meteoric in nature, retains some significance in the Islamic faith.)

B.   A Prophet is Born

Mohammed's Youth   Mohammed, who became the founder of the new faith of his people, was born into the Quraysh tribe around the year A.D. 570. Little is known about his early life, since no one had any reason to keep a careful record. Most of what is written was compiled after his death by followers whose views were rather one-sided in his favour. However, it has been established that Mohammed, whose name means "highly praised", was orphaned at an early age and raised mainly by an uncle, Abu Talib, who eventually became his adoptive father. As a youth, he contributed to his own upkeep by doing odd jobs, and apparently accompanied the occasional caravan to Syria. If this is so, it is possible that he was influenced by contacts there with both Christians and Jews. As we shall later see, there are strong traces of both of these religions in the beliefs of Islam.

His Interest in Meditation   By the time he reached his early twenties, he was a rather striking looking man — of medium height, but with strong, massive shoulders and a handsome face. At the age of twenty-five, he married Khadijah, a widow who owned a flourishing caravan business.

This new-found wealth and leisure afforded Mohammed the opportunity to indulge what for him was becoming a preoccupying interest, deep and serious meditation on the meaning of life. From his youth, Mohammed displayed a tendency toward brooding and introversion. He frequently had spoken critically of the evil he saw around him, and of the Arabs' lack of a coherent faith. Over the next few years, he made increasingly frequent visits to a particular cave on Mount Hira, a huge and barren rock some three miles outside of Mecca. Here, often in night-long vigils, he meditated on religious questions. So exhausting did these sessions become that his family began to worry about his health. But one of the most important events in the founding of Islam was about to occur.

C. The Revelations

The First Communication   One night in the year 610, when he was about forty years of age, Mohammed had an awe-inspiring experience in the cave on Mount Hira. There are many versions of the incident, but Moslems believe that God communicated with Mohammed through the angel Gabriel, who told him that he (Mohammed) was God's apostle and commanded him:

> Recite, in the name of thy Lord who has created,
> Created man from clots of blood.
> Recite, seeing that thy Lord is the most generous,
> Who has taught by the pen,
> Taught man what he did not know.[1]

Thus, the first fragment of Islam's holy book, the *Koran*, was revealed. Mohammed memorized the words, and rushed home to tell Khadijah of his experience. On hearing his account, she became his first convert.

Mohammed Declares His Role   Strangely enough, Mohammed received no further communication for a long time. But just when fear and self-doubt were about to overcome him, the messages commenced again and continued, with varying frequency, for the rest of his life. Moslems believe that this process revealed God's full and final truth. Mohammed himself announced that he had been commanded by God to preach his word to all mankind.

2. The Basic Beliefs and Practices of Islam

A. The Sources

The Koran   The core of Islam is contained within two principal sources — the Koran and, to a lesser extent, the *Sunnas*. The Koran, which means "the reciting" or "the reading", is the Moslem equivalent of the Bible. Being some 78,000 words in length, it is approximately four-fifths as long as the New Testament. Its length alone makes the reading of it a challenge; its heavy reliance on poetic symbolism and vague, obscure references make full understanding very difficult for the average person. Nonetheless, millions of Moslems have succeeded in memorizing it word for word. Moslems believe that the Koran was revealed by God, or Allah as they call him, to the prophet Mohammed through the angel Gabriel, over a period of some twenty-two years. Although Mohammed's followers wrote down some of the passages, a complete text was not compiled until after his death. Because of these circumstances, some critics doubt the full authenticity of the Koran; orthodox Moslems, however, accept it without question, believing that Allah's supervision preserved its literal accuracy, and caused it to be a perfect copy of the original Koran, which exists in Heaven.

Miller Services Ltd.

The Kaaba in Mecca. This is the very centre of the Moslem world and faith. It houses the Black Stone, and is the principal destination of pilgrims on the hajj. Non-believers are banned from the holy cities of Mecca and Medina.

The Nature of Its Content   The Koran is organized into one hundred and fourteen chapters, called *suras*. These, in turn, are arranged in almost exact order of decreasing length, with the exception of the short first sura, which is a kind of "Lord's Prayer of Islam" and reads as follows:

> In the name of God, the Merciful, the Compassionate.
>
> Praise be to God, the Lord of the Worlds,
> The Merciful One, the Compassionate One,
> Master of the Day of Doom.

Thee alone we serve, to Thee alone we cry for help.
Guide us in the straight path
The Path of them Thou hast blessed.
Not of those with whom Thou art angry
Nor of those who go astray.[2]

Generally speaking, the first suras are the most fundamental to the faith, and contain the essential teachings for the faithful. In addition, some are legalistic, laying down regulations concerning justice, property rights, family relations and so on. The shorter suras toward the end of the Koran tend to concentrate on the nature of the Judgment Day. They also contain comments on the events of the time, and stories to which morals are attached.

Overall, certain recurrent themes are evident — the total power of Allah, the inevitability of the Day of Judgment, the horrors of Hell and the bliss of Heaven.

Tradition   In addition to the Koran, there are the *Hadith*, or traditions. Since Mohammed was regarded as the perfect Moslem, believers wanted to know every detail about his life, so they could emulate him. This was difficult information to provide because, after the Prophet's death in 632, many false stories about him grew, and intermingled with more accurate ones. About two hundred years later, scholars collected all the alleged sayings, teachings, rulings and deeds of Mohammed, examined them, and recorded those they believed to be authentic. These are known as the Hadith. D. G. Bradley asserts that: "The teachings of Mohammed have been preserved with more accuracy than those of the founder of any other religion."[3] But it must be remembered that these teachings rank second in importance to the Koran, which alone contains the revelations of Allah to Mohammed.

B. The Basic Theological Concepts of Islam

The Main Articles of Faith   To be a Moslem a person must accept five main articles of faith:

1. Belief in Allah as the one true God
2. Belief in angels as the instruments of God's will
3. Belief in the four inspired books, of which the Koran is the final and most complete.
4. Belief in the twenty-eight prophets of Allah, of whom Mohammed is the last.
5. Belief in a final Day of Judgment.

The Nature of Allah   "La ilaha illa Allah; Muhammad rasul Allah." This is the *Shahada,* a call by which Moslems are beckoned to prayer five times a day. It means "There is no God but Allah; Mohammed is the prophet of Allah." Moslems believe in Allah as the eternal, all powerful Creator, who has no sons or daughters, or anyone else with whom he shares power. He has absolute unity, and is all-seeing, all-hearing and all-knowing. The lord of the worlds, Allah is unchanging, invisible and present everywhere at all times.

By tradition, there are ninety-nine epithets of praise for him. These include The Holy, The Merciful, The Generous, The Shelterer of Orphans, The Friend of the Bereaved, The Deliverer from All Afflictions and so on. The following passages from the Koran serve as illustrations of some of these characteristics:

> . . . He is God, One, God, the Everlasting Refuge, who has not begotten, and has not been begotten, and equal to Him is not anyone.[4]

> Is He not closer than the vein of thy neck? Thou needest not raise thy voice, for He knoweth the secret whisper, and what is yet more hidden. . . . He knows what is in the land and in the sea; no leaf falleth but He knoweth it; nor is there a grain in the darkness under the earth, nor a thing, green or sere, but it is recorded.[5]

> By the noonday brightness, and by the night when it darkeneth, thy Lord hath not forsaken thee, neither hath He been displeased. Surely the future shall be better for thee than the past; and in the end He shall be bounteous to thee, and thou shalt be satisfied.[6]

Angels   A belief in angels is essential to the acceptance of the manner in which Allah revealed himself to Mohammed, and to various other prophets before him. Moslems regard Gabriel as the chief angel. They also believe in a fallen angel called *Shaitan* and in the jinns or demons, who are the minions of Shaitan. The angel Michael was allegedly responsible for carrying out Allah's plans for the creation of the universe. Other angels, unnamed in the Koran, perform such tasks as assisting Moslems in battle, guarding the gates of Heaven and Hell, and recording men's thoughts and deeds for reference on the Day of Judgment.

The Prophets   Numerous similarities can be seen in Judaism, Christianity and Islam. According to Moslem belief, this is so because Islam is not the youngest but in fact the oldest religion in the world. It has existed since time began and was revealed to mankind in stages by Allah, who used various prophets as vehicles for making his truth known.

Twenty-eight prophets are specifically named in the Koran. These include Adam, Noah, Abraham, Moses, Isaac, Jacob, Ishmael, Joseph, David, Job and others from the Old Testament, plus Jesus, Zacharias, John the Baptist and others from the New Testament. The twenty-eight prophets are divided into two categories. Most important are those who introduced new teachings; the first was Adam, who was followed by Noah, Abraham, Moses, Jesus and Mohammed in that order. Abraham, for example, received God's revelation that there was only one God. To Moses were revealed the Ten Commandments and to Jesus the golden rule. The second group are of lesser significance, since they merely repeated the messages of earlier prophets.

The Inspired Books   Islam recognizes three sets of Scriptures as containing partial revelations of Allah's will. These are the Torah of Moses, the Psalms of David and the Gospel of Jesus. But, to repeat, the Koran represents the final and complete revelation, superseding all previous revelations or conflicting claims to truth. Furthermore, its message is for all mankind.

Mohammed   Of all the prophets, Moslems regard Mohammed as by far the most important. Revelations to preceding prophets were incomplete and furthermore were corrupted and disobeyed by the peoples to whom they were presented. Mohammed, or the Prophet, as he is known to Moslems, was the last and greatest prophet, to whom was revealed, in pure form, the complete truth of Allah.

It should be noted, however, that while Mohammed has come to be idealized by many zealous Moslems as the perfect human being, he has never been regarded as divine. He himself never claimed such status, nor did he associate himself with any miracles, except for the revelation of the Koran, in which case he was on the receiving end of a miracle from God.

The Day of Judgment   The concept of a Judgment Day is common to Christianity, Judaism and Islam, though the particulars may differ in each faith. For Moslems, the details of this day are vividly, indeed almost terrifyingly described in the Koran:

> When the sun shall be folded up, and the stars shall fall, and when the mountains shall be set in motion. . . . and the seas shall boil. . . . then shall every soul know what it hath done.[7]

The Day of Judgment will be prefaced by signs and portents, and then announced by a trumpet blast. Everyone will bodily rise from the grave, and will gather in a great plain, where they will be tortured by great heat and thirst. The record of the thoughts and deeds of each person will be examined, and the individual consigned to eternal Heaven or Hell. No one can escape this assessment.

Unbelievers and gross sinners will swelter in the fires of Hell, where they will be scourged by hot blasts, boiling liquids, foul smoke, molten metal and the like. On the other hand, those who reach Heaven will dwell in perpetual luxury and physical comfort, featuring abundant food, clear water, cool breezes, mansions, servants and lovely maidens. The Koran refers frequently to the Day of Judgment, and paints vivid pictures of Heaven and Hell, as these excerpts indicate:

> A banquet of fruits, and honoured shall they be,
> In the gardens of delight,
> Upon couches face to face.
> A cup shall be borne round among them from a fountain;
> Limpid, delicious to those who drink:
> It shall not oppress the sense, nor shall they therewith be drunken.
> And with them are the large-eyed ones with modest, refraining
> glances . . . .
> Truly great is their felicity![8]

> . . . But as for him who is given his book in his left hand,
> he shall say, "Would that I had not been given my book
> and not known by reckoning; Would it had been the end!
> My wealth has not availed me,

My authority has gone from me."
Take him, and fetter him, and then roast him in Hell,
Then in a chain of seventy cubits' length insert him!
Behold, he never believed in God the All-mighty, and
He never urged the feeling of the needy; therefore he
Has not here one loyal friend, neither any food
Saving foul pus, that none excepting the sinners eat.[9]

While conservatives still interpret these passages literally, more
modern, liberal Moslems tend to regard them as symbolic in nature.

Kismet   A sixth belief, which is not mandatory but still accepted by many
Moslems is the concept of *Kismet* or fate. This holds that all happenings,
including each person's death, and the Day of Judgment, are predetermined.
Thus, history is regarded as the unfolding of Allah's great plan, under his
control.

C. The Way to Heaven

To reach Heaven, Moslems believe that faith, and observance of ritual, are not
enough. The emphasis instead is on intent and action. A man must walk the
straight path, which means he must accept the beliefs of the faith as previously
described, perform the required duties and generally live according to the moral
precepts laid out in the Koran and Hadith. The terms "Islam" and "Moslem"
themselves afford a clue to the basic requirement for a believer. In Arabic,
"Islam" means "surrender to God" and "Moslem" means "one who surrenders".
Thus, the greatest virtue is complete submission to the will and authority of
Allah. Beyond this general principle, there are five specific duties, known as "The
Five Pillars", which are demanded of every Moslem. These are:

1. Recitation of the Shahada: *La ilaha illa Allah, Muhammad rasul
   Allah.* (There is no God but Allah; Mohammed is the Prophet of
   Allah.) This is the most important single statement a Moslem can
   make
2. Regular prayer
3. Alms-giving
4. Fasting
5. Pilgrimage to Mecca.

The Shahada   As stated previously, the Shahada is part of the call by which
Moslems are summoned to public prayer. The person whose job it is to make
this call five times each day is the *muezzin*. Most Moslems recite the phrase
themselves several times daily as a matter of course, but the faith requires that at
least once in his lifetime a Moslem must repeat the Shahada publicly, fervently
and with complete conviction. Otherwise, he is not a believer.
       Perhaps one reason for this great emphasis on the singularity of Allah
is to avoid what some Moslems believe to be a confusing point about Christianity
— the concept of the Trinity.

Prayer   In Islam, prayer is the most important of all duties. The basic purposes of prayer are to express gratitude and love to Allah the Creator, and to remind man of his inferiority, thereby teaching him humility. Thus, in Islamic prayer, the emphasis is on reverence, not on petition or requests for favours. Consequently, it might better be described as worship. There are two kinds of prayer: *du'a* is private or inner prayer, considered non-compulsory but still meritorious; *salat* is formal ritual prayer, which is compulsory, and precisely defined.

Salat must be performed five times daily. A Moslem can pray anywhere, either individually or in a group, and any good Moslem can lead the faithful in prayer. However, the usual place of prayer is a *mosque*, meaning "place of prostration". Since Friday is the nearest thing to a Moslem holy day, all believers should try to pray in a mosque at least once a week, on Friday at noon. While there is no official clergy standing between man and God, mosques usually employ a number of people to assist in the carrying out of the required ceremonies of worship. Here is the *azan*, by which the *muezzin* calls the faithful to prayer:

> God is most great
> I testify there is no god but Allah
> I testify that Mohammed is the Messenger of Allah
> Come to prayer;
> Come to salvation,
> God is most great;
> There is no god but Allah.[10]

To help rouse the tardy in the early morning, the muezzin frequently adds "Prayer is better than sleep". The *imam*, who holds his position as senior officer of the mosque by virtue of his recognized piety and scholarship, leads the faithful in prayer, and may also deliver a short sermon or Scripture reading. However, in a large mosque, the latter functions are performed by another official, the *khatib*.

There are five appointed times for prayer: upon rising in the morning, at noon, in mid-afternoon, after sunset and before retiring. This is not a completely rigid timetable. Travellers, for example, who might find it difficult if not impossible to go to prayers at the required time may make up the missed devotions at the next opportunity.

The place of prayer, as well as those who worship there, must be clean. Before entering a mosque, Moslems remove all footwear. Otherwise, they must be decently clothed and have their heads covered. All exposed parts of the body must be cleansed. If water is unavailable, then sand or dust is to be used. These ablutions purify physically as prayer cleanses spiritually, so that the believer is completely pure in the sight of Allah. Inside the mosque there are no statues or pictures, and no seats for the worshippers. A person may bring a prayer rug if he wishes. There is no singing or music during the service. Although there usually is no pulpit, a large decorated niche, called a *mihrab*, is set in one wall, indicating the direction of the Kaaba in Mecca. All prayers must be said while facing in this direction.

The Method of Prayer   The worshippers line up in rows, and enact the prayer ritual in unison, under the direction of an appointed leader, usually the imam.

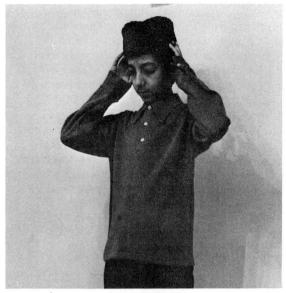

1. wuquf

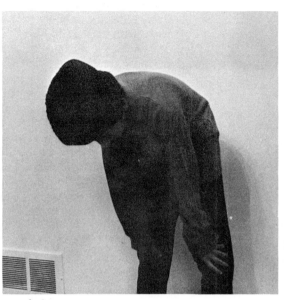

2. ruku'

A young Canadian Moslem demonstrates the four basic positions of prayer.

Riley E. Moynes

3. sujud

4. julus

Standing erect, with hands beside the head, palms facing forward, the Moslem
says silently, or in a low voice: *Allahu Akbar* — (Allah is the most great). He
then recites the opening sura of the Koran, and perhaps another sura as well.
Next, with back straight, he bows forward from the hips, resting his hands
on his knees and saying "Great God". Straightening up, he again says "Allah is
the most great". Then, he glides gently to his knees and touches his head to
the floor, saying "God the Highest". Following this, he raises himself and sits on
his heels, again repeating the phrase "Allah is the most great". He completes this
seven-stage procedure, known as a *rak'a*, by touching his head to the floor a
second time. Two rak'as are called for at the morning prayer session, four at
the second, third and fifth, and three at the fourth or sunset ceremony. They may
be interspersed with various other sayings or optional prayers. After the ritual
part of the worship is completed, an individual may add whatever special prayers
he pleases. The following prayers are fairly typical. The first stresses the worship
of Allah, while the second is more petitionary in nature.

> Thanks be to my Lord; He the Adorable, and only to be adored. My
> Lord, the Eternal, the Ever-existing, the Cherisher, the True Sovereign
> whose mercy and might overshadow the universe; the Regulator of the
> world, and Light of the creation. His is our worship; to Him belongs
> all worship; He existed before all things, and will exist after all that is
> living has ceased. Thou art the adored, my Lord; Thou the Master, the
> Loving and Forgiving. . . . O my Lord, Thou art the Helper of the
> afflicted, the Reliever of all distress, the Consoler of the broken-
> hearted; Thou art present everywhere to help Thy servants. . . . O my
> Lord, Thou art the Creator, I am only created; Thou art my Sovereign,
> I am only Thy Servant; Thou art the Helper, I am the beseecher; Thou
> art the Forgiver, I am the sinner; Thou, my Lord, art the Merciful, All-
> knowing, All-loving.[11]

> O Lord, grant to me the Love of Thee. Grant that I may love
> those that love Thee. Grant that I may do the deeds that win Thy love.
> Make Thy love to be dearer to me than self, family or than wealth.
> O Lord! Grant me firmness in faith and direction. Assist me
> in being grateful to Thee and in adoring Thee in every good way. I
> ask Thee for an innocent heart, which shall not incline to wickedness.
> I ask Thee for a true tongue. I pray Thee to defend me from that vice
> which Thou knowest, and for forgiveness of these faults which Thou
> knowest. O my Defender! assist me in remembering Thee and being
> grateful to Thee, and in worshipping Thee with the excess of my
> strength. Forgive me out of Thy kindness, and have mercy on me; for
> verily Thou art the forgiver of offences and the bestower of
> blessings on Thy servants.[12]

Alms   Islam places great emphasis on charity. There are two kinds of alms:
sadaqua can be voluntary, but *zakat* is compulsory. Those to whom Allah has
given abundance must share their good fortune with the needy. Mohammed
prescribed a minimum tax of $2\frac{1}{2}$ per cent on the revenues and holdings of those
who had more than enough to meet their basic needs. The assessment could be

paid in cash, precious metals or in kind, depending on the nature of a man's wealth. These alms were used to meet the needs of the faith, which included supporting widows, orphans and the poor, and equipping Moslem armies for holy war. Today, while various formulas of assessment are employed, the reasons for giving and the uses of the alms are much the same as before.

Fasting   The most important period of fasting is the month of *Ramadan*. This is the ninth month of the year, and since Moslems follow a lunar calendar, it can fall during any season. During Ramadan, Moslems must abstain from eating, drinking, smoking and sexual intercourse each day from before sunrise until after sunset. These sacrifices are designed to test the spirit, discipline the will, maintain a sense of religious duty and dependence, and act as a reminder of the hunger of the poor. Moreover, they signify recognition of the importance of the month of Ramadan, during which numerous important events took place in the past, including God's first revelation to Mohammed in A.D. 610, the latter's historic flight from Mecca to Medina in 622, and his victory in battle at Badr in 624.

Again in the matter of fasting, Islam demonstrates its great reasonableness and adaptability to local conditions and needs. Fasting is not required of young children, pregnant women, the elderly, the sick, soldiers engaged in holy war or travellers embarked upon essential journeys, though the latter are expected to make up at a later time the days of sacrifice missed. For those who do fast, in addition to their previously mentioned sacrifices, they are expected to be especially considerate to their fellow Moslems. Thus the unity and brotherhood of Islam are fostered. As might be expected, the end of the month of Ramadan is joyously celebrated, often with lavish feasts. When Ramadan falls during the hot summer months, this indulgence has been well earned.

Who Must Fast?

The Fasting of Ramadan is compulsory upon every Muslim, male or female, who has these qualifications:
1. To be mentally and physically fit, which means to be sane and able.
2. To be of full age, the age of puberty and discretion, which is normally from 14 to 15 up. Children under this age should be encouraged to start this good practice on easy levels, so when they reach the age of puberty they will be mentally and physically prepared to observe the Fasting.
3. To be present at your permanent settlement, your home town, your farm, your business premises, etc. This means not to be travelling on a journey.
4. To be fairly certain that the Fasting is unlikely to cause you any harm, physical or mental, other than the normal reactions to hunger, thirst, etc.

Exemption From Fasting

The above said qualifications exclude the following categories:
1. Children under the age of puberty and discretion.

Ramadan Time Table for Toronto and Vicinity

Ramadan 1392	Oct./Nov. 1972		Sahoor	Fajr	Sunrise	Zuhr	Asr	Sunset	Isha
1	Mon.	9	5:49	5:59	7:25	1:11	4:01	6:45	8:20
2	Tue.	10	5:50	6:00	7:26	1:11	4:00	6:43	8:18
3	Wed.	11	5:51	6:01	7:27	1:11	3:59	6:41	8:16
4	Thu.	12	5:52	6:02	7:28	1:10	3:58	6:40	8:14
5	Fri.	13	5:53	6:03	7:30	1:10	3:57	6:38	8:13
6	Sat.	14	5:54	6:04	7:31	1:10	3:56	6:36	8:12
7	Sun.	15	5:55	6:05	7:32	1:09	3:54	6:34	8:11
8	Mon.	16	5:56	6:06	7:33	1:09	3:54	6:33	8:10
9	Tue.	17	5:57	6:07	7:35	1:09	3.53	6:31	8:08
10	Wed.	18	5:59	6:09	7:36	1:09	3:52	6:30	8:06
11	Thu.	19	6:00	6:10	7:37	1:09	3:51	6:28	8:04
12	Fri.	20	6:02	6:12	7:38	1:09	3:50	6:26	8:02
13	Sat.	21	6:04	6:14	7:40	1:08	3:49	6:24	8:00
14	Sun.	22	6:06	6:16	7:41	1:08	3:48	6:23	7:59
15	Mon.	23	6:07	6:17	7:42	1:08	3:47	6:21	7:57
16	Tue.	24	6:08	6:18	7:43	1:08	3:47	6:20	7:55
17	Wed.	25	6:08	6:18	7:45	1:08	3:46	6:18	7:54
18	Thu.	26	6:09	6:19	7:46	1:08	3:45	6:17	7:53
19	Fri.	27	6:10	6:20	7:48	1:07	3:44	6:15	7:52
20	Sat.	28	6:11	6:21	7:49	1:07	3:43	6:14	7:51

EASTERN STANDARD TIME STARTS

21	Sun.	29	5:12	5:22	6:50	12:07	2:43	5:13	6:50
22	Mon.	30	5:13	5:23	6:51	12:07	2:42	5:12	6:49
23	Tue.	31	5:14	5:24	6:53	12:07	2:41	5:10	6:48
24	Wed.	1	5:15	5:25	6:54	12:07	2:41	5:09	6:47
25	Thu.	2	5:16	5:26	6:56	12:07	2:40	5:07	6:46
26	Fri.	3	5:17	5:27	6:57	12:07	2:39	5:06	6:44
27	Sat.	4	5:19	5:29	6:59	12:07	2:39	5:04	6:42
28	Sun.	5	5:21	5:31	7:00	12:07	2:38	5:03	6:41
29	Mon.	6	5:22	5:32	7:01	12:07	2:38	5:02	6:40
30	Tue.	7	5:23	5:33	7:02	12:07	2:37	5:01	6:39
	Wed.	8	SHAWWAL EID DAY						

Correction: To get exact local time for other locations add to or subtract
from this time table as noted below:
Hamilton +2 min. Niagara Falls −2 min. Waterloo +4 min. Guelph +3 min.

2. The insane people who are unaccountable for their deeds.

3. Men and women who are too old and feeble to undertake the obligation of fast, and bear its hardships. Such people are exempted from this duty, but they must offer, at least, one needy poor Muslim an average full meal or its value per person per day. This compensation indicates that whenever they can fast even for one day of the month, they should do so, and compensate for the rest. Otherwise they are accountable for their negligence.

4. Sick people whose health is likely to be severely affected by the observance of fast. They must postpone the fast, as long as they are sick, to a later date and make up for it, a day for a day.

5. People in the course of travelling. In this case such people may break the fast temporarily during their travel only and make up for it in later days, a day for a day.

6. Expectant women and women suckling their children may also break the fast, if its observance is likely to endanger their own health or that of their infants. But they must make up for the fast at a delayed time, a day for a day.

7. Women in the period of menstruation (of a maximum of ten days) or of confinement (of a maximum of forty days). These are not allowed to fast even if they can and want to. They must postpone the fast till recovery and then make up for it, a day for a day.

It should be understood that here, the intention must be made clear that this action is undertaken in obedience to Allah, in response to His command and out of love for Him.

How the Fast of Ramadan Becomes Void

The fast of Ramadan becomes void by intentional eating or drinking or smoking or indulgence in any intimate intercourses, and by allowing anything to enter through the mouth into the interior parts of the body; and if this is done deliberately without any lawful reason, the penalty is to observe the fast of sixty consecutive days or, as a second alternative, feed sixty poor persons sufficiently, besides observing the fast of one day against the day whose fast was made void.

When the fast of days other than those of Ramadan is broken for a lawful reason like those classified above under the heading "Exemption", the person involved must make up for that fast later, a day for a day.

If anyone, by mistake, does something that would ordinarily invalidate the fast, his observance is not nullified, and his fast stands valid, provided he stops doing that thing the moment he realizes what he was doing.

ON COMPLETION OF THE FAST OF RAMADAN, THE SPECIAL CHARITY KNOWN AS SADAQATUL-FITR (CHARITY OF FAST-BREAKING) MUST BE DISTRIBUTED.

General Recommendations
It is strongly recommended by the Prophet Muhammad (peace be upon him) to observe these practices especially during Ramadan:
1. To have a light meal before the break of dawn, known as Sahoor.
2. To eat three dates and have a drink of water right after sunset, saying this prayer: Al-lahumma laka sumtu, wa 'ala rizqika aftartu. (O Allah for your sake I have fasted and now I break the fast with the food You have given me.)
3. To make your meals as light as possible, as the Prophet put it, the worst thing man can fill is his stomach.
4. To observe Taraweeh prayer.
5: To exchange social visits and intensify humanitarian services.
6. To increase study and recitation of the Qur'an.
7. To exert the utmost patience and humility.
8. To be extraordinarily cautious in using the senses, the mind and especially, the tongue; to abstain from careless and gossipy chats and avoid all suspicious motions.

Pilgrimage   The fifth pillar of the faith is *hajj*, or pilgrimage. All Moslems who are able should make at least one journey to Mecca during their lifetime. While extra pilgrimages can be made at any time, the mandatory one must take place during the twelfth and sacred month of *Dhu'l Hijja*. If individuals cannot afford the hajj, a group of them might send one person to represent them all.

The hajj is a tremendous, unifying factor in Islam, developing a unique sense of brotherhood in Moslems of all classes, races and countries. The late Malcolm X, a prominent leader of American Negroes in the early 1960's, was only one of many Moslem converts who expressed amazement at the depth of religious community spirit fostered by this phenomenon. Many of the travellers must save money all their lives to be able to afford the journey. Arriving at the outskirts of Mecca, the tens of thousands of pilgrims shave their heads, bathe, and don white robes which they wear for the duration of the pilgrimage. All pilgrims undergo the same preparations and experiences. Kings and rich men walk shoulder to shoulder with people of every class, country and race. Once prepared, they all enter the holy city and proceed directly to the Kaaba. Here, they make seven circuits of the shrine, stopping each time to kiss the Black Stone, and reciting various prayers glorifying Allah. Next, the pilgrims run seven times between two nearby hills, preserving an Arab custom from pre-Islamic times.

The most important part of the hajj begins on the ninth day, at Arafa, in a valley nine miles from Mecca. Here, the pilgrims gather near a small hill, praying and listening to a sermon by a special dignitary. It was here that Mohammed preached his last sermon. The environment produces a moving atmosphere of great holiness. To many Moslems, this is the greatest moment in their lives. After sunset, they begin the return trip to Mecca, spending the night at the village of Muzdalifa. Early next morning, at Mina, the pilgrims throw stones at pillars representing the devil and temptation. With each throw

Courtesy M. Husain, Toronto

Modern-day pilgrims on the hajj prepare dinner outside their tents.

they cry: "In the name of God! Allah is almighty." Each person also makes a sacrifice to Allah by slitting the throat of a camel, sheep or goat. On the return to Mecca, the pilgrimage is completed by making seven final circuits of the Kaaba and running an equal number of times between the two nearby hills. Those who complete the hajj are promised special consideration on the Day of Judgment.

Holy War   These five pillars are the core of the *shari'a*, "the clear path to be followed". Unofficially, there is a sixth duty of Moslems. This is *jihad*, or struggle. In the narrow sense, this can be interpreted as "holy war", or the taking up of arms against an enemy, but it can also mean struggle within oneself to resist the temptation of sin. The Koran commands:

> Fight those who believe not in God and in the last day, and who forbid not what God and His Apostle have forbidden, and who do not practise the religion of truth from amongst those to whom the Book has been brought, until they pay the tribute by their hands and be as little ones.[13]

Moslems hasten to point out that the Koran expressly forbids aggressive acts of violence. On the other hand, they explain that the Koran requires them to defend themselves and fellow members of the Moslem community against injustice, and Islam itself against actual or threatened attack. Islam's promise of immediate transfer to Heaven for those who die in holy war has inspired incredible feats in battle by Moslems throughout the ages.

Asceticism   The practices of certain small sects notwithstanding, Islam generally condemns asceticism. Moslems believe that Allah meant man to enjoy moderately the good and proper things in life, and to stay in his community, serving his fellow Moslems to the best of his ability, rather than withdrawing from the world and scourging himself with all manner of punishments.

D. Other Ideas in Islam

Man and the Universe   The Islamic concept of God has already been described. Both man and the universe, of which Mecca is regarded as the centre, are God's creations. Mecca is also thought of as the navel of the earth; it was created first, and the earth developed around it. But God's supreme achievement was the creation of man himself. Thus, like the other major Western religions, Islam believes in the reality of the material world and the unique individuality of every human being. Many Eastern religions, however, regard this world as illusory, and stress the all-encompassing cosmic spirit in which individuals are totally absorbed.

Moslems further believe that man has but one life on this earth, during which time he will, through his thoughts and actions, earn his reward in either Heaven or Hell. But, while God's overall plan is complete, he still allows certain freedom to the individual, and also to Shaitan and his jinns. Man has been given freedom of choice and action and is thus the architect of his own destiny. Allah, in his unquestioned wisdom, may let misery or disaster befall anyone. After all, he has shown man the right path and provided the example of prophet Mohammed as a perfect guide by which to live. If a man gives in to temptation and wanders from the straight path, it is his own fault. Until he returns, his life will be without meaning or purpose.

The Status of Women   One of the most common misconceptions about Islam concerns the Moslem view of women. Among many false impressions held by Westerners are the beliefs that Moslem males regard women as inferiors, and that most of them have several wives. In fact, the Koran expressly states that Allah makes no distinctions between people on the basis of class, race, nationality or sex.

However, due to the influence of long-standing customs in many Moslem lands, there is a general belief in the Islamic community that men and women have clearcut and different roles to play in society. For example, men are regarded primarily as providers and protectors. Thus, as the members of the family who have professional careers, run the government, operate businesses and so on, women are regarded basically as homemakers and the raisers of children. The same generalizations hold true for most other societies in the world, past and present. Recent trends in the West perhaps have prompted some people to regard this female role as inferior, but no such inferiority is actually understood in the Moslem faith. Moreover, as industrialization, urbanization and other fundamental changes occur in Moslem countries, the trend has been, as elsewhere, for an increasing number of women to be "liberated" from the role of housewife and babysitter, and to enter the working world in whatever capacities they see fit.

Marriage is looked upon as one of the most important of all institutions in Moslem society, which still places great emphasis on the religious and social value of close family life. Although it is true that a Moslem male technically is allowed up to four wives, polygamy is in fact quite rare. The Koran permits the taking of more than one wife only in special circumstances, as when a widow, or an orphaned girl of marriageable age, requires security; when a wife becomes physically or mentally incapacitated; and so on. Moreover, a husband having more than one wife is required to treat them all equally, and no woman can be forced to marry against her will.

Divorce, although looked upon as a last resort, is permitted, and both sexes have equal rights in such action. Islamic law also permits divorced women to remarry.

Views on Conduct   Besides demanding observance of its basic beliefs and practices, Islam also encourages its followers to acquire certain virtues. Among these are humility, courage, fidelity, charity, hospitality and kindness. Parents and elders are to receive special consideration. The Koran teaches Moslems not to discriminate on the grounds of race, class or sex and, while it does not prohibit slavery, it encourages Moslems to free those in bondage. Today, most Moslem countries have outlawed the institution of slavery.

Among the evils specifically condemned in the Koran are: unbelief, murder, adultery, theft, lying, slander, cheating, usury, gambling, sorcery, eating pork or the flesh of scavengers and birds of prey, consuming intoxicants, deserting the armies of Islam in holy war and despairing of God's mercy. Most of these ethical values are summed up in the following passage from the Koran:

> Thy Lord has decreed that ye shall not serve ought but Him; and to parents kindness. . . . And give the kinsman his due, and the poor and the wayfarer. But do not lavish wastefully. . . . And slay not your children in fear of poverty. We will provide for them. Beware; to slay them is a great sin. And approach not to fornication; it has always been vileness and evil as a practice. And slay not the soul that God has made inviolable, save for just cause. . . . And approach not the possessions of the orphan. . . . And fulfill your compact. . . . And give full measure when you measure and weigh with just balance. . . . And make no charges of foul deeds where thou hast no knowledge. . . . And walk not on the earth with self-conceit; thou wilt neither split the earth nor touch the mountains in height.[14]

While the majority of these values are still held by Moslems, changes in modern life have caused certain teachings to be altered or de-emphasized. For example, some Moslems now tolerate moderate drinking. Also, the charging of interest is now permissible on loans made for business purposes, though not for loans used to relieve human suffering.

Death   In the Moslem faith, burial follows death very quickly. The corpse is washed and laid in the grave on its right side, facing Mecca. Prayers are then said over the grave. Some Moslems believe that if the person was evil the sides of the grave will topple in on the corpse. As stated previously, Islam teaches the Resurrection of the body on Judgment Day, and Koranic descriptions of the nature of Heaven suggest that those who enter paradise will do so in a youthful state.

Religious Toleration   The Koran offers guidance to Moslems on the question of their proper attitude toward followers of other religions:

> Unto you your religion, and unto me my religion.[15]

To every one hath we given a law and a way. . . . And if God had
pleased, He would have made you all [all mankind] one people [people
of one religion]. But He hath done otherwise, that He might try you
in that which he hath severally given unto you: wherefore press
forward in good works. Unto God shall ye return, and He will tell you
that concerning which ye disagree.[16]

When Moslems conquered new territories, they usually offered the
peoples there two alternatives: either to embrace Islam, or to retain their
particular religions but pay prescribed taxes to the Moslem state. For reasons
that have already been explained, the Moslems showed special favour to
Christians and Jews, some of whom were allowed to hold influential positions
in Moslem communities.

While the Koran enjoined the faithful to be tolerant, it did not advise
them to "turn the other cheek" when Islam was endangered or maligned. War
could righteously be fought if it was defensive in nature, or if it was necessary
to right a wrong done to the religion or its followers. Such a war was the right
and, indeed, the sacred duty of the faithful, who were promised immediate
entry into Heaven should they die in battle for Islam. Unfortunately, these
teachings of the Koran sometimes were used to justify aggressive wars plotted
by ambitious political leaders of Moslem lands.

3. The Establishment and Spread of Islam

A. Islam Is Established in Arabia

Mohammed Begins to Preach   When Mohammed began to receive God's
revelations, he recounted these experiences to his wife, Khadijah, and to a circle
of close relatives and friends. They listened to his impassioned arguments about
the coming of the Judgment Day, about Heaven and Hell, about the need to take
God's word to all the people, and they became his first converts. Soon, he was
making public speeches in Mecca. At the sacred Kaaba he was booed and
ridiculed while attempting to preach on the theme of Allah being the one true
god.

Undaunted, he pressed on, with such fervour that the authorities no
longer regarded him as a laughing matter. His claims that all believers were equal
in the sight of God, and that the rich must share with the poor, gave serious
offence to many prominent citizens. He was causing many pagans to doubt their
old beliefs and thus was interfering with the lucrative concessions operated in
conjunction with the pilgrimage trade in the city. Because he was drawing ever
increasing crowds, some even regarded him as a political threat. Accordingly,
the officials launched a program of persecution against his followers, many of
whom were covered with filth, stoned, beaten, tortured and even killed. The
wealth and connections of Khadijah's family probably helped to save the
prophet himself from serious harm.

The Flight to Medina   Fortunately for Mohammed, he was at this point invited by some people from Yathrib, a city 250 miles north of Mecca, to come to their city to preach. His flight in 622 from the dangerously hostile environment of Mecca is known as the *Hegira*. This event is looked upon by Moslems as the turning point in the history of the world, and is the year from which they date their calendar. In Yathrib, Mohammed quickly rebuilt his core of followers, and constructed the first mosque. His success in overcoming old and bitter tribal feuds demonstrated his leadership ability and this, coupled with the rapid growth of his religious following, thrust him into a pre-eminent position in the city. Yathrib became known as Madinat al-Nabi, "the City of the Prophet", now Medina in English.

Conquest of Mecca   In need of money, arms and supplies, Mohammed began to launch raids upon Meccan caravans, and soon found himself at war with his native city. His cause and personal reputation were greatly enhanced by a surprising victory over superior Meccan forces at Badr in 624. Interpreting this as a sign of God's favour, a number of Arab tribes joined Mohammed's army. Within six years he had captured Mecca itself. Entering the city in triumph, he proceeded to the Kaaba, where he destroyed all the idols and rededicated the Black Stone to Allah. Mecca was rapidly converted to the faith, and became the spiritual centre of Islam. Later, a tradition developed which prohibited non-Moslems from entering the Holy City. Medina, however, remained the centre of Moslem political power for some time.

Arabia Falls to Islam   Mohammed could not rest content with these successes and so he pressed on, aiming at nothing less than the unification of all the feuding tribes of Arabia. With a rare combination of persuasion, diplomacy and

The centre of Medina, as it appears today. Note the four minarets, from which muezzins call the faithful to prayer. The large dome-topped structure on the left houses the tomb of the Prophet Mohammed.

force, he succeeded in this hitherto impossible task in the amazing time of less than two years. When he died suddenly in 632, all of Arabia was under Moslem control, and most of its people had embraced the religion of the Prophet.

The Place of Mohammed   Although Mohammed had never laid claim to divinity, or to miracle-working power, he was idolized by his followers, and his death came as a severe shock. It is a tribute to his own inspirational ability, and to the strength of Islam itself, that his death was followed not by the disintegration of the newborn faith, but by its continued solidarity and expansion. Though not worshipped he is, to this day, revered by all Moslems as the final prophet to whom Allah revealed his complete truth. They rarely mention Mohammed's name without a benediction, such as "Salaam upon you, O Prophet of God". His life, though not free of error or sin, has been idealized by Islam's more zealous adherents, and his teachings have been incorporated into the main body of the faith. One author sums up Mohammed's role this way:

> [Mohammed] called forth out of unpromising material a nation never united before, in a country that was hitherto but a geographical expression; established a religion which in vast areas superseded Christianity and Judaism and still claims the adherence of a goodly portion of the human race; and laid the basis of an empire that was soon to embrace within its far-flung boundaries the fairest provinces of the then civilized world.[17]

B.   Islam Becomes a World Religion

The Successors to Mohammed   If the unity of Islam, and that of its growing empire, were to be preserved, it was essential that continued strong leadership be provided. Successors to Mohammed took the title of *caliph*, and were regarded as the spiritual and political rulers of the entire Moslem world. The first of these was Abu Bakr, one of Mohammed's best friends and the father of one of the several wives taken by the Prophet after the death of Khadijah. Abu Bakr was succeeded by Omar, who proved to be another strong and successful leader.

Unfortunately, in later times the immense power, wealth and prestige associated with the caliphate tempted various families to lay conflicting claims to that office, thus bringing about political intrigues, bloody wars, and division of the faith into several competing sects.

Abu Bekr   Abu Bekr was caliph from 632 until his untimely death in 634. Despite his short reign, he was able to consolidate Mohammed's achievements in Arabia, and to begin the first great wave of Islam's foreign conquests. After crushing a rebellion by several Arab tribes, he launched his armies against the neighbouring states of the Byzantine and Persian empires. Islam burst out of Arabia with such amazing force that the scope and speed of its expansion are unparalleled in the history of religions.

Omar   Abu Bekr personally chose Omar as his successor. Omar used the title "Commander of the Faithful", a designation retained by all the caliphs who succeeded him. Omar is regarded as one of the greatest caliphs because of his

The Spread of Islam

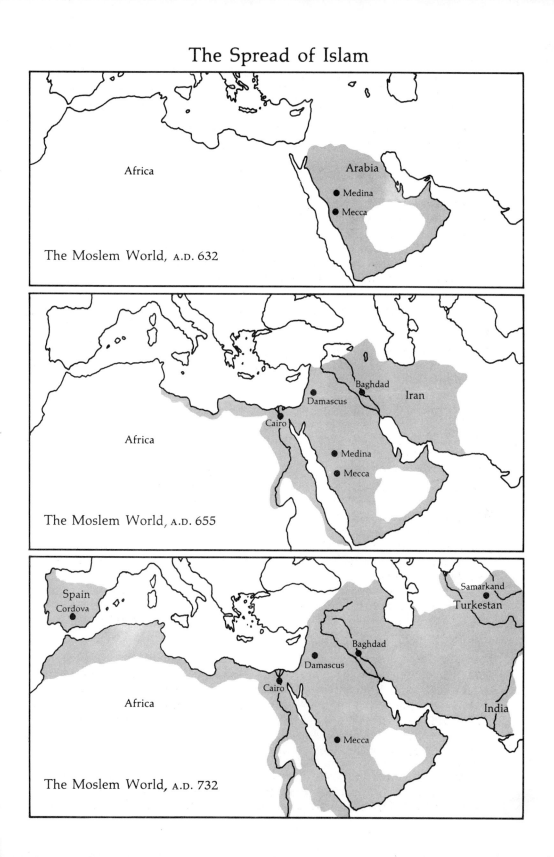

Africa

Arabia

● Medina

● Mecca

The Moslem World, A.D. 632

Africa

Damascus ●

Cairo ●

Baghdad ●

Iran

● Medina

● Mecca

The Moslem World, A.D. 655

Spain

Cordova ●

Samarkand ●

Turkestan

Baghdad ●

Damascus ●

Cairo ●

Africa

India

● Mecca

The Moslem World, A.D. 732

character, which was one of piety, honesty and courage, and also because he gave Islam its most outstanding conquests. Campaigns launched northward by Abu Bakr against Palestine and Syria were renewed. After these territories fell, the Moslem armies drove east into the heart of Persia and west into Egypt, thus opening the gates to India and North Africa respectively.

Islam was successful in winning victories over armies, but also over the hearts and minds of men. Three basic factors account for its rapid expansion: great military strength, firm and judicious administrative policies, and the appeal of the Moslem faith itself.

The Armies   The Arabs, and other peoples who later carried the banners of Islam, moulded themselves into an excellent fighting force, combining their exceptional horsemanship with the brilliant use of desert strategy.

Surprise attack by mounted swordsmen, supported by archers on foot, was the favourite Arab tactic, and was employed by a series of gifted military commanders. Effective motivation was provided by the Koran's teachings about the sinfulness of desertion, and the promise of immediate entry into Heaven for those who died for Islam.

Treatment of Subject Peoples   Omar, guided by the Koran, established many of the policies by which later caliphs governed the growing empire of Islam. Territories that surrendered peacefully were required to pay taxes, but usually their inhabitants did not suffer confiscation of their goods or property. Since this sort of treatment was often better than that which the people were receiving under their former rulers, thousands regarded the invading Moslem armies more as liberators than oppressors. But, when the Moslems encountered resistance, they were sometimes quite ruthless, inflicting physical violence and confiscation of property on their opponents, and then levying the usual taxes on top of this. Local political customs and institutions that were considered useful were integrated with the overall scheme of Moslem administration. As a rule, Jews and Christians paid fewer taxes because they were "people of the Book".

While conquered peoples were not forced to embrace Islam, their religious activities were often harassed or even severely curtailed. Moreover, within the empire, being a Moslem had several advantages: lower taxes, better legal protection and at least some educational and political opportunities. These considerations, plus the inherent attractions of Islam, caused the great majority of people in the conquered territories to convert to the Moslem faith.

The Attractions of Islam   These peoples were attracted to Islam for several reasons. Perhaps most important was the power, simplicity and cohesion of its message, summarized by the Shahada: "There is no God but Allah; Mohammed is the Prophet of Allah." Its basic teachings were easy to understand, and its devotional exercises simple to perform. Also enticing were the concepts of brotherhood and equality among all races and classes of the faithful. For those concerned about past sins, Islam taught that acceptance of the faith wiped out a man's past; errors committed in ignorance of the will of Allah would not be included in the reckoning on Judgment Day. No initial penalty, and no later sacrifices except for the observance of the five pillars, was necessary. A person could become a Moslem at any time, any place, simply by repeating earnestly and publicly the Shahada.

History of the Moslem Empire   Under a series of active caliphs, the armies of Islam won victory after victory. In the north and east, aided by the rivalry between the Byzantine and Persian emperors, they took Syria, Palestine, Iraq and Persia — eventually, they drove across the northern portion of the Indian subcontinent to the borders of China. In the west, they pushed through Egypt, across North Africa and into Spain. Subsequently, Moslem forces invaded France; if they had not been stopped by Charles Martel, the grandfather of Charlemagne, at the battle of Tours in 732, it is possible that much of Europe today might belong to Islam. At its peak in the ninth century, the Moslem Empire was the largest state and its caliph the most powerful man on earth. It had matched, if not exceeded, the Roman Empire at its zenith, and had made Arabic the common language of 90 million people.

The Caliphate   Omar was murdered in 644. He was succeeded by Uthman, who ruled for twelve years and was followed, in turn, by Ali. The succession of Ali was challenged by a rival faction, thus producing a split in Islam which persists to this day. Ali chose Kufa, in Iraq, rather than Medina as his capital, because it was more central to his burgeoning empire. When Ali was killed at Kufa in 661, his son, Hassan, relinquished his claim to the caliphate to Mu'awiya, Ali's former rival. Mu'awiya founded the Umayyad dynasty, which lasted from 661 to 750.

Operating from their capital at Damascus in Syria, the first Umayyads were good administrators and military leaders. During their reign, a distinctive Islamic culture began to form. Ultimately, the dynasty was undone by dissension, which stemmed in part from the growing autocracy and decadence of the later Umayyad caliphs. Scandals developed concerning their private lives, which featured lavish banquets and prolonged orgies conducted in their ornate palaces. In time, they were overthrown by a new dynasty, the Abbasids, who took the caliphate for themselves.

Under the Abbasid dynasty, which lasted from 750 to 1258, the Islamic Empire enjoyed its Golden Age. The capital was moved to Baghdad, which was transformed from a mere village into a heavily fortified yet beautiful city, the political and commercial hub of the largest, richest and most powerful civilization in the known world. Unfortunately, the Abbasid dynasty peaked early; its later caliphs steadily transformed the caliphate into a thoroughly autocratic position. No longer content to be the mere successors of the Prophet, they assumed the more exalted position of deputies of God himself. They became inaccessible to the people, surrounding themselves with aides, elaborate pomp and ceremony, and a general air of mystery.

As early as the ninth century, the Islamic Empire began to show signs of internal strife. Various provinces, including Spain, Morocco and Egypt, broke away and set up their own local dynasties. In 1055, the Seljuk Turks, themselves believers in Islam, swept in from Turkestan and conquered Baghdad. Thereafter, the Abbasids ruled only as figureheads. The Mongol invasion of the thirteenth century destroyed Baghdad, and ended the period when the caliph ruled over the entire Moslem world as both its political and spiritual leader. After the Mongols finally withdrew, the Ottoman Turks restored control over portions of the former Islamic Empire. They even conquered new territories, taking Constantinople in 1453 and later sweeping into south-eastern Europe, much of which they dominated until the late nineteenth century.

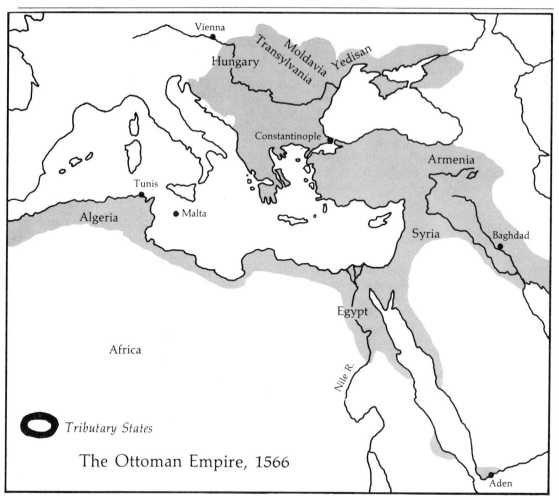

Vienna

Hungary
Transylvania Moldavia Yedisan

Constantinople

Armenia

Tunis
Algeria • Malta

Syria
Baghdad

Egypt

Africa

Nile R.

Tributary States

The Ottoman Empire, 1566

Aden

Trade contacts and missionary work brought new converts to the faith in such distant places as China, Borneo, Malaya, Indonesia and the Philippines. However, the Turks were unable to reunite all of the Moslem lands. It also proved impossible for them to recover the economic and cultural superiority which the Moslem world had formerly enjoyed. The Ottoman Empire, though large and a power in both European and Asian affairs, eventually declined. It finally collapsed in World War I. When Turkey was made a republic in 1922, the caliphate was abolished.

C. The Development of a Distinctive Islamic Civilization

The Nature of Islamic Culture   The fact that the Islamic world survived, and indeed flourished, despite the political misfortunes of its rulers, supports the view that the world of Islam had a vitality which made it independent of any institutional support of a political or military nature. This vitality was supplied by the religion of Islam itself, and the civilization that had developed around it. True, the political empire had been the vehicle by which both of these were spread and established, but once this had been accomplished, the Islamic religion and civilization proved capable of standing by themselves.

The Arab tribes that swept out of the Arabian peninsula to conquer what became the central portion of the Islamic Empire were religious zealots and good soldiers, but as a people they were still relatively uncivilized.

Originally, their only major cultural contribution to the new civilization that developed within the empire was the Arabic language. Byzantine and Persian influences were much stronger; the latter was particularly noticeable and was reflected in the areas of art, literature, philosophy and science. Other peoples who were incorporated into the empire contributed to its emerging culture in various ways. Islam's achievement was its ability to take these elements from several diverse cultures, synthesize them, and then develop a unique product from them.

Its Highlights   From the ninth to the twelfth centuries, Islamic culture flourished. Held together by a common religion, a common language, and a highly developed trading network, this civilization embraced such diverse and far-flung peoples as Spaniards, Moors, Egyptians, Turks, Arabs, Persians, Indians and Chinese. Progress was made in almost every conceivable field of cultural endeavour.

The construction of mosques became the principal vehicle for the development of a distinctive architectural style. In literature, works such as *The Arabian Nights,* and Omar Khayyam's *Rubaiyat* achieved international recognition. Lesser arts such as carving, ceramics, glassware, metalwork and carpet-making also produced some exquisite pieces. In all the arts, religious themes were a frequent source of inspiration.

Brilliant men from all parts of the Moslem world came to Baghdad, attracted by its pleasures and the excitement of being involved in the development of a new culture. These poets, artists, scientists and philosophers revived the thought of Greece and other ancient civilizations, made original contributions of their own, and thus rolled back the shrouds of ignorance from vast bodies of knowledge in mathematics, physics, chemistry, astronomy, medicine and other fields. Outstanding libraries and schools sprang up in Baghdad, Cairo, Granada and numerous other urban centres within the empire.

Its Significance   In addition to developing an outstanding culture in its own right, the world of Islam made contributions of virtually immeasurable value to modern Western civilization. This "cultural transfusion" occurred at three main points of contact: Spain, Sicily and the eastern shores of the Mediterranean. Moslem scholars brought "Arabic" numerals and indispensable mathematical concepts such as zero and decimals from India, paper-making and other important skills from China; they translated and transmitted the cultural legacy of ancient Greece and brightened parts of Europe during the Dark Ages. "While Europe north of the Pyrenees wallowed in the brutish conditions of the Dark Ages, Cordoba's citizens were enjoying public plumbing and illuminated streets."[18] Undoubtedly, the European Renaissance was inspired to a significant extent by Islamic civilization.

D. Theological Developments within Islam

How Moslem Theology has Developed   The main body of Moslem teachings rests, of course, on the Koran itself. But, like other religions, Islam has had to adapt to various peoples, lands and time periods. Over the centuries, its followers have found it necessary to decide what might be accepted as proper derivations from Mohammed's original teachings. Beyond those concepts to which all Moslem teachers throughout history have agreed, adherents of Islam also accept the Sunnas, or customs, which have been certified by a succession of scholars, and which are clearly based upon the Hadiths, or traditions, concerning Mohammed. Divisions more frequently appear when it becomes a matter of making inferences and deductions from original teachings. The Ulamas (learned ones), centred principally in North Africa and the Near East, have played a crucial role in the development of Moslem theology. Probably the greatest Islamic theologian of all time was Abu Homid al-Ghazzali, who synthesized Sunnite dogma and Sufi mysticism in the twelfth century.

Four Schools of Law   Various schools of thought have developed in Islam, each based on a particular way of establishing true belief. Most conservative is the Hanbali school, which demands strict conformity to the literal interpretation of the Koran. It is strongest today in Saudi Arabia. The Shafiite school, prevalent in Indonesia and southern portions of Arabia, is also fairly conservative. It preaches a return to the Koran and the Hadiths. It is therefore critical of the Hanafi school, which extends orthodox teaching by analogy, and adapts Islam to local conditions. Most Hanafites are found in India and China. A fourth school, the Malikites, while accepting the Koran and the Hadiths, also adapt their teachings to local conditions, relying on community consensus for verification.

Early Sects   The unity of Islam was first broken by a group known as the Kharijites (Secessionists) who charged that the caliph Ali was more interested in wealth and power than in practising religion. These religious fanatics were almost wiped out in battles with the caliph's forces. Other early splinter groups included the Murjites, who were quite liberal, tolerating Christians and Jews as well as all Moslem sects, and the Mutazilites, who were inclined to orthodox belief and missionary work.

The Shiites   Perhaps the most serious split today exists between the Shiites and the Sunnites. At the root of their original differences was the question of succession to the caliphate — whether it had to be hereditary, and restricted to the descendants of Mohammed, or whether it could be determined by election. The Shiites adhere to the former position, claiming that only Ali and his descendants had a legitimate right to lead the faithful. In their Friday prayers, they still curse the elected caliphs, such as Abu Bakr, Omar and Uthman. At the time of their origin, the Shiites resented the rule of the Umayyads, whom they regarded as usurpers. Politically, they were swept aside in the power struggle which produced the Abbasid dynasty. Numbering about 25 million, the Shiites are still prominent in India, Iraq and Iran. Both they and the more numerous Sunnites claim to be the most orthodox members of the Moslem faith.

The Shiites are somewhat pliable, adapting their beliefs as their life changes. Arguing that divine revelation expresses itself in the person of contemporary leaders, they believe that their imams are inspired by Allah. They also have the concept of a *Mahdi*, or divinely guided ruler. He is the last legitimate caliph, and will return to earth to unite the faithful under the true religion, conquer the world for Islam and reign in splendour for a thousand years. Predictably, several claimants to the title of "Mahdi" have arisen in Moslem history, with the result that several sub-sects, such as the Fatimites and the Ismailis, have developed within the Shiite movement.

The Sunnites   Because of their great numbers, the Sunnites are more dominant than the Shiites. They have tended to be more conservative, relying closely on the Koran and the Sunnas. Consequently, their movement has not suffered so many schisms. They did, however, produce a puritanical group known as the Wahhabis, who are discussed below.

Mysticism   The mystic movement in Islam is known as Sufism. A mystic is called a *sufi*, a name that probably is derived from the Arab word for wool, which was frequently worn by ascetics of various faiths, including Christianity. Sufism developed as a protest against tyrannical government by corrupt rulers, and against the formalism of worship which seemed to be for the sake of appearances only, lacking sincerity and conviction. Sufis tended therefore to disregard Moslem rules and to seek Allah through contemplation and direct emotional experience.

Often a zealous and perhaps gifted individual would leave his community to live as a hermit, and might gradually gather about him followers who would help him establish a religious order, complete with its own dress, rules and ritual. The great orders, known as dervishes, began to form in the later Middle Ages. One of the best known of these brotherhoods are the *Maulawiyah* or "Whirling Dervishes", who employ flute music and lengthy dance sequences to induce a feeling of religious ecstacy.

Other mystics forsook the relatively secure existence of an order, gave up their possessions, and travelled about as mendicants, preaching and living off the charity of their fellow Moslems. Some of them were fakes, but others were outstanding men of saintly stature. Understandably, the unorthodox habits and beliefs of these mystics did not endear them to the more conservative elements in the Moslem community, at least until the theologian Ghazzali made them respectable by championing their cause.

Among later orders, the *Wahhabis* are among the more familiar. They arose in Arabia in the eighteenth century; today, they control Mecca and are influential in southern Arabia. Austere, and rigidly orthodox, they represent a reaction against Western influence in the Moslem world and against degeneration within Islam itself. At the present time, there are literally hundreds of mystic orders, with millions of adherents. They are most prevalent in Egypt, Syria, Iraq, Turkey and Arabia. Many of them have been influenced by Christian, Hindu and Buddhist thinkers. Generally, the Shiites disapprove of the mystic orders, because they introduce novel ideas into Islam and tend to reduce the importance of the imams in religious life.

4. Islam in the Modern World

A. Recent Developments

The Trend to Reform   For centuries after its initial spectacular expansion, Islam tended to be rather conservative, and complacent in the belief that all truth had been revealed, that everything worth knowing was already known. Only the decline of Islam as a political force, with its attendant threat to the religious and cultural integrity of the Moslem world, caused this pattern to be broken. The nineteenth century brought encouraging new developments, chiefly in the persons of two dynamic thinkers, Jamal Din al Afghani and Mohammed Abduh.

      The latter was particularly influential, attacking conservatism and calling for, among other things, the modernization of Moslem education. He, and others like him, caused far-sighted Moslems to realize the necessity of change if Islam was to meet the challenges of the twentieth century, including the impact of Western technology, science, and political and social ideas upon Moslem countries. One result of such thinking has been a broader view of the proper role to be played by women in society. Progressive Moslems continue to press for extensive economic, social and legal reforms in their countries, and for greater tolerance and unity within the community of the faith.

Bahaism   On the theme of toleration, an interesting spin-off from the Shiite sect of Islam is the relatively new religion of Bahaism, founded in Persia in the late nineteenth century by Husayn ali Baha Ullah. This unusual man proclaimed his divine mission to unify all men and all religions. Persecuted and scorned, he nonetheless managed to create a devoted following, which continues to win converts in many places of the world, including North America. On this continent, the centre of Bahaism is located in Wilmette, Illinois. Among their other principles, the followers of this religion believe that all religions have a common base, that all prejudices must be eliminated, and that all mankind can be united through religion. Their goals include world peace, world government and a universal language.

B. The Situation of Islam Today

Continuing Difficulties   For many years, Islam has lacked an authority figure who could exert leadership over the entire Moslem world. This is reflected today in the religious and political disunity within Islam. Not only are there few indications of amalgamation among the various sects, but Moslem nations in the Middle East are having difficulty maintaining a united front against the state of Israel. Indeed, one of the foremost Moslem states, Pakistan, was split in two late in 1971 by a bloody civil war.

      Some Moslem authorities admit that the observance of the five pillars has become routine with many people, and that the community of the faithful lacks the fervour that it once had. Poverty, illiteracy and technological backwardness are contributing to a steadily mounting demand for sweeping reforms

Miller Services Ltd.

The Bahai International Temple at Evanston, Illinois, U.S.A.

in several Moslem countries. Until this demand is satisfied, Islam will probably go on losing ground among the more impatient members of the young generation. If they turn to Communism for a solution to their economic and social problems, Islam could be in rather serious trouble.

Encouraging Signs   On the brighter side, the numbers of the faithful continue to grow. This is partly because Moslem lands tend to have high birth rates, but it also reflects the success of missionary work, particularly in central Africa. Non-white peoples, many of whom have experienced Western imperialism in the last one hundred years, are currently more receptive to Islam than to Christianity. Moreover, despite the Russian efforts to strengthen ties between the Soviet bloc and the Moslem countries of the Middle East, there seems little likelihood that Communism will make significant inroads in the Islamic world in the near future.

     Although the Soviet Union may be somewhat less suspect than major Western countries as a potential friend, because it does not have a "colonial power" image to most Moslems, it still comes in for its share of criticism. One reason for this is that Moslems are the second largest religious group in the Soviet Union, and have been subjected to considerable persecution. Also, there obviously are too many fundamental differences between Islam and Marxism for them to be compatible to any great extent. Indeed, Communist parties are banned in many Moslem countries, some of which imprison local Communists for extended periods of time.

Islam is an optimistic and very practical faith. As the youngest of the world's major religions, it is proving itself to be at least as resilient as the others in the face of substantial problems, and appears to be more dynamic now than it has been for several centuries past.

Suggestions For Further Study

1. Investigate the various interpretations of how and when the Koran was compiled. Why are non-Moslems sceptical about the authenticity of the Koran and the Hadiths?

2. Authorities such as A. Bahm and A. C. Bouquet claim that, from conversations with pilgrims and travelling merchants, plus personal visits into areas such as Syria where substantial numbers of Jews and Christians lived, Mohammed became quite familiar with, and undoubtedly influenced by, the fundamental ideas of Judaism and Christianity. Yet another expert, G. E. von Grunebaum, remarks:

> . . . it can be said with certainty that he [Mohammed] had no close contact with the Christians there [Syria], nor did he attend a Christian service with any understanding.[19]

Investigate Mohammed's early life, to discover which viewpoint is more likely to be valid. In what ways do you think Islam was influenced by Judaism and Christianity?

3. Moslems believe that there is but one universal God, who has revealed one truth for all mankind. They also believe that prophets such as Abraham, Moses and Jesus received parts of this same truth, which was later revealed in its entirety to Mohammed. Yet there are conflicting views in the Scriptures of these men. How would Moslems account for these apparent contradictions in the Holy Scriptures which they recognize?

4. Why, in their prayers, do Moslems not emphasize petition, or asking God for favours and assistance?

5. What possible reasons might explain why Islam has no clergy or priestly class?

6. When Mohammed first went to Medina, many of its residents were of either Jewish or Christian faith. In his early teachings, Mohammed required Moslems to say their prayers facing Jerusalem. Why? What is suggested to you by the fact that he later persecuted Jews, and changed the direction of prayer from Jerusalem to Mecca?

7. One author, D. G. Bradley, claims: "The teachings of Mohammed have been preserved with more accuracy than those of the founder of any other religion."[20] Do you agree?

8. A. S. Tritton is sceptical of the motives behind Moslem expansion in the years following Mohammed's death. He states:

> The picture of the Muslim soldiers advancing with a sword in one hand and a Koran in the other is quite false. Not till seventy years after the death of Mohammed did a caliph arise who was more interested in converting his subjects than in taxing them.[21]

Investigate the accuracy of this criticism.

9. Would the advent of Communism in a Moslem country necessarily mean the end of Islam there? Explain your answer.

10. In what ways does Islam foster a strong sense of community and brotherhood among its adherents?

Notes

[1]*The Koran*, Sura XCVI, 1-5, as cited in Arthur Jeffery, ed., *Islam: Muhammad and His Religion*. New York: Bobbs-Merrill Co., Inc., 1958, p. 4. Copyright © 1958, by The Liberal Arts Free Press, Inc., reprinted by permission of the publisher, The Bobbs-Merrill Company, Inc.

[2]*The Koran*, Sura I, 1-7, as cited in J. A. Williams, ed., *Islam*. New York: George Braziller, 1962.

[3]David G. Bradley, *A Guide to the World's Religions*. Englewood Cliffs, N.J.: Prentice-Hall, 1963, p. 70.

[4]*The Koran*, Sura CXII, as cited in the Editors of the National Geographic Book Service, *Great Religions of the World*. Washington, D.C.: National Geographic Society, 1971.

[5]*The Koran*, Sura VI, 12, 59, as cited in Huston Smith, *The Religions of Man*. New York: The New American Library, Inc., 1958.

[6]*The Koran*, Sura XCIII, *ibid.*, p. 214.

[7]*The Koran*, Sura LXXXI, *ibid.*, p. 215.

[8]*The Koran*, Sura XXXVII, *ibid.*

[9]*The Koran*, Sura LXIX, Williams, *op. cit.*, p. 53.

[10]*The Azan*, as cited in Desmond Stewart and the Editors of Time-Life Books, *Early Islam*. New York: Time Incorporated, 1967, p. 142.

[11]Williams, *op. cit.*, pp. 220-221.

[12]*Ibid.*, p. 221.

[13]*The Koran*, Sura IX, 29, as cited in A. J. Bahm, *The World's Living Religions*. New York: Dell Publishing Co., Inc., 1964, p. 326; Carbondale: Southern Illinois University Press, 1971.

[14]*The Koran*, Sura VI, 151-153, as cited in A. S. Tritton, *Islam*. London: Hutchinson University Library, 1951, p. 124. Reprinted by permission of Hutchinson University Library, London.

[15]The Koran, Sura CIX, 6, Smith, *op. cit.*, p. 229.

[16]The Koran, Sura V, 48, *ibid.*, p. 229.

[17]Philip Hitti, *The Arabs: A Short History*. New York: St. Martin's Press, Inc., 1949, p. 32.

[18]Stewart and the Editors of Time-Life Books, *op. cit.*, p. 142.

[19]G. E. von Grunebaum, *Classical Islam: A History 600-1258*. London: George Allen & Unwin Ltd., 1970, p. 29.

[20]Bradley, *op. cit.*, p. 70.

[21]Tritton, *op. cit.*, p. 21.

Religion In Canada Today

Chapter Ten

Modern Christianity

Today, as in the age of the "Scientific Revolution", religion seems to be assailed on all sides. Faith seems to be placed in opposition to science. Old styles of worship are being pressured by the new. Churches are being asked more and more to take stands on issues about which they would have been silent even a few years ago. In these final chapters, some of the modern churches of Canada will be discussed regarding basic beliefs and with reference to their reactions to the pressures of the modern world. As will be seen, there have been sincere and honest efforts on the part of many churches to keep pace with the bewildering changes taking place in recent years and to meet the challenges which will no doubt be presented in the future.

In this chapter, a number of religious denominations in Canada today are to be discussed. Others which some consider to be significant have of necessity been omitted, but these are believed to be a small minority. Our guiding principle in selecting groups to be discussed has been to choose those which are the largest in terms of membership, those which most people would have at least heard of, and those which are growing in popularity today or which are also quite well established. Some of the newer or less well-known groups are discussed in the final chapter.

One of the things that will be most apparent after study of this chapter is the basic unity in belief and effort of these churches. The differences often seem relatively insignificant to the objective observer. As will be seen, some of the groups recognize this fact and are working towards some kind of united church, often through the Canadian or the World Council of Churches. Others, for reasons which they strongly believe to be valid, are opposed to the process.

The positions outlined here are the official positions of the churches in question, if the church publishes an official stand. Often, however, individuals or clergymen are more liberal than the official establishment and therefore are willing to accept wider interpretations of things than the church is officially willing to accept. We have attempted to indicate questions upon which there is a difference of opinion. Furthermore, within groups there tend to be widespread differences on even such basic questions as the existence of God; hence, the middle of the road approach taken here may be unacceptable to some. It is believed, however, that the information contained in this chapter reflects fairly the beliefs of most members of most groups on most issues most of the time. For further specific information, addresses are given where such can be obtained from each group.

Hopefully this chapter will be read with an open mind and a sincere attempt to understand the beliefs of others; efforts to ridicule others' sincere beliefs really accomplishes nothing. With an open mind, the basic similarity of these groups will become very clear.

1. Roman Catholicism

Sunday morning, St. Peter's Square, Rome. Thousands are gathered for the Sunday papal blessing. From his Vatican apartment high above the square, the frail figure of Pope Paul VI can be seen by the masses below. Here to many millions is the centre of Christendom. Here in these surroundings and at this moment the power of the Roman Catholic Church can be felt. But the church is also in rural Quebec as an old priest gives the last rites to an elderly farmer in the quiet of the farmhouse. It is in Germany, the Baltic states and Poland; it is in Spain, Portugal and Africa; it is in South America, the United States and Canada. Of a total population of about 22 million, over 9 million Canadians are of the Roman Catholic faith. Of 958,510,000 Christians throughout the world, 614,906,000 are Roman Catholic. In the true sense of the word "catholic" the Roman Catholic Church is "everywhere".

The Second Vatican Council originally called by Pope John XXIII was held in four sessions in St. Peter's Basilica in Rome and ran intermittently from September 11, 1962 to December 8, 1965. The council, sometimes called Vatican II, prepared and published sixteen documents which, taken together, marked some very significant departures from earlier statements of belief. As a general rule, the statements of belief discussed in this chapter have come from the documents of Vatican II. Books published before that council often follow a quite different method of presenting Catholicism than those published later. Vatican II has been regarded as a major watershed in Roman Catholic history. This will be clearly seen in the ensuing pages.

A. Basis of Authority and Government of the Church

What is the church? By way of a short, incisive definition, the church can be said to be that assembly of men and women which Jesus Christ called together to share in his life. The church has over the ages been variously and elaborately described by historians and theologians, and a recent (1968) description in the Creed of the People of God runs as follows:

> We believe in one, holy, catholic, and apostolic Church, built by Jesus Christ on the rock which is Peter. She is the Mystical Body of Christ: at the same time a visible society instituted with hierarchial organs, and a spiritual community; the Church on earth, the pilgrim People of God here below, and the Church filled with heavenly blessings: the germ and the first fruits of the Kingdom of God through which the work and the sufferings of Redemption are continued throughout human history, and which looks for its perfect accomplishment beyond time in glory. In the course of time, the Lord Jesus forms His Church by means of the sacraments emanating from His Plentitude. By these she makes her members participants in the mystery of the Death and Resurrection of Christ, in the grace of the Holy Spirit who gives her life and movement. She is therefore holy, though she has sinners in her bosom, because she herself has no other life but that of grace: it is by living by her life that her members are sanctified: it is by removing themselves from her life that they fall into sins and disorders that prevent the radiation of her sanctity. This is why she suffers and does penance for these offences, of which she has the power to heal her children through the Blood of Christ and the Gift of the Holy Spirit.[1]

The Church's Mission   What is the church's mission and its characteristics?

> Heiress of the divine promises and daughter of Abraham according to
> the Spirit, through that Israel whose Scriptures she lovingly guards
> and whose patriarchs and prophets she venerates; founded upon the
> Apostles and handing on from century to century their ever-living
> word and their powers as pastors in the Successor of Peter and the
> bishops in communion with him; perpetually assisted by the Holy
> Spirit: — she has the charge of guarding, teaching, explaining and
> spreading the Truth which God revealed in a then-veiled manner by
> the prophets and fully by the Lord Jesus. We believe all that is
> contained in the Word of God written or handed down, and all that the
> Church proposes for belief as divinely revealed, whether by a solemn
> judgment or by the ordinary and universal magisterium. We believe
> in the infallibility enjoyed by the Successor of Peter when he teaches
> *ex cathedra* as pastor and teacher of all the faithful, and which is
> assured also to the episcopal body when it exercises with him the
> supreme magisterium.
>   We believe that the Church founded by Jesus Christ and for
> which He prayed is indefectibly one in faith, worship and the bond of
> hierarchical communion. In the bosom of this Church, the rich variety
> of liturgical rites and the legitimate diversity of theological and spiritual
> heritages and special disciplines, far from injuring her unity, make it
> more manifest.[2]

Basis of Authority   What is the basis of authority in the church? Roman
Catholics, like all Christians, base their faith on the reality and authenticity of
God's revelation of himself to men in the Scriptures and especially in Jesus
Christ. Like some Christians, but not all, Catholics acknowledge Jesus Christ to
be God and their faith in his divinity is the only real basis of authority in the
church. This authority of "God revealing through Christ" is encountered, for
Catholics, in many places. It is first encountered in the words of writings of
those who heard Christ teach, or who knew men and women who heard Christ
teach; that is, it is encountered in tradition and Scriptures. These have become
the primary sources of the Catholic understanding of God's self-revelation
through Christ.

        There are other, though less primary sources, of the Catholic's
understanding of God's revelation through Christ: there are the interpretations
of the Bible made by great churchmen (sometimes called the Fathers) in the
early Christian centuries — John Chrysostom in the East, Augustine of Hippo in
the West; there are also the documents of early Church councils, like Nicaea;
and there are the treatises of theologians, all of whom are acknowledged,
whatever their competence, to be imperfect fallible witnesses to revealed truth,
and some of whom (e.g. Calvin) are acknowledged to have erred seriously.

        Roman Catholics go beyond this and say that a further important
source of authority in interpreting God's word is the college of bishops in
conjunction with the pope. And this brings a distinct divergence of opinion to
the fore. Non-Catholics usually do not accept the belief that the college of
bishops has an irreplaceable function in holding in balance the various factors
(Scripture, tradition, and contemporary experience, etc.) making it possible to

understand and express the Gospel. Catholics however insist that one must not only take into account these factors already mentioned, "but also the explicit and official positions adopted by the Church's college of bishops, both past and present."

Pope's Role   The role of the bishop of Rome or the pope (that is, Father, from the late Greek *papas*) in this process deserves some attention too. Non-Catholics are probably most familiar with the term "papal infallibility". Officially declared at Vatican I in 1870, it meant that when speaking on matters of morals or faith and when speaking in his capacity as pope (as opposed to speaking as a private individual) and when proposing a belief to be binding on the whole church, he was free from doctrinal error. It did not imply access to all truth. Many Christians maintain, in view of John 16:13, and Acts 15:28, etc., that the church is infallible. Vatican I declared that infallibility attaches even to certain papal declarations. Following that pronouncement an exaggerated importance came to be attached to the pope, so that many statements not within the bounds listed above have been popularly taken to be infallible pronouncements. In actual fact, a formally infallible statement has, since 1870, been issued only once, by Pius XII when in 1950 he defined the Assumption. The

Pope Paul delivers his 1972 Easter blessing to a large crowd gathered in St. Peter's Square. In his traditional message, he appealed to those people who practise violence and live by the laws of hatred and discrimination to mend their ways. He also assured the religiously oppressed in Communist and other lands that he had not forgotten them.

Religious News Service Photo

result of extravagant notions of the pope's power to make infallible declarations was that he came to be in the eyes of many people absolutely and totally dominant. In such a context, bishops (who as one large college, including the head bishop or pope, also speak for the universal church) came sometimes to be regarded as mere delegates of the pope, serving at his pleasure. The job of others in the church was supposedly one of explanation, defence, dissemination, and implementation of papal views and directives.

Since Vatican II, however, papal theory has been less narrowly understood. The pope is accepted as head of the church, acting for Christ as head of the church, and also as leader of the college of bishops. His normal mode of action is a collegial one, that is, he acts in collaboration and agreement with his fellow bishops. But it is misleading to refer to papal authority as "supreme and absolute" — only God himself has claim to that. A helpful comparison might be drawn between the relationship of the pope with the college of bishops and of the Canadian Prime Minister with the Canadian Cabinet. Bishops are not merely delegates of the pope; they possess real power as members of the college and as descendants of the college of Apostles. The two (pope and college) work together bound by the presence of the Holy Spirit and fraternal love. Technically ". . . the college of bishops is the possessor of supreme and full authority over the whole Church. This authority, although never independent of the pope, is not bestowed upon the college by the pope". In fact the pope's personal proposal to the Theological Commission in 1964 suggesting that the pope should be "answerable to the Lord alone in his action" was rejected.

Once these words on papal power and episcopal collegiality are understood, the practical controversies will be also, as in the case of the morality of birth control. When Pope Paul VI reaffimed that no presently known artificial means of birth control except the rhythm method should be used, it was made clear that this encyclical was not to be regarded as infallible. Though he is the leading moral authority of the church, the pope too is limited by his human condition, and like other men, experiences sin and error. The Catholic, however, in the difficult task of forming his own conscience "must pay serious heed to the pastoral and theological directives of his Church's principal bishop".

The point has been made above that the Catholic faith, which derives primarily from Jesus, is known through many channels: through the teachings of Jesus to the Apostles and written in the Bible, though interpretations of the Bible by churchmen and especially by the Fathers, through the decrees of Church councils, the writings of classical theologians, and scholarly disciplines, and in an especially living way through the teaching consensus of the college of bishops including the bishop of Rome, and by the teachings of the pope himself as successor of St. Peter and head of the church on earth.

Present Organization of the Church   Having seen the basis of authority in the church, let us now examine the organization of the Roman Catholic Church today. The pope is the single most important person in the church on earth. His responsibilities are to maintain authority in matters pertaining to faith and morals and to carry out the discipline and government of the church throughout the world. (See chart p. 297.) He has his own "civil service" to help him with his onerous duties. This civil service is called, in a term surviving from feudal times, his Court or Curia. He also appoints cardinals to serve as princely dignitaries and to elect his successor after his death or resignation.

Papal Election   The Roman Pontiff is elected by the cardinals in secret conclave, being chosen by a two-thirds majority vote. This procedure, a modification of older ones, was decreed by Pope John XXIII on September 5, 1962. The conclave is held in a sealed off area of the Vatican Palace and may begin on the fifteenth day after the death of a pope and must begin no later than the eighteenth day. Cardinals under the age of 80 may attend and vote. Voting takes place in the Sistine Chapel where four secret ballots are cast each day until one of the candidates obtains the required majority. The candidate so elected is asked by the dean of the College of Cardinals whether he accepts the office. He becomes pope immediately on giving an affirmative reply. The subsequent coronation is only a ceremonial recognition of the fact that he is the pope. In a ceremony called *adoratio*, the cardinals signify their obedience to the new pontiff in the Sistine Chapel before public announcement of his name is made from the main balcony of the Vatican. The fact of the election is signaled to the outside world by means of a puff of white smoke from a special chimney.

The pope is elected for life. If he should resign, which he may do, a new pope is elected. Any male Catholic may be elected, even one who is not a priest. If a layman were elected and he accepted the office, he would be ordained as a priest and bishop. If a priest were chosen he would be ordained as a bishop.

Cardinals   Cardinals (who nowadays are always bishops) are chosen by the pope to serve as his principal assistants and advisers in the central administration of church affairs. Collectively they form the Sacred College of Cardinals. From 1586 to 1959 the number of cardinals remained at 70. In 1959, John XXIII raised the number to 79, in 1960 to 85 and 1962 to 87. Paul VI increased membership to 118 in 1967 and to 134 (plus two *in petto*, that is, elected but name not released) in 1969. All cardinals must be priests and in 1962 John XXIII declared that all cardinals would henceforth be bishops. As of July 1, 1971 there were 122 cardinals from 45 countries or areas. Of these 9 were American and 4 were Canadian (Leger, McGuigan, Roy, Flahiff).

There are three categories of cardinals: cardinal bishops, cardinal priests, cardinal deacons. The cardinal bishops include the six titular bishops of the suburban sees of Rome and four major Eastern Rite Patriarchs. (Patriarch, a term originating in the Eastern Church, is the title of a bishop who, second only to the pope, has the highest rank in the hierarchy of jurisdiction. Subject only to the pope, an Eastern Rite Patriarch is the head of the faithful belonging to his rite throughout the world. The four rites are the *Copts*, the *Marionites*, the *Chaldeans* and the *Armenians*). These four were made cardinal bishops in February, 1965. (Two have since died). Cardinal priests who were formerly in charge of leading churches in Rome are bishops whose dioceses are outside Rome. Cardinal deacons are titular bishops assigned to full time service in the Roman Curia. They are selected by the pope and actually become cardinals on reception of the distinctive red biretta and ring (formerly sapphire, now gold). Their first public appearance as cardinals is to celebrate Mass with the pope.

The cardinals elect the pope (usually from their numbers) when the Holy See becomes vacant. They are major administrators of church affairs, serve in one or more departments of the Roman Curia, and enjoy a number of special rights and privileges. They are called Princes of the Church.

Age limits on the functions of cardinals were decreed by Pope Paul and took effect on January 1, 1971. Cardinal heads of curial departments and similar offices were asked to resign voluntarily at 75. At 80, cardinals automatically

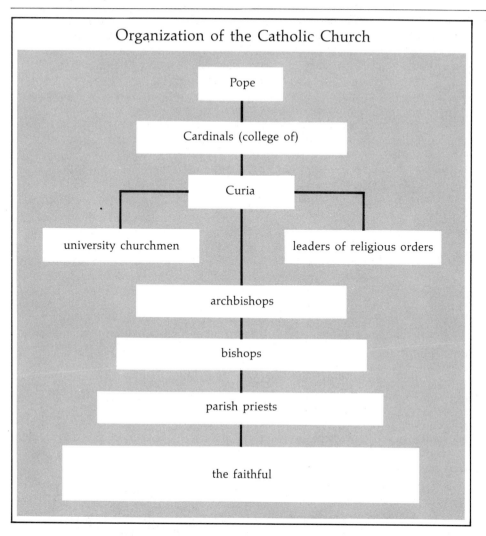

Organization of the Catholic Church

Pope

Cardinals (college of)

Curia

university churchmen

leaders of religious orders

archbishops

bishops

parish priests

the faithful

cease to be members of curial departments and similar offices and lose the right to take part in a papal election although they do retain membership in the College of Cardinals. (See chart above.)

The Curia The Roman Curia consists of a Secretariat of State, a Sacred Council for the Public Affairs of the church and a complex of ten congregations, five secretariats, three tribunals and six offices which handle the administration of church affairs at the highest level. This organization may be loosely compared to our Canadian Civil Service in that it carries out the practicalities of decisions after receiving them from the decision makers. The entire structure was reorganized in the 1960's to meet new and increased demands on its services. Among the changes were the appointment of several non-Italians to key curial positions, the admission of lay persons to serve as consultants to curial departments, increased independence of action within departments and use of modern languages instead of Latin in the day to day business schedule (though Latin remains the official language of the Curia).

The Secretariat of State provides the pope with the closest possible assistance in the case of the Universal Church and in dealings with all departments of the Curia; the cardinal secretary is the co-ordinator of operations. This official could be likened to a prime minister because of the role he plays in policy co-ordination at the highest level.

The Council for Public Affairs of the Church handles diplomatic relations with nations, other dealings with civil governments and matters connected with state law. With the Secretariat of State it supervises apostolic delegations and the Pontifical Commission for Russia. The council has the same head as the Secretariat of State.

Archbishops are prelates in charge of an archdiocese. The archdiocese is usually the major see in an ecclesiastical province consisting of a number of dioceses. As several Canadian counties unite to form a province, so do many dioceses unite to form an archdiocese. Presently Canada is divided into 18 archdioceses and there are 18 archbishops. The United States has 31 archdioceses and archbishops. Throughout the world, there are a total of 466 archdioceses and archbishops. (See chart p. 297.)

Bishops   In the hierarchy, the bishops follow archbishops. As archbishops rule large archdioceses, bishops rule the smaller and more numerous dioceses. Of a world total of 1,692 dioceses, Canada has 51 while the United States has 128.

It should be noted that bishops in hierarchical union with the pope and their fellow bishops (who include archbishops and cardinals) are thought to be the successors of the Apostles as pastors of the church. As such they have individual responsibility for the care of the local churches they serve and collegial responsibility for the care of the universal church. It is this group referred to when speaking of the council of bishops of whom the pope is the most important. (See chart p. 297.)

Priests   At the bottom of this pyramidal hierarchy is the church official with whom the masses have the closest direct contact: the priest (who has vowed to poverty, chastity and obedience). Though not always, he will probably be a parish priest — a parish being a subdivision of a diocese, as a township is a subdivision of a county. According to the 1972 *Catholic Almanac* there are 422,483 priests in the world of whom 276,293 are parish or diocesan priests. The other 146,190 are divided into teaching priests, missionaries, etc. In Canada there are some 4,958 parishes and a total of 14,187 priests. (See chart p. 297.)

University Churchmen   Fitting into the scheme somewhere, although where is not exactly clear, must be the Catholic university churchmen. Often extremely gifted theologians, they count among their number Rev. Gregory Baum and Professor Leslie Dewart of St. Michael's College in the University of Toronto. Through their writing and speaking they discuss points of theology, not uncommonly arguing against accepted doctrine. Though sometimes seen as rabble rousers and radicals by older more conservative churchmen, they do have a definite constructive ministry within the church. They consider it to be a valid task to test the present preaching, teaching and missionary activity of the church against the abiding tradition of the church whether expressed in Sacred Scripture, the documents of early councils or the writings of important theologians of the past. Thus, although there is sometimes obvious tension existing between the college council of bishops and these university theologians, the effects may be good. Though difficult to assess their influence precisely, many argue today that these men are influencing policy and must therefore be considered important. (See chart p. 297.)

B. Fundamental Theology: Some Basic Beliefs

The "Constitution on Revelation" promulgated by the Second Vatican Council is helpful in stating some of the basic concepts of the church.

I. Revelation Itself

"Through divine revelation, God chose to show forth and communicate Himself and the eternal decisions of His will regarding the salvation of men. That is to say, He chose to share with them those divine treasures which totally transcend the understanding of the human mind" (Art. 6).

"By this revelation . . . the deepest truth about God and the salvation of man shines out for our sake in Christ, who is both the mediator and the fullness of all revelation" (Art. 2).

From the start of the human race, God "manifested Himself to our first parents. Then, after their fall, His promise of redemption aroused in them the hope of being saved (cf. Genesis 3:15), and from that time on He ceaselessly kept the human race in His care, to give eternal life to those who perserveringly do good in search of salvation (cf. Romans 2:6-7). . . . He called Abraham in order to make of him a great nation (cf. Genesis 12:2). Through the patriarchs, and after them through Moses and the prophets, He taught this people (the Hebrews) to acknowledge Himself as the one living and true God . . . and to wait for the Saviour promised by Him, and in this manner prepared the way for the Gospel down through the centuries" (Art. 3).

Revelation in Christ

"Then, after speaking in many and varied ways through the prophets, 'now at last in these days God has spoken to us in his Son' (Hebrews 1:1-2). . . . Jesus perfected revelation by fulfilling it through His whole work of making Himself present and manifesting Himself; through His words and deeds, His signs and wonders, but especially through His death and glorious resurrection from the dead and final sending of the Spirit of truth. Moreover, He confirmed with divine testimony what revelation proclaimed, that God is with us to free us from the darkness of sin and death, and to raise us up to life eternal.[3]

Really, three key concepts are contained here. One is the belief that all people share in the sin of Adam and Eve, that is, the defying of God.

Original Sin

We believe that in Adam all have sinned, which means that the original offense committed by him caused human nature, common to all men, to fall to a state in which it bears the consequences of that offense, and which is not the state in which it was at first in our first parents, established as they were in holiness and justice, and in which man knew neither evil nor death. It is human nature so fallen, stripped of the grace that clothed it, injured in its own natural powers and subjected to the dominion of death, that is transmitted to all men, and it is in this sense that every man is born in sin. We therefore hold, with the Council of Trent, that original sin is transmitted with human nature, "not by imitation, but by propagation," and that it is thus "proper to everyone."

We believe that Our Lord Jesus Christ, by the Sacrifice of the Cross, redeemed us from original sin and all the personal sins committed by each one of us, so that, in accordance with the word of the Apostle, "where sin abounded, grace did more abound" (Romans 5:20).[4]

Second, there is the concept of *Incarnation,* that is, the belief that God's son Jesus was made man. Defined by the *1972 Catholic Almanac* Incarnation is:

The human coming-into-flesh or taking of human nature by the Second Person of the Trinity. He became human as the son of Mary, being miraculously conceived by the power of the Holy Spirit without ceasing to be divine.

Third there is the concept of *redemption.* According to this theory Jesus sacrificed himself by dying on the Cross so that the sins of men could be forgiven. By the fact that he was raised from the dead God's power over death was manifested. Thus by believing in him, man can be freed from the darkness of sin and death and can be raised to life eternal. These concepts are also stated, though in more concise terms, in the Apostles' Creed.

Because of her unique function Mary is specially venerated (though *not* worshipped) as one whose Immaculate Conception preserved her from Original Sin.

We believe that Mary is the Mother, who remained ever a Virgin, of the Incarnate Word, our God and Savior Jesus Christ, and that, by reason of this singular election she was, in consideration of the merits of her Son, redeemed in a more eminent manner, preserved from all stain of original sin, and filled with the gift of grace more than all other creatures.

Joined by a close and indissoluble bond to the mysteries of the Incarnation and Redemption, the Blessed Virgin, the Immaculate, was at the end of her earthly life raised body and soul to heavenly glory and likened to her risen Son in anticipation of the future lot of all the just; and we believe that the Blessed Mother of God, the New Eve, Mother of the Church, continues in heaven her maternal role with regard to Christ's members, co-operating with the birth and growth of divine life in the souls of the redeemed.[5]

Another very important belief is that of the *Trinity* — the belief that God is three persons, though one nature. Originally proclaimed at the Council of Nicaea in A.D. 325 it was more recently explained in the "Creed of the People of God", proclaimed by Pope Paul on June 30, 1968. The belief is as follows:

Profession of Faith

We believe in one only God, Father, Son and Holy Spirit, Creator of things visible such as this world in which our transient life passes, of things invisible such as the pure spirits which are also called angels, and Creator in each man of his spiritual and immortal soul.

The Holy Trinity

We believe that this only God is absolutely one in His infinitely holy essence as also in all His perfections, in His omnipotence, His infinite knowledge, His providence, His will and His love. He is He Who Is, as He revealed to Moses; and He is Love, as the Apostle John teaches us; so that these two names, Being and Love, express ineffably the same divine reality of Him who has wished to make Himself known to us and who, "dwelling in light inaccessible" (I Timothy 6:16), is in Himself above every name, above every thing and above every created intellect. God alone can give us right and full knowledge of this reality by revealing Himself as Father, Son and Holy Spirit, in whose eternal life we are by grace called to share, here below in the obscurity of faith and after death in eternal light. The mutual bonds which eternally constitute the Three Persons, who are each one and the same Divine Being, are the blessed inmost life of God Thrice Holy, infinitely beyond all that we can conceive in human measure. We give thanks, however, to the Divine Goodness that very many believers can testify with us before men to the Unity of God, even though they know not the mystery of the Most Holy Trinity.

God the Father

We believe, then, in the Father who eternally begets the Son; in the Son, the Word of God, who is eternally begotten; in the Holy Spirit, the uncreated Person who proceeds from the Father and the Son as their eternal Love. Thus, in the Three Divine Persons, coeternal and coequal with each other, the life and beatitude of God perfectly One superabound and are consummated in the supreme excellence and glory proper to uncreated Being, and always "there should be venerated Unity in the Trinity and Trinity in the Unity."

God the Son

We believe in Our Lord Jesus Christ, who is the Son of God. He is the Eternal Word, born of the Father before time began, and one in substance with the Father (homoousios Patri), and through Him all things were made. He was incarnate of the Virgin Mary by the power of the Holy Spirit, and was made man: equal therefore to the Father according to His divinity, and inferior to the Father according to His humanity, and Himself one, not by some impossible confusion of His natures, but by the unity of His person.

He dwelt among us, full of grace and truth. He proclaimed and established the Kingdom of God and made us know in Himself the Father. He gave us His new commandment to love one another as He loved us. He taught us the way of the Beatitudes of the Gospel: poverty in spirit, meekness, suffering borne with patience, thirst after justice, mercy, purity of heart, will for peace, persecution suffered for justice' sake. Under Pontius Pilate He suffered, the Lamb of God bearing in Himself the sins of the world, and He died for us on the Cross, saving us by His redeeming Blood. He was buried, and, of His own power, rose the third day, raising us by His Resurrection to that sharing in the divine life which is the life of grace. He ascended to heaven, and He will come again, this time in glory, to judge the living and the dead: each according to his merits — those who have responded to the love and piety of God going to eternal life, those who have refused them to the end going to the fire that is not extinguished.

And His Kingdom will have no end.

God the Holy Spirit

We believe in the Holy Spirit, who is Lord, and Giver of life, who is adored and glorified together with the Father and the Son. He spoke to us by the prophets; He was sent by Christ after His Resurrection and His Ascension to the Father; He illuminates, vivifies, protects and guides the Church; He purifies the Church's members if they do not shun His Grace. His action, which penetrates to the inmost of the soul, enables man to respond to the call of Jesus: "Be perfect as your Heavenly Father is perfect" (Matthew 5:48).[6]

Precepts   Besides these elements of theology there are some important moral and social obligations and certain precepts of the church. Those precepts are as follows. Roman Catholics must assist (that is, be present) at Mass on Sundays and holy days of obligations and must also desist from unnecessary servile works on these days. They must fast on appointed days — Ash Wednesday and Good Friday. Sins must be confessed at least once a year. Holy Communion must be received during the Easter time. Catholics must observe the laws of the church concerning marriage and must contribute to the support of the church.

Moral obligations are more difficult to state specifically though some are established clearly. Among these are adherence to the teachings of the Ten Commandments. These are broadened though to incorporate wider-ranging ideas: obedience to parents and others in authority; obligations of parents to children and of persons in authority to those in their care; respect for life, fidelity in marriage, justice and mercy, truth and love of neighbour. In this connection, many papal encyclicals have been issued expressing official church interest and involvement. In 1961 John XXIII issued "Christianity and Social Progress"; in 1963, "Peace on Earth". In 1967 Paul VI issued "Development of Peoples". These documents represent serious attempts to systematize the social implications of the gospel and the rest of divine revelation as well as the socially relevant writings of the Fathers of the church. Their contents are theological penetrations into social life, with particular reference to the rights of workers, the needs of the poor and those in underdeveloped countries, and humane conditions of life, freedom, justice and peace. In some respects, they read like legal documents; underneath however, they are gospel-oriented and intended to apply in daily life situations.

Vatican II   has brought some basic changes to Catholic attitude as well as to doctrine. The church no longer, for example, sees itself as the only visible expression of the gospel. There is the acceptance of the fact there are others within the "Body of Christ" besides just Roman Catholics. The "Dogmatic Constitution on the Church" promulgated by Vatican II states:

> The church recognizes that in many ways she is linked with those who, being baptized, are honored with the name of Christian, though they do not profess the faith in its entirety or do not preserve unity of communion with the successor of Peter . . . we can say that in some real way they are joined with us in the Holy Spirit, for to them too He gives His gifts and graces whereby He is operative among them with His sanctifying power . . . [Article 15].[7]

Furthermore it is now recognized that even the unbaptized may be saved.

> Finally, those who have not yet received the Gospel are related in various ways to the People of God. In the first place we must recall the people (the Jews) to whom the Testament and the promises were given and from whom Christ was born according to the flesh. . . . [cf. Romans 9: 4-5].

> But the plan of salvation also includes those who acknowledge the Creator. In the first place among these there are the Mohammedans. . . . Nor is God far distant from those who in shadows and images seek the unknown God. . . . Those who can attain to salvation who through no fault of their own do not know the Gospel of Christ or His church, yet sincerely seek God and, moved by grace, strive by their deeds to do His will as it is known to them through the dictates of conscience [Article 16].[8]

Thus, whereas it was once commonly thought that those who were not baptized members of the Roman Catholic Church could not attain salvation, such an opinion is no longer common among Catholics.

Two other changes must be mentioned also. There is now recognition that non-Christians often seek to serve God too. Thus, rather than ignoring other religious groups, the Roman Catholic Church now encourages dialogue though still firmly convinced that Jesus is the key, the focal point, and the goal of all human history. Secondly, no longer is the saving mission of the church seen only in terms of converting others. True, this is still an important task, but the socially oriented encyclicals mentioned earlier are proof that other factors are very important too.

C. The Sacraments and Liturgy

Catholicism teaches that Christ instituted seven sacraments: baptism, confirmation, Holy Eucharist, penance, anointing the sick (unction), holy orders and matrimony. He determined the substance of each sacrament but did not fix all the details of rite and symbolic activity. Christ is the priest or minister of every sacrament; human agents — an ordained priest, baptized persons entering into marriage, etc. — are secondary ministers. Sacraments have their power from Christ, not from the human who administers them. For example, during penance, the priest who hears confession and forgives, does so as the agent of Christ — only he can forgive sins against himself.

> The sacraments are actions of Christ and His Church which signify grace, cause it in the act of signifying it, and confer it upon persons properly disposed to receive it. They perpetuate the redemptive activity of Christ, making it present and effective.[9]

Baptism Baptism is the sacrament of spiritual regeneration by which a person is incorporated in Christ and made a member of His Mystical Body, given grace and cleansed of Original Sin. Actual sins and punishment due for them are remitted if the person baptized was guilty of such sins; this may be the case where a person is baptized after reaching the age of reason. As water is poured on the head of the person (infusion) the words, "I baptize you in the name of the Father and of the Son and of the Holy Spirit", are repeated. The usual minister of baptism is a priest, but in an emergency anyone, including a non-Catholic, can validly baptize. Natural water is sufficient, though specially blessed water is sometimes used. The church recognizes as being valid baptism by immersion, aspersion (sprinkling of the water) or infusion (pouring of the water) — though in the Roman Rite (that is, most of Canada and the Western world) infusion is used most often. The baptism of infants has always been considered valid and it may also be conferred conditionally where there is doubt about the validity of a previous baptism.
　　Baptism is necessary for salvation. If baptism of water is impossible, it may be supplied by baptism of blood where martyrdom is suffered for the Catholic faith or some Christian virtue, or by the baptism of desire (that is, perfect contrition joined with at least the implicit intent of doing whatever God wills that men should do for salvation). A person must be validly baptized before he can receive any of the other sacraments, and must have a sponsor in baptism.

Any Catholic in his fourteenth year or older may be sponsors or *godparents*. Only one is required, though two (one of each sex) is acceptable. Their role in the ceremony is secondary to that of the parents. They serve as representatives of the community of faith and with the parents, as proxies for the child, request baptism on his (or her) behalf, and perform other ritual functions. After baptism their function is to serve as proxies for the parents should they for any reason be unable to provide for the religious training of the child. At baptism, children are given Christian names, usually the name of a saint.

The Holy Eucharist (Holy Communion)   This sacrament is the one in which Christ is believed to be present and is received in the appearances of bread and wine. The matter is unleavened bread of wheat (leavened in the Eastern Rites) and wine of grape. The words of consecration are "This is my body. . . . This is the cup of my blood". Only a priest can consecrate bread and wine so they become the actual body and blood of Christ (transubstantiation — the conversion of the bread and wine to the body and blood of Christ). After consecration, however, the Eucharist can be administered by deacons or lay persons.

In the Roman Rite the faithful partaking of the Communion usually receive the bread only; in some circumstances, however, they may receive both bread and wine.

Sisters of the Precious Blood in Pembroke, Ontario, make Communion wafers.

Miller Services Ltd.

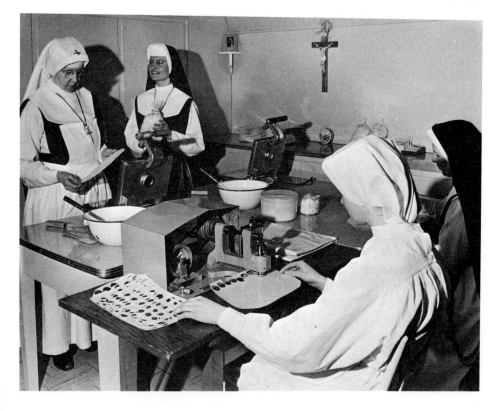

In Eastern Rite practice the faithful usually partake by reception of a piece of consecrated leavened bread which has been dipped into consecrated wine. Conditions for receiving the Eucharist are the state of grace, the right intention and observance of the Eucharistic fast which states that under normal conditions no food or drink (except water) should be consumed for one hour before taking the Eucharist. The faithful of Roman Rite are required by a precept of the church to receive Communion at least once a year during the Easter time (Lent).

Penance   Penance is the sacrament instituted by Christ for the forgiveness of sins committed after baptism. Its prime object is to restore to grace persons in the state of mortal sin. In the *Catholic Almanac* sin is defined as being "rejection of God manifested by free and deliberate violation of His law by thought, word or action". Mortal sin — involving serious matter, sufficient reflection and full consent — results in total alienation from God, making a person "dead" to sanctifying grace, incapable of performing meritorious supernatural acts and subject to everlasting punishment.

The first step is confession — the act by which a person tells or confesses his sins to a priest who is authorized to give absolution (or forgiveness) in the sacrament of penance. During confession all mortal sins must be confessed; lesser sins (venial) should be confessed but this is not technically a must. Such confessions of course are private, with the priest sworn to secrecy. Even before the actual confession, the person must be contrite, that is, he must be sorry for having sinned and must be sincerely desirous of amending his sin. Also the penitent must have the intention of performing the works of penance assigned by the confessor.

Absolution of sins is done by the priest by the words, "I absolve you from your sins; in the name of the Father, and of the Son, and of the Holy Spirit. Amen." Priests receive the power to absolve by virtue of their ordination, and the right to absolve by virtue of jurisdiction given them by their bishop. This so-called "power of the keys" is spiritual authority and jurisdiction in the church, symbolized by the keys of the Kingdom of Heaven. Christ promised the keys to St. Peter, as head-to-be of the church [Matthew 16: 19], and commissioned him with full pastoral responsibility to feed his lambs and sheep [John 21: 15-17]. The pope, as the successor of St. Peter, has this power in a primary and supreme manner. The bishops of the church also have the power, in union with the pope. Priests share it through holy orders and the delegation of authority. Thus, forgiveness of sin comes from Christ through the pope, bishops and priests. Any priest can absolve a person in danger of death, in the absence of a properly qualified priest; this includes a priest who is under the penalty of excommunication or suspension.

A precept of the church obliges the faithful of Roman Rite guilty of serious sin to confess at least once a year. However it is strongly suggested that the sacrament be taken more often, not only for forgiveness of sin but also for reasons of devotion when there are no serious sins to be confessed.

Confirmation   Confirmation is the sacrament by which a baptized person, through anointing with chrism (a mixture of olive or other oil and balm, blessed by a bishop) and the laying on of hands, is endowed with the gifts and special strength of the Holy Spirit for mature Christian living. The sacrament is the completion of baptism and can be received only once.

The ceremony consists of the anointing of the forehead with chrism and the imposition of hands by the minister. As the chrism is delivered the minister says, "I sign you with the sign of the cross and confirm you with the chrism of salvation, in the name of the Father and of the Son and of the Holy Spirit".

A sponsor — at least fourteen years of age, confirmed, and of the same sex — is required for the person being confirmed. This sponsor can not be the same as for baptism. In the Roman Rite, it has been customary for children to receive confirmation within a reasonable time after first Communion and confession. There is a developing trend however, to defer confirmation until later when its significance as the sacrament of Christian maturity becomes more evident.

In the Eastern Rites, confirmation is administered at the same time as baptism. Adult converts are confirmed as soon as conveniently possible after their reception into the church.

Anointing of the Sick (Extreme Unction)   This sacrament, promulgated by St. James the Apostle [James 5:13-15], is for the spiritual and physical welfare of persons who are seriously ill and in some danger of death from internal causes. By the anointing with blessed oil and the prayer of a priest, the sacrament confers on the person comforting grace, the remission of venial sins and unconfessed mortal sins, and sometimes results in an improved state of health.

Usually the eyes, ears, nose, mouth, hands and feet of the sick are anointed, or, in cases of emergency, a single anointing of the forehead will suffice. As this is done, the following words are spoken by the priest: "By this holy anointing and His most loving mercy, may the Lord pardon you for any sins you have committed by sight, hearing, etc." Anointing of the sick (formerly called extreme unction) may be received more than once, for example in new or continuing stages of serious illness. Ideally, the sacrament should be administered while the recipient is conscious and in conjunction with the sacraments of penance and the Eucharist. It may be administered conditionally even after apparent death.

Matrimony   The Catholic Church, in line with the belief that it was established and commissioned by Christ to provide and administer the means of salvation to men, claims jurisdiction over the baptized persons in matters pertaining to marriage, which is a sacrament. Some of the formalities include deciding the time and place of the ceremony, doctrinal and moral instruction concerning marriage and the recording of data in documentary form which prove the eligibility and freedom of the persons to marry.

Problems have sometimes been found to arise in mixed marriages where one of the partners is non-Catholic. To attempt to minimize these, there are programmes of instruction for the non-Catholic in the essentials of the Catholic faith for the purposes of understanding. Desirably, some instruction should also be given the Catholic party regarding his or her partner's beliefs. The Catholic party to a mixed marriage is required to declare his or her intention of continuing practice of the Catholic faith and to promise to do all in his power to share his faith with children born of the marriage by having them baptized and raised as Catholics. No declarations or promises are required of the non-Catholic party, but he (she) must be informed of the declaration and promise made by the Catholic. A non-Catholic minister may not only attend a marriage but may also address, pray with and give his blessing to the couple following the marriage ceremony. All of these points are radical departures from accepted norms of the pre-Vatican II era.

According to church teaching, a valid and consummated marriage of baptized persons cannot be dissolved by any human authority or any cause other than the death of one of the partners. There are some conditions then under which dissolution is possible. Among them: a valid but unconsummated marriage of baptized persons; a baptized and unbaptized person; a very seldom granted papal dispensation, and a few others.

Because of the unity and indissolubility of marriage, the church denies that civil divorce can break the bond of a valid marriage. However, because of the possibility of marital distress, the church permits an innocent and aggrieved party (husband or wife) to seek and obtain a civil divorce for the purpose of acquiring title and right to such civil effects of divorce as separate habitation, maintenance and custody of children. This divorce, if obtained, does not break the bond of a valid marriage. No remarriage is possible.

A decree of nullity, sometimes improperly called an annulment, may on occasion be granted. This is a decision by a competent church authority — a bishop, a diocesan marriage tribunal or the Sacred Roman Rota — that an apparently valid marriage was actually invalid from the beginning because of the unknown or concealed existence from the beginning of an essential defect in consent, or a condition placed by one or both of the parties against the very nature of marriage. In late 1971, Pope Paul instituted some new rules designed to speed the handling of such cases; previously such decisions were known to have taken years.

Children are considered to be the supreme gift of marriage; thus birth control is an area of major interest within the church today. On this issue, though not invoking papal infallibility, Pope Paul spoke authoritatively on July 29, 1968. Following are a number of key excerpts from the document called *Humanae Vitae*; this document was framed in the pattern of traditional teaching and statements:

> Marriage doctrine and morality were the subjects of the encyclical "Humanae Vitae" issued July 29, 1968, by Pope Paul VI. Following are a number of key excerpts from the document, which was framed in the pattern of traditional teaching and statements by the Second Vatican Council.
>
> ". . . each and every marriage act ('qulibet matrimonii usus') must remain open to the transmission of life" (Art. 11).
>
> "Indeed, by its intimate structure, the conjugal act, while most closely uniting husband and wife, capacitates them for the generation of new lives, according to laws inscribed in the very being of man and of woman. By safeguarding both these essential aspects, the unitive and the procreative, the conjugal act preserves in its fullness the sense of true mutual love and its ordination toward man's most high calling to parenthood" (Art. 12).
>
> "It is, in fact, justly observed that a conjugal act imposed upon one's partner without regard for his or her condition and lawful desires is not a true act of love, and therefore denies an exigency of right

moral order in the relationships between husband and wife. Hence, one who reflects well must also recognize that a reciprocal act of love which jeopardizes the responsibility to transmit life — which God the Creator, according to particular laws, inserted therein — is in contradiction with the design constitutive of marriage and with the will of the Author of life. To use this divine gift, destroying, even if only partially, its meaning and its purpose, is to contradict the nature both of man and of woman and of their most intimate relationship, and therefore it is to contradict also the plan of God and His will" (Art. 13).

". . . the direct interruption of the generative process already begun, and, above all, directly willed and procured abortion, even if for therapeutic reasons, are to be absolutely excluded as licit means of regulating birth.

"Equally to be excluded . . . is direct sterilization, whether perpetual or temporary, whether of the man or of the woman. Similarly excluded is every action which, either in anticipation of the conjugal act, or in its accomplishment, or in the development of its natural consequences, proposes, whether as an end or as a means, to render procreation impossible.

"To justify conjugal acts made intentionally infecund, one cannot invoke as valid reasons the lesser evil, or the fact that such acts would constitute a whole together with the fecund acts already performed or to follow later and hence would share in one and the same moral goodness. In truth, if it is sometimes licit to tolerate a lesser evil in order to avoid a greater evil or to promote a greater good, it is not licit, even for the gravest reasons, to do evil so that good may follow therefrom; that is, to make into the object of a positive act of the will something which is intrinsically disorder, and hence unworthy of the human person, even when the intention is to safeguard or promote individual, family or social well-being.

"Consequently, it is an error to think that a conjugal act which is deliberately made infecund, and so is intrinsically dishonest, could be made honest and right by the ensemble of a fecund conjugal life" (Art. 14).

"If, then, there are serious motives to space out births, which derive from the physical or psychologica conditions of husband and wife, or from external conditions, the Church teaches that it is then licit to take into account the natural rhythms immanent in the generative functions, for the use of marriage in the infecund periods only, and in this way to regulate birth without offending the moral principles which have been recalled earlier" (Art. 16).

Pope Paul called the foregoing teaching authoritative, although not infallible. He left it open for further study. As a practical norm to be followed, however, he said it involved the binding force of religious assent.

With pastoral concern, the Pope said: "We do not at all intend to hide the sometimes serious difficulties inherent in the life of Christian married persons; for them, as for everyone else, 'the gate is narrow and the way is hard that leads to life.' But the hope of that life must illuminate their way, as with courage they strive to live with wisdom, justice and piety in this present time, knowing that the figure of this world passes away.

"Let married persons, then, face up to the efforts needed, supported by the faith and hope which 'do not disappoint . . . because God's love has been poured into our hearts through the Holy Spirit, who has been given to us.' Let them implore divine assistance by persevering prayer; above all, let them draw from the source of grace and charity in the Eucharist. And, if sin should still keep its hold over them, let them not be discouraged but rather have recourse with humble perseverance to the mercy of God, which is poured forth in the sacrament of penance."

Exception was taken to the binding force of the encyclical — notably by the bishops of Belgium, Austria and France, and many theologians — for several reasons: rights of conscience; questions concerning the natural law concept underlying the encyclical; the thesis of totality; the proposition that contraception may in some cases be the less of two evils. All agreed, however, that conscientious objection to the encyclical could not be taken without serious reasons and reflection.

Pope Paul, since publication of the encyclical, has not moved to alter its contents or to mitigate its binding force.[10]

Holy Orders

Holy orders is the sacrament by which spiritual power and grace are given to enable an ordained minister to consecrate the Eucharist, forgive sins, perform other pastoral and ecclesiastical functions, and form the community of the People of God. Holy orders confers a character on the soul and can be received only once. The minister of the sacrament is a bishop.

Holy orders, like matrimony but in a different way, is a social sacrament. As the Second Vatican Council declared: "For the nurturing and constant growth of the People of God, Christ the Lord instituted in His Church a variety of ministers which work for the good of the whole body. For those ministers, who are endowed with sacred power (by ordination), serve their brethren so that all who are of the People of God . . . may arrive at salvation. . . . Bishops . . . with their helpers, the priests and deacons, have taken up the service of the community, presiding in place of God over the flock, whose shepherds they are, as teachers for doctrine, priests for sacred worship, and ministers for governing" ("Dogmatic Constitution on the Church," Arts. 18, 20).

The fullness of the priesthood belongs to those who have received the order of bishop. Bishops, in hierarchical union with the pope and their fellow bishops, are the successors of the Apostles as pastors of the Church: they have individual responsibility for the care of the local churches they serve and collegial responsibility for the care of the universal Church. In the ordination or consecration of

Courtesy of Catholic Truth.

Consecration of a bishop: Bishop Hubert O'Connor, O.M.I., of Whitehorse, Yukon. Note the "laying on of hands", a gesture stressing the line of authority down through the years from the time of Christ.

bishops, the essential form is the imposition of hands by the consecrator(s) and the assigned prayer in the preface of the rite of ordination.

A priest is an ordained minister with the power to celebrate Mass, administer the sacraments, preach and teach the word of God, impart blessings, and perform additional pastoral functions, according to the mandate of his ecclesiastical superior.

Concerning priests, the Second Vatican Council stated:

". . . the divinely established ecclesiastical ministry is exercised on different levels by those . . . called bishops, priests and deacons. Priests, although they do not possess the highest degree of the priesthood, and although they are dependent on the bishops in the exercise of their power, are nevertheless united with the bishops in sacerdotal dignity. By the power of the sacrament of orders, in the image of Christ the eternal High Priest (Heb. 5:1-10; 7:24; 9:11-28), they are consecrated to preach the Gospel and shepherd the faithful and to celebrate divine worship, so that they are true priests of the New Testament. . . . Priests, prudent cooperators with the episcopal order, its aid and instrument, (are) called to serve the People of God . . ." (Op. cit., Art. 28).

In the ordination of a priest of Roman Rite, the essential matter is the imposition of hands on the heads of those being ordained by the ordaining bishops. The essential form is the accompanying prayer in the preface of the ordination ceremony. Other elements in the rite are the presentation of the implements of sacrifice — the chalice containing wine and the paten containing a host — with accompanying prayers.

Regarding the order of deacon, the constitution stated:

"At a lower level of the hierarchy are deacons, upon whom hands are imposed 'not unto the priesthood, but unto a ministry of service'. For, strengthened by sacramental grace and in communion with the bishop and his group of priests, they serve in the diaconate of the liturgy, of the World, and of charity to the People of God.

"It is the duty of the deacon, according as it shall have been assigned to him by competent authority, to administer baptism solemnly, to be custodian and dispenser of the Eucharist, to assist at and bless marriages in the name of the Church, to bring Viaticum to the dying, to read the Sacred Scripture to the faithful, to instruct and exhort the people, to preside over the worship and prayer of the faithful, to administer sacramentals, to officiate at funeral and burial services. (Deacons are) dedicated to duties of charity and administration. . . .

". . . the diaconate can in the future be restored as a proper and permanent rank of the hierarchy. It pertains to the competent territorial bodies of bishops . . . with the approval of the Supreme Pontiff, to decide whether and where it is opportune for such deacons to be established for the care of souls. With the consent of the Roman Pontiff, this diaconate can, in the future, be conferred upon men of more mature age, even upon those living in the married state. It may also be conferred upon suitable young men, for whom the law of celibacy must remain intact" (Ibid., Art. 29).

The Apostles ordained the first seven deacons (Acts 6:1-6): Stephen, Philip, Prochorus, Nicanor, Timon, Pharmenas, Nicholas.

The Church later assigned ministerial functions to men in the orders of subdeacon, acolyte, exorcist, reader and porter.

A subdeacon has specific duties in liturgical worship, especially at Mass. The order, which was mentioned for the first time about the middle of the third century, was regarded as minor until the 13th century; afterwards, it was called a major order in the West but not in the East. Together with the following minor orders, it is of ecclesiastical origin.

An acolyte serves in a minor capacity during acts of divine worship.

An exorcist is empowered to perform services of exorcism for expelling evil spirits. This function, however, has been reserved to specially delegated priests.

A reader takes part in the Liturgy of the Word by reading assigned passages of Sacred Scripture.

The order of porter originated in the early Church; it was

his function to guard the entrance to an assembly of Christians and to ward off undesirables who tried to gain admittance.

Tonsure is the ceremony in virtue of which a man is raised to the clerical state and made capable of receiving orders; it is not an order but a sacramental. In this ceremony, the hair of the candidate is clipped and he is vested with a surplice.[11]

Recent Changes in Liturgy   Many changes, mostly emanating from Vatican II, have considerably altered Roman Catholic services from what they were prior to 1962. In 1964, revised rituals for administration of the sacraments in popular languages were approved and passed into general use in many countries. By the end of the year popular languages were being used at Mass. In 1966, a number of bishops in the United States were granted permission for the celebration of Mass in private homes and other places. In some places, bishops allowed stringed instruments and permitted "folk" Masses for young people. In 1971, revised funeral services began to stress more clearly the theme of Resurrection. In some areas that same year, bishops were permitted to allow laymen to distribute Holy Communion under certain conditions of pastoral need. In addition, many dozens of other minor changes were made in an attempt to allow the church to be more fully in tune with the changing conditions of today.

D. Salvation and the Afterlife

Salvation is (1) the liberation of men from sin and its effects, (2) reconciliation with God in and through Christ and (3) the attainment of union with God forever in the glory of heaven as the supreme purpose in life, and as the God-given reward for fulfillment of his will on earth. Salvation-in-process begins and continues in this life through union with Christ in faith professed and in action. Its final term is union with God and the whole community of the saved in the ultimate perfection of God's Kingdom. The church teaches that: God wills the salvation of all; people are saved in and through the church; membership in the church established by Christ is necessary for salvation; people with this knowledge and understanding who deliberately reject this church, cannot be saved. In the context of Catholic belief, the Catholic Church is the church founded by Christ.

This very strong final sentence is softened slightly though, by a decision made by Vatican II:

> Those also can attain to salvation who through no fault of their own do not know the Gospel of Christ or his [Catholic] Church, yet sincerely seek God and, moved by grace, strive by their deeds to do His will as it is known to them through the dictates of conscience. Nor does Divine Providence deny the helps necessary for salvation to those who, without blame on their part, have not yet arrived at an explicit knowledge of God and with His grace strive to live a good life. Whatever good or truth is found among them is looked upon by the Church as preparation for the Gospel. She knows that it is given by Him who enlightens all men so that they may finally have life. ["Dogmatic Constitution on the Church", Article 16.][12]

Those referred to here of course would constitute the vast numbers of people who are members of other religions and would therefore not know "the Gospel of Christ or his [Catholic] Church". This may well include Moslems, Jews, Hindus, Buddhists, etc. It may also include large numbers who belong to other Christian sects and who therefore do not fully know the teaching of the Catholic Church on certain points. Therefore, it should not be understood that one cannot be saved unless a member of the Roman Catholic Church — this is not a teaching of that church.

Judgment   Upon death, there is an immediate Judgment to decide where the person's soul will go. Hell is the state of punishment of the damned, that is, those who die in mortal sin, in a condition of self-alienation from God and of opposition to the divine plan of salvation. The punishment of Hell begins immediately after death and lasts forever. Purgatory is the state or condition in which the souls of those who have died in the state of grace suffer for a time before they are admitted into Heaven. This is in order that they may be cleansed of unrepented venial sins and/or to make satisfaction for temporal punishment still due for his sins. The "limbo" of the Fathers was the state of rest and natural happiness after death enjoyed by the just of pre-Christian times before and until they were admitted to Heaven following the Ascension of Christ. Belief in this matter is stated in the Apostles' Creed. The existence of limbo for un-baptized persons of infant status — a state of rest and natural happiness — has never been formally defined. After Purgatory has achieved its purpose, the soul may then move on to Heaven which is the state of those who, having achieved salvation, are in glory with God. At the Second Coming of Christ, Final Judgment will take place in which all people who have ever lived on earth will be bodily resurrected and judged finally for all eternity. At this time, official doctrine states, the body will be re-united with the soul in the state of Heaven or Hell.

Conclusion

Outlining these doctrinal beliefs of the church is not to say that all of the faithful must obey and accept all of them. *Many* are the areas of grave dispute today within the church. Some today doubt that because of Jesus' divinity he was all-knowing from birth. Others doubt the concept of Original Sin being placed on all people because of the sin of Adam and Eve. Many doubt that the pope can be infallible under any circumstances. But this does not mean that these people are not "good" Catholics; nor does it mean that they will be removed from membership in the church. Do not forget, there were those who doubted the need of conducting the Mass in Latin — and recently their views have been accepted. The same may be true of these other situations — in time.

The lack of haste with which changes have come is one of the major criticisms of the church, although Vatican II went a long way to defuse that argument. Another criticism is that the church does not seem relevant to people today, particularly the young. All churches seem to be experiencing this phenomenon. However the Catholic Church has been hit particularly hard, for it is losing many of its key officers — priests and nuns. In 1971 Father Francais Houtart, director of the Institute of Social and Religious Studies at Louvain University reported that 3,800 priests made application to be absolved of their priestly vows in 1970. The total number of such requests from 1962 to 1970 was more than 14,000 mostly from priests between 30 and 45 years of age. During the same time, he estimated that 25,000 had left the active ministry without formally requesting release from their clerical obligations.

So great is the church's concern over this trend that Pope Paul VI felt obligated to speak pointedly about it. On Holy Thursday 1971 he deplored the "moral mediocrity" of priests who abandon the priesthood and called them "runaway brothers" who scandalize their communities. "How", the Holy Father asked, "can one fail to weep for the conscious defection of some? How can one fail to deplore the moral mediocrity which seeks to justify as natural and logical the breaking of a real promise which has been thought over for a long time and solemnly professed before Christ and the Church?" His remarks were exceptionally striking because they followed a reference to the flight of Judas (Jesus' betrayer) from the Upper Room during the Last Supper. He said:

> I cannot think of this tragic Easter drama without also in my spirit as a bishop and a shepherd associating it with the memory of the abandoning, of the flight, of so many brothers in the priesthood.

But there has been much effort exerted recently to overcome justified criticism; much is being done to speed warranted change; much is being done to realize the goal of a Christendom united under Christ. Worthy of note too is the fact that, oftentimes, official doctrine tends to be a little more conservative than the practice of many of the priests and the faithful. Stated otherwise, official doctrine is not always the strict practice. Sometimes the practice is closer to the needs of the flock. The Roman Catholic Church has proven itself to be capable of relatively speedy change; there is reason to believe that it will continue to be so and hence remain a vibrant faith for years to come.

Summary *

Membership Requirements:
Adequate information in and commitment to the beliefs and practices of the Roman Catholic Church.

Essentials of its Nature and Purpose:
It is a community of the baptized who freely believe in Christ, worship in common and agree to live under the leadership of bishops and pope. Its aim is to help bring the Kingdom of God to fuller realization through living the gospel.

Key Difference(s) from Other Religious Groups:
The unique feature is acceptance of the bishop of Rome as Vicar of Christ, endowed with that infallibility with which Christ wished his church to be gifted in passing on the gospel.

How Man Was Created:
The church does not specify, only insists that the spiritual aspect of man's life is divinely given, neither necessarily, nor merely, the product of evolution.

Dietary Restrictions:
None

*This summary and others following are based on information compiled by Barry Conn Hughes for an article in *The Canadian Magazine*, August 5, 1972.

Position on Birth Control:
Advocates responsible parenthood; artificial birth control to achieve this is officially discouraged; exceptions for particular reasons are increasingly condoned.

Canadian Membership and Recent Trend:
About 10,000,000. Up 15 per cent in last five years

For Further Information:
Catholic Information Centre,
830 Bathurst Street,
Toronto 179, Ontario.

Notes

[1]"Creed of the People of God", United States Catholic Conference, Washington, D.C., as cited in the *1972 Catholic Almanac*. Reprinted by permission of Our Sunday Visitor, Inc., Huntington, Indiana, pp. 248-50.
[2]*Ibid.*, pp. 248-50.
[3]"Constitution on Revelation", *ibid.*, p. 226.
[4]"Creed of the People of God", *ibid.*, p. 250.
[5]*Ibid.*, p. 249.
[6]*Ibid.*, p. 249.
[7]"Dogmatic Constitution of the Church", *ibid.*, p. 224.
[8]*Ibid.*, p. 224.
[9]*Ibid.*, p. 272.
[10]*Humanae Vitae*, United States Catholic Conference, *ibid.*, pp. 280-81.
[11]*Ibid.*, pp. 276-7.
[12]"Dogmatic Constitution of the Church", *ibid.*, pp. 221-24.

2. United Church

The United Church of Canada came into existence on June 10, 1925 as a result of a union of the Presbyterian, Methodist and Congregational Churches of Canada. Though encountering difficult days during the Depression, the new church survived and expanded rapidly after World War II. In 1972 it claimed membership of 1,016,706 adult confirmed members and 2,777,446 adherents under pastoral care (including children) thus making it the largest Protestant church in Canada. According to the 1961 census, about 20 per cent of the population of Canada claimed adherence to it.

Today its work covers the whole country except for the strongly French-Canadian Roman Catholic sections of rural Quebec, and it ministers to all Canadians except the Eskimos. Strongly in favour of the ecumenical movement, it is a member of the World Council of Churches, the Canadian Council of Churches and others.

A. Basis of Authority and Organization of the Church

Authority comes from God whose holy redeeming love was revealed in Jesus Christ, declared in Scripture and testified to by the universal church. Further doctrine of the United Church is stated in the *Basis of Union*. This is a conservative confession which tried to do justice to the basic beliefs of the uniting churches. Whereas this remains the official statement of the church's doctrine (with which ministers are required to be "in essential agreement"), the *Statement of Faith* (1940) which is quoted widely here, and the *Catechism* (1944) are contemporary in style and distinctly liberal in content. One of the distinctive marks of the United Church is that it attempts to be tolerant of all shades of doctrinal opinion consistent with the acceptance of Jesus Christ as Lord.

Organization   The foundation of government was laid down in the *Basis of Union* and the specifics of the system as it developed over the years is set forth in *The Manual*. The system is distinctly *presbyterial*. Each local congregation has a Session consisting of the minister and elected lay people which is responsible for the discipline and the spiritual interests of the congregation. The congregation is also served by a Committee of Stewards who look after financial matters and the Official Board which is a general consultative body. The Presbytery (of which there are about one hundred in Canada) has oversight of the churches within its bounds and is responsible for the discipline of ministers and the supervision of candidates for the ministry.

The next highest body, the Conference, consists of an equal number of ministers and lay people, and there are eleven Conferences in Canada. The Conference oversees the Presbyteries within its bounds, ordains ministers and, through its Settlement Committees, considers the placement of ministers.

The General Council is the chief legislative and policy-making court of the church; it meets every two years. It too is made up of an equal number of ministers and lay people. It is presided over by the moderator who also presides over its executive committees during the two years between councils. As can be seen, the type of organization is almost identical to that used by the Presbyterian Church.

In August, 1972 at the United Church's twenty-fifth council held in Saskatoon, 43-year-old Reverend Bruce McLeod was elected moderator. One of the new breed of churchmen, Mr. McLeod has some rather unorthodox things to say about the church in general today. For example he says: "The church should stop worrying about dropping membership or about trying to fill its buildings. We have too many churches anyway." He also believes that change is essential and that "the best place to change it is from within".

Other opinions that might startle fellow clergymen:

On legalizing marijuana: "It's going to happen anyway. I'm not in favour of smoking pot myself, but prohibition is not the answer."

On Rochdale College, the controversial student residence on Bloor Street in Toronto: "It gets a lot of bad press, but some of it is undeserved. There are raids that take place there which wouldn't be tolerated anywhere else in the city."

On changing sexual mores: "I believe a lot of young people can handle their sexuality a lot better than their elders, who are so critical of them."

On the Vietnam War: "I am totally opposed to it. I was in Vietnam for a time in 1966 and saw things I'll never forget."

On union with the Anglican Church: "I am in favour, but this is just a family affair. Ecumenical to me means world-wide scope."

McLeod also wants "more abrasive, rude kids in the church. They should leave their sing-songs and become more political. We've obviously trained young people to be over-polite. . . ." And he says the same should be true for ministers: "We don't want any more of the passive dependent type who want to be prima donnas over a congregation. We need people who will work alongside people rather than give orders from above, people who will take risks, and be prickly, even shocking, when conviction leads them." The result, he said, will bring more joy into the United Church.

B. Fundamental Theology: Some Basic Beliefs

In this instance, since the *Statement of Faith* (1968) is so concise, it is best to let the church speak for itself:

I. God.

We believe in God, the eternal personal Spirit, Creator and Upholder of all things.

We believe that God, as sovereign Lord exalted above the world, orders and overrules all things in it to the accomplishment of His holy, wise, and good purposes.

We believe that God made man to love and serve Him; that He cares for him as a righteous and compassionate Father; and that nothing can either quench His love or finally defeat His gracious purpose for man.

So we acknowledge God as Creator, Upholder, and Sovereign Lord of all things, and the righteous and loving Father of men.

II. Jesus Christ.

We believe in Jesus Christ, the Son of the Father, Who, for us men and our salvation became man and dwelt among us.

We believe that He lived a perfect human life, wholly devoted to the will of God and the service of man.

We believe that in Him God comes face to face with men; so that they learn that God loves them, seeks their good, bears their sorrows and their sin, and claims their exclusive faith and perfect obedience.

We believe that in Jesus Christ God acted to save man, taking, at measureless cost, man's sin upon Himself; that the Cross reveals at once God's abhorence of sin and His saving love in its height and depth and power; and that the Cross is for all time the effectual means of reconciling the world unto God.

We believe that Jesus was raised victorious over death and declared to be the Son of God with power; and that He is alive for evermore, our Saviour and our Lord.

So we acknowledge Jesus Christ as the Son of God Incarnate, the Saviour of the world.

III. The Holy Spirit.

We believe in the Holy Spirit by whom God is ever at work in the minds and hearts of men, inspiring every right desire and every effort after truth and beauty.

We believe that the Spirit of God moves men to acknowledge their sins and accept the divine forgiveness and grace.

We believe that the Spirit was present with power at the beginning of the Church, enabling the disciples to bear witness to what they had seen and heard, filling them with love of the brethren, and hope of the coming Kingdom, and sustaining them in the sense of Christ's continuing presence in their midst.

We believe that by the same Spirit the Church is continually guided and empowered, and her members fortified against temptation, fear and doubt, and built up in faith and holiness unto salvation.

So we acknowledge the Holy Spirit as the Lord and Giver of life, through whom the creative, redeeming love of God is ever at work among men.

IV. *The Holy Trinity.*

Knowing God thus, as Creator and Father, as Redeemer in Christ, and as Holy Spirit working in us, we confess our faith in the Holy Trinity.

So we acknowledge and worship one God, Father, Son, and Holy Spirit.

V. *Man and Man's Sin.*

We believe that God gave to man, as he did not to the lower creatures, capacity to share His thought and purpose, and freedom to choose whether he would or would not love and serve Him.

We believe that man has used his freedom of choice for low and selfish ends, thus estranging himself from God and his brother man, and bringing upon himself the judgment and wrath of God, so that he lives in a world of confusion and distress, and is unable of himself to fulfil God's high purpose for him.

So we acknowledge man's sin, God's righteous judgment, and man's helplessness and need.

VI. *Redemption.*

We believe that in the greatness of His love for man God has in Christ opened up a way of deliverance from the guilt and power of sin.

We believe that Christ, by living our life without sin, by dying at the hands of sinful men with faith unshaken and unfaltering love, has done for man what man could not do for himself. On the Cross He bore the burden of sin, and He broke its power; and what He did there moves men to repentance, conveys forgiveness, undoes the estrangement, and binds them to Himself in a new loyalty.

We believe that by his resurrection and exaltation Christ stands victorious over death and all evil, and that He fills those who commit themselves to Him with such grace and strength that in Him they, too, are conquerors. His redemption of man is at once an awful mystery and a glorious fact; it is the Lord's doing and marvellous in our eyes.

So we acknowledge the unmerited love and the mercy of our God in giving His only-begotten Son that we might not perish, but have everlasting life.

VII. The Church.

We believe that the Church, the society of the redeemed, was brought into existence by God himself through the work and risen power of Christ, Who in calling men into fellowship with Himself calls them by the same act into fellowship with one another in Him.

We believe that the Church is the organ of Christ's mind and redemptive will, the body of which He is the Head. Under Him the Church is called to the proclamation of the everlasting Gospel with its offer of Salvation, to the worship of God, Creator and Redeemer, to the loving service of mankind, and to the care and nurture of the flock.

We believe that all members of the Church are one in Him, and that the life of the Church in every age is continuous with that of the first apostolic company. The groups commonly known as "churches" are called to share in the life of the whole Church, of all ages and of all lands, entering freely into the full heritage of thought, worship, and discipline, and living together in mutual confidence.

We believe that for the fulfilment of her mission in the world God has given to the Church the Ministry, the Scriptures and the Sacraments.

So we acknowledge one holy, catholic, apostolic Church, the Body of Christ, the household and family of God.

VIII. The Ministry.

We believe that God has appointed a Ministry in His Church for the preaching of the Word, the administration of the Sacraments, and the pastoral care of the people.

We believe that the Church has authority to ordain to the Ministry by prayer and the laying on of hands those whom she finds, after due trial, to be called of God thereto.

We believe that, for the due ordering of her life as a society, God has appointed a government in His Church, to be exercised, under Christ the Head, by Ministers and representatives of the people.

So we acknowledge the Holy Ministry appointed by God for the spread of the Gospel and the edification of His Church.

IX. The Holy Scriptures.

We believe that the great moments of God's revelation and communication of Himself to men are recorded and interpreted in the Scriptures of the Old and New Testament.

We believe that, while God uttered His Word to man in many portions progressively, the whole is sufficient to declare His mind and will for our salvation. To Israel He made himself known as a holy and righteous God and a Saviour; the fullness of truth and grace came by Jesus Christ. The writings were collected and preserved by the Church.

We believe that the theme of all Holy Scripture is the redemptive purpose and working of God, and that herein lies its unity.

We believe that in Holy Scripture God claims the complete allegiance of our mind and heart; that the full persuasion of the truth and authority of the Word of God contained in the Scripture is the work of the Holy Spirit in our hearts; that, using Holy Scripture, the Spirit takes of the things of Christ and shows them unto us for our spiritual nourishment and growth in grace.

So we acknowledge in Holy Scripture the true witness to God's Word and the sure guide to Christian faith and conduct.[1]

C. The Sacraments

X. The Sacraments.

We believe that the Sacraments of Baptism and the Lord's Supper are effectual means through which, by common things and simple acts, the saving love of God is exhibited and communicated to His people, who receive them in faith.

We believe that in Baptism men are made members of the Christian society. Washing with water in the name of the Father, the Son, and the Holy Spirit signifies God's cleansing from sin and an initial participation in the gifts and graces of the new life. The children of believing parents are baptized and nurtured in the family of God so that they may in due time take upon themselves the yoke of Christ.

We believe that the Lord's Supper perpetuates the fellowship between Christ and His disciples sealed in the upper room, that at His table He is always present, and His people are nourished, confirmed, and renewed. The giving and receiving of bread and wine accompanied by His own words signifies the gracious self-giving of Christ as suffering and living Lord in such wise that His faithful people live in Him and He in them.

So we acknowledge Baptism as God's appointed means of grace at initiation into the Christian fellowship; and the Lord's Supper as His appointed means of maintaining the fellowship in health and strength, and as the act of worship in which the whole soul of man goes out to God and God's grace comes freely to man.[2]

Penance is not considered a sacrament, but rather a personal, individual drawing of one person unto God with no intermediary. Marriage is a ceremony of the church and is conducted as such. The United Church does confirm candidates for admission to communicant membership. This usually takes place around Easter.

Baptism usually takes place during the Sunday morning service. The Lord's Supper is celebrated usually four times a year, though the frequency is increasing in many churches.

D. Salvation and the Afterlife

XI. The Consummation.

We believe that the resurrection and exaltation of Christ, following on His crucifixion, gives assurance that the long struggle between sin and grace will have an end, the Kingdom be revealed in its fullness, and God's eternal purpose accomplished.

We believe that God will judge all men by Jesus Christ, the son of man.

We believe that, while salvation is offered to all, God does not take away or override the freedom with which He has endowed men. If they stubbornly refuse His mercy and prefer sinful ways they shut themselves out from the light and joy of salvation and fall under the righteous judgment of God.

We believe that those who accept the offer of salvation and persevere in the Christian way do after death enter into the joy of their Lord, a blessedness beyond our power to conceive. They see God face to face, and in the communion of saints are partakers with the Church on earth of its labours and prayers.

So we acknowledge the righteous and merciful judgment of God and we wait for the coming of the Kingdom which shall have no end.

"We know Whom we have believed, and are persuaded that
He is able to keep that which we have committed to Him."

"To the only wise God our Saviour be glory and majesty, dominion and power, both now and ever."[3]

Exact interpretation of Heaven and Hell and even the use of the terms vary with individuals. Some deny the literal existence of Heaven and Hell; others see those who "shut themselves out from the light and joy of salvation" as going to Hell while those who "enter into the joy of their Lord" are seen as entering Heaven. Whether physical, spiritual or symbolic Resurrection is accepted is to be determined by each individual. The essence of the church is the acceptance of Christ as Lord. Other beliefs are variable.

Conclusion

The United Church placed on its seal, in Latin, the words: "That they may all be one" [John 17:21]. This statement along with its efforts to be not only a united but a uniting church, have placed it in the forefront of the ecumenical movement. Serious talks have been conducted for example over the last few years with the Anglican Church and the Christian Church (Disciples of Christ) with the goal of organic church union in mind. In fact, in 1971 the United and Anglican Churches published a common hymn book. In view of the demand of Christ on the whole man and on the whole of society it has championed certain moral and social principles, often making its views known through the sometimes provocative publication, the *United Church Observer*. Officially it advocates voluntary total abstinence from alcoholic beverages and it is opposed to legalized gambling though not all members necessarily agree with or conform to these stands. It is a national church in respect of its concern for the unity and well-being of the nation, and an international church in view of its world-wide missionary programme in co-operation with churches in India, Japan, Brazil, Trinidad and elsewhere.

Summary

Membership Requirements:

Affirmation of belief in God as known in Jesus, and of ourselves as children of God. Membership can also be by baptism, and baptized children are considered members.

Essentials of its Nature and Purpose:

Belief in Christ as the supreme revelation of God. A desire to worship, celebrate, find friendship, and act in accordance with our understanding of the meaning and purpose of life as found in Christ.

Key Difference(s) from other Religious Groups:

An attempt to include a wide variety of interpretations in the basic Christian faith, to encourage personal, social and political action on the basis of the United Church faith.

How Man was Created:

It could well have been God's plan to create man through evolution.

Dietary Restrictions:

None.

Position on Birth Control:

Birth Control is encouraged.

Canadian Membership and Recent Trend:

1,016,706 — down two per cent in last five years.

For Further Information:

News Services, United Church,
85 St. Clair Avenue E.,
Toronto 290, Ontario.

Notes

[1]*Statement of Faith of the United Church of Canada.* Toronto: The United Church of Canada, 1968. Reprinted by permission of the Division of Mission in Canada, The United Church of Canada.
[2]*Ibid.*
[3]*Ibid.*

3. Anglican Church

The Anglican Church of Canada is an autonomous religious denomination comprising a part of the worldwide Anglican Communion. Since 1955 it has held its present name; before then it was called the Church of England in Canada. Like the United Church its work extends over all of Canada and it shares in the work of the Anglican Communion in parts of Africa, India, Hong Kong, Malaya and Japan, the West Indies and Latin America.

Today the Anglican Church of Canada adheres to the decision of the Lambeth Conference of 1930. It stated that four conditions must be preserved;

they are (1) Holy Scriptures as the record of God's revelation of himself to man and as the rule and ultimate standard of faith; (2) the Nicene Creed as sufficient statement of Christian faith, and either it or the Apostles Creed as the baptismal confession of faith; (3) the divinely instituted sacraments of baptism and of the Holy Communion as expressive of the corporate life of fellowship in Christ; (4) and a ministry acknowledged by all parts of the church as possessing not only the inward call of the spirit, but also the commission of Christ and the authority of the whole body.

As will be seen the Anglican Church is something of a "bridge church" standing between and overlapping the Catholic and the Reformed or Protestant branches of Christendom. Its doctrine places it in this position, and so does its strong position in favour of ecumenism. In fact, for the past few years there have been discussions going on between the Anglican and United Church with the ultimate possibility of organic union between the two.

As of 1968 (the most recent figures available) there were about 40 million adult and child believers; Canada in 1971 had about 700,000 confirmed members and 1,100,000 believers; in the United States the church is called the Episcopal Church and in 1970 there were about 2,270,000 members. Obviously, the heaviest concentration of Anglicans is in the British Isles.

A. Basis of Authority and Government of the Church

The Anglican Church takes as its standards of worship and doctrine the Bible, *The Book of Common Prayer*, and the *Thirty-Nine Articles*. Changes have taken place over the years, so that whereas once it was felt that no deviation should be made from these two latter sources, now revision of the Prayer Book is done and a definitely liberal attitude has emerged towards acceptance or rejection of some or all of the *Thirty-Nine Articles*. The Prayer Book can be altered to suit local needs. The *Articles* are viewed while taking into account the fact that they were adopted at a time when religious feeling ran extremely high, and much was made of the differences between the Anglican and Roman Catholic Churches after the English Reformation. Today, though it outlines basic beliefs of the church, many Anglicans are unaware of the contents of the *Thirty-Nine Articles*. Some Anglicans say that they are bound only by the creeds, that is, the Apostles' Creed, the Nicene Creed and the Creed of Athanasius. Some Anglican congregations are even rewriting the creeds to suit their own circumstances and needs.

Thus it is not surprising that Anglican congregations differ widely in attitude and mode of worship. It is entirely possible to hear two Anglicans argue whether or not the *Thirty-Nine Articles* are part of Anglican doctrine. But more likely still would be a discussion, not about doctrine at all; more likely would it be to hear a discussion as to how the church can achieve and maintain a relevance to the present. To a majority of concerned Anglicans today, these questions are of infinitely greater significance than any rigid list of beliefs.

Despite their declining significance however, the *Thirty-Nine Articles* (found in the *Book of Common Prayer*) do outline rather clearly the traditional church position on most matters of importance.

As most other Protestant churches, Anglicans agree that the Bible is the inspired final standard of faith and life — it is the Word of God and as such contains all things necessary to salvation [Article VI]. Thus God, as manifested in the Bible, is the basis of authority. The church has:

> . . . power to decree Rites or Ceremonies and power in Controversies of Faith; And yet it is not lawful for the Church to ordain anything that is contrary to God's Word written. . . . Wherefore, although the Church be a witness and a keeper of Holy Writ, yet, as it ought not to decree anything against the same, so besides the same ought it not to enforce anything to be believed for necessity of Salvation. [Article XX].[1]

General Councils or Synods (as referred to in Canada) are also believed capable of error, so that "things ordained by them as necessary to salvation have neither strength nor authority, unless it may be declared that they be taken out of holy Scripture". This is the exact opposite of the traditional Roman Catholic position. Clearly then, God's word is afforded primacy in the Anglican Church.

Like Roman Catholics, Anglicans believe that Christ organized a church while on earth and inspired his Apostles to further organize and extend it. Thus the church is in existence today and has been since the time of Christ; the Anglican Church is part of this catholic (that is, universal) church. Stemming from this is the corollary that ecclesiastical authority has come from Christ through the Apostles and that the bishops of the Anglican Church (as well as Catholic bishops) are their successors. However, they agree that there was no divine favouritism shown to any particular type of ministry and Anglicans are quite willing to admit that other churches may have the same authority from the same source.

Organization   The Anglican Church of Canada is an independent organization and is structured as such in that the supreme authority, the primate, is a Canadian and resides here. Individual Anglican Churches are grouped together in *dioceses*, the basic organizational unit. There are 28 dioceses in Canada today, each ruled by a *bishop*. There is also the Episcopal District of Mackenzie. In this, the organization is similar to the Roman Catholic Church. Unlike the Catholic Church whose next largest unit is the archdiocese, the Anglican Church has ecclesiastical provinces; presently there are four of them: British Columbia, Ontario, Canada and Rupert's Land. The ecclesiastical province of Ontario is comprised of the Dioceses of Toronto, Huron, Ontario, Niagara, Algoma and Ottawa. The ecclesiastical province of British Columbia comprises the dioceses of British Columbia, New Westminster, Caledonia and Kootenay. The other 18 dioceses and episcopal district of Mackenzie fall under either the ecclesiastical province of Canada (in the East) or Rupert's Land (in the West).

Each ecclesiastical province meets at regular intervals in a provincial synod attended by representatives of both the clergy and the laity. The provincial synod is presided over by a metropolitan with the title of archbishop. Then there is the General Synod of the Anglican Church of Canada which meets usually every two years; the most recent session, the 25th, met in late Janaury 1971 in Niagara Falls, Ontario. It consists of the bishops of the church and members chosen by the clergy and the laity.

The General Synod is the supreme authority of the church in Canada. It is responsible for the "national character, constitution, integrity and autonomy of the Anglican Church in Canada", relations of the church to other religious bodies in Canada and elsewhere, the revision and publication of a *Book of Common Prayer*, and a host of other concerns. The president of the General Synod is the primate of the Anglican Church of Canada. The primate holds the ecclesiastical position of "archbishop". The present primate is the Most Reverend E. W. Scott.

As the position of prime minister is the most powerful in Canada today, so is the primate of the Anglican Church in Canada the most powerful churchman in that church. However, as Canada recognizes a titular head in the Queen, so does the Anglican Church of Canada recognize the figurehead rule of the Archbishop of Canterbury as the Head of the Anglican Communion.

B. Fundamental Theology: Some Basic Beliefs

God is seen by Anglicans as an infinite, transcending spirit without form or body who created the earth and all things in it. As Article I describes it:

> There is but one living and true God, everlasting, without body, parts or passions; of infinite power, wisdom and goodness; the Maker, and Preserver of all things both visible and invisible.

Anglicans also accept the Trinity:

> And in unity of this Godhead there be three Persons, one of substance, power, and eternity; the Father, the Son, and the Holy Ghost [Article I].[2]

> The Son, which is the word of the Father, begotten from everlasting of the Father, the very and eternal God, and of one substance with the Father, took Man's nature in the womb of the blessed Virgin, of her substance; so that two whole and perfect Natures, that is to say, the Godhead and Manhood, were joined together in one Person, never to be divided, whereof is one Christ, very God and very Man; who truly suffered, was crucified, dead and buried, to reconcile his father to us, and to be a sacrifice, not only for original guilt, but also for all actual sins of man [Article II].[3]

Here a number of key concepts are stated: the belief in the Virgin Birth is affirmed (that of Immaculate Conception is rejected by Anglicans); the essence of the Nicene Creed, that is, God and Jesus are of one substance is also stated; the Atonement of Christ for all of our sins is affirmed, and lastly, so is the concept of Original Sin.

Original Sin is seen not so much as stemming from Adam as from the fault and corruption of the nature of every man. Article IX states in part:

> . . . man is very far gone from original righteousness, and is of his own nature inclined to evil, so that the flesh lusts always contrary to

the spirit; and therefore every person born into this world deserves God's wrath and damnation.[4]

Christ's Atonement for us made salvation possible.

Taking the undeservedness of man and Atonement of Christ one step further, Article XI states:

> We are accounted righteous before God, only for the merit of our Lord and Saviour Jesus Christ by Faith and not for our own works and deservings: Wherefore, that we are justified by Faith only is a most wholesome Doctrine, and very full of comfort . . . .

Here the Lutheran influence through his doctrine of "Justification by Faith Alone" can be seen. Though not necessary to Salvation, good works "are pleasing and acceptable to God in Christ" [Article XII].

In opposition to Catholicism and in harmony with other Protestant groups, Anglicans have been in favour of speaking to the congregation in the vernacular since early days. Article XXIV states:

> It is a thing plainly repugnant to the Word of God, and the custom of the Primitive [that is, Early] Church to have public prayer in the church, or to minister the Sacraments in a tongue not understood by the people.[5]

On the question of clerical marriage, Anglicans are closer to Protestants than to Roman Catholics.

> Bishops, Priests, and Deacons are not commanded by God's Law, either to avow the estate of single life, or to abstain from marriage: therefore it is lawful for them, as for all other Christian men, to marry at their own discretion, as they shall judge the same to serve better to godliness [Article XXXII].[6]

C. The Sacraments

Article XXV states clearly that there are two Sacraments ordained of Christ in the Gospel: baptism and the Lord's Supper. Baptism can be done by sprinkling or immersion and can be given to infants or adults. Baptism is

> . . . not only a sign of profession, and mark of difference . . . but it is also a sign of Regeneration or new Birth, whereby, as by an instrument, they that receive baptism rightly are grafted into the Church; the promises of forgiveness of sin, and of our adoption to be the sons of God by the Holy Ghost are visibly signed and sealed; Faith is confirmed, and Grace increased by virtue of prayer unto God. The Baptism of young children is in any wise to be retained in the Church, as most agreeable with the institution of Christ [Article XXVII].[7]

Baptism is held by many Anglicans to be essential to salvation. In an emergency any Christian may perform the baptism.

The second sacrament is the Lord's Supper.

> The Supper of the Lord is not only a sign of the love that Christians ought to have among themselves one to another; but rather is a Sacrament of our Redemption by Christ's death: insomuch that to such as rightly, worthily, and with faith, receive the same, the Bread which we break is a partaking of the Body of Christ; and likewise the Cup of Blessing is partaking of the Blood of Christ [Article XXVIII].[8]

They say here that Christ is a real Presence in Communion; however Anglicans do not go so far as to accept the Roman Catholic theory of transubstantiation for it cannot be proven, they say, by Holy Scripture. The body of Christ is given, taken and eaten in the Supper, only in a heavenly and spiritual manner; the means by which Christ's body is received and eaten in Communion is faith. Though not usually done, the Communion may be celebrated daily.

Five other significant ceremonies are also regarded as sacraments, "outward and visible sign of an inward and spiritual grace" [Catechism, *Prayer Book*, p. 550] either instituted or blessed by Christ in his earthly life.

Confirmation takes place in childhood or early teens. Penance is the rite through which sin is absolved by Christ, and both public general confession and private confession in the presence of a priest are practised by Anglicans. Ordination, as in the Roman Catholic Church, is the sacrament of holy orders. Prayers for healing are practised in the belief that prayer is valuable for all souls, and unction, or anointing with oil, is called the "sacrament of healing". The celebration of marriage also is a sacrament.

D. Salvation and the Afterlife

There is a definite belief among Anglicans that there is an afterlife. Many believe that there is an intermediate state between death and the Final Judgment and that there is growth possible in one's spiritual life after death. There is also a widespread belief in the Second Coming of Christ to judge all people dead and alive. This is stated in Article IV:

> Christ did truly rise again from death, and took again his body, with flesh, bones and all things appertaining to the perfection of Man's nature; wherewith he ascended into Heaven, and there sitteth, until he returns to judge all Men at the last day.

There are differences of opinion as to the conditions under which he will reappear. Some Anglicans for example believe that his coming will only take place through a growing holiness on the part of Christian people.

The *Articles of Religion* state that Anglicans reject the concept of Purgatory. Article XXII puts it clearly:

> The Romish [that is, Roman Catholic] Doctrine concerning Purgatory, Pardons, Worshipping and Adoration, as well as of Images as of Relics,

and also invocation of saints, is a fond thing vainly invented, and grounded upon no warranty of Scripture, but rather repugnant to the Word of God.[9]

A belief in physical Resurrection is part of church belief although some hold that it will be spiritual only. After Resurrection these people held that the spiritual body will be in continuity with the life of this earth, though without identity with the body laid in the grave.

Of Heaven and Hell there seems to be a general acceptance, though the nature of the two locations is open to varying interpretation. They agree that it is impossible for the good and evil to enter the same place; hence Heaven is sometimes described as being in the Presence of God and Hell as being alienated from God. Salvation comes through repentance and faith in Christ; Hell may be the result of lack of repentance and lack of faith in Christ.

Conclusion

The Anglican Church has always placed a high premium on education and thus has been responsible for the establishment of some of the finest schools and colleges in Canada. In 1827 King's College was established at York (later Toronto); in 1848 the name was changed to the University of Toronto. In 1852 Trinity College was founded and became part of that university in 1904. Other schools were founded in Fredericton, New Brunswick; Lennoxville, Quebec (Bishop's College); London, Ontario and elsewhere. There are now also fine

St. Bartholomew's Anglican Church on the island of New Guinea in the South Pacific.

Courtesy of the Anglican Church House.

Anglican theological colleges including Wycliffe College in University of Toronto.

The Anglican Church is also involved in missionary work both at home among Canada's native people and abroad. This is particularly true in Japan, India, West Indies, and Africa. Members of the St. John the Evangelist Society devote themselves especially to the preaching of missions and conducting retreats. The Order of St. Faith's in Manitoba is occupied in rural areas with religious education and youth; and this is only a partial picture.

Since the completion of the first Anglican Church in Halifax in 1750, the group has made numerous and continual contributions to the political, economic, cultural and religious development of Canada. Fortunately there is no indication that this will cease in the years to come.

Summary

Membership Requirements:

Baptism in water in the name of the Trinity following a declaration of faith by the individual or if an infant, by parents or godparents.

Essentials of its Nature and Purpose:

It is part of the reconciled and reconciling community of the followers of Jesus Christ. Its purpose is to receive the tradition and the mind of Christ, and to express him as adequately as possible in the world today.

Key Difference(s) from Other Religious Groups:

It is both catholic (universal) and reformed. The church is episcopal (that is, bishops are part of the hierarchy) and decentralized; it values order without rigidity. It has an appreciation of reason, for the biblical basis of the faith, and for a variety of schools of thought within the one church.

How Man was Created:

They do not know, nor do they believe biblical narratives of Creation to be concerned with How questions.

Dietary Restrictions:

None

Position on Birth Control:

Advocate responsible parenthood.

Canadian Membership and Recent Trend:

1,180,000 believers; down ten per cent in last five years

For Further Information:

Anglican Church of Canada,
600 Jarvis Street,
Toronto 285, Ontario.

Notes

[1]*Thirty-Nine Articles of Faith.* Reprinted by permission of the Anglican Church of Canada.
[2]*Ibid.*
[3]*Ibid.*
[4]*Ibid.*
[5]*Ibid.*
[6]*Ibid.*
[7]*Ibid.*
[8]*Ibid.*
[9]*Ibid.*

4. Lutheran Church

When the austere Augustinian monk Martin Luther nailed the Ninety-five Theses to the church door over 450 years ago, he probably never dreamed that in time a huge church would be formed and bear his name. Yet such is the case. In fact, if all branches of Lutheranism are included, membership is about 60 million — the largest Protestant body on earth. In Canada in 1971 there were 302,465 baptized Lutherans; in North America there are about 10 million.

Though bearing Luther's name, this church sees its roots in earlier history. Its history really goes back to the Pentecost and the days of the Apostles. The designation "Lutheran" does not really mean a follower of Luther; it more accurately defines a believer in Christ within the tradition of Luther, or in a harmony with the rediscovery of the gospel through Luther.

Luther lived in an age of controversy and like many key figures was under pressure from several directions. His writings reflect this and sometimes are overstrong. Lutherans today tend to somewhat temper the positions held in Luther's day and thus have adopted a middle-of-the-road course. Worship preserves many elements common to Roman Catholics — a church-year cycle, responses and chants coming from the same ancient sources and similar Bible readings. Luther preserved what he felt was worth preserving, and eliminated what he thought of as abuses. The Lutheran faith has something of a middle position between Protestantism and Roman Catholicism.

A. Basis of Authority and Government of the Church

As many other groups, Lutherans state strongly that the Bible is the inspired Word of God and the only guide to religious truth. Beyond Holy Scripture a few other significant documents are regarded as authoritative. Luther's *Small Catechism* is a discussion and interpretation of such important things as the Ten Commandments, the Apostles' Creed, the Lord's Prayer, the Sacrament of Baptism and the Sacrament of Communion. This *Small Catechism* still provides the core of instruction prior to confirmation for Lutherans around the world. The unofficial constitution of the Lutheran Church is the *Augsburg Confession*. It originated as a statement setting forth the Lutheran position on matters of faith at issue between Lutherans and Roman Catholics. Some Lutherans interpret it literally while others see it as a statement to be interpreted and understood within its historic setting; but all regard it in one way or another as their distinctive confession of faith. All such writings, of course, are measured against Holy Scripture and if the two should part company, there is no question among Lutherans as to which has the final say.

Organization As far as organization is concerned Lutherans are flexible. They tend to follow the pattern of the political government. Where governments are monarchies, Lutheran churches usually have bishops and archbishops ruling dioceses and archdioceses; where democracy or representative government prevails, synods and presidents are structured for the church in something fairly closely resembling the Presbyterian or United Church method of organization. As in this system, local congregations have some autonomy and local synods and national conferences decide general, overall policy.

Lutherans believe Christ committed the ministry to the whole church, all the people of God, not merely to those specially trained. This theory is usually referred to as the "priesthood of all believers" and is used to mean man can approach God directly without need of intermediaries (a reference to the priests of the Roman Catholic Church) for either confession or prayer. However, for specific functions, certain ministries are established and recognized by the church in the rite of ordination. This has traditionally been defined as the "Ministry of Word and Sacraments" requiring special training and the calling of men to serve in fulltime capacities. However, there are ministries for teaching, merciful work, music and administration which do not require ordination but which are still considered essential for the church's well being.

B. Fundamental Theology: Some Basic Beliefs

In their basic beliefs Lutherans are very much like most Christians. They accept belief in the Trinity — God is three distinct persons in one Divine Essence. Jesus is the second person being God manifest in the flesh. The Holy Ghost is the third person, through which God is manifested. They also accept (officially) the concept of the Virgin Birth, that is, Christ was conceived of the Holy Ghost and born of the Virgin Mary. This belief is not held by all Lutherans and is the subject of some discussion today. Lutherans do not officially accept the doctrine of Immaculate Conception. This is the theory that Mary's soul in the first moment of its existence (nine months before her birth) was free from Original Sin.

Lutherans do not believe that Christ organized a church while on earth (as do Mormons and Roman Catholics). This organization came later and they believe that the Lutheran Church most nearly approaches the ideal of Christ.

They do believe in the doctrine of Original Sin. They also believe that Christ, by his innocent suffering and death upon the Cross, made complete satisfaction for all the guilt of all mankind for all time and carried away all our guilt. He thus reconciled us to God and purged all our sins, including our inherited Original Sin.

C. The Sacraments

Lutherans regard only Baptism and Holy Communion as sacraments. Other rites and ceremonies, like confirmation, ordination and marriage are merely rites of the church, not sacraments. To qualify, a sacrament must be commanded by Christ and serve as a means of grace. Lutherans emphasize God's imparting of himself; here God approaches man and communicates himself to man in a special way. Man's part is that of trust and grateful receiving. Baptism therefore is God's way of making a person his own, and the Lord's Supper the communion at which the Lord himself is host, imparting himself through bread and wine to all who will receive in trust. The body and blood of Christ are believed to be "in" and "with" and "under" the bread and wine, though they themselves are not changed. Thus, here Lutheran belief falls midway between Catholic belief in transubstantiation and belief of some Protestants in the pure symbolism of the bread and wine.

Congregations are free to determine the frequency of the sacrament just as they are free to determine the mode of communing. Thus the sacrament of Holy Communion may have a festive tone on Easter or Christmas, a solemn tone on Holy Thursday and Good Friday (the Thursday and Friday before Easter) and a social tone on Worldwide Communion Sunday. The basic belief remains however that as a congregation celebrates communion, Christ is present in a mysterious, and yet in a very real way.

D. Adiaphora

Lutherans have few rules. No canon law governs their life. They tend to allow considerable leeway, relying on guidelines provided by the church for the exercise of Christian concern and love. In matters of worship and practice, a sense of fitness and decency are controlling principles. On ethical and social questions, the church sets no hard-and-fast answers, but provides guidelines for its people, leaving it up to the enlightened Christian conscience to form its own judgments.

Lutherans regard many practices and ways of doing things as of minor importance, so long as they are done decently and in good order. Such things are called "adiaphora" which means they make little difference one way or the other. Into this category Lutherans would group many worship practices (vestments worn by the clergy) and patterns of organization (congregational or highly structured with bishops and archbishops). Baptism by sprinkling is just as valid as by immersion. Communing by common cup is as valid as by individual glasses. No official position is taken, yet often practices in different areas tend to be very similar.

E. Distinctiveness

Whatever distinctiveness there may be in Lutheranism lies in its emphases — these elements of belief seen slightly differently from other groups as being more important than others. One such emphasis is the weight given the God-to-man approach. What God does is paramount, what man does is seen largely as response. In the sacrament of Holy Communion, for example, we come as guests invited by the Lord to his table. The validity of the sacrament lies in Christ's presence, not in our being there or our eagerness to receive. The church too is seen from this light. Members belong not by right but by God's invitation. The rules for admission are those God establishes. Man too is seen in this way — judged by what God has created for him and sees him to be. In the light of God's demands, man is a condemned sinner; in the light of God's love, man is a redeemed saint. Lutherans view man as standing before God, made to respond to him in love and obedience.

These statements may explain why Lutherans give such attention to God's grace and man's sin, to a theological stance on social questions, to a high view of the church, to Scripture and the sacraments. It may also explain why Lutherans often react unfavourably to regarding the church as a social club or to thinking man can save himself or lift himself by his own bootstraps.

A second point of emphasis is the Word of God as the supreme authority in religion. But the Word of God is not Scripture alone. It is a living Word transmitted through Scripture, through Christ, through the sacraments, through preaching and through the life of the church. Thus the "Word" is almost anything that communicates God — and this is precisely the function of the Scriptures according to Lutherans.

The Word is communicated through teaching and preaching as long as it is faithful to the Bible message. Tradition too enters the picture, for essential truth revealed in Christ needs application and interpretation from age to age. And the Word is communicated through the sacraments. As we express our feelings at times silently with a smile or a hug, so does God's Word come through the sacraments, silent means of God's communication.

Third, there is great emphasis in Lutheranism on Christ and the Cross. Acknowledgement that Christ sacrificed himself for us accounts for the importance given Lent, with its six weeks' remembrance of the sufferings and death of Christ and for the singing of hymns with frequent reference to the Cross and for the prominence of the empty Cross as a symbol of worship.

Man is basically self-centred, which causes a gap between man and God. This gap Lutherans call "sin". God wills the gap to be closed, and in this context the redemptive contribution of Christ is more fully seen and appreciated. Through his actions, he made it possible to be pardoned and to be reunited with God. Hence the importance attached to Christ and the Cross.

F. Salvation and the Afterlife

By attempting to overcome one's self-centredness (though impossible to do) by faith in Christ, and through God's grace (granted through repentance and faith in Christ) man can be saved. Salvation begins today, in knowing Christ and in striving to do his will. Upon death we will dwell with God. As for those who reject Christ, their ultimate fate we do not know. God knows. God judges. Heaven is to be with God. Hell is to be without God. No effort is made to locate either of these places as being spiritual or temporal locations. In one form or another, the belief in a life after death is adhered to.

It is also held that, in time, Christ will return to earth to judge all men, both living and dead. Some believe that he will appear everywhere at the same time. When he resurrects men God will miraculously resurrect — bring to life — our dead persons (consisting of body and soul) into a final perfect and incorruptible form.

Conclusion

Two aspects of Lutheranism are particularly noteworthy. One is the position halfway between Catholicism and other Protestant groups on some questions of theology and practice. The other is the somewhat stronger emphasis on the power of God and the utter inability of man to save himself held by Lutherans than some other Protestant groups.

An interesting social note is that many Lutherans in Canada are of German or Scandinavian descent. In 1964, 41.6 per cent of all Canadian Lutherans lived in Ontario, and a large concentration of these Ontario Lutherans reside in Waterloo County. Their influence in the area is readily visible when one notices the great number of Lutheran churches in the area, the large number of German place names and the fact that many Lutheran educational and social institutions are congregated in the area including Waterloo Lutheran University.

Summary

Membership Requirements:

Course of instruction leading to baptism (if not previously baptized), or to confirmation or to profession of faith.

Essentials of its Nature and Purpose:

A church consisting of those who accept the Christian faith as elaborated by the confessions of the Lutheran Church. A worshipping and serving church.

Key Difference(s) from other Religious Groups:

Heavy emphasis on that which Christ has done for us. Nothing within us merits any of God's gifts. This was a main issue in the Lutheran Reformation over 450 years ago.

How Man was Created:

By God.

Dietary Restrictions:

None

Position on Birth Control:

Leave decision to parents.

Canadian Membership and Recent Trend:

302,465.

For Further Information:

Lutheran Council in Canada,
550-364 Hargrave Street,
Winnipeg 2, Manitoba.

5. Presbyterian Church

As of December 31, 1971 the membership of the Presbyterian Church in Canada was 182,559 — the third largest Protestant group in the nation. American membership is about four million; worldwide there are about fifty million Presbyterians, largely concentrated in Great Britain, particularly Scotland.

The roots of Presbyterianism are in the sixteenth-century Protestant Reformation especially as acted out by John Calvin in Geneva. Here he set up a form of organization which appealed very much to a former Catholic priest, John Knox. This system emphasized the teaching ministry of the church and provided a closely knit system of theology outlined in his book *The Institutes of Christian Religion*. When Knox, a Scot, became a Protestant much of Calvin's organization was transferred to Scotland where the Presbyterian Church was established in 1560. Today the Presbyterian Church of Canada states itself to be in "historic continuity with the Church of Scotland as reformed in 1560".

A. Basis of Authority and Government of the Church

Like other Reformed churches, the Presbyterian Church in Canada acknowledges Jesus Christ to be the only king and head of the church, and the Scriptures of the Old and New Testaments to be the only infallible rule of faith and practice. More than some other groups, Presbyterians have traditionally been scrupulously faithful to the teaching of Scripture.

Presbyterians also accept the Westminister Confession of Faith (1646) as a subordinate basis of authority — subordinate in the sense of being less important than the Scriptures. The Confession stresses the universality of the church and states:

> "[The] visible church, which is also catholic or universal under the Gospel (not confined to one nation as before under the Law) consists of all those throughout the world that profess the true religion, together with their children: and is the Kingdom of the Lord Jesus Christ, the house and the family of God, out of which there is no ordinary possibility of salvation."

Few Christian churches today confine themselves to a particularistic interpretation of the gospel stressing peculiar doctrines or practices as necessary for salvation — Presbyterians are in this mainstream. As one Scottish Presbyterian put it, "the true catholic, as his name implies, is the well read, the open-minded, the hospitable hearted" because he "belongs to all sects and all sects belong to him".

Other confessions and creeds also form part of the Presbyterian basis of authority. In many congregations, the Apostles' Creed is repeated in worship services. In some the Nicene Creed is used at services of Holy Communion. The Scots Confession of 1560 is also used; it stresses the universality of the church, and the belief in the Trinity.

Presbyterianism derives its name from its form of church government. The name is derived from the Greek word *presbuteros* meaning "elder". Church government is built around two types of elders: ruling elders are elected by congregations and hold office (in Canada) as long as they are members of that congregation; ministers are called to rule and teach and are licensed and ordained by a Presbytery. (See below.)

Elders are appointed to fulfill what were taken to be the duties assigned to the elders referred to in the Apostolic Church. Elders are referred to many times in the New Testament as being people set apart or overseers of the church. The model is similar to the Jewish *Sanhedrin*. Wherever there was an organized Jewish community there was a Sanhedrin composed of elders of the community who were given authority to settle disputes arising within the community and to be responsible for the functioning of the synagogue. Later, members of local Christian churches formed Sanhedrins of their own with elders chosen from their midst. When speaking to the elders of the Church of Ephesus, St. Paul exhorted them to take heed to themselves, and the flock of God over which the Holy Spirit had made them overseers [Acts 21:28]. These are the basic obligations of those called to be elders in the Presbyterian Church. Presbyterians do not claim that

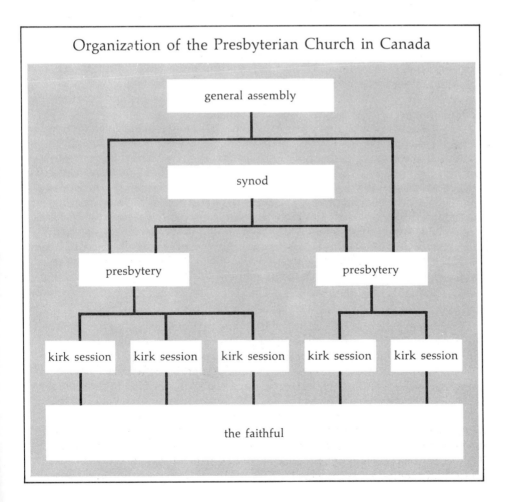

Organization of the Presbyterian Church in Canada

this system of government is the only form of church organization sanctioned by the New Testament. It is claimed though that this form has New Testament authority and precedent and that it has proven useful for over four centuries.

The system of government by *presbyters* (ruling elders elected by the congregations) and ruling and teaching elders who are ordained ministers functions through a graded system of church courts: the Kirk Sessions are associated with individual church congregations; a Session consists of the minister who presides at all Session meetings as Moderator, and the elders elected by the congregation. The Kirk Session makes provision for the administering of the sacraments of baptism and Holy Communion, admits people to membership in the church, supervises the work of Christian Education within the congregation and encourages the congregation's participation in the activities of the church.

Each congregation is represented in the Presbytery by the minister and an elder appointed by the Kirk Session. The Presbytery consists of Kirk Session representatives from a specified area and supervises the work of congregations within that area. There were 49 Presbyteries in Canada in 1972. It provides for the licensing, ordination, induction or transfer of ministers. It receives petitions and appeals made to it by Kirk Sessions. The powers of the Presbytery may be generally compared to those of a Roman Catholic or Anglican bishop. Ministers within its bounds are subject to its discipline and the congregations within its bounds are subject to its oversight.

The Synod consists of the ministers and representative elders of the Presbyteries within its bounds. Presently there are eight Synods in Canada. Ordinarily Synods meet once each year to receive petitions and appeals from the Presbyteries on all aspects of the church's work.

The highest of the courts or councils of the Presbyterian Church is the General Assembly which usually meets once a year, most often in June. It comprises one-sixth of the number of ministers on the rolls of the Presbyteries, and an equal number of elders. It is authorized to deal with all matters, respecting the doctrine, worship, discipline and government of the church. It prescribes and regulates the courses of study of students preparing for the ministry. It determines the policy of missionary work within the church at home and overseas. In general it "adopts such measures as may tend to promote true godliness, to repress error and immorality, to preserve the unity of the Church, and to advance the Kingdom of Christ throughout the world." The Moderator of the most recent ninety-eighth General Assembly is Reverend M. V. Putnam.

B. Fundamental Theology: Some Basic Beliefs

Presbyterians maintain a considerable freedom of religious thought and interpretation. Thus, beliefs indicated here are general only and are in some instances either altered or contradicted by individual Presbyterians. As most Christians, Presbyterians emphasize the sovereignty of one God in three persons (that is, they accept the belief in the Trinity). This God is supremely revealed in Jesus Christ His Son and in the power of the Holy Spirit.

Most Presbyterians accept the belief in the Virgin Birth. Most do not agree that Jesus organized a church while on earth. Rather, he appointed Apostles and others and taught Christian living which needs no organization. Most do agree that Jesus' Atonement was for the sins of the entire world as well as our personal sins. Sin, they believe, results in death which is separation from God; this sin came through Adam, and Jesus atoned for it for all mankind.

Presbyterians practise two sacraments: baptism and Holy Communion. Baptism may be by sprinkling or pouring water or by immersion, depending on the will of the applicant. Baptism in other churches is accepted as being valid. Infant baptism is performed as is adult baptism. Contrary to some faiths, Presbyterians do not all believe that baptism is necessary to salvation.

Holy Communion is regarded as a means of grace, and is administered with bread and wine in remembrance of Christ's death — the bread and wine are symbolic of the body and blood of Christ, and he is present in spirit.

One distinctive feature of Presbyterianism has traditionally been the great simplicity of its worship form. Hand in hand with this has been a strong Calvinist emphasis on the reading and preaching of the word, that is, the Bible. The austerity of worship came partly from a desire to rid the church of all traces of "the dregs of popery". The early reformers took as a rule of thumb the belief that in the practice of worship, what was not expressly commanded in Holy Scripture should be regarded as forbidden. Thus in its early years Presbyterians did not observe the Christian year in regard to celebrations associated with Christmas, Easter, etc. They also consciously rejected such practices as the vow of chastity, forswearing of marriage, the observance of fasting days and prayer for the dead: these were not expressly commanded by the Bible. On the same principle, for three centuries there was no musical accompaniment to psalms sung in church. Some of these usages were carried over into the early Canadian church.

Now however many have been abandoned. Music was allowed in 1862, provided it was used prudently. Observances of the main festivals of the Christian year are now the rule rather than the exception in Canadian Presbyterian Churches. However in comparison to Roman Catholic or Anglican Churches, most Canadian Presbyterian Churches are rather subdued in architecture and adornment.

C. Salvation and the Afterlife

Presbyterians believe that faith in Christ as the Son of God and Saviour of Man is the only thing necessary to Salvation. This faith is made effective by a personal commitment to him. Those with faith in Christ will be in the presence of God and will be happy — this is Heaven. Those without faith in Christ will not be in the presence of God — a state referred to by some Presbyterians as being in Hell.

Most believe that Christ will come again, though whether it will be before or after the millenium is the subject of some controversy. On Judgment Day, many believe that the body will be physically resurrected and that there will be individual identity and a continuation of personality.

Conclusion

In 1925 the Methodists, Congregationalists and some Presbyterians combined to form the United Church of Canada. Today the United Church of Canada is recognized as a member of the Presbyterian Church throughout the world. Some Presbyterians who believed their duty was to preserve their name and

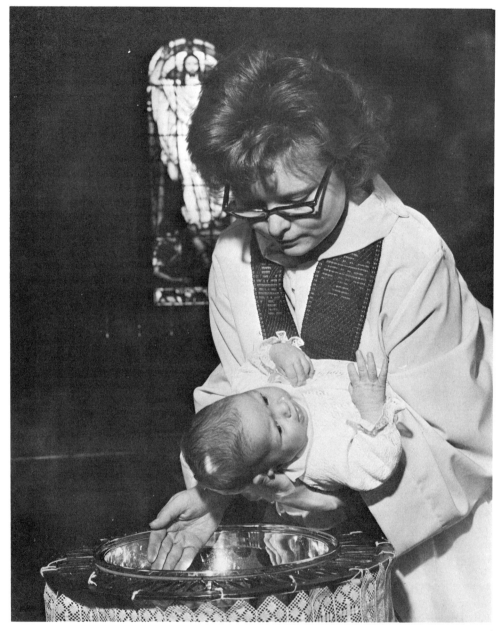

Despite bitter opposition from conservative elements, the Church of Sweden now allows women to be ordained. There are now about sixty officiating women priests in the country and they put an entirely new complexion on religious rites like Baptism.

organization refused to join the new church and were often derided for obstructing a large-scale experiment in ecclesiastical unity. The entire organization had to be rebuilt and for a period of time the Presbyterian Church in Canada experienced acute difficulty. For example, the number of men graduating from the theological colleges maintained by the church (eg. Knox College in the University of Toronto) was inadequate to meet the church's needs.

However since World War II things have improved considerably. Between 1950 and 1959, 27 new congregations were formed in Canada and 30 new church buildings were erected. Now there are 182,559 members in Canada, and though this is down slightly from numbers in the past five years, the Presbyterian Church in Canada is confident of future growth.

Summary

Membership Requirements:

Baptism and profession of faith in Jesus Christ.

Essentials of its Nature and Purpose:

It is a reformed church following the Presbyterian system whose purpose is to bring people to God through Christ.

Key Difference(s) from Other Religious Groups:

Presbyterians believe the church is the body of Christ, and Christ is the only head of the church. Thus the Presbyterian Church is not *the* church, but only part of the holy catholic church.

How Man was Created:

God created man in his own image.

Dietary Restrictions:

None.

Position on Birth Control:

They do not discourage birth control.

Canadian Membership and Recent Trend:

182,559 — down about five per cent in last five years.

For Further Information:

The Presbyterian Record,
50 Wynford Drive,
Don Mills 403,
Ontario.

6. Baptist Church

Within the Baptist Church there is a wide divergence of practice and ritual, though the basic beliefs are more or less constant. There are Baptist Churches in the southern states which do not allow negro membership; although the Southern Baptist convention is officially opposed to segregation there are all-black Baptist congregations in the north and south. Martin Luther King Jr. was a Baptist minister; so was Congressman Adam Clayton Powell; so today is Billy Graham. Some Baptists display extreme energetic fervour in their services; others are much more subdued; the majority like Billy Graham, stress the evangelical aspects of the church.

As of January 1972 Baptists claimed membership of 31,432,130 in 130 countries of the world. Of this number the United States has about 27,527,000 and Canada about 174,000. As they point out, each unit of these figures represents a man or woman who has personally professed faith in Jesus Christ as Saviour and Lord and has followed him in the believer's baptism, that is, baptism by immersion.

A. Basis of Authority and Government of the Church

The foundation truth upon which Baptists build is the Lordship of Christ over the individual believer. All other authorities are judged by the authority of the Son of God. Ultimate loyalty, therefore, is given to a person, rather than to creeds, books, historic patterns and effective procedures. Christ's will is mandatory for the believer. Just as Christ is confessed as Lord of the individual believer, so also Baptists recognize him as head of the church. He is the head of the church in its expression within a local congregation. He is likewise head of the church in its wider expression which includes all those redeemed in him, through his grace. Baptists state clearly their belief that no vicar, pope, bishop, prophet, elder, minister, priest, council, synod or convention can usurp the pre-eminence of Christ's authority. Neither may anyone or anything interfere with the directness of that authority to the church. In the imagery of Scripture, Baptists confess that the body must submit to the head.

The Bible is recognized by the Baptists as having a unique role and character. For them, the inspired Scriptures possess authority in all matters of faith and practice — they are, after all, God's word. Though not particularly known as creedal people, they have at times found it helpful to use creeds or confessions of faith in worship. They have been used principally as instruments to systematize and summarize certain biblical truths. However, such statements have never been accorded the same status as Scripture nor have they been used to determine orthodoxy. They have always been recognized as deriving their authority from the Bible, and their validity is always judged by the Scriptures.

As in other aspects of the Baptist Church a wide variety of interpretation is applied to the Scriptures — some interpret the Bible literally, others are at the other end of the scale and see it as being symbolically significant, and of course many more pursue a middle course.

Church Government   The church is composed, as will be seen, of the redeemed who have equal access to the presence, mind and will of God. Hence, Baptists are convinced that the local church must be governed democratically by its own congregation. While not assuming that decisions democratically arrived at will always reflect the will of God, it is believed that a spiritually sensitive congregation is less likely to misinterpret the divine will than might an individual observer. The New Testament gives prominence to the congregation and the local expression of the priesthood of believers.

The pattern of individual local church organization has been undergoing change in the twentieth century. Traditionally the *pastor* was the leader and moderator of the congregation; more recently there has been a trend to regard him as a leader of the congregation in its witness and service and to elect a lay moderator to preside at corporate meetings of the church. Traditionally the *deacon's* functions were to assist the pastor and to serve as agent to execute the will of the congregation in both temporal and spiritual affairs; more recently there has been a tendency to multiply the number of church officers by creating boards of trustees, boards or committees of education, boards of mission and boards of evangelism. Traditionally decisions were made by the congregations in a church meeting; more recently church meetings have become less frequent and there has been a tendency to delegate decisions to the various boards or committees.

An ordained ministry is an integral part of Baptist structure. Ordination is a formal recognition that God has given a set-apart ministry to the church, that he has specifically called a man to his service, endowed him with spiritual gifts to bless the church, and further, that the candidate has taken seriously the divine call by giving proof of thorough preparation and a holy life. Different from the United and Presbyterian Churches, Baptist ordination is an act of the local church and is conferred following the recommendation of a council composed of ordained and lay representatives of sister churches, which examines the candidate at length.

Though each church is seen to be fully equipped to minister in the name of Christ, and need not derive authority from a higher source, Baptists have not interpreted this to mean that each church is isolated and detached from all others. The local church is but one manifestation of the catholic church, and as individual Christians are bound to pray for one another and to maintain communion with one another, so particular churches are under like obligations. Thus, many churches belong to associations and conventions through which they can seek counsel and advice and co-operate in common concerns. In the United States for example the Southern Baptist Convention has nearly 10.5 million members; the National Baptist Convention, U.S.A. about 5.5 million members, and there are others. In Canada, the Baptist Convention of Ontario and Quebec has about 48,000 members; the Baptist Union of Western Canada has 17,200 members; and the United Baptist Convention of the Atlantic Provinces has 68,400 members and the Union of French Baptist Churches in Canada has 450 members. Other Baptist groups have about 50,000 members.

The Baptist World Alliance is composed of "any general union, convention, conference or association of Baptist churches which desires to co-operate in the work of the Alliance". In 1928 the Baptist World Congress met in Toronto. In 1970 it met in Tokyo and between July 8 and 13, 1975, the thirteenth Baptist World Congress will meet in Stockholm, Sweden.

B. Fundamental Theology: Some Basic Beliefs

Within Baptist beliefs there are certain basics acceptable to most, but also some specifics interpreted very differently by different groups. We shall begin by examining some of the former. As stated earlier, all Baptists agree that Jesus was indeed the Son of God who was empowered to and did atone for our sins. Thus the way was opened for our being able to enjoy everlasting life. Virtually all Baptists accept the concept of the Trinity — that God, the infinite eternal spirit, the source and support of all things, entered history as Jesus the Son, and entered experience as the Holy Spirit, the third person of the Trinity. Most also believe in the Virgin Birth — God desiring to link himself to man was born of the Virgin Mary, thus entering human history as the Christ. Also, as previously indicated, the Bible is the supreme authority in all matters of faith and practice. The Bible contains the supreme revelations of God to man and is authoritative in all matters of faith and conduct.

Baptism   Another belief held by most Baptists, and the one which originally made them a distinctive group, is their attitude towards baptism. Baptists understand the Bible to teach that it is by a personal rebirth that one becomes a member of the family of God. Though salvation is the gift of God, the individual must make the proper response to the divine provision for his need. His response begins with an acknowledgement of his sin and his estrangement from God; it continues with his sincere repentance and his trust in Christ as Saviour and Lord. For new believers, the ordinance of baptism is the act of entry into the fellowship of the local church.

Study of the New Testament has led Baptists to conclude that only immersion has Scriptural authority as a mode of baptism. The symbolism of baptism revealed in the New Testament which portrays death, burial and Resurrection, has confirmed Baptists in their conviction that only immersion speaks clearly of the meaning of this ordinance. They also baptize none but believers. Since baptism is an outward sign or expression of an inward experience, the former has no meaning apart from the latter. Thus, baptism of infants who are incapable of personal faith, mass baptism of peoples without due regard for their personal relationship to God, and baptism of the unconscious or dead have not been practised. (Compare with Mormons and Roman Catholics.)

Baptism is not viewed by Baptists as mediating in any way the saving grace of God to the individual. Salvation is through the finished work of Christ. Baptism is seen as one of the significant first acts of obedience to be performed by the individual who has already experienced spiritual rebirth. In the baptismal waters, one thus symbolically declares his death to an old life and his Resurrection by God's spirit to a new life in Christ. This act is attended by God's blessing upon the one who so confesses his faith and also upon the community of believers who witness his profession.

The Lord's Supper   The second ordinance administered by the church is that of the Lord's Supper. In that it celebrates only two ordinances (some call them sacraments) Baptists can be compared to many Protestant groups. While Baptists reject the doctrines of transubstantiation (of Roman Catholicism) and consubstantiation (of Lutheranism), they nevertheless find spiritual renewal through the observance of this memorial feast in which Christ is truly present in spirit.

The memory of Christ's sufferings and death bring to the believer the desirable experiences of self examination, repentance, a new-found sense of communion with God, a renewed dedication to the divine will and a new loyalty to the body of Christ. This celebration is offered usually about once a month.

Individual and Church Liberty   Baptists stress the desirability of religious liberty for all men. Although zealous in the propagation of their own beliefs, they hold back from the use of physical, economic and political intimidation, and protest the use of these tactics by others. Hence, the Soviet government's attitude toward religion is a continual source of potential danger to the 550,000 Baptists in the Soviet Union. It is not only Russian Jews who are intimidated by the Communist regime.

Baptists also believe that every follower of Christ is free to come to God without the mediation of a priestly class which has exclusive control over the dispensing of divine favour (an obvious allusion to Roman Catholicism). They believe Christians should be free to read the Bible and be guided to its meaning by the Holy Spirit. (However, in becoming a member of a local church, an individual's freedom of personal behaviour and doctrinal interpretation must obviously be tempered by the convictions and needs of the congregation.) This conviction does not however rule out the need for an ordained ministry. Members of the ministry (pastors or deacons) have special responsibilities to be sure; but they come from the consent of the congregation.

As individuals are free, so are local churches. They are believed able to make and carry out the policies and programmes which best reflect and fulfil God's purpose for the church.

The church has always had the obligation to give heed to the directions of Christ, and must be free to do so.

Separation of Church and State   Closely related to the ideas of individual and church freedom, is the conviction that there must be a basic separation of church and state. The state's primary functions are to exercise civil authority, keep law and order, and promote public welfare. The church's primary functions are to witness to the gospel of Jesus Christ and to build up believers in the faith. Since the expressed responsibilities are not identical, Baptists hold that each must therefore maintain separate administrations, separate sources of support, and separate educational programs. The church must be free from any entangling alliance which will prevent it from serving as the conscience of the state.

Missionary Efforts   Most Baptists agree that the proclamation of the gospel is central to their task in the world, since they recognize the gospel to be God's good word to man. Thus, traditionally Baptists have possessed a strong missionary spirit — one that has taken them to the ends of the earth. This is evidenced by the fact that in addition to large numbers in North America and Europe, there are also Baptists today in little-known and out-of-the-way places like Botswana, Malawi and Rwanda in Africa; Bangladesh, Macao and Burma in Asia; El Salvador, Haiti and the Leeward Islands in Central America.

C. Theological Differences

But all is not sweetness and harmony in the Baptist Church. On some very crucial issues there are distinct and sharp differences of opinion among individuals. For example while all Baptists acknowledge the inspiration of the Scripture, there is difference of opinion regarding the precise way in which Scripture is to be understood in light of the final authority of Christ himself. There are also differences of opinion over the authorship of Biblical books, the nature of Biblical language, and the legitimacy of a scholarly approach as to whether certain passages of the Bible are to be regarded as literal or symbolic truth.

Many Baptists hold to some form of millenial (that is, the end of the world) doctrine, but this is by no means true of all, and such differences often exist within the same convention. There are also differences of understanding concerning eternal punishment and the possible salvation of all men; there are contrasting views concerning the universal scope of the Atonement of Christ or its limitation to an elect group. Then there are the Seventh Day Baptists who have their own special emphasis concerning the observance of Saturday as the Sabbath.

Important differences also appear in regard to believers' baptism and its relation to church membership. Some churches limit membership to immersed believers only (closed membership); others admit membership on profession of faith and leave the question of baptism to the conscience of the believer (open membership), although none would practise infant baptism.

In recent years, a middle position has been adopted where Christians from other denominations, although not baptized as believers, are admitted to a more active membership but are not generally given the privileges of voting for the call of a minister or of acting as a delegate to associations or conventions. This practice, often called "associate membership", is found in some churches both in the United States and Canada.

The *ecumenical movement* (of which more will be said in the next chapter) is the cause of one of the most serious recent discussions among Baptists. While Baptists have a form of ecumenicity in the Baptist World Alliance, some feel that this is not enough and that Baptists cannot refuse to consider their relationship to other Christian bodies.

Others feel that membership in the World Council of Churches will lead in time to the organic union of all existing churches with the consequent disappearance of Baptists as a separate denomination and the danger of an eventual "superchurch" which would be a threat to religious liberty. Presently, with the exception of the large Southern Baptist Convention and some others, the majority co-operate fully in interdenominational and ecumenical bodies including the Canadian Council of Churches.

Lastly, differences of opinion are strong regarding the manner of conducting services in different churches. Some stress the freedom of the spirit and the informed nature of the service; others believe that the reality of the Spirit's presence is not incompatible with a more formal and liturgical form of service. Some incline more to the "mass evangelism" of Billy Graham (himself an ordained Baptist minister) and others like him. These factors result in differences of attitude and atmosphere from one local church to another and between geographical areas and countries. However they are not considered to be so significant as some of the other doctrinal differences of opinion.

D. Salvation and the Afterlife

In this connection too there are differences of opinion. Many believe that Christ will return to the earth in person as it is believed he ascended. Salvation is to be achieved through the grace of God, personal faith in Christ, and a life of discipleship.

All Baptists hold that there is a future life in which a distinct identity and personality will exist. Again there are variations in the understanding of what the future life is like. Some say that there are various levels in the future life according to one's degree of spiritual development, providing for the possibility of advancement. Others however accept the theory that there is a fixity of character which makes advance impossible. Some say that there is a physical Heaven and Hell; others see Heaven as a state of being in the presence of God and Hell as being without the presence of God. When final Judgment is passed, the separation of people will take place, thus fixing our final state.

Conclusion

It must again be stated that Baptist belief varies extremely widely; probably more widely than almost any other Protestant group. This is the logical outcome of the Baptist belief in individual freedom of conscience and religion. Statements here have attempted to reflect the majority view which is often a middle of the road between two extremes. Some Baptists would reject statements made here; it is believed that the majority would not. This wide diversity of belief is interpreted by some as a source of weakness, and by others as a source of strength. Certainly the Baptist future is not completely rosy, but with continuing efforts being made to find common understanding within the church, there are indications that the Baptist Church will continue to make significant contributions both in Canada and the world for the foreseeable future.

Summary

Membership Requirements:

In most churches, a personal confession of faith in Christ, symbolically expressed in the baptism of the believer.

Essentials of its Nature and Purpose:

A return to the New Testament as the supreme standard. A doctrine that only those who have experienced a personal responsible relationship with Jesus Christ should be members. Hence, belief in believers' (not infant) baptism.

Key Difference(s) from other Religious Groups:

They see the local church as a group of believers baptized after their experiences of conversion to Jesus Christ, and banded together as a self-governing and competent church, though inter-connected.

How Man was Created:

There is no *one* Baptist view but all affirm that whatever the manner, man is made in the image of God, and by God.

Dietary Restrictions:

None, though the use of alcoholic beverages is definitely discouraged.

Position on Birth Control:

Most accept that it may be practised within marriage.

Canadian Membership and Recent Trend:

174,264 (Jan. 1972); down five per cent in last five years.

For Further Information:

Baptist Federation of Canada,
Box 1298, Brantford, Ont.
or
Baptist Convention of Ontario and Quebec,
217 St. George St.,
Toronto 180.

7. Mormons

You have probably heard them often: Three hundred and seventy-five voices
accompanied by one of the largest and finest organs in the world; they
have a weekly radio broadcast received in parts of Canada; and have made
best-selling record albums. They are the world-famous Mormon Tabernacle
Choir. This choir and the worldwide missionary activity has led, according
to Mormon sources, to a 94 per cent membership growth between
1960 and May, 1972. There are now about 3,090,900 Mormons throughout the
world with some 54,680 in Canada. Heavily oriented to the United States
(2,133,760 members) they now have won converts in Mexico, Central and South
America, Europe, Asia and the South Pacific.
      According to Mormon belief, the Prophet Mormon who was one of
God's prophets in the Western Hemisphere was commanded by God to gather
the sacred records of ancient America and abridge them on thin sheets of gold.
He collected these inspired writings called the *Book of Mormon* into one volume
— writings containing a thousand years of religious history, telling of the first
colonizers in the Americas and how God led them here from the Holy Land.
Then Mormon gave the plates to his son, the great warrior and prophet Moroni
who, under direction from the Lord, deposited them in a stone box and buried
them in the Hill Cumorah (in western New York State), until such time as the
Lord should bring them forth — in the latter days.
      In the latter days a religious young man named Joseph Smith was to
receive them. Born in 1805 in Vermont, and moving soon to New York State,
Smith's family was caught up in the religious fervour of the times.
      Methodists, Baptists and Presbyterians were all intent on converting as
many as possible, and religious discussion was widespread. While most of his
family became Presbyterian, Joseph, by this time fifteen, was unable to decide.
In 1820 while praying in the woods one day he saw a vision and two person-

Miller Services Ltd.

The Mormon Temple, Cardston, Alberta.

ages: God and Jesus. One said, "This is My Beloved Son. Hear Him!" — and
told him not to join any of the contending sects.

One night in September, 1823, Smith saw another vision, this time of a
man calling himself Moroni who said he had been sent by God to command
young Joseph to find the plates and the accompanying stones which were the
keys to translation. Their location was made clear to him, as was the fact that
he was to tell no one of them until commanded to do so. To do so was to be
destroyed. When he found the plates, he was forbidden to take them since the
messenger told him he must wait four years. Finally, four years later on
September 22, 1827 Smith was given the plates by the messenger Moroni. Then
came the work of translation.

Assisting Smith in this work was a friend named Oliver Cowdery.
On May 15, 1829 they went to the woods to pray and ask the Lord about
certain passages pertaining to baptism. While there a messenger from Heaven
descended and gave them each the power to baptize, but first they baptized each
other. This messenger from Heaven claimed to be John the Baptist. After
baptism their minds were enlightened and the true meanings of some of the
mysterious passages were made clear.

Continuing with the translation, they understood that three special
witnesses were to be provided by the Lord to see the plates from which the

Book of Mormon was being translated. These three men were Oliver Cowdery, David Whitmer and Martin Harris. Having given the original plates back to Moroni, Smith and the three had to pray and ask him to show the plates. This they did and were shown the plates by an angel. A voice from Heaven then said:

> These plates have been revealed by the power of God. The translation of them which you have seen is correct and I command you to bear record of what you now see and hear.[1]

They thus prepared a statement:

The Testimony of Three Witnesses

> Be it known unto all nations, kindreds, tongues, and people, unto whom this work shall come: That we, through the grace of God the Father, and our Lord Jesus Christ, have seen the plates which contain this record, which is a record of the people of Nephi, and also of the Lamanites, their brethren, and also of the people of Jared, who came from the tower of which hath been spoken. And we also know that they have been translated by the gift and power of God, for His voice hath declared it unto us; wherefore we know of a surety that the work is true. And we also testify that we have seen the engravings which are upon the plates; and they have been shown unto us by the power of God, and not of man. And we declare with words of soberness, that an angel of God came down from heaven, and he brought and laid before our eyes that we beheld and saw the plates, and the engravings thereon; and we know that it is by the grace of God the Father, and our Lord Jesus Christ, that we beheld and bear record that these things are true. And it is marvelous in our eyes. Nevertheless, the voice of the Lord commanded us that we should bear record of it; wherefore, to be obedient unto the commandments of God, we bear testimony of these things. And we know that if we are faithful in Christ, we shall rid our garments of the blood of all men, and be found spotless before the judgment seat of Christ, and shall dwell with Him eternally in the heavens. And the honor be to the Father, and to the Son, and to the Holy Ghost, which is one God. Amen.
>
> Oliver Cowdery, David Whitmer, Martin Harris.[2]

While the Book of Mormon was in the hands of the printer, Smith and his associates made known the fact that they had received a commandment to organize the church; such was begun on April 6, 1830.

Shortly thereafter Smith moved to Ohio and built a temple and began missionary work. Soon the church body moved to Missouri but there found much intolerance and antagonism. Hence another move was made to Illinois which was peaceful for a time. Before long though intolerance again bloomed and one night in June, 1844, Smith and his brother were shot and killed.

Brigham Young succeeded to the headship of the church and organized an historic trek across the country to the Rockies where in Salt Lake City, Utah, the Mormon Church flourishes today.*

A. Basis of Authority and Church Government

Referring back to Biblical times, Mormons point out that Apostles appointed by the Lord were considered essential if the church was to survive. They were to receive current revelation from the Lord for the direction of the people as their needs arose. However, by about A.D. 100 the original Apostles had died and therefore, according to the Mormons the church was left to drift without any valid authorities.

Great persecutions were experienced; Greek philosophy distorted original concepts of God; jealousies, intrigue and personal ambition within the church weakened it. Men like Constantine protected and advanced the church's interests for political rather than religious reasons. Bishops' rivalry helped split the two principal Christian churches; Henry VIII's interest in church affairs was political rather than religious at its heart. Luther was protected by John of Saxony, a man whose only authority was political and therefore who had no divine authority to establish the Church of God.

> In no case was a new revelation from heaven even claimed. In no case was any restoration of divine authority in the ministry professed. It was admitted on every hand that where the state religions were organized, they were developed and authorized by the political agencies who ruled the land, and therefore possessed only political but not divine authority.[3]

Other churches sprang up too but none declared or claimed divine authority for their acts. Hence, Mormons believe God will reject the unauthorized ministers of these sects as he has in the past [I Samuel 13:8-15; Matthew 7:21-29; Acts 19:1-6; Acts 19:13-16].

They say that the pattern for calling men to the ministry is clear. God will give a revelation to his prophet and the prophet under that direction will call to the work the individual thus designated. The implication for Mormons is that in the true church there must be a prophet. Thus, in this context Joseph Smith's importance is magnified greatly. Mormons believe that Smith and his successors are the Apostles called by the prophet Moroni. Given the power of the higher or Melchizedek Priesthood by the Apostles of old, Peter, James and John, all the gifts and powers of former days have been restored. This power came not from any existing organization, and did not come from any political unit. It came from Heaven; it came from God.

Thus, the restored church, known as the Church of Jesus Christ of Latter-Day Saints, meets all the specifications of Scripture: it possesses the

*When Joseph Smith was killed and Brigham Young took over, there came a split in the church. Some people believed that a blood relative of Smith should have become the new prophet. These believers for the most part did not make the long trek west; they remained in the east where they are today known as the Reorganized Church of Jesus Christ of Latter-Day Saints.

divine priesthood of God and is headed by prophets and Apostles as was the church in the days of Peter and Paul.

The Bible and the Book of Mormon are basic Scriptures to the Mormons; other sacred works are the *Pearl of Great Price* and *Doctrine and Covenants*. Along with the authorities there are human authorities who comprise the government of the church. According to the Bible there are two levels of priesthood. The lesser is the Aaronic [Exodus 28:1; 29:1-46; 30:30]. New male adult members and youths 12 years of age are ordained into the Aaronic priesthood. At 12 years of age a young man, if worthy, can become a deacon of the lesser priesthood; at 14, a *teacher* and at 16 he can become a *priest* of the Aaronic priesthood. Females do not hold the priesthood.

At this time, preparation can be begun for the higher or Melchizedek priesthood [Hebrews 5:4-10]. At 19, a person can be received into this higher priesthood as an *elder*. All male missionaries serving in different areas of the world are elders. Another office in the Melchizedek priesthood is that of a "Seventy": there are seventy of these groups and in a quorum they are responsible for missionary work. High priests are bishops. At the same level are stake presidents (see below).

Finally, there are twelve apostles and one prophet, who is the seer and revelator. All members of the higher priesthood have the same power. However, each calling or position in the church has specific keys of authority which only the person chosen can exercise with his priesthood power. The apostles have most of the keys of authority, but only the prophet has all the keys of authority. The newly-annointed prophet (July, 1972) is Harold B. Lee.

Co-existent with these offices, is a worldwide organization. Presiding over a ward is a bishop; usually wards include areas similar to a parish in other churches. Eight to ten wards comprise a stake, of which there are 581 in the world. The stake president has the keys of authority and thus a significant power. Comprising two to ten stakes is a region — there are thirty regions in the world. Finally the world is divided into twelve geographic areas with one of the twelve apostles in charge of each. Through organization such as this the church can function efficiently from headquarters in Salt Lake City, Utah.

B. Fundamental Theology: Some Basic Beliefs

Articles of Faith   The basic beliefs of Mormonism are summed up clearly by the "Articles of Faith" written by Joseph Smith:

1. We believe in God, the Eternal Father, and in His Son, Jesus Christ, and in the Holy Ghost.

2. We believe that men will be punished for their own sins, and not for Adam's transgression.

3. We believe that through the atonement of Christ, all mankind may be saved, by obedience to the laws and ordinances of the Gospel.

4. We believe that the first principles and ordinances of the Gospel are: first, Faith in the Lord Jesus Christ; second, Repentance; third, Baptism by immersion for the remission of sins; fourth, Laying on of hands for the gift of the Holy Ghost.

5. We believe that a man must be called of God, by prophecy, and by the laying on of hands, by those who are in authority, to preach the Gospel and administer in the ordinances thereof.

6. We believe in the same organization that existed in the Primitive Church, viz.: apostles, prophets, pastors, teachers, evangelists, etc.

7. We believe in the gift of tongues, prophecy, revelations, visions, healing, interpretation of tongues, etc.

8. We believe the Bible to be the word of God as far as it is translated correctly; we also believe the Book of Mormon to be the word of God.

9. We believe all that God has revealed, all that He does now reveal, and we believe that He will yet reveal many great and important things pertaining to the kingdom of God.

10. We believe in the literal gathering of Israel and in the restoration of the Ten Tribes; that Zion will be built upon this (the American) continent; that Christ will reign personally upon the earth; and, that the earth will be renewed and receive its paradisiacal glory.

11. We claim the privilege of worshipping Almighty God according to the dictates of our own conscience, and allow all men the same privilege, let them worship how, where, or what they may.

12. We believe in being subject to kings, presidents, rulers, and magistrates, in obeying, honoring and sustaining the law.

13. We believe in being honest, true, chaste, benevolent, virtuous, and in doing good to all men; indeed, we may say that we follow the admonition of Paul—We believe all things, we hope all things, we have endured many things, and hope to be able to endure all things. If there is anything virtuous, lovely, or of good report or praiseworthy, we seek after these things.[4]

It should be noted that belief in God, Jesus and the Holy Ghost is not to Mormons what it is to Roman Catholics or Anglicans. Whereas these groups see the Trinity as one being, the Mormons do not. To them, God and Christ are two personages; the Holy Ghost is a spirit. They are three and distinct, though united in purpose. Christ is the mediator between God and man; and the Virgin Birth of Christ is acknowledged. Notice, however, in these "Articles of Faith" that original sin is rejected; man will be punished for his own sins, not those of someone else.

C. The Sacraments

Rather than calling them sacraments, Mormons refer to four "first principles and ordinances" indicated in the fourth "Article of Faith". By means of these, a person may place himself within the reach of divine mercy. The first is faith in Jesus Christ; that is acceptance of his gospel and allegiance to his commandments, and to him as the one and only Saviour of men. The second is repentance embracing genuine contrition for the sins of the past and a resolute turning away therefrom with a determination to avoid, by all possible effort, future sin. This repentance is done by the individual directly to God — there is no intermediary who can help. Third is baptism by immersion, usually at about eight. This is so because without original sin, man creates his own. At a younger age than eight, it is thought that a child does not understand maturely the difference between right and wrong. Since the purpose of baptism is to remit sins, there is no need before age eight. Baptism must be administered by one having the authority of the priesthood, that is, the office of "priest" in the lower Aaronic priesthood or any officer in the Melchizedek priesthood. Fourth, there is "Laying on of hands for the gift of the Holy Ghost". This higher form of baptism is referred to as "confirmation" and is received with baptism, and must be performed by a member of the Melchizedek Priesthood. In the laying on of the hands the person being baptized actually receives the Holy Ghost and comes in close relation to God.

Communion (or The Sacrament, as Mormons call it) is taken with bread and water, both of which are only representative of Christ's body and blood.

Mormons practise an interesting rite called *baptism for the dead*, and cite I Corinthians 15:29 as the authority. It is done on behalf of those who were unable to be baptized themselves before death and it is essential, for baptism is believed to be necessary in order to enter God's Kingdom.

Marriage is an area of special interest since polygamy was practised by some two per cent of the Mormons in their early history — it was sanctioned by the teachings of the Old Testament. However, since 1890 it has been forbidden on pain of excommunication. Today, there are two types of marriage. One is called "marriage for eternity". It must be performed in the temple, which itself is a restrictive measure since not all Mormons may enter the temple and is only open to those who are extremely worthy. Each of these marriages is solemnized through the authority of the President of the Church and is based on the precept that as God is eternal and God is love, so is love eternal. The other marriage is similar to other church views of marriage, that is, "till death do you part". This ceremony can be performed by anyone in the higher level priesthood, that is, the Melchizedek.

D. Concepts of Salvation and the Afterlife

Mormons believe that salvation can come from good works as outlined in the Articles of Faith, and from faith, thanks to the Atonement of Christ. The highest level of glory is *celestial* — comparable to the great beauty of the sun. Secondly there is *terrestrial* glory — comparable to the moon, that is, secondary in beauty to the sun. Thirdly there is *telestial* beauty — beauty comparable to the stars in relation to the sun and moon. Those who have been worthy of telestial beauty only, will realize when they see celestial beauty what they could have attained had they been better people. This will be the discomfort of the afterlife. Mormons reject the fire and brimstone connotation of Hell in their views of afterlife. The doctrine of Mormonism is relatively straightforward — it appeals to man's responsibility. Any sin committed is yours alone and you must bear that responsibility. There is no original sin. This simplicity combined with a vigorous missionary work has brought many converts. Indications are that such will continue in the foreseeable future.

Summary

Membership Requirements:

Course of instruction leading to baptism (if not previously baptized), or to confirmation or profession of faith.

Essentials of its Nature and Purpose:

The Scriptures indicate that before the Second Coming of Christ, his church would be restored in its original form and through it the sacred gospel preached anew to the world and "then shall the end come".

Key Difference(s) from Other Religious Groups:

It is not a fragment of any other denomination. It is distinct from all others as a restoration of original Christianity with apostles and prophets at the head, guided by current modern revelation.

How Man was Created:

Man was created by an act of God in his own image. How this was done has not been revealed.

Dietary Restrictions:

Mormons advocate wholesome food and prohibit tobacco, liquor and stimulants.

Position on Birth Control:

They discourage it.

Canadian Membership and Recent Trend:

58,683. Up by 8,660 in last five years.

For Further Information:

Church Information Committee
338 Queen St. E.,
Suite 205,
Brampton, Ontario.

Notes

[1]*The Prophet: Joseph Smith's Testimony*. Salt Lake City: The Church of Jesus Christ of Latter-Day Saints. Information Service, The Church of Jesus Christ of Latter-Day Saints, p. 24.
[2]*Ibid.*, pp. 25-6.
[3]Mark E. Petersen, *Which Church Is Right?* Salt Lake City: The Church of Jesus Christ of Latter-Day Saints. Information Service, The Church of Jesus Christ of Latter-Day Saints, p. 21.
[4]"Articles of Faith". Salt Lake City: The Church of Jesus Christ of Latter-Day Saints. Information Service, The Church of Jesus Christ of Latter-Day Saints.

8. Jehovah's Witnesses

Two people stand at a busy downtown intersection. Calm and quiet amid the noise and confusion, they hold up copies of small publications called *Awake!* Most people hurry by hardly noticing them; a few stop. The two standing there are Jehovah's Witnesses.

A knock comes at the door. Two people are outside with copies of *Awake!*, *The Watchtower* and other religious literature. They would like some of your time to explain to you the blessings that will come by means of God's Kingdom. Persistent missionaries, these people too are Jehovah's Witnesses. In the world today their membership is approaching 1,500,000 and their basic belief is that the Kingdom of God is ruling now from Heaven and will replace earthly governments which should not be obeyed if they go contrary to the law of God.

A. History

Today, according to their own statistics, there are 790 congregations in Canada and about 50,166 ministers involved in a house to house campaign. Worldwide, they exist in 208 countries and 27,154 congregations. Numbers involved in an active (though not necessarily full-time) ministry are about 1,590,000.

The Witnesses say that they are not a denomination, but rather an association of men and women who put God's service first. Thus they say the first time witness of God was Adam's son Abel. However, for practical purposes one can go back to 1881 and agree that the founding in that year of the Watch Tower Bible and Tract Society of Pennsylvania was the real beginning in North America. In 1879 the first *Watchtower* was published with the basic idea (then as now) that the uninterrupted rule of the Gentile nations would be brought to an end in 1914 and that Christ's kingdom would begin to rule amidst the chaos. In 1909 the headquarters were moved to their present location in Brooklyn, New York. In 1931 the present name, Jehovah's Witnesses was adopted, and in 1942 the current president, Nathan H. Knorr, was elected.

Like all Christians, Jehovah's Witnesses believe in the absolute supremacy of God and the role attributed to Jesus as the Son of God; they do not see Jesus as a member of the Trinity with equal status with God. However, they interpret these figures in ways a little different from some other Christian sects. The basic problem of the world today, as they see it, is that the majority of nations are deeply concerned with attempting to establish world domination. However, only God has world sovereignty. Nations seem to be unwilling to give up their claims and therefore a collision between man and God is inevitable. The Holy Bible, God's inspired word, explains clearly what world domination by God would be like, but people do not read the Bible sufficiently to know; otherwise all would be on the side of God.

Witnesses are able to interpret the entire Bible from this point of view. The Garden of Eden was not extended to the whole world as was originally the intent because Adam and Eve had a collision with God — they ignored God's ownership of Paradise and ignored him by eating the fruit. Thus they were punished and ejected from Paradise [Genesis 2:15-17; 3:16-24]. However, a few people have "walked with God" and have not collided with him. Enoch was saved by God from a violent death [Hebrews 11:5]; Noah survived the flood which removed the original Paradise, but it can be restored and will be, through Jesus.

When God brought the Jews to Palestine, the "Land of milk and honey" he told them that they were settlers only [Leviticus 25:23]. However, the Jews acted as though they owned the land. Amos warned of a confrontation [Amos 4:11-13]. In 609 to 607 B.C.E. (Before the Common Era) Babylon defeated Palestine and depopulated the land. Today Christendom claims to be the Spiritual Israel. Again today Christendom is warned through the Bible and yet fails to listen.

Destruction   According to the Witnesses, the Biblical timetable for this destruction is quite clear. The Gentile Times are considered to have begun in 607 B.C. with Jerusalem's destruction and desolation. They were to run for 2,520 years and come to an end in the early autumn of 1914 C.E. (Common Era). Though the Biblical reference is to Luke 21:24, it is a general reference and not specifically stated there to be 2,520 years. (For a more complete description of the dating see *Awake* March 22, 1960, pp. 4-8). In Daniel 2:1-43, there is reference to a dream being interpreted by Daniel for the King of Babylon. The Witnesses take this interpretation to be symbolic of the collision between a stone cut from a universal mountain and the "clay besmeared feet" of a terrifying metallic

Converts to the Jehovah's Witness faith are baptized by total immersion. Often these baptisms take place at Witness conventions and are done on a mass scale using public swimming pools for the ceremony.

Miller Services Ltd.

image — the nations of the earth. This stone was cut in 1914 — this was the end of the Gentile Times, for in this year war broke out worldwide over the issue of world domination.

> "Hence the symbolic 'stone', God's Kingdom by Christ, did not strike the symbolic 'image' of political power in 1914. It merely began to rule in the midst of its enemies. So it has been hurled forth by divine power. It is now on its way, headed toward that political 'image'."[1]

The "image" of course is the worldwide system of politics.

Revelation [17:11] speaks of an "eighth King" — interpreted by the Witnesses as an eighth world power. The first seven world powers were Egypt, Assyria, Babylon, Medo-Persia, Greece, Rome and the Anglo-American world power. This eighth power is the United Nations which is "the international organization for world peace and security and so for keeping the feet of the idolatious 'image' standing where they ought no longer to stand."

How do these nations oppose Jesus, the Lamb of God who takes away the sin of the world? First, they refuse to yield national sovereignty to God. Secondly, they oppose and persecute those who are "ambassadors for Christ" and in effect fight the "Lamb Jesus Christ, the King of Kings." The "ambassadors" are Jehovah's Witnesses. Armageddon is imminent! On this earth, the only place of safety is on the side of Jehovah. Here, one will have everlasting life. Any other position will bring obliteration.

Personal Life   As is often the case, religious teachings strongly influence the Witnesses' personal life. Generally their moral tone is very strict. They reject the assertions of some Protestant (Christian) clergymen that under certain conditions pre-marital sex may not be bad. Nor do they tolerate what they consider to be a too casual attitude to divorce. They accept the statement that what God yokes together let no man put asunder. Accepting the concept of original sin the Witnesses see it as our duty to follow Jesus as closely as possible, for Jesus is the means by which man can be saved from not only the power of sin but also from death. Fleshly desires are always to be avoided. Hence, the reading of pornographic materials or seeing films heavily oriented to sexual license are things from which to refrain. Remember, says *The Watchtower*: "The destruction of an immoral generation by the great deluge in Noah's day stands as a pattern of what Jehovah will do to the debauched generation of today."

Family Life   Family life, too, is guided by these moral precepts. Discipline and the teaching of right habits are very important parental responsibilities. Proverbs are quoted to prove the wisdom of physical punishment: "The rod and reproof are what give wisdom; but a boy let on the loose will be causing his mother shame" [Proverbs 29:15]. Punishment is linked to love of the child: "The one holding back his rod is hating his son, but the one loving him is he that does look for him with discipline". [Proverbs 13:24]. The Bible is also used and followed to teach respect for parents and older persons as well as respect for law and order. "Easy money", that is, money gained in gambling is ruled out, even though it may have been won at a church bingo. Homosexuals, say the Witnesses, can not attain the Kingdom of Heaven for so it is written

[I Corinthians 6:9-10]. Businessmen are exhorted not to cheat their customers for this violates the Golden Rule. As can be seen then, the Bible's teachings are adhered to closely to attempt to produce a high moral tone in individual Witnesses and in their family life.

B.   Organization and Basis of Authority

That the news of the establishment of God's Kingdom is of extreme importance is the primary reason for the organization's existence. Since the Kingdom is God's, he clearly is the basis of all authority. Only God can ordain a Witness minister — only God can make it valid. They believe that those who are ordained by an organization of men are ministers of such an organization, and that those ordained by God are his ministers. Ordination requires a personal dedication to God's will [Romans 12:1] made in private prayer to God through Christ. Then to symbolize such dedication one must be baptized by immersion in water as Jesus was [Matthew 3:13-17]. Then a person is God's ordained minister. Seminary training and written documents are not considered necessary [John 7:15; Acts 4:13]. Furthermore, every Witness is to be a minister, "minister" being used in the sense of being a public servant of Jehovah who follows Jesus' footsteps by spreading the news. Basically the spreading of the news is done by preaching from house to house — a practice which may well have brought you into contact with the Witnesses by now.

Witness organization is not democratic. All presiding ministers are "servants" appointed by the governing body in Brooklyn in harmony with God's spirit as expressed in his Word, the Bible. In the final analysis, leadership comes from Jehovah God as exercised through Jesus.

Administration of the organization is handled by headquarters in Brooklyn and operating through approximately 95 branches worldwide. Zones (largest areas), circuits and districts (smaller areas) are the basic units used to structure the organization. A number of individual congregations form a district in a structure not totally unlike the parishes, dioceses and archdioceses of the Roman Catholic Church.

Individual congregations have a residing minister called a "presiding overseer". He is not the leader of the other ministers of the congregation; he is the shepherd of the flock whose job it is to care for his charges [Matthew 23:10-12]. It is not seniority necessarily that counts in his appointment; rather it should be his spiritual maturity which is important. To aid him in his tasks, there are ministerial assistants whose responsibility it is to help both the elder and the other ministers of the congregation. Neither officer is paid for his job; money necessary to maintain buildings and to pay for printed materials comes from donations from the congregation.

Kingdom Hall   Each Witness meeting place is called the "Kingdom Hall of Jehovah's Witnesses" in an effort to advertise God's Kingdom as the hope of the world. Since the congregations split in two when they reach a total membership of 200, most buildings are small and modest. But inside, there is activity much of the time. A "Theocratic Ministry School" is held once a week to train people to be better speakers and also to help them become more familiar with the Bible. Both of these skills will help when speaking to people door to door. Usually on the same night as the "Theocratic Ministry School" is held, so is the "service meeting" — an effort to discuss with the hope of improving all-round services of missionary work, etc. On Sunday, usually in the morning or afternoon, there is a "public meeting" in which Bible study is conducted. Following the public meeting there is usually a *"Watch Tower* meeting". At this most important meeting, copies of the *Watch Tower* are discussed as they relate to fulfilling God's purpose on earth, and the Bible is studied in conjunction with *Watch Tower* articles.

C. Salvation and the Afterlife

To fully understand Witness beliefs about the afterlife, one must first understand why man dies. God created earth, Witnesses say, and his purpose was to make man fruitful, to fill the earth and subdue it, and to have dominion over the lower animals. As a test of appreciation God told man, who was perfect (being created in God's image) and possessed of free will, not to eat a certain fruit. Man was fully able to obey that command [Genesis 1:1, 26-8; 2:15-17; John 17:17; Deuteronomy 32:4].

However, lacking in appreciation, man and woman disobeyed God and were thus sentenced to die; had they not disobeyed they would have lived forever. On death they were returned to the ground [Genesis 3:1-19; 5:5]. As their children were not brought forth until after they had sinned, they were born sinners with the condemnation of death hanging over them. Hence, it can be seen that Jehovah's Witnesses accept the doctrine of Original Sin (in the sense of disobedience to God.)

"Little Flock"   Many people believe that the soul is immortal and lives on after bodily death. Witnesses say that there is not one text in the Bible which states that the human soul is immortal. Jesus brought the idea of immortality to light with the gospel that a "little flock" would be with him in the heavenly kingdom and that they would be changed from mortal to immortal, divine creatures [Luke 12:32; I Corinthians 15:53, 54; 2 Timothy 1:10; 2 Peter 1:4]. But, the doctrine of inherent immortality of all human souls is based on ancient Babylon's belief in the immortality of the human soul [Genesis 10:8-10].

This "little flock" is believed to be 144,000 in number and will consist of the people who once lived in any era from the first century until the present. They will be those who most closely adhered to Jesus' teachings and most faithfully carried out his work. Their job will be to help Jesus rule the new world of peace and happiness and everlasting life which God has planned for us [Revelation 5:10; 7:14].

The hope of other good people is in the Resurrection of the person's personality and characteristics in a body on Judgment Day — a Resurrection made possible by Christ's ransoming of himself for us to fulfill God's plan for the earth. Billions of those now dead will be raised to life again right on this earth in a righteous new order [Matthew 20:28]. Paul's entire argument in I Corinthians 15 is to the effect that Jesus was raised from the dead and that, since that is so, there is also hope for others who have died. The wicked will also be resurrected [Acts 24:15] and will have the opportunity to respond to the education God will provide through his Kingdom government. After the thousand-year reign of Jesus it will be established whether an individual's Resurrection was a Resurrection to life or to adverse Judgment [John 5:20-29]. On the other hand, the everlasting life of the righteous will bring honor to Jehovah's name and endless joy to them [Psalm 37:10; Romans 6:23; Revelation 4:11; 21:1-4].

Witnesses see themselves today as throwbacks to the early Christians. They are proud of their neutrality in political matters — a stand so strongly felt that they refuse to salute the flag of any country. They see themselves as *in* but not *of* this world — rather they are zealously preparing for the rapidly approaching end of the present unrighteous system.

D. Special Characteristics

Two elements of belief are probably better known than any other among non-Witnesses. One is the refusal to fight in war. This stems from the Biblical statements in John 13:34 to "love one another" and in Matthew 5:9 to be "peaceable". But, while taking this position individually they are not to interfere with the affairs of the government under which they live. Nor are they to tell others what they should do in matters of conscience. Hence, Jehovah's Witnesses can be classified as "conscientious objectors" to war, though they also claim exemption on the basis that they are all ministers and thus claim ministerial exemption. Doing so though, they have been dealt with harshly. In 1941 they were banned in Australia. Even in the United States thousands were sent to prison because they refused to take up weapons of war in World War II. In Germany they were placed in concentration camps for refusing to fight.

Blood Transfusions   The other well-known belief is the refusal to accept blood transfusions, though this is part of a larger concept. In an interesting publication called *Blood, Medicine and the Law of God,* they explain the larger belief. Genesis 9:34 and Deuteronomy 12:23 are interpreted to mean that the soul is the blood, and is not to be taken as food. Leviticus states the same thing, [Leviticus 3:17; 17:13-14] and it is reconfirmed in the New Testament [Acts 15:28-9]. This means to Witnesses that no animal with blood in it is to be eaten and that food containing blood (e.g., blood sausage) is to be avoided.

> Since it is forbidden to take the blood of another creature into one's body, it will necessarily follow that it would be wrong to give one's blood to be infused into the body of another.[2]

Since, "Our life is dependent upon obedience to him" and his will is known to us through the Bible, then in actual fact it is believed to be better to refuse the blood and die (and yet be saved by obeying Jehovah's will) than to take the blood, return to health, and yet later be punished for disobedience.

Though the Biblical rules are the most important, there are other reasons for not accepting transfusions. Many medical sources are cited to back up the claim that there can be serious hazards in using transfusions including contracting all kinds of diseases (including syphilis and hepatitis) and dangers from the mixing of incompatible blood. Furthermore, they say, doctors often use a transfusion before exploring all other possibilities — thus transfusions are not always necessary. For all these reasons Jehovah's Witnesses will not allow blood transfusions to be given to themselves or their children.

Using the Holy Bible as a handbook containing God's will, the

Witnesses make it part of their life work to explain to people why they must repent. "Awake" they say, "the end is near!"

Summary

Membership Requirements:

One must accept the Bible as the infallible Word of God and be willing to bear witness to Jehovah and preach.

Essentials of its Nature and Purpose:

The preaching of the good news of God's Kingdom and the making of willing persons into disciples. Further, there is a desire to help persons serve God and thus gain his approval and eternal favour.

Key Difference(s) from other Religious Groups:

The acceptance of the Bible as the inspired and infallible Word of God. The performance of the public house-to-house ministry.

How Man was Created:

Man is the direct creation of Jehovah.

Dietary Restrictions:

No eating of blood in any form such as blood puddings and blood sausages, and in some cases wieners.

Position on Birth Control:

A personal matter for each married couple.

Canadian Membership and Recent Trend:

50,166 active workers; 19.7 per cent increase in last 5 years.

For Further Information:

Watch Tower Bible and Tract Society,
150 Bridgeland Avenue,
Toronto 390, Ontario.

Notes

[1]*When All Nations Collide Head On With God.* New York: The Watch Tower Bible and Tract Society of New York, Inc., 1971, p. 21. Reprinted by permission of the Watch Tower Bible and Tract Society of New York, Inc.

[2]*Blood, Medicine and the Law of God.* New York: The Watch Tower Bible and Tract Society of New York, Inc., 1961, p. 7. Reprinted by permission of the Watch Tower Bible and Tract Society of New York, Inc.

9. Church of Christ, Scientist

Founded in 1879 by Mrs. Mary Baker Eddy, the Church of Christ, Scientist now boasts over 3,200 branches in 56 countries in addition to numerous informal groups not yet organized to the extent of founding a church, and about 500 organizations at colleges and universities. The church does not publish membership figures in the belief that there is an over-accentuation on numbers and that it really matters little how many people are actual members of the group. Of greater concern is the quality of the people in the pews. This was felt by the Canadian government to be a valid claim and hence Christian Scientists

Mrs. Mary Baker Eddy, founder of Christian Science.

The Christian Science Publishing Society.

are exempt from the census. World headquarters is The Mother Church, The First Church of Christ, Scientist in Boston, Massachussets.

A. Basis of Authority and Government of the Church

Christian Science states itself to be a religion based on the words and works of Jesus. Its authority comes from the Bible. Its basic teachings are set forth in Mrs. Eddy's book entitled *Science and Health with Key to the Scriptures* written in 1875.

Born in New Hampshire in 1821, Mrs. Eddy was widowed early, experienced much sickness and suffered long separation from her only child. These factors no doubt contributed to an increased desire on her part to find a deeper understanding of God. In time she came to believe that the origin of all disease is mental. In 1866 she was healed of the effects of a serious accident as she sat pondering one of Jesus' healings as recorded in the New Testament. She believed this to have been a revelation, a belief which led her to greater study and an ensuing deeper understanding of God. Slowly, students began to come to her and in 1875 her major book was published, *Science and Health with Key to the Scriptures*. After establishing the church in 1879, she continually strove to perfect its organization and its counsel, and carried on publishing new books and improving *Science and Health*. Throughout this time she consistently stressed that the church was established on God as divine Principle, not an individual human personality. Hence, though she is thought very highly of, she is not deified or worshipped in any sense. Many biographies of the lady are available in Christian Science Reading Rooms across Canada.

Organization   Mrs. Eddy provided for the government of the church today by writing the *Church Manual*. A Board of Directors consisting of five people administer the affairs of The Mother Church. Each branch of this church has its own democratic government and is not subject to official control of the Mother Church except in those relations with it governed by the *Church Manual*. However, each such church or society derives its legitimacy from its recognition as a branch of the Mother Church. A Christian Science Society is an organized branch which has not yet met the full requirements. The first branch in a community is designated, for example, as First Church of Christ, Scientist, Toronto; the second as Second Church of Christ, Scientist, Toronto; and so on. The first Church of Christ, Scientist, Toronto is located in the Spadina-Bloor Street area of the city, and there are seven other Christian Science Churches in the metropolitan Toronto area. Each church must provide a reading room in the area of its location so that people may study the Scriptures; in this practice, there is a throwback to early days of Judaism when the synagogue was a place of study and knowledge.

B.   Fundamental Theology: Some Basic Beliefs

As outlined by Mrs. Eddy in *Science and Health* the basic teachings are as follows:

> 1. As adherents of Truth, we take the inspired Word of the Bible as our sufficient guide to eternal Life.

2. We acknowledge and adore one supreme and infinite God. We acknowledge His Son, one Christ; the Holy Ghost or divine Comforter; and man in God's image and likeness.

3. We acknowledge God's forgiveness of sin in the destruction of sin and the spiritual understanding that casts out evil as unreal. But the belief in sin is punished so long as the belief lasts.

4. We acknowledge Jesus' atonement as evidence of divine, efficacious love, unfolding man's unity with God through Christ Jesus the Way-shower; and we acknowledge that man is saved through Christ, through Truth Life and Love as demonstrated by the Galilean Prophet in healing the sick and overcoming sin and death.

5. We acknowledge that the crucifixion of Jesus and his resurrection served to uplift faith to understand eternal Life, even the allness of Soul, Spirit, and the nothingness of matter.

6. And we solemnly promise to watch, and pray for that Mind to be in us which was also in Christ Jesus; to do unto others as we would have them do unto us; and to be merciful, just and pure.

A closer analysis of some of these statements will help to further explain the Christian Science position. The first of the statements does not mean that the Bible is to be interpreted literally. It is held that the Bible is a history of man's growing recognition of the spiritual nature of God and that there is a development from the Old to the New Testament of the theme of God's love for man. Because of God's love, he provides man with the means to be saved.

The second statement acknowledges the Trinity and has some similarity to Catholic, Anglican and United Church beliefs, though different from the Mormon view.

The third statement is the most difficult to understand and to explain. God is Love, the divine principle of all that is good. He creates only good. Man was made in the image of God and is therefore capable of expressing God's attributes. Obviously, Christian Science dismisses the Roman Catholic concept of Original Sin. Sin is regarded as the acceptance of another power opposed to the one consistent, loving, good God, a power such as greed, infidelity, dishonesty, arrogance, etc. Furthermore, this third statement points out that evil is unreal — even though it may seem very real to us. Only that which is unchanging, ever-present, and created by God is real. The suffering caused by evil is like that of a person who receives two telegrams, one at a time. The first arrives and informs him that a loved-one has died tragically. Based on this news, he feels sorrow, loss, sadness and maybe bitterness. Soon, however, the second telegram arrives and explains, with apologies, that the first one was a mistake, an error, not true. The first telegram contained news that was not real — but it still evoked strong response. Similarly, the bodily senses may report suffering or evil of any sort, but the "good news" of the gospel comes to tell man that God never created these conditions. They are not "real", and man can be freed from their illusory power by knowing this truth. But he will suffer from evil as long as he accepts it. This is illustrated by the following example.

A student working out a mathematical problem who misunderstands, misuses or disregards the relevant mathematical principle, will come out with a wrong answer. A failing mark may be the "punishment" for his error; in order to escape this punishment he must detect, correct and eliminate the error.

But the error has not the "reality" of the mathematical principle, which requires his recognition and obedience in order to produce the right result but which exists independent of anything he may do. The error has no place — no necessity, legitimacy or potency — in the ordered structure of mathematics. It has not even the "reality" that the right answer has, for the right answer follows inevitably from the right understanding and application of the relevant mathematical principle. Mrs. Eddy wrote in *Science and Health*, "It is our ignorance of God, the divine Principle, which produces apparent discord, and the right understanding of Him restores harmony."

This analogy does not hold at all points, but it suggests the metaphysical reasoning behind the third tenet. The professor does not "forgive" the error; he forgives the student by giving him the understanding that corrects it. Thus Jesus, demonstrating to the woman taken in adultery the true nature of divine Love, could end by saying to her, "Neither do I condemn thee. Go, and *sin no more.*"

These beliefs put Christian Science in the mainstream of Christianity, even though they differ in some respects from traditional doctrines.

In other ways however Christian Science is unique, for its adherents rely on spiritual means alone to heal all physical disease; and they see a very close relationship between their religious teachings and the healing work of the church. Genesis I says that God made man in his own image and pronounced all that he had made "very good". Hence, it is argued, man created in the image of God (Spirit) must be wholly spiritual and as perfect as his Creator. It follows that the sick and sinning mortal who appears to the physical senses is really a false representation of man — a material misconception of man as he really is. As Mrs. Eddy wrote in *Science and Health*:

> Jesus beheld in Science the perfect man, who appeared to him where sinning mortal man appears to mortals. In this perfect man the Saviour saw God's own likeness, and this correct view of man healed the sick.

Sickness Sickness is not spiritually real; thus it can be spiritually healed and display human aspects of cure. The crux of the problem is to achieve a proper relationship with God, *not* to want to be cured. The cure can come from the former. Man must experience reformation and regeneration of himself through an awareness of his spiritual nature. By so doing, the false evidence or sickness may be destroyed. Such healing is possible for any Christian; one need not be a Christian Scientist.

But Christian Scientists quietly point out the differences between their healing and faith cures and suggestion or psychotherapy. The basic difference is, they say, that their healing does not rest on blind faith; rather it rests on an enlightened understanding of God as infinite, divine Mind, Spirit and Soul. It recognizes God as acting through universal, spiritual law, an understanding of which constitutes the Science of Christianity. This Science distinguishes between relying on the divine Mind (God) and those types of cure which employ the human mind as a curative agent (including the use of suggestion, will power, and hypnotism). Jesus said; "Ye shall know the truth, and the truth shall make you free" [John 8:32]. *Science and Health* declares:

> It is our ignorance of God, the divine Principle, which produces apparent discord, and the right understanding of Him restores harmony.

Christian Scientists admit that one of the reasons for placing special emphasis on the healing of the sick is that it is the most conspicuous proof of the validity of Christian Science, and one of the natural results of drawing closer to God in one's thinking and living. As Jesus' healing miracles were significant but not pre-eminent to his mind, so is it true with Christian Science. However, much documented evidence of healing is published in the monthly *Christian Science Journal*, the weekly *Christian Science Sentinel* and the quarterly *Herald of Christian Science*, published in 12 languages. The following excerpt from the May 6, 1972 edition of the *Christian Science Sentinel* is one of many. In each case the editors say, "The statements made in this testimony with regard to healings have been carefully verified. The original testimonies and their respective verifications are on file for reference with The Christian Science Publishing Society."

Testimonies of Christian Science Healing

Christian Science has meant much to me and my family for many years. I have received invaluable inspiration and encouragement from the testimonies published in the periodicals, and am writing this in the hope that it will help others.

When one of our sons was in kindergarten, his teacher told us that the school psychologist, the principal, and she herself found him to be mentally retarded and did not believe that he could be taught in the public schools. They advised that we have him examined and tested by a well-known children's neurological expert to determine the extent of his retardation. Even though I had been a longtime student of Christian Science, I was quite shocked and fearful at the claim they had made about this dear little one. My husband, who is not a student of Christian Science, lovingly left to me the decision as to what should be done.

I immediately called my teacher in Christian Science for help and spent all the available time studying references from the Bible and from the writings of Mary Baker Eddy on *Mind, completeness, intelligence, man,* and *reflection*. The school had told me that with the report of the neurologist they could place the child in an educational program outside the public school, but without this report they could not put him anywhere in a learning position.

Through my study it became clear that this loving concern on the part of the school officials was their highest sense of good for the child. A feeling of peace replaced the resentment in my thinking. Turning completely to God for guidance, I prayed humbly to know the right steps to take. I realize now that as the fearful, resentful thoughts melted away, the healing began. I lived with the definition of Mind in the Glossary of *Science and Health with Key to the Scriptures*, particularly the part where Mrs. Eddy writes, "not that which is *in* man, but the divine Principle, or God, of whom man is the full and perfect expression" (p. 591). That powerful statement just didn't leave any room for incompleteness or retardation.

In view of the stand that the school had taken, I now felt it was right to make the appointment with the neurologist, leaving all in

God's hands. In phoning his office I found that it would be three months before this busy man could see us. This gave us more opportunity to prepare our thinking for the interview.

When I finally met the doctor, I told him that I was a Christian Scientist and explained to him why I had come. I found this man to be loving and kind, and genuinely interested in learning something about Christian Science. My son had a cold that day, and the doctor said that he preferred to test him when he was perfectly free. He asked if we could have him healed of the cold in two days and made another appointment for that time.

We left with joyful hearts and returned with joyful hearts two days later. The cold had vanished. He examined the boy and said that he would not think of suggesting any other method of healing than that he was already receiving, that we should just keep up the good work and he would write a report to the school that would satisfy all concerned.

The doctor expressed a desire to know more about Christian Science and eagerly accepted an offer of the textbook, *Science and Health*. I received a wonderful letter of thanks and appreciation after he had received the book, and I know that the good it brought him is going on to bless all those hundreds of people that come to him for help.

My son went back to school in the fall on a trial basis. His progress was steady, and much loving support was given by a Christian Science practitioner in moments of discouragement. We were grateful for each expression of kindness and love from his teachers over the next two years. Our son will soon complete the sixth grade, a happy, eager-to-learn little boy who is even ahead of his class in some areas.

Can we ever be grateful enough to God, for the ever-present activity of the Christ, and to Mrs. Eddy for her faithful obedience in setting forth the Principle of Christ Jesus' healing works. For all the consecrated practitioners, for membership in a branch church and The Mother Church, and for the privilege of class instruction, my heart overflows with gratitude.

(Mrs.) Patricia B. Young
Hastings-on-Hudson, New York

Christian Science cannot be combined successfully with a reliance on medical aid; Jesus never used medical remedies of any sort, and Christian Scientists believe that to try to combine spiritual and material means lessens the effectiveness of both. Of course, when the law demands certain medical treatment (such as child innoculation against certain diseases), Christian Scientists comply with the law. Also it is acceptable to allow a surgeon to set a broken bone, so long as no medication is used. Christian Scientists do not ignore or neglect disease; on the contrary, they believe they heal in accordance with Jesus' promise: "He that believeth in me, the works that I do shall he do also." [John 14:12]. Or as Mrs. Eddy puts it, "Only through radical reliance on Truth can scientific healing power be realized".

To help attain this reliance on truth, people read and study *Science and Health*, pray sincerely to God and can be helped by another Christian Science practitioner and/or a Christian Science nurse who will come to the home to offer assistance.

Since the purpose of Christian Science is to achieve full salvation for all mankind attained by a scientific understanding of God, much more must be done than just healing the physically ill. Psychological tensions and moral confusions exhibiting themselves in family or business problems or social injustice are also dealt with. Besides this, relief to all faiths in time of war or disaster, charity for people in need, the old, and the infirm are provided. Ministries are maintained in the Armed Forces. Though there is no missionary activity in the usual sense of the word (as practised by many other Christian sects), there are an average of 4,000 free public lectures given per year under the auspices of Christian Science churches throughout the world. And of course, the faith is spread by the example of individual adherents.

In another sense healing is also attempted among nations by the daily publication of the world-renowned newspaper, *The Christian Science Monitor*. Known and admired in all circles for its lack of sensationalism, its editorial balance, its accuracy and impartiality, it is among the finest newspapers published anywhere.

C. The Individual Congregation

There is no ordained Christian Science clergy; any layman (male or female) may rise to any position as long as they demonstrate fitness for the task. In a branch church, services are conducted by a First and Second Reader elected by and from the membership for a specific period of time. The Sunday service consists in part of the reading of a lesson-sermon composed of related passages in the Bible and *Science and Health*. Mrs. Eddy chose 26 subjects for these lesson-sermons and they are repeated twice a year. Among the 26 subjects are Life, Truth, Love, Spirit and Soul — all synonyms for God. However, readings chosen to illustrate the themes are always fresh and new. References to these passages are listed in the *Christian Science Quarterly* so that Christian Scientists can study each lesson during the week preceeding the Sunday service.

On Wednesdays there are meetings held which include testimonies of the healing and saving power of God. Also on Wednesday, the First Reader of each branch chooses a timely topic of his own and builds up his own readings from the Bible and *Science and Health*. He may choose any subject that seems appropriate — pollution, sex morality, racial justice, occultism, weather, sports, employment, the raising of children, etc. — and with ingenuity and inspiration can bring to bear the timeless truths of revelation on the needs and interests of the moment.

D. The Sacraments

Christian Science does not ritualize the sacraments as most other Christian churches do, but like all Protestant churches it recognizes two sacraments: baptism and communion. These are not church ceremonies but daily individual experiences. Baptism is regarded as the inward purification of thought from all error, leading to a regeneration and cleansing of character and resultant activities. Hence, it is practised continually by each individual. Similarly, communion is celebrated by Christian Scientists as an inner process of finding one's conscious unity with God through the example of Jesus Christ.

The second chapter of *Science and Health* is entitled "Atonement and Eucharist" and discusses this subject in depth. Twice a year, the weekly lesson-sermon is entitled "Sacrament" and the Sunday services at which this lesson is read include a period during which the congregation is invited to kneel in silent communion with God. No visible elements are used in these services. The true act of worship is done by the individual before God, not necessarily in the church. Not even marriage is performed in Christian Science churches. With no ordained clergy, a person vested with the power to marry is called upon to conduct the service, which usually is a civil ceremony, or conducted in a Protestant church.

In this context Christian Scientists point out that the lack of reliance on symbolism and ceremony does not in any way suggest a lack of feeling for the things which these ceremonies stand for. Since God is infinite, all-present, consistent and all-pervading, we must continually look for God's manifestations in all aspects of our lives all the time. Hence these sacraments must be practised always, everywhere and must not be reserved for special occasions.

Conclusion

Christian Scientists feel themselves to be in spiritual fellowship with all who worship a supreme and righteous Deity. This obviously includes many non-Christians. But they see themselves as being rooted firmly within Christianity and fully accept Jesus' words, "I am the way, the truth and the life: no man cometh unto my father but by me."

Christian Science they see as Christianity in its most practical and scientific form, and they accept its new insights into the nature of reality. As Mrs. Eddy wrote:

> What is the cardinal point of difference in my metaphysical system? This: that by knowing the unreality of disease, sin and death, you demonstrate the allness of God. This difference wholly separates my system from all others. The reality of these so-called existences, I deny, because they are not to be found in God, and this system is built on Him as the sole cause. It would be difficult to name any previous teachers, save Jesus and his disciples who have thus taught.

Hence, the Christian Scientist is different from other Christians in denying the reality and power of evil, but is united with other Christians in worshipping God as the supreme power whose infinite love for man was revealed to the world through the life of Jesus.

Summary

Membership Requirements:

Acceptance of the teachings of Christian Science; be free from the use of alcohol, drugs and tobacco.

Essentials of its Nature and Purpose:

Mrs. Eddy and a small group of students voted to "organize a church designed to commemorate the word and works of our Master, which should reinstate primitive Christianity in its lost element of healing."

Key Difference(s) from Other Religious Groups:

Followers rely on prayer alone for physical healing. There is no clergy or religious hierarchy. Designated pastor of the church is the Bible and *Science and Health with Key to the Scriptures.*

How Man was Created:

They find theories of evolution and the Adam and Eve allegory insufficient to explain inner spiritual identity of man.

Dietary Restrictions:

None.

Position on Birth Control:

It is a personal matter.

Canadian Membership and Recent Trend:

The church does not publish this information.

For Further Information:

Christian Science Committee
on Publication for Ontario,
Room 403,
696 Yonge St.,
Toronto 285, Ontario.

Notes

[1]Mary Baker Eddy, "The Tenets of Christian Science" from *Science and Health with Key to the Scriptures.* Boston: the Christian Science Publishing Society, 1968. Used by permission of the Christian Science Board of Directors.
[2]Excerpted from the *Christian Science Sentinel*, May 6, 1972, pp. 822-4. Used with permission of the Christian Science Publishing Society, Boston.

10. Unitarianism

A very different group from those examined previously is that which calls itself Unitarian. The name comes from the belief that the universe, nature and man are one — a belief in the organic wholeness of the universe. Originally expressed as the "Unity of God", the name "Unitarian" evolved. Belief in one world means a rejection of the dualism of Heaven and earth, spirit and matter, natural and super-natural. Those Unitarians who believe in God see him within the universe, within nature, within man. Belief in the unity of nature is expressed by saying that nature is the product of an age-old development and that nature includes very simple one-celled molecules, plants, animals and man. Each is dependent on the others and all are built of the same basic stuff. Man being part of nature, they believe therefore in the unity of mankind-human brotherhood, emancipation from ignorance and starvation, and the need for a world government.

Unitarians refer to such religious pioneers as the prophets of ancient Israel, Buddha, Socrates, Jesus, Voltaire, Spinoza and Jefferson as men who may properly be regarded as spiritual ancestors of Unitarianism. As an organized movement, the faith began in the sixteenth century and is most easily understood as the liberal wing of the Protestant Reformation. In the seventeenth and eighteenth centuries it was closely identified with the Enlightenment. Modern Science, modern democracy and modern religion (Unitarianism) had much the same background and have always had much in common.

Unitarians see it as no accident that Unitarianism began in the United States about the same time as the American Revolution and that some famous Americans of the period either belonged to Unitarianism or expressed their sympathy for the beliefs. Some of the names included in this list are John Adams, Thomas Jefferson, Benjamin Franklin and Thomas Paine.

Generally speaking, each Unitarian Church is independent. There is, however, a Canadian Unitarian Council which meets annually. Each congregation is entitled to send one voting delegate, though any interested individual is invited to attend. Also in 1961 in the United States the Unitarians and the Universalists (those who believed that salvation would be universal) united to form the Unitarian-Universalist Association. Headquarters are in Boston and this voluntary association has about 1,100 churches and fellowships in North America. By working together the association members can pursue a wide variety of endeavours that would be impossible if each congregation worked by itself. Each congregation is eligible to send delegates to the annual North American Unitarian-Universalist Association meeting, and in this way the Association is controlled by its churches and fellowships.

Unitarianism has no ecclesiastical authority. The churches are governed by ministers and boards of trustees. In fact, fewer and fewer Unitarian Churches each year have ministers at all. Those that do have often come from other organized churches. There is however a Canadian Unitarian Council which meets annually. Each congregation is entitled to send one voting delegate, though any interested individual is invited to attend.

A. Basic Beliefs

The basic principle of Unitarianism is freedom of belief. Unitarians do not have or require assent to any creed or statement of belief. Instead they maintain that each person has an obligation to seek truth as he best understands it, and to follow that truth wherever it may lead him. A widely used statement declares that Unitarian-Universalist Churches are dedicated to human betterment "through religion, in accordance with the advancing knowledge and the growing vision of mankind. Bound by this common purpose and committed to freedom of belief, we hold in unity of spirit a diversity of convictions".

God   Keeping in mind the freedom of belief mentioned above, Unitarians are free to believe about God whatever seems to them to be true and most meaningful. Some are *agnostics* who prefer to put theology aside and be concerned with moral and ethical questions. For others, however, the concept of God has many deep and sustaining meanings, again varying with the individual. Some see him as the creative process, the life force, the organizing principle of the universe or the ideal of love, justice, goodness and perfection.

Jesus   Two thousand years ago, a brilliant young Jewish teacher and prophet appeared in Palestine. Basing his message on the time-honoured moral and religious precepts of his people, he preached a relationship of man to God that was psychologically and spiritually full of insight, and remarkable for the nobility of its moral and ethical commands. Unitarians regard him as one (and in terms of influence, the greatest) of the master saints and prophets of the human race. He is thought very highly of as are Moses, Buddha, Confucius, Mohammed and other of the world's outstanding religious leaders.

However, Unitarians do not regard him as a supernatural creature, the literal son of God who was divinely sent to earth as part of a master plan for the salvation of men's souls. A summary way of putting it is to say that Unitarians are more inspired by the historical Jesus than the theological Christ. The necessary corollary of this, of course, is a rejection of the usual Christian belief in the Trinity, for such a belief would be contrary to their belief in the unity of things. Furthermore, Biblical references to the Holy Ghost are not to be understood literally; this belief is rejected. Also, Unitarians do not accept the concept of the Virgin Birth. Jesus was not the son of God in any literal sense; spiritually we are all sons of God. If Christ was not the literal son of God, he did not have the power to atone for our sins. Furthermore, say Unitarians, the human race has never fallen and therefore no Atonement is necessary. Most Unitarians accept the theory of evolution and therefore see man as ever-improving and hardly in need of Atonement.

The Bible   Unitarians regard the Bible as a collection of many books written by many men over a 1,300-year period, the sum of which is our greatest single treasury of religious teaching, literature and moral precepts. A basically human document, the Bible is to them a record of man's never ending search for meaning in the universe. Unitarians or "religious liberals" as they sometimes refer to themselves, do not regard the Bible as being in any sense the word of God or as representing any unique, exclusive truth. Nevertheless, it is held in reverence because of its many values and because of what it has meant to Jews and Christians for centuries. But it is not the only book held in reverence; the religious and sacred Scriptures of other religions are regarded in the same way, and include the Vedas of Hinduism, the Koran of Islam and the Tripitaka of Buddhism among others.

Prayer   Can a person have a rational attitude toward prayer? Can a man pray who does not believe in supernaturalism? Does prayer have meaning and value in a scientific age like ours? Yes, say Unitarians, although they reject the magical conception of prayer as a force that can persuade God to change his mind or interfere in the natural order of the universe to answer personal or specific requests.

Instead Unitarians see prayer (or "meditation" as they sometimes call it) as a means by which man brings into focus his finest aims and reaffirms them; is purged of the mean and ignoble; achieves a fresh sense of confidence and inspiration or feels a sense of connection with the eternal realities of the universe. "To whom do you pray?" seems irrelevant to religious liberals. For them, the purpose of prayer is not to change or influence God, it is to motivate and inspire men.

Baptism, and other ceremonies   Many Unitarian churches have ceremonies of

dedication during which parents are reminded of their obligations and children
are dedicated to the service of the highest good, but these ceremonies have
nothing in common with the orthodox notion of the necessity of baptism to wash
away sin. Of course, Communion or the Eucharist is not nearly as significant to
Unitarians because of the lack of acceptance of Jesus as being divine. It is
offered occasionally, only upon request and then as symbolic of love as manifest
in worship. Marriage, a ceremony of the church, is performed, of course. Other
of the seven sacraments known to Roman Catholicism are not practised by
Unitarians even as official ceremonies.

Christmas and Easter   Nearly all Unitarian Churches celebrate Christmas and
Easter but for different reasons and in different ways from their orthodox
neighbours. At the time of the winter solstice toward the end of December
when the days begin to grow longer again, and in the spring of the year when
new life peeks out from a winter-weary earth, men throughout the ages have
held festivals of rejoicing and thanksgiving. It is within this largest universal
context that most Unitarians celebrate Christmas and Easter. If they retain some
of the symbolism traditional to the festivities, it is because they appreciate
symbolism as poetry without accepting it as literal fact.

Christians?   To decide if Unitarians are Christian one must first decide the
meaning of the word. No, if one defines a Christian as a person who accepts the
traditional creeds of 1,500 years ago and the dogmas associated with Christ and
the Trinity. Yes, if you mean that Unitarianism has been an integral part of
Christian history; uses the vocabulary and many of the customs, ceremonies and
ideas (though often somewhat modified) of Christianity; and prizes the teachings of Jesus rather than the theological ideas about Jesus. Some say yes; others
say no.

B. Salvation and the Afterlife

The concept of Original Sin and the doctrine that man has to be saved from the
consequences of that sin are utterly foreign to the thinking of religious liberals.
They believe that although man is conditioned by heredity, environment and
other influences, he is still sufficiently free to shape the world to the pattern of
his greatest dreams. "Salvation by character" — the conviction that our hope lies
in the maturation of man and the continuing improvement of society — is their
faith and their aim.

On the question of immortality, the very large amount of freedom
granted by Unitarianism allows people to believe whatever they personally find
most meaningful. Some are persuaded that death is the end of individual life
and let the matter rest at that. Others believe in an immortality of the spirit, or
that something uniquely and distinctively personal survives the fact of death.
It does seem safe to say though that no Unitarians believe in a Resurrection of
the body, a literal Heaven or Hell, or any kind of eternal punishment. Christ
will not come again to resurrect all men; Christ was a great moral teacher, but
nevertheless mortal and hence subject to death. Heaven and Hell are seen merely
as myths coming to us from the primitive lore of early peoples. The terms are
used only to denote good to be attained and evil to be overcome.

Conclusion

Unitarians believe they put less emphasis than most people on specific, formal beliefs and more on practical, concrete action. Hence, they were early members of the struggle for integration and racial equality in the United States. They have also been leaders of civil liberties, mental health, United Nations and other large social and humanitarian causes of our time.

In this field they have established the Unitarian-Universalist Fellowship for Social Justice, the Departments of Social Responsibility and of Overseas and Interfaith Relations and, the most famous, the Unitarian Service Committee. This Committee was organized in 1940 to assist refugees from Fascist Spain and Nazi Europe. Today it is developing projects at home and abroad in medicine, social work, education, community development, and leadership training based on the concept of self help. Unitarians are proud of the fact that they are basically "this worldly".

Summary

Membership Requirements:

The formal act of joining is usually just a matter of signing a membership card or book.

Essentials of its Nature and Purpose:

Stresses the importance of the freedom and the responsibility, and the goodness of man.

Key Difference(s) from Other Religious Groups:

Reject divinity of Christ. Believe natural law rules the universe.

How Man was Created:

Man evolved from lower forms of life.

Dietary Restrictions:

None.

Position on Birth Control:

A decision of husband and wife.

Canadian Membership and Recent Trend:

6,500 members at last census, 1961. Trend is upward.

For Further Information:

Canadian Unitarian Council,
175 St. Clair Avenue W.,
Toronto 7, Ontario.

11. Other Groups

A. Pentecostal Assemblies of Canada

Origins:

No single founder; related to Pentecostal revival beginnings in parts of North America in early 1900's. Incorporated in Canada in 1919.

Membership Requirements:

Must repent sin and believe Christ has forgiven you and accepted you through his death and Resurrection.

Essentials of its Nature and Purpose:

To perpetuate the teachings, spiritual experiences and practices of the first-century church in the twentieth century.

Key Difference(s) from Other Religious Groups:

Presence of present day reality of the New Testament experience and a belief in the pre-millennial personal return of Christ.

How Man was Created:

Man came from the hand of his Creator.

Dietary Restrictions:

None.

Position on Birth Control:

No official position.

Canadian Membership and Recent Trend:

About 160,000. Up over 10 per cent in last 5 years.

For Further Information:

Pentecostal Assemblies of Canada,
10 Overlea Blvd.,
Toronto 354,
Ontario.

B. Salvation Army

Origins:

Started by William Booth in the East End of London in 1865. Converts from England started work in London, Ontario, in 1882.

Membership Requirements:

Profession of faith in Christ. Must sign a statement making declarations regarding experience, belief and behaviour.

Essentials of its Nature and Purpose:

A Christian movement whose acceptance of Jesus Christ as Lord and Saviour is the source of service, of love to others; characterized by devotion to Christ and practical concern for the needs of others.

Key Difference(s) from Other Religious Groups:

Internationalism: soul saving and social services spread all over the world with no distinction of class, creed or colour. Practical Christianity: serves with heart to God and hand to man. Organized as a military operation with colonels, captains, etc.

How Man was Created:

He was created by God in the image of God.

Among the most significant objects in any Christian church: the Communion cup and wafers. Interpreted by different denominations in different ways, they still symbolize the sacrifice made by Christ for mankind.

Miller Services Ltd.

Dietary Restrictions:

Soldiers are total abstainers from alcohol. They are opposed to tobacco.

Position on Birth Control:

This is an individual matter.

Canadian Membership and Recent Trend:

About 100,000. Slight upward trend.

For Further Information:

Salvation Army,
Information and Special Efforts Department,
20 Albert Street,
Toronto, Ontario.

C.   Seventh Day Adventists

Origins:

Grew out of the extensive worldwide religious movement of many Protestant churches in 1843-44.

Membership Requirements:

To accept Christ as the personal leader of one's life, and to demonstrate this by living by the teachings of the Bible.

Essentials of its Nature and Purpose:

A basing of faith and practice wholly on the Bible. Purpose is to help all people be ready for the imminent return of Christ to this earth.

Key Difference(s) from Other Religious Groups:

A conviction that the seventh day of the week (Saturday) is the only day of religious worship mentioned in the Bible; and its teaching of the literal, visible and physical return of Christ to this earth.

How Man was Created:

God created man.

Dietary Restrictions:

A milk product and vegetarian diet is recommended.

Position on Birth Control:

The church promotes family planning.

Canadian Membership and Recent Trend:

20,450 adults. Up about 20 per cent in last five years.

For Further Information:

Review and Herald,
6840 Eastern Ave. N.W.,
Washington, D.C. 20012.

D. Disciples of Christ

Origins:

Founded by Jesus Christ. All-Canada Committee formed in 1922 by individual Christians associating to advance the cause of Christ.

Membership Requirements:

Faith in Jesus Christ. Repentance from sin. Baptism in water a commitment to the Christian way of life.

Essentials of its Nature and Purpose:

Its aim is to promote unity rather than disunity among Christians, and to restore the simplicity and vitality of the land of Christian experience evidenced in the church of New Testament times.

Key Difference(s) from Other Religious Groups:

Emphasis on the personal nature of Christian faith. Personal commitment to Christ. An effort to be undenominational and emphasize the wholeness of the Christian church in love for the fellowship of *all* Christians.

How Man was Created:

By God, perhaps by evolution or perhaps by other means.

Dietary Restrictions:

None.

Position on Birth Control:

Encourage it.

Canadian Membership and Recent Trend:

About 5,000. Constant.

E. Christadelphians

Origins:

Organized by Dr. John Thomas, an English doctor, in 1832 in the United States. "Christadelphian" means "brethren in Christ".

Membership Requirements:

Faith in Jesus Christ. Repentance from sin. Baptism in water and commitment to Christian way of life.

Essentials of its Nature and Purpose:

They are lifelong Bible students who try to live "in the world but not of it," and whose daily lives are governed by Bible teachings and the example of the elder brother, Jesus Christ.

Key Difference(s) from Other Religious Groups:

They believe in the imminent tangible return of Christ to rule the world in righteousness. They reject as pagan superstition such ideas as "immortal souls" and "going to Heaven when we die". The true Christian's reward will be immortal life here on earth. Read the Bible daily; read the whole Bible at least one and one-half times per year. Refuse to serve in the armed forces or police.

How Man was Created:

God created man from the dust of the ground, and breathed into him the spirit of life.

Dietary Restrictions:

None.

Position on Birth Control:

A private matter for each to decide.

Canadian Membership and Recent Trend:

About 2,000. Constant.

For Further Information:

The Christadelphians,
728 Church St.,
Toronto 285.

F. Society of Friends (Quakers)

Origins:

Grew out of the Christian witness of a young Englishman named George Fox, and his friends in the mid-seventeenth century.

Membership Requirements:

The applicant must be a humble learner and an active seeker who finds spiritual aid in the meetings.

Essentials of its Nature and Purpose:

The Society of Friends is a free religious association. Its purpose is to help people find religious truth as seen by the society and take part in activities related to peace and social concerns.

Key Difference(s) from Other Religious Groups:

Based on what they call the "Inner Light" and the belief that there is "something of God in every man". They wish to stress certain definite values not stressed by other denominations. They have no dogma, creed or liturgy. Most Quakers do not take the Bible literally, and accept a scientific rather than strictly biblical line. They believe the Bible is one Word of God but not the only Word, and that he is still speaking to men of each generation. Most believe that all men are divine and the children of God, but that Jesus was able to rise to the full heights of his divinity and be fully aware of the will of God. They believe there is no need for an intermediary between man and God; thus there are no clergymen. Meetings are based on silent worship.

How Man was Created:

By God's will through evolution.

Dietary Restrictions:

None, aside from moderation.

Position of Birth Control:

An individual matter.

Canadian Membership and Recent Trend:

943. Up slightly in recent years.

For Further Information:

Society of Friends,
60 Lowther Avenue,
Toronto 180.

Conclusion

If the membership figures given by the churches as printed here are accurate, there is very little basis upon which to say that religion is declining in importance in Canada. In fact, if anything there appears to be renewed interest as manifested by the youthful appearance of many adherents especially in some of the newer groups. If one of the reasons for earlier decline in interest was that the churches did not relate to young people, most would agree that there is a definite attempt to do so now. Hence the churches are involved in many youth and social programs outlined in the next chapter.

Suggestions For Further Study

1. What are some of the specific points upon which the United and Anglican Churches of Canada have found agreement in their discussions on church union? What are some of the remaining differences?

2. Some people who are members of one church or another do not know what the official beliefs of that church are; for example, some United Church members are not aware of the existence (let alone the contents) of the *Statement of Faith*, and the same is true in other instances. How can these people consider themselves true members of a church under these conditions? Do you feel that such people should be allowed to join? Defend your position. If unaware of the basic tenets of a church, on what basis do they join? Conduct an informal poll among those you know to find out.

3. What formal educational training has been completed by the clergy of the individual groups discussed in this chapter? What is their annual salary? Do they pay income tax? To what extent are their expenses paid for by their congregations? Should a clergyman be able to afford two cars, a cottage and a colour T.V.? Defend your position.

4. How much latitude do clergymen have in interpreting their church's beliefs? How much are they consulted as to where they will be sent to take a congregation?

5. "The only difference between the Anglican and Roman Catholic Church is that they are led by two different men. In all other major areas they are virtually identical." Decide upon major areas (ritual, organization, etc.) and decide to what extent this statement is true.

6. "Of all the major Christian churches, Christian Science demands the most intellectual concentration to be properly understood." Do you agree? Defend your stand.

7. "Any Christian who fails to actively attempt to bring others into the fold is not a *true* Christian." Defend or refute this statement. Which Christian group is, in your opinion, the most zealous in its missionary work?

8. It is said that there has traditionally been a connection between the "Establishment" in Canada and a particular Christian church. The tradition goes back to at least the 1830's and is present, though in less obvious form, still today. John Porter's *Vertical Mosaic* is helpful on this question. What Christian group is being referred to? To what extent is the allegation true?

9. "A little philosophy inclineth man's mind to atheism, but depth in philosophy bringeth man's mind about to religion" [Francis Bacon]. Do you accept this view? Defend your stand.

10. "Sir, I think all Christians, whether Papists or Protestants, agree in the essential articles, and that their differences are trivial, and rather political than religious" [Samuel Johnson]. To what extent is this an accurate view today?

Chapter Eleven

Religion In Canada Today

At this moment, established religious groups in Canada are under greater stress than they have ever been before. The pressures come both from outside and from within. There are gigantic problems which challenge, and at times seem to contradict, the deepest religious convictions of Canadians. As citizens of the world, they share its concern about pollution, overpopulation and the possibility of nuclear extermination. At home, they see increasing crime, violence, drug use and sexual permissiveness — trends which some people interpret as evidence of the declining moral authority of the church. More and more Canadians are becoming aware of, and concerned about, the continuation of poverty, injustice and public corruption. New questions, such as the morality of birth control, abortion, organ transplants, and test-tube babies, arise almost daily. The faithful turn to their religious leaders for guidance in their conduct, and in some cases for direct action, while the cynics dismiss whatever efforts are made as inadequate or hypocritical, or both.

   In fairness, it should be pointed out that, in attempting to meet these and other challenges, the established religions experience many trying problems. Sometimes they are trapped between traditional teachings and the insistent demands of their members for change. To complicate matters, churches often find their membership seriously divided, not only over whether or not changes should be made, but also over how far-reaching they should be. For good or ill, the major consequences of this whole situation have been the rise of new religious sects, declining attendance in some of the older, more established churches, and a general increase in the number of agnostics in Canada.

1. Church Attendance

The Anglican Church of Canada — in 1931, 15.8% of the population;
                    — in 1961, 13.2%

The Presbyterian Church of Canada — in 1931, 8.4% of the population;
                    — in 1961, 4.5%

The Baptist Church of Canada — in 1931, 4.3% of the population;
                    — in 1961, 3.3%

The above has the familiar ring of a Bay Street report when the market has had a black day. The declining membership, the waning attendance, the increasing defection of the young, the dissatisfaction of many in the ministry with their vocation — the figures speak of these things. To the casual observer, these are symptoms of a malady which has shaken the Christian church in Canada to its roots. It would appear, on the surface at least, that the traditional forms of worship are losing their appeal to more and more of the faithful.

The Canada Census of 1961, cited above, clearly indicated the extent of the losses suffered by the Christian churches, especially those of the major Protestant denominations. Indeed, among the larger Christian churches, only Roman Catholicism showed a significant increase in its membership enrollment in the three decades prior to 1961. In 1931 for example, Catholics comprised 39.5 per cent of the population of Canada; by 1961 this figure had grown to 45.7 per cent. Of perhaps even greater significance was the fact that Catholics made up 50.2 per cent of the all-important under-15 age group. Augmented by generally higher birth rates among its constituents, and continuing immigration from the predominantly Catholic European nations, the Catholic Church seems to be ascendant. It was with these facts in mind that Carleton Professor John Porter remarked: "Canada seems to be on a path to becoming increasingly more Catholic and less British."

The non-Christian churches in Canada have also fared well. The Canadian Bill of Rights guarantees freedom of worship for all religions and this permits even the smallest denominations to thrive and expand their membership. The growing immigration from Eastern countries in recent years has also tended to swell the ranks of the Moslem, Buddhist and Hindu communities in Canada, although they remain comparatively small.

Jews form the largest of the non-Christian denominations in Canada, with approximately 1.5 per cent of the population, the largest portion of which is concentrated in Toronto and Montreal. Moslems number approximately 30,000 with the largest group also residing in Toronto, although a sizeable membership also exists in Montreal, Vancouver and Edmonton, where the first mosque in Canada was erected. The Hindu and Buddhist Churches each number approximately 15,000 members, with the large metropolitan areas again proving popular as homesites among these groups.

The combination of factors noted above seems to augur well for the growth and development of the non-Christian community in Canada.

But among the liberal Protestant churches there is further evidence that the decline has not yet abated. The membership of the United Church reached its highest peak in 1965, but subsequently suffered a steady erosion in its membership. The trend may be seen clearly in areas outside of actual church membership. Both the United and Anglican Churches of Canada reported substantial defections from the ranks of their ministry in recent years. In 1969 alone, the Anglican Church sustained a loss of nearly 100 clergymen and 1,000 Sunday School teachers.

Nor do the figures tell the whole tale. Churchmen of all faiths frankly concede that attendance does not always reflect the official enrollment. In typical congregations, many attend religious services only on important occasions such as Christmas or Easter, and ignore the traditional Sunday worship. To a great extent this attitude seems to be reflected among young people, many of whom avoid participation in religious services, or abandon altogether the religion of their fathers for the novel appeal of the Eastern faiths, or the renewed Christian appeal of the evangelist movement and the Jesus revolution.

The irony of these developments was accentuated by Dr. A. C. Forrest, editor of *The United Church Observer,* following a recent trip to Russia. Dr. Forrest remarked:

In Russia, where the state has officially preached atheism and opposed the Church for 50 years — at the same time permitting freedom of worship — the churches are full. . . . I think it is possible that in North America now with its many churches and its freedom of religion we have fled further from God than anywhere in the Christian world.

Have these trends created shock waves in the religious community, or merely surface ripples? In many ways a minor revolution has already overtaken many Christian churches. In an effort to recapture their audience and rid themselves of the image of dullness, many congregations have completely changed their traditional services — modernizing, updating, streamlining, in short bringing "relevance" to their forms of worship. In recent years the Roman Catholic Church introduced the use of the vernacular — the language of usage in the country — to replace the traditional Latin in the Mass. It also encouraged the participation of laymen in the conduct of the service, and more recently the performance of the "folk mass", where the ceremonies are carried out to the beat of folk or rock groups.

The Protestant churches have also worked to dispel the signs of boredom among their congregations. Rev. Paul Smith of the People's Church of Toronto once brought a horse into the church to enliven his sermon; many churches now purchase ads in newspapers to broaden their appeal; and where the flock has scattered, as in the resort areas, ministers take their pulpits to the beaches and cottages to preach the Word of God.

What effect these innovations are having on attendance is open to question. Enrolment continues to be down and the renewed enthusiasm among the young appears ephemeral. Separate polls conducted at Runnymede Collegiate in Toronto and Emery Collegiate in North York showed that while the majority of students considered themselves religious, only 30 per cent attended church services regularly. When asked why he attended the "folk mass", one youth replied: "The music is a gas."

Many churchmen, however, are optimistic. They view the new trends as a challenge, and an opportunity to re-examine their position, and re-evaluate their doctrines. Some foresee the abandonment of the massive church structures of the past as meeting places for their congregations. These would be replaced by smaller, more flexible neighbourhood "cells", with meetings taking place in local homes, libraries or schoolrooms. Others see the common use of church buildings by several different faiths as a distinct possibility in light of attendance problems.

On one point there is agreement; in light of these trends organized religion must re-examine its function and role if it is to serve the needs of Canadian society.

2. The Changing Role of the Churches

The major religious organizations of Canada have abandoned the notion that they are meeting the needs of Canadian society simply by conducting weddings, baptisms, funerals and regular church services. In the face of the crises, noted previously in this chapter, they could do little else. Today, they are engaged in an ever-increasing variety of social and political activities that are having a significant, positive impact on problems that matter to Canadians.

Social Services   In the realm of social services, hundreds of illustrations could be offered. For example, the Canadian Council of Churches lists the following among its many recent enterprises:

1. a study of the possibility of a guaranteed income scheme
2. a study of penitentiary reform
3. a committee to combat racism in Canada
4. a conference on ecology
5. a commission to study ways of improving English-French relations
6. a study of mixed marriages.

Throughout Canada, ministers are serving as marriage counsellors, legal advisers to minority groups, social workers in slum neighbourhoods, chaplains in prisons, hospitals, and other institutions and in many other capacities. Many churches operate drop-in and recreation centres, coffee-houses, day-care centres, hostels, and so on, usually on their own premises. "Rendezvous" is a recently created co-operative venture among five different Toronto churches, who provide, on a rotating basis, an open-house for distressed or lonely people. "Street Haven", for female drug addicts and prostitutes, and

An informal Eucharist is celebrated by delegates to an Anglican Youth Work Tour Orientation. Caribbean and Canadian youth took part. After the orientation these young people took part in community and youth activities under church auspices during the summer months.

Courtesy Anglican Church House.

the Scott Mission for the indigent and unemployed, are other Toronto-based services which have their counterparts in most large cities across Canada. Several churches co-operate with Alcoholics Anonymous and also with drug-addiction centres, or in a few cases set up their own such centres. Jewish communities, in addition to contributing to general charities such as the United Appeal, are also well known for their own self-help organizations. Of course, the long-established activities of the Salvation Army in such matters as youth centres, maternity homes, camps, clinics, homes for the aged, and the like, are familiar to most Canadians.

Political Activities and Influence   Like other large interest groups, most of Canada's major religious organizations are keenly interested in acquiring and increasing their influence with government. This is partly because the authority and money required to deal meaningfully with the economic and social problems of the country lie with the federal and provincial governments. Also, influence with government is deemed necessary by most churches to uphold their spiritual and ethical values, and to protect their substantial economic interests. Legislation on a wide range of questions like abortion, homosexuality, divorce, censorship, and aid to separate schools, to name but a few, is of great concern to religious groups.

Naturally, the largest denominations are usually the most effective in making their views known and heeded by government. While church leaders can no longer control the voting preferences of their members, as they occasionally did in the nineteenth century, they can still offer "guidance" on keenly felt issues. Moreover, some church-sponsored magazines or journals, such as *The United Church Observer*, provide very lively, controversial journalism and, with their wide circulation, are undoubtedly influential. Through such publications, and through the speeches of their leading officials, many religious organizations have called upon governments to recognize Communist China, legalize therapeutic abortions, stop, or continue, aid to separate schools, stop trading with racist South Africa, reform divorce laws, refrain from taxing church property, and so on.

In addition to various forms of direct influence, many religious organizations have an impact on the thought and action of Canadians in other ways. For example, Catholic Action is a Quebec-based institution, formerly directed by the highly respected Claude Ryan, which has affected the thinking of Quebeckers of all ages and classes. Catholic Action also has had a considerable impact on the reform policies of both Liberal and Union Nationale governments in that province, particularly in the field of education.

Some clergymen and ex-clergymen have entered the arena of politics in order to effect change in government policy. J. S. Woodsworth, an ex-Methodist minister who helped to instigate the Winnipeg General Strike in 1919, also founded the c.c.f. party, which was absorbed into the n.d.p party in 1961. The founder of the Social Credit party, William "Bible Bill" Aberhart, was a Baptist lay preacher, as is T. C. Douglas, the recent leader of the n.d.p. Another prominent figure in the c.c.f.-n.d.p. party, Stanley Knowles, who for many years has been regarded as one of the foremost experts in Canadian parliamentary law, is an ordained United Church minister.

Many of Canada's most outstanding scholars and teachers are active or retired members of the clergy. Canon Lionel Groulx is a highly regarded

Canadian historian. Northrop Frye and E. J. Pratt, both ordained United Church ministers, have been brilliant professors of English at Victoria College, University of Toronto. The well-known media journalist and commentator, Charles Templeton, was once a bigger name in evangelism than Billy Graham.

The "Credibility Gap"   In their efforts to help Canadian society cope with its many problems, religious establishments have had to wrestle with what some people refer to as a "credibility gap". To begin with, the many churches of Canada collectively possess assets valued in the billions of dollars. These take the form chiefly of real estate, buildings, stocks, bonds, art treasures and precious metals or gems. Moreover, few of the governing boards of Canadian churches give significant representation to the underprivileged elements of society, to the young, or to racial and ethnic minorities. Thus, some people have difficulty believing in the sincerity of church efforts to combat poverty, racism, alienation of youth and other ills of today's society, no matter how enthusiastic the speeches of church leaders might be. These sceptics suspect that the large churches are controlled by very conservative elements whose efforts are devoted more to the maintenance of the material interests of the churches themselves than to the betterment of Canadian society as a whole. This was one of several critical comments made by Canadian author Pierre Berton in his best-selling book, *The Comfortable Pew*.

3. The Growth of New Sects and Movements

One of the most interesting phenomena, and perhaps the most significant in Canada and indeed most of the Western world today, is the growth of new cults and sects. An increasing number of young Canadians, joined by smaller numbers of the middle-aged, are turning away from traditional Christianity and Judaism to new "religions", some of which show strong traces of Eastern and even occult influences.

Reasons for this Trend   Although many of today's youth are disillusioned with the outmoded rules and seemingly meaningless ritual of the established faiths, most of them still sense a fundamental spiritual need. The so-called "hippie" philosophy of "free love" and the highly publicized "drug culture", to the extent that they have been attempts to fill this void, have failed to hold large numbers of young people. At the same time, young people have become more aware of other philosophies, because of the continuing impact of the communications media, and because of the influence of prominent figures admired by today's youth.

Interest in the East   Virtually all teenagers have been aware for some time of the interest of the Beatles in Transcendental Meditation, led by Maharishi Yogi, and many of them purchased recordings of George Harrison's "Hare Krishna" song. Bob Dylan and Arlo Guthrie both claimed to be advocates of "I-Ching", an ancient Chinese method of foretelling the future. Timothy Leary, the high priest of drugs, and Allen Ginsberg, a new-left poet, both became deeply involved in Eastern philosophy and managed to communicate this interest to some of their admirers. For these and other reasons, the Eastern religions, or new cults inspired by them, are on the upswing throughout North America. Buddhism and the Baha'i faith are among the leaders in this trend.

Hare Krishna   One of the most recent sects to attract attention is that of Krishna Consciousness, which is led by His Divine Grace A. C. Bhaktivedanta Swami Prabhupada, and which has been strongly influenced by the Vedic literature of India. For example, it shares Hinduism's belief in the ideas of Reincarnation and karma, and that all religions are merely different variations on the same basic theme. Krishna Consciousness teaches that Krishna is the supreme deity. It also contends that humans are the highest form of consciousness, and that a person's goal should be to transcend his physical body through meditation and through living an exemplary life. Drugs and sex outside of marriage are forbidden, and a vegetarian diet is recommended. Devotees wear saffron robes resembling Indian dress, and the males shave their heads, except for a pigtail which Lord Krishna may use to pull them into greater consciousness, and knowledge of him. Their rituals include the use of prayer beads, a sort of rosary, swaying back and forth in group dances, and chanting rhythmic hymns from Vedic scriptures. By chanting the phrase "Hare Krishna", they believe they free themselves from "false ego", and very often they reach high levels of ecstasy. Followers of this philosophy can sometimes be seen in public places, explaining their beliefs or distributing their literature to passers-by.

Krishna-conscious devotees chanting Hare Krishna on a downtown street.

Iskcon Press

The Church of Scientology   One of the fastest growing new religions in North America is the Church of Scientology, which was founded by L. Ron Hubbard in Phoenix, Arizona, around 1950. Its broad aim, according to its own literature, is to create "a civilization without insanity, without criminals and without war, where the able can prosper and honest beings can have rights, and where Man is free to rise to greater heights."[1] It claims to have nine million members throughout the world, including over thirty thousand in Canada, where it is led by the Rev. Bryan G. Levman of Toronto.

The Church of Scientology believes in the basic goodness of man, and places its greatest emphasis on helping people to achieve complete spiritual health, so that they can gain greater insight into themselves and a closer relationship with God. This is done by having disciples relate their problems, and the unpleasant events of their past life, to an "auditor" or counsellor-confessor, who helps them see their difficulties in a new light. Through the "auditing" process, which costs approximately $30.00 per hour, the disciple is then led up through a series of grades of personality development until he is "clear" (cleansed). In this state, the believer in Scientology is a well-balanced, secure, happy individual who is free of all unwanted emotions. The Church of Scientology claims this process to be a unique and exact technology, developed by its founder. It is highly critical of handling what it regards as spiritual problems with hypnosis and drugs. (Medical drugs *are* advised for physical problems.) Also, the Church of Scientology has spoken out against some types of brain surgery, the use of shock treatments, and conditions in prisons and mental hospitals. *Narcanon* is a successful programme for heroin addicts sponsored by the Church of Scientology.

The Process—Church of the Final Judgment

> But CHRIST said: Love your enemies.
> CHRIST'S enemy was SATAN and SATAN'S enemy was CHRIST.
> Through Love enmity is destroyed.
> Through Love saint and sinner destroy the enmity between them.
> Through Love Christ and SATAN have destroyed their enmity and come together for the End;
> CHRIST to Judge, SATAN to execute the Judgment.
> The Judgment is WISDOM; the execution of the Judgment is LOVE.

Thus is explained one of the basic tenets of The Process.

The church was founded by Robert de Grimston, a 35-year-old Englishman, in London, England, in the mid 1960's. The founder is described as being of Anglican background and as having studied religion, architecture and philosophy. He is said to be a visionary and a prophet. The Process was born out of a series of prophetic dreams in which he saw the state of the world and suffering of mankind — a situation which must lead to eventual destruction. After this destruction, he believed a new civilization would be born — one ruled by Christ in love and harmony rather than by man in fear and conflict. As of December 1971, the Processeans claimed a membership around 100,000, though *Time Magazine* in September 1971 placed the membership at 5,000.

What They Do   Processeans carry out a number of services. For example,

almost every afternoon and evening of the week (except Saturday) there are
activities carried on at all Process chapters. Then there are "free shops" and
"free kitchens" where clothes are collected, sewn, cleaned and given to those in
need; food is donated by supermarkets, shops, hotels, etc., and cooked and
served to those in need. "Customers" at these shops may give a donation for
required items in cash or kind, or in helping with the work. Processeans also
visit hospitals, mental institutions, orphanages, old people's homes, prisons,
reform schools and anywhere they feel they can contribute. Money is raised by
Process Disciples giving one-tenth of their income and in some cases by
government grants. In the spring of 1972 the Toronto Chapter of The Process
was awarded a $25,000 grant to specifically fund wages for some of their
volunteer social workers. Money is also raised through the sale of literature in
the chapters, through the mail, on the streets by Messengers (part of the training
programme) and from people who just give donations.

Beliefs   The basics of Processean belief are contained in a small booklet entitled
The Unity of Christ and Satan by Robert de Grimston. Basically it is concerned
with the reconciliation of opposites; Christ said, "Love your enemies" and
Processeans see this as the ultimate reconciliation. They know however that such
reconciliation cannot take place within the present structure of human society.
Thus, they see that the destructive elements of society will destroy *themselves*
and give way to a new and enlightened culture which will be open to the
concept of universal harmony.
        In religious terms this reconciliation of opposites is manifested in the
coming together of Christ and Satan. Satan, the Adversary, redeemed like the
prodigal son, was brought back to the Aura of God through the power and the
love of Christ. What greater conflict can there have been, they ask, than that
between these two Great Beings, Christ and Anti-Christ; the power of good and
the power of evil; the power of right and the power of wrong; the power of light
and the power of darkness? The Process teaches that, in like manner through
the power of love, through acceptance and through healing, all human conflicts
can also be resolved.
        In today's world of strife between rich and poor, Arabs and Jews,
black and white, management and labour, male and female, religion and science,
no one is a winner. But Christ said that these things must be and that we should
not be troubled by them and throw up our hands in despair. Nor, say
Processeans, should we take part in this strife. They say one must be concerned
and involved, but not associated with either side of the conflict; one must
understand and appreciate the points of view on both sides and thereby rise
above the points of difference and disagreement to find and consolidate the
points of mutual agreement.
        Once understanding the importance of Satan and Christ to The Process,
one can see the significance of their Unity Cross. This is a large silver cross with
a scarlet and black serpent engraved on it — Satan, the spirit of healing. If
Christ can heal Satan then he can heal us all, they say. All men must, in their
own minds, understand and balance the extremes in their lives — by so doing,
the conflicts of society can be healed.

The Jesus Revolution   THE BIBLE IS TRUE! MIRACLES HAPPEN; GOD
REALLY DID SO LOVE THE WORLD THAT HE GAVE HIS ONLY

BEGOTTEN SON! This is the essence of the message presently sweeping across
North America. It is a startling development for a generation that has been
constantly accused of "tripping out" or "copping out" with sex, drugs and
violence.

Of course, many have simply adopted a belated hero worship of a
"rebel", the first great martyr to the cause of peace and brotherhood.

However, if one very clear mark identifies adherents to the group, it
is a seemingly total belief in an awesome, supernatural Jesus Christ; not just a
marvelous man who lived 2,000 years ago, but a living God who is both Saviour
and Judge, and the ruler of their destinies. Many theologians who a year or so
ago thought it was a fad, have changed their minds. The devotion and sincerity
of these young people has impressed many. Truly, some say, it is a "Jesus
revolution".

Why did it start? Many of the converts have no doubt turned to Christ
from the fraudulent promises of drugs. For others, the decline of authority led
to a feeling of insecurity. Often security was sought in the oriental, the mystical,
the occult or even in Satanism before familiar roots were once again tapped.
Still others believe that Jesus is seen as a father figure by thousands of young
people whose fathers have never said "I love you."

The movement seems to be divided in two: the Jesus People (also called
Street Christians or Jesus Freaks) who trace their beginnings to San Francisco
in 1967 and who are the most visible; and, the so-called Straight People who are
far larger in numbers and are mainly active in interdenominational, evangelical
campus and youth movements. Together they are making waves in the Christian
communities of North America.

The most obvious example of the presence of the Jesus revolution is in
popular music where such religious tunes as "Amazing Grace", "My Sweet
Lord", and "Put Your Hand in the Hand" have fared well on pop music charts
and also are being incorporated into the services of many churches as hymns.
Godspell, a bright moving musical, written by students and based on the
Gospel according to St. Matthew, was a huge success both in New York and
Toronto; a similar story is true of *Jesus Christ Superstar*, the record album of
which was a huge success. Recently at Fifth Avenue Presbyterian Church in
New York a minister smilingly baptized an infant "In the name of the Father,
the Holy Ghost, and Jesus Christ Superstar". Pat Boone is an enthusiastic
leader of the movement; he baptized more than 200 converts in his own
swimming pool in 1971. Johnny Cash is a Jesus movement convert; so is Paul
Stookey of Peter, Paul and Mary fame.

So sure of the sincerity of the movement is Bill Bright, the founder of
the Campus Crusade for Christ that he recently commented: "Our target date
for saturating the United States with the gospel of Jesus Christ is 1976 — and
the world by 1980. Of course, if the Lord wants to work a bit slower, that's
O.K.".

Susan Alamo conducts a mass baptism at Venice Beach, California, as the Jesus Revolution
sweeps across North America.

Miller Services Ltd.

4. Christian Evangelism

One of the more predictable consequences of the general turmoil which exists in North American religion today has been the revival of evangelism. This trend has been most noticeable in the United States, where gifted preachers, through the expert use of mass media, have converted or reconverted millions of people to a fundamentalist, almost "old-time" religion based on a very strict interpretation of the Christian Bible. Because of their regular use of network radio and television, and their many tours or "crusades" abroad, these American evangelists have become the most prominent leaders of the evangelical movement, not only in their own country, but in Canada and much of Europe as well.

From the time of Christ there have been evangelists. Most are unknown or forgotten; a few became world famous. In ancient times, St. Paul was successful and well known. Today there are Billy Graham, Rex Humbard, Oral Roberts and a host of lesser knowns. Some evangelists today, especially among the lesser knowns, are frauds and hucksters — some have been exposed, while others, such as the celebrated "Marjoe" have admitted the fact. Some people today think very highly of Graham, Roberts or Humbard; others see them as big-time entertainers who have become wealthy under the guise of evangelism. One critical cartoonist portrayed Billy Graham as a grasping materialist and the caption read, "God is bread."

Billy Graham   It is argued by some that Billy Graham is the greatest preacher since St. Paul, and probably for the same reasons, though 2,000 years separate them. Now as then, the world is in confusion. St. Paul spoke to people seeking comfort from the oppression of the Roman Empire, and to those who were concerned with its licentiousness. Billy Graham speaks to those who are seeking an identity and assurance of stability in a modern mixed-up world. But the modern crusader has all the marvels of twentieth-century technology at his command. He faces his audience behind a battery of microphones and he puts on his own colour T.V. programmes which are broadcast at regular intervals throughout Canada and the United States. He is a speaker with a magnetic appeal as one immediately discovers when watching or attending one of his services. Born in 1918, his appearance, energy and dynamism make him seem younger than his years. World-famous now, he appeals to large numbers of Christians of all denominations. Graham is married and has five children.

Born in North Carolina, he was ordained a minister of the Southern Baptist Union in 1939. He soon developed his evangelical zeal and held his first crusade in 1947 in Grand Rapids, Michigan. Six thousand people attended and so successful was his preaching that 500 of them came forward to make a "decision for Christ" — Billy Graham's way of interpreting the desire to know more about Christianity. Something in his message caught on, for when he held another meeting one month later, the attendance figures shot up to 42,000. In 1950 he faced audiences totalling 350,000 in an eight-week campaign in Los Angeles. In 1955 he toured Great Britain and continental Europe where well over one million people attended services. In 1956 he toured the Far East and in 1960 a long pilgrimage took him to Australia, New Zealand, Africa and the Holy Land. Now he has campaigned in every American state and nearly

Miller Services Ltd.

Billy Graham speaking before 51,000 people during one of his crusades in Northern California. A One Way sign appears behind Dr. Graham who, according to one youth, was getting through when he said, "Man, Jesus Christ is where it's at and Billy Graham tells it like it is." Total attendance for the ten-day crusade was 367,200 with 21,670 people making decisions for Christ.

every major city in the Western world as well as some in Eastern Europe.

His books *Peace with God, The Secret of Happiness, My Answer,* and *World Aflame* have been read by millions. His column *My Answer* appears in many United States newspapers every day, and he has been named "Man of the Year" by *Time* magazine. Each week 800 radio stations around the world broadcast his "Hour of Decision" programme and he now sponsors a T.V programme with money collected in 1970 and 1971 campaigns. Thus after 20 years his audiences are still growing; in 1970 he revisited Europe to speak to vast numbers.

The Billy Graham Evangelistic Association is big business. At his meetings he pleads for $1.00 from everyone in the audience. Few of his workers are salaried, but for a major campaign he can always recruit 5,000 volunteer workers to run his "secretariat" which puts every person who comes forward in touch with a church near his home. Books, pamphlets and records are another major source of income. Big crowds are drawn to his crusades by show business personalities like singer Ethel Waters and British pop singer Cliff Richard, backed by choirs of up to 5,000.

No one knows how lasting Billy Graham's success will be. Many people are hypnotized by the crowds, the choirs and the passionately exclaimed simple message. They move forward to the rostrum to announce their religious beliefs. A brief history of every man, woman and child is noted and these particulars sent to a pastor in their hometown. Many fall by the wayside, but for most of them, at least for a time, they live their lives with renewed hope.

Rex Humbard   Another very popular though less well-known evangelist is Rex Humbard. In his early fifties, Alpha Emmanuel Rex Humbard is pastor of two congregations. One numbers about 2,800 families who are members of his Cathedral of Tomorrow in Akron, Ohio. The other, his "television ministry", spans the continent and is claimed to be the largest congregation in the world. On Sundays Humbard holds an hour-long, interdenominational service in his church which is video-taped and distributed for broadcasting 14 days later to, at last count, 215 American and some 100 Canadian television outlets. Its audience is about the size of Canada's population — 21,000,000. This is staggering exposure, the largest in television history and thus Humbard is now seen by more people than is Billy Graham. Since this exposure is paid for by the viewers, it is clear that many millions of Canadians and Americans believe in Rex Humbard.

Once a month Humbard and his T.V regulars go on the road for a week of one-night rallies somewhere in the United States or Canada. Humbard says: "We must meet the people." In the spring of 1971, for example, they flew into Ontario — to Chatham, Peterborough, Orillia, Kingston and Ottawa. The mood at Humbard meetings is a happy one; hot dogs, cokes and chips sell well. There are lots of songs and many short prayers. Humbard looks fit and is the centre of attention, with hair brushed and sprayed to perfection. A dynamic speaker, he hammers home the simple message — Seek the Saviour! Repent! Be born again! He talks of the "three dimensions" — mental and physical man is doing fine he says, but spiritual man is not. That is the neglected third dimension.

There is an offering as in all churches and then finally there is "altar call". Folks, often 200 of them, assemble before Humbard. He gets down on one knee, squeezes his eyes shut and they all pray — the service is thus brought to a close.

The Humbard Empire   Rex Humbard, 51, was born in Little Rock, Arkansas, the oldest of six children. He came by his fundamentalism naturally: his parents, both evangelists, brought their children into religious work early.

A high school graduate, Humbard received no religious training. He was ordained by his father.

After the Sunday night service in 1942 at Cadle Tabernacle in Indianapolis, Humbard married his beautiful Texan wife, Maude Aimee Jones.

The family was still travelling in 1952 when Humbard decided to settle in Akron, Ohio, because "God had work for me there."

"He gave me an idea," Humbard states in his book. It was to build a great church and bring the gospel via television to all the United States and Canada. "I had $65 at the time", he says.

Humbard built the church, created the "television ministry" and, in the process, developed a multi-faceted, multi-million-dollar religion-business empire.

The Cathedral of Tomorrow in Akron is the largest interdenominational church in the world, and seats nearly 5,000. It is a huge, domed, circular, glass and marble structure that cost $3.5 million. A special feature is a 100-by-50 foot cross suspended from the dome with 4,700 light bulbs that can be illuminated in 60 patterns of red, white and blue.

1. The operation's colour television equipment is estimated at over $2 million.
2. Humbard said the television ministry is paid for by viewer's donations, and that this year's budget would be around $7 million.
3. This corporation, Cathedral of Tomorrow, Inc., owns an ad agency, a girdle manufacturing company, an electronics company, a multi-million-dollar fully equipped college, and a 52-seat Viscount turboprop.

    The corporation is building a television station next to the church. This will include a 1,300-seat restaurant and a $4-million, 750-foot tower with a revolving dining lounge modelled after Calgary's Husky Oil Company Tower. Humbard says it is a non-profit corporation created to spread the gospel. He said that, as president, he draws a salary of $500 a week. The operation has a staff of nearly 200.

4. The organization's latest acquisition, purchased in June, 1971 reportedly for $10 million, was a complex of new structures in downtown Akron, including a 24-storey office building, a 2,150-car parking lot and a 14-storey motel.
5. He said that while company profits may go to help the television work, viewers' contributions are never used by the corporation. He said the operations are kept strictly separate as is the church's own $500,000 budget. This goes for his Canadian office in Toronto, which spends $60,000 a month on the cause. "All the money taken in Canada must stay for our work there", he said.

5. Ecumenism

From the time of the great split in Christianity created by the Protestant Reformation, responsible churchmen on both sides have looked forward to the day when the "separated brethren" on both sides would be reunited or at least be capable of working together in a spirit of brotherhood. It was not until the nineteenth century, however, that this spirit of co-operation and unity among Christian churches, now commonly referred to as the ecumenical movement, began to take serious shape.

Pope Paul and Dr. Arthur Ramsay, Archbishop of Canterbury, exchange gifts at their first meeting in 1966. The head of the world-wide Anglican communion gave the Pope a pectoral cross and several volumes of his writings; in return the pontiff gave Dr. Ramsay a twelfth-century painting of Christ and a series of Church Council decisions. Also present is Bishop Jan Willebrands of Holland, secretary of the Vatican Secretariat for Promoting Christian Unity.

Organizations such as the Y.M.C.A, founded in 1844, and the Y.W.C.A, founded in 1855, performed valuable pioneer work in this field among young people. Soon the churches caught the enthusiasm and the movement quickly spread worldwide.

In Canada too there was great hope. The first significant fruits of the ecumenical movement in Canada were seen in the creation of a new church union. In 1925 "three great streams of religious life", the Methodist, Presbyterian and Congregational Churches of Canada, merged to form the United Church of Canada. Its purpose was expressed in these terms:

It shall be the policy of the United Church to foster the spirit of unity in the hope that this sentiment of unity may in due time, so far as Canada is concerned, take shape in a Church which may fittingly be described as national.[2]

While certain problems were created and some congregations, notably a minority among Presbyterians, rebelled, in general the union proved a great success, and other Protestant denominations began to examine seriously the possibility of further union.

The heightened ecumenical spirit fostered during the period of World War II, possibly as the result of the widespread use of army chaplains of all religions to minister to the religious needs of the Canadian army, created the atmosphere for the next important step. At Yorkminster Baptist Church in Toronto in September 1944, as the direct result of "the movement of inter-Church co-operation within Canada" and the international ecumenical movement, ten Canadian Christian churches met to form the Canadian Council of Churches.

The council did not represent an actual union, for each church retained the freedom to choose its own course of action. Rather, the council sought to urge joint action by the member churches in areas of legitimate concern, particularly in areas of social action. The constitution of the council states that its purpose "shall be to serve God in His mission to the world to give expression to the unity which is offered to the world through Jesus Christ, to witness to the continuing renewal of the Church by the Holy Spirit, to promote the growth of ecumenical and missionary obedience among all Christians, and to facilitate common action by the member churches."

The current membership of the council consists of the following churches:

The Anglican Church of Canada
The Armenian Church of Canada — Diocese of Canada
The Baptist Federation of Canada
The Christian Church (Disciples) — All-Canada Committee
The Greek Orthodox Archdiocese of North and South America — Ninth District
The Lutheran Church in America — Canada Section
The Presbyterian Church in Canada
The Reformed Church of America — Classis of Ontario
The Salvation Army — Canada and Bermuda
The Religious Society of Friends — Canada Yearly Meeting
The United Church of Canada

From the beginning however, it was clear to many that the future of ecumenism in Canada would be determined by the attitude of the Catholic Church. It was futile to speak of Christian co-operation without the active participation of one-half the Christian population of Canada. The initial reaction from Rome proved disappointing; Pope Pius XI's statement in 1928 that Christian unity could best be served "by furthering the return to the one true Church of Christ those who are separated from it" which would include adopting the belief in the infallibility of the Roman pontiff, cooled Protestant advances and seemed to permanently exclude Catholicism from the mainstream of the ecumenical movement.

Some were relieved to see Roman Catholicism remain outside of the movement, fearing a Catholic takeover of the decision-making process among Christian churches should they become involved. This attitude is still operative to some extent. Charles A. Tipp, editor of the *Evangelical Baptist* voices these reasons for his apprehension of Catholic motives:

> Rome may be very happy to reach *rapprochement* with the Orthodox and Anglican communions of the world and few other denominations. They would then claim over 75 per cent of all Christians. This would leave most of the Presbyterians, Baptists and various other denominations outside their jurisdiction and on the defensive. Yes, Rome could have another Francis of Assisi or Luther. But I believe they and their followers would receive the same treatment as their predecessors. They would be persecuted or excommunicated or their movement would be absorbed and modified.[3]

The unexpected revolution in the Catholic attitude was brought about with the accession of John XXIII to the papal throne and his subsequent convocation of Vatican Council II in 1962. At that time the pontiff called for the revival of Christian morality and spoke of the need to bring the Catholic Church "into closer accord with the needs and conditions of our times." Pope John hoped that this would in itself "provide an outstanding example of truth, unity and love". He also said:

> May those who are separated from this Apostolic See, beholding this manifestation of unity, derive the inspiration to seek out the unity which Jesus Christ prayed for so ardently from his heavenly Father.

This was a clear call to renewed efforts for ecumenical dialogue, this time with the blessing and assistance of the Catholic Church and with every hope for its future co-operation.

The Protestant approach and answer may well be found in the words of A. B. Moore, President of the Canadian Council of Churches. In his 1971 address to the council, Dr. Moore remarked:

> The isolated individual is a myth, the isolated church is an anachronism. The individual who lives to himself is sick. The Church that

lives to itself is blasphemous. Only within fellowship may we be and do what Christ asks us to be and do in this generation. Only in fellowship which crosses the lines of division will the strength of the whole vision be brought to the local and individual.[4]

Conclusion

What the future holds for the church in Canada, and indeed organized religion throughout the world, will largely be determined by its response to the issues facing contemporary society: family planning, poverty, racism, mass education, the increasing participation of women in church councils — these are but a few of the social problems which will have to be met and solved if organized religion is to survive in its present form. In a world which is increasingly viewed as a "global village" and where the actions of individual men and nations can no longer be considered in isolation, the desirability for all religions to act in unison becomes all the more apparent.

One proposed solution — the idea of religious unity not only of Christian churches but of all religions — strikes a responsive chord in many people whose philosophy is one of tolerance and respect for the faiths of other men. The obstacles to such union are perhaps insurmountable; but to its advocates, the movement is nonetheless necessary. The noted historian Arnold Toynbee calls the major religions "variations on a single theme", and from the East the keynote call for a union of faiths comes from Indian philosopher S. Radhakrishnan. Whether one embraces the universal concept or maintains his devotion to an individual faith, it is a statement which should give all men reason for thought:

> In a restless and disordered world which is unbelieving to an extent which we have all too little realized, where sinister superstitions are setting forth their rival claims to the allegiance of men, we cannot afford to waver in our determination that the whole of Humanity shall remain a united people, where Moslem and Christian, Buddhist and Hindu shall stand together, bound by a common devotion not to something behind but to something ahead, not to a racial past or a geographical unit but to a great dream of a world society with a universal religion of which the historical faiths are but branches. . . .[5]

Suggestions For Further Study

1. Investigate the nature and variety of church-sponsored social services in your community.

2. Develop a chart on which you can list the position of Canada's major religious groups on controversial issues facing today's society. Include in your chart whatever laws exist pertaining to each issue.

3. As a general rule, should a religious faith alter its basic teachings or doctrines to "fit the times" and please people, or adhere closely to its long-established beliefs? Defend your point of view.

4. Because of certain articles written in the last few years in *The United Church Observer* there has been noticeable tension between that church and some

parts of Canada's Jewish community. Read back issues of *The Observer* to find what the controversy is about. Do you feel that a church publication should be speaking strongly on this? Does *The Observer* reflect official United Church thinking?

5. Neither church land nor buildings (of any denomination) are taxed in Canada today. What would be the effects of taxation on the churches of Canada? After investigating this question debate whether or not they *should* be taxed.

6. Many churches advertise in Canadian newspapers today. How do you react to the charge that, by advertising, these churches prove themselves to be little more than business ventures? What arguments can be used to defend the policy of advertising?

7. One of the problems confronting organized religion in Canada is the question of racial or religious discrimination. What is the official position of your church on these issues? What was the policy of Canada's Christian churches regarding anti-Semitism during the pre-World War II period? What is their current policy toward apartheid in South Africa?

8. There has been concern expressed over the future of the ecumenical movement. What roadblocks stand in the way of a possible Catholic-Protestant union? Of union between Christian and non-Christian churches?

Notes

[1]L. Ron Hubbard, *The Aims of Scientology*. Saint Hill Manor, Sussex: Hubbard College of Scientology, 1965.
[2]*Constitution*, Article III, The Canadian Council of Churches, Toronto, Ontario.
[3]Philip LeBlanc and Arnold Edinborough, eds., *One Church Two Nations*. Toronto: Longman, 1968, p. 59. Reprinted with permission.
[4]"The President's Address", "The Minutes", p. 4, Central Committee Meeting held in Kitchener, Ontario, November 23-25, 1971. Used by permission of the Canadian Council of Churches, Toronto, Ontario.
[5]The Editors of Life, *The World's Great Religions*. New York: Time, Inc., 1957.

Appendices

Glossary

Note: In explaining the terms listed below, the authors have attempted to give definitions acceptable to the majority of the adherents of the particular religions concerned. They realize such explanations might be considered incomplete, or even, in a few instances, unacceptable to certain followers of those religions.

Abhidhamma Pitaka (Buddhism): a major section of the principle Scripture, the Tripitaka.

absolution (Christianity): the act by which a priest of the Roman Catholic or Greek Orthodox Church, acting as an agent of Christ, grants forgiveness of sins.

adiaphora (Christianity): a Lutheran term meaning that many practices and ways of doing things are of little importance, so long as they are done decently and in good order.

Adonai (Judaism): a Hebrew word meaning "Lord". Used because the name "Yahweh" is considered by some Jews too holy to utter.

Adoratio (Christianity): in the Roman Catholic Church, a ceremony in the Sistine Chapel during which the cardinals vow allegiance to a newly elected pope, before the announcement of the election is made public.

agnostic: a person who holds that man cannot have certain knowledge of immaterial reality, especially the existence of God and things pertaining to Him.

ahimsa: the doctrine of non-violence emphasized in Jainism, and also practised by Hindus and Buddhists.

aliyah: (Judaism): a call to come forward to recite a portion of the Torah, during the Bar Mitzvah ceremony.

Allah (Islam): God.

Amaterasu (Shinto): the sun goddess.

Analects, The (Confucianism): thoughts and sayings of Confucius, collected and written down by his disciples.

anatta (Buddhism): the no-soul doctrine. Buddha rejected the idea of a human soul.

angels: purely spiritual, immortal beings with intelligence and free will, whose name indicates their mission as ministers of God and ministering spirits to men.

animism: the belief that all objects in the world, living and non-living, possess souls or supernatural spirits.

anthropomorphism: the belief held most commonly in the religions of the ancient world that the gods possessed human form.

Apocrypha: fourteen miscellaneous books which form a bridge between the Old and New Testaments.

Aranyakas (Hinduism): Scriptures commenting on the Vedas.

archbishop (Christianity): a prelate in charge of an archdiocese.

arhat (Buddhism): holy man who has freed himself of all desires and thus has achieved enlightenment.

Arjuna (Hinduism): the hero of the Hindu epic, the Bhagavad-Gita.

asana (Hinduism and Buddhism): a bodily position assumed during meditation. There are several such positions.

asceticism: the practice of very strict or severe devotions, usually involving self-denial, eg. fasting.

Atharva-Veda (Hinduism): a section of the Vedas, consisting of various charms and incantations.

atheist: one who believes that there is no God.

atman (Hinduism): a Sanskrit word for soul. Hindus believe an atman to be a part of the world soul, Paramatman.

Australopithecus: a species representing the first stage of human evolution, believed to have existed two million years ago.

avatar (Hinduism): an incarnation of the God Vishnu.

Avesta or *Zend-Avesta* (Zoroastrianism): the sacred literature of the Zoroastrian religion.

azan (Islam): the call used by the muezzin to summon Moslems to prayer.

ba (Egyptian): the true soul of a person which left the body at death. It was depicted as a human-headed bearded bird.

baals: nature gods of the Canaanites; baal worship was adopted by some Jews in ancient times.

Babylonian captivity: the exile of the Jews deported by Nebuchadnezzar into Babylonia, 597 B.C.

baptism (Christianity): a sacrament symbolic of spiritual regeneration in which, through the use of water or oil and the recitation of a few words, the recipient is cleansed of Original Sin, and admitted into Christianity or a specific Christian church. In Christian Science it means a submergence in Spirit or purification by Spirit.

Bar Mitzvah (Judaism): means literally a Son of the Commandment. It is a ceremony by which a boy becomes a full member of the Jewish community; symbolizes the coming of manhood and religious responsibility.

basilica (Christianity): a title assigned to certain Roman Catholic Churches because of their antiquity, dignity, historical importance or significance as centres of worship.

Bhagavad-Gita (Hinduism): a famous portion of the great epic, the Mahabharata. The Gita fully develops Brahmanism.

bhakti (Hinduism): intense devotion or love shown toward a particular god or gods.

Bhakti Yoga (Hinduism): the way to union with God through intense devotion to one or more manifestations of God (lesser deities).

bishop (Christianity): churchmen believed to be (in union with fellow bishops) the successor of the Apostles as pastor of the church; the head of a diocese.

Black Stone (Islam): a small rock, possibly part of a meteorite, which Arabs have regarded as sacred since before the birth of Mohammed. It is housed in the Kaaba in Mecca (see also Kaaba).

bodhi (Buddhism): perfect wisdom, or enlightenment.

bodhisattva (Buddhism): a saviour who has attained bodhi or enlightenment but who remains in the world to help others toward the same goal.

Brahma (Hinduism): god of creation, a member of the trimurti and the personification of Brahman.

Brahman (Hinduism): the eternal, unchanging cosmic force underlying all existence. All things come from and ultimately return to Brahman.

Brahmanas (Hinduism): Scriptures forming part of the Vedas, and containing rules for sacrificial rituals.

Brahmanism (Hinduism): the Hindu belief in Brahman as the supreme principle of life.

Brahmin (Hinduism): a member of the priestly caste; the first class in Hindu society.

Buddha: the founder of Buddhism (*see* Gautama).

Caliph (Islam): the title taken by successors to Mohammed as the spiritual and political leaders of the Moslem world.

caste system (Hinduism): a principal feature of Hindu society, dividing the majority into four basic classes, each with its own rules, duties and social and religious status.

cathedral (Christianity): the principal church in a diocese, the one in which the bishop has his seat, cathedra.

celibacy (Christianity): in the Roman Catholic Church, the unmarried state of life required of candidates for holy orders and of men already ordained to holy orders, for the purpose of chastity and total dedication to the service of people in the ministry of the church.

Chaos (Greek): the formless void from which the universe sprang.

chih (Confucianism): the ideal of wisdom.

circumcision (Judaism): the act of cutting off the foreskin, performed on the eighth day after birth; originally a sign of the faith in the flesh intended to show a bodily sign of spiritual belief.

collegiality (Christianity): the Roman Catholic statement by which the bishops of the church in union with and subordinate to the pope, have supreme teaching and pastoral authority over the whole church.

confession (Christianity): the sacrament by which a person tells or confesses his sins to a priest who is authorized to give absolution in the sacrament of penance.

confirmation (Christianity): the sacrament by which a baptized person, through the anointing with oils and the laying on of hands is endowed with the gifts and special strength of the Holy Spirit for mature Christian living.

cosmology: a theory relating to the structure of the universe and the principles which govern it.

Covenant (Judaism): an agreement made at Sinai in which God swore to show everlasting love in return for the obedience of the Jews to his Law.

Cro-Magnon Man: the first true man who emerged about 30,000 years ago and developed elaborate burial rites for his dead.

Dalai Lama: ruler of Tibet, and God-King of Tibetan Lamaism.

Deism: the belief that God, though he created the world does not interfere in its affairs; belief in the existence of God.

dharma (Hinduism and Buddhism): moral

or sacred duty; the path to be followed depending on one's nature and position in life.

Dionysia (Greek): a festival in honour of the god of wine, Dionysus.

dispensation (Christianity): the relaxation of a law in a particular case; the pope is dispensed from all ecclesiastical laws.

du'a (Islam): private or inner prayer.

dukka (Buddhism): the idea of suffering, one of the chief characteristics of existence.

Ebionites or Nazarenes: zealous early Jewish-Christian sect.

ecumenism (Christianity): the movement of Christians and their churches toward the unity believed to be willed by Christ.

Elysian Fields (Greek): the land of the blessed dead, where souls favoured by the gods led a pleasant and peaceful existence.

Epicureanism: the teachings of the Roman philosopher, Epicurus, that the chief good in life is the pursuit of pleasure and the avoidance of pain.

Essenes (Judaism): members of a Jewish religious order (second century B.C. to second century A.D.) who believed in immortality but not Resurrection, and who practised ceremonial purity.

ethics: the study of man's moral behaviour.

Eucharist (Christianity): the sacrament commemorating Christ's Last Supper in which Christ is present and received through the consecrated elements of bread and wine. In Christian Science, spiritual communion with God.

evangelism: (Christianity): the zealous preaching and dissemination of the gospel.

evolutionism: a theory which suggests that all religions develop through stages from primitive origins to the major modern faiths.

Exodus (Judaism): a book of the Pentateuch in the Old Testament; contains some of the most important events in Biblical history, including the deliverance of the Hebrews from bondage in Egypt, institution of the Passover and the giving of the Ten Commandments.

extreme unction (Christianity): a Roman Catholic sacrament, now called "anointing of the sick", by which a person is given comforting grace, remission of venial sins and some mortal sins.

fetish: any object which is thought to possess special supernatural powers.

Gathas (Zoroastrianism): songs or hymns ascribed to Zoroaster. They form part of the Avesta.

Gautama: the founder of Buddhism.

Gemara (Judaism): the second part of the Talmud, consisting of a commentary on the Mishna.

genius (Roman): the spirit or soul, believed by ancient Romans to be each man's true nature or spiritual double.

ghetto (Judaism): originally a street or sector of a city enclosed by walls and a gate in which Jews were compelled to live; existed from the eleventh century in Italy to the late nineteenth century in Italy, Germany, Russia, etc; any city section inhabited by a minority.

godparents (Christianity): men and women whose function after baptism is to serve as the proxies for the parents if they should be unable or fail to provide for the religious training of the child.

Granth (Sikhism): the holy Scriptures of the Sikhs.

guru (Hinduism): a religious teacher or spiritual guide, who can help a person attain Nirvana.

Hadith (Islam): the authentic teachings, sayings and deeds of the Prophet Mohammed.

Haggadah (Judaism): the fables and proverbs of Talmudic literature, as distinct from the Law; the story of the Exodus read at the beginning of Passover.

hajj (Islam): pilgrimage to Mecca.

Hanafites: a Moslem sect.

Hanukkah (Judaism): Festival of Lights.

hara-kiri (Shintoism): Japanese term for ritual suicide.

Hasidim (Judaism): originally the most rigid adherents of Judaism. When Antiochus IV decreed that the Jews must offer sacrifices to Greek gods, the Hasidim led the resistance.

Heaven: in Roman Catholicism, the state of those who, having achieved salvation, are in glory with God. Heaven is a feature of other religions as well, and is seen in different ways by different peoples, groups and sects.

Hegira (Islam): the flight of Mohammed and his followers from Mecca to Medina in 622 A.D.

Hell: in the Roman Catholic Church, the state of punishment of those who die in mortal sin, in a state of alienation from God and in opposition to the divine plan of salvation. Hell is a feature of other religions as well, and is seen in different ways by different peoples, groups, and sects.

Hinayana Buddhism: (See Theravada Buddhism).

holy orders (Christianity): the sacrament by which spiritual power and grace are given to enable an ordained minister to consecrate the Eucharist, and perform other church functions; principal orders of the clergy in Christian churches.

Holy Spirit (Christianity): Third Person of the Trinity.

homa (Hinduism): a form of worship, in which an offering is placed in a fire that has been blessed by a priest.

Homo erectus: a species representing the second stage of human evolution. It existed 500,000 years ago, and is believed to have possessed the ability to make fire.

hsin (Confucianism): the virtue of honesty.

I Ching: the Confucianist "Book of Changes".

idolatry (Christianity and Judaism): worship of any but the true God; a violation of the First Commandment.

imam (Islam): the senior official of a mosque.

Immaculate Conception (Christianity): Roman Catholic belief that Mary, in view of her calling to be the mother of Christ, was preserved from the first moment of her conception from Original Sin.

incarnation (Christianity): the taking on of human nature by the Second Person of the Trinity, who became human as the son of Mary.

indulgence (Christianity): in the Roman Catholic Church, the remission before God of the temporal punishment due for sins already forgiven (as far as their guilt is concerned), which a follower of Christ acquires through the intervention of the church.

Jainism: a religion of India founded in the sixth century B.C., that teaches the immortality and transmigration of the soul, and denies the existence of a perfect or supreme being.

japa (Hinduism): a form of worship featuring the chanting of the name of a favourite deity.

Jataka (Buddhism): part of the Buddhist Scriptures. The Jataka Tales are a collection of over 500 stories of former lives of Buddha.

jen (Confucianism): brotherly love, or compassion, the highest of all Confucian virtues.

Jihad (Islam): struggle against evil; it may include a holy war to defend the faith.

Jina (Jainism): a term meaning "conqueror", which is applied to Vardhamana, (the founder of Jainism) and to those sharing his beliefs.

jinns (Islam): spirits capable of assuming human or animal form.

jiva (Jainism): the concept of a soul.

jnana-yoga (Hinduism): the way to union with God through supreme knowledge.

ka (Egyptian): a person's second soul; it was thought to be his exact replica or double.

Kaaba (Islam): a small, rectangular shrine at Mecca which houses the Black Stone and is the main centre for pilgrims.

kami (Shintoism): any type of supernatural being or force.

kami-dana (Shintoism): a god-shelf on which a Shintoist keeps religious artifacts, and which serves as an altar for prayer.

karma (Hinduism and Buddhism): the accumulation of good or evil, depending on conduct, which brings rewards or punishments to a soul in its next life.

karma yoga (Hinduism): the way to union with God through good actions and thoughts.

Kashruth (Judaism): the Jewish dietary laws.

Kharijites (Islam): a Moslem sect.

kismet (Islam): the concept of fate.

koan (Zen Buddhism): a puzzle or riddle presented to a novice by his master for the purpose of mental discipline.

Kojiki (Shintoism): an important text of the Shinto faith.

Koran: the holy book of Islam.

kosher (Judaism): a Jewish term meaning "fit to eat"; a prescribed method of killing that must be followed before meat is declared "kosher".

Krishna (Hinduism): a god, usually portrayed as loving and compassionate (and one of the many avatars of the god Vishnu).

Kshatriya (Hinduism): a member of the ruler-soldier caste, the second class in Hindu society.

Lao-tzu: founder of Taoism.

Laws of Manu (Hinduism): Hindu texts establishing principles of social and religious life.

li (Confucianism): the virtue of propriety.

limbo (Christianity): in the Roman Catholic Church, an as yet formally undefined state held to be a condition of rest and natural happiness for unbaptized infants.

liturgy (Christianity): the rituals or established formulas for public worship.

maat (Egyptian): the ethical principle which maintained that good deeds would produce good results.

Magi (Zoroastrianism): members of the Persian priestly class before Zoroaster.

magic: the attempt to manipulate the forces of the universe through the practice of prescribed rituals.

Mahabarata (Hinduism): the larger of the two great Hindu epics, developing the universal themes of good versus evil, and individual conscience in conflict with the rules of society.

Mahavagga (Buddhism): a part of the Scriptures of Buddhism.

Mahayana Buddhism: the largest school of Buddhist thought, more liberal than the older Theravadin school.

Mahdi (Islam): a divinely guided ruler who according to Moslem belief, is the last legitimate caliph and will return to earth to unite the faithful and conquer the world for Islam.

Malikites (Islam): a Moslem sect.

mana: a term of Melanesian origin which refers to an impersonal supernatural force thought to exist in some types of animate and inanimate objects.

manitou: a sacred power or force of nature, either good or bad, similar to the Melanesian mana, revered by the Algonquin and other North-American Indians.

mantra (Hinduism): a sacred word or phrase.

Mara (Buddhism): the Buddhist equivalent of the devil.

matrimony: marriage, a sacrament of the Roman Catholic and Anglican Churches.

matzah (Judaism): unleavened bread eaten especially during the festival of Passover.

Maulawiyah (Islam): the "Whirling Dervishes", a well-known M o s l e m brotherhood.

maya (Hinduism): a word in Hindu philosophy suggesting a temporary, illusory nature; applied to this present world.

Mechitza (Judaism): a partition used in Orthodox congregations to separate the women from the men.

Meng-Tze (Confucianism): the Book of Mencius; a principal source of Confucianist ideas.

minyan (Judaism): the quorum of ten men essential for public prayer.

Mishnah (Judiasm): interpretation of original Torah in the light of second-century A.D. conditions.

Mitzvot (Judaism): Commandments of Divine Law; originally there are believed to have been six hundred and thirteen of them, now reduced to the Ten Commandments.

Mohammed: the founder of the Moslem faith.

moksha (Hinduism and Buddhism): release from samsara, or the cycle of rebirths.

monism: the belief that a single element or principle underlies all reality. This principle is conceived of as mind or matter, rather than a god.

monotheism: belief in and worship of one god.

mortal sin (Christianity): in the Roman Catholic Church, rejection of God manifested by free and deliberate violation of his Law, sufficient to result in *total* alienation from God, making a person "dead" to sanctifying grace and subject to everlasting punishment.

muezzin (Islam): the person who summons the faithful to prayer.

Murjites (Islam): a relatively liberal Moslem sect.

Mutazilites (Islam): a Moslem sect.

Mysteries, The: in the time of ancient Greece, certain religious cults whose rites were kept secret from all but initiates.

myth: explanation of the world by ascribing the phenomena of nature to supernatural or immortal beings, but superhuman heroes.

Nanak: the founder of Sikhism.

Neanderthal man: a kind of man who lived about 150,000-30,000 years ago.

Nihongi (Shintoism): an important text of the Shinto faith.

Nirvana (Hinduism and Buddhism): self-annihilation, or the extinguishing of all traces of desire, which represents final enlightenment and which releases a person from the cycle of rebirths.

numina (Roman): the powerful, invisible forces, believed by ancient Romans to exist everywhere in nature.

Okipa: four-day religious ritual of the Mandans, an extinct tribe of Indians who were located in what is now the north-western United States.

oracles (Greek): individuals who were believed to have the power to communicate with the gods and foretell the future.

orenda: a sacred power, similar to the Melanesian "mana" or the Sioux "wakan", worshipped by the Iroquois Indians.

original sin (Christianity): the sin of Adam, with consequences for all men.

Pali: a dialect of Sanskrit and the sacred language of Buddhism. It was allegedly spoken by Buddha himself, and is the language in which the main Buddhist Scripture, the Tripitaka, was originally written.

Panathenaea (Greek): a festival held in Athens in honour of the goddess Athena.

papal infallibility (Christianity): In the Roman Catholic faith, the belief that when the pope makes a statement of policy regarding faith or morals he is immune from error.

Paramatman (Hinduism): the world soul, and a dimension of Brahman.

Parentalia (Roman): a festival which commemorated the souls of dead ancestors.

Parvati (Hinduism): a goddess who has many manifestations, including Shakti, Kali and Durga.

Pentateuch (Judaism): the first five books of the Old Testament.

Pharisees (Judaism): extreme wing of the Hasidim; basing all upon the Law, they insisted upon the strictest observances of the ordinances of Judaism in all aspects of life.

pilgrimage: a long journey, usually arduous in nature, by devotees of a particular religion. This is undertaken to demonstrate or re-affirm faith, and frequently has a shrine or other holy place as its destination.

polytheism: belief in many gods.

Pontifex Maximus (Roman): the High Priest in Roman society. Traditionally he was elected to this position.

prakriti (Buddhism): matter, one of the two essential elements of the universe, along with purushas (spirits).

presbyterial (Christianity): the system of organization in the United Church.

Presbyters (Christianity): in the Presbyterian Church, the ruling elders elected by the congregation.

Presbytery: (Christianity): in the Presbyterian Church, a form of church government combining ruling elders elected by the congregation with ruling and teaching elders who are ordained ministers. In the Roman Catholic Church, the residence of a priest.

priesthood of all believers (Christianity): a doctrine of Martin Luther enabling all men to approach God on an individual basis; an attempt to deny the necessity of the mediation of a priest in communicating with God.

puja-place (Hinduism): a place in the home for worship.

Puranas (Hinduism): Hindu texts of lesser importance than the Vedas. The Puranas tell stories about various gods and heroes, and are thus part of Hindu folklore.

Purgatory (Christianity): in the Roman Catholic Church, the condition in which the souls who have died in the state of grace suffer for a long time, in order that they may be cleansed of unrepented sins, before they are admitted into Heaven.

purushas (Buddhism): spirits, one of the two essential elements of the universe,

along with prakriti (matter).

rabbi (Judaism): the spiritual head of a Jewish community.

raja-yoga (Hinduism): the way to union with God through meditation.

rak'a (Islam): a seven-stage procedure unique to Moslem prayer.

Rama (Hinduism): hero of the epic Ramayana, and an avatar of the great god Vishnu.

Ramadan (Islam): the ninth lunar month during which fasting is observed to commemorate the revelations given by Allah to the Prophet Mohammed.

Ramayana (Hinduism): the shorter of the two great Hindu epics which recount the exploits of the heroic figure, Rama.

Rauana (Hinduism): the chief of the demons.

redemption (Christianity): saving from sin through the Atonement of Christ.

reincarnation: being born again.

relic (Christianity): the physical remains and effects of saints, which are considered worthy of veneration because they are representative of persons in glory with God.

Rig-Veda (Hinduism): the oldest of the Vedas, consisting of a large collection of hymns addressed to various gods.

Rosh Ha-Shanah (Judaism): the festival of the New Year.

sacraments: actions of Christ and his church which signify grace, cause it in the act of signifying it, and confer it upon persons properly disposed to receive it. They perpetuate the redemptive activity of Christ, making it present and effective.

sadaqua (Islam): alms.

Sadducess (Judaism): the predominately priestly party among the Jews at the time of Christ; noted for extreme conservatism.

sadhu (Hinduism): a Hindu holy man.

salat (Islam): formal, ritual prayer.

salvation (Christianity): in the Roman Catholic Church, the liberation of men from sin, reconciliation with God in and through Christ, the attainment of union with God forever in the glory of Heaven.

samadhi (Hinduism): a trance-like state of superconsciousness, the ultimate goal of yogic meditation when the mind loses all consciousness of self and becomes one with Brahman.

Sama-Veda (Hinduism): a section of the Vedas, consisting mainly of chants to be used at sacrifices.

samsara (Hinduism and Buddhism): the endless cycle of rebirths which brings man suffering, and from which he should seek release.

Sangha (Buddhism): the monastic order founded by Buddha.

Sanhedrin (Judaism): highest judicial and ecclesiastical council of the ancient Jewish nation, composed of from 70 to 72 members.

Sanskrit: the classical language of India, used in the holy Scriptures of Hinduism.

satori (Zen Buddhism): the rare and brilliant flash of insight which brings enlightenment.

Saturnalia (Roman): a festival in which the traditional roles of masters and servants were reversed.

Seder (Judaism): a feast held on the eve of Passover.

Sedna: in Eskimo religion, one of four major deities, the goddess of the water who is queen of the sea mamals and grants luck in hunting.

Semites: people whose original home was probably Arabia and who later spread out to Mesopotamia, the Eastern Mediterranean and the Nile delta.

Shafiites (Islam): a Moslem sect.

Shahada (Islam): the most important, fundamental statement of faith, and a call by which the faithful are summoned to prayer.

Shaivites: (Hinduism): devotees of the god Shiva.

Shaman: a person believed to possess special powers and the ability to deal with supernatural matters. He is sometimes known as a "witch doctor" or "medicine man".

Shari'a (Islam): the path of conduct to be followed by Moslems.

Shebuot (Judaism): Jewish holiday coming fifty days after Passover.

Shema (Judaism): the daily prayer of Judaism (Deuteronomy 6: 4-9).

Shiites (Islam): a Moslem sect.

Shin Buddhism: a prominent Buddhist sect found principally in China; a variation in concept of Amida Buddhism, "the easy way".

Shiva (Hinduism): the god of destruction and reproduction; a member of the Hindu trimurti, along with Brahma and Vishnu.

Sikhism: a religion founded in India in the late fifteenth century by Nanak.

Shiva (Hinduism): the Hindu god who destroys and restores life. A member of the trimurti.

shofar (Judaism): a horn, (usually a ram's) used during the services of the New Year and the Day of Atonement.

Sila: in Eskimo religion, one of the four major deities; lord of the air who has the power to punish man's sins.

sin: the rejection of God manifested by free and deliberate violation of his Law by thought, word or action.

sorcerer: a practitioner of black or harmful magic.

Ssu Shu (Confucianism): an important collection of Confucianist writings.

Stoicism (Greek): philosophy founded by Zeno about 308 B.C., holding that wisdom lies in being superior to passion, joy and grief, and in unperturbed submission to the divine will.

stupa (Buddhism): a sacred shrine, usually containing relics of Buddha or his disciples.

Sudra (Hinduism): a member of the peasant-servant caste, the fourth class in Hindu society.

sufi (Islam): a Moslem mystic.

Sukkoth (Judaism): Feast of Booths or the Feast of Tabernacles; originally a harvest festival.

Sunnas (Islam): actions of the Prophet Mohammed, or traditions pertaining to the same.

sura (Islam): a chapter heading in the Koran.

Sutras (Hinduism): Hindu Scriptures establishing rules based on interpretations of the Upanishads.

Sutta Pitaka (Buddhism): a major section of the principal Buddhist Scripture, the Tripitaka.

suttee (Hinduism): a Hindu rite, now outlawed in India, wherein a wife threw herself on her husband's funeral pyre.

synagogue (Judaism): building where Jews gather for worship.

tabu or *taboo:* a rule established by a group or community to set apart a person or thing as accursed or sacred, which neutralizes possible evil effects of supernatural forces.

Talmud (Judaism): compilation of the oral Law of the Jews with rabbinical commentaries (as distinct from the Scriptures or written Law); the accepted authority for orthodox Jews everywhere; comprising the Mishnah and the Gemara.

tanha (Buddhism): the idea of desire, which brings suffering and leads ultimately to rebirth.

Tantras (Hinduism): Hindu Scriptures of lesser importance, telling how to win the favour of the gods, and stressing the worship of Shakti.

Tantrism: a unique blend of certain features of Mahayana Buddhism and popular Hinduism. Tantrism has greatly influenced Tibetan Lamaism.

Tao: in Chinese philosophy "the way", which Lao-tzu claimed all forms of life should follow.

Tao Teh-ching (Taoism): a small book of poems containing the basic ideas of Taoism.

tarpana (Hinduism): a form of worship featuring an offering, usually of food or flowers, to a particular deity.

Tartarus (Greek): caverns in the underworld where the souls of men who had offended the gods were sent for punishment.

T'fillin (Judaism): black leather straps laced to the body; used in conjunction with weekday morning worship.

Theravada Buddhism: the older, smaller and more conservative of the two major schools of Buddhist thought.

Torah (Judaism): Hebrew name for the first five books of the Bible called also the Law of Moses of the Pentateuch.

totemism: the belief that all members of a family or clan have a common ancestor, either plant, animal or object, which serves as an emblem of the clan.

transmigration of souls: the passing of a soul into another body after death.

transubstantiation (Christianity): in the Anglican and Roman Catholic Churches the change of the whole substance of the bread and wine of Communion into the body and blood of Christ; not perceptible to the senses; commonly called a miracle.

Trimurti (Hinduism): the group of three major Hindu deities, Brahma, Shiva and Vishnu.

Trinity (Christianity): belief in Three Divine Persons—Father, Son and Holy Spirit—in one God.

Tripitaka (Buddhism): the principal Buddhist Scripture.

"Twice-born": a collective term referring to the top three castes in Hindu society.

Untouchable (Hinduism): a member of the outcastes, the lowest-ranking level in Hindu society, who is considered unclean by Hindus of higher castes.

Upanishads (Hinduism): Hindu Scriptures forming a key section of the Vedas. Because they contain the l..ghest spiritual concepts of Hinduism, they are said to be the basis of "orthodox" Hindu beliefs.

Vaishnavites (Hinduism): devotees of the god Vishnu.

Vaishya (Hinduism): originally a member of the merchant-farmer caste, the third class in Hindu society, now largely made up of merchants and businessmen.

Vedanta (Hinduism): literally "the end of the Vedas". A collective term referring to the philosophy of the Upanishads and subsequent interpretations thereof; all reality is a simple principle, Brahman, and the believer's goal is to transcend the limitations of self-identity and realize union with Brahman.

Vedas (Hinduism): the oldest, most sacred Scriptures of Hinduism, including the psalms, incantations, hymns and formulas of worship in four collections called the Rig-Veda, the Yajur-Veda, the Sama-Veda and the Atharva-Veda.

veneration: a high respect or reverance held towards a person or an object; not to be confused with worship.

venial sin (Christianity): in the Roman Catholic Church, a sin less serious and with less serious consequences than mortal sin; pardonable.

Vinaya Pitaka (Buddhism): a major section of the principal Buddhist Scripture, the Tripitaka.

Virgin birth (Christianity): belief that Jesus was miraculously begotten of God, and born of Mary, who was a Virgin.

Vishnu (Hinduism): the god who protects and sustains life; a member of the Trimurti along with Brahma and Shiva; chief deity worshipped by the Vaishnavites.

Wahhabis (Islam): a Moslem brotherhood formed in the eighteenth century and noted for austerity and orthodoxy.

wakan: a supernatural force revered by the Sioux Indians, similar to mana.

Wu Ching (Confucianism): the "Five Classics"; a major collection of classical Chinese literature.

wu-wei (Taoism): the idea of avoiding thoughts or actions which are not in harmony with Tao, the natural order of the universe.

Yahweh (Judaism): a name for God.

Yajur-Veda (Hinduism): a re-arrangement of the Rig-Veda to facilitate chanting.

yang: in Chinest philosophy, one of the two principal forces in the universe; the active, masculine cosmic principle.

Yengishiki (Shintoism): important document of the Shinto faith.

Yin: in Chinese philosophy, one of the two principal forces in the universe; the passive, female cosmic element.

Yom Kippur (Judaism): the Day of Atonement, the holiest Jewish holiday.

zakat (Islam): obligatory alms.

Zealots (Judaism and Christianity): a political party opposed to Roman control of Judea during the first century A.D.; advocates of armed rebellion against Rome.

Zen (Buddhism): a particular form of Buddhism, stressing intense meditation; most prevalent in Japan.

Zoomorphism: the belief held in ancient times that the gods took on the physical forms of animals.

Bibliography

GENERAL

Bahm, A.J., *The World's Living Religions*. New York: Dell Publishing Co., 1964.
Bouquet, A.C., *Comparative Religion*. Harmondsworth: Penguin Books Ltd., 1962.
Bouquet, A.C., *Sacred Books of the World*. Harmondsworth: Penguin Books, Ltd., 1954.
Bradley, D.G., *A Guide to the World's Religions*. Englewood Cliffs, N.J.: Prentice-Hall, 1963.
The Editors of Life, *The World's Great Religions*. New York: Time Inc., 1963.
The Editors of the National Geographic Book Service, *Great Religions of the World*. Washington, D.C.: National Geographic Society, 1971.
Hoffer, Eric, *The True Believer*. New York: Harper and Row, 1951.
Hume, Robert, *The World's Living Religions*. New York: Charles Scribner's Sons, 1952.
James, William, *The Varieties of Religious Experience*. New York: New American Library, 1958.
Noss, J.B., *Man's Religions*. New York: The Macmillan Co., 1964.
Parrinder, E.G., *What World Religions Teach*. London: George Harrap & Co. 1968.
Radhakrishnan, S., *East and West in Religion*. London: George Allen & Unwin Ltd., 1949.
Schoeps, Hans-Joachim, *The Religions of Mankind*. Garden City: Anchor Books, Doubleday and Co., Inc., 1968.
Siu, R.G.H., *The Tao of Science: An Essay on Western Knowledge and Eastern Wisdom*. Cambridge, Mass.: Massachusetts Institute of Technology, 1957.
Smith, Huston, *The Religions of Man*. New York: New American Library, 1958.
Smith, W.C., *The Faith of Other Men*. Toronto: CBC Publications, 1964.

Chapter One: The Foundations of Religion

Allegro, J.M., *The Dead Sea Scrolls*. Harmondsworth: Penguin Books Ltd., 1959.
Baker, Liva, *World Faiths*. London: Abelard-Schuman, 1965.
Banton, M., *Anthropological Approaches to the Study of Religion*. London: Tavistock Pub., 1968.
Bellah, R.N., *Beyond Belief: Essays on Religion in a Post-Traditional World*. New York: Harper & Row, 1970.
Blackham, H.J., *Humanism*. Harmondsworth: Penguin Books Ltd., 1968.
Bouquet, A.C., *Sacred Books of the World*. Harmondsworth: Penguin Books, 1962.
Brandon, S.F., *Creation Legends of the Ancient Near East*. London: Hodder and Stoughton, 1963.
Eliade, Mircea, *From the Primitives to Zen*. New York: Harper & Row, 1967.
Jaspers, Karl, *Socrates, Buddha, Confucius, Jesus*. New York: Harcourt, Brace and World, 1957.
Keller, Werner, *The Bible as History*. New York: Wm. Morrow and Co., 1964.
O'Dea, T.F., *Sociology of Religion*. Englewood Cliffs, N.J.: Prentice-Hall, 1966.
Potter, C.F., *The Great Religious Leaders*. New York: Washington Square Press, 1962.

Quennell, P., and Hodge, A., eds., *History Today*, Oct. 1963, March, August, 1964.

Russell, Bertrand, *Why I Am Not A Christian*. New York: Simon and Schuster, 1966.

Sahakian, Wm., ed., *Philosophies of Religion*. Cambridge, Mass.: Schenkman Publishing Co., 1965.

Sandars, N.K., *The Epic of Gigamesh*. Harmondsworth: Penguin Books Ltd., 1966.

Smith, Ruth, *The Tree of Life*. New York: Viking Press, 1969.

Wach, J., *The Comparative Study of Religion*. New York: Columbia University Press, 1958.

Walker, E.D., *Reincarnation*. New York: University Books, 1965.

Weber, Max, *The Sociology of Religion*. Boston: Beacon Press, 1956.

Chapter Two: The Origin of Religion

Barbeau, Marius, *Medicine Men on the North Pacific Coast*. Ottawa: Information Canada, 1958.

Eliade, Mircea, ed., *From the Primitives to Zen*. New York: Harper & Row, 1967.

Feldman, Susan, ed., *African Myths and Tales*. New York: Dell Publishing Co., 1970.

Hopkins, E.W., *Origin and Evolution of Religion*. New York: Cooper Square Publishers, 1969.

Howells, William, *The Heathens*. New York: Doubleday & Co., 1948.

Lowie, Robert, *Primitive Religion*. New York: Liveright Pub. Corp., 1952.

Malinowski, B., *Magic, Science and Religion*. London: The Society for Promoting Christian Knowledge, 1954.

Maringer, Johannes, *The Gods of Prehistoric Man*. London: Weidenfield and Nicolson, 1960.

Mowat, Farley, *People of the Deer*. Boston: Little, Brown and Co., 1952.

Owen, R., Deetz, J. and Fisher, A., eds., *The North American Indians*. Toronto: Collier-Macmillan Co., 1967.

Ringgren, H., and Strom A., *Religions of Mankind, Today and Yesterday*. London: Oliver & Boyd, 1967.

Spencer, Robert, *The North Alaskan Eskimo*. Washington: Smithsonian Institution, 1969.

Symington, F., *The Canadian Indian*. Toronto: McClelland and Stewart, 1968.

Chapter Three: The Religions of the Ancient World

Albright, F.A., *From the Stone Age to Christianity*. New York: Doubleday & Co., 1957.

Breasted, J.H., *A History of Egypt*. New York: Charles Scribner's Sons, 1967.

Bullfinch, T., *Mythology of Greece and Rome*. New York: Collier Books, 1962.

Carcopino, J., *Daily Life in Ancient Rome*. Harmondsworth: Penguin Books Ltd., 1964.

Durant, Will, *Caesar and Christ*. New York: Simon and Schuster, 1944.

———, *Our Oriental Heritage*. New York: Simon and Schuster, 1935.

———, *The Life of Greece*. New York: Simon and Schuster, 1939.

Frankfort, Henri, *Ancient Egyptian Religion*. New York: Harper, 1961.

Glanville, S.R.K., *The Legacy of Egypt*. Oxford: Clarendon Press, 1963.

Graves, Robert, *The Greek Myths*, Vols. I and II. Harmondsworth: Penguin Books Ltd., 1958.

Hamilton, Edith, *Mythology*. Boston: Little, Brown and Co., 1942.

Hawkes, J., *Dawn of the Gods*. New York: Random House, 1968.

Herodotus, *The Histories*. Harmondsworth: Penguin Books Ltd., 1968.

Homer, *The Iliad*. Harmondsworth: Penguin Books Ltd., 1964.

————, *The Odyssey*. Harmondsworth: Penguin Books Ltd., 1963.

Legge, F., *Forerunners and Rivals of Christianity*. New York: University Books, 1964.

Murray, Gilbert, *Five Stages of Greek Religion*. New York: Doubleday Anchor Books, 1955.

Nilsson, Martin, *A History of Greek Religion*. New York: W.W. Norton & Co., 1964.

Noss, J.B., *Man's Religions*. New York: The Macmillan Co., 1963.

Chapter Four: Hinduism

Bouquet, A.C., *Hinduism*. New York: Hutchinson's University Library, 1948.

Eliade, M., *Yoga: Immortality and Freedom*. New York: Pantheon Books, Inc., 1958.

Gandhi, M.K., *The Story of My Experiments with Truth*. Washington, D.C.: Public Affairs Press, 1948.

Goetz, H., *Five Thousand Years of Indian Art*. New York: McGraw-Hill Book Co. Inc., 1959.

Isherwood, Christopher, *Ramakrishna and His Disciples*. New York: Simon and Schuster, Inc., 1965.

————, *Vedanta For the Western World*. Hollywood: Vedanta Press, 1952.

Kramrisch, S., *The Art of India: Traditions of Indian Sculpture and Architecture*. New York: Phaidon Publishers, Inc., 1965.

Morgan, Kenneth, *The Religion of the Hindus*. New York: Ronald Press, 1953.

Nikhilinanda, Swami, *The Essence of Hinduism*. Boston: Beacon Press, 1948.

————, *The Upanishads*, Vols. I, II and III. New York: Harper and Bros., 1956.

Radhakrishnan, S., *The Hindu View of Life*. London: George Allen and Unwin, 1960.

————, *The Bhagavad-Gita*. New York: Harper and Bros., 1948.

————, *Indian Philosophy*, Vols. I and II. London: George Allen & Unwin Ltd., 1951.

————, and Moore, C.A., *A Source Book in Indian Philosophy*. Princeton: Princeton University Press, 1957.

Rawlinson, H.G., *India, A Short Cultural History*. New York: Frederick A. Praeger, Inc., 1952.

Ross, N.W., *Three Ways of Asian Wisdom*. New York: Simon and Schuster, Inc., 1966.

Rowland, Benjamin, Jr., *The Art and Architecture of India*. Harmondsworth: Penguin Books Ltd., 1953.

Vivekananda, Swami, *Jnana Yoga and Karma Yoga and Bhakti Yoga*. New York: Ramakrishna-Vivekananda Center, 1945.

Wood, Earnest, *Great Systems of Yoga*. New York: The Philosophical Library, Inc., 1954.

Zimmer, H., *The Philosophies of India*. New York: Pantheon Books, 1951.

Chapter Five: Early Religions of China and Japan

General:

Creel, H.G., *Chinese Thought from Confucius to Mao Tse-tung*. Chicago: University of Chicago Press, 1960.

Croizier, R.C., ed., *China's Cultural Legacy and Communism*. New York: Praeger Publishers, 1970.

Day, Clarence, *The Philosophers of China*. New York: Citadel Press, 1962.

Fang, T. H., *The Chinese View of Life*. Kowloon: Citadel Press, 1962.

Fung, Yu-lan, *A Short History of Chinese Philosophy*. New York: The Macmillan Co., 1962.

Waley, A., *Three Ways of Thought in Ancient China*. Garden City: Doubleday and Co., 1956.

Taoism:

Bynner, W., translator, *The Way of Life: According to Lao-tzu*. New York: The John Day Co., Inc., 1944.

Welch, H., *The Parting of the Way; Loa-tzu and the Taoist Movement*. Boston: Beacon Press, 1957.

Confucianism:

Creel, H.G., *Confucius and The Chinese Way*. New York: Harper and Row, 1960.

————, *Confucius, The Man and The Myth*. New York: John Day and Co., 1949.

Waley, A., *The Analects of Confucius*. London: George Allen and Unwin Ltd., 1938.

Ware, J.R., translator, *The Sayings of Confucius*. New York: New American Library, 1955.

————, *The Sayings of Mencius*. New York: New American Library, 1960.

Shinto:

Anesaki, Masaharu, *History of Japanese Religion*. London: Kegan Paul, Trench, Trubner and Co., Ltd., 1930.

Benedict, R., *The Chrysanthemum and The Sword*. Boston: Houghton Mifflin Co., 1946.

Bunce, W.K., *Religions in Japan*. Tokyo: C.E. Tuttle Co., 1955.

The Japanese Agency for Cultural Affairs, ed., *Japanese Religion*. Tokyo: Kodansha International Ltd., 1972. (Available through Fitzhenry and Whiteside, Toronto.)

Chapter Six: Buddhism

Bahm, A.J., *Philosophy of the Buddha*. New York: Harper and Bros., 1958.

Benoit, H., *The Supreme Doctrine: Psychological Studies in Zen Thought*. New York: Pantheon Books Inc., 1955.

Burtt, E. A., *The Teachings of the Compassionate Buddha*. New York: New American Library, 1955.

Chang, Chen-Chi, *The Practice of Zen*. New York: Harper and Bros., 1959.

Conze, E., *Buddhism: Its Essence and Development*. New York: Harper Torchbooks, 1959.

Dumoulin, H.S.J., *A History of Zen Buddhism*. New York: Pantheon Books, 1963.

Eliot, Charles, *Japanese Buddhism*. New York: Barnes and Noble, 1959.

Evans-Wentz, W.Y., *The Tibetan Book of the Dead*. London: Oxford University Press, 1951.

Grousset, Rene, *In the Footsteps of the Buddha*. London: George Routledge and Sons, Ltd., 1932.

Humphreys, C., *Buddhism*. London: Penguin Books, 1951.

————, *Zen Buddhism*. London: William Heinemann Ltd., 1949.

Kapleau, P., *The Three Pillars of Zen*. New York: Harper and Row, 1966.

Minamoto, H., *An Illustrated History of Japanese Art*. Kyoto: K. Hoshino, 1935.

Morgan, K., ed., *The Path of Buddhism; Buddhism Interpreted by Buddhists*. New York: The Ronald Press Co., 1956.

Pratt, J.B., *The Pilgrimage of Buddhism*. New York: The Macmillan Co., 1928.

Ross, N.W., *Three Ways of Asian Wisdom*. New York: Simon and Schuster, Inc., 1966.

Seckel, D., *The Art of Buddhism*. New York: Crown Publishers, Inc., 1964.

Shattock, E. H., *An Experiment in Mindfulness*. New York: E.P. Dutton and Co., Inc., 1960.

Suzuki, D.T., *The Essentials of Zen Buddhism*. London: Rider and Co., 1962.

————, *Zen and Japanese Culture*. New York: Bollingen Foundation Inc., Pantheon Books Inc., 1959.

Waley, Arthur, *The Real Tripitaka, and Other Pieces*. London: George Allen and Unwin Ltd., 1952.

Watts, A.W., *The Way of Zen*. New York: Pantheon Books, Inc., 1957.

Chapter Seven: Judaism

Applebaum, Morton M., *What Everyone Should Know About Judaism*. New York: Philosophical Library, 1959. (Answers to the questions most frequently asked about Judaism.)

Daiches, D., "What is a Jew?" *Horizon*, Summer, 1971.

Dimont, Max I., *Jews, God and History*. New York: Simon and Schuster, 1962.

Encyclopedia Judaica. New York: The Macmillan Co., 1970. (The authoritative source for all aspects of Judaism.)

Herberg, W., *Protestant, Catholic, Jew*. New York: Doubleday and Co., Inc., 1960. (Re. religious sociology in the U.S.)

Hertzberg, A., ed., *Judaism*. New York: George Braziller, 1962.

Hexter, J.H., *The Judaeo-Christian Tradition*. New York: Harper and Row, 1966.

Lamm, Maurice, *The Jewish Way in Death and Mourning*. New York: Jonathan David Publishers, 1969.

Learsi, Rufus, *Israel: A History of the Jewish People*. New York: World Publishing Company, 1949.

Marshall, J., "City's Jews: Equal in most places, in most cases," *Telegram*, Toronto, August 7, 1971.

Michener, J., *The Source*. New York: Random House, 1965.

Mohs, Mayo, "What it Means to be Jewish," *Time*, Cover Story, April 10, 1972.

Plaut, W. Gunther, *Your Neighbour is a Jew*. Toronto: McClelland and Stewart, 1967.

Rosenberg, Stuart E., *To Understand Jews*. Toronto: Paperjacks, 1972.

Roth, Leon, *Judaism: A Portrait*. London: Faber and Faber, 1960.

Sack, B.G., *History of the Jews in Canada*. Montreal: Harvest House, 1965.

Sandmel, Samuel, *We Jews and Jesus*. New York: Oxford University Press, 1965.

Schwartz, L.W., ed., *Great Ages and Ideas of the Jewish People*. New York: Random House, 1956.

Steinberg, Milton, *Basic Judaism*. New York: Harcourt Brace, 1947.

Waxman, Meyer, *A Handbook of Judaism*. Chicago: L. M. Stein Publisher, 1953. (Subsequently enlarged and published by Thomas Yoseloff under the title *Judaism: Religion and Ethics*.)

Wouk, H., *This Is My God*. New York: Doubleday and Co., 1959.

Zeitlin, Solomon, *Who Crucified Jesus?* New York: Bloch Publishing Company, 1964.

Chapter Eight: Early Christianity

Baly, D. and Tushingham, A.D., *Atlas of the Biblical World*. New York: The World Publishing Co., 1971.

Bultman, R., *Primitive Christianity*. London: Colliers, A Fontana book, 1959.

Cross, F.L., *The Oxford Dictionary of the Christian Church*. London: Oxford University Press, 1957.

Durant, W., *Caesar and Christ*. New York: Simon and Schuster, Inc., 1944.

———, *The Age of Faith*. New York: Simon and Schuster, Inc., 1950.

———, *The Reformation*. New York: Simon and Schuster, Inc., 1957.

Fosdick, H.E., *The Man From Nazareth*. New York: Harper and Row, 1949.

French, R.M., *The Eastern Orthodox Church*. London: Hutchinson, 1967.

Hackel, S., *The Orthodox Church*. London: Ward Lock Educational, 1971.

Schonfield, H.J., *The Passover Plot*. New York: Bantam Books, 1968.

Spraggett, Allen, "Is This a Photo of Christ?" *Toronto Star*, April 13, 1968. (Re. the Shroud of Turin.)

"Death of a Patriarch", *Time*, July 17, 1972. (Re. the death of Athanagoris.)

Chapter Nine: Islam

Abdulla La Maududi, S., *The Meaning of the Koran*, Vols. I-IV. Lahore: Islamic Publications Ltd., 1967.

Al-Ati, Hammudah A., *Islam in Focus*. Edmonton: The Canadian Islamic Centre, 1963.

Ali, Ameer, *The Spirit of Islam*. London: Christophers, 1922.

Brockelmann, Carl, *History of the Islamic Peoples*. New York: G.P. Putnam, 1947.

Cragg, K., *The Call of the Minaret*. New York: Oxford University Press, 1956.

Durant, Will, *The Age of Faith*. New York: Simon and Schuster, Inc., 1950.

The Editors of Time-Life, *Early Islam*. New York: Time, Inc., 1967.

Farah, C.E., *Islam*. Woodbury, N.Y.: Barron's Educational Series, Inc., 1968.

Gabrieli, F., *Muhammad and the Conquests of Islam*. New York: McGraw-Hill Book Co., 1968.

Guillaume, A., *Islam*. Harmondsworth: Penguin Books, 1954.

Hitti, Philip K., *History of the Arabs from the Earliest Times to the Present*. London: The Macmillan Co., 1967.

Irving, Dr. T.B., trans., *Al Qur'an: Selections from the Noble Reading*. Cedar Rapids, Iowa: Unity Publishing Co., 1968.

Pickthall, Mohammed, M., *The Meaning of the Glorious Koran*. New York: New American Library, 1953.

Qutb, Sayyid, *This Religion of Islam.* Palo Alto, California: Al Manar Press, n.d.

Roolvink, R., *Historical Atlas of the Muslim Peoples.* Cambridge, Mass.: Harvard University Press, 1958.

Saunders, J.J., *A History of Medieval Islam.* London: Routledge and Kegan Paul, 1965.

Tritton, A.S., *Islam.* London: Hutchinson University Library, 1951.

von Grunebaum, G.E., *Classical Islam: A History 600-1258.* London: George Allen and Unwin Ltd., 1970.

Wensinck, A.J., *The Muslim Creed, Its Genesis and Historical Development.* London: Frank Cass and Co., 1965.

Williams, J.A., ed., *Islam.* New York: George Braziller, 1962.

Chapter Ten: Modern Christianity

Roman Catholic:

A New Catechism. Montreal: Palm Publishers, 1872.

"Catholic Church Did Not Always Condemn Divorce", *Toronto Star*, June 2, 1969.

"Catholic Freedom vs. Authority", *Time*, November 22, 1968.

"Ecumenism", *Time*, June 20, 1969.

The Editors of the National Geographic Society, *Great Religions of the World.* Washington: the National Geographic Society, 1971.

McBrien, R.P., *Who Is a Catholic?* Denville, N.J.: Dimension Books, 1971.

1972 Catholic Almanac. Huntingdon, Indiana: Our Sunday Visitor, Inc.

"Nuns Change Their Dress and Their Lives", *Toronto Star*, May 24, 1969.

"Nuns and Priests: Going Their Way", *Time*, February 23, 1970.

"Removal of Saints 'Routine' ", *Telegram*, Toronto, May 10, 1969.

Ryan, J.J., *The Jesus People.* Chicago: Life In Christ, 1970.

"The New Mass: More Variety for Catholics", *Time*, January 26, 1970.

"Why 69 Countries Have Envoys at the Vatican", *Toronto Star*, October 6, 1969.

Wilhelm, A.J., *Christ Among Us: A Modern Presentation of the Catholic Faith.* New York: Newman Press, 1967.

(All of the above are available at the Catholic Truth Society, 67 Bond St., Toronto 5, Ontario.)

United Church:

The Manual of the United Church of Canada. Toronto: The United Church Publishing House, 1972.

The Observer. Toronto: The United Church Publishing House.

The Statement of Faith of the United Church of Canada. Toronto: The United Church of Canada, 1940.

(These and many other sources are available at the United Church House Book Store, 85 St. Clair Avenue East, Toronto, Ontario.)

Anglican Church:

The Canadian Churchman. Toronto: The General Synod of the Anglican Church of Canada.

Moorman, J., *Episcopalians and Anglicans.* Glen Park, N.J.: Paulist Press, 1966.

Williams, D., *Why I Am an Anglican*. St. Thomas, Ontario: Sutherland Press,
    1950.

The Parish Question Box.

(These and many other sources are available at the Anglican Church House
Book Store, 600 Jarvis St., Toronto, Ontario.)

Lutheran Church:
Cronmiller, C.L., *A History of the Lutheran Church In Canada*. Philadelphia:
    Fortress Press, 1970.
Horn, W.H., *What Lutherans Believe Today*. Philadelphia: Fortress Press, 1970.

The Church of Jesus Christ of Latter-Day Saints:
The Articles of Faith. Salt Lake City: The Church of Jesus Christ of Latter-Day
    Saints.
The Book of Mormon. Salt Lake City: The Church of Jesus Christ of Latter-Day
    Saints.
Doctrine and Covenants. Salt Lake City: The Church of Jesus Christ of
    Latter-Day Saints.
Pearl of Great Price. Salt Lake City: The Church of Jesus Christ of Latter-Day
    Saints.

Jehovah's Witnesses:
The Watchtower. Toronto: Watch Tower Bible and Tract Society.
Awake. Toronto: Watch Tower Bible and Tract Society.
"The Nations Shall Know That I am Jehovah" How? New York: Watch Tower
    Bible and Tract Society of New York, Inc., 1971.

(These and many other sources are available from the nearest Jehovah's
Witnesses congregation.)

Christian Science:
"The Christian Science Journal" (monthly). Boston: Christian Science Publishing
    Society.
"The Christian Science Monitor" (daily). Boston: Christian Science Publishing
    Society.
"The Christian Science Sentinel" (weekly). Boston: Christian Science Publishing
    Society.

(These and many other sources including several biographies of Mary Baker
Eddy are available at the nearest Christian Science Reading Room. This can be
located in the telephone directory.)
(Many sources for further information on the Presbyterian Church can be
obtained by contacting the Presbyterian Publications Book Room, 52 Wynford
Drive, Don Mills, Ontario.)
(Further information and sources for more detailed study of the Unitarian
Church may be obtained from the Information Centre of the Unitarian Council
of Metropolitan Toronto, 14 Esther Lorrie Drive, Toronto, Ontario.)
(For a list of sources for the Baptist Church, contact any of these addresses:
Baptist Book Room, Box 1053, Saint John, N.B.; Baptist Resource Centre,
217 St. George St., Toronto 180; Supply Centre, Baptist Union of Western
Canada, 8925 - 82nd Avenue, Edmonton 82, Alberta.)

Chapter Eleven: Contemporary Trends In Religion

Berton, Pierre, *The Comfortable Pew*. Toronto: McClelland and Stewart Ltd.,
    1964.

Blishen, B.R., ed., *Canadian Society—Sociological Perspectives*. Toronto: The
    Macmillan Co., 1971.

"Donating: As You Give, So Shall You Receive". Toronto: Process-Church of
    the Final Judgment.

Doyle, Barrie, "Empty Pews: A Challenge for New Worship Forms", *Telegram*,
    Toronto, July 24, 1971.

"Fellow Travelling with Jesus", *Time Magazine*, September 6, 1971. (Re. The
    Process.)

Graham, Billy, *My Answer*. New York: Doubleday & Co., 1960.

Graham, Billy, *Peace With God*. New York: Doubleday & Co., 1953.

Graham, Billy, *Secret of Happiness*. New York: Doubleday & Co., 1955.

Graham, Billy, *World Aflame*. New York: Doubleday & Co., 1965.

Harpur, T., "Study Tells What Protestants Think of the Church", *Toronto Star*,
    Saturday October 14, 1972.

———, "Former U.S. Child Revivalist Admits He Was a Fake", *Toronto Star*,
    Saturday September 16, 1972. (A study of Marjoe Gortner.)

Hillen, E., "Rex Humbard: He's Called 'King of the Soul Savers' ", *Weekend
    Magazine*, Toronto, August 7, 1971.

"Hollow Holiness", *Time Magazine*, August 14, 1972. (Re. Marjoe.)

Honeyford, Hal, "Jesus Revolution Sweeps Across the Continent", *Telegram*,
    Toronto, July 17, 1971.

"How Can I Become a Field Disciple of the Process?" Toronto: Process-Church
    of the Final Judgment. (Toronto Chapter, 99 Gloucester St., Toronto 5,
    Ontario.)

"How Can I Become a Processean?" Toronto: Process-Church of the Final
    Judgment.

"The Jesus Revolution", *Time Magazine*, June 21, 1971.

Kilbourn, W., ed., *The Restless Church*. Toronto: McClelland and Stewart Ltd.,
    1966.

Leblanc, P., and Edinborough, A., eds., *One Church, Two Nations?* Toronto:
    Longman's, 1968.

Mann, W.E., ed., *Canada: A Sociological Profile*. Toronto: Copp Clark, 1971.

"Miracle Woman", *Time Magazine*, September 14, 1970 (Re. Kathryn Kuhlman).

Pollock, J., *Billy Graham*. Grand Rapids, Mich.: Zondervan, 1966.

"The Process". Toronto: Process-Church of the Final Judgment.

"The Process—'Fax 'n Figgers'." Toronto: Process-Church of the Final
    Judgment.

"The Process—Foundation." Toronto: Process-Church of the Final Judgment.

"Street Christians: Jesus as the Ultimate Trip", *Time Magazine*, August 3, 1970.

"To Discover the Church," *Time Magazine*, December 14, 1970. (Re. Pope's
    Visit to Asia, Australia and Oceania.)

"The Unity of Christ and Satan." Toronto: Process-Church of the Final
    Judgment.

Wilson, D.J., *The Church Grows in Canada*. Toronto: Committee on Missionary
    Education of the Canadian Council of Churches, 1966.

Index

		Judaism	Christianity
2000 B.C.	Ancient Egypt flourishes in its "Middle Kingdom" Stage Shang Dynasty brings order to Chinese civilization The great age of Mycenae Dorian invasions of Greece	Abraham leads people from Ur Biblical story of Joseph (Genesis 37-50) Exodus (1300) Ten Commandments at Sinai	
1000 B.C.	Founding of Rome Emergence of Zoroastrianism	Solomon builds temple — Jerusalem becomes centre of Hebrew life Period of the prophets Babylonian captivity	
500 B.C.	The "Golden Age" of Greece The rise of Rome	Alexander the Great captures Palestine (332) Maccabean period of independence Pompey makes Palestine a Roman province Christ born	Christ born
Time of Christ	The fall of Rome	Christ crucified (30) Jerusalem destroyed (70)	Christ crucified Christian persecutions New Testament completed (c.180) Edict of Milan — Christianity legal Christianity official state religion (383)
A.D. 500	The start of the "Dark Ages" Tang Dynasty ("Golden Age" of China) The "Middle Ages"	Karaite heresy	Church becomes organized and well established
A.D. 1000	The Renaissance Discovery of America	Moses Maimonides (1135-1204) Jews expelled from England (1290) Jews denied residence in France (1394) Unconverted Jews expelled from Spain	Eastern and Western Churches split (1054) Crusades Height of Medieval Papacy under Innocent III First Bible printed from movable type (1458)
A.D. 1500	The Reformation The Enlightenment The Industrial Revolution The rise of Western Imperialism The world wars The "Atomic Age"	United Nations Assembly votes to partition Palestine to create a Jewish State (1949) Six Day War (1967)	Martin Luther's 95 theses (151_ Calvin establishes church in Geneva Henry VIII breaks with Church of Rome — makes king head of the church in England (1534) Society of Jesus established Council of Trent — defines Catholic dogma King James version of Bible published (1611)

Islam	Hinduism	Religions of the Far East
	Aryan invasion of India	
	Formulation of Vedas and Upanishads Mahavira founds Jainism	Development of Shinto Lao Tzu & Confucius born in China Birth of Buddha in India
	Emperor Ashoka converted to Buddhism Emergence of Great Epics (Ramayana and Mahabharata)	Growth of Buddhist monasteries in India Buddhist expansion begins Confucianism instituted as state religion in China
		Great Council organizes Buddhist Scriptures Buddhism spreads to China
	Development of the Puranas.	
Birth of Mohammed (570) Arabia converted to Islam Expansion of Moslem empire Beginning of Abbasid (750) Dynasty (the "Golden Age") Growth of sects	Continued growth of Bhakti cults	Buddhism reaches Japan Compilation of Shinto Scriptures
Turks capture Damascus Struggle against Christian crusades Moslems recapture Jerusalem Mongol invasion Ottoman Turks take Constantinople (1453)	Mogul Dynasty begins Sikhism founded by Nanak	
Western imperialism reaches Moslem lands Growth of Wahhabi sect World War I ends Ottoman Empire — Caliphate abolished (1922) Moslem lands regain independence Expansion of Islam into Central Africa	British conquest of India Birth of Ramakrishna (1836) Abolition of Suttee Caste system declared illegal Ghandi leads fight for independence	Fifth Great Buddhist Council Manchus elevate Confucius to equal status with Heaven and Earth Religion in China challenged by Communist takeover (1949) Sixth Great Buddhist Council